LIST OF CONTENTS

ACKNOWLEDGEMENTS

As with all of our publications, the History Club acknowledges that they would not be possible without the help and support of a team of dedicated people who are willing to generously give up their time so that memories of our past can be chronicled to produce a further volume for future generations.

Once again our major thanks go to Owen Rowland, who has spent many, many hours in the Durham Record Office, looking through old newspaper articles - and if it were not for his dedication, then I am quite sure this series of books would not have been possible.

Our word processor operators on this occasion were:

1947	Sheila Brown
1948	Margaret Hedley
	Joan Scott
1949	Mary Walker
1950	Janet Thomas
1951	Margaret Hedley
1952	Sheila Brown
1953	Edith Rose
	Joan Scott
1954	Mary Walker
1955	Sheila Brown
	Margaret Hedley

The onerous task of proof-reading was undertaken by Alf Carr.

Images have been provided by a range of people and most scanned and/or restored by Bill Burrell at The Wheatley Hill Heritage Centre.

We thank you all for your interest and dedication.

INTRODUCTION

The history of our villages continues in this, the fourth edition of our books charting the development from the opening of the collieries to their closing, the information coming mainly from newspaper articles.

This book shows how the villages of Thornley, Ludworth and Wheatley Hill continued to develop after 1947 and Nationalisation of the pits. This was an optimistic time for the villages - rationing and food shortages were over and despite an overall decline of the coal industry, Thornley and Wheatley Hill pits continued to provide most male employment throughout the villages.

The book is full of what life had to offer people living in the villages in the late 1940's and early 1950's. The pit was still the major employer, and employed most men in the village. Most women still stayed at home and looked after her husband and family. However times were changing. Factories were beginning to develop in the local area of Hartlepool, Peterlee and Durham and pit work was not the only option open to boys leaving secondary school.

The new town of Peterlee was becoming a reality and named after miners leader, Peter Lee, it offered many opportunities for people from the colliery villages.

The content of this book will be within the living memory of many of our readers and provide a nostalgic look at their own past.

1947

WHEATLEY HILL OBSERVANCE

Vesting day was celebrated at Wheatley Hill on Sunday, when a parade through the village of workmen employed in all sections of the colliery was headed by Wheatley Hill Miners' Lodge banner and Wheatley Hill Colliery Band (under the conductorship of Mr W Forrest). The unfurling of the flag in the colliery yard by the oldest workman, Mr William Snaith, JP (77), was attended by a record gathering. Previously the village had been circularised about the celebrations by Mr E Cain, JP, secretary, on behalf of Wheatley Hill Miners' Lodge.

"The sweat, blood and tears of the old miners have at last brought freedom from the owners," stated the circular. "A silent revolution has taken place and now we are about to witness the great change-over. We must all play our part in the great transformation, and we must show the nation that we are capable and willing to work the industry not in the interests of the few, but in the interests of the nation as a whole."

Boys Unveil Plaque

The two youngest colliery employees, Clarence Connor and George Reay, both aged 14, erected the wooden plaque announcing that the colliery was now owned by the National Coal Board. Coun E Wharrier, chairman, miners' lodge, presided, and Mr J Simpson (manager) and Mr E Cain, JP, also spoke. Mr Simpson appealed to the workmen for their co-operation in increasing production and stamping out absenteeism. Particular reference to the pioneers of the miners' trade union movement – Keir Hardy, Bob Smillie, H Smith, A J Cook and Peter Lee – was made by Mr Cain, who emphasised the noble part they had played in setting the seed for the nationalisation of the industry. Mr Snaith, who unfurled the flag, is still employed at the colliery on the surface as a pick sharpener. He has taken an active part in political and trade union matters in the village for many years.

BOY'S PLEA AT THORNLEY

At Thornley Colliery the ceremony went off without a hitch. Mr W T Roper (82), oldest worker at the colliery, unfurled the flag. Pulling a rope, the flag ran up to the top of the pulley wheel and there unfurled and fluttered in the breeze. Mr John Williams (chairman of the miners' lodge) called for cheers.

This followed a procession headed by the Thornley Lodge banner and the Thornley Colliery Band. Mr A Welsh, jun, acted for his father, who is recovering from an operation. He was accompanied by other colliery officials. In the gathering were Mr W Dowding (miners' secretary), Mr Jos Cherry (treasurer), Mr D Swallow (financial secretary), Mr James Adamson (compensation secretary), Mr James Webb (delegate) and members of the committee. Enginemen were represented by Mr Bert Pattison (secretary, just out of Durham Hospital after being severely burned when his home was destroyed in October) and Mr W Henderson (treasurer). Deputies' representatives were Messrs J Johnson and R Milburn, and the mechanics had Messrs W Straughan (secretary) and J Ulatt (treasurer). Messrs C Alderson, E Green and C Woodward were amongst representatives of the Officials' Association.

Mr Welsh, jun, before calling upon Clifford Miller, Ludworth, one of the youngest workers, to unveil the plaque erected above the gates at the colliery fence, said the opportunity was not often given to an individual, and much more seldom to an undertaking, to wipe the slate and start afresh. "The coal industry has been given that opportunity," he said, "and what it makes of that opportunity rests mainly with us. In the past there has been enmity, bad feeling and distrust. Let the new era which opens now see the end of these things. Let us wash them out and start afresh. The job in hand is for us to get coals out. If we tackle that job together we can do it and will make a success of this new order."

"Do Your Duty"

Young Clifford, standing on a chair so that he could be seen, read out his speech in a ringing voice. "Please note the last word on the board – the word 'people,'" he said. "Who are they? We, the youth of the day, are part. And in his new era we have our duty to do. We will try. We ask you to think and then do your duty. To all miners, we say co-operate, produce and progress. To the aged miner, whose duty is done, we say 'Thank you.' And to all we say 'Let us all progress together.' Thank you.

After Clifford had been well cheered for his speech, the ceremony of unfurling the flag at the pit-head was carried through and then the gathering moved back to the public clock in the Market Place, where Mr John Williams called upon Mr M Fleming (chairman of the Parish Council) to speak. Mr Fleming said "I want to thank the local officials

5

and the management for this celebration. Thornley has always had historic sense, and I am sure that historical sense has been exemplified today. As a trade unionist myself I was much struck by the number of officials walking under the banner today."

Mr Hubert Tunney

Mr Hubert Tunney, former chairman of Thornley Miners' Lodge and now assistant labour director of the Coal Board at Newcastle, said "This is a very important event, not only in the lifetime of Thornley, but in the lifetime of the whole mining community. Thirty years ago a lot of us saw in the far distance a dream of the public ownership of the mines. Now we have realized that ownership we have the important duty of making that venture a success. You are now privileged to work for a model employer. You have had holidays recently with pay and without conditions attached to them, the Board taking the view that there is a value in stressing and expressing the human side of the industry. The responsibility is now upon the management and the men to recognize that they also must play their part as far as production is concerned. Absenteeism must be reduced; lightning strikes must be cut out. There is no necessity for these things. You have the necessary machinery to deal with every possible aspect, and it is up to us to make a success of this venture. I hope we will in the future put this celebration into practical form by increasing production at the colliery."

A vote of thanks to speakers and others taking part was moved by Mr C Alderson and seconded by Mrs B Bosomworth. Mrs Bosomworth mentioned that Thornley Colliery banner was on the platform at the first "Big Meeting" of the Durham miners.

10 January 1947

FOOTBALL FAMILY- WHEATLEY HILL RECORD

Wheatley Hill's local football team – Wheatley Hill Welfare SC – which has tasted defeat only once since 5 October, is more or less a family affair, but no "family squabbles" have upset its run of success, and big things are expected this season. In the regular team play two sets of two brothers and an uncle and his nephew. Members of the Ferryhill and District League, the team has won six of its league games, lost four and drawn one, with 27 goals for and 15 against. They have reached the second round of the Ferryhill Nursing Cup, Thornley Aged Miners' Cup and the League Knock-out Cup, and only recently were dismissed from the Durham Amateur Cup by Gilesgate Labour Party at the third attempt. In October the club had three victories over Whitworth Park – in the Ferryhill Nursing Cup, Thornley Aged Miners' Cup and a league game.

James Wylie, their regular goalkeeper, who was recently demobbed from the Forces, is a nephew of their right-back, Joseph Wylie. Related to the Wylies are the two Bean brothers, who also play regularly for the football team. William Bean, who occupied the centre-half berth, played for Trimdon in the Northern League when he was 17, and his brother, George William, who started for Wheatley Hill as a full-back, has lately done good work as leader of the attack.

The Bean family's association with the football team does not end there, for another brother. James, who played several games last season, is treasurer of the club as well as trainer, and yet another brother, Joseph, is a member of the committee. They are all sons of Mrs Bean, of Stephen's Terrace, Wheatley Hill. James formerly played for Trimdon and was with the Northern League team when he broke a leg. James and Joseph are employed at Wheatley Hill colliery and William and George at Trimdon colliery.

More Brothers

Two other brothers who turn out regularly for the football team are Robert William and Raymond Carr, sons of Mr and Mrs F Carr, Stockton Street, Wheatley Hill. Robert, a putter at the local colliery, plays left-half and his brother, a mason at the same colliery, outside-left. Another brother, Bertie, is also on the team's books, having played several games this season both as right-half and centre-forward.

Yet another brother, Teddy Carr, has made a name for himself as a professional footballer. Starting with Wheatley Hill Juniors he was signed up by Arsenal and went to their "nursery" at Margate. He played regularly as an inside forward for Arsenal and was with them when they won the League. A knee injury then gave him considerable trouble and during the war he returned to his work at Wheatley Hill colliery and turned out as a "guest" player at Bradford, Huddersfield and Newcastle. In one of his games with Newcastle he scored six goals. Last season he was transferred from Arsenal to Huddersfield, and at the beginning of the present season went to Newport County, where he now captains the team.

In Murton Side

Another popular member of the Wheatley Hill team, Jack Scott, has a brother, Sammy, who has played for Murton CW in the North-Eastern League. Sammy was with Teddy Carr in Wheatley Hill Juniors' team which had a remarkable run of success in the early 1930s. In 1933 the team won the Junior Challenge Cup and were joint holders with Fatfield of the Junior Divisional Cup (NE Division), a cup which the previous year they had won outright.

Jack Urwin, another keen player who is often among the goals, is also well known as a cricketer. His brother, Tommy, formerly played football for Ferryhill in the Northern League.

With nine of their regular players living in Wheatley Hill itself, the Welfare can truly boast that it is a local team; the other two "regulars" live in the neighbouring villages of Thornley and Shotton. One of their forwards, Slack, who is a clever right-winger, last season had a trial with Newcastle United.

To complete the record of this "family" football team it must be mentioned that the goalkeeper, James Wylie, as well as having an uncle playing in front of him, has his father as a member of the committee.

Injuries handicapped the team at the beginning of the season, but they are now making excellent progress, and with such a "family" atmosphere prevailing they are hoping to bring home several trophies by the end of the season. Officials of the club are:- President, Mr A Baldasera; chairman, Mr George Hall; secretary, Mr Robert Patterson jun; treasurer, Mr James Bean; committee, Messrs F Smith, J Dunn, G Armstrong, T Armstrong, J Wylie and Joseph Bean.

10 January 1947

LIBRARY RE-OPENED – After a lapse of many years a branch of Durham County Library has been re-opened at Wheatley Hill, largely through the efforts of Mr E Cain. Books are issued every Monday between 6 and 7 pm in the Welfare Hall, Wheatley Hill. Mrs L M Bellis is the voluntary librarian, and Mr Cain is assistant.

LABOUR PARTY – Coun E Wharrier presided at the annual meeting of Wheatley Hill Local Labour Party, when a satisfactory financial statement was given, and Coun T Taylorson gave a report on council matters. It was decided to place on record appreciation of the long service of Mr E Cain, who has held an official position in the party for

8

the past 29 years. For 20 years he has been secretary and before that was chairman. The following officers were elected: Chairman, Coun E Wharrier; secretary, Mr E Cain; treasurer, Mr James Harper; delegate, Mr John Harper.

NEW LEGION HEADQUARTERS – By permission of the manager of Wheatley Hill colliery, Mr J Simpson, the men's and women's sections of Wheatley Hill British Legion have acquired new headquarters in what served as Home Guard headquarters during the war. The women's section, which is flourishing, meeting fortnightly, has hitherto held its meetings in the DDSS hut at Wheatley Hill. The men's section was re-formed only recently after a lapse of some ten years, and it is felt that the new headquarters will encourage a big increase in membership.

17 January 1947

MODERN MINING METHODS – URGENT NEED IN DURHAM COALFIELD

Urgent need of modern mining methods in our Durham collieries is alluded to this week in an article from the inspired pen of Mr W Wakefield Adam, MIMechE, the well-known consulting engineer of London.

Fruits of Past Neglect

Perhaps the most difficult problems facing the National Coal Board, he writes, relate to the introduction of modern methods of coal mining. In this country, over a long period of years, with a few notable exceptions, colliery owners have been content to take profits out of the mines, and have neglected to spend money on modern equipment. During the autumn of 1944, an American mission of coal experts visited this country and gave a report on the state of the British coal mining industry. No information could be extracted from Major Lloyd George about the contents of this report, but it must have been unfavourable. Major Lloyd George immediately appointed the Reid Committee, and the first time in the history of coal mining, competent mining engineers, with an expert knowledge of the investigations they had to make, were appointed to investigate and report to the Minister on the state of the industry. The report was issued in March 1945 - the first actual report by experts. (Great credit is due to Major Lloyd George for instituting this enquiry.) The report confirmed the antiquated methods used in many of the mines and the urgent need for improvements, and concluded with the words "There is no time to be lost".

It was estimated that the cost of modernising the industry might be about £310 million.

Much to be Done

A vast amount of work requires to be done, not only the application of mechanization, but underground transport, ventilation and lighting, the electrification of existing steam winders, etc, etc.

There are at present about 15,000 miles of underground roadways in British mines. Sir Charles Reid has estimated that it may take about 20 years to modernise the coal industry, and the reconstruction of underground roadways and their electrification will be the greatest task of all. Electric locomotives for mine haulage are certainly more suitable than Diesel locomotives which are heavier for the same power and pollute the air with exhaust gases.

Electrification of existing steam winders would effect a substantial annual saving in the operating costs of the nation's coal industry and at the same time contribute greatly to the much desired conservation of "workable" coal reserves, which are Britain's greatest asset. Let us remember, however, that it is a wasting asset, which is irreplaceable.

WHEATLEY HILL

SHOWS SUCCESSES - Well-known East Durham breeder of prize rabbits, Mr George Ford, Wingate Lane, Wheatley Hill, added to his long list of successes last week-end when, at Croydon Fanciers' Society open show, he won two firsts and a challenge certificate and special for the best Dutch in the show.

MR W FOSTER – Funeral took place at Wheatley Hill cemetery on Saturday 18, of a familiar figure in the district, Mr William Foster (44), 39 Quetlaw Road, Wheatley Hill, who died nearly 12 years after breaking his spine when caught by a fall of stone at Thornley Colliery, where he was employed as a filler. Since the accident, on 1st August 1935, Mr Foster had only been able to get about in an invalid chair but had remained remarkably cheerful and had a wide circle of friends in and around Wheatley Hill. He was an affiliated member of Wheatley Hill Workmen's Club and previously a member of Cassop Workmen's Club. Surviving him are his wife, two sons and two step-sons. Funeral service was conducted in All Saints' Church, Wheatley Hill, by Rev P T Casey (vicar). At the inquest at Thornley on Friday, medical evidence showed that death was due to cerebral haemorrhage and increased blood pressure caused as a direct result of a fracture of the spine received in an accident at Thornley Colliery and a verdict in accordance with this evidence was returned.

WILL OPEN 75th HOUSE –
EASINGTON CHAIRMAN'S CEREMONY

Coun T Laing, Hutton Henry, chairman of Easington Rural District Council, is to open the 75th permanent house erected under the Council's direct labour scheme, on the Wheatley Hill site, tomorrow. Members of the Council have been asked to attend, and the house, which has been furnished by a local firm, will be open for inspection. It is designed to be either a three bedroomed parlour or four bedroomed house as desired, the fourth bedroom being on he ground floor. The most up to date amenities are included, with convector air heating from the back-to-back range providing warm air supply to two bedrooms on the first floor, a calorifier worked from the back boiler to the range providing all domestic hot water, fitted cupboards to the kitchen giving ample storage accommodation, pram space conveniently situated in the hall, built in wardrobes in two bedrooms and built in wireless aerial and earth.

Novel arrangement is that rainwater falling on the roofs is collected in a storage tank built into outbuildings and provides soft water on tap at the laundry sink unit.

24 January 1947

J D Johnson 1947

Durham County
Colliery Enginemen's, Boiler-Minders'
and Firemen's Association.

This Certificate of Competency

is given to any member who has been under instruction Twelve Months from the date of his Certificate of Authority, and found to be a competent Winding Engineman according to Rule 29, particulars of which are set forth on the back hereof.

This is to Certify

THAT Mr. JOHN DAWSON JOHNSON a financial

Member of the THORNLEY Branch of this Association, is now a competent Winding-Man, and has been legally instructed under our care and supervision.

Date JANUARY 30th 19 47.

ENGINEMEN BY WHOM TAUGHT:

John Richardson Thornley Colliery
John Lawson Thornley Colliery

Manager's or Engineer's Signature:

ASSOCIATION'S STAMP.

General Secretary.

THORNLEY PARISH AFFAIRS –
ROAD SAFETY IN SCHOOLS
Councillor Questions Education Committee

Producing pamphlets from the Royal Society for the Prevention of Accidents, Coun Mrs D Roper, at Thornley Parish Council meeting, said that Durham County Education Committee were reported as having refused to allow police instruction in schools. She moved that the County Education Committee be asked their reason for refusing police instruction, whether they had any intention of reconsidering that decision, and what steps they are now taking to ensure that children are taught road safety. This motion was carried.

The Time and Place

Mrs Roper added that she understood the County Committee did not object to children being taught road safety by police officers outside school. If that were so, she failed to see why they objected to teaching being given by police officers inside school. "The time for teaching anything is in youth and the place is school," said Mrs Roper. "Could anyone be more qualified to do this teaching than police officers?"

In reply to a question by Coun T Strong, who asked why so many houses were being completed at Wheatley Hill while none was being completed at Thornley, Coun J H C Scott, a member of the Easington Rural District Council, said the houses completed at Wheatley Hill had their foundations laid before the war. He added that before the war Thornley got more houses than Wheatley Hill.

BRAVED THE STORM

Several workmen from Blackhall employed on the building site at Wheatley Hill thought they would have to find shelter for the night on Tuesday when the buses ceased running. However, they set off to walk and managed to hitch-hike a ride home in a lorry – one of the few to brave the snowstorm which started in the early hours of the morning following a day of blustering winds and rain.

7 February 1947

MISFORTUNE BEFELL WILLIE CURRY, youngest of the three Curry boxing brothers, Wheatley Hill, when, in a recent fight at the Baths Hall, Darlington, be broke his nose. Willie, who is only 19 is to undergo an operation at Hartlepools Hospital today. His two bothers, Charlie (29) and Johnny (27), have made quite a name for themselves locally with the gloves. Their father, Mr William Curry, of 3 Fourth Street, Wheatley Hill, was also a well-known local boxer in his younger days, and has played a big part in training them to their present standard. The brothers also pay tribute to famous Paddy Gorman, who gave them their initial training and valuable hints which have stood them in good stead.

Charlie, a "regular" in the Army Physical Training Corps, who is stationed at Brancepeth as a sergeant PT instructor, had several big fights before joining up eight years ago. He fought Ronnie James, lightweight champion of Great Britain, but had to retire in the ninth round. Another opponent was Tom Smith, Northern featherweight champion, who beat him on points. During the course of their Army career, Charlie and Smith, by a coincidence, were stationed on the same camp for about three years and boxed many exhibition matches in various parts of the North, as a result of which a considerable sum of money was raised for war charities. Recently Charlie has been acting as a sparring partner for Smith, who is training for the British featherweight title.

Johnny, who is employed as a bricklayer, last week made a comeback after two years, with a points victory over Nipper Price at the Baths Hall, Darlington. Working away from home in the South interfered with his training, but now he is back into harness again and hopes to do big things. He has another fight fixed up for Monday at Darlington. In his eight professional fights to date, Willie, who is gradually coming into the limelight, has only been beaten once. Six of his seven victories were knock-outs. He is employed as a datal hand at Thornley colliery.

The two elder brothers, with their father, are running a successful gymnasium for young boxers in the Soldiers' and Sailors' Cub at Wheatley Hill. Inaugurate four months ago by Mr Curry, the boxers' club now has a membership of 30. Ages of the young boxers range from 13 to 20, and instruction is given every night in the week except Sundays, when the gymnasium is open in the afternoon only. Membership fee is a shilling a week. One of the young trainees, Dessie Bell, of Ludworth, is on the same boxing programme as Johnny Curry at Darlington on Monday. "Enthusiasm is high," Charlie told me, "and I can see the makings of some good boxers among our present members".

21 February 1947

MINERS' MEMORIAL IN CATHEDRAL
"Those Who Work in Darkness and Danger"

One of the worst blizzards for half a century was raging when, in the eight-centuries-old Cathedral Church at Durham on Saturday, the Bishop of Durham (Dr Alwyn Williams) was dedicating to the memory of Durham miners a memorial which bears the inscription: "Remember before God the Durham miners who have given their lives in the pits of this county, and those who work in darkness and danger in those pits today." Significantly enough the memorial consists largely of a magnificent fireplace which was for many years a treasured object at Ramside Hall, and was a gift to the Cathedral by the Pemberton family.

COLLIERY BANDSMEN PLAY "COMRADES IN ARMS" – Attending the service were representatives of the National Coal Board, ex-coal-owners, including Sir Richard Pease and Mr Austin Kirkup, sen, Fence Houses; representatives of Durham mineworkers Mr E Moore, president Durham Branch, NUM; Mr W S Hall, Ald J W Foster, Mr W Chesterton, Ald J Gilliland, Mr C Thompson, Mr Gibson French, Mr F Fakes, Mr George Peart and Mr Jack Adair. There were also the Mayor (Coun F Foster) and other members of the Corporation, and Professor J F Duff, representing the University of Durham. Many miners and their families were in the congregation despite the wintry weather and the drifting snow which cut off some of the colliery districts from the city.

Originally the service was announced to take place at three o'clock, but the fuel crisis caused it to be put back half an hour, by which time it would be possible to light the interior. It was significant that at such a time the vast congregation should be concerned in the dedication of a memorial which, for generations, had been a fireplace in an ancestral home on the outskirts of the city.

Spanish Mahogany

It has been placed near to the south-west wall, a conspicuous object in skillfully carved black Spanish mahogany, with an ornate mantel in the form of laurel wreath. The whole thing has been assembled by the craftsmen of the Dean and Chapter under the direction of Mr Walter Hollis, who made the base, inserted the centre panel upon which there is a representation in gilt of a Davy lamp, and himself inscribed the lettering. The memorial will be the shrine for Durham mineworkers for generations to come.

The idea of it came from a letter sent anonymously to the Dean by one who signed himself "Durham Geordie," and was readily adopted by the Dean and Chapter. Thus miners of Durham are given an honoured place in the great Mother Church.

Beneath the dedicatory sentence appear the words "He breakth open the shaft away from where men sojourn: they are forgotten by the foot that passeth by."

Banners in the Cathedral

Bandsmen from Craghead, Boldon, Horden, Harton, Crookhall, Bearpark and Blackhall were to be seen just before the service ploughing their way through the snow from buses, carrying their banners and instruments into the Cathedral to play their part in the service. The banners were placed near the west wall, the one from Bearpark bearing a life-like portrait of Alderman William Kingston; that from Boldon proclaiming, "Each for all and all for each"; Horden, with its picture of a college and lads from the colliery villages walking towards it, and, underneath, "As it should be"; Craghead, "Comrades in every clime"; and Blackhall banner with the portraits of A J Cook, Peter Lee and Keir Hardie.

The bandsmen occupied seats round and about the font at the west end of the Cathedral, and, conducted by Mr Dennis Scoins, Horden, they gave an impressive rendering of "Comrades in Arms," and then, under the direction of Mr Conrad W Eden, organist of the Cathedral, played the processional hymn, "O God our help in ages past". The Bishop, the Dean and clergy moved to the west end of the great church, where Dr Williams unveiled and dedicated the memorial. This ceremony completed, they returned to the choir, singing "Great Master Worker of us all".

Days of Strain

"It is fitting," said the Bishop in his sermon, "that these men of Durham should be lastingly remembered in our cathedral, a cathedral whose grim yet glorious majesty is a fitting symbol of the struggles, the sacrifices and aspirations of all sorts, and conditions of men. Today we are thinking of the men of one great industry."

Speaking of the contrasts that could be seen within our country, Dr Williams said that in Durham County they talked of the drabness of modern life, of drab villages and drab streets – and indeed, they are often very drab – but the thoughts in their minds today took them far below the surface.

"The occasion of this commemoration is in more ways than one significant. We are passing through days of strain and peril which will not pass away with the melting of the snow or with the coming of the spring. That peril is bringing home to multitudes of people the long-known but often forgotten truth that upon this great industry, whose martyrs and servants we have in mind today, there rests the strength and the material hope of our nation, and not of our nation alone.

Solid Ground for Hope

"Then, again, at this very time, the industry is entering upon a new stage in its long history. Deeper than all differences and controversies over controls, management and organisation there lies the consciousness to us all that the future depends on the quality of the effort of mind, body and spirit which can be found to sustain a great responsibility. We may believe that the story of endurance, of readiness to face danger, and of frequent heroism which have been so large a part of our country's history gives solid ground for hope.

"'The mining community has produced a great race of men.' These are words of the writers of the Reid Report of two years ago. They used words the truth of which is borne out by our own knowledge. Courage and constancy are, after all, the foundation of all the other virtues. They have been found here among our own people in full measure, both in war and in peace. The Chapel of The Faithful Durhams reminds us of the character shown in the mine as well as on the battlefield. We pay our tribute today to that great army, and take strength from the remembrance of past victories and of much endurance, praying that for the future God will grant new gifts of the same courage and a new gift of the vision of our country's need without which the people perish."

Another hymn, "Praise my soul," and a memorable service was at an end.

28 February 1947

VITAL NEED IS PRODUCTION – SAYS MR SAM WATSON

Mr Sam Watson, leader of the Durham miners, does not leave anything to the imagination in his comments on the subject of the White Paper. "Produce – or accept the consequence" is his summing-up of the implications the Paper contains.

16

The Naked Truth

Mr Watson writes: "The White Paper issued by the Labour Government, and presented to Parliament in February, is one of the most important surveys of our economic position ever published. It ought to be read and studied by every man and woman who has the interest of the country at heart and believes in the necessity for sound economic planning on the basis of Public Ownership of Essential Industries and Transport, with the preservation of the democratic liberties of the people.

"It is the duty of any democratic Government," states the Prime Minister in the Preface to the White Paper, "to take the people frankly into its confidence however difficult the position of the country may be." The Government has not shirked its responsibility, and we ignore at our peril the blunt, out-spoken warning contained in the White Paper. Either we increase production in every sphere of our economic life, or we accept the inevitable lowering of our standard of living and social services. Unless the present level of productivity is increased, our future remains insecure and uncertain, with the possibility of recurring crises every time production is slowed down by wintry weather conditions.

The long term problem to increase production is capable of solution much easier than the short term policy, but is, nevertheless, linked up with our immediate production problems.

Let us improve the working conditions in industry; let us pay the highest economic wage possible; but let us, in the name of common honesty and individual responsibility, preach the doctrine of **increased production**, for we cannot retain the improvements in conditions and wages unless we increase production to the limit. How else can we pay for the imports we need? We import more than half of our food – that is to say every other meal we eat has to be paid for by an exchange in goods and services produced in Britain. Nearly all the basic raw material we need in our industries for manufacturing the finished article for home and export markets come from abroad.

Think of some of the imports we need: meat, food, butter, eggs, bacon, hides, cotton, tea, coffee, fruit, timber, iron ore and many more. We do not get these for nothing. We have to pay for them and we cannot pay for them in "tons" of pound notes, but only in tons of coal, other goods and services.

THORNLEY VICAR'S OFFER TO CELEBRATE
TARGET BEATING

Thornley Colliery, the first colliery to ship coals at Hartlepool docks 112 years ago, succeeded last week in beating its Shinwell target of 7,000 tons, with 75 tons to spare.

To mark his pleasure and appreciation of this success, the Vicar of Thornley, the Rev W A Lathaen, ex-POW padre, offered the colliery management the Union Jack he had used at the burial of 13 British prisoners of war who had died at the camp in Poland where Mr Lathaen officiated in captivity. This historic flag came into the hands of Mr Lathaen by way of the Red Cross. As the war was closing, and the camp was reached by the Russians, the Vicar, his colleagues and fellow prisoners, had to pack their few belongings and get away quickly. In what "he stood up in," and with a very few personal belongings, including his communion vessels and the flag, Mr Lathaen got safely home after a perilous journey.

The generous offer of the flag was accepted by Mr A Welsh, the colliery manager, with the result that the flag waved along-side the NCB flag over the pit pulleys during the week-end.

For his services as a padre in the POW camp, the Vicar was awarded the British Empire Medal.

In spite of the bad weather the output at Thornley Colliery had been near the target figure during previous weeks of the storm period, the men who helped in this success, including those who worked on the difficult job of clearing the railway lines after repeated drifting up, were thanked by notices displayed on the colliery premises.

VOTE OF CONFIDENCE – Members of Thornley Labour Party, at their annual meeting, passed a vote of confidence in Mr Shinwell, the Minister of Fuel and Power, and Member of Parliament for the Seaham Division. The motion moved by Mr T Stoker (chairman), said the Thornley Labour Party was prepared to give him all possible support. Officers elected: Chairman, Mr T Stoker; secretary, Mr W F Whitehead; treasurer, Mr W Brereton; delegate, Mrs I Johnson.

MRS A E PARK – Funeral of Mrs Ann Elizabeth Park (93), Thornley's oldest resident, took place on Thursday, interment being at Ludworth Road burial ground following service in St Godric's Church. Mrs Park, one time landlady of the Dun Cow Inn, had lived for many years with her late daughter, Mrs Riley, and afterwards with another daughter, Mrs McCoy. Mrs Park remembered the famous Thornley "Putt Pay", when a large body of police had to be called in to prevent a feared riot when the colliery owners, becoming bankrupt, were unable to pay the workmen's wages. Ultimately the wages were paid, and the story goes that in at least one case the money was sent to a former workman who had emigrated to America.

7 March 1947

"NEW WORLD FOR MINERS" – SAYS MR R JOHNSON, WHEATLEY HILL "People talk of days long past as the 'good old days', but I call them 'damn bad old days'." So declared Mr Richard Johnson, 21 Peter Lee Cottages, Wheatley Hill, who celebrated his golden wedding with his wife, who is 71, same age as himself. A retired veteran of the mines, Mr Johnson, in an interview, said conditions had vastly improved for the miner compared with his early days, and he "wouldn't mind starting all over again". "It is a new world for the miner compared with conditions at the end of the Great War", he added.

Married at St John's Church, Meadowfield, by the late Rev J J Lawson, on 6 March 1897, Mr and Mrs Johnson, who both enjoy good health, have lived at Wheatley Hill for 30 years. Born at Shincliffe Village, Mr Johnson started work in the brickyards at the age of 13 but three years later stared his mining career at Bowden Close. "I was just in the pit three weeks when I started putting", he said. "I used to work ten hours a day, and later, when I was coal-hewing, I thought I was doing very well if I got 50s for 12 shifts. Shortly after I was married I was getting 30s for ten shifts."

Beer 2½d a quart

Though he complained of miners' wages and conditions in his younger days, Mr Johnson said money certainly meant a great deal more than it did at the present day. "It was surprising what ten shillings could buy in those days," he went on, "but nowadays it is scarcely worth having in your pocket. You could get a quart can running over with beer for twopence half-penny, and if you paid twopence for half an ounce of tobacco when it was 3½d an ounce you were generally given a box of matches with it."

After employment at Bowden Close, Mr Johnson worked at Craghead, Brandon, Sunnybrow and Shotton collieries before going to

Wheatley Hill colliery in 1916. He retired on shift work nearly two years ago. He is a member of Wheatley Hill Workmen's Club.

Does her housework

A native of North Wales, Mrs Johnson came to Durham County as a young girl. She does all her own housework, and most of her spare time is spent making mats. "I am busy making my fourth mat this year," she said. The couple have living a son and daughter and one grandchild. The daughter (Mrs Lucy Strother, Amble) celebrates her silver wedding next year. The won (William) is a driller at Wheatley Hill colliery. Two of Mrs Johnson's younger brothers live abroad – Mr George Jones at Buenos Aires and Mr Sam Jones in Vancouver. They may be visiting England this year.

WHEATLEY HILL COLLIERY STRIKE – OF BRIEF DURATION

After a lightning strike at Wheatley Hill colliery on Monday morning, miners decided at a mass meeting later in the day to return to work immediately in the night-shift, pending the miners' lodge officials and representatives of the Durham area of the National Union of Mineworkers meeting the colliery management and settling all outstanding grievances within a few days.

Putters in the main coal seam, No 2 Pit, complained of low wages and bad working conditions and refused to go in-bye. The rest of the miners, numbering about 1,100 men and boys, came out in sympathy. Despite appeals from the management and DMA representatives the decision remained unaltered. Failing to get satisfaction they refused to start work. The colliery's target is 6,000 tons.

The alleged grievance of the putters concerning the wages will be investigated by representatives of the Northern Divisional Coal Board and the Durham area of the National Union of Mineworkers on Monday.

HOUSEWIVES REBELLIOUS – WHEATLEY HILL'S NEW HOUSES
No electricity provided

Accustomed as they have been to no electricity in their houses since they became first tenants several months ago, people living in the latest houses and bungalows to be built by Easington RDC at Wheatley Hill, have found no additional hardship in the recent cut in the domestic use of electricity enforced by the Government.

The houses first began to be occupied four months ago and the opening of the 75th post-war house was marked by a speech-making ceremony in January. Though the houses are modern in every detail, electricity has not yet been laid on with the result that householders are becoming more and more discontented as the days go by and lighting facilities are still unavailable.

When I visited the new housing estate this week (writes our reporter) all the housewives I interviewed were in a rebellious mood. All complained of the hardship and inconvenience created by the lack of electrical power, and declared emphatically it was "high time" something was done in the matter. Not only had they to put up with oil lamps and candles – when they could get them – for lighting their homes, but they were also unable to use any of their electrical appliances. Biggest grouse among some of the women was that they had no place to boil their clothes on washing-day.

"Biggest Bug-Bear"

Washing-day is my biggest bug-bear," said Mrs Ralph Woodward, 44 Liddell Terrace, who has lived in her new house for the past three months. "It's not much use having a beautiful electric boiler in the house if you are unable to use it. We are all getting fed-up being without lights, and it is the main topic of conversation here – When are we going to get our electricity? It costs a small fortune to keep oil lamps burning – the lamp glasses are always cracking and have to be renewed, and it is sometimes a difficult job to get sufficient oil for our needs. It seems to me that by the time they do get the lights switched on it is going to be in the middle of summer when we won't need them so much!"

Mrs Woodward said that the recent spell of severe weather had taxed the patience of them all. "For quite a while," she added, "we were snowbound and unable to get out for any lamp oil; I had to rely, on candles. It is a big strain on the eyes, and after I have had a night at mat-making, either by oil-lamp or candle I feel a wreck the next morning through sore eyes and headaches. What with the blackout, the storm, and no lights during recent weeks, I have been glad either to go to bed early or to leave the dismal oil lamp and go out to the pictures."

One of the tenants in the first houses to be opened four months ago, Mrs Edward Ord, 40 Liddell Terrace, told me she had no complaints to make about the house itself, but the lack of electricity had certainly been a great handicap. "We have put up with these conditions a long time now," she said, "and after being used to electricity for almost everything in the house, including the wireless and electric iron, we seem lost without it. Luckily, up to now, I haven't been without oil or candles!"

Mrs Woodward with
Colin & Connie, Liddell Terrace

Twenty-Three in One House

Perhaps the greatest sufferer from the lack of electrical power is Mrs John Williams, 13 Stoker Terrace, who has one of the biggest families I have ever come across. Living with herself and her husband are seven sons and seven daughters, two sons-in-law, two daughters-in-law and three grandchildren, a grand total of 23! "With so many workers in the house and young children attending school," she told me, "there is a constant coming and going all day long. Often some of the men folk have had to have a bath and a meal in the dark when they have come home at the end of their day's work. We need a light from five o'clock in the morning, when the first worker goes out, until two o'clock the next morning when the last one comes in."

Mrs Williams added that she had only one oil-lamp and this had to be carried from room to room as required. "It will be a great day when the power is switched on," she said, "for we are tired to death of burning candles. Sometimes, when we have been without both oil and candles, we have just had to rely on matches when we can get the matches! Match ends are lying about the house from top to bottom, and it is a good part of our day's work sweeping them up every morning. A lot of the family, after they have had their tea, are glad to get outside again to go to the pictures, and for my own part I am ready to go to bed when the candles are brought out." Mrs Williams, who has lived in Wheatley Hill for four years, has occupied her new home for the past month.

"Just a Song at Twilight"

The old people's point of view was simply put by 77 year old George Cowell, widower, 6 Ryan Terrace, when he said, "The plain fact is it is far too dangerous for old men and women to have to grope their way around in the dark or with a little oil lamp in their hand."

Mr Cowell, a man with over 60 years' service in the mines, who lives by himself, his wife having died ten years ago, moved into his new bungalow in January. He has a small lamp but the light is too poor for him to read at night. "I do all my reading in the day-time," he said, "for it's useless trying to read by means of a lamp, I just content myself sitting around the fireside at night.

"It will be a grand thing when we have electricity and there will certainly be less danger of the house being set on fire by a lamp burning too high."

Mr Cowell's neighbour, Mrs Albert Mather, who has occupied her bungalow at 7 Ryan Terrace, for nine weeks, said she and her husband, who is employed at Easington colliery, had had to sit without a light in the house many a night. "It is no easy task getting oil and candles these days," she said, "and generally when the oil comes in the shop there is quite a queue for it. Often, to save oil for my husband going out to work at night, we have sat in the dark, and after he has gone out I like to go straight off to bed for there's no pleasure sitting without either light or wireless."

And so, in similar strain, story after story was related by housewives who said the recent severe weather had not improved matters – or their tempers. All were unanimous in their praise of the houses themselves but, as one put it, "We won't feel really settled down in our new homes until we can press a switch and find the power really there."

Reason for the Delay

Mr William Stoker, clerk to Wingate Parish Council, which controls most of the lighting in the area, spoke to me about the lighting in the newest council houses at Wheatley Hill. "The lighting arrangements," he said, "are in the hands of Easington Rural Council who propose having an underground cable for the purpose of domestic and street lighting. It was only after prolonged negotiations and arguments with the rural authority that the parish council finally agreed to their method of installing the electricity.

"Had we had our own way in the first place, the electricity would have been laid on before the people moved in, for it was simply a matter of transferring the lighting overhead from existing poles on the same estate. The difficulty at present, of course, is getting the necessary underground cables, that is where the hold up lies."

14 March 1947

EASINGTON RURAL COUNCIL – NEW TOWN "PETERLEE"

In honour of the later Mr Peter Lee, who was described by Mr G Henderson (chairman), as a strong dominant personality who spent his life in the service of his fellows, the Council decided to name the new town, which they propose to build between Horden and Shotton, Peterlee.

Mr Lee was for many years a member of Easington Rural Council and occupied the chair. He was later a member and chairman of Durham County Council and a headquarters agent of Durham Miners' Association. The town which, if approved by the Government, will bear his name, will cover 1,500 acres, provide accommodation for 32,500 people and cost nearly £14,000,000.

The town was named at the suggestion of Mr C W Clarke (engineer and surveyor) who said he wished to include it in the printed copies of the development plans for the area.

It was also agreed that the three neighbourhood units in the new town be named Howletch, Oakerside and Yoden.

Praise For The Council

In a report of a conference on the proposed new town, submitted by Mr J W Gray (Clerk), Mr Max Tetlow, Regional Controller of the Ministry of Town and Country Planning, says that the proposal was one which to some extent surprised him, but very much pleased him. "Normally, one finds that it is the Government officials in an area who are pressing the elected representatives to concentrate development. You will realise then with what great pleasure I find the largest rural district in England coming forward and saying 'We want a new town'."

The Council's idea was to build the town in 15 to 20 years, but his idea was to do it in a much quicker time. The main factors controlling the speed of development were labour and materials. "You are in a happy position in that you have a direct labour organisation. You have the labour which you can put on to this new town, and that will give you a fine start. It would have a big effect upon the speed of building the new town."

28 March 1947

73, AND STILL WORKS IN MINES –
THORNLEY MAN'S RECORD

Mr Joseph Luke, 53, High Street, Thornley, now nearly 73 years old, very fit, and still working underground at Thornley Colliery, has completed 60 years as a miner, all his working life having been spent underground. Born at Cassop, he started work at the neighbouring East Hetton (Kelloe) Colliery before he had reached his 13th birthday. This wage as a trapper was 10½d a day and his shift 10 hours. As a putter and filler he earned £2 a fortnight, which was then considered a good wage. His father was killed at Kelloe Colliery in June 1898, leaving six sons and five daughters. The loss of their father induced the family to move to Thornley in September 1898. He takes a good deal of interest in trade union and public affairs.

EASINGTON RURAL DISTRICT COUNCIL

Tenders for Dance Bands, Brass Bands or Military Bands and Choirs, at Crimdon Park.

(1) Tenders are invited from Dance Bands (8-10 players) to perform at Public Dances at Pleasureland Dance Hall, Crimdon Park, on Wednesday and Saturday evenings, commencing 24 May 1947, for Summer Season 1947.

(2) Tenders are invited from Brass Bands or Military Bands and Choirs to give concerts on Sunday afternoons and evenings at Crimdon Park during the Summer Season 1947.

The Council do not bind themselves to accept the lowest or any tender.

Offers, giving full details and endorsed "Bands" should be addressed to the undersigned to be received not later than Monday 28 April 1947.

Tenders for Trading Rights and Amusements at Crimdon Park Seaside Resort.

Tenders are invited for permission to exercise the following rights at Crimdon Park during Season 1947:

(1) Ply Motor and Rowing Boats for hire.

(2) Ply Beach Donkies and Ponies.

(3) Take Beach Photographs.

(4) Sketch Silhouettes.

(5) Sell Ice Cream.

(6) Provide Children's Roundabouts and Swings.

(7) Provide Ventriloquial and Punch and Judy Entertainment.

The Council do not bind themselves to accept the highest or any tender. Offers, giving full details and endorsed "Trading Rights," should be addressed to the undersigned to be received not later than Monday 28 April 1947.

OFFICIALS' GROUSE – Dissatisfied because the £1 a day bonus paid to miners on Good Friday and Easter Monday was not applicable to colliery officials, the 40 odd officials at Wheatley Hill Colliery this week notified the Ministry of Labour that they were handing in the statutory 21 days' notice to cease their employment with the National Coal Board. If that matter is not settled by the end of that period a further 14 days' notice will be given to cease work. It was at Wheatley Hill Colliery that miners staged a lightning day's strike a month ago in sympathy with the putters who were demanding better wages and conditions.

11 April 1947

DARK NIGHT – Wheatley Hill was plunged into darkness on Tuesday night, and householders made a quick hunt for candles and oil lamps when the electricity supply was cut off as a result of the storm. Output was seriously affected at Wheatley Hill colliery because of the breakdown in electrical power, and most of the miners who went to work in the night shift at 4.20 pm were compelled to return home a few hours later. Work in ten o'clock shift was also affected, but by 2.30 am on Wednesday electricity supplies were restored and the fore shift was able to work as usual.

18 April 1947

WHEATLEY HILL CHILD KILLED – SHOCK FOR PARENTS

Only a short while after he had been seen by his father, who was on his way to the mass meeting of Thornley Miners' Lodge, where the miners were to consider the strike situation, a two-year old Wheatley Hill child, Richard Purvis, fourth son of Mr and Mrs Matthew Purvis, 7 Third Street, was knocked down by a bus on the Wheatley Hill-Thornley road on Wednesday morning and received severe injuries from which he died soon afterwards. The child, who would have been three in September, was one of a family of five sons and one daughter.

Mr Purvis, who is employed as a coal cutter at Thornley colliery, told our reporter that he saw his son walking homewards on the footpath while he was walking in the opposite direction on his way to Thornley Club Hall. "I did not attract his attention," said Mr Purvis, "for he would have wanted to go with me and, of course, I couldn't take him to the meeting." Soon after he had reached Thornley Mr Purvis was informed of the tragedy and rushed home.

Mrs Purvis said that her little boy had gone out to play with two others, John Waller and Robert Lincoln. They had been warned not to go on the road, but a favourite playing spot was a heap of sand near the Catholic School. "Richard was picked up by a neighbour, Mr Thomas Hutchinson, and carried home," she said, "but he was unconscious and died before the arrival of the ambulance which had been summoned."

WHEATLEY HILL FIRE –
PROMPT ACTION BY FIRE BRIGADE

Only the prompt action of a passer-by and Wheatley Hill NFS, under J Poulson, prevented what might have been a disastrous fire at the home of Dr W G MacLean, Front Street, Wheatley Hill, on Saturday night. When flames were seen pouring from the wooden eaves of the doctor's house, which faces the main road, a young man, John Million, who was near at hand, dashed up a ladder with a hosepipe and helped to fight the flames until the arrival of Wheatley Hill NFS, some of whose members were summoned by a message flashed on the screen of the local cinema.

Horden NFS were also summoned, but the fire had been put out by the time they arrived. As a precautionary measure, Mrs MacLean, the doctor's wife, who was alone in he house with her three children, got her family out of bed. "Had it not been for the fire brigade's quick arrival on the scene," she told our reporter, "the house would most probably have been burned to the ground." Mrs MacLean added that once before the eaves had caught fire, but the cause of the outbreak was a mystery.

Apart from the burned eaves, the only damage was that done by water to the furnishings of one of the bedrooms.

25 April 1947

WHEATLEY HILL

ON TARGET – Some weeks ago, when Wheatley Hill Colliery had a lightning strike, it was stated that the Northern Divisional Coal Board was anxious about output at the colliery The output was being hindered by "rolls" and "hitches," and this has continued for about three months. Last week, however, the colliery hit its target of 6,000 with 200 tons to spare. Moreover, a colliery official said they were hoping that when the five-day week comes into operation they will still equal their target.

DRAMA GROUP – Excellent talent was displayed by members of Wheatley Hill Drama Group when they presented Noel Coward's "This Happy Breed," in the Welfare Hall, Wheatley Hill, on Wednesday and again last night (Thursday). Producer was Mrs Vera Fairclough, Shotton, and parts were taken by: Mesdames Thackerley, R Woodward, Kenny and Pryor, Misses G Ranson, E Carter and M Robinson, and Messrs F Bowes, G Marshall, K Dowson, T Kelly and J Tunney. Mr M Fleming (Thornley) was in charge of the lighting effects, and secretarial duties were by Mrs Wharrier.

LEGION BIRTHDAY – About 100 members were entertained to supper at the 17th birthday party of Wheatley Hill women's section of the British Legion, when Mrs M Forster, who presided, wished the Legion every success. Included in an entertainment, organised by Miss E Richardson, was a comedy sketch, "Agatha's Spirit," played by Mrs R Maughan, Mrs D Jackson, Mrs M E Richardson and Miss E Richardson. Winner of the "quiz" competition was Mrs R Maughan, and other prize-winners were: Mrs L Cowey (musical parcel), Mrs E Stainsby and Mrs L Cowey (musical arms), Mrs H Carter (lucky chair) and Mrs Sunley and Mrs I Carter. Music was by Mr T Richardson and his accordion. Four new members were enrolled.

CONSTITUTIONAL CLUB – Mr Wm Fenwick presided at last annual meeting of his 25 years' service as chairman of the Wheatley Hill Constitutional Club. After the ordinary meeting he was presented with a wallet and a cheque for £25, as a mark of appreciation by the members for his devoted service. Another presentation was that to Mr and Mrs George Gradon, who have been steward and stewardess for 26 years. Mr Gradon received a gold hunter watch and Mrs Gradon a chiming clock. They also are retiring, and Mr J A Simpson, president of the club, said the members were deeply grateful to the three recipients for their faithful service. New chairman is Mr A S Johnson, Mr G Poulson is treasurer and Mr R Woodward was unopposed as secretary. Entertainment was given by Mr John Quinn's Party, who are well-known in the North-East. Refreshments were handed round and evening's entertainment was concluded with the singing of "Auld Lang Syne". Arrangements were made by Mr R Woodward (secretary) and Mr W Cowie, a member of the committee. Committee elected: Messrs W Cowie, R Crosby, R Graham, G Carter, W O Greenwell, J Fishwick, W Newby, S Scott, J Wrightson and A Nicholson.

EMBASSY CLUB EFFORT – First annual whist drive and dance organised by the newly-formed Wheatley Hill and District Embassy Maids' and Bachelors' Club, in the Embassy Ballroom, Wheatley Hill, on Tuesday were a success. Novel attraction was the search for "Mr Sunshine" and "Miss Sunshine," and prizes were awarded to Miss M Jordan, Ludworth, who identified Mr Barnett (Thornley) as "Mr Sunshine, and Mr George Hornsby (Shotton), who identified Miss Wilson (Wheatley Hill) as "Miss Sunshine," Messrs G Carr and Longstaffe (Shotton) were MCs for the whist, and stewards for the dance were Messrs L Hetherington and J Durkin. Mr E Ward presented prizes to the following whist winners: Miss E Dixon (Wheatley Hill), Miss J Storey (Blackhall), Mr T Hall and Mr K Kendall (Wheatley Hill) and Mr T Alderson (Thornley). Spot dance prizes were won by Mr T Cowley and Miss A Pearce (Shotton), Miss M Pattern (South Hetton), Miss N Miller (Blackhall), Mr L Dyer (Hartlepool), Miss M Jordan (Ludworth) and Mr L Dean (Wheatley Hill). Supper was served, and music for dancing was by Reg Bushby and his full broadcasting band. Arrangements were made by Mr J Tunney (chairman), Mr J A Burnside (secretary) and Miss M Cook (treasurer), supported by a committee.

2 May 1947
WINGATE AND WHEATLEY HILL COLLIERIES - WINDERS' STRIKE

Idle since the week-end through the Durham Winders' Union strike, production was partly resumed at Wingate and Wheatley Hill collieries in the ten o'clock shift on Wednesday night. No 1 Pit at Wheatley Hill colliery restarted with two workmen, both with winding experience, manning the cages. This pit employs 600 of the colliery's 1,100 men and boys. "These men are keen to get back to work," Mr E Cain, secretary of Wheatley Hill Miners' Lodge, told our reporter, "for they feel they have been badly let down by the strikers."

Wingate colliery resumed work in the Busty seam of the Lady Pit. This seam absorbs more than three-quarters of the colliery's 900 men and boys. The colliery's weekly target of 4,300 tons was passed in the five working days last week by a margin of six tons and the miners had hoped to repeat this achievement this week. At a special meeting of Wingate Miners' Lodge on Tuesday, Coun P McMann presiding, members unanimously resolved to support any move to retain the services of the trainee winders permanently if they so desired, to replace the six strikers.

9 May 1947

POSITION OF MECHANICS –
DISCUSSION AT WHEATLEY HILL

General agreement with the hours now being worked by the mechanics under the new five-day week was expressed at a meeting of the Durham Colliery Mechanics' Federation in Wheatley Hill Welfare Hall on Sunday. Seventeen of the 93 mechanics' lodges in the county were represented, and a report of the previous day's Council meeting at Durham was given by the Federation secretary (Mr E Longley, Boldon).

After particulars of the shifts now being worked at their collieries had been given by the delegates, the chairman (Mr E York, Ferryhill) said that the eight-hour shift appeared to be "pretty well" established in the afternoon and night shift. Dissatisfaction was expressed by the Thornley delegate, who stated that the mechanics at his colliery were having to work a night shift of 8½ hours, exclusive of meal-times. Because of this grievance they had tendered 21 days' notice to the Ministry of Labour that a dispute existed, but they were meeting the management again the next day to try and establish an eight-hour shift. At the moment they were working "under protest".

COALFIELD STRIKE ENDED

The strike of members of the Durham Winders' Union which caused serious disruption in the Durham Coalfields last week terminated at the week-end. The men accepted the recommendation of the Executive Committee of the National Union of Winding Enginemen to return to work and later acceded to the conditions of re-employment laid down by the Durham County Mining Federation Board.

These were that they should join the Durham Colliery Enginemen's, Boilerminders' and Firemen's Association, which is affiliated to the National Union of Mineworkers, and complete the training of substitute winders who took their places during the strike.

16 May 1947

CHURCH WORKER RETIRES

Mr John Spence, after 25 years of earnest service as superintendent of the Church Street Methodist Sunday School, Wheatley Hill, has retired from his work at Thornley Colliery and is moving to Nelson, Lancashire, where members of his family are residing. Tribute to his work was paid by the Sunday School teachers when they presented him with a wrist watch. Previous to his service at Wheatley Hill, he was superintendent at Thornley Waterloo Street Sunday School. He held several other church offices. Thornley people will remember that he and two others (Messrs W Scott and the late J Parker) were injured in a shot-firing accident several years ago. Since then Mr Spence had worked on the surface at Thornley Colliery.

MINERS' LODGE

At the annual meeting of Wheatley Hill Miners' Lodge, officers were returned unopposed, viz Secretary, E Cain, JP; card marker, R Sayers; treasurer, Coun T Taylorson; financial secretary, N Cook; compensation secretary, H Bradshaw; delegate, R Watson; auditors, G Bishop and G Buxton; crakeman, R W Hird; death fund committee, N Cook, J Frost and R Watson; check-weigh fund secretary, G Robinson; assistant weighman, T Knowles and F Burnside; band committee, M Cain, J Frost, R Watson and S Mitchison. The welfare, canteen and pit production committee were all re-elected pending the formation of a joint consultative committee. Nominations were received for other positions and a pit-head ballot will be held shortly.

30 May 1947

GALLANTRY REWARDED –
RESCUE FROM BURNING HOUSE RECALLED

Thornley miners presented Mr Edward Cooper, Thornlaw South, Thornley, with an illuminated certificate and a cheque in recognition of his gallantry in rescuing Mr Bertram Pattison from his burning house on the night of 21/22 October of last year. Mr John Williams, chairman of the lodge, making the presentation, said that Cooper's fellow workmen were proud of him and they wished him long life and happiness to enjoy the honour.

When Mr Pattison's home was destroyed, his daughter Doreen (18), a shop assistant, lost her life, Mr Pattison was critically ill with burns for many weeks, and his son was also in hospital. The people of Thornley and district, and enginemen in all parts of the county, joined in subscribing to a fund which assisted Mr and Mrs Pattison to set up another home provided for them by the Easington RD Council.

Presentation

A pleasing ceremony took place in Workmen's Club Hall, Thornley, on Saturday, when Mr J Williams, chairman of Miners' Lodge, presented a member, Mr E Cooper, with a suitably inscribed plaque and a cheque in recognition of "the coolness and courage he displayed on the occasion of a fire at Thornley".

MR L CARLIN – Death has taken place of Mr Lewis Carlin (78), a well-known Wheatley Hill man, who for many years was closely identified with social and artistic activities in the village. He taught at Wheatley Hill Boys' School for a long period and was musical director when the operatic society gave a number of successful performances. He was also actively associated with Wheatley Hill Cricket Club.

LODGE ELECTIONS – At the nomination meeting of Thornley Miners' Lodge, following were re-elected:- Financial secretary, Mr D Swallow; compensation secretary, Mr J Adamson. 20 were nominated for lodge committee with 12 wanted. Other nominations are:- Chairman, Mr J Williams and Mr F Walker; correspondence secretary, Mr W Dowding and Mr W Whitehead; treasurer, Mr J Cherry and Mr S Hargreaves; delegate, Mr J Webb and Mr R Hedley.

DROWNING TRAGEDY AT CRIMDON PARK

While on a visit to Crimdon Park, Blackhall, on Sunday, a Wheatley Hill miner, William Harward Batty (26), third son of Mrs Barnes and the late Mr H Batty, 4 Fifth Street, Wheatley Hill, was drowned. Batty left home shortly before noon on Sunday to meet a girl friend, Irene Donnison (18), Wall Street, Trimdon Colliery, who accompanied him to the lido. They reached the beach shortly after one o'clock and Batty went in bathing. About 3.45 pm he told his girl friend he was going in for another swim and that was the last she saw of him. Miss Donnison became increasingly concerned when some time later Batty still had not returned and told a woman he was missing. The beach life-guard (Mr William Richardson) was notified at 7.30 pm and began searching the beach in company with PC W Duggan (Blackhall). Shortly after nine o'clock Batty's body was discovered lying in shallow water near the edge of the beach.

Mr Richardson told our reporter that he heard a rumour shortly after four o'clock that someone was in trouble in the sea, but nobody knew anything definite and he himself had seen nothing. He went into the sea and swam around, but nobody had heard of anything amiss except one swimmer who said he, too, was searching, as he had heard the same rumour.

Rumour That Proved True

"Still not satisfied," said Mr Richardson, "I swam out to a boat some 300 yards distant, but the owner said he had neither seen nor heard anything. I could only surmise, therefore, that it had been a false rumour." The life-guard returned to the shore and still kept continuous patrol but though there were thousands of people on the beach, no incident was reported to him until 7.30 pm.

Mr Batty's mother told our reporter that her son was "not much of a swimmer". "If he could swim, it was only a little bit," she added. Batty's step-sister, Miss Rita Barnes, said she and her young man visited the lido the same afternoon and, knowing that Batty and his girl friend were going there also, they searched the sands in vain for them. They returned home, knowing nothing of the tragedy, though they had seen the life-guard swim out to the boat.

Batty was employed as a shifter at Thornley colliery and during the war he served in the Home Guard. He had lived at Wheatley Hill since 1935, moving there from Thornley.

6 June 1947
MANAGER'S APPOINTMENT
After nearly 40 years' service at Wheatley Hill colliery, first as under-manager and later as manager, Mr J A Simpson has left to take up a new appointment with the National Coal Board in No 5 Area of the Northern Division. He has been succeeded as manager at Wheatley Hill by Mr T H Dobson, Workington, Cumberland.

TREACHEROUS ROOF – FATALITY AT SHERBURN HILL
INQUEST ON THORNLEY HEWER

Comments on the alleged treacherous roof of the Busty seam at Sherburn Hill Colliery were made at a Sherburn Hill inquest on Friday on Thomas William Race (39), coal hewer, East View, East Street, Thornley. When giving evidence of identification, his father, William Race, unemployed coal hewer, stated that his son was an experienced man and knew his job.

John Simpson, pony putter, 23 Plantation Avenue, Littletown, stated that at 10.15 am on 21 May he began work in the Second West district of the Busty seam at Sherburn Hill Colliery. About two hours later he took an empty tub to the place where Race was working. That was the first time he had visited that place during the shift.

After backing his pony into the place, he shouted, "Are you full?" but got no reply. He then noticed that Race's tub was half empty. Witness looked under the canch and saw loose coals lying, and then discovered Race lying under a big stone. Witness immediately summoned the deputy. Race had been working alone, the nearest man being 30 yards or so away.

The deputy-overman, Samuel Satterley, 5 Heather View, Littletown, stated that he did not examine the place until after the accident. It had been inspected by his "marra," Samuel Davidson, between nine and ten that morning, and deputies were supposed to examine their district every five hours at least. On the previous day witness had observed that the timbering at the scene of the accident was well within the rules.

Previous Falls Question

He had no knowledge of any extensive previous falls at that particular place. Although he knew that the Busty seam was liable to faults, he was not aware of this fault.

He was informed of the accident by a putter boy. Witness found Race with his head and part of the shoulders buried under a huge stone. After 10 to 15 minutes Race was extricated, but was found to be dead. There was no timber under the stone, which had broken off quite close to the timber. The next pair of gears were about two feet from the stone.

Good Timberer

In reply to Mr W A Boam, HM Inspector of Mines, Satterley stated that Race was a good timberer and most experienced. Although it would help the work of the deputies if the timber rule was reduced, most men already set their timbering close together.

Coroner (Mr T V Devey) submitted a medical note, giving the cause of death as multiple fractures of the skull. The jury returned a verdict of "Accidental death". Expressions of sympathy to Race's relatives were made by the Coroner, Mr Boam, Police Inspector H Valks, Mr W L Lowerson (colliery manager), Mr Gibson French (representing Durham

Deputies' Association), and Messrs M H Lee and J Leonard (representing the workmen).

13 June 1947

LODGE BALLOT

As a result of a ballot the following officers have been elected by Wheatley Hill Miners' Lodge for the ensuing year: Chairman, Coun E Wharrier; average takers, Messrs J Bradley and M Cain; pit inspector, Mr R Watson; lodge committee, Messrs T Buxton, J Brandling, J W Burrell, J Hedley, T Knowles, H Peacock, J Richardson and H Trees; aged miners' committee, Messrs T Buxton, J W Burrell, J Frost, R Sayers, H Trees and R Watson; Checkweigh Fund committee, Messrs J Richardson, J Bradley and M Telford. Officials returned unopposed have already been reported.

CRICKET TEAMS

Wheatley Hill CCs first 11 to visit Boldon tomorrow in the Durham Coast League (Division 1) has been chosen as follows: G Hughes (captain), R H Poole, G Gribbens, H Simpson, R Robson, S Wilson, G Carr, W Smart, L S Lee, T Hall, N Herron; reserve G Kent. Second 11, at home to Boldon Seconds, is S Peaceful (captain), W Ferry, T Ayre, G Kent, J Davis, J Jordan, L Maddison, T Carr, T Kelly, E Snowden, J Nicholson; reserves, R Patterson, sen, R Patterson, jun. On Monday Wheatley Hill entertain Mainsforth in the first round of the Mathew Oswald Cup with the following team: G Hughes (captain), R H Poole, J W Moore, G Gribbens, H Simpson, R Robson, W Smart, S Wilson, E Smart, L S Lee, N Herron; reserve, T Hall. Wickets pitched 6.00 pm.

ROAD FATALITY – WHEATLEY HILL VICTIM

A verdict of "Accidental Death" was returned at Ferryhill on Wednesday, at an inquest on Peter Carter Redshaw, a labourer employed at the Ministry of Supply factory at Aycliffe, who was killed while jumping from a lorry at the Thinford Cross Roads on Thursday of last week.

Albert Redshaw, 17 Chapel Street, Thornley, said that his brother Peter, who lived at 2 Luke Terrace, Wheatley Hill, had been very active until he had an accident in the mines a few years ago when he broke his thigh.

George C Ramsey, 3 Martin Street, Thornley, told the coroner that after finishing work at Aycliffe on Thursday afternoon, he, together with about 12 other men, one of whom was Redshaw, got a lift from a lorry which had been unloading at the factory. The lorry stopped at the Thinford Cross Roads.

Dragged under Wheels

The driver, William Henry Watson, 24, Denton Avenue, Leamington-on-Tyne, said that he had been driving for about 12 years. After picking up some men at the factory he stopped at Ferryhill, and was asked to stop at Thinford Cross Roads.

As the vehicle was coming to a standstill the men jumped to the ground. Redshaw, however, seemed to be in some difficulty, and he was dragged underneath the wheels. Witness did not know that there was anything wrong until he came to a complete stop, about six yards farther on.

A medical report stated that Redshaw had died from cardiac failure due to a fracture of the skull.

The jury returned a verdict of accidental death, and exonerated the driver from all blame.

20 June 1947

WHEATLEY HILL

NSPCC – As a result of a house-to-house collection in Wheatley Hill, organised by the local committee with Miss Jackson as secretary, £20 was raised for the National Society for the Prevention of Cruelty to Children.

AID FOR BLIND – Sum of £15 15s was raised for Sunderland Royal Institution for the Blind as the result of a "Black Cat" flag day organised at the weekend by Wheatley Hill WI. Mrs R Woodward was organising secretary and collectors were Mesdames Snowden, Flower, Atkinson, Poole, Henderson, W Raffell, J Raffell, Tyson, Hutchinson, English, Thackeray, Armstrong and Woodward.

ANNIVERSARY – Sunday School anniversary services were concluded in Patton Street Methodist Church, Wheatley Hill, on Sunday, when Mr Joseph Scrafton presided afternoon and evening. In the afternoon a demonstration "The Light Ship" was given, and at night a programme of special singing and recitations. Mr J Mann was organist and Mr W Williams, choirmaster. Collections for the day amounted to over £18 in aid of Sunday School funds.

WOMEN'S LEGION

Mrs M Forster presided at the fortnightly meeting of Wheatley Hill women's section, British Legion, when arrangements were made to meet the men's section with a view to raising funds for a new building to serve as headquarters for both sections. Five new members were enrolled and final arrangements were made for the annual outing to Harrogate on 14 July. A gift of a silver butter dish, sent by an ex-Serviceman to raise funds for the Legion, was won by Mrs Metcalfe. Winners of the prizes given by Mrs Luke and Mrs Robinson were Mrs M Cowell and Mrs Forster.

MR J H RAFFELL – MISS L CONNER

Rev J W Thurlby (resident minister) officiated at the wedding in Patton Street Methodist Church, Wheatley Hill, of Miss Lena Conner, daughter of Mr F and the late Mrs Conner, 8 Wordsworth Avenue, Wheatley Hill, and Mr Joseph Hartley Raffell, son of Mr and Mrs J Raffell, 12 Stanhope Street, Wheatley Hill. Given away by Mr J Cain (Thornley), bride wore a green costume with hat and shoes to match, and was attended by Miss Olive Raffell (bridegroom's sister), who was in fawn and brown. Best man was Mr H F Horner. After the ceremony a reception was held at the home of the bridegroom, and later the happy couple left for Scarborough. The bridegroom was "demobbed" a year ago after six years' service in the RAF.

MR W FLOWERS – MISS H FAIRHURST

At Patton Street Methodist Church, Wheatley Hill, on Wednesday, the wedding took place of Miss Harriet Fairhurst, eldest daughter of Mr and Mrs T Broughton, 6 Wheatley Terrace, Wheatley Hill, and Mr William Flowers, elder son of Mr and Mrs A Flowers, Grayswood, Hamble, Southampton. Rev J W Thurlby (resident minister) officiated. Given away by her step-father, the bride wore a beige two-piece with brown hat and shoes to tone, and was attended by her step-sister, Miss Peggy Broughton, who wore a green two-piece. Best man was Mr Jack Ball (bride's uncle). Small attendants were Sandra Parker and Maureen Ball, cousins of the bride. Reception was in the Methodist Schoolroom and later the happy couple left for Kendal and the Lake District.

SPORT IN HORDEN

Main sporting event at Horden on Saturday was a boxing programme, arranged by Mr Fred Simm, the Sunderland promoter, in the open-air at the Ball Alley, Horden Workmen's Club. There were 12,000 spectators, but they were disappointed by the non-arrival of Stan Hawthorne, who was to have boxed six rounds exhibition.

Top liners were D Brock (Newcastle) and D Davis (Darlington) in a cruiserweight contest. The crowd was satisfied with the draw verdict. Referee stopped the middleweight match between Alf Rock (Choppington) and G Casson (North Shields) in the first round in favour of Rock. The fight between Len Graham (Wheatley Hill) and Mike Casey (Sunderland) was similarly stopped in favour of Graham.

Billy Williamson (Thornley) knocked out Jim Muirhead (Choppington) in the eighth round. W Curry (Wheatley Hill) beat Les Thorpe (Norton) on points. S Woodhouse (Darlington) knocked out C Evans (Wheatley Hill) in the second round.

YOUNG BANDSMEN - SUCCESSES IN RECENT CONTESTS

Recent successes at the Northern Area Musical Festival have crowned a long prize-winning record at contests in Durham County by five young members of Thornley Colliery Silver Band, whose ages ranges from 9 to 18 years, viz, the brothers Alf (18) and Dennis Hood (16), Thornley; Jackie Youll (14), Thornley; Ernest Murray (16), Wheatley Hill, and Donald Lavery (9), Spennymoor. Among them these keen musicians have won many certificates and cups for solo and duet playing, and are to be congratulated on the fine performances they have given in competition with some of the best players in the North.

Donald Lavery, the youngest player, gained an award within twelve weeks of starting to play the cornet, when he was placed third in 1945 in the solo competition for "under 14s" at Easington and District Youth League Festival at Wheatley Hill. At the solo championship for players under 14 at Gateshead this year, he won fourth prize and a certificate.

Premier Award

Euphonium player Dennis Hood this year carried off the premier award in the Northern Area championship for players aged 14 to 18 years. In 1945 he won third prize and a certificate in the Easington and District Youth Festival for players under 17, and last year was sixth in the Durham Band League competition. His brother, Alf, a cornet player, has a long list of successes to his credit. Last year he won first prize and a cup in the Easington and District Youth League Festival, as well as a medal for the best cornet player in a quartette. In Durham Band League competitions he won first prize and a shield in 1943, fourth prize in 1944, and fourth prize (competing with seniors) for solo playing, and third prize in a duet last year. Competing in the Tyneside Championship Festival for players under 16, he won second place both in 1942 and 1943, and the following year won first prize and a cup.

Cornettist Ernest Murray was awarded third prize and a certificate in the Northern Area Solo Championship at Gateshead this year for players 14 to 18. Last year, in the Durham Band League Festival, he and Jackie Youll were awarded first prize and shield in the duet section, and the year previous they gained the second award and a cup in a similar contest. Last year also Ernest was placed first in the solo competition of the Durham Band

E Murray, D Hood, D Lavery, J Youll, A Hood

League of players under 16 and was presented with the shield. In 1945 Ernest and Jackie also carried off first prize in the duet section of the Easington and District Youth League contest, and Ernest was awarded first prize in the solo section for players under 14.

Other Successes

Jackie Youll, who plays the euphonium, achieved a great success last year when he was placed third out of 41 competitors in the Northern Area Solo Championship for players under 14, held at Bradford. In addition to the honours he shared as a duettist with Ernest Murray, he won fourth prize and a certificate at the Easington and District Youth League contest in 1945 for players under 14.

These young bandsmen have received every encouragement from their fellow members of the Thornley Colliery Band and from their conductor, Mr Edward Kitto, who last year completed 25 years' service in this capacity. Mr Kitto, who is employed as a stoneman at Thornley

Colliery, is also conductor of Shotton Colliery Band, and during the winter months is a tutor for Durham County Council evening classes at the Spennymoor Centre, giving instruction in brass instruments.
27 June 1947
PRESENTATION
At a representative gathering of officials and workmen of Wheatley Hill colliery and various local organisations, in the Nimmo Hotel, Wheatley Hill, a presentation was made to Mr J A Simpson, OBE, who has left the district to take up a new appointment with the NCB in No 5 Area of the Northern Division, after having been manager of Wheatley Hill colliery for many years. Mr F Simpson (colliery under-manager) presided on behalf of the colliery officials and workmen, Mr John Welsh, chief engineer at Wheatley Hill colliery, presented Mr Simpson with a silver cigarette box and a cheque for £69. Tributes to the work of Mr Simpson, who had spent the last 40 years at Wheatley Hill colliery, were paid by the following: Dr A P Gray, Mr T H Arnold, Mr W Snaith, JP, Major Gibson Sherburn (formerly of the 22nd Batt Home Guard, of which Mr Simpson was OC), Mr F Quin (retired county councillor), Mr T W Allan (on behalf of the Enginemen's Association), Mr R Simpson (representing the cricket club) and Mr J White (on behalf of the colliery officials). Suitable words of thanks and appreciation of their parting gift were voiced by Mr Simpson. Refreshments were served during the evening, and vocal items were contributed by Mr T Kelly and Mr H Peacock, with Mr J Hogg at the piano. Arrangements for presentation were made by Mr J White.
4 July 1947
PERMANENT RELIEF FUND, WHEATLEY HILL
At the quarterly meeting of the Wheatley Hill branch, Permanent Relief Fund, the balance sheet, submitted by Mr F Quinn, gave the total income as £251 14s 3d. Payments were: to 25 women and children, £51 10s 5d, 24 permanently disabled cases £69 18s 4d, 58 minor accident cases £89 12s 8d.
11 July 1947
ROYAL GARDEN PARTY – Sister Mary E Dunn, SRN, SCM, of General Hospital, Walsall, Staffs, was chosen by the staff to be present at the Royal garden party at St James Palace, London. Walsall's was one of 50 hospitals in the kingdom who sent up a fair sum of money (£300)

for the British Empire Nurses War Memorial Fund. Sister Dunn, whose mother lives at Wheatley Hill, was trained at the Ingham Infirmary, South Shields.

18 July 1947

DURHAM MINERS' PLEDGE TO SUPPORT
THE GOVERNMENT

Durham Area Executive Committee of the National Union of Mineworkers and Durham County Mining Federation Board, at special meetings on Saturday, pledged support to the Government and the NUM in whatever measures agreed upon to secure maximum coal production.

A united Council meeting will be held on 23 August to hear a report of the national conference and ballot on the recommendations to secure additional output.

Lodges are being requested to make preliminary arrangements in every colliery with the colliery manager in order to operate whatever decision is agreed nationally as and from 6 September.

Winding Enginemen

The County Federation Board discussed the question of the 24 winding enginemen who had not yet rejoined the official union. Steps are being taken in conjunction with the NCB and the newly-appointed Colliery Consultative Committees to interview each of these workmen to give them an opportunity of carrying out the undertaking they gave to re-joint.

RETIRED MINERS' SUGGESTION

Easington RDC have had before them the question of accommodation in the shape of bungalows of some description for retired miners and it was suggested the National Coal Board should be asked to provide suitable accommodation for 50 retired miners at Thornley. The Committee appreciated that this was a problem not only for Thornley but throughout the whole area but did not feel that an application to the Coal Board would meet with success.

After discussion it was agreed that the Clerk report the whole matter to the National Coal Board and ask for their assistance.

OLD PEOPLE'S TRIP – First trip provided by Wheatley Hill Workmen's Club for retired aged members over 65 and their wives and widows of members over 60 was held to Whitley Bay on Saturday. Six buses conveyed the party of 250 and each tripper was given £1 pocket money as well as being provided with a lunch. Arrangements were

Winner of Durham County Press Cup - George Charlton

made by club secretary (Mr T Storey).

15 August 1947
DURHAM COUNTY PRESS CUP AWARDED TO WHEATLEY HILL GARDENER

Mr G Charlton, 13 York Street, Wheatley Hill, has been adjudged the winner of The Durham County Press Allotments Cup which was held in the first year by Mr John W Robinson, 41 Salisbury Place, Bishop Auckland. Judging was by Mr Thomas Pattison, 42 Ladywell Road, Winlaton (formerly of Murton), and Mr W Knaggs, Stockton. The cup will be presented at The Durham County Press Show in the Town Hall, Durham, on Friday 5 September.

Judge Sees "Perfect Garden"

Mr Pattison is one of the most skilled gardeners in the North of England, and though he has been retired from market gardening for 14 years he has probably never been so busily engaged as he is today. His services are in constant demand at shows in all parts of the county, and what he does not know about the soil and its produce is not worth knowing.

With Mr Knaggs he visited the garden of every entrant, and is enthusiastic in his comments upon the fine displays he saw on every hand. Colliery workers have once again proved that they are just as adept in vegetable and horticultural production as they are in winning the coal the country so urgently needs, and, indeed, in these days, it is a matter for speculation as to which is of the greater importance.

The sole object of The Durham County Press competition, as well as the show to be held at Durham on 5 and 6 September, is to stimulate food production, and anyone who has studied the facts of the crisis now shadowing the country, will fully realise that the need for such stimulus is of paramount importance.

Pittington Challengers

Asked his views upon the gardens he had inspected, Mr Pattison said that on the night before they reached South East Durham they were quite certain that either Mr John Gibson, "South End", Pittington, or Mr

Albert Juniper, 16 Hallgarth Lane, Pittington, was a likely winner of the coveted trophy, but Mr Charlton's garden, which they saw on the following day, easily captured the maximum points and therefore the cup.

"Not a single fault could be found with this garden," said Mr Pattison. "It was perfect in every detail, and from the point of view of the rotation of crops was the ideal to which all gardeners should aim. The whole plan of cultivation was so arranged that there is produce available the whole year round.

Rotation Won the Extra Points

Mr Charlton has a movable greenhouse which can be taken with little difficulty to any part of the garden where most needed. His tomato plants were a revelation to the judges and show how growth of the fruit begins almost at ground level and continues to the top of the plants. In the garden were potatoes, celery, leeks, vegetable marrows, carrots, turnips, parsnips, beet, cabbages, beans, peas and, indeed, every kind of produce, arranged in a rotation that ensures a constant supply for the kitchen. It was in the matter of rotation, providing for the winter and spring, that Mr Charlton won the points that made him a certain winner of the cup, which is one of four that he has carried off this year.

The judges spoke in glowing terms of the gardens they saw in the Shotley Bridge area, and also in the Bishop Auckland district, and, indeed, throughout they were much impressed by the general excellence of the work. Mr Robinson, last year's cup winner, was at the head of his section.

Prizewinners – Section A – West of the Great North Road

Novices 1 £10 William Forrester, 7 Ashfield, Shotley Bridge.
2 £7 John N Porter, sen, 70 High Street North, Langley Moor.
3 £5 Wilfred Hogarth, East View, Tenters Street, Bishop Auckland.
4 £3 John N Porter, jun, 58 High Street North, Langley Moor.

Open 1 £10 John W Robinson, 41 Salisbury Place, BishOop Auckland.
2 £7 William Greig, Summerdale, Shotley Bridge.
3 £5 Frederick W Bowe, 36 The Briary, Shotley Bridge.
4 £3 Robert Hagger, 7 Alexander Street, Shildon.

Prizewinners - Section B – East of the Great North Road

Novices   1   £10   Allan Hutchinson, 2 Albert Street, Thornley.

          2   £7   William G Pickering, Coopers Terrace, Thornley.

          3   £5   John H Johnson, 3 Fatherley Terrace, Colliery Row, Fence Houses.

          4   £3   John Nattrass, 12 Lynn Terrace, Wheatley Hill.

Open   1   £10   George Charlton, 13 York Street, Wheatley Hill.

          2   £7   John Gibson, 11 South End, Pittington.

          3   £5   Albert Juniper, 16 Hallgarth Lane, Pittington.

          4   £3   George Mossom 30 Gill Crescent (South), Fence Houses.

GOLDEN WEDDING AT THORNLEY

A disastrous fire which ravaged Thornley pit in 1875 was recalled in an interview with our reporter this week by 83 year old Mr John Kirk, 28 Aged Miners' Homes, Thornley, who celebrated his golden wedding on Tuesday. He and his wife (72) were married at Easington Register Office on 2 September 1897, and both still enjoy good health.

Recalling the pit fire, which, he said, started in the pumping house, Mr Kirk said that so fierce was the blaze that people were able to read a newspaper a good distance away by the light of the flames. "Fortunately," said Mr Kirk, "no one was killed. Just as the last miner reached the surface the cage which had brought him to the top of the shaft crashed to the bottom. When told of the surface fire, many of the miners underground made their way to the nearby Wheatley Hill colliery shaft and reached the surface from there." Later Mr Kirk well remembers watching the sinking of the new pit.

Mr Kirk has lived in Thornley all his life, being the oldest resident, and, as a young man, was in the greengrocery business. Later, because business was not so good, he started work at Thornley colliery, where he remained until his retirement at the age of 70.

"Toiling Life"

A native of Wingate, Mrs Kirk is quite active and able to do all her own housework. "People nowadays," she said, "have a much better time of it than we older people have had. My husband and I have had a toiling married life, but it has been a happy one. We have lived through three wars and three miners' strikes, and for many a year my husband never earned more than 6s 6d a day at the pit. We can always look on the bright side of life, however, for it's no use grumbling."

The couple have had a family of 12, but only one son and two daughters are now alive. They have six grandchildren. A family celebration party is to be held tomorrow.

"PRE-FABS" TENANTED – Local members of Easington Rural Council, Couns W Brereton and J H C Scott, presented the keys for the first 20 pre-fabricated houses to be completed on the Park Street Estate, Thornley, to the new tenants. "The new tenants," Coun Brereton told our reporter, "are all young married couples with no more than two in family who have been living in overcrowded conditions." Fourteen more "pre-fabs" on the Cooper's Terrace site are to be let next week and Coun Brereton stated that it is expected that 12 of the 48 steel houses under construction on the Gore Hall Estate will be completed by the end of the month. "These houses," he added, "will be let to those with large families living in condemned houses."

THORNLEY PARISH COUNCIL – OBJECTION TO NEW TOWN

The first note of criticism of the proposal to build the new East Durham town of Peterlee was heard at a meeting of the Parish Council.

Describing the proposal as a "whim and a fancy," Coun M Fleming said that because of the idea of concentrating on the new town, Thornley was going to be stopped from having any more new houses or amenities for years and years to come.

"For fifty years we have suffered in Thornley from derelict streets covered in mud and rubbish," said Coun Fleming. "Thornley colliery has a good many years of life left in it, and we are not willing to sacrifice our good life to the whim and fancy of this new town."

In the past there had been a lot of talk about derelict South-West Durham, but they in Thornley would have to look out or they would be allowed to become derelict as well.

Referring to an offer of aluminium houses if sites could be provided by 1 October, Coun W Brereton, a member of the Easington RDC, said there was a considerable number of derelict sites in Thornley that houses could be place upon.

Coun Whitehead (Chairman): It means that if we take extra men on at the colliery they will have to travel from the new town. I think it is outrageous.

A resolution to send in a protest against concentrating on the new town at the expense of the older places was carried unanimously.

SUCCESS OF WHEATLEY HILL BAND

In the Northumberland dance band championship at the Oxford Gallieries, Newcastle, the Gordon Kitto quintette (Wheatley Hill) were awarded second prize. "Specials" were awarded to Derek V Humble, clarinet and also sax; John Humble, bass; and Gordon Kitto, diploma of merit for leader; Edward Kitto, piano, and Thomas Hargreaves, drums, complete the quintette. Each member received a medal. The Quintette was only beaten by a band from Ashington by a small margin.

5 September 1947

TOWN COUNCIL

Easington Rural Council's proposed new £14,000,000 town, Peterlee, came in for both criticism and praise at the meeting of Wingate Parish Council, presided over by Coun Mrs L Smith, on Monday.

"Farewell Squalor"

During a discussion which followed the receipt of a complimentary copy of "Farewell, Squalor" – the book dealing with the new town – Coun R Hird (Wheatley Hill) said the Council should protest against the idea.

"At the last meeting of Wheatley Hill Labour Party," said Coun Hird, "it was decided to forward a resolution to Easington Council protesting against this new town. A more useful purpose would be served if factories were built near or in our villages instead of people having to travel to this proposed new town. They are not looking after these little villages – only those down the coast."

Declaring he had heard much adverse criticism against the town, Coun J T Gilchrist (Wingate) said that although they were bound to admit it was a good scheme, people were asking how, "when it suited certain people," they could get the materials and labour to build such a huge town, whilst for years people in the villages had been "crying out for a habitation." "I would have been more satisfied," added Coun Gilchrist, "had the Council tried to alleviate village housing problems before tackling this idea of a new town."

New Town an Asset

Coun. E Wharrier (Wheatley Hill), declaring he was in favour of the town, said he was thinking about the children of today and of what they would have to look forward to. "From an economic point of view," he said, "it is not wise to build a factory here, there and everywhere. If we can put the factories in one place and made a nice place of it, people will be able to live and work there under ideal conditions. You cannot make anything nice out of unsightly pit-heaps such as we have at Wheatley Hill and Thornley. I feel the new town will be an asset to our villages. We are looking at the matter from a little parochial view when we talk of scattering factories all over the place." ·

Prefers Closely Knit Community

Supporting Coun Wharrier, Coun G Pugh (Deaf Hill) said he had heard of no adverse criticism in his village. "Personally, I think a closely-knit community is the best," he said, "and the new town is a good idea." Coun A Crossley (Wingate) said Peterlee represented what the Labour Party had lived for – better living conditions, a better community life and better employment. Coun J Madrill (Deaf Hill) declared that some of the people living in the smaller villages were prejudiced against the scheme simply because the town was not being built beside their own particular village. "This attitude is entirely wrong," he said, "Peterlee will, I think, be a good town, and we should give it our support."

Coun Mrs Smith said that although she was by no means against the proposed new town, she thought that more should have been done in the matter of housing for young married couples in the villages throughout the area. Coun Pugh proposed that the Council should fall in line with the Easington scheme, but when the Clerk (Mr William Stoker) said no motion was asked for, it was decided to let the matter rest, Coun Wharrier remarking that in any case the older members of the Council would probably never live to see the fulfilment of the plan.

PRESENTATION – Presentation of The Durham County Press Cups by Mr Arnold Rowntree (President of the show) at Durham Town Hall on Friday. Mr G Charlton, Wheatley Hill, received the cups for best display of chrysanthemums and the Allotments Cup, and also the trophy for best collection of vegetables on behalf of Thornley Allotment Society.

12 September 1947

NEW HEADMASTER – Mr Joseph Thomas Andrews (Tudhoe), who has been on the teaching staff of Middlestone Moor County School for the past 19 years has begun his new duties as headmaster of Wheatley Hill Senior Boys' School. He succeeds Mr T H Arnold (Wheatley Hill), who retired a year gone March after 27 years as headmaster at the school. Educated at the Alderman Wraith Secondary School, Spennymoor, and later at the City of Leeds Training College. Mr Andrews's first appointment was at Middlestone Moor and he remained there until this new appointment. During the 1939-45 war Mr Andrews, who is married, served in the army for five years, first in the RAC and later in the Army Educational Corps. He is actively interested in youth and WEA activities, and a keen sportsman, has played both cricket and hockey.

10 October 1947

CO-OPERATIVE SOCIETY – Half-yearly meetings of Sherburn Hill Co-operative Society on Saturday were presided over by Mr Peter Cairns (Wheatley Hill), who said a pleasing feature of the past six months was that sales amounted to three-quarters of a million pounds, an increase of £117,521 on the preceding half-year. Another achievement was the fact that £1,000 had been transferred to the reserve, something which had never been done during the war. A dividend of 3s in the £ was declared. Reports were given by the delegates, Mr W Dowding (Wheatley Hill) and Mr J Shield (Blackhall), on the Congress at Brighton. Following nominations were received for the committee in the Wheatley Hill district:- Messrs W Dowding, E Dean, J Williams, J Gray, J Hughes, J Johnson and J Harrison.

MR W H O'CONNOR

A married partnership of 56 years was broken by the death at 17 Burns Street, Wheatley Hill, of one of Wheatley Hill's oldest standards, Mr William Henry O'Connor, who was in his 80th year. Mr O'Connor had lived in the village for over 35 years and was employed at Wheatley Hill colliery until injuries received in an accident compelled him to terminate his career. He held a diploma for 50 years' membership of the Durham Miners' Association. Surviving Mr O'Connor are his wife and six sons and five daughters. All six sons – Robert, Nicholas, Ernest, Michael, Jack and Lawrence – acted as underbearers at the funeral, which took place at Wheatley Hill cemetery on Monday following a service at the graveside conducted by Rev Fr B Sharratt (Thornley).

EXTENDED HOURS IN THE PITS
DURHAM MINERS TO CONSIDER AGREEMENT

The extended hours agreement for miners will be explained at a special meeting of the United Council for the Durham Coalfield in the Miners' Hall, Durham, on Saturday. Special meetings of lodges and branches are being arranged for the same purpose not later than 26 October. In the event of the agreement being accepted, collieries desiring to work the additional Saturday shift will start on 1 November. Those choosing to work the extra half hour on each of the first five days of the week will commence to do so on 3 November.

Durham Miners' Council on Saturday resolved that, in view of the Whitehaven and Morrison Busty pit disasters, provision should be made at every colliery for the workman to travel by the return airways, accompanied by a colliery official, at least once every three months. The matter was brought before the council in the form of a resolution by the Kimblesworth Lodge, in which it was pointed out that, following the recent explosion at Whitehaven, a workman saved the lives of several comrades by travelling the return airways.

17 October 1947
WHEATLEY HILL MINERS – MAY AGREE TO TRANSFER
Having heard a report from their chairman, Coun E Wharrier, and secretary, County Coun E Cain, who are members of the Wheatley Hill Pit Consultative Committee, that there was no alternative but to close down Wheatley Hill colliery if they were not agreeable to 91 workmen being transferred to other collieries because the colliery was already overstaffed, members of Wheatley Hill Miners' Lodge, at a special meeting on Sunday morning, said they would agreed to the transfer provided that they themselves were allowed to put in "cavils" to decide who would have to leave the colliery.

"Though they agreed in principle with the transfer," Coun Cain told our reporter after the meeting, "they were not prepared to accept a list of 114 names already selected by the management to leave the pit, and felt they had every right to ballot among themselves, since, naturally, none is keen to have to travel out of the place to another distant colliery. Twenty-three of the 114 men who are described as redundant are over 65 and will be given their notices, but the rest, by a scheme drawn up by No 3 Area of the Northern Division of the NCB, are to be transferred to Blackhall, Easington, Shotton, Thornley, Horden and South Hetton collieries. Blackhall was scheduled to claim the largest number, namely, 34.

NCB View
Coun Cain said that officials of the NCB met the Pit Consultative Committee at Wheatley Hill on Friday, and at that meeting it was stated by an NCB official that unless the miners accepted the transfer the

colliery would have to close, but if they agreed there was no reason why the colliery should not go on working for some years. Different categories of workmen, both on the surface and underground, will be affected," added Coun Cain, "and arrangements will be made for their transport to their new pits. The men's decision will now be conveyed to the management for their consideration, for our members are definitely against the names having been already chosen."

With a weekly target of 6,000 tons, Wheatley Hill colliery employs 1,100 men and boys.

24 October 1947

EAST DURHAM SPORT

Thornley Youth Club Juniors, who have been granted the use of Wheatley Hill football ground for their home games, lost by the odd goal in five when visited by East Rainton Juniors on Saturday in Division II of the Hetton Junior League.

Now well in the running for league honours, Wheatley Hill Welfare SS maintained their unbeaten record on Saturday in the Ferryhill and District League when they visited Sedgefield St Edmund's and won by four clear goals despite the fact that for last 20 minutes they played with only ten men, Carr being carried off injured. With a drive from 20 yards out Carr opened Wheatley Hill's account after 20 minutes.

The game was fought at a fast pace, with both goals being visited in turn until 15 minutes from the end when Wheatley Hill gained complete supremacy and scored three quick goals through G W Bean and C Laverick (2).

Wheatley Hill's team to visit Ferryhill Station SC in the first round of the Ferryhill and District League Challenge Cup tomorrow, has been chosen as follows: Gibson, Stokoe, G W Bean, Goynes, W Bean, Hall, Urwin, C Laverick, Buck, Carr, J Laverick.

31 October 1947

EAST DURHAM'S OUTPUT

Highest output since nationalisation was recorded by the eight collieries in No 3 Area, Northern Division, NCB last week, when every colliery exceeded its target. Total output amounted to 85,741 tons, equivalent to 107.27 per cent of the combined target. Individual figures were:- Horden, 23,584 tons (107.19 per cent of its target); Easington, 16,691 tons (107.19 per cent); Blackhall, 13,421 tons (107.54 per cent); Shotton,

9,698 tons (103.16 per cent); Wheatley Hill, 6,377 tons (106.29 per cent); Thornley, 7,131 tons (101.87 per cent); Wingate, 4,785 tons (111.27 per cent); Deaf Hill, 4,054 tons (124.73 per cent). Indeed, a magnificent achievement.

WHEATLEY HILL MINERS – PROPOSED TRANSFERS

Following their decision a fortnight ago to agree to 114 redundant workmen being transferred from Wheatley Hill colliery to neighbouring collieries only if they were allowed to ballot as to who would have to go, members of Wheatley Hill Miners' Lodge, at a mass meeting in the Regal Cinema on Sunday, accepted the recommendation of their lodge officials to agree to the original list drawn up by the colliery management in conjunction with officials of No 3 Area, Northern Division, NCB, on condition that individual cases of hardship would be fully investigated.

Original List Reduced

It was stated that the original list of 114 had now been reduced to 76. Twenty-three miners over 65 were to be retired, and a number of youths between 16 and 18, who were considered indispensable, as well as several hardship cases, had been removed from the list.

Coun E Wharrier presided at Sunday's meeting, addressed by Mr N F Nattrass, labour director for the Northern Division, and Mr Sam Watson, agent for Durham Area, NUM. Mr J H Blackwell, Labour Relations Officer, Seaham, was also present.

Serious Situation

After Coun Wharrier had reported that the management had refused to allow the men to compile their own redundancy list by a ballot, Mr Watson stressed the seriousness of the situation as the future of Wheatley Hill colliery, which was at present overstaffed, was "not bright". He advised the men to accept the list of names already prepared, and gave an assurance that cases of individual hardship would be fully examined by local lodge officials in conjunction with himself and NCB officials.

"Out of a gathering of about 400 miners, only two voted against the transfer," County Coun E Cain, secretary of Wheatley Hill Miners' Lodge, told our reporter after the meeting. "The date of the transfer has not yet been fixed. Men listed for transfer, who are in receipt of light rate compensation, will be paid their compensation at the collieries they are transferred to, and the money will be debited to Wheatley Hill colliery. The case of composite workmen, who are now having to do datal work, is also to be investigated.

To be Retired

Coun Cain added that in addition to the 23 miners who were to be retired, five colliery officials over 65 were also to be finished.

Regarding transport for the miners who will have to travel to neighbouring collieries, Mr Nattrass said that full arrangements would be made by the NCB. "The workmen transferred," he said, "will be expected to pay the normal fare for the transport, but the difference between the normal fare and the cost of the transport will be subsidised by the NCB."

THORNLEY "GOLDEN" – HOUSEWIFE NEVER RETIRES

Well-known in Thornley, where they have lived all their married life, Mr and Mrs John H Dower, 26 Aged Miners' Homes, celebrated their golden wedding on Thursday. They were married at St John's Church, Hesleden, by the Rev J Little, on 30 October 1897. Both still enjoy good health and Mrs Dower, who was born at Lumley 72 years ago, does all her own housework. "There's no retirement for the housewife," she declared, in an interview with our reporter.

A native of Hesleden, Mr Dower (73), began work at Castle Eden colliery soon after he reached his twelfth birthday. "I began as a trapper boy," he said, "and received 1s 1d for a ten hour shift. In those days that was better money than they paid at Thornley colliery." He remained at the colliery until it closedown, through flooding, on his 20th birthday and claims that, as a putter, he took the last two tubs in-bye before work creased altogether. For two years he worked at pits in Northumberland and then started at Thornley colliery where he was employed in different capacities until he retired on shift work when he was 68.

Still Active

Mr Dower is still quite active and walking is his favourite pastime. "There's nothing I enjoy better than a few miles' walk," he said. For many years Mrs Dower has been actively associated with Thornley Waterloo Street Methodist Church and Sisterhood and on Saturday a celebration party was held in the church schoolroom for her family, and Methodist friends.

The couple, who have lived in the Aged Miners' Homes for the past four years, have two sons and one daughter, six grandchildren and two great-grandchildren.

7 November 1947

A THORNLEY HERO – RECIPIENT OF GIFTS

A hero of the Japanese prisoner-of-war camps, Cpl John Hamilton Williamson, Shinwell Crescent, Thornley, received an electric clock and an illuminated address at Thornley. Cpl Williamson had been one of the principal witnesses at the war crimes trial in Tokio, in September, when the "Mad Doctor" Hisakichi Tokuda was sentenced to death.

Tokuda had been charged with performing cruel and bizarre medical experiments on Allied prisoners of war, and Williamson told the American court how Tokuda had injected a milk made from soya beans into several prisoners, causing them to die. He also related how the "mad doctor" began to perform operations with no training in surgery and had to be pushed aside by Allied doctors so that they could save the lives of the prisoners.

Another part of Cpl Williamson's evidence was the story of how he himself was beaten on several occasions by a Jap named Arai, known to prisoners as "The Man from Mars". Arai was also sentenced to death.

No News

Cpl Williamson served in the Royal Scots Regiment for 12 years and was captured at Hong Kong on Christmas Day of 1941. For a long time his family were without news of him. For his outstanding services to sick prisoners in the hospital camp, described in a report as a "veritable medieval torture chamber," Cpl Williamson was awarded the British Empire Medal.

The presentation by Thornley War Committee was made at short notice because Cpl Williamson had to return after two days to his work as an attendant at a West Riding Hospital. Mr H E Cox (treasurer) complimented him on the honour he had brought to Thornley.

Apologising for the unavoidable absence of Mr J H C Scott (chairman), Mr T H Holder (hon secretary) handed the gifts to Cpl Williamson and congratulated him on returning from his ordeal.

After Cpl Williamson had briefly replied, Mr W Scott and Mrs Brewster added their tributes to the corporal. Among those present was

Cpl Williamson's mother, who is a member of the Thornley War Committee and a valued worker for poor Children's Holiday Association.

WINDERS THREATEN STRIKE –
CLAIM FOR WAGE INCREASE

Twenty-one days' notice to cease work, operating from 15 December, will be given by members of the National Union of Colliery Winding Enginemen if the National Coal Board will not recognise them as a negotiating body in their claim for an increased wage of 37s 6d per shift or grant them an immediate advance, pending negotiations, of 10s on the present minimum day rate.

This was learned by our reporter from Mr Joseph Walton, Blackhall Colliery, Chairman of the National Union, who said this course of action in their quest for a wages advance to be negotiated by their representatives was a normal procedure which would be followed by any section of workers who felt they had a real grievance. The general secretary of the National Union had sent a letter, dated 5 November, with the union's decision, to Lord Hyndley, Chairman of the NCB. The decision to hand in notices was reached, said Mr Walton, at a recent meeting of the executive council at Leeds. "If a favourable reply is not received within ten days," added Mr Walton, "action will be taken."

The letter forwarded to Lord Hyndley concludes with the hope that "reason will prevail in all our joint undertakings and that a stoppage with be averted by justice being meted out to colliery winding enginemen on a basis differing from the raw deal they have had since the coal mines came under Government control."

Strike Recalled

The National Union, said Mr Walton, now had over 2,000 members in England, Scotland and Wales. One of its branches, the Durham Colliery Winders' Trades Union, of which Mr Walton is secretary, staged a strike for better wages in May, which crippled output at many collieries in Durham for nearly a week. About 100,000 tons of coal were lost as a result of that stoppage.

The Durham Union, which "broke away" from the Durham County Enginemen's, Boilerminders' and Firemen's Association, had increased in strength since May by about 25 per cent, said Mr Walton, and now had a membership of over 200. Since May also the strength of the

National Union had increased by about 50 per cent, and only recently Cumberland winders had become members.

14 November 1947

WHEATLEY HILL COLLIERY TRANSFERS
NO MORE REDUCTION TO BE MADE

Following negotiations between officials of Wheatley Hill Miners' Lodge and officials of the Northern Divisional Coal Board (No 3 Area) and Durham Area of the National Union of Mineworkers, a final figure of 53 redundant workmen to be transferred from Wheatley Hill colliery to neighbouring collieries has been agreed upon and no further reduction will be made.

This information was given to our reporter this week by County Coun E Cain, JP, secretary of Wheatley Hill Miners' Lodge, who said that in addition to the 53 men who would have to leave the colliery, 30 men over 65, including five colliery officials, were to be retired.

"By agreement with the National Coal Board," said Coun Cain, "the pensioners who are to be finished will be paid 12 weeks' wages each as redundant workmen."

Closing Danger

Originally a list of 113 redundant workmen was drawn up, as it was stated that the colliery was overstaffed and there was a danger of it having to close down altogether if the men did not agree to the transfer. Agreement was reached a fortnight gone Sunday on condition that individual cases of hardship would be fully investigated. Since then 17 boys between the ages of 15 and 18 have been retained and 13 cases of proved hardship.

"Those on the redundancy list who complained of hardship," said Coun Cain, "personally presented their cases to the officials, who gave them a sympathetic hearing." Of the 53 men now redundant, 34 are to be transferred to Blackhall colliery 14 to Easington, two to Thornley, and one each to Horden, Shotton and South Hetton collieries. The date of transfer has not yet been fixed nor has the date when the over-65s are to cease their employment.

COUNCILLOR WITHDRAWS OBJECTIONS –
MR W BRERETON EXPLAINS

Opposition to the construction of the proposed new town of Peterlee in the Easington rural district, emanating from some of the parish councils in the area, received a check at a meting of Easington Rural District Council on Thursday when Coun W Brereton, a member of the District Council and also of Thornley Parish Council, withdrew their objection to the scheme.

In a personal statement made at the close of the meeting Coun Brereton said: "I wish to withdraw any statement of mine that has appeared in the Press interfering with the development of Peterlee and I want to assure this Council that I abide by its constitution."

Coun Gordon Henderson (chairman of the Labour Group on the Council): I move that we accept the statement of Coun Brereton. As far as this Council is concerned I think we are all agreed that the development of Peterlee is of paramount importance to all the inhabitants of Easington rural district and not to any particular isolated village.

"If we can get the sanction of the Minister of Town and Country Planning to proceed with this scheme for the whole district, then there is a greater prospect of bringing new industries into the area than there would be if we were proceeding as isolated or individual villages. We therefore hope that those who have supported this scheme in the past will continue to do so because we believe it will be of immense value to the progress of Easington rural area."

After the meeting Coun Henderson, together with Coun M Purcell (secretary of the Labour Group), approached by a "Durham Chronicle" representative, said there was a unanimous decision of the Labour Group supporting the construction of Peterlee. Recently, in several villages in the area, objections had been raised and certain members of the Council had lent some support of these objections. He wished to remind members of the Labour Group that, as loyal members, they must adhere to the majority decision.

Won't Attend Protest Meeting

Coun Brereton, to a "Durham Chronicle" representative, said that at a recent meeting of Thornley Parish Council he had associated himself with a decision of the Parish Council to protest against the development of the new town and he, along with the other members of the Parish Council, agreed to attend a protest meeting to be held at Thornley on 3 December, but he now wished to disassociate himself with opposition to the scheme.

21 November 1947

NEWS FROM THE COALFIELD –
WAGES AGREEMENT ACCEPTED

By a very large majority the lodges of miners, colliery enginemen and mechanics in the Durham coalfield have accepted the recommendation of the United Council and voted in favour of the new wages agreement for day-wage underground and surface workers. This provides for the weekly minimum in the case of adult underground men to be increased from £5 to £5 15s and that of surface men from £4 10s to £5. The weekly minimum of juveniles underground is advanced by 15 per cent, and that of juveniles above ground by 11 per cent.

The increases, if accepted by other coalfields in the country, will be retrospective to the first week in November. Back money, it is hoped, will be included in the Christmas pay packets.

Negotiations have been opened in London between the National Coal Board and the National Union of Mineworkes in respect of the claim of shotfirers for increased wages and the request for the designation of collier craftsmen, including winding enginemen, for whom new wage scales are sought.

Cokemen's Threat

Meanwhile there is a threat to render idle most of the by-product plants in the county if not in the country because the cokemen are dissatisfied with the delay in having their claims for a shorter working week and higher wages considered.

Fourteen days' notice to cease work was handed in on Monday on behalf of workmen on 18 of the 21 coking plants in the Durham coalfield and ten in Yorkshire. Cokemen at Evenwood, Brancepeth (Willington) and Victoria Garesfield, as well as the men engaged on the acid plant at Dean and Chapter have not taken this step.

If the threat to stop work is carried into effect, serious consequences will result. Some plants may go out of commission and gas supplies in several areas will be greatly curtailed.

5 December 1947

COKEMEN'S STRIKE CALLED OFF –
GRIEVANCES TO BE CONSIDERED

The threatened strike on the part of cokemen and by-product workers has been called off. This step follows an announcement by the union secretary, Mr T W Tindale, that the grievances would be considered this week by the National Conciliation Board if the notices to cease work were withdrawn.

Dissatisfied with the delay in setting up machinery to deal with claims for a shorter working week and higher wages, representatives of all but one or two of the cokemen's branches in the Durham coalfield last month called for a special meeting of the Council of the Cokemen's Union. This was convened and held at York. Against the advice of the president and the secretary, who walked out of the meeting with three Scottish delegates, it was resolved to tender 14 days' notice to cease work on behalf of the whole Union.

Offer Accepted

Although such action was denounced as unconstitutional, notices were handed in by workers engaged on 18 plants in Durham County, eleven in Yorkshire and one in Lancashire. They were due to expire this weekend. Last Thursday the Divisional Coal Board undertook to meet representatives of the Durham cokemen and discuss their grievances if the notices were withdrawn. Two days later came notification that the National Conciliation Board would consider the complaints on the same terms.

In the light of these statements and after a protracted discussion at Garden House Hotel, Durham, on Monday, it was resolved, by the narrow majority of two votes, to withdraw the notices handed in by Durham cokemen.

The meeting, attended by delegates from all but one of the 21 Branches in the county, was presided over by Mr P Purcell, of Horden, with Mr R W Rowe, of Shotton, as secretary. At the close Mr Purcell told our representative that ten lodges voted for the withdrawal of the notices and eight against. The decision has been conveyed to the rest of the districts in the Cokemen's Union.

Mr Tindale, who has urged the men throughout to proceed along constitutional lines to secure a solution of their grievances, expressed his pleasure at the result of the Durham meeting and hoped that the negotiations would proceed quickly.

Shotton Cokemen Not to Withdraw Notices

Shotton Cokemen's branch decided on Tuesday night not to withdraw notices handed in on behalf of 85 workers on the plant to cease work early on Monday. All but one of the remaining lodges in the county have notified Mr T W Tindale, the national secretary, that notices have been withdrawn. Similar action has been taken by ten branches in Yorkshire and one in Scotland. Shotton branch will hold a further meeting today.

THORNLEY PRESENTATION – MANAGER'S RETIREMENT

Mr A Welsh, sen, who retired from the managership of Thornley Colliery, was presented with gifts from the officials, the staff, deputies and the Miners' Welfare Fund, at a gathering in the Church Hall, Thornley, on Saturday. Mr C Alderson presided on behalf of the officials, staff and deputies, and Mr W Atkin, for the Welfare. Two solid silver Georgian tankards, dated 1761 and 1778, were handed to Mr Welsh by Mr Amos Robinson (72), the oldest deputy on the colliery, and 60 years a worker underground. A silver bowl from the Welfare was presented by Mr T H Holder. In returning thanks, Mr Welsh recalled his mining career had extended over 53 years.

Other Speakers

Others who spoke were Messrs T Tunney, W Henderson, G Peel, J H Pattison and C Woodward. Entertainment was given by Messrs John Pattison (Shotton), W Potts, W Potts, jun, J Orange, B Pattison, H and W Hetherington, F Bradley, jun, and R Pattison.

Mr Welsh served part of his apprenticeship at the Rainton pits and when they closed he completed it at Seaham Colliery. He was assistant manager for 11 years at Silksworth Colliery before going to Ryhope as under-manager. For a few months he was manager at Adelaide Colliery and then became manager at Usworth Colliery. From Usworth he went to Thornley in 1930. He has been chairman of the Welfare, the Pithead Baths and the Aged Miners' Homes Committees.

12 December 1947

TEACHER RETIRES – After holding post of head teacher at Thornley Junior Mixed School for the past 20 years, Mrs A Temple has retired. At a gathering of the staffs of the two Thornley schools, Mrs Temple was presented with an oak sewing cabinet and a handbag, the gifts being handed to her by Miss F Berriman. A cushion was presented on behalf of the kitchen staff. Mr E Cox, head of senior school, and Mr W Nixon spoke of the happy relations which had always existed between the schools. Misses V Holmes, F Cook and M Hodgson, former pupils of Mrs Temple, and now teachers there, were amongst those present.

THORNLEY WI – At the annual meeting, presided over by Mrs J H C Scott, reports of the past year's work was presented by Mrs Miller (secretary), Mrs Todd (treasurer) and Miss Kirk (treasurer of the War Memorial fund). Miss Willans spoke on future activities and how members could help in the present crisis by producing more food. She was thanked by Miss Elliott. It was agreed to send donations to various hospitals and Thornley Aged Miners' Christmas Fund. Mrs Scott was re-elected president, Mrs Miller secretary, and Mrs Todd treasurer. Committee will be:- Mesdames Brandling, Bosomworth, Carlson, Dowson, Hetherington, Inman, Local, Lindsay, Muir, Sawdon, Tully and R Walton (senr). Pantomime, produced by Mrs Clark, was presented by Mesdames Bonar, Dowson, V Bosomworth, B Henderson, Lincoln, Orange, Sanderson, Winter and the Misses Orange and Oswald.

19 December 1947

SILVER WEDDING – Mr and Mrs Christopher Brown, 51 Jack Lawson Terrace, Wheatley Hill, celebrated their silver wedding on Tuesday with a party in the Welfare Hall, attended by over 200 guests. The couple, who were married at All Saints' Church, Wheatley Hill, have lived in the village all their married life. Mr Brown is employed at Wheatley Hill Colliery and they have an only son (Kenneth). Their anniversary coincided with the birthdays of two nephews, Robert William Storey (27), Wheatley Hill, and Raymond Halsall (12), Wingate, and they were both present at the party.

PIT VICTIM – Funeral took place at Wheatley Hill Cemetery on Monday 22, of Mr Herbert Jones (34), younger son of Mrs Jones and the late Mr E Jones, 7 Shop Street, Wheatley Hill, who died in Sunderland Infirmary the day after being injured in an accident at Easington Colliery, where he was employed as a shifter. It appears that while at work he had slipped and been crushed by the first of a set of tubs which were drawn by a "rather flighty" pony. "Accidental death" was the inquest verdict. Before being transferred to Easington Colliery four years ago Jones, who was unmarried, was employed at Wheatley Hill Colliery. A younger brother, Ebenezer, was drowned at sea during the war while a prisoner in Japanese hands, and his father was killed during the 1914-18 war. The funeral service was conducted in All Saints' Church, Wheatley Hill, by Rev P Casey (Vicar), and chief family mourners were: Mrs Jones (mother), Mr and Mrs E Jones (brother and sister-in-law), and Mr and Mrs E Almond (brother-in-law and sister).

WHEATLEY HILL'S "BEVIN" BOYS

A Christmas card conveying "compliments of the season" to the manager and workmen at Wheatley Hill colliery and recalling "happy memories" has been received by the manager of Wheatley Hill colliery (Mr W H Dobson) from three former Bevin Boys at the colliery, who sign themselves "Reg, Ron and Arthur". On the completion of their service in the mines some months ago the boys returned to their homes in the south. "The card reveals the fine spirit which prevailed between these boys and the management and workmen and we are proud to think they have remembered us in this way," commented County Coun E Cain, secretary, Wheatley Hill Miners" Lodge, who told our report of the receipt of the card.

26 December 1947

1948

MR LAWTHER'S M ESSAGE
UNION TO PRESS FOR A PENSION

In a New Year message to miners, Mr Will Lawther, President, National Union of Mine-workers, writes:-

We enter 1948 with more than ordinary hope. We have passed the first milestone in our nationalised industry. All the fears of the ultra-pessimists have been smashed by your actions. Your faith in the era that began a year ago was as intense as the diehard's hatred of the change. Your deeds, the records you have broken, entitle you to an honourable place in the community. At long last, everyone realises that the salvation of this country depends upon your efforts. Only by your efforts can coal be mined.

Despite the hollow arguments of the critics of the National Coal Board, you know from experience that during 1947 more changes have taken place to improve your lot than in any one year in the history of this industry. You have the assurance of the Board that steps will be taken by way of increased supplementary compensation payments to improve the position of those of you who meet with injury or who suffer from industrial disease. The union will also press for payment of a pension from the industry in addition to that provided by the State to those of you who have spent your lives in Britain's premier industry.

Further Improvements

These are further improvements that a nationally owned industry will give to those who provide the heat and energy for Britain's industry. Your efforts are an example to a stricken world struggling to rehabilitate itself. You have done a grand job during 1947; continue the good deeds of 1947 into the coming year. Let everyone in the industry, in whatever sphere he operates, resolve that no action of his during 1948 shall interfere with the productive capacity of the supply of coal needed by Britain for her recovery.

2 January 1948

COMPLAINED "FOR 25 YEARS"

Complaining that many streets in Thornley were badly in need of being made up, Coun M Fleming said that he believed it would be 25 years since the council began to make protests to the County Council of the condition of the streets. In spite of this, however, little had been done. He had seen cows grazing in one street.

It was agreed to write to the County Council on the matter.

A letter from the County Education Director acknowledge receipt of the Council's request for a nursery school to be provided and stated that a further communication on the subject would be sent in due course.

A draft agreement for the supply of electricity by the North Eastern Electric Supply Company for street lighting at the Park Street and Gore Hall housing sites was approved as far as the price was concerned.

The Thornley Parochial Church Council wrote complaining of the state of the footpath outside the church hall and the road leading by Church Street to the church. A member said other paths had been left in an unsatisfactory state after the recent laying of an electric cable. It was agreed to refer these matters to the highway authority.

MR S FAIRBURN - MISS N KENNY

Monsignor Jeffreys officiated at the wedding in Thornley Church of the English Martyrs of Nora, daughter of Mr and Mrs T Kenny, 13 Darlington Street, Wheatley Hill and Stephen, son of Mr and Mrs Fairburn of Morpeth. Given away by her father (who won the VC during the 1914-18 war), the bride was in white satin beaute with bridal veil and coronet of orange blossom. Bridesmaid, Miss Monica Barber (bride's niece), Station Town, was in blue taffeta and a small attendants, Patricia Matthews and Kathleen Barber (bride's nieces), in blue satin. Brian Bell and Thomas Kenny, bride's nephews were pages. Best man was Mr Thomas Beresford, Wallsend (bride's brother in law). Reception was in Wheatley Hill Temperance Hall, and later the couple left for Redcar.

WHEATLEY HILL WI

Mrs Hutchinson presided at the monthly meeting and extended New Year's greetings to members. Mrs R Smithson was elected delegate to the Produce Guild meeting at Houghall, and final arrangements were made for the children's party to be held in the Welfare Hall on Saturday from 2 – 5.30pm. Mrs Hutchinson was MC for a whist and domino drive and prize-winners were: Mesdames Starke and J White (whist), Whinn (dominoes). Homemade mince pies competition: Mrs Smithson. Members of West Cornforth WI, who were cordially thanked, presented the pantomime "Dick Whittington". Tea hostesses were Mesdames J Robinson, Armstrong, Baxter, Weirs and Pryor. Officers elected were: President, Mrs Hutchinson; vice presidents, Mrs Baxter and Mrs Wharrier; secretary,

Mrs Poole; assistant secretary, Mrs Pryor; treasurer Mrs Atkinson; assistant treasurer Mrs Poulson; handicrafts secretary, Mrs Weirs; produce guild secretary, Mrs Smithson; press correspondent, Mrs Tyson.

LUDWORTH R S -v- EASINGTON LANE

A great game took place at Ludworth, when the Rising Star entertained Easington Lane in the Durham Amateur Cup competition, fourth round. It was always a great struggle, with the visitors winning by the odd goal in seven. Burnside put the home side in the lead, but within 15 minutes of the start, Shanks had equalised. At half-time another goal from Smith had put the Lane into a 2-1 lead. The issue seemed sealed when Purvis and Williams added other goals in the first half of the second period, but Ludworth fought back hard and by ten minutes from the end, Lofthouse and Hughes had brought the deficit to only one goal. In the last minutes the Rising Star men fought desperately hard for an equaliser. Over £9 was taken at the gate.

COUNCIL'S OBJECTIONS TO PETERLEE

The Parish Councils of Haswell, Hutton Henry and Thornley have all had acknowledgments of the objections they have sent in to the new town of "Peterlee." In reply the Ministry of Town and Country Planning state that the councils will be notified of the date of the public inquiry. The three objecting councils have decided to confer on the question of putting their objections to the representative of the Ministry at the inquiry.

It is understood that all the objections are on similar lines, the main one being that after houses now under construction are completed all house-building will be concentrated on Peterlee. The Councils feel that improved amenities, such as the making-up of streets, the clearing up of rubble from demolished houses, and the building of new houses to take the place of old houses, is not likely to be carried out when work is concentrated on the new town.

One of Thornley's objection is that miners will be compelled to travel from Peterlee when this could be avoided by providing houses at Thornley.

9 January 1948

HOLIDAYS AT THORNLEY

Mr J R Kilburn at the talk on "Peterlee," given by Coun G Roseby, said that many people had differences of opinion as to where they thought they should live. He related a story of a time 40 years ago when he brought a young lady from Shotton to Horden by pony and trap conveyance and pulled up at the top of Ellison's Bank where by far the best view of Horden in the valley is always obtained.

He asked the young woman if she did not think that it was a beautiful sight. "I don't see anything more beautiful about it than I see at Shotton," she replied, "and in fact I can see nothing nice about Horden."

Mr Kilburn was so surprised that he asked her where she spent holidays each year. He was amazed when she said "I go every year to spend my holidays with my grandmother at Thornley."

GERMAN BRIDE AT THORNLEY

A German girl, Miss Waltrout E Beyer, who came to this country from Essen, in Germany, to marry her fiancée, Mr John W. Hill second son of Mr and Mrs T H Hill, of The Villas, Thornley, had the company of her brother, Heinz Beyer, at the wedding at Thornley Parish Church. He travelled from his POW camp near Edinburgh to attend the wedding . The bride was given away by the bridegroom's father and Mr George Hill bridegroom's brother was best man. Rev J M How, Vicar of Thornley, officiated. Couple met while the bridegroom was serving with HM Forces in Germany. The bridegroom is in business with his father as butchers at Thornley.

23 January 1948

LEGION WOMEN'S SECTION

Mrs R Slater, Thornley British Legion (women's section), has won a competition for standard bearer at Durham. She now becomes county standard bearer for the second time, and will shortly visit York to compete for area position.

WORKMEN'S CLUB

Of six candidates for the office of Chairman of Thornley Workmen's Club, Mr John French was elected. Mr R Bosomworth was elected secretary for the 13th year, defeating three opponents. Mr W Walls (treasurer) and Mr M Soppitt (doorkeeper) were re-elected without opposition. Committee elected: Messrs F Walker, A Bullock, W Hall and J Frost

30 January 1948

EAST DURHAM SPORT

Visiting Trimdon Grange on Saturday in the third round replay) of the Hartlepools Hospital Cup, Wheatley Hill Welfare qualified to visit Fishburn Athletic in the semi-final as the result of a 2-1 victory. Though kicking off against a strong wind, the Welfare were soon on their attack and from Wardell's centre Buck grazed the crossbar. Trimdon improved, but during a series of dangerous attacks the visiting defence stood firm and Gibson dealt smartly with several good shots. Soon after the interval Ross gave Trimdon the lead, but the Welfare's persistent pressure resulted in G W Bean equalising. Ten minutes from the end Gaskell headed the winning goal from Carr's beautiful pass. Home team were well served by W Thompson and Wardell, Wheatley Hill, was the best forward on view.

HOUGHTON FOOTBALL LEAGUE

Only Houghton and District League game to take place was that between Meadows CW and Ludworth RS. The wind ruled the game from start to finish and football was scrappy. Ludworth scored four goals through Soppit, Burnside, R and A Hooper. Meadows, well served by Gallon and Lawrence, could do nothing in attack, and could not reply to the Ludworth score.

WINGATE PARISH COUNCIL - A "SMASHING" EPIDEMIC
WANTON DAMAGE TO LIGHTING

Following the receipt of a letter from the head electrician at Wheatley Hill colliery requesting a supply of 100 watt and 60 watt lamps for street lighting as there was a "serious" epidemic of lamp-breaking, several members of the council, at the monthly meeting, expressed deep concern at the wanton damage being done to the public lighting at Wheatley Hill. The Clerk (Mr William Stoker) alleged that children with toy weapons resembling "pop guns" were puncturing the lamps and putting them out of action.

"New lamps have been fitted on a Tuesday or Wednesday," said the clerk, "but by the week-end had been broken. As fast as we put them on they are being knocked off and the whole place is crying out because of the darkness." Coun .A .Crossley proposed that they issue warning posters to try and remedy the matter, and was supported by CounR Hird. The motion was finally agreed upon and the Clerk was instructed to order the necessary posters.

13 February 1948

WHEATLEY HILL

PLAY - Great appreciation was expressed of the play, "Caste", presented by the Arts Council of Great Britain, in conjunction with the Miners' Welfare Commission, at Wheatley Hill. Local arrangements were made by County Coun E Cain, secretary, Wheatley Hill Miners' Lodge.

NEW AMBULANCE - At the annual meeting of Wheatley Hill Colliery Hospital and Ambulance Fund it was reported that the new ambulance, which had been bought for £1,076, would be publicly exhibited in the welfare ground at Wheatley Hill on Sunday from 11 a.m. to 2 p.m. A new garage was nearing completion to house the ambulance and one of the two old ambulances was to be sold. A balance of £300 still remained in the fund, and during the year the following donations had been made: Hartlepools Hospital, £200; Newcastle RVI, £100; Sunderland Eye Infirmary, £60. Mr R Hird was re-elected president for the 27th successive year, Mr H Bradshaw treasurer for the 14th year and Mr. J J Harrison secretary for the 13th year. Other officers elected were: Auditors, Messrs N Cook and T Taylorson; governor to Hartlepools Hospital, Mr T Bradley ; governor to Newcastle RVI, Mr A Hardy; committee, County Coun E Cain and Messrs J Frost, J Mawson, H Smart, H Peacock and J Brandling.

20 February 1948

WHEATLEY HILL FUNERAL –
BODY BROUGHT FROM AMERICA

The body of a former Wheatley Hill woman, Miss Mollie Lee (60), niece of the well-known Durham Miners' Leader, the late Mr Peter Lee, reached this country on Tuesday from New York for burial at Wheatley Hill cemetery. Miss Lee left Wheatley Hill in 1922 to be a children's nurse in America. Since leaving this country she had returned for three holidays, her last visit being 15 years ago.

"It was always her expressed wish to be brought back to Wheatley Hill when she died", a brother, Mr Thomas Lee, told our reporter, "and when we were notified by cable of her sudden death we immediately cabled back asking for the necessary arrangements to be made for her body to be sent here for burial. My brother and I met the ship which brought my sister's body over, when it docked at Liverpool and we saw the coffin put on the railway for Darlington, from which place it was brought to Wheatley Hill by road.

Mr Lee said they were very grateful to American friends of his sister in New York who had helped with the arrangements for the transport of the body.

The funeral of Miss Lee took place from the home of her brother-in-law and sister, Mr and Mrs M Rowley of 19 Shinwell Crescent, Wheatley Hill and Requiem Mass was conducted in Thornley RC Church by Monsignor Jeffreys.

27 February 1948

PETERLEE

Now that the Minister for Town and Country Planning has approved the scheme for the new East Durham Town, Peterlee, it is interesting to note the reactions.

Coun George Barnes, chairman of Easington RDC said, "I am pleased. This is the council's reward for their pioneering efforts during the past three or four years in their housing programme."

Mr L Rudd, secretary of the Durham County NFU, deplored the sanction because he says, it will mean that many acres of valuable agricultural land will no longer be available for food production.

12 March 1948

WHEATLEY HILL YOUTH CLUB

It is proposed in the near future to inaugurate a Youth Club at the Senior Boys' School, Wheatley Hill, open to boys attending school from the age of 13 years and nine months. Classes in physical recreation will be held, leading eventually to football, basketball ball and cricket and competitions with other Youth Clubs in the district.

Other games will include shinty and table tennis and other varieties of indoor games, and instruction will be given in P T (and advance forms leading up to pyramids, vaulting and agility).

Arts and crafts are also to figure in the club's curriculum. These will include woodwork, metalwork and plastic work. Girls will also have a part in the club, where they can join in suitable activities, and especially in the mixed drama group and mixed junior choir, which it is proposed to form.

"Excursions will be held during the summer month," Mr G Hornsby , member of the teaching staff, told our reporter, "and these should prove popular with the cycling and hiking clubs." When the club is in full swing the age limit will be raised to 18 years.

MOTHER FOUND CHILD IN FLAMES
Wheatley Hill Tragedy

How a mother found her two-year-old daughter in flames was described at an inquest at Durham County Hospital on Joan Mary Cain (2), daughter of Wm. Patrick Cain (44), council labourer of 21 Wordsworth Avenue, Wheatley Hill.

Norah Cain, the child's mother, stated that at 11.10am on Friday, Joan was playing on the mat in front of the kitchen fire, dressed in a nightdress. Witness removed the fireguard from the fire in order to put on some more coal. She went across the yard to the coal-house and on her return found her daughter on the mat with her nightdress ablaze. Witness pulled off the nightdress but found that the shirt underneath was also on fire and the child was burned about the body. Mrs Cain called for her daughter, Norah, aged 19, who was downstairs, and also summoned a neighbour, Mrs Gibson. Witness and Mrs Gibson smeared the child's body with castor oil, pending the arrival of Dr A P Gray (Wheatley Hill), who ordered the child's removal to hospital.

Mrs Elspeth Gibson, 92 Wordsworth Avenue, corroborated evidence of previous witness. She stated that there was not much fire in the grate and the guard was standing nearby.

Dr V S Metgud, resident surgical officer at the County Hospital, gave the cause of death as severe shock and acute toxaemia due to extensive burns. The child died two days after the accident.

The Coroner (Mr W Carr) returned a verdict of "Accidental Death".

19 March 1948

PREACHERS WED AT WHEATLEY HILL

Local preachers in Thornley, Methodist Circuit, Miss Dorothy Kent, second daughter of Mrs Powell and the late Mr J W Kent, 7 Wordsworth Avenue, Wheatley Hill, and Mr Fred Mitchell, son of Mr & Mrs J G Mitchell, 433 New Cross Row, Wingate, were married in Church Street Methodist Church, Wheatley Hill, on Saturday. Rev J W Thurlby officiated, assisted by Rev Arnold Skelding (Surrey). The bridegroom, a preacher for five years, is actively associated with Wingate North Road Methodist Church, where he is assistant Sunday School superintendent, and the bride, who was received on to the "plan" a year ago, has been a keen worker in the Church Street Church, Wheatley Hill, where she is a chorister. Bride received a wedding gift of blankets from the church choir and the bridegroom was presented with a fruit bowl from the Sunday School.

Given away by her step-father (Mr N Powell), bride was in white satin with a bridal veil and coronet of orange–blossom. She was attended by the Misses Peggy Kent (sister), Irene Mole (cousin), Marjorie Kent (sister), and Chrissie Mitchell (bridegroom's sister), all in blue with head-dresses to match. Best man was the groom's brother (John) and the bride's brother (George) was groomsman. On leaving the church the bride, who carried a gold sovereign in each shoe, was presented with a silver horse-shoe by the bridegroom's niece (Daphne Foster). Reception was in the Welfare Hall, Wheatley Hill, and later the couple left to take up residence in their new home at Station Town.

Bride has been employed on the staff of Wheatley Hill Infants' School canteen and from her colleagues received a gift of a statuette.

26 March 1948

WHEATLEY HILL FIRE ALARM

What might have proved a disastrous fire in Smith Street, Wheatley Hill was averted by the prompt action of Wheatley Hill NFS on Easter Monday night. Shortly before he was going to retire, Mr Harold Todd, a member of the NFS, 15 Smith Street, smelt something burning. Rushing outside to investigate, he discovered smoke coming from the roof of his neighbours, Mr and Mrs J Ellward who live in No 16.

After warning the occupants, Mr Todd raised the alarm and drove the fire unit to the scene, under Section Leader Stanley Poulson, who had been quickly summoned from a nearby dance. The flames, coming through the slates of the roof, were fanned by a strong wind towards neighbouring houses, but the NFS quickly had the fire under control and did not need the services of Horden NFS who had also raced to the scene.

As a precautionary measure furniture was taken from both houses, and Mr Ellwards's two young children were awakened and brought downstairs. With their parents they watched the fireman fighting the flames. Damage was not extensive.

It is believed that the fire started in the chimney of Mr Ellward's house.

WHEATLEY HILL WELFARE were right among the goals at Easter when they played two home games in the Ferryhill and District League. On Good Friday they beat Leasingthorne 7-0 and the following day scored five goals against Bishop Middleham without reply.

FOOTBALL TEAM – Wheatley Hill Welfare, strong challengers for the championship of Ferryhill and District League through winning five points out of a possible six during the Easter holidays, have chosen the following team to entertain Sedgefield tomorrow in a league game: Gibson, G W Bean, J Carr, Veitch, W Bean, Goyns, Buck, Gaskell, Wardell, R Carr, Temple.

NFS SUCCESS – For the second year running, Wheatley Hill NFS have been awarded a silver cup for being the most efficient "retained station" in No 1 Fire Force Areas, which covers all Northumberland and most of

Durham. The unit, which is under Section Leader, Stanley Poulson. has also won a cup for similar efficiency in the "D" sub-area, this being the second successive year also that they have won this trophy.

2 April 1948

MINERS' RELIEF FUND – Mr J Frost presided over quarterly meeting of Wheatley Hill branch of the Northumberland and Durham Miners' Permanent Relief Fund, when the secretary (Mr R Patterson, jun) reported that the quarterly income of £536.15s.3d included members' contributions of £279.5s.3d. Following disbursements were made during the quarter; Widows and children (23), £57.15s: permanently disabled miners (35), £94.9s.2d; minor accident cases (68), £80.12s.

WHEATLEY HILL WI – Mrs Hutchinson presided over monthly meeting, when members, after discussing the proposed increase of 2s.6d in the yearly subscriptions, voted in favour of the proposal. Mrs Poole reported on the county meeting at Gateshead, and collection, in aid of the Hospital for Sick Children, realised £3.19s. It was decided to provide entertainment during the Wheatley Hill Road Safety Week. Dyed egg competition, judged by Mrs Dobson, was won by Mrs Tyson. Entertainment was provided by 17 "granny" members, the accompanist being Mrs Snaith. Hostesses were Mesdames Willis, J Wilson, Thackeray, Wharrier and Ord.

9 April 1948

CASTLE EDEN POLICE AWARDS

Hundred per cent pass was recorded in a St. John Ambulance Brigade examination at Thornley Police Station in connection with Castle Eden sub-divisional police. Dr. A Todd was examiner, Mr C Woodward instructor and Sgt R Lander, secretary.

Awards were as follow:- Medallions, Police Constables Douglas (Wheatley Hill), Jackson (Castle Eden), Pedley (South Hetton) and Thorn (Thornley), labels, Insp. R Robinson (Castle Eden), Sgt R Lander, PC Todd (Trimdon Grange) and PC Alderson (Wingate) vouchers, PC's Bayes (Haswell), Peacock (Shotton), Barkes (Shotton) and Hardman (Wheatley Hill).

16 April 1948

THORNLEY PARISH AFFAIRS
Plea for Nursery

Coun Mrs Roper at Thornley Parish Council meeting made a strong appeal for everything possible to be done for the provision of a nursery or a nursery school. She said the ideal would be to combine the two. "If a Victorian came back and looked round she would be pleased with certain of our improvements, but she would eventually ask: "Where are your nurseries?" Mrs Roper said they ought not to be afraid of the expense of providing a nursery, as the expense would be amply repaid in future years by the better bringing up of the children.

It was decided that Mrs Roper and Coun Whitehead were to attend an area meeting of the Parish Councils' Association, when it was expected the matter would be considered before going before the meeting of the County Association.

A letter from Easington RDC thanked women members of the Council for raising £21.6s.4d for the Children of Europe Fund. It was mentioned that a collection arranged by Monsignor G J Jeffreys had raised a further £9.

There was a complaint of rubble being left lying about the entrance of the burial ground and it was decided to ask the authority responsible to clear it away.

Land Reclamation
Reclamation of a stretch of low lying land between Thornley and Wheatley Hill was considered on the suggestion of County Coun E Cain, who recommended that the parish councils of Thornley and Wingate should go into the question. Coun J H C Scott said it would be very desirable to have the land reclaimed, but as the estimate cost was £58,000 it seemed hopeless to expect that anything could be done at the present time.

Easington RDC wrote stating that they would go into the matter of leasing to the Parish Council a piece of land near the Welfare Hall site as a playing field. It was stated that the leasing of other land in the vicinity for the same purpose had been held up pending the decision of the Northern Town and County Planning Authority.

7 May 1948

INQUEST ON WHEATLEY HILL CHILD
A verdict of "Accidental Death" was returned by the jury at the Hartlepools inquest on Derek Carr (6) of 14 Weardale Street, Wheatley Hill, who died in Hartlepools Hospital from multiple injuries received when he was knocked down by a 'bus near St Godric's RC School on the Wheatley Hill-Thornley road. The driver of 'bus was exonerated.

11 year old Joan Carr, Derek's aunt, said they both dismounted from a Triumph 'bus at a stop near the school about 8.45am on 5 May. A

72

'bus was approaching from the opposite direction of Thornley and she held Derek's hand and told him to stand.

Broke Loose

Some children on the opposite side of the road, however, called out, "Derek Carr is a baby", and the boy broke loose and ran towards them. Joan shouted to him to stop and Derek appeared to halt as if undecided in which direction to go, but ran the wrong way and was hit by the 'bus.

Frederick A Cuthbertson, 23 Linden Road, West Cornforth, driver of the 'bus, said it was his intention to stop at the school barrier, but the bell did not ring and, noticing the 'bus stop ahead, he carried on. The boy suddenly darted across the road from behind a stationary 'bus, and he immediately applied his brakes and did all that was possible in the short time that remained.

14 May 1948

THORNLEY WI

At the 23rd birthday party president, Mrs J H C Scott, welcomed about 150 members and friends. Each person received a portion of a birthday cake, which was presented to the Institute by Mrs Scott, who was thanked by Mrs Tully. Winners of the whist and domino drive were:- Whist: Mesdames Winter, Kellet, E Henderson and Cass, Mr Potts and Mr Winnard. Dominoes: Mrs Taylor. Refreshments were served and an excellent entertainment was provided by Mr and Mrs Galley, of Horden, the accompanist being Mrs G Wilson (Thornley).

WHEATLEY HILL PIT FIRE

Morning Alarm

Awakened by the fire alarm siren at Wheatley Hill shortly before 4 o'clock on Whit Monday morning, 25 year old Leading Fireman Frank Horner, 2 Stanhope Street, dashed out of bed, wondering where the fire was, to take charge of the local fire unit. He soon discovered the cause of the alarm for as he opened his back door to rush across to the nearby fire station a clear picture of the fire at Wheatley Hill No 2 Pit heapstead, confronted him a few hundred yards distant.

"When our unit of nine firemen reached the scene", Horner told our reporter, "flames nearly 40 feet high, were shooting through the roof of the tippler, house and licking up the legs of the pulley wheels of the shaft. The heat was intense and dense smoke and sparks were flying in all directions. Until the arrival of two fire units from Horden we attacked the fire with two jets from the north and south side of the pit shaft to prevent the flames from spreading down the shaft itself".

Horden Fire Units, under sub Officer J R Ellwood, and Houghton Fire and Rescue Brigade, under Supt A J G Coulshed quickly reached the fire and the combined efforts of all the fireman had the blaze under control within an hour. Chief Fire officer C V Hall of the Durham County Fire Brigade and Assistant Chief Officer C Tozer directed the operations, and the scene was visited among other officials by County Councillor G E Pritchard (Blackhall), Chairman of the County Fire Brigade, and County Councillor E Cain, Wheatley Hill Miners' Lodge secretary.

Raised Alarm

The alarm was raised when Thomas Kears, the ash-wheeler at the boiler plant, discovered fire and smoke coming from the No 2 Pit heapstead. Many workmen were quickly drafted to the shaft entrance to start repair work as soon as the flames had been subdued so that the minimum time would be lost before normal production was resumed. Above them was a twisted mass of roof supports, and charred timber surrounding them was ample evidence of the trail of damage left by the fire. NCB officials paid high tribute to the work of the fireman whose combined quick action undoubtedly prevented greater damage to the pit shaft itself. The fire is believed to have been caused by a spark from an oxyacetylene cutter used during repair work the previous afternoon.

21 May 1948

THORNLEY BRITISH LEGION

Mr J W Waite was re-elected Poppy Day organiser at a meeting of Thornley branch of

The British Legion. This year's collection will be on 6th November.

The branch is to seek a meeting with the manager of the local Labour Exchange to discuss ex-Servicemen's problems. A report was given on a recent meeting of representatives of Thornley War Memorial Committee and Thornley Miners' Welfare Committee on the question of providing a memorial in the new Welfare Institute, building of which is expected to begin soon.

Legion members were informed that the Ministry of Pensions has agreed to increase the annual grant for wear-and-tear of clothing from £3 to £5 per year for single amputation cases and £5 to £8 for double amputation cases. A concession in education grants has also been made for ex-Servicemen's children.

A circular revealed that the British Legion is desirous of providing financial help to relatives wishing to visit war graves in France, Holland and Belgium.

28 May 1948

FOOTBALLER WEDS
AT WHEATLEY HILL

Sunderland footballer, W Stanley Lloyd, eldest son of Mr and Mrs W Lloyd, 83 Thornlaw North, Thornley, who has played for the First Division club for a number of seasons, was married in All Saints' Church Wheatley Hill, to Miss Margaret Trees, only daughter of Mr and Mrs H Trees, 114 Wordsworth Avenue, Wheatley Hill. Rev P T Casey (Vicar of Wheatley Hill) officiated.

W Stanley Lloyd

Given away by her father, bride was in white lace, with a bridal veil and coronet of orange blossom. The bridesmaids Misses Bessie Galley and Hilda Dixon, were in blue and pink lace respectively, with picture hats to match, and the small attendants, Ann Trees (bride's cousin) and Freda Bradwell, wore white net over satin, with white satin poke bonnets to match, Geoffrey Lloyd (groom's brother) was page-boy, wearing blue velvet trousers and white satin blouse. Mr George Harris (Thornley) was best man and Mr Robert Robinson (bride's uncle) groomsman. Reception was in the Welfare Hall, and later the happy couple left for London.

During the war the bridegroom served in the Royal Navy for 3½ years. For the past seven years the bride has been employed at Moore's Stores, Wheatley Hill, having been manageress for the past two years. From members of the staff she received a wedding gift of a wicker stool

4 June 1948.

75

SOUTH AFRICA BOUND
THORNLEY FAMILY SEEKS NEW LIFE

When they board the "Arundel Castle" at Southampton on Tuesday, a young Thornley couple will be taking the first step in a new adventure abroad, for which they have been making preparations during the past few months. The couple, Mr and Mrs George Kime Oswald, 118 Thorn-law North, Thornley, who with their six year old only child, Judith, are leaving for Natal, South Africa, where work in the mining industry has been found for Mr Oswald, who is 35.

The couple first began to think of a new life abroad when they read glowing accounts of South Africa's prospects from Mrs Oswald's 34 year old brother, Jonathan, who went to live there last July. When he was wounded while serving as a paratrooper during the war, Jonathan was sent to a hospital in South Africa and there met his future wife. They were married in Durban and the young bride followed her husband to this country when he was "demobbed." After a year in England, however they decided to return to Durban. Jonathan has since been working in the Utrecht mines

In Same Mines

Mr Oswald has been guaranteed work in the same mines and it was partly through the efforts of the mine manager that he obtained a priority passage for both himself and his family.

"We are going straight to a home of our own in Utrecht," Mr Oswald told our reporter, "and naturally my wife and I are looking forward very much to a happy future in a new country". Until two years ago, when he became a male nurse at Winterton Hospital, Sedgefield, Mr Oswald was a miner for 18 years at Thornley Colliery. For the past 25 years he has been a member of Thornley Colliery Silver Band, being the principal cornet player, and he has also appeared in many dance bands in the area.

Since selling up their home a few weeks ago, Mr and Mrs Oswald have been living with Mrs Oswald's parents, Mr and Mrs R Richardson, 8 Darlington Street, Wheatley Hill. Mr Oswald's parents also live at Wheatley Hill in Wordsworth Avenue. Mrs Oswald is a grand-daughter of 84 year old Mrs Catherine Cowie, 55 Wordsworth Avenue, who, with the rest of her family, wish Mrs Oswald and her husband every success in their new life overseas.

11 June 1948

WHEATLEY HILL'S "NUT-CRACKER" CLUB

Formed six months ago to provide cultural and social activities for young people of Wheatley Hill and district over 18 years of age on a Sunday evening, Wheatley Hill "Embassy Nut-Cracker" Club has made rapid progress and at an "open night" in the Embassy Ballroom on Sunday, over 120 people were present. Mr R Crosby, manager of the ballroom, was compere for an enjoyable variety programme and Mr W Horne accompanist.

A short play, "Man Power," was presented by Mr Alf Watson and Mr Robert Greenwell and Messrs L Etherington, W Watson and T Hall took part in a humorous sailor sketch. Humour was also provided in large doses by Mr J Lamb, "The Conjuror Who Forgot". Choral items were given under the conductorship of Mr G Hornsby, Miss Watson sang, and Mr "Andy" Hardy sang and played the piano accordion.

Members of the, "Nut-Cracker" Club, now numbering 70, meet at 8pm every Sunday and different tastes are catered for in a programme of discussions, debates, dramatic shows, music and dancing. Membership fee is 1s.6d a quarter, and the hall is generously loaned free by Mr Crosby. Mr F Lamb is secretary of the club.

9 July 1948

AGED PEOPLE'S TRIP – Annual outing for retired aged miners at Wheatley Hill Colliery and their wives and widows of superannuated members over 55 or those with sons working at the colliery, is to be held at Whitley Bay on Tuesday 20 July. This was decided upon at a meeting of Wheatley Hill Aged Miners' Homes committee, representative of all sections of workmen and officials at the colliery. It is expected that about 300 will go on the trip and each will receive 7s.6d pocket money. County Coun E Cain, JP is in charge of arrangements.

OUTING – About 300 Sunday School scholars and friends of Church Street Methodist Church, Wheatley Hll, went by train for their annual outing to South Shields. Arrangements were made by Sunday School Secretary, Mr M Nixon.

BANNER CARRIERS – At a meeting of Wheatley Hill Miners' Lodge the following banner carriers (each of who will be paid 30s and his travelling expenses) were chosen for Durham Miners' Gala Day: Messrs. F Wales, G Pryor, F Alderton Jnr, J R Walton, J Fawkes, D Thackeray, J Bartley and W Galley; reserves Messrs S Burnside and T Harper Jnr. It was decided to give each full member working at the colliery 7s for Gala Day and each half member 3s.6d.

WHEATLEY HILL WI – A film show was given by Newcastle representatives of the Central Office of Information at the monthly meeting. Mrs Hutchinson presided and collectors were chosen for a flag day this weekend in aid of the Sunderland Blind Institute. It was decided to enter next year's county bulb competition, and Mrs Poole was chosen to grow the tulips and Mrs Atkinson the hyacinths. In response to an appeal, a donation of £10 was made towards a village memorial clock to be erected by the local women's war committee. Mrs P H Galley won the snapshot competition and games were held during the social half-hour. Hostesses were Mesdames R Chisholm, J Chisholm and Craggs.

9 July 1948

DURHAM MINERS GALA
SCENES TO BE FILMED

Yet another Durham miners' gala is at hand, the 65th of a long series beginning in a small way in Wharton Park.

With the passing of time have come many sweeping changes, the foremost of which was the nationalisation of the industry. But while the era of agitation has gradually subsided the miners' Big Meeting loses nothing in the way of popularity, so that given fine weather, the streets of the old world city will on Saturday re-echo the tread of a myriad feet and the music of scores of bands as the miners and their wives pass in orderly processions to the race-course to listen to the speakers.

Innovation

Several innovations are announced for Saturday's pilgrimage. The gala, including the Cathedral service, is to be filmed: trainees from the New Kyo and Easington Centres are to march in the procession and the miners will receive a civic welcome from the Mayor (Coun H C Ferens).

In memory of those who have lost their lives in the mines of the county since the last gala massed bands from Hetton, Kibblesworth, South Moor, Silksworth, Ravensworth, Dawdon, Craghead, Blackhall, Beamish, Thornley, Washington and Boldon (nearly 400 instrumentalists) will play the hymn, "Gresford," under the conductorship of the composer, Mr R Saint, Hebburn. The copyright of this composition, which was inspired by the mine explosion in Gresford, South Wales, twelve years ago, is now vested in the Durham Miners' Association.

23 July 1948

"SAFETY QUEEN"
AT THORNLEY

Miss Denie Hitch, daughter of Mr and Mrs N Hitch, Hartlepool Street, Thornley, was elected as Thornley's "Road Safety Queen" at a dance at the Embassy, Wheatley Hill. The judges were Dr Monica Felton (Chairman of Peterlee Corporation), Mrs Carr (wife of Mr G Carr, headmaster of Wellfield A J Dawson School) and Mrs Dobson (wife of Mr T H Dobson manager of Thornley Colliery).

Mrs Carr presented the sash (Miss Thornley) to Miss Hitch, and Dr Felton handed her a prize. She also presented a prize to Miss Monica McGuinness, winner of the second place.

A vote of thanks to the judges and to Mr Crosby (manager of the Embassy) was moved by Coun W Brereton, seconded by Coun J H C Scott. The sash was provided and made by Mr W Hetherington and Mr and Mrs H Hetherington.

Mr J H Pattison (chairman of the road safety entertainments committee) presided.

Short talk on road safety was given by PC Jackson, accidents prevention officer, Castle Eden. Arrangements were made by Mr W Davies, entertainments organiser.

30 July 1948

WINGATE PARISH COUNCIL
CRITICISM OF PETERLEE BOARD

When, at the monthly meeting of Wingate Parish Council, a letter was read from the Peterlee Development Corporation Board, saying that the technical staff would appreciate advice to "determine the appropriate standard of public open spaces to be provided in the new town," the council decided to reply that the Corporation's first consideration should be houses for the workmen travelling to Peterlee from the surrounding villages.

"They seem to be starting at the wrong end first," declared Coun G B Hobbs (Wingate). "There's a lot of chatter about nothing and they are getting nothing done. They want to get on building the houses!"

The letter from the Corporation stated that the standard of public open spaces must be based on local experience. A survey was being made of existing open spaces, but to complete the picture they wished to discover present needs as reflected in plans to provide further open spaces approved by the council, but not yet carried out, plans favourably discussed, but not formally approved, and any evidence for playing fields and other facilities.

"I think," said the Clerk (Mr William Stoker), "that the Corporation are engaging a sufficiently high staff with handsome wages and salaries to conduct this business themselves." Coun A Crossley (Wingate) said it appeared to him that the Corporation were seeking information as to the needs of the community who would be moving into Peterlee. The chairman, Coun E Wharrier (Wheatley Hill), emphasised the need for homes to be built for workmen travelling into the new town area. "People travelling should have the first choice," he declared, "and that will leave houses in our villages for the big lists we have waiting for them."

13 August 1948

COLLIERY ACCIDENT

Following an accident at Thornley Colliery, Stanley Cooper (43), 20 Morris Crescent, Thornley, was admitted to Durham County Hospital early on Saturday morning. He had sustained a compound fracture of the right fibula.

20 August 1948

CELEBRATION AT THORNLEY
Legion "Birthday"

The women's section of Thornley British Legion held their 23rd "birthday" party in the club hall, when over 200 members and friends were entertained to tea. Mrs Bovill (president) welcomed those present and spoke of the work done by the branch. She appealed to non-members to join the Legion and help in the good work. "Our motto", she said, "is service, not 'self'".

Mrs Clark presented the speaker with a bouquet. Mrs Bovill cut a cake iced in Legion Colours, made by Mrs T Bosomworth (late treasurer) and iced by Mrs S Parker (late secretary).

After tea the Legion concert party, trained by Mrs Slater and Mrs Bosomworth, gave a concert. Accompanist was blind Jackie Toye, with his piano accordion, and soloists were Mesdames Millington, K Ord and Slater. Mrs Hedger (county secretary) was guest, and spoke to Mrs Slater (branch standard-bearer), who has won the county and area competitions for two years in succession, and has been presented with a silver cup and gold badge. Speaker wished her luck in this year's competition.

Sketches and singing followed, with M Chapman, E Convery, H Mitchell, E Barrass, M Anderson, S Hyman, M Dobbin, M Mitchell and S Baldasera taking part.

HASWELL PLOUGH MINERS DEATH

While working as a datal hand near the shaft bottom at Wheatley Hill Colliery on Monday morning, John William Williams (43), married, 44, Gloucester Terrace, Haswell Plough, collapsed and died before reaching the surface. The Coroner for the district has been notified.

3 September 1948

CHECKWEIGHMAN RESIGNS

So that he can work underground as a stoneman and, in his own words, "make more money", 47-year-old Mr Horace Bradshaw, 14 Stoker Crescent, Wheatley Hill, has resigned the position of checkweighman at Wheatley Hill Colliery after 14 years service. "The present wage paid to the checkweighman at Wheatley Hill Colliery", Mr Bradshaw told me, "is not commensurate with the job's responsibilities. With the colliery now only working a five-day week, my weekly wage has only been £6.1s, less 6s.6d off-takes. This is insufficient to support a wife and four children and, knowing that I can make more money down the pit, I decided to give up my job as checkweighman".

Mr Bradshaw, who finishes as checkweighman tomorrow and starts down the pit on Monday, has worked at Wheatley Hill Colliery since leaving school at 14. He was a datal lad, then putter and coal-hewer, and left the latter work, when, in 1934 he was appointed checkweighman out of more than 20 applications. A keen trades unionist, he has been compensation secretary of Wheatley Hill Miners' Lodge for five years, and before that was lodge delegate for ten years. For nearly 15 years he has been treasurer of Wheatley Hill Hospital and Ambulance fund.

Members of the Wheatley Hill Checkweigh Fund, at a meeting on Sunday, decided not to appoint a successor to Mr Bradshaw, but to carry on with only one checkweighman, County Coun E Cain, JP, who has filled the position for many years. Coun Cain incidentally is still in Hartlepools Hospital making a slow recovery from his recent operation.

UNLUCKY THORNLEY ST GODRIC'S

Thornley St. Godric's had Ferryhill Station S.C. as visitors in the Ferryhill and District League and, in an even game, were unfortunate to lose by two goals to one. There was not much football to see but thrills there were aplenty.

After a great deal of midfield play, Thornley went ahead through P Tonks, who converted a penalty. Just before half-time Ferryhill were on terms, also from the spot.

P Tonks had another penalty chance in the second period, but his low drive was well saved. Then M Taylor, their centre forward, failed to get control of the ball when only three yards from the goal line. All were expecting a drawn game, when C Harle scored a fortunate goal for the visitors. He kicked a high ball towards the goal and when A Bonar, the 'keeper, came out too far, the ball bounced over his head into the net.

Tonks did well at left half for Thornley while R Waller and F Carraghan were good inside forwards.

In another Ferryhill and District game, Wheatley Hill gained a 4-1 victory over Coxhoe, who had won their first two games.

10 September 1948
PRIZE GARDENER AT WHEATLEY HILL

When reminded that Mr A Rowntree speaking at the Durham County Press and Houghall Show, had said that some of the vegetables displayed at that show were good enough to win prizes at Southport Show, Mr George Charlton, well-known Wheatley Hill exhibitor, said it did not pay him to compete there, owing to the distance and the fact that it was a three-day show. "It pays me better to show at Halifax" he said. "The prize money is better than at Southport. Recently I left home about 5.30 in the morning for Halifax, arrived there at half-past eight, and was back at home about 10.30 at night, after having picked up £18 in prize money".

Mr Charlton is quite a famous Halifax winner. This year, with seven entries, he took six firsts and a second. He won the Halifax trophy this year for the most meritorious display in the show. Once he has won first prize for the best allotment in Durham County and twice he has been second – an excellent record.

WHEATLEY HILL CRICKET

Though halfway through the season, they had been hit by injuries, both Wheatley Hill cricket teams finished third off top in their respective divisions of the Durham Coast League. Reporting this at the annual meeting of the cricket club on Saturday night, the secretary, Mr A Stark, said that the season's best bowling feat was, strangely enough, that of a recognised batsman, George Gribbens, who took five wickets for only seven runs against Jobling's Welfare. With an undefeated innings of 68 against Chilton Moor, G Smart had the best individual batting performance.

Best batting averages were: First XI – G Smart (26.8), T Urwin (17.77), J W Moore (17.70). Second XI – E Snowden (29), R H Poole (26), W Smart (17). Topping the bowling averages were: First XI – R Patterson

(8), W Woodhead (9.81), G Carr (11.57). The bowling of Woodhead who is only 16, was particularly praiseworthy in view of the fact that it was his first season in league cricket.

It was decided to again compete in the Durham Coast League and to advertise for a match professional. Officers were elected for next season as follows: President, Mr T H Dobson. Patrons: Messrs. J H B Forster, R Crosby, H Smith and A Cairns; Chairman, Mr R Simpson; vice-chairman, Mr W Snowden; Secretary, Mr A Stark; Treasurer, Mr T E Turner; Auditors, Messrs E Ward and R Jordan; League Representatives: Messrs R Simpson and A Stark. Committee: Messrs G Hughes, T Hall, R Patterson sen., G Harper, W Pyecroft, T Hird, J Soulsby, R Blacklock, W Vincent and S Wilson. Captain – First XI J W Moore; Captain Second XI T Cowie, vice captain T Ayre.

17 September 1948

DRAW FAIRER

One of the best games seen for a long time was that between Ryhope C. W. Reserves and Ludworth R.S. on the latter's ground, and though Ryhope won by the odd goal in three, a draw would have been more fitting to this hard- fought game.

It was a case of the visiting forwards fighting for supremacy over the home defence, with Hooper, left-half, one of the famous brothers in first-class football, and Harrison and Youll outstanding. On the Ryhope left flank, Tolchard and Fitzsimmons were always dangerous and each netted. Gradon scored for Ludworth.

1 October 1948

RINGWORM FROM A PIT PONY
Unusual Case from Wheatley Hill

A claim for loss of earnings by a Wheatley Hill miner who alleged that he contracted ringworm from a pit pony at Thornley Colliery was dealt with by Judge Gamon at Durham County Court on Monday, when he awarded Alfred Huntington (35), South Side, Wingate Lane, £5.6s.8d by way of workmen's compensation. Plaintiff had claimed £22.16s damaged against the NCB for loss of earnings, the claim being based on the alleged negligence of defendants in not taking proper care of the workmen.

When the case first came before the Court in July, plaintiff said he had been putting with two ponies, "Silver" and "Topsy", and when putting he wore a sleeveless vest, so that his shoulder came in contact with the ponies' hindquarters. Red blotches appeared on his left arm and later

83

spread all over his body. He went to Dr Gray, who diagnosed animal ringworm.

Giving judgement, His Lordship said he was satisfied that plaintiff did contract ringworm in the pit, and as a result was off work for three weeks. The action for damages would fail, and on that claim he gave judgement for the NCB.

1 October 1948

GATHERING AT WHEATLEY HILL
Presentations to Club Secretary

Many tributes to the work of Mr Thomas Storey, as secretary of Wheatley Hill Workmen's Club, were paid at a gathering in the club when he was presented with a cheque for £50 inside an inscribed wallet from the members of the club, and a certificate of merit and silver badge from the Club Union and Institute, in recognition of his 23 years' unbroken service as club secretary. Mr T Cowie, 29 year old chairman of the club, presided.

Making the presentations, Mr Stan Hall, assistant secretary Durham County Club Union, declared that Mr Storey's record was a "terrific achievement" in a workmen's club where the secretary is elected yearly by the members. "Mr Storey has carried on the job successfully", added the speaker, "and deserves a lot of credit for a lot of work".

"Behind the Scenes"

A Club Secretary, like many another secretary, said Mr Hall, "was always working behind the scenes. "It is all very well for us to have our communal leisure, our glass of beer, our entertainment, our tournament games – in fact, all those things that go to make up club life", he continued, "but we must remember that there is a lot of work going on all the time behind the scenes. Tonight you are expressing thanks for that work in a magnificent way".

Concluding, Mr Hall said he was very proud of their secretary and of the members who had kept him in that position. "We not only salute him as secretary of the club", he added, "but also as a working man and primarily as a club man".

Expressing thanks for the gifts, Mr Storey said he had 30 years' practical experience of club life. His early experiences when he took over the secretaryship in 1925, he said were "not very pleasant ones". The position of the club at that time was very precarious he said. It wasn't an easy task to surmount the difficulties.

The club today, said Mr Story, was in the pleasing position of having many thousands of pounds invested.

WHEATLEY HILL MEMORIAL

Permission has been granted to Wheatley Hill Women's War Committee for the erection of an electric clock on the outer wall of Wheatley Hill Senior Boys' School, facing the front street, as a memorial to Wheatley Hill Servicemen who lost their lives in the second world war. Giving me this information this week, the secretary, Mrs J Atkinson, said it had been agreed to erect a bronze memorial plaque at each side of the clock with the names of the 30-odd Servicemen who died. As a result of a recent appeal about £50 has been donated by various village organisations towards the cost of the

memorial, bringing the total in the fund to £170. More money is still required, however and anyone wishing to contribute is asked to communicate with either the secretary or treasurer, Mrs G Carter.

WHEATLEY HILL TRAGEDY
Two Died in a Bath

A double tragedy was revealed at Wheatley Hill about six o'clock on Monday night, when a well-known local dentist, Mr J Paley Yorke, 6 The Avenue, Wheatley Hill entered the upstairs bathroom of his home and discovered his one-year-old daughter, Joan and the housemaid, 17-year-old Miss Christina Mitchell dead in the bath. Miss Mitchell was grasping an electric kettle and it is believed that she and the baby were electrocuted.

Mr Yorke's wife and his other young daughter were not at home at the time and before the discovery, Mr Yorke and his assistants had been working in another part of the house entirely unaware that anything was amiss upstairs. Police and skilled electricians were immediately summoned to the scene to make a full investigation into the sad affair and the facts have been forwarded to the coroner for the district. Mr Yorke, who has not long been living in the district, is a popular member of the Wheatley Hill Drama Group and had been given a part in their next production in December.

Bright Personality

Miss Mitchell, who was 17 in June, was the youngest of the family of four sons and four daughters of Mr and Mrs John George Mitchell, 433 New Cross Row, Wingate. Described by all her friends as always full of vitality and a bright personality, she had been in domestic service with Mr and Mrs Yorke for 14 months.

BATH VICTIM'S FUNERAL

Large representative cortege attended the funeral at Hutton Henry cemetery of Miss Christina Mitchell (17), daughter of Mr and Mrs J G Mitchell, 433 New Cross Row, Wingate, whose death in the bathroom of her employer's house at Wheatley Hill was reported in last week's issue. Miss Mitchell who lived at Wingate all her life, was formerly a Sunday School scholar at North Road Methodist Church and had shown an interest in the village's youth movement. Rev J W Thurlby (Wheatley Hill) conducted the funeral service in the North Road Methodist Church, and among the general mourners was Mr J Paley Yorke, Dentist, of Wheatley Hill, whose baby daughter lost her life with Miss Mitchell and was cremated two days previously.

LUDWORTH'S TWELVE GOALS

Ludworth Rising Star had their best gate of the season when they had the 426th Coast Regiment (West Hartlepool) as visitors in the first round of the Hartlepools and District Cup competition. Outstanding for Ludworth were Edwards, Gradon, Whiting and John Hooper (captain).

Hooper opened the scoring for Ludworth, heading in from a corner kick placed by Hughes. Five minutes later he scored again following a pass from Gradon, and then the visitors reduced the arrears. Before half-time Hughes shot a great goal to put Ludworth 3-1 up.

Second period was only five minutes old when Rowe scored from 30 yards. Other goals followed in regular succession from Peachey, Edwards (2), Gradon (2), Lofthouse and Whiting. Coast Regiment did not give up and replied with their second before Lofthouse concluded the scoring with the twelfth for the home team.

It was a good game full of interest with the visitors better than the margin suggested. Mr Parks was a good referee –prompt in his decisions

22 October 1948

SERVICE TO WOMEN'S LEGION

Chairman of Wheatley Hill Section for 12 Years

After 12 years service as Chairman of Wheatley Hill women's section, British Legion, Mrs Mary Forster, 23 Cain Terrace, Wheatley Hill has been succeeded by Mrs M Brain. Since the 1914-18 war during which her husband, Mr Thomas Forster, served in the army, Mrs Forster has always shown an active and enthusiastic interest in the work of the British Legion. She joined the Wheatley Hill section shortly after its formation and served as vice-chairman for three years before her election as chairman. For 12 months she served on the North-Eastern Area committee, then for five years was a member of the Durham County women's committee.

"I have many happy memories of my membership of North-Eastern Area committee", Mrs Forster told our reporter this week. "The outstanding incident was when I was chosen a member of the British Legion Guard of Honour for the present Queen – then the Duchess of York – when she visited the North East in 1936. She had a word for each one of us and I shall never forget the thrill of meeting Her Majesty personally".

Six of Mrs Forster's nine sons have served in the Forces. Five of them during the late war. They are Thomas (Royal Artillery), now manager of the Grapes Inn, Easington Lane; Matthew, a lance-corporal in the RASC, who is now manager of Quarrington Hill branch of the Sherburn Hill Co-operative Society (he was recently secretary of the Wheatley Hill men's section of the British Legion); Robert (RAMC), in business as a barber at Thornley; William (RASC), a miner at Wheatley Hill Colliery and Alfred (RAF) who is employed by Easington Rural District Council. Sidney, Mrs Forster's youngest son, who is the only one of the family unmarried, is still serving in the Somerset Light Infantry which he joined a year past January.

The other three sons of Mrs Forster are also well known in the district. They are James (her eldest), licensee of the Fleming Hotel, Flemingfield. Charles, a miner at Wheatley Hill Colliery and Jack who is employed as a deputy at Dean and Chapter Colliery.

Got Back

Mrs Forster also has three daughters, all married. "My sons who served in the Forces", she said, "all got back home safely without a scratch, for which I was very thankful".

Mrs Forster's husband, a victim of chronic asthma, has worked very little since his demobilisation after the first world war. Though no longer chairman of the Wheatley Hill women's section, Mrs Forster who is 64, is continuing her interest in Legion affairs as a member of the committee.

THORNLEY PARISH AFFAIRS

"The boy and the football seem to go together. It is a pity we have not a village green where the boys could kick a ball about," said Coun Mrs Roper at a meeting of Thornley Parish Council. She was suggesting that the Education Authority be asked to allow their sports field at Thornley School to be thrown open on Saturday afternoon for boys to play upon.

Coun Whitehead thought they would get very little help from the Education Committee, this matter having previously been put to them. If they would agree, said Coun Whitehead, he hoped that it could be used on the summer evenings as well as on Saturday afternoons.

On the suggestion of the chairman (Coun W Brereton) it was decided to put the request to the Divisional Education Committee.

An application by the War Graves Committee to place gravestones to the memory of LACJ McEnaney, ACR Armstrong, and Pte. J Atkinson was granted. The Council agreed that no charges be made.

Coun Fleming reported that the occupier of a house close to a 'bus stop at the east end of Hartlepool Street was complaining of disturbance caused by waiting passengers. It was agreed the Traffic Authority be asked to sanction the removal of the stop to an open space a short distance away.

Six lamp-fittings are to be ordered for Thornlaw North, where there is no street lighting at present.

THORNLEY

SKELETON WANTED - The miners' ambulance class at Thornley, County Durham, lost their demonstration skeleton when their Welfare Institute was burned down in 1944. Now in the market for another skeleton, they find the price is £40, about four times the cost of the old skeleton

RETIRED - After working in the mine for 61 years, except for four years when he served in the1914-1918 war, Mr Amos Robinson, 66 Shinwell Crescent, Thornley, has retired. He began work at Haswell Colliery when he was 12 years old, his wage being 1s a day. Mr Robinson as a hewer worked at Whitworth and East Howle Collieries for 4s a day. Moving to Thornley Colliery 50 years ago, he was appointed a deputy in 1913 and continued in this work until his retirement. Interested in sport, Mr Robinson attended the recent Sunderland –Arsenal match, but found the crowding rather trying. He has seen six Derbys run.

5 November 1948

THORNLEY'S CHOICE FOR RURAL COUNCIL

Mr Joseph J Johnson, of Wheatley Hill, returned unopposed as Labour member of the Easington RDC, is descended from trade union pioneers in Thornley and Wheatley Hill district. When the Northumberland and Durham Miners Permanent Relief Fund was formed, Tom Park, Mr

88

Johnson's grandmother's brother, went from door to door collecting contributions. Today, and for many years past, these contributions have been deducted from the miners' pay-notes. A brother of Tom Park, "Boxer" Park, had his head 'split open' (to use Mr Johnson's words) during the troubles which arose from Thornley "Putt Pay", when the workmen's wages were not forthcoming through the colliery firm becoming bankrupt. Mr Johnson and his late wife were closely associated with the Labour movement at Thornley, and Mr Johnson was chairman of the Thornley Parish Council.

THORNLEY CENTENARY
WATERLOO STREET CHURCH

Members of Thornley Waterloo Street Methodist Church are celebrating the centenary of their church with great enthusiasm. Starting off on 31 October with a visit from Rev Percy S Carden, Chairman of Sunderland District, they are continuing to have special services and social events through November. The sisterhood, choir and Sunday School are all making their contributions and a vast amount of work has been done to prepare the programme. The interior of the building has been re-decorated in honour of the centenary.

The buildings used to be known as the "Wesleyan" buildings but since the joining together of the "Primitives" and the "Wesleyans" in one church the word has naturally been dropped, and residents of the village now refer to the Waterloo Street Church. Since the Thornley Welfare Institute was unfortunately burned down in 1944, the people of the village have learned to appreciate the great value of the accommodation there is in the building, and the trustees have always been generous in placing rooms at the disposal of organisations which have been hard pressed for accommodation. There is the cosy chapel with gallery, a pipe organ, well furnished vestry, guild room and classroom on the ground floor. Upstairs there is a commodious schoolroom. These details are mentioned because it is fitting that tribute should be paid to those past members of the church who in hard times worked for the upkeep and the extension of the premises.

In an interesting souvenir compiled at the request of the trustees, Mr Harry E Cox, head teacher of the Thornley senior school, and a leader in the church, tells how the church arose from the influx of people to Thornley when the colliery was opened. In 1831 there were 50 people in Thornley, all agricultural workers, but in 1841, after the colliery was opened, the number had increased to 2,700. Now it is near 5,000, and it is

89

confidently anticipated that the colliery will continue to work for 70 or 80 more years, which means that the population will probably stay at something like that figure unless transfers are made to Peterlee if and when inferior houses at Thornley are demolished.

Mr Cox says that when Thornley was being pegged out for the erection of houses, cottages and shops in 1837, the early members bought a site for £19, and at once set about building the chapel, even before the legal documents were completed. Such was the enthusiasm that women as well as men carried stones across from the quarry to the site.

In 1844, when Thornley miners were involved in a bitter fight with the colliery owners, which resulted in some men going to gaol, a number were evicted from their homes. These included members of the church. Mr Cox says that up to recent years there was a close relationship between the church and the colliery and that this must have been uncomfortable and distressing at times, as many of the colliery owners and officials were closely associated with the church. Mr Cox leaves it to be imagined how distressing it would be for members of the church to have to inflict the distress of eviction on fellow-members, showing that every generation has its mental as well as its economic anxieties.

Thornley Wesleyan Church was accepted into the Durham Circuit. Preachers had to walk from places as far away as Durham, Chester-le-Street and Brancepeth. Those who were miners would probably get up about 4a.m. on Sunday and would not get home until it was nearly time to go to work on Sunday night or Monday morning.

Enlargement of the chapel took place in or soon after 1865, when the gallery was added, allowing for accommodation for 500, the calculation being at the rate of 18 inches per person. Building had to go upwards because the site was hemmed in by other buildings. In 1876, however, further extensions were made by purchasing two cottages for £470, and in 1910 another cottage, purchased for £300, gave site room for the Sunday School and Institute. The Institute provided recreation and culture for young people-not without heart-burning to the older generation-but it closed when the Miners' Welfare Institute came into being. The pipe organ, costing £650, was dedicated in 1923, free of debt.

The leaders of the church are already facing the difficult problem of more extension, proving that they are actuated by the same enthusiasm as that which enabled their forebears to surmount great difficulties.

12 November 1948

LETTER TO THE EDITOR
AGED MINERS' COAL

Sir, There is much indignation being expressed by mineworkers because retired miners, many of them living in aged miners' cottages, after next Christmas are to receive no more free coal as was customary in previous years. This concession, which before nationalisation provided about a ton of coal free every Christmas, is curtailed to 5 cwt this year after which the Coal Board has announced its complete cessation. It is a commentary upon the past accusations of miners that the late owners were selfish, to find that the present owners, or at least their representatives, are not prepared to be so generous to the veterans of the industry. **EC**

19 November 1948

WHEATLEY HILL VC'S PASSING
Gained Award in First World War

After a six-month illness, Mr Thomas Kenny, 13 Darlington Street, Wheatley Hill, the first Durham County man to win the Victoria Cross during the 1914-18 war, died on Monday at the age of 66. He won the coveted award on 4 November 1915, when as a private in the 13th DLI he made a noble, but vain attempt to save his officer's life in France while under rifle fire.

With Kenny as his observer, the officer, Lieut. P A Brown, of Beckenham, Kent, left the trench to visit a working party in front. They over-ran the wire, were lost in the fog and the officer was shot through both thighs. Kenny took him on his back and for more than an hour ploughed his way through deep mud and debris with bullets whistling over his head. Time and time again Lieut Brown beseeched Kenny to go on alone, but the soldier refused and struggled on until the comparative safety of a ditch was reached.

After making his officer as comfortable as possible, Kenny went to seek medical assistance. It was not until late at night that he discovered a listening post and though almost exhausted, he insisted in guiding a stretcher party to the officer who died, however, before reaching the dressing station.

Met Officer'S Mother

Mr Kenny served throughout the whole of the war and rose to be a sergeant-major. When he left Buckingham Palace after receiving his VC from King George V, he was met at the gates by a middle-aged woman in black. She was Lieut. Brown's mother and, though he had never seen her before, he recognised her by her strong resemblance to her son. Mrs Brown took him to her home in Beckenham and from then onwards until her death 13 years ago, kept up a regular correspondence with Mr Kenny and his wife.

Every year, on the anniversary of Mr Kenny's heroic deed, he received a gift of money as an expression of gratitude from Mrs Brown, and after her death, from her daughter who now lives in Chelsea. The last gift arrived a month ago.

In Home Guard

During the last war Mr Kenny served in the Home Guard. A native of Hart Bushes, South Wingate, he was a miner at Wingate and Wheatley Hill collieries for the greater part of his life until he finished work at the latter pit two years ago. He had lived at Wheatley Hill for the past 21 years and was a member of the local Workmen's Club, where formerly he served on the committee.

Surviving Mr Kenny are his wife, three sons and seven daughters. Funeral took place at Wheatley Hill Cemetery yesterday (Thursday), following Requiem Mass in Thornley RC Church.

3 December 1948

THORNLEY PARISH AFFAIRS

When Coun W Brereton, chairman of Thornley Parish Council, gave a report on a meeting held at Durham for the purpose of re-forming the Durham County Playing Fields' Association, Coun Martin Fleming remarked that he was glad they were getting back to their old democratic way of life. "Everything seems to be in the hands of the State departments. We might soon be getting State ice-cream sandwiches," he said.

Coun C Woodward said there were strong complaints of the fouling of footpaths by dogs at the Half-Way House dog track. The chairman agreed that it was "a barbaric state of affairs," and Coun Whitehead said he had kept dogs all of his life and he knew there was no need of such filthy fouling of the footpaths. It was agreed to ask the proprietor of the track to take the matter up with the owners of the dogs.

Thornley Miners' Lodge wrote asking for better lighting on the Thornley –Wheatley Hill Road. Coun Fleming thought there was good reason for the complaint. It was decided that, while there were still restrictions on street lighting, a useful improvement could be made by fixing new wing-reflectors and increasing the power of the lamps from 60-watt to 100-watt.

It was reported that Mr T H Strong, a member of the Council, had left the district, and it was agreed a letter of good wishes be sent to him.

10 December 1948

"SOUNDING BRASS AND VOICES" AT THORNLEY

Described in their programme as a concert of "sounding brass and voices," Thornley Colliery Silver Prize Band, led by Mr E Kitto, and Thornley District Welfare Male Voice Choir, led by Mr N Strong, joined together.

The audience in Bow Street Methodist Church was a large one, and the performance was highly successful. Items by the band alone were "Punchinello," which opened the concert, selections from Beethoven and "Echoes from Schubert." A horn solo by L Saunders, trombone solo by J Merifield, and a cornet duet by the brothers George and Edward Kitto (sons of the conductor) were well received. Mr Billy Williams sang "Nirvana," and Messrs Williams and A Curry sang "Watchman!, What of the Night?" by special request.

In his remarks, Mr J H C Scott (chairman) said the proceeds were to provide Christmas cheer for the patients in Durham County Hospital.

DEATH FUND OFFICIAL RESIGNS

Mr Joseph Howe, until recently a member of Wheatley Hill Colliery office staff and now cashier at Wingate Grange Colliery, has resigned the post of secretary of the Workmen's and Officials' Death Fund at Thornley, Wheatley Hill and Ludworth collieries. He has held the post for 23 years. Altogether he served the fund for 26 years as secretary, committee member and honorary auditor.

A short time ago he gave up the office of honorary treasurer of Wheatley Hill Aged Miners' Homes Fund after 26 years, being on the committee longer than any other member. Another office Mr Howe has given up is that of chairman of Haswell Moor District County Homes Committee. He was also on the County Homes Committee for 20 years. His public service also includes 10 years as honorary auditor of Wheatley Hill Nursing Association.

THORNLEY PRIZE BAND

Mr Tom Tunney (secretary) reported a successful season at the annual general meeting of Thornley Colliery Prize Band, one of the oldest brass bands in the country.

Out of six contests entered, they had been first on four occasions and second on another. In Durham County Band League, the brothers J and L Merrifield won first prize in the duet competition, while the quartet gained second place in their section.

Juveniles J Youll, E Murray and D Hood also gained awards. The Band had been much sought after for shows, park and seaside concerts.

Mr Tunney spoke of the work done by Mr Waite (chairman for the past 13 years) who was retiring because of ill-health and of the valuable services of Mr E Kitto (bandmaster).

Officials elected are: Secretary, Mr T Tunney, Theodore House, Thornley; Treasurer, Mr R Mitchell; Librarian, Mr S Saunders; Assistant Bandmaster, Mr B Luke; Chairman, Mr L Saunders; Committee – Messrs G Kitto, E Kitto and J
Mitchell; Hon Members – Messrs R Robinson, T Dyke and J Archer.
17 December 1948

1949

LUDWORTH

Annual Dance –Ludworth Rising Star held their third annual dance in the Church Hall. Messrs C Campbell and T Williams were MCs and music was supplied by Cochrane's band. Spot prizes, given by Messrs J G Barnett, S Cook and A Baldasera (Thornley), were won by Misses E Biblingey, J Betts, V Bowman, Mrs D White, Messrs R White and C Robinson. Mrs Appleby was winner of the "lucky dip." Mr C Campbell thanked the guests for the support they were giving to the club and led the singing of "Auld Lang Syne" and other old-time songs after the New Year had been "danced in."

THORNLEY AFFAIRS
Playing Field Request Turned Down

Thornley Parish Council's request, for the school playing field to be used by children outside school hours, has been turned down by Durham County School Buildings Committee. This decision was conveyed to a meeting of the Council in a letter from the Divisional Education Officer. Coun Mrs Roper, who proposed the motion that the request be made, said she thought the reasons ought to be given.

Coun W F Whitehead (presiding in the absence of Coun W Brereton) said he agreed with Mrs Roper. If the Parish Council knew the reasons they might find some way of getting over the difficulties.

It was agreed to ask the Education Authority to state the reasons for turning down the request.

Lighting Request

Making a complaint about the poor electric lighting in houses, Coun J H C Scott said the present standard of lighting was bad for the eyes, "We had better lighting in the tallow candle days," he said. Mrs Roper did not agree with this and said "I well remember doing lots of homework by the light of a paraffin lamp.

Stressing the national difficulties of providing sufficient electricity Coun M Fleming reminded the Council that while they had load shedding they did not have complete cuts like many other parts of the country.

"Nauseating Smell"

Referring to "the nauseating smell from the pit-heap." Coun Scott began a discussion on ways and means of dealing with the trouble. Councillors

Whitehead and Woodward, who have practical knowledge of mining, said the present day methods of machine mining made it necessary to bring refuse to the surface.

Coun Woodward said he knew the officials of the NCB were very concerned about the heap and were taking various steps to reduce the trouble about which people were complaining.

When Mrs Todd said the fumes must be bad for the people's health, Coun Woodward said he knew men who had worked many years on such heaps and were amongst the fittest men employed at the colliery. He said the problem of pit-heaps was very difficult and he had sometimes thought that the very large quarries at Trimdon might be used for dumping pit waste by means of overhead carriers.

The Council did not pass a resolution on this subject.

7 January 1949

THORNLEY COLLIERY OFFICIALS' RETIREMENT

On 1 January 1947, Vesting Day, the National Coal Board's flag at Thornley Colliery was unfurled by Mr Tom Roper, oldest employee of the colliery. He has just retired after working 72 years in the mining industry, 55 of which were spent underground. When 12 years old he began work underground at Wingate Grange Colliery, and in 1892 he went to Thornley as a deputy-overman. Since then he has served as master shifter, back-overman and fore-overman. In 1931 he was given a surface post at Thornley Colliery and has remained in this until his retirement.

Another well-known Thornley Colliery official who has retired is Mr Joseph Box, Gowland Terrace, Wheatley Hill, who has been foreman plumber at Thornley and Wheatley Hill collieries for the past 36 years. He started his apprenticeship at Hetton Lyons in 1893. A native of the district, he intends to live there in his retirement.

14 January 1949

AFTER EXTRA TIME

Spectators at the Wheatley Hill SC v Whitworth Park cup-tie on Saturday, certainly got value for their money. A dramatic last-minute goal by Wheatley Hill made extra time necessary and in this later period the "Hill" scored twice to win one of the most exciting matches seen at Wheatley Hill for many season.

The game was the first round (replay) of the Ferryhill and District League Cup.

Soon after the start the "Hill" nearly went ahead, when, following a centre by Temple, Goynes had his powerful shot kicked off the line. At the other end Gibson did well to hold a great effort by Wray, the visitors' inside-left. Halftime arrived with the score sheet blank, and Wheatley Hill resumed the stronger side.

Half-backs Cudlip, Billy Bean and Carr frequently set the attack in motion, but the forwards could do anything but find the net. The ball frequently stuck in the mud spoiling the home team's efforts to open their account. Seven minutes from time Whitworth broke away and, to the amazement of the home side, went ahead through Juler.

This was a cruel blow to Wheatley Hill, who had definitely been on top, but with only a minute to go a centre from Carr was headed goal-wards by Billy Bean. Again the ball stuck in the mud and in one mad rush, with twelve players in the goalmouth, it was suddenly discovered in the net. No one yet knows who scored, but it was the equaliser and led to extra time and ultimate victory for the "Hill," who took the lead through Goynes and G W Bean.

Wheatley Hill's team to entertain Leasingthorne to-morrow in the Ferryhill and District League is: Gibson: G W Bean: Scott; Cudlip: W Bean: J Carr; M Carr: Laverick: Gaskell: Goynes: Temple.

ILL-LUCK FOR LUDWORTH

Dispute Over Lumley Ground. What is believed to have been a dispute between Lumley Juniors and Lumley Rovers as to who should play on the one ground in their village resulted in misfortune for Ludworth Rising Star. But when the case arising is heard by the committee of the Lumley Nursing Cup competition, it may be a little unfortunate for the Rovers. Ludworth had been due to play Lumley Rovers in the Cup competition, but their secretary received a telegram at 11am on Saturday cancelling the game. Mr C Campbell, chairman, and two committee-men went to Lumley and discovered that the Juniors had claimed the ground for a cup-tie with Broom YC.

A Rising Star official writes, "We saw the Lumley Rovers secretary who showed us a letter from the Juniors secretary. It said if the Rovers occupied the pitch the Juniors would take up the goal posts, which belonged to them. The goal nets also belonged to the Juniors."

It is stated that Ludworth intended to claim expenses incurred, the price of a bus to convey the players and committee.

As two buses were engaged, Ludworth will have to stand the cost of one. In addition, as Ludworth are still in three cups and have 12 league games to play, the loss of a Saturday is also unfortunate.

It is understood that there is but one ground at Lumley and it seems unfortunate that the respective officials had not come to some agreement about the ground sooner than they did.

The obvious course seemed to have been the toss of a coin to decide whether the Rovers or the Juniors should have been at home, and the loser should then have forfeited ground advantage to their cup opponents.

If the facts are as reported then Ludworth Rising Star might then be fully justified in claiming the tie- so late was the cancellation.

21 January 1949

SPORTING LUDWORTH
Lumley Rovers Lose Cup-Tie

When committee of Lumley Nursing Cup competition was held to consider claim of Ludworth Rising Star to be awarded the second round tie against Lumley Rovers for non - fulfilment of their fixture, Mr W H Lark presided and was supported by Mr S F Stokoe (president of the competition) and Mr C E Milburn (D F A Council).

After hearing the evidence of the Lumley and Ludworth secretaries, Messers. T Dobson and C Campbell, the committee awarded the tie to Ludworth and called on the Lumley club to pay 10s towards expenses.

The chairman of the committee generously paid this amount on Lumley's behalf, and then Mr Campbell asked the committee to accept the money as a gift to the competition from the Ludworth club.

Mr Milburn said that in his 40 years football experience he had never witnessed a more sporting action.

Vote of thanks to Messrs Milburn and Stokoe was accorded on motion of Mr G P Williams.

28 January 1949

FIRE IN WHEATLEY HILL PIT CANTEEN

An electrical fault is believed to have been the cause of a fire, which broke out in Wheatley Hill colliery canteen shortly before three o'clock on Sunday morning and did damage estimated at £600. The fire originated in the managerial office, where most of the damage was done.

Seeing smoke and flames pouring out of a ventilator of the canteen building on his way to work, a colliery deputy, Owen Rowlands, immediately informed a member of Wheatley Hill Fire Brigade, Leading Fireman R G Horner, who summoned his colleagues. When the brigade reached the scene colliery workmen were fighting the fire with a hose from the nearby pithead baths.

Sub-Officer S Poulson, in charge of the Brigade, and Leading Fireman F Horner broke down the office door and inside found furniture and shelving ablaze. The fire was prevented from spreading to an adjoining storeroom, containing a refrigerator, and the dining room, but severe damage was done to the office and some foodstuffs were destroyed.

The fire was under control in less than ten minutes. Assistance was given by the Horden Fire Brigade, under Sub-Officer J R Ellwood and Leading Fireman G Price, and Houghton NCB Fire Brigade, who were also summoned, stood by as an emergency measure. Many tributes were paid to the firemen, whose prompt work saved the whole of the building from being destroyed.

BOW STREET METHODIST OVER 20 CLUB
Dave Harris, Mr Brewster, Robert Wigham, George Watson, Florrie Waite, Harry Watson, Stan Fort, George Gretton, Curry
Tommy Lincoln, Bella Watson, Nancy Hesit, Dorothy Watson, Sally Gretton, Jimmy Plant, Eric Farrell, Vera Curry, Isabel Watson, Clive Lincoln

WOMEN'S SECTION

At The Fortnightly meeting of Wheatley Hill women's section British Legion, presided over by Mrs Brain, arrangements were made to visits two Newcastle pantomimes. One new member was enrolled. Winners of special competitions were Mesdames Robinson, Foster and Alderton.

"THE MISER" A Full House in the Welfare Hall, Wheatley Hill, on Monday enjoyed Miles Malleson's version of Moliere's comedy, "The Miser," presented by the Northern Theatre Company of the Arts Council of Great Britain in co-operation with the Divisional Miners' Welfare Committee. Arrangements were made by County Coun E Cain, secretary, Wheatley Hill Miners' Lodge.

11 February 1949

SHOTTON COLLIERY - 18 year old boxer, Terry Cullen, is attracting notice by his stylish displays in the professional ranks at West Hartlepool, Middlesbrough, Newcastle and Ryhope. In three years he has had 14 fights, only one of which was amateur, and of those he won 12, drew one, and had one defeat. He is being nursed with a view to reaching top-line class, and is under the wing of Mr Pat Ibbensen. His victories to date have been five knockouts, four on points, one retiring, two stopped by the referee.

His home training is done under the watchful eye of his father, Mick Cullen, who in his 20's was hailed as Northern welter weight pitman's champion and is himself the winner of 60 fights, which included Alex McBeth, Jim Lawson and Harry Buxton. Terry's last fight was a week ago at Newcastle, when he scored an easy points victory over Jimmy Muirhead and was booked to meet Billy Kane, Newcastle, there on 28th February.

25 February 1949

STARTED SCULPTURE: BECAME A MINER
EDWARD KITTO'S INFLUENCE AMONG
COUNTY BANDSMAN
"MUSIC IS IN HIS SOUL"

Mr Edward Kitto, Thornley, talks, breathes and even dreams of music. Such a man, if he had had the chances in his early years of the young men of the present day, would have held high office in musical circles.

He could not have helped it because music is in his soul, and what is more, he has imparted a love of it to thousands who have come within the sphere of his influence as a bandsman and as the master of Thornley Prize Silver Band for 27 years.

He has inspired a musical interest in his own family Gordon, is principal cornet in the Thornley band and Edward assistant solo cornet. Edward holds a record as a prizewinner in solo competitions but six years in the Army had a deleterious effect upon his health. Gordon has a dance band. Both are gold and silver medallists, and prolific winners of certificates.

Judged Juniors In Oxford

Recently Mr Kitto has been at Oxford judging for the fourth successive year the juniors in their contest under the auspices of the Oxfordshire District Brass Bands Association. Competitors numbered 58 soloists, five in the duet section and seven quartettes.

For seven hours he was engaged in the task, and was able to tell the Association that there had been a greatly improved standard of playing. During his stay in Oxford he was the guest of Mr and Mrs G H Giles, of Headington Band, and he speaks highly of the kindness and hospitality shown to him during an all-too brief stay.

Early Inspiration At Spennymoor

"Where did you get your inspiration?" our representative asked Mr Kitto.

He told him his early intention was to become a sculptor and, as a youth, he served under Robert Swinburn, of Spennymoor, who was conductor of Whitworth Band. He became deeply interested and studied the conductor's technique.

"In later years," he said, "I found that his methods were A1 and a guide to me in my work as a conductor."

About the same period in his young life he came under the influence of Mr Mutton, who was conductor of Spennymoor Temperance Band, and Coun J E Bell (now of Tow Law) who led the Salvation Army Band at Spennymoor, and gave him lessons on the cornet.

Is there any wonder that with such a background Edward Kitto has made his mark in the world of prize bands? His name is known and respected throughout the length and breadth of the land, and stands for all that is good in the world of "good bandsmanship."

The work of a sculptor did not greatly appeal to him and soon he was working in the mines. He found his way to Thornley where he joined the colliery band that was formed in 1919 and two or three years later he was chosen as conductor, an office he has held with distinction ever since.

It would scarcely be possible to enumerate all the young people who have passed through his hands in the last 41 years, but he must have influenced at least 800.

Fifteen of them have been or are conductors of bands in various parts of the country.

Thornley Band has won 200 prizes, and almost as many have gone to the juniors.

In 1929 Thornley Band won the BBC contest among 28 competitors. Fifteen of the Thornley instrumentalists had not produced a note four years before the contest and some of them not even a year before.

His many friends all over the county will wish him many more successes, and many useful years of "happy banding."

4 March 1949

SUDDEN DEATH – Mr George Iddon, 223 Thornlaw South, Thornley, a 56 year old labourer employed by Sedgfield Rural District Council, collapsed and died almost, immediately while digging a trench on the council's building site at Trimdon Village shortly before noon on Saturday. A "veteran" of both world wars, Mr Iddon served in the 1914-18 war in the Border regiment and was awarded the French Military Medal. Shortly after the outbreak of the last war he joined up again in the Northumberland Fusiliers, serving throughout the conflict, and finishing in the DLI as a corporal. A native of Trimdon Colliery, Mr Iddon had lived at Thornley since his marriage. Before starting work for Sedgefield Council some nine months ago, he was employed at Billingham ICI works. He leaves a widow, four sons and two daughters. Funeral took place at Thornley cemetery yesterday (Thursday) following a service in the Parish Church.

FOOTBALLERS' VICTORY – Wingate Lane brought their total of points to five from their last four games when they visited Byers Green in the Ferryhill and District League and won 4-0. Though they faced the wind and snow in the first half the Lane netted all their goals in this period, their marksmen being Patterson, Carter, and Armstrong (2). In the closing stages, Nicholson, Wingate 'keeper, saved a penalty. Tomorrow's opponents were not known at the time of writing, but selected

102

team is : Nicholson; Peacock; Walker; Bosomworth; Smith; Weatherall; Peacock; Carter; Patterson; Stonehouse; Armstrong.

MGR G JEFFERYS
Seventy Priests at Thornley Funeral

Over 70 priests, headed by the Bishop of Hexam and Newcastle (Rt Rev J Macormack), attended the funeral on Friday at Thornley of the Very Rev Mgr George Jefferys (74), priest at the Church of the English Martyrs, Thornley, since 1942, and previous to that headmaster for 20 years of St Cuthbert's Grammar School, Newcastle.

Requiem Mass was sung to a crowded congregation by Fr. L Landreth, of St. Cuthbert's Grammar School, Newcastle, assisted by Rev. A Hannon and Rev P Roache (Ushaw College).

The panegyric was delivered by Fr Marshall, who spoke of Mgr Jefferys' great work in the diocese.

At the graveside in Ludworth Road burial ground the Bishop offered the prayers. Mr Edward Jefferys (London), brother of Mgr Jefferys, represented the chief mourners. Amongt the priests in attendance were Canons Dicks (Stanley), Forkin (Hebburn), F Wilkinson (Darlington), E Wilkinson (St. Mary's, Newcastle), Corcoran (St. Mary's, Newcastle), Pippett (St. Godric's, Durham), and Burke (St Hilda's Hartlepool).

Fr.F Dunn (St. Joseph's, West Hartlepool) arranged the service.

11 March 1949

COXHOE FUR AWARDS

Coxhoe Fur Society held an open table show on Saturday at the old Red Lion Hotel, which attracted over 70 entries. Mr George Foord (Wheatley Hill), with a black Dutch Rabbit, won four first prize awards. Mr B Smith (Middlesbrough) was judge.

600 AT THORNLEY MEETING
"Unfinancial" Men Substituted

More than 600 miners from Thornley Colliery attended a meeting at the Hippodrome Cinema, Thornley, on Sunday, to hear a report by their lodge secretary, Mr W Dowding, on recent negotiations in connection with the proposed re-organisation scheme.

It was revealed that instead of the 129 men to be dispensed with, the number has now been reduced to 115. The Colliery management have decided that 26 "unfinancial" men will be substituted for a corresponding number on the original list.

The lodge secretary intimated that a number of recommendations from the lodge had been laid before the Colliery Consultative Committee and had been substantially agreed. This resulted in a revision of the original list and a consequent reduction in the number of men to be affected by the scheme. Mr Dowding pointed out that of the 115 men, 56 who were 65 and over would get redundancy pay for 26 weeks and would also qualify for State pension.

The remainder would, in addition to 26 weeks redundancy pay, be entitled to unemployment benefit until such time as they could fine work. It was expected that a number of men would be transferred to other pits, but prospects in this direction were not too bright because many collieries appeared to have a redundancy.

Thornley Colliery is more than 100 years old and about 1,500 are employed in the pit. It has a weekly target of 7,000 tons.

It is understood that the reason for the proposed changes is the introduction of new methods of face working.

The meeting was presided over by Mr F Walker, lodge chairman.
18 March 1949

LUDWORTH R S FOUGHT HARD
But Lost In Semi-final

A large crowd saw a grand game at Trimdon between Wheatley Hill SC and Ludworth Rising Star in the semi-final of the Hetton Charity Cup. The gate was a good one, £14 7s. No member of the cup competition committee seemed to be present, and this was commented on by several officials.

A Ludworth supporter claims that the "man in charge" had a poor game.

End to play was a feature of the first 20 minutes, with both sides showing good football. Then came a period of 10 minutes when Wheatley Hill were complete masters. A centre from Temple reached Gaskill, who lobbed the ball into the net.

Wheatley Hill attacked again, and a pass by Slack sent Topping away along the right wing. He crossed the ball right over to Temple and from his centre Laverick scored. Ludworth, although two goals down, fought back valiantly and after Lofthouse had sent Edwards through the latter beat three men before sending in a grand shot had Gibson well beaten.

The leaders put themselves two up again when a mistake by the Star defence let in Temple who recorded an easy goal.

'Keeper In Action

The Star side began the second period in grand style, and Gibson, Hill 'keeper, was often in action. A shot by Brunton hit the upright and one from Orton hit the 'keeper in the chest. Edwards and Martin were doing grand work on the right wing and Martin, with a fine shot from 20 yards, again reduced the deficit to one.

It now seemed as if the Ludworth men were going to draw level, but Wheatley Hill were awarded a free kick and this was taken by Jackie Carr from 30 yards. To the dismay of the Star supporters. Aylesbury allowed the ball to trickle through his hand and put the Hill 4-2 up.

Penalty Action

Ludworth again were not done with and when Edwards scored from a penalty, once again it seemed they were destined to draw level. It seemed all Ludworth, with Gibson saving just under the bar from Harrison. He fell back and the Ludworth appeals that he was over the line were turned down. While they were still appealing, Hill's right wing got away and Gaskitt put them 5-3 in the lead.

Ludworth fought hard, but the issue was settled when Cudlip collected the Sixth goal.

Wheatley Hill were slightly the better on the day's play, but were a little fortunate in that Aylesbury had an off day. He made two mistakes at critical times.

Best for Ludworth were Youll, Edwards, and Lofthouse, while for Wheatley Hill Jackie Carr, Slack, and Temple did well.

COUNTY COUNCILLOR E F PEART
New Member for Thornley Division

Mr Emmerson Featherstone Peart will take the place of County Coun Edward Cain, who was elected during the past triennial period when Coun, Francis Quin retired. Coun Cain, however,recently intimated that he did not seek re-election to the County Council.

Mr Peart was formerly a teacher at Crook, when he took a leading part in a dispute between the Crook Football Club and the Durham Football Association, which involved court proceedings.

He came to Thornley as headmaster of the Mixed School, later resigning to take up the clerkship of Easington and Durham Rural District Councils' Assessment Committee. He joined up early in the last war and served in Germany for about two years after the war ended.

His Son An MP

Formerly a member of the Easington RD Council and secretary of the Seaham Divisional Labour Party, he is now treasurer of the newly formed Easington Divisional Labour Party.

By a coincidence his son, Capt T F Peart MP for Workington, gave the radio talk on "The Week in Westminster" on the same day as Mr E F Peart was nominated for the Durham County Council.

DINNER - At the second annual dinner of Thornley branch of Durham County Enginemen's, Boilerminders' and Firemen's Association, on Saturday, in Thornley Workmen's Club Hall, about 70 members and guests attended. The members were from Thornley, Wheatley Hill and Ludworth pits, and included seven retired members Messrs W Elliott, T Holmes, R Thomas, S Peaceful, J Bulmer, J Lawson and C R Long. Local officials responsible for the arrangements were Messrs. T Allen (chairman), B Pattison (secretary) and W Henderson (treasurer). After an excellent meal and an entertainment by Billy Campbell's (Sunderland) Concert Party. Mr W Henderson, who presided, expressed the pleasure of the Association in having the presence of representatives of the various colliery organisations. He was particularly pleased at the presence of their old members. Mr A Welsh, on behalf of the visitors, thanked the Association for a happy evening.

LEGION PRESENTATIONS - Thornley, Wingate and Ludworth women's sections of the British Legion were represented at the 19th birthday party of Wheatley Hill women's section, attended by more than 200, on Tuesday. An excellent birthday tea was served, and a beautiful cake, surmounted by 19 candles and decorated in the section's colours of blue and amber, was cut by the vice-president (Mrs P Galley). The cake was made by Mrs E Richardson (vice-chairman) from ingredients given by members, and decorated by Mrs Sinclair. For their long service as officials of the section, three members, Mrs M Forster (formerly chairman for 11 years), Mrs M E Richardson (recently resigned as secretary after 17 years) and Mrs M Straughan (treasurer for 12 years), were presented with inscribed biscuit barrels. Presentations were made by Mrs Galley, introduced by the chairman of the section, Mrs M Brain. Mrs Galley paid a tribute to their devoted work over such a long period and wished them health and happiness. At night the entertainment party gave an enjoyable programme of sketches and vocal and musical items. Mrs Straughan was compere and accompanist Mrs E Richardson.

25 March 1949

THORNLEY'S REMARKABLE MAN
VARIETY OF JOBS MUST BE UNIQUE

Mr George Graham, 11 Rosberry Crescent, Thornley, well-known at the pit as "Doctor" Graham (he dosen't know why) remembers when he started work because it was a month after the water broke away at Kelloe Colliery, when several men lost their lives.

Mr Graham has done all sorts of jobs-far more than most men venture to try. He started at the pit as a bank lad, and before long he left the pit and went to work for a farmer near Haswell "cleaning middens out for 3s 6d a week." "Aa swapped my fiddle for a gewgaw," said Mr Graham.

He worked for another farmer when self-binders first came into use. Then, at 16, he tried his hand as a postman at Haswell for a wage of ten shillings and sixpence a week. A little later, at Shotton, he was a navvy at 5½d an hour. At Shotton Colliery he teemed stones, and was a "bait-setter" and banker-out. One day he blundered while banking-out and the cage rope slackened and hung in the street, through the cage remaining on the "keps."

The young banksman didn't know what had happened until his wife brought his "bait" and said: "What's thoo being deein Geordie? The cage rope's hanging in the street."

Beat His Own Tub

Geordie got the sack for that and went down the pit to "put." One day, not long afterwards, he was ordered out-bye in a hurry to bank out once more.

"Aa put me token on the tub and hurried to bank," he said, "Aa beat me aan tub to bank, took the token off and sent the tub down again." The shortage of banksmen at the time was so great that he worked three days without being "lowsed."

In 1908 he came to Thornley Colliery. Before 1920 he had worked in the lamp cabin, token cabin, powder magazine, on the stoneheap and underground as a horsekeeper, pumper, putter and hewer. If experience was anything he was certainly entitled to his appointment as a deputy. He kept at this work until 1942, but owing to pains he had to take a lighter job.

Mr Graham is one of the men over 65 years old who finished their employment on Saturday because of the reduction of the number of employees. But he isn't upset. "Aa think Aa've done my bit," he said, and all reasonable folk will agree with that.

THORNLEY

INQUEST - A post-mortem on George Iddon 56, labourer, 223 Thorn-law South, Thornley, who collapsed and died while digging a trench on a new housing estate at Trimdon Village on 5th March, revealed that heart failure was the cause of death. This was stated at the inquest at Easington on Wednesday, when a verdict in accordance with the medical evidence was returned.

CHRISTIAN ENDEAVOUR – Bow Street Methodist Church Christian Endeavour, held anniversary services, when Rev G K Fawell (Durham) was speaker. In the evening a rally was held, presided over by Mr Stephenson. Mr Fawell was speaker and Mrs Dowding was soloist. Rev W T Rose took the roll-call. Mr A Curry was soloist on Sunday, when Rev S Rose (Wesley College, Leeds) gave the address. Following young members took part, Misses D Robinson, E Blackett, M Harris and Miss B Jordan (soloist).

1 April 1949

NEW INDUSTRIES
Letter From President of Board of Trade

Mr Harold Wilson, President of the Board of Trade, has written to Mr E Shinwell, secretary of State for War and MP for Seaham, in reply to a letter from the local Labour Party at Wheatley Hill, concerning the lack of new industries there.

Mr Wilson says: "I think I should explain that, although no new factories have been built in Wheatley Hill itself we are developing a substantial industrial estate at Dragonville, near Sherburn, which is not more than five or six miles from Wheatley Hill. We expect the seven factories there to employ 400 men and 600 women when they are in full production (they already employ 110 men and 310 women) and they should provide ample opportunities for the present for people living in Wheatley Hill.

"I appreciate, as the secretary of the Labour Party points out, that this means daily travel of up to ten miles, but I am sure you will agree with me that it is not always practical to set up factories everywhere in the development areas. An industrial estate should be established at a focal point on a good site, which is within fairly easy reach of the different centres where labour is available, is generally a much more effective means of promoting new industries to set up their factories in each and every small community."

Peterlee Development

"In time, as you point out, we hope that the new factories and all the 'service' trade which will be developed at the new town of Peterlee, will provide further opportunities and work for people living in Wheatley Hill much nearer at hand. In the meantime, I do not consider it would be right for us to promote new industries in Wheatley Hill itself. With the present restrictions on capital investment our scope is strictly limited to new projects which will make a substantial and early contribution to exports and import saving. And, as you no doubt know, we cannot build any more factories in advance of demand for the time being. Rather than disperse our building resources I should much prefer to see them concentrated in getting ahead with the new town.

"Naturally I have much sympathy with the disabled persons who are compelled to travel considerable distances to work but here again it is probably not possible for the Disabled Persons' Employment Corporation to do more than set up their Remploy factories at central points where there are sufficient numbers of severely disabled persons to warrant the building of such factories.

"I understand that the nearest remploy factories are at Pallion, near Sunderland, and at Hartlepools, but the Minister of Labour, to whom I am sending a copy of this letter, will be able to tell you more about his plans for these factories.

"Mr Shinwell has taken up the question of factories for disabled persons with the Ministry of Labour."

THORNLEY LAMBS HIGH PRICE

Record price of £14.5s.1d each was paid by the Ministry of Food for two fat lambs, 115lbs estimated dead weight each, at Castle Eden Collecting Centre. They were the property of Miss Olive Gilson, Croft House Farm, Thornley.

15 April 1949

LUDWORTH REACH FINAL
BY BEATING WASHINGTON SIDE

Ludworth Rising Star earned the right to meet Burnside United in the final of the Lumley Nursing Cup by a two goal win over their Houghton and District league opponents, Washington Glebe Welfare, on the Banks Head United ground on Saturday.

The game had many thrills although the football never reached a high standard. Ludworth have played much better football and will, indeed, need to return to their high standard before 30th April if they hope to overcome their strong Burnside opponents.

Washington won the toss and elected to play with the wind. Though they were first to go into the attack, it was from Ludworth that the first real scare came. A movement started on the left sent Edwards through and his terrific drive shook the woodwork amid a roar of "Oohs."

End-to-end play followed and in a spirited attack Wilkins had his feet hooked from under him in the penalty area, but despite the appeals of the attackers, the referee waved play on. George Lofthouse gave a brilliant defensive display in this half and broke up many well-planned raids of the young Washington forwards.

In successive Ludworth attacks Hughes struck the upright and Edwards headed over when well placed. After Ranson had a strong shot saved by Nicholson, play switched to the other end and Ludworth went into the lead in the 30th minute.

Edwards raced Short for possession and the ball crashed out to Dick Hughes, who beat Ingleby from an almost impossible angle. Against the wind Washington fought hard and were indeed the better side during the second period but poor finishing spoilt many scoring chances.

Heroic Game

Halse, their left-half, was playing a heroic game, falling back to defend and then going right up with the forwards when an attack was initiated.

Lofthouse, now suffering from a back injury, still continued to foil the Glebe forwards. Ludworth never really shone in this period, but on one occasion when Bradley hit the upright Edwards caught the ball on the rebound and to everyone's surprise blazed it over the bar from about two yards out with Ingleby beaten.

Washington had opportunities to equalise and Ranson with a glorious chance shot over the bar. With only a minute to go, and when many had left the ground, came the best goal of the game. Laverick gained possession in midfield and hotly pursued by two opponents, raced through to beat the Washington 'keeper with a beautiful drive.

Halse Starred

Most outstanding player on view was Halse, the Washington half-back, while for Ludworth Lofthouse gave a magnificent display, ably backed up by Whiting and Youll. Wingers Petrie and Green, for Washington, were superior in a good forward line and had they adopted the same first-time tactics of their opponents and overcome that hesitancy when in possession, then a different tale may have been told.

Washington Glebe, a colliery welfare side have been functioning for two seasons and, like their opponents, are members of the Houghton and District league. While no big successes have yet come their way, they have always held their own, and only a fortnight ago held league leaders, Houghton SC Rovers, to a draw.

Mr Joe McBurnie is the club secretary, with Mr B W Barron chairman and Mr J Lyle treasurer. With the side on Saturday were committee men Messrs. J Short, J Minto, jun., T Scorer and R Short.

Washington were represented by Ingleby, Kennyon, Wood, Bestford, Short; Halse, Petrie, Cullinan, Wilkins, Ranson, Green.

LUDWORTH TEAM

Mr Harry Meek, secretary of the Lumley Nursing Cup committee, along with treasurer, Billy Milburn, were fully engaged attending to the "gate" and finances, and unfortunately failed to get into the picture with the cup as they desired.

The Ludworth side did not, as is generally believed, take the "Rising Star" from a public house of that name. In fact their headquarters

111

in Ludworth are at the Standish Arms, and "mine host" Mr Jack Gibson is club treasurer.

Secretary is Mick Phenny and chairman of this club is sportsman Charlie Campbell, well known throughout the area.

It was on a suggestion of Charlie's, when the club was formed three years ago, that they add Rising Star to the club's name, for it was with Thornley that he saw service in pre-war years. Mr Campbell was 12years old when he played schoolboy football for Castletown and was a member of the successful Wheatley Hill Juniors in 1913-14, when they were runners up in the Hetton Junior League.

Along with other two players he was the only survivor of that side who served in the First World War. After the war he continued to play football for local sides and on coming to Ludworth 23 years ago threw in his lot with Ludworth Athletic becoming chairman.

Charlie also served in the last war and was a prisoner for five years but continued to play soccer and was 48 years old when he played his last game in Poland. Previous to his escape in1944, he won a veteran's race over 80 yards in 10 seconds, which at the age of 48 is not bad going.

With such a sporting personality as an example it is small wonder that the Ludworth side are acclaimed sportsmen, and wherever they go they have a good following, their away supporters often numbering around the hundred mark.

On Saturday they arrived by cycle, motor-cycle and bus. One of the club's keenest supporters is Billy Redfern, and though injured in a mining accident at Horden 13 years ago, follows the fortunes of the team each week from the seat of his invalid carriage. Next is 68-year-old Bob Lofthouse, who since the formation of the club three years ago, sees the lads play at home and away.

Winning team on Saturday consisted of: Jack Nicholson, I Peachey, Joe Harrison, Sandy Whiting, G Lofthouse, Jack Youll, Dick Hughs, Stan Edwards, Bradley, "Nipper" Martin, Laverick. First Aid man, (with a string of medals) "Darkie Forster," has had over 20 years experience at ambulance work and is always ready to hand in the care of bruises or injury.

HETTON CHARITY CUP FINAL
Fatfield Down to Wheatley Hill
Teams: Wheatley Hill, Gibson, Bean, Watson, Cudlin, W Bean, J. Carr, Topping, Laverick, W Gaskell, Goyns, Temple. Fatfield, Gatenby, Mason, Wright, Mitchell, Pearson, Seager, Carr, Barrass, Escott, Exott, Stevenson.

This Hetton Charity Cup Final was keenly contested and was smartly refereed by Mr T McDermott (Houghton). The cup went to the team that turned their chances into goals and Wheatley Hill won by five goals to one.

Fatfield began well, the outside right's effort being fouled just outside the box. The ball was blazed over the bar, and then Seager, a useful link between attack and defence, also shot over.

After five minutes however, Goyns put Wheatley Hill into the lead.

Two minutes later Wheatley Hill were two up, Topping fastening on to a loose ball and scoring. Sporting Fatfield continued with constructive football, but found Wheatley Hill were moving quicker and taking every chance.

After another shot over the bar for Fatfield, Gaskell recorded the first goal of his hat-trick for the winners. At the Wheatley Hill end Gibson was in action several times but remained safe. After Wheatley Hill missed a penalty, Gaskell made it 4-0 after 25 minutes.

Fatfield generally had the better of the second half but their only goal was recorded by Pearson, Gaskell replied for the winners.
22 April 1949
WHEATLEY HILL
Serving in Malaya - Corporal W A Young (34) taken prisoner by the Japanese in Burma when the King's Own Yorkshire Light Infantry faced overwhelming odds on the Sittan River, near Moulmein, is back again with his old unit. Today he is the Regimental Provost Corporal at the Battalion HQ on Panang Island, Malaya. Corporal Young's wife now living at 17 Wordsworth Avenue, Wheatley Hill, hopes to join her husband in Malaya shortly. When I saw the Corporal at Glugor Barracks in Penang, writes a Military Observer, he had one special request to make: "Can you find whether Bandsman Hiscock, who escaped in 1942 from the prison in which I was at Rangoon, ever reached India? He left

with a friendly Burmese who was imprisoned with me." Asked if there were any striking difference between 1939 and 1949, he replied: "Probably there are more young soldiers now. But they are just as keen."
6 May 1949

THORNLEY MINE DISASTER
THREE WORKMEN WERE DROWNED
MOURNING IN THE DISTRICT

When water flooded the Hutton seam of Thornley Colliery, on Friday, resulting in the death of three miners, memories of a similar disaster at nearby Kelloe (East Hetton) pit, exactly 52 years before to the very day, were revived in the minds of veterans living in East Durham. In the Kelloe disaster ten lives were lost.

The three miners drowned at Thornley were, William Kelly (37), Younger son of Mrs Prudence and the late Mr James Kelly, 20 Wheatley Terrace, Wheatley Hill: Matthew Purvis (42), husband of Mrs Elizabeth Ann Purvis, 1 Second Street, Wheatley Hill; and Walter Rudkin (35), son of Mr and Mrs W Rudkin, 53 Morley Crescent, Kelloe. Mr Rudkin lived with his brother-in-law and sister, Mr and Mrs Thomas Hutchinson, 7 Fifth Street, Wheatley Hill.

Were Trapped

Late on Friday night Rudkin's body was recovered, but the bodies of his two workmates were not recovered until Sunday. The three men made up a coal-cutting team and, with another, Robert Holder, deputy over-man, School Square, were trapped when the water broke through. In a desper-ate, but vain, attempt to reach the three victims, Holder battled against the onrush of water, but found himself being carried along then thrown on one side. Twice he went back in an attempt to reach the trapped men, but he saw nothing of them. Five hours after the disaster occurred Holder was

L-R *Matthew Purvis, William Kelly & Walter Rudkin*

found in an exhausted condition and suffering from shock by a rescue party. He was taken home, where he is now recovering.

The Hutton seam, where the water broke away, is about 1,100 feet deep, and the men were trapped about 2¼ miles from the shaft. It was estimated that the water broke through at the rate of 5,000 gallons per minute. Over 30 men at work in the same district safely reached the surface.

Work began on Sunday with the installation of new pumping apparatus to take the place of the permanent pumps, which are submerged, and concentrated efforts have been made all this week to drain the pit and get it back into production.

Effect at Wheatley Hill

As well as the miners at Thornley Colliery being idle since the disaster, miners employed in No.1 Pit, at the neighbouring colliery of Wheatley Hill, were laid idle this week as a "precautionary measure." It was stated that one of the districts in the Busty seam of this pit was close to the flood waters in Thornley Colliery. When men arrived for work in the ten o'clock shift on Sunday night they were sent back home. Work was similarly stopped in the pit on Monday and Tuesday, though several miners were transferred to No.2 Pit. About 500 men are employed in No.1 Pit and a Coal Board official told our reporter he could not say when normal working would be resumed.

Mr Walter Rudkin, one of Friday's three victims, was buried at Wheatley Hill Cemetery, on Tuesday afternoon. As the large cortege proceeded from his home, through Front Street to Patton Street Methodist Church, crowds of people lined the route and, bare headed and with tear-stained eyes, paid simple homage to the young miner. The cortege was headed by the colliery band, officials and members of the Miners' Lodge and Wheatley Hill Workmen's Club, with the Miners' Lodge banner. Patton Street Methodist Church was filled to capacity for an impressive service, conducted by Rev J W Thurlby. Mr Rudkin had worked at Thornley Colliery since leaving school.

His Father Was Killed

The two other victims, Mr Matthew Purvis and Mr William Kelly, were buried at Wheatley hill Cemetery, on Wednesday, when again crowds of people attended the funeral services. Mr Kelly, who was unmarried, was one of a family of two brothers and two sisters. His father was killed on his 37th birthday while fighting on the Somme, on 1st July, 1916-by a tragic coincidence Mr Kelly was also 37 when he met his death. He had worked at Thornley Colliery since leaving school and formerly served on the committee of Wheatley Hill Workmen's Club. Mr Kelly was buried following a service at "The Rest," Wheatley Hill, conducted by Father Sheridan, Thornley RC Church.

A native of Ludworth, Mr Purvis had like his fellow victims, been employed at Thornley Colliery from leaving school, and he too, formerly served on Wheatley Hill Workmen's Club committee. He leaves a widow and seven children. His 2½ year old son, Richard, was killed by a bus near the Catholic School, on the Wheatley Hill-Thornley Road two years ago. Mr Purvis was well known as a singer at many clubs in East Durham – he had been engaged to sing, at Horden Workmen's Club, on Sunday last. His funeral took place following a service in Church Street Methodist Church, Wheatley Hill, conducted by Rev J W Thurlby.

Mr Purvis's widow told our reporter that her husband and the other two victims were inseperable companions, both in and out of the mine.

All three had paid their fares and lodgings to join a party going for a week's holiday to London in a fortnight's time. "They went about everywhere together," said Mrs Purvis.

Memories of Kelloe

One of the veteran miners in East Durham who vividly remembers the flood in Kelloe Pit, on 6th May, 1897, is 68 years old Mr Robert Lister, Wave Crest, Coast Road, Blackhall Rocks, now retired. "At the time," Mr Lister told our reporter this week, "I was working as a landing boy at the pit, I arrived at the colliery at 6 am to start my shift, but was told water had broken in two hours earlier." The water said Mr Lister, came from old workings at Cassop Colliery it is from these same workings that the water is said to have entered Thornley Pit on Friday.

In the Kelloe disaster, recalled Mr Lister, ten lives were lost, but one miner, the late Mr Jack Wilson, who died about two years ago, had a miraculous escape. He was imprisoned, said Mr Lister, for about 100 hours before rescue parties found him.

"When I reached the pit that fateful day," continued Mr Lister, "they were already bringing the ponies out. Work was stopped at the pit for several weeks after the disaster."

" By a remarkable coincidence," said Mr Lister, "he was discussing the Kelloe disaster with his wife on the eve of the Thornley flood last week. The date of the Kelloe disaster is clearly stamped in my mind," he added, "for I remember carving it on a tree near Kelloe Pit."

Mr Lister eventually was employed as a deputy at Kelloe Pit but left there at the age of 32 for Dean and Chapter Colliery. He was then an official at Trimdon Grange Colliery for five years and later an official for 19 years at Blackhall Colliery until his retirement as back overman four years ago.

13 May 1949

WOMEN'S LEGION - At the fortnightly meeting, Wheatley Hill women's section, British Legion, presided over by Mrs Brain, it was announced that the men's section were now taking over the Poppy Day arrangements, and Mrs Brain and Mrs Jackson were chosen to represent the women's section on the Poppy Day committee.

PIT RESTART - Idle all last week as a precautionary measure because of the nearness of one of its districts to the flood waters in the adjoining colliery at Thornley, where three miners lost their lives on 6th May. No.1 Pit at Wheatley Hill Colliery restarted work on Monday. Approximately 500 men are employed in the pit. They were all idle on the first day that the pit ceased working, but later most of them were found jobs on bank and in No. 2 Pit. It is estimated that between 3,000 and 4,000 tons of coal were lost through the pit being idle.

20 May 1949

WORK AGAIN AT THORNLEY

Coal drawing operations up the shaft at Thornley Colliery, which were stopped on 6 May when three miners lost their lives in a pit flood, were resumed on Monday. "The pit will not be back to full production for a while yet," an official of the Coal Board told me, "but at the start it is expected that approximately 900 tons of coal will be drawn a day against an average of 1,400 tons before the flood disaster." Coal drawing was actually restarted on Thursday last week, but the small amount produced - 256 tons- was taken up the shaft at the neighbouring Ludworth colliery. Practically all the men employed at Thornley colliery are back at work again, those unable, for the time being, to resume their jobs at Thornley, have been transferred to neighbouring collieries. Thornley colliery's weekly "target" is 7,000 tons. Before the flood this figure was regularly passed.

THORNLEY PARISH COUNCIL

After being elected Chairman of Thornley Parish Council for the ensuing year, Coun Martin Fleming commented on the fact that women were in the majority as members of the Council. He said to the women; "You have come into a heritage of which you can be proud."

Coun Mrs Roper, after remarking that she was the daughter of a suffragette and the neice of two women who suffered in the cause of women's suffrage, said the presence of women on the Council would help to make life easier for the men.

The following were elected - Vice-chairman, Coun Mrs Brewster ; Easington RDC Rating Committee, Couns F A Walker and Mrs E Bosomworth ; school managers, Coun F Walker and Mrs H Slater ; representative to Annual Conference of National Association of Parish Councils, Coun W F Whitehead ; Annual Conference of County Association of Parish Councils, Chairman and Clerk ; County Playing Fields' Association, Mrs S Gott.

27 May 1949

LUDWORTH HOMING

Ludworth Homing Society's old bird race from Peterborough has resulted: Appleby and Partners,1141 (3d, 6d, and 1s pools); Brain and Partners, 1129 and 1121; Vasey and Partners, 1118 (2s 6d, pool); Cordner and Partners, 1085 (5s pool).

3 June 1949

CHOIR TRIP – Members and friends of the choir of Church Street Methodist Church, Wheatley Hill, went by bus for their annual outing to Scarborough on Whit Monday. Arrangements were made by Miss Bessie Galley.

SUNDAY SCHOOL ANNIVERSARY – Services were conducted in the Church Street Methodist Church, Wheatley Hill, on Sunday, by Mr J Hughes (superintendent). During the morning the scholars, teachers and friends sang through the streets of the village, Mr T McCartney providing musical accompaniment. In the afternoon a demonstration, "The Building of the Church," was given by the scholars, assisted by the

118

choir under conductorship of Mr T Christopher. At night scholars took part in a programme of singing and reciting. Mr T McCartney being organist. The services will be continued on Sunday when Mr G Poulson will preside.

CRICKET CUP VICTORY – Visited by South Hetton on Tuesday night in the first round of the Richard Murray Bowl, Wheatley Hill had a comfortable win. After scoring 131 for eight in the set number of overs, they dismissed South Hetton for 105. G Lumley (43 not out) was Wheatley Hill's top scorer, and for the visitors T Hellyn took seven wickets for 48. H Batey, with 57, was chief contributor to South Hetton's total, whilst R Robson claimed five wickets for 31 and T C Williams three for 67.

LATE MR J GAIR – One of Wheatley Hill's oldest residents, Mr John Gair (82), 23 Aged Miners' Holmes, who died on Saturday after a brief illness, was buried at Wheatley Hill Cemetery on Wednesday afternoon, following a service at "The Rest." A member of the Salvation Army for 60 years, Mr Gair had been connected with the Thornley Corps since moving to Wheatley Hill 41 years ago, and for more than 20 years was bandmaster of the S A Band. Before going to Wheatley Hill he lived at Tudhoe and Felling. He was a miner all his working career, retiring at Wheatley Hill colliery at the age of 68. He is survived by his second wife, formerly a Salvation Army Officer at West Cornforth, and three sons.

10 June 1949

APPRECIATION – Miss Bessie Bosomworth, of Thornley, has had the honour of being a guest at the anniversary celebrations, at the Mansion House, London, of the British Soldiers' Society. This was in recognition of the work she has done as flag-day organiser and collector for the society.

CONSULTATIVE COMMITTEE – As a result of a ballot the following members of Wheatley Hill Miners' Lodge have been elected to serve on the local colliery consultative committee for the ensuing year: Messrs T Knowles and J Richardson (representing the face workers), H Bradshaw (contract workers), J Cowie (underground haulage workers), T W Buxton (surface workers), and W S Ruth (tradesmen).

FOOTBALLERS' PRESENTATION – At a dance in the Embassy Ballroom, Wheatley Hill, organised by Wheatley Hill SC Football Club, miniature cups were presented to members of the football team successful in winning the Hetton Charity Cup last season. Mr A Baldesera, president of the club, presided and introduced Mr "Bobby" Gurney, manager of Horden CW club, who made the presentations. Thanks to Mr Gurney were expressed by the club secretary, Mr F E Smith. Dance music was played by Reg Bushby's band.

AWARDED TUC SCHOLARSHIP
Mr Alan Cairns, Thornley

Mr Alan Cairns (22), Percy Street, Thornley, now an underground worker at Easington Colliery, having been transferred after an inrush of water at Thornley Colliery on 6th May, has been awarded a TUC Scholarship at the London School of Economics. He will leave the pit when he takes up residence in London in October.

Mr Cairns, son of Mrs Cairns and the late Mr Joshua Cairns, started the pit on leaving Thornley Council School. When he was about 20 he "felt a thirst for knowledge" (to use his own words), and since then, helped by correspondence courses, he has won three summer school scholarships awarded by the Durham Area of the National Union of Mineworkers. He is to attend a Labour Youth rally at Filey in September as the nominee of the Thornley Miners Lodge. His ultimate aim is to take a degree in economics.

LUDWORTH FOOTBALL FUNCTION

Officials and players of Ludworth Rising Star F C were entertained to supper by the ladies' Supporters' Club to celebrate the winning of miniature cups for each player in recognition of being runners up in the Fence Houses and Lumley Cup competition. Mr C Campbell, who has been chairman of the club for the last three seasons, presided.

Mr Campbell thanked the ladies and complimented the players on their fine displays during the past two years. The club was successful from a financial point of view, and they had a balance in hand of over £26.

The secretary, Mr M Phenny, and the treasurer, Mr J Gobson, were thanked for their work for the club.

Mr A Welsh, manager of Thornley Colliery, said that though he had not seen the team he had followed their progress from week to week, and was pleased with the reports he had had about them. He presented cups to Ray Whiting (captain), Jim Nicholson, Isaac Peachey, Joe

Harrison, Jackie Youll, George Lofthouse, Dicky Hughes, Fred Bradley, Stan Edwards, Ronald Martin and Jackie Laverick.

Mr J Briggs moved a vote of thanks to Mr Welsh for making the presentation, and he then moved another vote of thanks to Mr Campbell for his work during the past three seasons. He congratulated Mr Campbell on his appointment as chairman of the Houghton League.

24 June 1949

LONG SERVICE RECOGNISED

The long service of five employees of the firm of Messrs J T Scott and Sons, Thornley, was recognised by presentations made by Mrs J H C Scott following lunch at Scarborough, in the course of the annual staff outing provided by the firm. Mr Joseph Hall, who started work for the firm when he was 13½ years old, and rose to the position of director and manager of the Langley Moor branch, received a gold watch and chain in recognition of 52 years service. His wife, Mrs Hall, who has served the firm for 43 years, received a silver salver.

Mr T T Ridley, of Thornley, with 27 years service, received a gold watch. Mr J C Fellows, of Darlington, who has been travelling representative for 25 years, received a gold watch and Mr Wilfred Allison, of theLangley Moor branch, chose a solid silver cigarette case. Mr J H C Scott, managing director, told the gathering of 60, which included wives of employees, that the firm appreciated faithful and willing service, and he hoped they would always continue to be a happy family.

1 July 1949

MINERS' WELFARE – Annual meeting of the Thornley Miners' Welfare members and users of the pithead baths and canteen were held on Sunday. Mr W Atkin presided over an attendance of about 80. Answering a question as to the possibility of starting to build a new welfare institute, Mr W Henderson (secretary) said there had been delay because of negotiations regarding a grant from the Ministry of Education, whose first offer of £2,000, subject to conditions, including representation on the management board, had been turned down. A later offer of £9,600, with the same conditions, had been agreed to, and it is hoped that this would clear the way for an early start with building. The accounts showed a profit of £408 for the year to 31st December, 1949. The pithead baths showed a profit of £493, but there was a heavy loss on the canteen. This caused a good deal of criticism. Messrs F Walker and J Williams, members of the committee, gave information on the steps being taken to improve matters. Messrs W Heale and E Carter were elected to the baths and canteen committee in place of Messrs J Williams and R Gibson.

THORNLEY PARISH AFFAIRS

Thornley Parish Council dealt with a variety of matters at their monthly meeting. One was the charges made by the North-Eastern Electricity Board for electricity for domestic use in some of the council houses. Coun Mrs Gott said they understood when the charges were increased for the winter there would be a corresponding reduction in the summer.

Coun M Fleming, who presided, said if appeared there had been a 50 per cent increase, which might become permanent. "If such things are going to be rushed upon our people without our being in a position to appeal we are going to be in a bad way," remarked Coun Fleming. It was agreed the matter be investigated.

An enquiry by Coun Whitehead about the parish clock in the Market Place, brought a reply that the face had been sent away for renovation. When several members said they missed the clock, it was decided the clockmakers be asked to expedite the reinstatement of the face.

An extension of the Northern bus terminus from the R C Church to the top of Dunelm Road was favoured and it was agreed to make the necessary application to the Traffic Commissioners through Easington Council.

The council were informed that the outdoor seats asked for by retired miners was being arranged, part of the arrangement being the obtaining of sanction by the Highway Authority to place the seats. Other seats are to be applied for after an inspection to fix suitable places.

During discussion on road safety matters, following a report of a meeting of Easington RDC Road Safety Committee by the Chairman, Mrs Roper, the propaganda agent for the parish committee, said that some posters were displayed, but were covered up with other bills.

8 July 1949

LUDWORTH

AGED MINERS' OUTING – Ludworth aged miners and their wives went to Whitley Bay for their annual outing, which was arranged by Wheatley Hill Miners' Lodge.

BRITISH LEGION – At a joint meeting of both sections of Ludworth British Legion it was decided to have the War Memorial re-dedicated in September. Mrs Winter, who presided, hoped that all county branches would co-operate in this venture, and an appeal was made by the branch chairman (Mr Winter) to all members asking for their co-operation in making it a success.

GALLANT DEED – Alfred Ingram, 28 year old miner, 29 Moor Crescent, Ludworth, was responsible for saving the life of a 12 year old boy, Trevor Smith, who had drifted away from the shore at Crimdon in a rubber dinghy. Mr Ingram, after swimming nearly a mile out to sea, dragged the dinghy back by means of the towrope held tightly between the teeth. This was not the first time his services had been needed, about two years ago he saved a boy and girl from drowning within a short time of each other at Seaton Carew.

22 July 1949

EAST DURHAM CRICKET
Wheatley Hill's Narrow Defeat

The Durham Coast League (Division 1) game between Wheatley Hill and Chilton Moor at Wheatley hill on Saturday retained the spectators' interest until the last over, for Chilton won with their last pair at the wicket. Wheatley Hill's opening wickets fell fast, only 19 were on the board when their sixth man was sent back to the pavilion, but a bright 37 by Bobby Patterson and an undefeated innings of 22 by R Robson made the score more respectable, the innings closing at 105.

The visitors' ninth wicket fell with the total at 94, but their last pair batted cautiously on and all the wiles of the home bowlers failed to separate them before they passed the "Hill" score, T C Williams, the home "pro," had six wickets for 39 and R Robson 3 for 42. Details:-

WHEATLEY HILL: J W Moore b Moyes 0, E Snowdon b Moyes 3, H Simpson run out 8, T Hall b Moyes0, G Lumley c Moyes b Walton 0, E Ward c Gill b Tippens 18, J Jordan lbw b Walton 3, J Graham c Bainbridge b Walton 4, R Patterson c Bainbridge b Walton 37, T C Williams b Tippens 0, R Robson not out 22; extras 10- total, 105.

CHILTON MOOR: 107 for nine.

Seconds' Revenge

Wheatley Hill II atoned for their seniors' narrow defeat by doubling the score of Chilton Moor II, whom they visited in Division 2 of the Coast League. After losing their first four wickets for 19 runs, Wheatley Hill improved and finally reached 113, T Cowie contributing 28, G Carr 26 and E Simpson 25. For the home team J Wilson took five wickets for 21. Chilton Moor could only muster 66, their last three wickets falling for no runs, S Brentley gave a grand display with the ball, taking six wickets for 28 and G Carr took three for 30.

Wheatley Hill's cricket teams for to-morrow's league games are first eleven (to visit Washington), J W Moore, H Simpson, G Lumley, J Jordan, R Robson, E Ward, E Snowdon, G Gribbens, R Patterson, T Hall, T C Williams, reserves, G Kent, G Carr, second eleven (Home to Washington II), T Cowie, T Ayre, W Gibson, G Carr, S Brentley, J Nicholson, G Kent, E Simpson, W Turnbull, G R Patterson, D Henderson, reserves, R Scarth, B Carr. These teams will also be on duty on Monday against Castle Eden.

29 July 1949

WHEATLEY HILL

MINERS' HOLIDAYS - Miners at Wheatley Hill colliery and the neighbouring colliery of Thornley have been on holiday this week.

APPOINTMENT - From a short list of four, Easington R D C has appointed Mr John William Moore, Alexandra Terrace, Wheatley Hill, as cleansing superintendent at a salary of £550-£610. Mr Moore is a clerical assistant to the Council.

SCHOOLBOY CAMP - Forty scholars from Wheatley Hill Senior Boys' School returned home on Monday after an enjoyable week's camping at Wolsingham with their headmaster, Mr J Andrews, and members of the teaching staff.

RAOB OUTING - Children of members of Wheatley Hill and Thornley lodges of the R A O B, went by bus for their first annual outing to South Shields. Each received 14s 3d "pocket money." The outing was organised by Bro Micheson, who, however, was unable to accompany the party owing to injuries received in an accident at work a few days previously.

WED AT NORTHAMPTON - Mr John Atkinson, only son of a well-known Wheatley Hill butcher, Mr J M Atkinson and Mrs Atkinson, of Front Street, was married at Northampton on Saturday to Miss Yvonne Chambers, daughter of Mrs Chambers and the late Mr W E Chambers, Maidford, Northampton. The bridegroom is a pilot in the R A F, in which he has served for the past seven years, and the bride is a nurse at Northampton General Hospital.

LUDWORTH

Ludworth Miners have been on holiday this week. Outings have been arranged by Mrs Kell and Mrs Phenny to Redcar, Seaburn and South Sheilds.

ON HOLIDAY - IN HOSPITAL - Mr Sid Youll (24), 157, Barnard Avenue, Ludworth, on holiday at Blackpool, was admitted to Blackpool Victoria Hospital with a broken leg and other injuries. In response to enquiries, it was stated that he is "fairly comfortable." His father and mother, Mr and Mrs J Youll, left for Blackpool on Tuesday.

AID FOR THORNLEY FOOTBALLER

As a result of a recent dance in The Embassy Ballroom, Wheatley Hill, organised by Thornley St. Godric's Football Club, for the benefit of one of their players, James Hoban, a well-known local footballer who broke a leg while playing for St. Godric's last season, the sum of £80 was raised.

12 August 1949

DEATH OF REV P T CASEY
Vicar of Wheatley Hill for 40 years

Funeral of Rev Philip T Casey (76), Vicar of Wheatley Hill, took place on Sunday afternoon. Except for seats reserved for the members of the Mothers' Union, the Parish Church of All Saints (in which Mr Casey had officiated for the past 40 years) was full half an hour before the cortege arrived from the Vicarage, which is nearly half a mile from the church.

The robed choir, formed of a majority of young women who showed clearly that they were grief stricken by the loss of their Vicar, led the way. The coffin came next carried by servers who were robed in red.

Clergy were the Ven Archdeacon E de Grey Lucas (Durham), Canon R H Tillard (Rector of Shadforth and Rural Dean of Easington),Rev G Baker (Vicar of Trimdon) and Rev G Beckwith (Vicar of Shotton). Rev Earnest Casey (Vicar of Chilton Moor), one of Mr Casey's four sons by his first wife, escorted Mrs Casey, the widow.

The churchwardens (Messrs J White and W Marshall were in the choir), who led the hymns, "For all the Saints" and "The Saints of God, their conflict passed," and the 90th Psalm "Lord, Thou has been our refuge." The Archdeacon read the lesson from the funeral service, and the Rural dean said the prayers. Leaving the church to the singing of the Nune Dimittis, the choir led the cortege to Wheatley Hill Cemetery, where Canon Tillard officiated and the choir sang the hymn, "The Church's One Foundation."

LUDWORTH RS, at home to Horden Rovers, had to fight all the way to win by the only goal of the game. The Rovers were one of last season's shock teams, and with a little more steadiness in front of goal should do well again this term.

RYHOPE CW travelled to Wheatley Hill to meet newcomers from Ferryhill and District League, Wingate Lane, and after a keen tussle took both points with a 2-1 margin.

MURTON WANDERERS GO "NAP"

Murton Wanderers at home accounted for the newly formed Ludworth Boys' Club, netting five times without reply. Skinner (2), Waters (2) and Butt, were the marksmen. Bell and Winstanley did well for the Ludworth side

26 August 1949

OLD PEOPLE'S TRIP - A 91 year old widow, Mrs Sarah Mole, 24 Aged Miners' Homes, Wheatley Hill, was the oldest guest of the Workmen's Club when on Saturday the club organised its third annual outing for aged members and their wives and widows of members over 60. The day at South Shields will long be remembered by the old folk. A fleet of ten buses conveyed over 320 trippers, who were accompanied by officials and committee members. Lunch and tea were provided free for them, and each tripper received £2 pocket money. Many were the words of appreciation passed on to the club management for an excellent outing. Arrangements were carried out by the club secretary (Mr Thomas Storey).

NEW TENNIS COURTS - Work is nearing completion on two new green tarmac tennis courts which have been laid out in Wheatley Hill Welfare ground to meet the greatly increased demand of local tennis enthusiasts. The total cost of the work, Mr E Cain secretary of the Welfare, told our reporter this week, is £846, all of which has been met by the Miners' Welfare Commission, except for the sum of £22 10s, half the costs of the posts, which has been paid by the local Welfare committee. At present there is only one tennis court in the grounds, a grass court which was converted a year ago from a croquet lawn. The new courts, said Mr Cain, were expected to be ready to play on before the end of the present tennis season.

HOUGHTON FOOTBALL LEAGUE

Houghton C W travelled to Wheatley Hill, and gave Wingate Lane their first points of the season. The home side have a good combination with quite a nippy forward line, in which Monaghan, Craggs and Carr stand out. Pick of the Houghton side was Oliver and Slater, with Greenwood and Smith best of the forwards.

Washington Glebe's forwards were goalshy on their visit to Ludworth and failed to reply to the Rising Star's three. The home side were well served by Hughes, Lofthouse and Peachey.

THORNLEY FOOTBALL

Thornley St. Godric's celebrated the opening of their new field by completing the double of Sedgefield St. Edmund's. The game, however, left the large crowd little to enthuse over. Chance after chance was missed and the only goal scored was a scrambled affair. Hoban, Tonks and Higgins alone lived up to their reputation.

What a change on Monday! Showing only two changes St Godric's visited Horden Reserves in an Orphanage Cup tie and gave the strong home team a severe tussle, only losing by 2-1. Thornley defence was on form Taylor, at half-back, being the man of the match.

The superior stamina of Horden prevailed in the end, although Brown nearly forced a draw for Thornley in the closing minutes. To shock a team of Horden's calibre however, stronger wing-men will have to be found.

Thornley C W came away pointless from Dawdon, the local Rangers scoring four times without reply. Thornley forwards were disappointing, Richards also showing the required initiative. Miles, Les Williamson and goalkeeper Orton were the pick of the defence.

9 September 1949

DIED OF GUNSHOT WOUNDS
SAD AFFAIR AT HART

From gunshot wounds received in an accident at Hart, on Tuesday, a well-known Thornley motor engineer and garage proprietor, Mr Walter George Linton (43), New Road Garage, Thornley, died in Hartlepools Hospital the same night. The accident occurred while Mr Linton was shooting with a friend on the farm of his brother, Mr J Linton, Whelly Hill Road Farm, Hart. It is understood that he shot a hare and, finding that it was not quite dead, clubbed it with the butt of his double-barrelled gun, which went off, shooting him in the stomach. Mr Linton is survived by his wife and a daughter.

CASTLE EDEN COURT TUESDAY 13TH
BUS DRIVER'S LICENCE ENDORSED

Told by the Chairman of the Bench (Mr C H Wreford) that the magistrates thought he was "absolutely" to blame, Frederick Allen Cuthbertson (40), 23, Linden Road, West Cornforth, was fined £5 for driving a bus without due care and attention on 14th July at Wheatley Hill. He was also ordered to pay 7s costs, and his licence was endorsed. Cuthbertson, who was represented by Mr S Levinson, pleaded "Not guilty."

The summons arose, said Supt W J Pearson, prosecuting, as a result of a collision on the main road between a bus driven by the defendant, and owned by the G and B Motor Services, Quarrington Hill, and a private car owned by Mr John F Henderson. of Wingate. About 4 pm on 14th July the bus was carrying scholars from Wellfield Grammer School. The driver overshot the junction between the main road to Durham and the road leading into Wheatley Hill, and it was alleged that he stopped his vehicle and reversed, without any warning, into Mr Henderson's car. Slight damaged was done to the car, but there were no serious results.

In evidence, Mr Henderson said he was driving behind the bus as it approached the junction. When saw the bus stop shortly after passing the junction he thought that passengers would be alighting, so he pulled up a distance behind the bus. "Nobody got off the bus," continued witness, "and the bus started to reverse very slowly towards me. Suddenly the bus stopped, then it started to reverse slowly again. As I could see no reason for this I sounded my horn vigorously, I never made any attempt to get out of the way for I hadn't time. The next thing I knew the bus had struck the front of my car."

In an alleged statement made to P C Lambton, defendant said that when he stopped his bus he looked through his reflecting mirror and saw that the road was clear to reverse. "I told my conductress to look out while I reversed," continued the alleged statement, " and as I received no warning from her, I started to reverse slowly. After I had travelled a short distance I felt a slight impact and immediately stopped my bus. I found I had collided with the front of a stationary car, I had expected a signal from the conductress if the road was not clear, but I received none. In my opinion it was a pure accident."

Cuthbertson told the magistrates he had never heard any hooting of the motor horn. Cross-examined by Supt Pearson, he admitted he was solely responsible for the driving of the bus, but said the drivers always expected assistance from the conductresses travelling with them. In this instance he had received no indication from the conductress that a car was behind him and he himself would not be able to see it through his mirror if it was not more than five or six yards away.

STACK FIRE - despite the efforts of Horden and Wheatley Hill Fire Brigade a 20 ton hay stack, valued at £160, was destroyed by fire at Mr Roper's farm, near Dunelm Road, Thornley. Last week.

ACCIDENTAL GUN DEATH

The tragic death of Mr George Linton at the early age of 43, came as a great shock to his numerous friends in Thornley and district and much sympathy is felt for his widow and daughter. He was accidentally killed by his gun while out shooting on his brother's farm near Hart. Though fond of this sport in his later years he was a great enthusiast of motor-cycling in his earlier years and for this was well known widely in East Durham. As a boy he came to Thornley to reside with his uncle and aunt, the late Mr and Mrs T H Ashford, and was educated at Barnard Castle School. He then opened a garage on the Ludworth new road and kept this until his death. During the last war he was a special constable. Funeral took place at Thornley on Friday and the respect in which he was held was shown by the large attendance of relatives and friends from all parts of the district. Following the service in Thornley Parish Church interment was at Ludworth Road burial ground.

WHEATLEY HILL

New Tennis Courts - The two new green tarmac tennis courts recently built in Wheatley Hill Welfare ground through grants from the Miners' Welfare Committee and the local Welfare committee were opened for play on Saturday. There are now three courts in the grounds, the other being a grass court.

Local Football - Wheatley Hill S C maintained their unbeaten record in the Ferryhill and District League this season when they visited Sedgefield St. Edmund's on Saturday and won 6-3. Three of their goals were scored by their captain, Goyns, two from the penalty spot, while Wardell scored two and Temple one. In their five games to date Wheatley Hill have dropped only one point and stand at the top of the league. To-morrow they entertain Bishop Middleham. At home to New Brancepeth Juniors on Saturday, Wheatley Hill Juniors won 3-2 in a Durham City and District Junior League game. Scorers for Wheatley Hill were Robson, Willis and Walker.

23 September 1949

LUDWORTH WAR MEMORIAL UNVEILED

A big crowd on Sunday attended the unveiling ceremony of Ludworth War memorial to the memory of five local men who gave their lives in the second world war. Thirty British Legion branches and women's sections, with their standards, took part. The unveiling was performed by Major General C F Loewens.

Dedication ceremony was performed by Canon R H Tillard, assisted by Rev. W Rose, superintendent of Thornley Methodist Circuit. Music was supplied by Thornley Colliery Silver Band (conductor, Mr E Kitto). The "Last Post" and "Reveille" were sounded. Major General Loewens gave an address. The branch president (Dr. Gray) and the women's section president (Mrs Barnes) laid wreaths on the memorial.

After the service a march past of members of the legion and other organisations took place and the salute was taken by Major General Loewens. The parade was led by the parade marshal (ex-Sgt. "Mick" Morgan, DCM), and branch chairman (Mr A Winter). Members of the women's sections were led by the section chairman (Mrs S J Winter).

After the parade tea was served to 200 people in Ludworth Church Hall by members of the women's section.

THORNLEY FOOTBALL

Thornley St. Godric's staged another goal rush when they defeated Sunderland St. Benet's in a county Catholic cup game. St. Godric's with eight in this match have now reached 19 in the last three games without reply. In fact the defence has yet to concede a home goal.

High spot of the afternoon was a 50 yards run by Niles on the left wing to beat three men and score. Smith (2), Regan, Scott, Tonks and Niles were the other scorers.

Thornley C W gained their first win of the season on Saturday when they accounted for Dawdon by four goals to one in a league match. Rickard, Wilson, and Wilson (2) scored. Bushby had a splendid game at right back as had Orton in goal. The latter saved a penalty.

St Godric's team to entertain Leasingthorne is: Burdess, Higgins, Hoban, Taylor, Regan, Tonks, Scott, Smith, P Wilson, Waller, Niles.

Niles showed his running ability in the Thornley mine accident for his speed enabled him to beat the falling stoned by seconds.

30 September 1949

FROM HOUGHTON TO WHEATLEY HILL

The Bishop of Durham has appointed Rev Arthur Preston, BD, MA Curate of Houghton-le-Spring, to the perpetual curacy of Wheatley Hill, vacant by the death of Rev P T Casey (76). Mr Preston gained his MA at Glasgow University in 1928, and his BD at St Andrew's University in 1931. He also obtained the Berry scholarship at Gottingen University in 1932. Ordained in 1943, he has been Curate of Houghton-le-Spring for the past six years.

14 October 1949

WINGATE LANE BEATEN – Entertaining Houghton SC, unbeaten leaders of Houghton and District League, on Saturday, Wingate Lane lost by five goals to one. The visitors scored twice in the first 20 minutes. Before half-time Kirby reduced the lead, Wingate failed to show the same form as the first half when they resumed and Houghton had little difficulty in adding three more goals. Teams again meet to-morrow in Hetton Charity Cup at Houghton. Wingate Lane's side being: Collinson, O'Brien, Scott, Slack, Kirby, C Peacock, Craggs, Evans, Patterson, Bradley, Richardson.

MINERS' RESOLUTION – At the close of a well-attended meeting of miners at Wheatley Hill colliery, convened by the local pit consultative committee in connection with the drive for increased output in the mines, in the Welfare Hall, Wheatley Hill, on Sunday morning, a resolution was passed that the workmen would make an all-out effort to reduce absenteeism, increase output and produce cleaner coal. Mr T H Dobson, manager of the colliery, presided, and the meeting was addressed by Mr F W Fry, No 3 Area general manager, Mr W Murphy (Murton), a member of the Executive Committee, Durham Area, N U M , and Coun T Knowles and Mr E Cain, chairman, and secretary of Wheatley Hill Miners' Lodge. A demonstration of new methods of cleaning coal was given by Dr D A Ruell, Castle Eden, scientific advisor to No 3 Area, N C B, and so interested were the miners in this that many stayed behind after the meeting to learn further details from Dr Ruell. "A fine spirit prevailed throughout the meeting," Mr Cain told our reporter afterwards, "and Wheatley Hill miners can be depended upon to support to the utmost this special drive for more coal,"

21 October 1949

THORNLEY PRESENTATIONS

Trophies won by Thornley Colliery Cricket and Rifle Clubs during the past season were presented to them at a dinner and social evening in the Workmen's Club Hall, Thornley, on Saturday night, by Mr T Scollen, No3 Area Welfare Officer of the Northern Divisional Coal Board.

The cricket club, competing against 33 other teams, won the Mainsforth Welfare Cricket Knockout Cup, and the Rifle Club, for the first time in their history, were champions of the second division of the Durham County Rifle Clubs' Association League.

In presenting the cricket cup to Mr George Parker, chairman of the cricket club, Mr Scollen said their performance was particularly meritorious in view of the fact that the club had only been formed this year. Before they could start playing cricket they had had many obstacles to overcome, and much hard work was put in to make the pitch playable.

The Rifle Club also had every reason to be satisfied, especially as it was one of their members, Jack Laverick, who had obtained the highest aggregate in the County. The rifle championship trophy was received by Mr Arthur Welsh jun., manager of Thornley Colliery, who is president of the Rifle Club.

Mr Scollen mentioned that the area welfare committee had made representation to the sub-divisional Welfare Committee for the provision of a rifle range in the basement of the proposed community hall at Thornley. Nothing definite had been promised, but they were hoping that the riflemen would get their wish.

The gathering was presided over by Mr A Welsh jun., and among those present were Mr A Atkin, colliery engineer, and Mr W Henderson, local welfare secretary. After dinner entertainment was provided by Messrs R Oswald, D Dove, R Dove, J Dickinson, P Dover and A Cooper. The accompanist was Mr R Sandywell.

28 October 1949

THORNLEY WOMEN'S BRITISH LEGION

Officers and committee have been re-elected, one new member being added to the committee, Mrs Gavanah, Ludworth. Mrs Hilda Mitchell was chosen as standard bearer, and Mrs Hilda Slater, assistant. Mrs Clark (presiding) thanked all for their co-operation and hoped for a still more successful year.

For Poppy Day efforts one member said she was making "stotty cakes" and selling them, another was making toffee. Members were reminded of the non-stop revue by their concert party in Safety First week.

Sympathetic reference was made to the deaths of Mrs Soppitt, Ludworth and Mrs Williamson, Thornley. Mrs Williamson, the president said, had been a member of the Legion from its earliest days and always very loyal. A poppy wreath was carried by the Legion chairman at both interments, the section forming a guard of honour at the cemetery gates.

DEATH OF "CHARLIE THE DRUMMER"
Founder Member of Thornley Band

Bandsmen from Wheatley Hill, Thornley and Shotton bands, under the conductorship of Mr W Forrest (Wheatley Hill's bandmaster), played at the funeral at Thornley Cemetery on Tuesday of a well-known Wheatley Hill bandsman, Mr Charles William Brown (71), 7 Alexandra Terrace, Wheatley Hill, whose death occurred with tragic suddenness on Friday. After tea, Mr Brown had gone to bed for a rest, apparently in his usual heath, but an hour and a half later was found dead in bed by his son-in-law, Mr Rowland Dickman. Familiarly known in the area as "Charlie the Drummer," Mr Brown had been a life-long bandsman. One of the founders of Thornley Colliery Band, he was their drummer until moving to Wheatley Hill 11 years ago, when he joined the band there in a similar capacity.

It was not until after this year's "Big Meeting" at Durham that he gave up playing in the Wheatley Hill band, but he continued his interest in the band's activities, and as recently as a week past Sunday paraded with them on Remembrance Day.

Born at Bishop Middleham, Mr Brown lived at Thornley for most of his life before moving to Wheatley Hill, and retired at Thornley Colliery three years ago after working there from the age of 24. In his younger days he served on Thornley Parish Council. Mr Brown is survived by his wife, six sons and two daughters.

Funeral service in Thornley Waterloo Street Methodist Church was conducted by Rev. W T Rose (resident minister).

18 November 1949

NEW HEADQUARTERS FOR WHEATLEY HILL LEGION
Voluntary work in digging the foundations for their new headquarters is to be started in the near future by members of Wheatley Hill men's section of the British Legion.

"We have obtained the lease of a site behind the Royalty Theatre in Front Street, Wheatley Hill," Mr James Robinson, secretary of the section, told our reporter this week, "and as we received no replies to an advertisement for tenders for the preliminary foundation work, the members themselves have decided to go ahead with it during their spare time, for they are very keen to have their own headquarters."

The section, with some 60 fully paid members, has been holding its weekly meetings in the old Home Guard headquarters at Wheatley Hill. "With a building of our own," said Mr Robinson, "we will be able to hold social evenings and entertainments, and we are hoping then that more ex-Servicemen of the last war will be encouraged to join the Legion.

As soon as the foundations are ready a new corrugated asbestos hut measuring 48 ft by 18ft is to be put up. The estimated cost is £100. The Legion already had the required money in the building fund said Mr Robinson , for this fund was started by the Women's section some years before the men's section was inaugurated two years ago.

"The women's section has given us valuable help," continued Mr Robinson, "and, of course, they will have the use of the new headquarters as well as us. They were the founders of the building fund and since our section was formed they have helped considerably in the organising of special efforts to raise money for the fund."

The new headquarters will consist of a hall and the usual outhouses and lavatories, and it is expected also that there will be a small kitchen.

"We are hoping," concluded Mr Robinson, "that the building will be completed and officially opened shortly after the turn of the year."

25 November 1949

THORNLEY CUP DRAW

Thanks to the initiative of Mr C Campbell, of 2, Margaret Street, Ludworth, the Thornley Aged Miners' Cup Competition has been revived after lying dormant for three years. Mr Campbell, former chairman of Ludworth Rising Star has reorganised the contest after being approached recently by members of Thornley Aged Miners' Committee Officers appointed are. Mr T H Holder (Thornley), vice-chairman, Mr J Miller (Ludworth), treasurer, Mr J Cherry (Ludworth), secretary, Mr C Campbell.

Draw for the first round, to be played on 17th December, has resulted, Ludworth Rising Star v Shotton Shamrocks, Shotton Mechs. V South Hetton Rovers, Old Shotton S C v Shotton S C, Horden Swifts V Wheatley Hill Mechs, Haswell Plough Reserves v Chester Amateurs, Hetton Athletic v Ludworth Y C, Old Lyonians O S C v Horden, Wingate Lane v Thornley C W.

2 December 1949

PRIZE PIGEONS AT HETTON

Hetton Homing Society's open pigeon show in the Workmen's Club was judged by Mr J Graham, Hetton and Mr R McLaren, Sunderland. Awards, 200 miles old,1, Hill (Thornley), 2 Metcalfe Bros, 3 Bradley Bros (Wheatley Hill); hen, 1 Bradley Bros, 2 and 3 Hill; young, Bradley Bros, Lawson and Son, Hill; hen Bradley Bros, Graham and Partners. Hartshorne; members' class G Harrison, Smith Bros, D Hartshorne.

9 December 1949

CASTLE EDEN COURT, SATURDAY 10TH
Rode On Moving Set of Tubs

For riding on a moving set of tubs at Wingate Colliery on 17th October, three miners were fined £2 each. They were, Norman Robinson (24), 19

Wolmerhausen Street, Wheatley Hill, Derek Thompson (18), 404, New Row, Wingate and William Baldwin (20), 11, Vicarage Estate, Wingate. All pleaded "Guilty," but Robinson said he was ignorant of breaking the law.

The case against a fourth miner involved in the same charge, John Tarren, 10, Walton Terrace, Wingate, was adjourned after it had been stated he had not yet recovered from a broken leg received at the time of the alleged offence.

Matthew Taylor, back-overman, gave evidence as to the offence.

Robinson, asked if he anything to say, declared that before 17th October he had never seen any notice forbidding anybody to ride on the set. The following day, he alleged, a notice board appeared to this effect, and a further notice appeared on the 12th November. "I put one of the notices up myself," he added.

Thomas Bryson, manager, said there were notices posted at the shaft and the surface before 17th October forbidding men to ride while the tubs were in motion.

Mr E Chicken (chairman) said every miner underground should know it was a breach of the law to ride on a full set.

16 December 1949
AMBULANCE DEPOT AT WHEATLEY HILL
It was disclosed at a meeting of No 8 area health sub-committee at Easington on Tuesday, that the new ambulance central depot will be located at Wheatley Hill. Heretofore control was at Easington, where all requests for ambulance transport were dealt with and the bulk of the vehicles and personnel were operated from that point. The new premises at Wheatley Hill are the property of the R D C and for some time past negotiations had been going on with a view to buying the property for use as a central control depot.

When it was stated by Coun Johnson that many people did not know where to make enquiries regarding home help, the M O pointed out that if application was made to the County M O H every effort would be made to provide help where needed. Should the case not be urgent the local health visitor could be consulted at her home or enquiries made at the welfare centre.

23 December 1949

POLICE TREAT

The second annual New Year's party for children of the policemen stationed in Castle Eden Division of the Durham County Constabulary is to be held in the Embassy Ballroom, Wheatley Hill, on Tuesday (3rd January) from 2 to 6pm.

Arrangements are in the hands of a sub-committee of the Divisional Sports Club, and if the first effort last year is anything to go by the children are in for a rollicking time. Tea, lemonade and ices will be provided, and Santa Claus will be there to distribute gifts from a Christmas Tree.

WHEATLEY HILL GENEROSITY

Retired members of Wheatley Hill Workmen's Club have every reason to be grateful to the club management for the way they look after them in their declining years. On Thursday night last week, they and their wives, as well as the "over 60" widows of members, were entertained to an excellent party in the Welfare Hall, Wheatley Hill.

The men in addition, received Christmas gifts of £2 each at the week-end.

This Christmas treat, the first to be organised by the club, follows an enjoyable outing the club provided for the retired members, and their wives, and widows in the summer. Not only were they given a free trip to South Shields, but dinner and tea were provided for them and every "tripper" received £2 spending money.

The club certainly believes in looking well after its faithful old members. Its generosity must rank high among the clubs of Durham County, all of which are noted for the interest they take in the welfare of the old folk especially at Yuletide.

Mr R Storey, Wheatley Hill Club's hard-working secretary, deserves a special word of praise for his efficient handling of last weeks treat. Everything went off without a hitch and this must have entailed much preliminary work on his part.

NEW VICAR – Rev Arthur Preston, who was inducted vicar of Wheatley Hill last week by the Bishop of Durham, succeeds Rev P T Casey, who died in August. Clergy present at the induction ceremony in All Saints' Church, Wheatley Hill, were, Canon Tillard (Rector of Shadforth) and Revs O N Gwilliam (Rector of Houghton), R A Beddoes (Vicar of Easington Colliery), J M How (Vicar of Thornley), G Beckworth (Vicar of Shotton) and L G Russell, of Jamaica, who has been carrying out clerical duties in All Saints Parish until the new vicar's arrival. Mr Preston who is married with a four-year-old son, studied for the ministry at Glasgow University, where he graduated as Master of Arts. Later, at the University of St Andrew's, he gained his BD degree, then followed a year's studies at the University of Gottingen, Germany. Mr Preston's education was completed at Lincoln Theological College, and Houghton-le-Spring was his first church appointment. Until his appointment as Vicar of Wheatley Hill, he served as curate at Houghton-le-Spring from 1943.

30 December 1949

1950

MR T BALDASERA – MISS R PALMIERI - An Italian girl, who came to live with her sister at Wheatley Hill two years ago, was married in Thornley RC Church to a well-known Thornley business man, Mr Thomas Baldasera, son of Mr and Mrs A Baldasera, Roseneath, Thornley. She was Miss Rose Palmieri, daughter of the late Mr and Mrs G Palmieri, Bari, Italy. She was married from the home of her brother-in-law and sister (Mr and Mrs W Tuttle, Castlemoor House, Front Street). Given away by Mr Tuttle, the bride was in white taffeta, with a bridal veil and coronet of orange blossom. She was attended by Miss Winifred Hart, Thornley, who wore blue lace, with head-dress to match. Best man was Alfred (bridegroom's brother). Reception was in the Embassy Ballroom. Bridegroom is a partner in the business of Baldasera and Sons, who have ice-cream and confectionery shops at Wheatley Hill and Thornley.

BACK FROM AUSTRALIA

Mr and Mrs C H Fisher, 7 Aged Miners Homes, Wheatley Hill, had their most welcome "first-foot" on New Year's Eve when their son, Rev Robert Henry Fisher, arrived home from Australia on a ten weeks' visit.

As a young man of 25, Mr Fisher left his native village of Wheatley Hill during the 1926 strike to carry out missionary work in Australia and this is his first trip back since emigrating.

Shortly after reaching Australia, where he is now stationed as a Methodist minister at Wonthaggie, Victoria, Mr Fisher began studying for the ministry, and after three years at Melbourne University, gained his LTh degree. He married an Australian girl and the couple now have a five-year-old daughter.

Before going to Australia, Mr Fisher was employed as a miner at Wheatley Hill Colliery. He was actively associated with Patton St Methodist Church, where his father and mother, aged 76 and 74 respectively, are members. Special "Welcome Home" for Mr Fisher is to be held in the church on Saturday evening, 14 January. Mr Fisher will preach in the afternoon, and, following a public tea, will be welcomed back to Wheatley Hill by Mr William Snaith, JP. The following day Mr Fisher will conduct special services. He is also to preach in Patton Street Church on Sunday evening.

WHEATLEY HILL "DERBY" - It was a "battle of the giants" when the two top teams in the Ferryhill and District League, Wheatley Hill SC and Thornley St Godric's, met at Wheatley Hill on Saturday in the third round of the Hetton Charity Cup, of which the "Hill" are the holders. The "derby" atmosphere prevailed throughout and Thornley could count themselves somewhat fortunate to win by the odd goal in three.

Anderson opened Thornley's account in the first half, and after the change over Smith added a second. Wheatley Hill were well on top in the later stages and after reducing the lead through Slack stormed the visitors' goal in an all out effort to draw level. Thornley, however packed their goal whenever the "Hill" got near and stubbornly kept them out.

This week I learned that Wheatley Hill have lodged a protest to the cup management committee against Thornley, alleging that the latter fielded an ineligible player.

On Monday Wheatley Hill had a runaway 10-0 victory when they entertained East Howle in a league game. East Howle provided feeble opposition and the "Hill" won as they liked, four goals coming in the first half and six in the second. The last goal, from the penalty spot, was netted by Gibson, Wheatley Hill's goalkeeper. Other marksmen were Fishwick (4), Featonby (8) and Slack (2). It was Fishwick's first game – his former club was Easington Albions – and he has every reason to be proud of his debut.

WHEATLEY HILL SOLDIER MEETS WAR MINISTER

"Where do you come from?" asked Mr Shinwell. "Wheatley Hill, Durham, Sir," said 37-year-old Sergeant James Cain, whose home is at 13 Shinwell Terrace. The street is named after Mr Shinwell and is in his constituency.

This took place at Fayid in the Canal Zone of Egypt, when the War Minister paid a visit to the 1st Regiment Royal Horse Artillery during his recent tour of the Middle East.

Educated at St Godric's Roman Catholic School, Sergeant Cain worked for a time at Wheatley Hill Colliery. He joined the Army in 1930 and went out to India with the Royal Artillery in 1939.

He was transferred to the Middle East two years later and after serving in Persia and Iraq joined the 1st Armoured Division in North

Africa. Later his regiment played a prominent part in the battle of the Gothic Line in Italy.

Returning home to England he was an instructor, training potential officers before returning to the Middle East and joining his present regiment two years ago. Sergeant Cain's uncle, Edward Cain, is Durham County and Urban District Councillor for Wheatley Hill.

20 January 1950
CASTLE EDEN JUSTICES TURN DOWN APPLICATION
Two-Hour Extension Claimed

Castle Eden magistrates, at the annual licensing session on Saturday, rejected an application by six cinemas in the Division for earlier opening on Sunday evenings. The applicants were the Palace (Wingate), Regal (Wheatley Hill), Hippodrome (Thornley), Hippodrome (Easington) and the Ritz and Empress Electric (Horden), all belonging to DRC Cinemas, Ltd.

For the applicants, Mr Lyall Wilkes said that at present the cinemas were open from 7.30pm till 10pm on Sundays – an arrangement which had obtained for many years. Now they were asking permission to open from 5.30pm till 10pm. In many of the towns said Mr Wilkes, cinemas were allowed to open as early as 4.30pm, and it was felt by the applicants, as well as by the general public, that facilities on a similar footing should be afforded the villages.

At present, continued Mr Wilkes, queues for the cinemas he represented began to form about 6 pm, as there was only one show, but if earlier opening were permitted, two shows could be put on and queuing would be greatly minimised. There was evidence that people sometimes wanted to go earlier to the cinema and so they were going to West Hartlepool and other towns. "If the application is granted", added Mr Wilkes, "the new hours will still be more restricted than many of the towns in the county."

Impatient Queues

Mr Leslie Muir, manager of the Regal Cinema, Wheatley Hill, said that sometimes there were as many people in the queue as could get into the cinema. On several occasions they had had trouble with the queues because they became impatient.

Declaring that queues began to form outside his cinema at six o'clock, Mr George Cole, manager of the Hippodrome, Easington Colliery, said that sometimes between 100 and 200 people were turned away after the cinema had been filled. Miners who had to be up for the early shift next day had asked for an earlier opening so that they could get to bed sooner.

The Objections

Objection to the application was voiced by four ministers of religion in the villages concerned, namely, Rev J W Thurlby (Methodist minister, Wheatley Hill), Rev Arthur Preston (Vicar of Wheatley Hill), Rev Harry Allen (Methodist minster, (Horden), and Rev J M How (Vicar of Thornley). Not only, they said, would the earlier opening clash with their church services, but they felt that it would not be in the "best moral interests" of the community.

Mr Thurlby said he was chiefly concerned about its effect on the young people, as it was largely a young people's audience which attended the Sunday evening cinemas. They were all concerned about juvenile delinquency. "At present," he added, "there is no problem of the streets at 5.30 pm – that problem comes later. Yet this proposal to open the cinemas earlier would turn out between 400 and 500 young people into the streets at eight o'clock and create a problem of the streets which at present does not exist!" The magistrates decision to refuse the cinemas' application was reached after a brief retirement

WHEATLEY HILL'S NEW BANNER - A new banner purchased by Wheatley Hill Miners' Lodge, to replace one which has been in use for the past 15 years, is to be unfurled at a ceremony in Wheatley Hill Welfare Hall on Sunday morning (11 o'clock) by Mr Jack Lawson, Lord Lieutenant of the County, and Mr Sam Watson, the well-known miners' leader.

On one side of the new banner is a portrait of Peter Lee, whose earlier life was spent at Wheatley Hill, while a scene depicting "Christ blessing the children" has been painted on the reverse side.

DRAW FOR WHEATLEY HILL

In their bid for the championship of the Ferryhill and District League, Wheatley Hill SC won a point on Saturday when, visiting Coxhoe, also league aspirants, they figured in a 2-2 draw. Both goals were quickly visited in turn and Wheatley Hill took the lead after 20 minutes when, from Billy Ball's long throw-in into the centre of the goalmouth, Sid Slack netted. Midway through the second half three quick goals gave the spectators a thrill. A long shot from Pennock appeared to be well covered by Gibson, Wheatley Hill's custodian, but the ball dropped out of his hands and entered the net to give Coxhoe the equaliser. Coxhoe went straight down the field after the ball had been centred and took the lead through Campbell. This spurred the "Hill" into action and Sid Slack had the ball int he net, but Featonby had moved slightly and Slack was given offside. Shortly after this Featonby was brought down just outside the penalty area and Jack Carr scored direct from the free-kick to earn Wheatley Hill a division of the spoils.

DEATH OF FORMER THORNLEY HEADMISTRESS

Death of Miss Eliza Augusta Hill at the age of 86 has removed one of the most outstanding women the Thornley and Wheatley Hill districts has ever known. A Scotswoman, and very proud of it, she came to Thornley as a young woman and was headmistress of the infants' school until she retired.

Her small sprightly figure was known to almost everybody. Two generations of parents were taught by her as children and it is safe to say that she remembered every one of them. On her retirement she paid a prolonged visit to British Columbia, with a view to settling there, but in a few months she was back at Thornley.

In the First World War, as secretary of the Thornley Savings Association, she was the main figure in making this effort a big success. Her long association with Thornley Parish Church was kept up after she took up residence at Wheatley Hill. For a period she was a member of Thornley Parochial Church Council.

After her retirement she gave numerous talks to Women's Institutes in all parts of the county. One she gave about a hundred times. Except for a few years when a nephew resided with her, she lived alone, but this had no effect on her buoyant temperament. Interment was at Darlington on Thursday following a service in Thornley Parish Church.

WHEATLEY HILL DEDICATION – New altar furnishings presented to All Saints' Church, Wheatley Hill, by Mrs Casey, in memory of her husband, Rev Philip T Casey, who until his death last year was Vicar of Wheatley Hill for 35 years, have been dedicated in the church by the present Vicar, Rev Arthur Preston. On Sunday morning the Rev Preston is to dedicate a pair of churchwarden's wands, made of oak and brass – these have been bought from church funds.

10 March 1950

FAREWELL TO WHEATLEY HILL

After spending three months with his aged parents, Mr and Mrs C H Fisher, 7 Aged Miners' Homes, Wheatley Hill, Rev Robert H Fisher left on Tuesday on the first stage of his journey back to Australia, where he is a Methodist minister stationed at Wonthaggie on the south coast. It was Mr Fisher's first return visit to England since going to Australia from Wheatley Hill during the 1926 strike. In his own words he has spent "a wonderful time back home," and it has been a delight to him to renew acquaintances with his many friends, to say nothing of the happy re-union he has had with his parents.

Mr Fisher does not set sail until Tuesday. His time since leaving Wheatley Hill on Tuesday is being spent visiting his three sisters at Cardiff, Bewdley (Worcs) and Watford. They all came to see him when he arrived at Wheatley Hill at Christmas, and now he is visiting their homes to bid them farewell.

Mr Fisher has been appointed to serve as chaplain on the ship taking him back to Australia. His passage to England was paid by the members of his church, such a high place does he occupy in their affections, and they also made him a gift of £50 worth of foodstuffs to bring here on his holiday. Patton Street Methodist Church, Wheatley Hill, where Mr Fisher worshipped before going abroad, was filled to capacity on Sunday, when Mr Fisher preached farewell sermons and warmly thanked the members.

CRICKET CLUB PRESENTATION - At the annual whist drive and dance organised by Wheatley Hill Cricket Club in the Embassy Ballroom, Wheatley Hill, an inscribed chiming clock was presented to Mr T E Turner, in recognition of his services as treasurer of the club. The presentation was made on behalf of the club by the president, Mr G H Dobson. Presentations were also made to Mesdames T E Turner, H Simpson and Blacklock in appreciation of their work in looking after the cricket teas during the season. Mr S Wilson (secretary) was whist M C, and prizes were presented to the following whist winners by Mr Dobson: Mrs Scott, Mrs Monaghan, Mrs Hodgson, Mr H Smart, Mr R Patterson jun, (Thornley) and Mr T E Turner. Dance music was played by Reg Bushby and his Band, and winners of the spot dances were Mr J Robinson and Mrs Heightley, (Kelloe) and Miss E Parks and Miss M Simpson.
31 March 1950

BRITISH LEGION. – Members of women's section are having a mystery trip in July and children are to have a free trip to Redcar. One new member was accepted. Prizes were won by Mesdames Leathers, Harper and Stannard.

OVERMAN INJURED – As a result of a fall of stone in the main coal seam of Wheatley Hill colliery on Tuesday, a back shift overman, Norman Garbutt, of Shotton, was taken to hospital suffering from spinal injuries.

VICTORY SOCIAL – To celebrate the return of Mr E Shinwell as M P for their Division, Wheatley Hill Labour Party held a whist drive and dance in the Embassy Ballroom. Messrs J Cowie and F Heele were M C's and prizes were presented to the following whist winners by Coun J Johnson: Mesdames Hodgson, Newton, Griffiths, Greenwell and Parsley and Mr J Fishwick. Coun S Hughes (secretary) thanked all who had helped locally in the election.

A BRAVE PIT DEPUTY
MR HOLDER HONOURED AT THORNLEY

Mr Robert Holder of Thornley, who was awarded the British Empire Medal for his attempt to save three of his workmates when water broke into Thornley pit at 12.30 p.m. on 6 May, 1949, was presented with a further award on Thursday night at the Hippodrome Cinema, Thornley.

The award was an oak framed certificate from the Carnegie Hero Trust, bearing the words, "Presented by the Trustees to Robert Holder, Thornley, Durham, in recognition of heroic endeavour to save human life on 6 May, 1949."

Accompanying the certificate was a cheque for £63.11s. from the Carnegie Trust. This amount was made up of £10 as special award and £53.11s to cover loss.

The awards were handed to Mr Holder on the platform of the cinema by Mr F W Fry, general manager of No 3 Area of the NCB, in the presence of Mr H F Wilson (District Inspector of Mines), Mr T N Sneddon (Production Manager, Group C), Mr E Gascoigne (Area Safety Manager), Supt W J Pearson (Castle Eden Police) and officials of the local branches of the trade unions. Mr A Welsh (Manager of Thornley Colliery) presided.

Water Up To Armpits

Mr Fry congratulated Mr Holder on having been awarded the B E M by the King, and then went on to outline the story of the disaster which overtook Thornley on 6 May, 1949. He said that Mr Holder might have given up the men as lost and got outbye much sooner, but instead, with water up to his armpits and all alone, he went towards the danger, and did not get out of the pit until 5.30pm.

Mr Wilson, who said that Mr Jones (H M Chief Inspector of the Northern Division) was unable to attend, congratulated Mr Holder on carrying on the highest traditions of the pit deputy.

Mr Holder, replying, said he had only a few words to say. He thought it was an occasion when they should remember the three men who were lost and their families. "They were all good men," he said. "I got on well with them." He finished by thanking "my friends" for making the presentation possible.

Mr F Walker (Miners' Lodge chairman) said Mr Holder's action illustrated the comradeship which was part of the miner's life

EAST DURHAM COLLIERIES' OUTPUT -

Only two of the eight collieries in No 3 Area (East Durham), Durham Division, N C B – Shotton and Thornley – failed to reach their targets last week. The area's total output of 88,428 tons was an increase of 264 tons on the previous week and represented 104.46 per cent of the combined target of 84,650 tons. Deaf Hill, the smallest colliery, was again credited with the best achievement, beating its target of 3,250 tons by 10.01 per cent.

Individual outputs, with targets in brackets, were: Horden, 24,011 tons (22,500 tons); Easington, 17,882 (16,500); Blackhall, 15,356 (14,500); Shotton 9,339 (9,600); Thornley, 7,203 (7,500); Wheatley Hill, 6,031 (6,000); Wingate, 5,032 (4,800); Deaf Hill, 3,575 (3,250).

7 April 1950

"COLLECTED" FRIEND'S PAY

CASTLE EDEN COURT, TUESDAY 11TH
CHAIRMAN, MR C H WREFORD

For two years, Thomas Hoole (39), 3 Fifth Street, Wheatley Hill, collected the weekly pay of a mining friend, William Curry, and promptly handed it to Curry's mother. On Thursday morning, last week, he collected the pay, amounting to £6.10s.11d. At Thornley Colliery, as usual, but this time the money was not handed over and Hoole disappeared from the district.

This story was told to the magistrates when Hoole was charged with the theft as bailee of Curry's pay. Hoole, who pleaded "Guilty," asked for a similar case, involving 16s, to be taken into consideration. He was fined £2 and ordered to repay the total sum of £7.6s.11d within two months. The alternative punishment was a month in prison.

Two days after Hoole had vanished with the pay, said Supt Pearson, he returned and went to Thornley Police Station. When told by Sergt Lander of the complaint against him, Hoole replied: "That's right. I have been drawing the pay for three years and never spent a penny of it until Thursday. I got tight, and gambled a lot." When charged with the offence, Hoole admitted he had done a "daft thing."

In court, Hoole expressed his regret at what had happened.

AMBULANCE MAN PROMOTE

Mr James Orange, foreoverman at Thornley Colliery, has been promoted from Serving Brother to Officer (Brother) of the St John Ambulance Association. When he was secretary of the Durham, Cleveland and Westmorland Ambulance League, he arranged realistic tests for the finals. Actual pit conditions were copied. Men pinned down by falls of roof cried out for help. Some even chided the "rescuers" for not going more quickly about the rescue business.

During his time as secretary of Thornley Colliery ambulance class, 817 students gained awards at examinations. His largest class was in 1930 when 157 students were examined by four doctors on two successive Saturdays. All the students passed.

He was secretary of the ambulance league which ran the well known Donald Bain and Elizabeth Bain shield competitions from 1928 until it was taken over by the National Coal Board last year.

Mr Orange has been foreoverman at Thornley Colliery for several years and holds the Home Office Second-class Certificate qualifying him to be a colliery under-manager. He has the distinction of serving for a record period as a colliery rescue worker, retiring last year after 29 years' service, including some time as captain of the local rescue team.

He obtained his First Aid certificate in 1917 and now holds the medallion and 23 labels of the St John Ambulance Association.

MATTHEW OSWALD CRICKET CUP

When the annual meeting of the Durham Aged Miners' (Matthew Oswald) Cricket Cup competition was held in the Liberality Tavern, Easington Village, Mr R Simpson (Wheatley Hill) presiding, reference was made to the death of Mr William Coburn (Horden), one of the founder members of the competition in 1920.

Two additions to the rules were agreed as follows: Rule 3, A player must be a bona fide member of the competing club and have seven clear days registration wit the cup competition; Rule 6, subject to umpires and captains agreeing, 25 overs may be played by reason of a late start through inclement weather.

Mr J Moore (Wheatley Hill), secretary and treasurer, reported, that since the inception of the competition, the sum of £663 has been raised for the Durham County Aged Mineworkers Homes Association.

Nearly forty entries were received and, to avoid excessive travelling, it was decided to play the preliminary first and second rounds in two divisions, East and West.

JUBILANT WHEATLEY HILL

Jubilation reigned high among supporters of Wheatley Hill SC when the "Hill" after a thrilling struggle, defeated their Wearside League neighbours, Wingate C W, by the only goal of the match in the re-played final of the National Orphanage Cup at Shotton on Saturday.

Quicker to take their chances and more accurate in their distribution of the ball, Wheatley Hill were worth their success which, considering that their opponents are well in the running for Wearside League championship honours, must rank as the best performance in the history of the club.

In the "Hill's" first attack Slack set Featonby away on the left wing, but the winger was brought down and the resultant free kick, was headed out of danger by Levitt. After only seven minutes, however, Wheatley Hill scored the goal which proved to be the winner.

A throw-in by Ball was headed across to Featonby, whose right foot drive had Scott well beaten. Wingate came into the picture with some good midfield play, but their forwards wasted chances by keeping the ball too close. In contrast the "Hill" forwards were using the long pass to advantage and in another raid Featonby again had the ball in the net, but was ruled offside. The best work for Wingate was coming from their half-backs, Brown, Levitt and Thompson, who supplied the attack with some good passes, but the forwards could not find an answer to the rock-like "Hill" defence.

Second Half

The second half saw Wingate mostly on the defensive. Featonby was playing a great game on the "Hill's " left wing and his side seemed certain to increase the lead when he sent a beautiful centre into the goal-mouth – Fisher ran in and scored but the referee again blew for offside. Towards the end Wingate looked a well beaten team. Wheatley Hill displayed team work from the start and none could begrudge them their victory. They were ably captained by Jack Carr and Fishwick was the brains of the attack. Apart from their middle line and goal-keeper Albert Scott, Wingate was only a moderate side.

Wheatley Hill are hoping to bring off a cup "double" to-night (Friday) when, on Trimdon Grange ground, they meet another Wearside League team, Horden Res in the final of the National Orphan Aid Cup. Selected team is Nicholson, Scott, Bowden, Ball, Robinson, Carr, Fisher, Fishwick, Sleeman, Slack, Featonby. Kick off 6.20 pm.

21 April 1950

"EASY MONEY" AT WHEATLEY HILL

Thornley Drama Group made a big success of their two performances of Arnold Ridley's three-act comedy "Easy Money" at the Wheatley Hill Welfare Hall. Full houses showed deserved appreciation. The players were Nancy Watson, Enid Dobbinson, Lilly Dowson, Ralph Jackson, Jean Oswald, James Bewick, Mary Orange, John Waite and Tom Woodward, with Vera Fairclough as producer, John English in charge of lighting and Norah Potts and Jane Clark as stage managers. The Group are looking forward to their next effort, "Dog for Delmont," Joseph Colton's amusing play about Durham miners' pastimes.

WHEATLEY HILL'S SUCCESS

By overcoming Wearside League opposition for the second time within a week, Wheatley Hill SC won their second cup this season when, on Trimdon Grange ground on Friday night, they defeated Horden Reserves 2-1 in the final of the National Orphan Aid Cup. The previous Saturday they had won the National Orphanage Cup by a 1-0 victory over Wingate CW at Shotton.

The game against Horden was keenly contested and some good football was seen. The "Hill," however, were superior in attack and fully deserved their success. The Wearside Leaguers showed some fine constructive football in midfield, but when they approached the goalmouth area could find few loopholes in a strong defence, in which Scott and Ball were outstanding.

Within 15 minutes Wheatley Hill had the ball in the net, but the goal was ruled offside. Sid Slack had headed against the bar, and when the ball rebounded at the feet of Featonby, the left winger had it in the back of the net in a flash. Play quickly changed from end to end, both defences being kept at full stretch, but half-time arrived with the score sheet blank.

Seven minutes after the interval Wheatley Hill opened their account, but it was a Horden player who scored. Jack Carr centred the ball right into the goalmouth and Frankland, a Horden defender, in heading back to his keeper to try and evert a dangerous situation, had the misfortune to see the ball enter the net.

Eight minutes later the "Hill," whose attack was in dazzling form, were two goals up following a long free kick taken by Ball. Maddison got the ball but dropped it close to Fishwick, whose return shot gave the keeper no chance.

Horden fought back in gallant fashion and there were some thrilling moments in the "Hill" goalmouth when Nicholson came to his side's rescue with a series of brilliant saves. McPherson, Horden's leader, was persistent in his efforts, but found himself up against a stubborn centre-half in Robinson.

Shortly before the end Horden's efforts were rewarded when Smith, their inside-right, reduced the lead with a grand shot from over 25 yards out, despite Ball's desperate effort to head the ball clear. Horden tried hard to level the scores but their attacks were repelled long before the forwards got a chance to shoot at goal.

Wheatley Hill whose "tails" are well and truly up following their two brilliant cup successes, are hoping to bring off a "hat-trick" tomorrow when on Ferryhill ground, they meet the winners of the semi-final between Winterton Hospital and Byers Green in the final of the Ferryhill and District League Cup. This will be their last cup game of the season.

PIT VICTIM'S FUNERAL – Thornley Parish Church was filled at the funeral service on Wednesday 26, of Mr William H Heale (25), who died from injuries received at Thornley Colliery on Friday. Rev J M How (Vicar) officiated. Young miners were underbearers, and the cortege to Thornley cemetery was headed by the colliery band. Among those attending were Messrs F Walker, J Williams and J Cherry (miners' lodge officials), Mr A Welsh (colliery manager) and Mr T Mackey (undermanager).

PINNED BENEATH STONE 8ft LONG
INQUEST ON YOUNG THORNLEY MINER

How a 25 year old miner was pinned beneath a stone eight feet long for close on a quarter of an hour was told at the inquest at Durham County Hospital, on Monday, on William Henry Heale, 73 Dunelm Road South, Thornley, a stoneman at Thornley Colliery.

The dead man's father, Mr William Henry Heale, of the same address, gave evidence of identification and told the Coroner (Mr W Carr) that his son had no physical disabilities.

Arthur Armstrong a deputy, 13 Seventh Street, Wheatley Hill, said that he went down the pit last Friday at 3.45pm. He was in the South Way district of the main coal seam and met Heale and his mate, Edward Lowther, at the kist about 5.30pm when he set them their normal work of advancing the face belt conveyor and attending to the roof supports. About three hours later he was with Heale and Lowther, working on the coal face opposite the middle left side gate.

First Aid On The Spot

After attending to the conveyor Heale was setting an extra prop under a wood plank when a stone fell from the roof without any warning and pinned him, face down, to the floor. He was liberated in less than 15 minutes and first aid was carried out on the spot. Armstrong added that he had examined the place about half an hour before the accident and was satisfied that everything was in order. The stone was about 8ft long, 4ft 6in wide and 14in thick. The seam was only 2ft 6in high which had made the lifting of the stone more difficult.

Edward Lowther, 7 Fourth Street, Wheatley Hill, corroborated this evidence and said he was only about two yards away from his mate when the accident occurred.

Resident surgical officer at the hospital, Dr V S Metgud, told the court that Heale was admitted about 11.15 on Friday night and died some two hours later. In his opinion, death was due to mass internal haemorrhage caused by ruptured organ or organs in the abdomen.

After the jury had returned a verdict of "Accidental Death," the Coroner expressed sympathy with the dead man's relatives, adding: "It was one of these cases where every caution had been taken, but notwithstanding that, the accident took place."

HAPPY COUPLE AT THORNLEY
CELEBRATE THEIR GOLDEN WEDDING

Well known at Thornley, where they have lived for 35 years, Mr and Mrs Thomas Long, 10 Aged Miners Homes celebrated their golden wedding on Friday and the following day entertained their family of four daughters and one son to a party at their home. The couple, married at Durham Register Office on 21st April 1900, have 11 grandchildren and four great-grandchildren.

Mr Long, who was 70 in December, was born in Worcestershire, but came north to Sherburn Hill as a baby. Shortly before his 13th birthday he started work at Littletown colliery being paid a shilling a day as a trapper boy. Before he was 16 he was "hand putting" at the colliery. Leaving Littletown, he worked at various collieries including New Brancepeth, Waterhouses, Willington and Craghead, before starting work at Thornley colliery a year and a half after his marriage. When at Willington colliery he was coal-hewing at the age of 19.

Loves Reading

Mr Long remained at Thornley colliery until ill-health compelled him to retire when he was 59. During the First World War he served in the 1st East Yorkshire Regiment and was wounded in France. Most of his time now is spent reading.

"I love a good book, especially a cowboy story," Mr Long told our reporter, "and pass away a lot of my time in the old age pensioners' reading room at Thornley. At home I'm happy if I have a book in my hand, and I don't mind a good love story either, and often I am up as late as two o'clock in the morning reading.

Mrs Long, who is two years younger than her husband, was born at Washington and when she was eight moved to Shadforth. She enjoys fairly good health and, except for the washing, does all her own housework. Though she herself was married when she was only 18 she thinks this age is "just a little bit too young." "The best time for a girl to get married is about 20," she said.

Their many friends wish Mr and Mrs Long many more years of good happiness.

28 April 1950

WHEATLEY HILL LEAGUE CHAMPIONS – Though, 20 minutes from the end of their home game with Coxhoe Athletic in the Ferryhill and District League on Wednesday night, Wheatley Hill S C were losing 2-1 and had two of their players – goalkeeper Carter and full-back Bowden - carried off, they won 3-2 to make them champions of the league for the first time since the club was re-formed after the war. The game attracted a record gate.

The "Hill's" determined drive when they played with only nine men deservedly gave them victory. Their marksmen were Featonby, Fisher and Sleeman.

Wheatley Hill's team to entertain Broom Y C tomorrow is: Turnbull, Scott, Cowie, Ball, Robinson, Carr, Fisher, Fishwick, Sleeman, Slack and Featonby.

5 May 1950

"SUFFERING FROM THE GHOST OF PETERLEE"
Vigorous Comments at SE Durham Conference

Scathing comments on the new East Durham town of Peterlee were made at a conference in the Embassy Ballroom, Wheatley Hill, on Saturday, convened by Wingate Parish Council, to consider the question of introducing light industries into the area. At the invitation of the Council, representatives of Thornley, Shotton, Haswell and Hutton Henry Parish councils attended, as well as local members of Durham County Council and Easington R.D.C.

New Industries Pleas

Several times there was heated discussion when Peterlee was mentioned and when towards the end, County Coun A Crossley, Wingate, declared that they should press for light industries coming into the area covered by the parish councils, in preference to Peterlee. Coun Gordon Henderson (Shotton), member of Easington Council, threatened that if an amendment to this effect was put to the conference he and his colleagues on the council would withdraw.

Extending a welcome to the visiting councils Coun G B Hobbs, chairman of Wingate Parish Council, said his council more than once discussed need of light industries for the area. "Housing, I quite agree, is priority No 1," declared Coun Hobbs, "but we are very concerned about the lack of light industries in our area, and we thought by calling the five parish councils together we might be better able, as a united body, to make progress in the matter. We are also concerned about our young people. Many of them are having to travel to different parts of the county to work – that is another reason why we want industries brought into the area. The migration of young people from our mining villages is reaching serious proportions and we have come to the conclusion that the question of work has a great deal to do with it.

Shotton's Future

Coun S Hughes, Wheatley Hill, mover of the resolution convening the conference for the discussion of light industries coming into this area, said he was anxious for the matter to be dealt with because of statements in the Press concerning the life of some of the pits in the neighbourhood. "Only recently," he added, "I read that the future of Shotton Colliery was very uncertain."

The "grim spectre of depression" was hanging over them, went on Coun Hughes, and the question of light industries was of "vital importance." I think it is the duty of everyone here today to try and establish security for the people," declared the speaker.

County Coun E F Peart, Thornley, deplored the fact that though industries had been established in neighbouring areas – there were no fewer than 21 in Bishop Auckland – not one had been introduced in Easington rural area. "This is because we are suffering from the ghost of Peterlee," declared Coun Peart. "Everything has to be sacrificed for Peterlee. In 1947 the Regional Planning Officer declared it was quite easy to get industries into the area – we were well on the way to getting a trading estate at Station Town. Up to March, 1947, Easington Council were making every effort to get light industries here. Now there is a change of policy!"

Will Villages Be Left Behind?

"The reason we didn't get the trading estate or factories at Shotton, Haswell and Wheatley Hill," went on Coun Peart, "was because they decided they had to have a new town, and everything had to be sacrificed for it. There are differences of opinion about Peterlee – but it seems as though the villages are going to be left behind."

"It was the bounden duty of every representative of the villages covered by the parish councils present to see that they got light industries', Coun Peart declared. "We have the labour and the sites," he continued, "and there is no agricultural or mineral problem. At present busload after busload of workers is leaving our villages for industries in other parts of the county when we could have the facilities here to employ them."

"Irrespective of whether "Peterlee goes on or not," said Coun Peart, they had prior claim for industries in the villages".

"I don't want you to be led away by the people connected with the Peterlee Development Corporation," continued the speaker. "If they agree with our claims they are going to put themselves out of a job!"

"We were in the queue for light industries long before Peterlee was. No planner has yet said that you should put industries in a place where other problems are not settled as opposed to a place where you have ideal conditions, labour, land and where you are satisfying the needs of the local people!"

A Comfortable Existence

Coun Peart declared he didn't want the villages to die, but it seemed that the Board of Trade's motto was "Who cares who dies if Peterlee lives. I don't blame Lord Beveridge or any other member of the Peterlee Corporation putting up a case for industries for the new town," continued Coun Peart. "If they didn't argue that way they are going to argue themselves out of existence – it was a long time before it leaked out, but they have a very comfortable existence, especially for a part-time job!"

Concluding, Coun Peart said he wanted the conference to say they were in favour of light industries for their villages before Peterlee. "Why should we take second place to a town which hasn't even a house built?" he asked.

Coun J Johnson, Wheatley Hill, a member of Easington Council, said he would rather that Peterlee was not mentioned in the discussion for they were concerned about industries in the villages covered by the councils and not in Peterlee. He believed they had better facilities for light industries in their part of the area, which was on the western border of the new town, than anywhere else. Everyday 17 bus-loads of girls from Thornley and Wheatley Hill were travelling to work in industries outside the area.

Another member of the Easington Council, Coun R W Rowe (Shotton), said the problem was not one of light industries alone, but mixed industries for in the area they had the basis for chemical industries and coke and by-product plants. In reply, Coun Hughes said he quite agreed that other industries as well as light industries could be introduced.

Station Town Site Rejected?

Coun T Aikenhead, a Wingate representative of Easington Council, said he would not like people to get the impression that the council was standing in the path of progress. Long before Peterlee was thought of the council had discussed the question of light industries for the area. They had had Sir Stafford Cripps out inspecting a site at Station Town for a trading estate, but the Minister had gone on to Hartlepool, and given his sanction to the trading estate there. The Station Town site was turned down.

Coun Gordon Henderson, Shotton, said that one would think Easington Council had been the "nigger in the wood pile," "I want to assure this conference," he went on, "that as far as Easington Council is concerned they have not put anything in the way of industries coming into the villages, nor will they do so in the future, but they want a consensus of opinion as to which is the most suitable site. Our major concern is not so much of travel as to see that there is some alternative employment for people unfit to work in the mining and heavy industries. Even if to go to work means a two or three-mile journey this is much better for a person that being in perpetual dread of unemployment.

What About Haswell?

Capt Swinburne Robinson, clerk to Haswell Parish Council, said he was perturbed about what was going to happen to the people left in the villages after a big percentage of their numbers had been transferred to Peterlee.

"The question of Peterlee," he added, "comes very strongly into this discussion. At Haswell we have over 50 acres of derelict land that would be suitable for light industries, but nothing has been done in the matter. Peterlee seems to be the stumbling block. It is the dream of the planning consultants and the only people receiving any benefit are those being paid large salaries!"

One of the women councillors present, Coun Miss E Bellinger, Wheatley Hill, who serves on Easington Council, declared that many of the planners forgot the "human side" of everything. Many people did not like the idea of being "uprooted" from their villages and "planted" somewhere else.

"We like our villages," continued Miss Bellinger, "and many prefer living in them to living in a town. I know we have to think of tomorrow, but today is the most important time as far as we are concerned, and we need light industries in this area for the women folk. During the depression period we had a mass migration of young people from this area – we don't want that to happen again. We don't want to see a very beautiful Peterlee with derelict villages round about."

Is it a Mistake?

County Coun A Crossley declared they "sold their rights" for factories when they accepted Peterlee. At first he was one of the strongest supporters of the new town, but he now realised he had made a "mistake." "Our duty today is to say we made a mistake," he declared, "and before Peterlee goes any further we want to see life in the villages round about!"

When Coun Crossley, strongly supported by Coun Peart proposed that they ask the Board of Trade for industries for the villages in preference to Peterlee, as an amendment to Coun Hughes's motion that industries be requested for the villages immediately, Coun Henderson rose from his seat and prepared to leave the meeting. "If that amendment is put to the conference," declared Coun Henderson, "I am prepared to ask my colleagues to withdraw from the meeting.

Coun Henderson was prevailed upon by his colleagues on Easington Council to remain and when Coun Hughes's resolution was put to the meeting it was carried by 16 votes to 14.

A copy of the resolution – "That this conference asks the Board of Trade to introduce industries into the area immediately" – is to be sent to Mr Shinwell, MP for the Division, Durham County Council and Easington Rural Council.

WHEATLEY HILL ROAD SAFETY WEEK

Wheatley Hill Children's Road Safety Week, for which an ambitious programme was drawn up by a local committee, with Mr William Stoker, clerk to Wingate Parish Council, as Hon Secretary, got off to a good start on Sunday night with an excellent concert in the Welfare Hall, Wheatley Hill, by Wheatley Hill Colliery Silver Prize Band.

Band started their programme with the hymn, "Rymington", then followed the march "West Riding," overture, "Prince and Peasant" and "Will o' the Wisp" waltz. The selection, "White Horse Inn," concluded a feast of good music. Also taking part in the concert were Mr Oswald (soloist), Mr Bestford (yodeller), Miss Joan Lewis (pianoforte solo) and Miss Bessie Galley (soprano), while a posthorn solo was given by Cliff Midgley and a trombone solo by his brother, John.

Coun J W Moore presided over an appreciative audience and during the interval PC, J L Jackson, Accidents Prevention Officer for Castle Eden Division, gave a brief talk on road safety, urging children to take the utmost care when crossing the road, not only during their special "safety" week, but during the weeks that followed.

Monday night's programme started with a procession and "Road Safety" tableau through the village. A decorated lorry, with illustrated road signs and road safety "tips," was a big attraction and heading the procession was the Road Safety Queen, for Wheatley Hill, 17 year-old Miss Joan Dodds, and her two attendants Miss Margaret Muir and Miss Margaret Moore, who were chosen from Wheatley Hill Infants' and Junior schools. Musical accompaniment was provided by Shotton Boys' Brigade Band.

The procession started from Wingate Lane Tavern and after touring the principal streets, proceeded to the Welfare ground. Wheatley Hill Welfare Hall was later filled to capacity for a concert by Houghton High Jinks. Party Coun T Knowles presided and Coun J W Moore spoke on road safety.

CHORAL SOCIETY'S CONCERT

So great was the attraction of Thornley St. Godric's Choral Society, who gave a concert in Wheatley Hill Welfare Hall on Tuesday night in connection with Wheatley Hill Children's Road Safety Week, that the hall was packed and many people were turned away. Mr E Cain, JP, presided and Sgt Moore of the Accidents Prevention Division of the County Constabulary, spoke on road safety.

The Choral Society gave a delightful programme of vocal items and individual items were contributed by the well known local tenor, Mr "Johnny" Quin and Mrs Doris Surman. Mr James Wilson, Miss Anne McCoy, Mr Anthony Gavaghan, Miss Teresa Morton and Jack Toye, Thornley's blind piano accordionist. A dancing display was given by a team of Irish dancers, with Mr J Surman as compere and M Scully as accompanist.

Another large crowd filled the Welfare Hall on Wednesday night when excellent entertainment was provided by the children of Wheatley Hill Junior School. Children of the Infant's School also pleased with a programme of road safety songs. Coun Miss E Bellinger presided and Mr F W Nightingale, County Education Officer, was the speaker on road safety.

26 May 1950

KNOCKED DOWN BY BUS
Inquest on Thornley Colliery Official

Evidence that just before he was knocked down and killed by a bus on his way to work at Thornley Colliery on Thursday morning last week, he was seen by the driver of the bus to "lower his head and stagger quickly on to the road," was given at an inquest at Thornley on Saturday night on George Richard Parker (40), 12 Garden Terrace, Thornley. Parker who was married, was employed as a keeker at the colliery.

The driver of the bus, Henry S Atkinson, 70 St. Leonard Street, Sunderland, said that about 8.55 am he was driving in an easterly direction along High Street, on the Thornley-Newcastle route, when, about 20 yards ahead, he noticed Parker standing on the kerb.

When he was about 12 yards off, Parker suddenly lowered his head and staggered quickly on to the road in front of the bus. "I foresaw the possibility of an accident," continued the driver, "and so I braked hard and veered towards the right. The man then appeared to turn slightly towards the bus, and when I was almost on to him he stumbled and disappeared from view beneath my front nearside mudguard." When the bus pulled up the driver found Parker underneath the rear nearside wheel.

Medical evidence showed that Parker died instantly from a fracture of the spine and multiple injuries.

The jury returned a verdict that Parker was "accidentally killed," and exonerated the driver from blame.

Sympathy with the deceased's widow and relatives was expressed by that coroner (Mr T V Devey). Mr Crute (representing the Sunderland and District Omnibus Company and the driver) and Mr Stanley Cook (foreman of the jury).

THORNLEY PARISH COUNCIL
Eight Houses Let: 385 on Waiting List

In a discussion on Thornley Parish Council meeting on Wednesday on the letting of Council houses, Coun J Williams, member of Easington RDC, the local housing authority, said that in 13 months Coun Mrs Peart and himself had let eight houses against a waiting list of 385. "We would formulate a scheme today if we had a number of houses to let," said Coun Williams, "and we would go through the whole list."

Coun Williams said he had always been in favour of a points system. A public meeting considered this but decided to leave the letting with the councillors. In the various areas of the Easington rural district there were variations in the manner of letting.

On the suggestion by Mrs Roper that the medical officer should have a number of points allowed to him for letting, Coun Williams replied that owing to the large number of applicants of every kind of case the medical officer would be in the same dilemma as we are.

Housing Superintendent

Coun F Walker thought that the best way in which the medical officer could help today was to examine the old houses at Thornley and tell the owners to put them in a fit state for habitation.

Coun J H C Scott: Not only do we want a points system – we want a housing superintendent.

Coun Fleming said there was a rumour that the National Coal Board had scheduled the "Hilly" to be filled up with pit refuse within the next two years. The "Hilly" was a beauty spot and he hoped that every possible step would be taken to save it.

9 June 1950

GOING TO NIGERIA
Wheatley Hill Miners' Leader

Signal honour has been conferred upon a well-known Wheatley Hill miners' leader, Mr Edward Cain, JP, who has been chosen as one of four Government advisors on Trade Union relations to visit Nigeria for a period from nine to ten months. With the other three selected men from different parts of the country, he will fly to Nigeria next Thursday.

"Needless to say," Mr Cain told our reporter on Wednesday, "it will be a thrilling experience. It came as a complete surprise to me when I first heard that I had been chosen as a Government advisor. There should be good relations between the miners of this country and those of Western Africa and I firmly believe we should strive for a better understanding and stronger unity."

Only once before has Mr Cain been out of this country – that was in 1930, when, as a representative of the National Union of Mineworkers, he attended the Miners' International Congress at Cracow in Poland for a fortnight.

Mr Cain had a serious operation two years ago, but has now fully recovered and feels no qualms about his long stay in Nigeria. He already ahs his tropical kit, few, if any, can be better informed than Mr Cain as an advisor on Trade Union affairs, for he has always been actively associated with the movement. He has served as secretary of Wheatley Hill Miners Lodge since 1934 and before that was chairman from 1921 to 1927.

WHEATLEY HILL VICTORIES

Both Wheatley Hill cricket teams registered victories in the Durham Coast League on Saturday against West Hartlepool. The first eleven, visiting West Hartlepool seconds, won by 45 runs. Taking first knock they had 94 on the board with only half the side out but the remaining five wickets added only 14 runs. Opening bat, H Simpson, came along with a good innings of 37, while E Snowden contributed 31. For the home team Lindridge took four wickets for 19 and Hall three for 25.

West were soon in trouble, four men being back in the pavilion with only 11 runs showing, and the side was dismissed for 63. Only one of their batsmen reached double figures. Bowling unchanged, Wheatley Hill's "pro," G Allison and R Robson had five wickets each for 25 and 29 runs respectively. Details:-

WHEATLEY HILL: H Simpson b Hesleton c Thompson 37, G Allison b Lindridge 10, E Snowdon b Hall 31, J W Moore b Sprott 11, G Gribbens c Telfer b Hall 3, E Ward c Sprott b Hall 0, E Smart c Sherwood b Lindridge 2, G Lumley b Lindridge 5, J Jordan 1bw b Lindridge 1, S Wilson c Telfer b Hall 1.

Record Season

Last season was Wheatley Hill SC football clubs most successful since they joined the Ferryhill and District League at the end of the war. This was reported by the secretary, Mr F E Smith, at the club's annual meeting at the weekend. Not only did they win the championship of the league, but they also won the league challenge cup – a "double" never before accomplished by a club in the league.

In addition to these honours the club won both the National Orphanage and the National Orphan Aid Cups.

Of the total number of 42 games played during the season only tow were lost. Thirty-two were won and eight drawn, while 154 goals were scored against 51. Top goal-scorers were Fishwick 25 (five of which were scored in one game). Temple 17, Sleeeman 13, Laverick 13, Featonby 12.

It was decided to resign from the Ferryhill and District League and seek admission to the Durham Central League.

Officers elected for the ensuing year were: President, Mr A Baldasera: vice-president, Mr R Cowan: chairman, Mr C Williams: vice-chairman, Mr T Young: treasurer, Mr J Bean: assistant secretary, Mr E Jones: committee, Messrs J Bradshaw: G Worthington, A Atkinson, A hardy, W Ponting, W Turnbull, J Hinton, G W Peacock, J Nicholson, R Carter, L Jefferson and F Burnside.

The financial statement showed a balance in hand of £28.2s.9d at the end of the season.

Next Friday night (23 June), the club are holding a dance in the Embassy Ballroom, Wheatley Hill, at which the four miniature cups won by each player will be presented by Mr H Dobson (manager of Wheatley Hill Colliery). The three cups and the shield won by the club will be on view. A record crowd is expected.

THORNLEY CRICKET – It was a jubilant week for Thornley cricket supporters last week for both first and second teams had victories.

On Thursday in the allotted 25 overs, East Hetton second XI compiled 52, and Thornley, batting right through their 25 overs, scored 79 for 9, Les Maddison being top scorer with a bright 27.

On Saturday Thornley first XI also had a victory, scoring 103, thanks mainly to a brilliant 43 by Jimmy Nicholson. Then the visitors, Stanley, were dismissed for 47.

THORNLEY'S CHARMIAN WINS TITLE
Durham High School Girl's Success

A 12 year-old Durham High School girl confounded the swimming critics at Gateshead, last Saturday, in the centralised championships of the Northumberland and Durham ASA by winning the ladies one metre springboard diving event. She was Charmian Welsh (Thornley) member of the Durham City ASC.

Her success is all the more notable since a week previous to the event, Charmian injured herself during training at Durham City Baths, and had to have several stitches inserted in a mouth wound. She was not expected to compete in the championships, but won her spurs at the expense of the reigning champion, Miss J A Royle (Sunderland), obtaining 109 points to her rival's 98. By her win Charmian made history in Durham City swimming circles because she is the first member of the gentle sex to bring Northumberland and Durham championship honours to the City Club.

Prior to carrying off the title, she competed in the junior ladies' 50 yards freestyle event and reached the final, but was placed third. Well done, Charmian!

16 June 1950

BEAUTY QUEENS
To Compete at Crimdon Park

The Embassy Ballroom, Wheatley Hill, was packed on Friday night when a dance – one of the most successful of the series organised by Easington Rural Council – was held to choose village "Beauty Queens," to compete for the title of "Miss Crimdon, 1950" at the council's lido at Crimdon Park on August Bank Holiday Monday.

Young ladies from the two villages of Wheatley Hill and Thornley, escorted by their male partners, paraded round the centre of the dance floor while the judging took place and nobody envied the judges their difficult task.

Miss Myra Davis, the 20 year old youngest daughter of Mrs D Davis and the late Mr Henry Davis, 7 Jack Lawson Terrace, Wheatley Hill, was a popular choice for "Miss Wheatley Hill ." She was presented with the prize of £2 by County Coun E F Peart, while the runner-up Miss Mary O'Brien (22), 2 Sixth Street, Wheatley Hill, received £1. Miss Davis is employed as manageress of the boot and shoe department of Wheatley Hill branch of Sherburn Hill Co-operative Society.

The only daughter of a stoneman at Thornley Colliery, Miss Monica Elliott (21), was chosen "Miss Thornley." Miss Elliott who was also presented with £2, lives with her parents Mr and Mrs T Elliott at 21 Thornlaw North, Thornley. The runner up was Miss Rose Evans (17), 1 Nelson Street, Thornley – she received £1.

Judges were members of Easington Rural Council, Coun J J Johnson, Mrs E F Peart and Miss E Bellinger, together with Mrs J J Johnson and County Coun E F Peart and Coun R W Rowe, chairman of Easington Council's Parks Committee. Mr Gilbert Oliver, Crimdon's entertainments manager was compere and, amid loud cheering announced the winners. Dance music was played by Gilbert Ridley and his band.

23 June 1950

GOLDEN WEDDING AT WHEATLEY HILL
Mr and Mrs William Turnbull

Well known figures in Wheatley Hill, where they have lived throughout their married life, Mr and Mrs William Turnbull, 8 Shop Street, celebrated their golden wedding on Friday, and two days later held a family party at their home. They were married at Easington Register Office on 23rd June, 1900.

The couple, who are both 72, enjoy fairly good health though Mr Turnbull, because of a war injury which still affects his left leg, is unable to get about much. Mr Turnbull served from 1914 to 1917 in the Northumberland Fusiliers and was wounded three times.

A miner for 55 years until his retirement at the age of 67, Mr Turnbull started his career at Castle Eden colliery, but when he was 15 transferred to Wheatley Hill colliery, where he remained until he finished work. Mr Turnbull is a member of Wheatley Hill Workmen's Club, where formerly he was librarian for 12 years.

Active Methodist

Mrs Turnbull was born in North Wales, but went to Rainton as a girl of five then moved to Wheatley Hill a few years before her marriage. She has been actively associated with Church Street Methodist Church, Wheatley Hill, for some 50 years, and for 27 years has been a hard-working member of the Sisterhood. Only last year, after many years' service, she resigned from the positions of Sisterhood vice-president, missionary president, and Trip Fund secretary, and at that time a party was held in her honour.

Mrs Turnbull is able to do a good part of her housework herself, though, she confessed her daughter helps her a lot. She is proud of the fact that she and her husband are the only couple in the past four generations of each of their families to celebrate their golden wedding.

Of a family of seven, Mr and Mrs Turnbull have living three sons and two daughters, 12 grandchildren and three great-grandchildren. They also each have tow brothers and a sister.

Many congratulatory cards and telegrams arrived at the couple's home and one of their most treasured gifts was a budgerigar from one of their daughters. That they may enjoy many more years of good health and happiness together is the sincere wish of their many friends in the district.

WOMEN''S FOOTBALL – Despite the poor weather a good crowd was attracted to Wheatley Hill football ground on Saturday afternoon, when a football match was played between two women's teams, Hesleden "Hurricanes" and Siemen's "Spitfires," in aid of an injured Wheatley Hill miner, Henry Hall. Hesleden won 4-2, their goalscorers being Alice Cooke (2), Hetty Rochester and Nora Graham.

INQUEST – Following a report by Dr G E Stephenson, the Newcastle pathologist, who conducted a post-mortem, that death was due to cancer, the Coroner (Mr T V Devey) returned a verdict of "natural causes," at the inquest at Thornley on Tuesday night, on Robert Berry (40), 6 Durham Street, Wheatley Hill, who died at home on 12 May. Evidence revealed that Berry sustained a fracture of the pelvis while working as a miner at Wheatley Hill colliery on 27 January, 1944. He was off work for nearly four years, then started light duties at the colliery, but was compelled to cease work for a further 18 months.

PRESENTATIONS – At a well-attended dance in the Embassy Ballroom, Wheatley Hill, on Friday night, organised by Wheatley Hill SC Football Club, miniature cups were presented to members of the team successful last season in winning four trophies – the Feryhill and District League championship Cup, league challenge cup, National Orphanage Cup and National Orphan Aid Cup. The following received four miniature cups each: W Gibson, S Scott, K Bowden, W Ball, J Robinson, J Carr, R Fisher, R Fishwick, J Sleeman, S Slack and A Featonby. Two other players. J Nicholson and R Temple, each received two miniature cups. In making the presentations, Mr T H Dobson, manager of Wheatley Hill colliery, who was introduced by the club secretary, Mr F E Smith, wished the club continued success next season when they would be competing in a new league, the Durham Central. Mr J Cowie was MC for the dance, music for which was supplied by Don Warner and his band, **30 June 1950**

CHLTON MOOR BATSMEN COLLAPSE

Chilton Moor paid the penalty of fielding a weakened side, owing to the holidays, and were heavily beaten by Wheatley Hill. Winning the toss, Wheatley Hill had first knock and reached 101. Bassett, to the surprise of the spectators, was taken off after he had sent down four overs for one wicket and five runs.

In reply the home side made a disastrous start and were all out for 37, including nine extras. George Allison, the Hill professional, had a field day for he took seven wickets for two runs in nine overs. Scores:-

WHEATLEY HILL: 101

CHILTON MOOR: J Willey, 5 Allison 0, H Bainbridge c Simpson b Robson 2, B Lowerson b Allison 0, G Bainbridge b Allison 0, W Bassett b Robson 6, G Meyes c Allison b Robson 15, C Harbron b Allison 0, N Hiley b Allison 5, R Walton b Allison 0, J Elliott b Allison 0, W Patterson not out 0, extras 9, total 37.

Chilton Moor bowling: Walton 2-36, Bassett 3-7, Moyes 4-42

CHILTON MOOR II lost by 129 runs to 127 against Wheatley Hill II. T Thompson 28 was best batsman in the Moor's total.

7 July 1950

THORNLEY BAND RUNNERS-UP

Under the leadership of Mr E G T Kitto, Thornley Colliery Band gained second prize in the selection contest, won by Crookhall (Mr J Stobbs). They were also placed third in the hymn tune class.

Thornley have a splendid record to date, for they were placed first in the County Brass Band Leagues' second section competition, as well as first in the northern area of a national second section contest at Newcastle in March. They were also awarded premier honours at a quartette contest at South Bank.

The Thornley men will compete in the final of the national contest at Belle Vue, Manchester, on 23 September. Mr Kitto, their conductor, also conducts   Sunderland Police and Shotton Colliery Bands.

STONES FROM COAL
EASINGTON RURAL DISTRICT COUNCIL

On the question of stones from coal left lying in the streets, the Clerk, Mr J W Gray, stated that this difficult matter was one of many years standing and opinions had been asked for from all quarters but, to the best of his knowledge, final opinion all pointed to the fact that if a nuisance was committed by leaving stones in the streets, the responsibility rested entirely with those who left the stones there.

It was observed from recent Press reports that the question was gaining momentum throughout the country. The question as to whether the local authority should bear the cost of abating the nuisance was another matter. It might be possible to come to some amicable arrangement with the NCB for shouldering a substantial portion, if not the whole of the cost of removal.

It was decided that a deputation should meet the Coal Board on the subject.

THORNLEY CRICKET - The secretary of Thornley Welfare Cricket Club wrote stating that they were perturbed about the future of their cricket field at the "Hilly" as it had been surveyed and scheduled for stone disposal by the Coal Board.

The "Hilly", it was observed, was a beautiful grass covered valley popular with the residents, and children used the surrounds as a playground. With further development, the Club claimed, it could be made into a creditable sports and health centre. On the recommendation of the Health Committee it was agreed that a deputation from the Council should meet the Area General Manager of the NCB to discuss the matter.

Coun M Purcell presided.

14 July 1950

AGED MINERS' TRIP – Nine buses were needed to convey 280 retired miners at Wheatley Hill colliery and their wives to South Shields on Tuesday. The trip was organised by the Aged Miners' Committee, and funds were raised by a voluntary levy by all the workmen. Each tripper received 10s pocket money. The arrangements were in the hands of Messrs N Cook (president), J Hedley (treasurer), J Harrison (acting-secretary) and E Cain.

WHEATLEY HILL WI – Mrs Hutchinson presided and satisfactory finances were reported by Mrs Atkinson. Three members agreed to complete a questionnaire on "Ideal Homes." Report of the London conference was given by Mrs Hutchinson. A demonstration on "Sweets and Savouries" was by Mrs Simpson, who was thanked by Mrs Wilson. During the social half-hour a "Have a Go" programme was organised by Mr T King. Taking part were Mesdames Armstrong, Woodward, Wharrior, Bishop, Hodgson and Thackeray and Miss B Galley. Mrs C English was pianist and Mrs Ranson won the "Jack Pot" question. Winner of the competition for the best apron made out of an old shirt, which was judged by Mrs Simpson, was Mrs Wears, sen.

WHEATLEY HILL CEREMONY

A large public clock erected on the outer wall of Wheatley Hill Senior Boys' School in the main street of the village was unveiled on Wednesday19 July as a memorial to the 31 Servicemen of Wheatley Hill who lost their lives in the 1939 – 45 war.

The clock, with a small brass plaque at each side bearing the names of the fallen, cost £180 10s and was bought from the balance of a comforts fund run during the war by Wheatley Hill United Women's War Committee, supplemented by recent donations from various organisations in the village.

Miss Annie Hutchinson, president of the funds, performed the unveiling ceremony and a service of dedication was conducted before a large crowd by Rev Arthur Preston (Vicar of Wheatley Hill), Rev J W Thurlby (resident Methodist Minister) and Lieut Taylor (Salvation Army). The arrangements were made by Mrs J Atkinson, secretary of the fund, and Mrs Carter (treasurer).

21 July 1950

GERMAN BRIDE AT WHEATLEY HILL

A German girl he met shortly after being posted to Germany a year ago became the bride of a Wheatley Hill regular soldier at a ceremony in All Saints' Church, Wheatley Hill, on Saturday. The soldier, Pte John D Woodward, second son of Mr and Mrs R Woodward, 44 Liddell Terrace, Wheatley Hill, who is on a month's leave from Germany, was married to Miss Rose Marie Voss, elder daughter of Mr and Mrs E Voss, Taarstedt, Scheswig, Northern Germany.

Given away by the bridegrooms father, the bride who, because of travelling difficulties, had no relatives at the wedding, was dressed in white crepe, with a bridal veil and coronet of orange blossom. She was attended by the bridegroom's cousin (Miss Joyce Cummings) wearing white floral silk, with a pink headdress to match, and two sisters of the bridegroom (Maureen and Constance) who wore white figured satin with blue headdresses to match. Best man and groomsman were Ralph and Colin bridegroom's brothers. After the ceremony, conducted by Rev A Preston (Vicar of Wheatley Hill), reception was held at the home of the bridegroom.

The bride, who reached England a fortnight before her wedding, first met the bridegroom's parents in February this year when she paid a three week visit while working as a children's nurse for a German family. Her employers allowed her time off to spend a few days with her prospective "in-laws." She speaks English quite fluently, and when her husband returns to Germany after his leave she is to continue to live with his parents. She hopes ultimately, while he remains in the forces, to get a post as a children's nurse in this country.

The bridegroom has served in the RASC for two years.

28 July 1950

KILLED BY FALL OF STONE

About three hours after the start of his shift, Arthur Patrick Mullen (49), 10 Fifteenth Street, Wheatley Hill, was killed by a fall of stone in the Busty seam, Wheatley Hill Colliery, yesterday. Mullen was employed as a coal hewer and had gone to work in the fore-shift with his son, Arthur, who is employed in another part of the pit. Mullen, who had arranged to go away for his annual holiday in a week's time, leaves a widow, two sons and two daughters. During the war he was head ARP warden at Wheatley Hill and had only recently volunteered again for civil defence. The colliery was laid idle for the rest of the day.

FIFTY YEARS' SERVICE – During an interval in a concert given by Thornley Colliery band at "the Hilly," Mr Arthur Welsh (manager of Thornley Colliery) accompanied by Coun John Williams (secretary of Thornley Miners' Lodge) presented NCB certificates for 50 years service in the mining industry to Messrs C Alderson, A Anderson, T Foster, W Greenwell, T H Holder, W Hurton, J Loftus, T Blanch, T Beddell, E Gair, Mark McDonnell, J W Murray, T Stephenson, N Smithson, J W Richardson, T Tunney and A Willans. The Presentation was arranged by the Colliery consultative committee.

18 August 1950

INQUEST ON WHEATLEY HILL MINER

How a Wheatley Hill miner, described by his work mate as "so very careful that he gave confidence to anybody working with him," was buried by a fall of stone while putting an extra support in the roof of the Busty seam of Wheatley Hill Colliery, was told to the deputy coroner at an inquest at Thornley Police Station on Monday.

The inquest was on coal-hewer, Arthur Patrick Mullen (49), 10 Fifteenth Street, Wheatley Hill, who was killed by the fall on 17 August. A verdict of "accidentally killed" was returned by the jury.

Robert Willis, 63 Jack Lawson Terrace, Wheatley Hill , said he and Mullen, who were workmates, went down the pit about 3am and started work in the Busty seam about half an hour later. They had filled three tubs when Mullen left him to get some more timber.

Without Warning

"I was only two yards away," said Willis, "and Mullen was knocking in a prop when suddenly the roof came away. The fall came without any warning whatever. I shouted, 'Are you all right, Pat'? but got no answer. There was a lot of dust about and I could not see a thing. When it cleared I started to scratch at the stones, but soon knew it was impossible to clear the fall by myself and so ran for the help of some other workmen. It took about quarter of an hour for us to get Mullen out."

Questioned by the deputy coroner, Mr L A Hope, about the timbering, Willis said it was "quite satisfactory."

Mullen, he added, was a very careful workman and before starting work always made a careful examination of the timber. "There was a fault in the seam where we were working," said Willis, "and that made him extra careful. HE decided to put in an extra support and it was then that the fall occurred."

Sympathy with Mullen's widow and family was expressed by the deputy coroner, Mr T H Dobson (assistant agent for the NCB), Mr N J Laverick (workmen's Inspector of Mines), Mr J U C Chester (H M Inspector of Mines) and Mr J Atkinson (on behalf of the jury).

"Mr Mullen," said Mr Dobson, "was regarded by us as a very valuable and experienced workman."

WHEATLEY HILL'S FINE START Making their debut in the Durham Central League on Saturday Wheatley Hill S C were full value for their 5-0 victory over Horden Reserves at the Welfare Park, Horden. The first half was keenly contested and the interval arrived with the score sheet blank. The "Hill," however, piled on the pressure in the second half, goals coming from Fishwick (2), Sleeman, Robinson and Luke.

For their home game with Brandon C W tomorrow Wheatley Hill have chosen: Nicholson, Scott, Bowden, Waller, Ball, Carr, Luke, Fishwick, Sleeman, Slack, Fisher. Kick off 3.15 pm.

HOLIDAY SAVING LOST
In Fire at Wheatley Hill

A Wheatley Hill miner and his three sons lost their holiday savings totalling £37 when fire broke out in the front kitchen of their home at 58 Wordsworth Avenue, Wheatley Hill, on Friday afternoon. The savings were in a drawer of the kitchen sideboard, where the fire originated.

The fire was discovered by the miner's wife, Mrs John Ryan, on her return from a two hours' shopping expedition. No one was at home at the time, Mrs Ryan's husband and three sons all being at work.

"I left home just after dinner to do my shopping," Mrs Ryan told out reporter, "and as I was walking up our street on my way back home about two hours later I noticed a lot of smoke coming from my house. I couldn't see the curtains for smoke. I dropped my shopping bag and ran for help, but was so distressed I could give little help myself."

Horden and Wheatley Hill units of the Durham County Fire Brigade were summoned, but until they arrived a neighbour of Mrs Ryan, Mr James Wylie, 60 Wordsworth Avenue, organised a chain of water buckets to help to subdue the blaze in the kitchen.

Women from surrounding houses gave valuable help and there was no doubt but what their prompt action helped considerable to prevent the house from being burned to the ground. The firemen quickly reached the scene and had the fire under control within a quarter of an hour. They remained on duty for an hour and a half.

Cherished Possessions Destroyed

The fire is believed to have been started by a spark from the kitchen fireplace flying out on to some inflammable material on the sideboard.. The top half of the sideboard was burnt out and damage was done to the floor coverings, other furniture in the kitchen, and the walls and ceiling.

Plaster on the wall near where the sideboard stood was stripped off to the bare bricks and the whole of the walls and ceiling were blackened. The walls of the adjoining back kitchen and bathroom were also smoke-blackened.

In addition to the money which was destroyed, Mrs Ryan lost many of her most cherished possessions, which she kept in the sideboard. New shirts bought for her son's holidays were also destroyed, together with three pocket watches and band instruments belonging to her sons, Jack and Christopher, who are members of Thornley Colliery Band, were damaged beyond repair. The instruments had been on top of the sideboard.

Though their savings had gone said Mrs Ryan, her sons were still going on holiday next week, the miners' holiday week at Wheatley Hill. Jack the eldest, was going to Bradford, Christopher to Filey and Michael to Blackpool. "We had the furniture and effects insured," said Mrs Ryan "so you can guess how thankful we are for that!"

25 August 1950

WHEATLEY HILL HOLIDAYS

There was a general exodus from Wheatley Hill on Saturday, when the miners' annual holiday week started. Blackpool seemed to be the most popular holiday choice – early in the morning three buses left packed for this resort – but quite a number of miners and their wives journeyed to London, some to visit relatives and others for their first sight of the capital.

Two clubs catered well for their members, whether they were staying at home or going away. As a holiday gift Wheatley Hill Workmen's Club gave £5 to each of their 560 members from an auxiliary fund of the club. The money was distributed each night last week by the club treasurer, Mr J Dunn, and members of the committee. Ten free pints of beer was the holiday gift of Wheatley Hill Constitutional Club for its members, some of whom got well through their "allocation" on the first day of their holidays.

Wheatley Hill's neighbour, Thornley Colliery, was also on holiday this week, and here too, many miners seized the chance to take their families for a seaside or country holiday. Quite a number went to camp at Crimdon, Easington's holiday lido.

FESTIVAL OF PLAYS:- In aid of the Arthur Bonar Appeal Fund – a fund launched some months ago to aid a young Thornley footballer who lost both legs in a pit accident on 10 March at Thornley Colliery, he was an apprentice fitter age 19 years.   Members of Wheatley Hill and Thornley Drama Group took part in a festival of one-act plays in the Welfare Hall Wheatley Hill. All the plays were produced by Mrs Vera Fairclough of Easington, and some excellent talent was revealed. The following took part in the plays presented by the Wheatley Hill Group:- "It Won't Be a Stylish Marriage" (a comedy), Evelyn Kenny, Simon Hedley, Dorothy Robinson, Maureen Abbs and Eve Wharrior; "Vindication" (drama), Emily Thackeray, Minnie Galloway, Frank Bowes, Ivy Scott and George Wilson. Plays presented by Thornley Group were:- "Dark Brown" (drama), Nancy Watson, Mary Brass, Jean Dowson, Margaret Walton, John Waite, Eunice Bewick, Ralph Jackson; "Nicodemus" (comedy), James Bewick, Mary Orange, Kenneth Dowson, John Waite, Ralph Jackson and Alice Winter. Supper was provided each night for the players by members of Thornley Catholic Women's League who were thanked on the first night by Mr R Woodward, secretary of Wheatley Hill Group, and on the second night by Mr J Waite, a member of Thornley Group.

1 September 1950

THORNLEY

STACK FIRE:- Damage estimated at £240 was done when a stack of baled hay was destroyed by fire at Roper's Gore Hall Farm, Thornley, shortly after midnight on Sunday. Horden and Wheatley Hill units of the Durham County Fire Brigade were summoned to the outbreak and had it under control within half an hour. They remained on duty for nearly three hours to prevent any danger of the scorched undergrowth breaking out into fire again. Cause of the blaze is unknown.

LEGION WOMEN:-To commemorate the silver jubilee of the women's section of Thornley British Legion, a birthday party was held in Thornley Club Hall. Mrs Clark welcomed Miss Todd and Mrs Ledger (county officials). They both gave short addresses. President, Mrs Bovil, said she had been a member from the inception and had held an official capacity for 25 years. After a knife and fork tea an iced cake (made by Mrs Parker) was cut and a piece handed to each one present. In the evening the chairman welcomed visitors from the men's section. To conclude the celebrations the Legion concert party entertained. Organisers were Mesdames Bosomworth and Slater.

8 September 1950

THORNLEY MINERS' LODGE CHANGES

Chairman, secretary and delegate of Thornley Miners' Lodge failed to retain their posts at the annual ballot. Mr Frank Walker, chairman, lost to Mr Edward Carter by 343 votes to 374. Mr William Dowding, a former secretary, became secretary again with 606 votes against 113 for Coun John Williams. Mr D Gott, a young member of the Lodge, was elected delegate with 422 votes against 257 for Mr Reginald Heale. Mr Joseph Cherry retained the post of treasurer by defeating Mr W H Heale.

15 September 1950

BACK FROM NIGERIA
WHEATLEY HILL MAN'S EXPERIENCES

After three months in a country where, he declared, "time and distance seem to have no meaning," Mr Edward Cain, JP, Burns Street, Wheatley Hill, returned home a few days ago to present a report to Mr James Griffiths, Secretary of State for the Colonies, about mining conditions in Enugu, a town in Nigeria, West Africa.

On 22 June this year, Mr Cain, who is employed as checkweighman at Wheatley Hill Colliery and is secretary of Wheatley Hill Miners' Lodge (though someone else is carrying on this job in his absence), was one of five members of a Labour Relations delegation who flew to Enugu to examine conditions in two mining drifts there. Last November, during trouble over wages among the natives employed at one of the drifts - the Iva Valley - 21 miners were shot.

When he left this country Mr Cain expected to be away some nine or ten months, but was recalled, and on Tuesday he left for London to present his report to the Colonial Secretary. He expects to return to Enugu again in the near future.

Miners In Bare Feet

Looking fit and well, despite the big change in climate - the atmosphere in Enugu, said Mr Cain, was "very humid" - Mr Cain said he had seen more in three months than many men who had gone there had seen in 20 years. That, at least, is what Government officials had told him.

The native miners, no matter what their job was, whether on the surface or below ground, worked in their bare feet, even when hewing or putting, and some, said Mr Cain, had as many as ten miles to walk to their work. The two drifts in Enugu - the Obwetti and the Iva Valley - employed about 7,000 natives, and the daily output of coal was about 2,000 tons.

Accompanied by an interpreter, Mr Cain visited the men at work, often underground, and had many opportunities of speaking to them in their rough straw made homes. "Everywhere I went," said Mr Cain, "I was received cordially by the natives. They were very approachable and eager to tell me about their job and any grievances they had."

Mr Cain lived in a chalet with all modern conveniences, but the homes of the natives, he said, were very primitive. There were lizards – some of them a foot long – everywhere. "They ran about the house like flies," declared Mr Cain, "but, though they had me scared stiff at first, I soon found out they had their uses – they helped considerably to keep down the flies and mosquitoes, so we never wanted to get rid of them. One morning at the beginning of my stay I nearly fainted – I found I could not get my foot in my shoe, and when I looked for the cause discovered that a lizard had made its home there!"

The whistling of the crickets and croaking of the bull-frogs throughout the night kept Mr Cain awake during the early part of his visit. But, he said, he got used to the noise, "and, believe me, it was a deafening one", and soon he could sleep as well as he could at home in England.

The natives main enjoyment, said Mr Cain, was their dancing and drinking "palm" wine. Mr Cain saw several of their quaint dances, including the Ju-ju dance which, it was claimed, few white men had ever seen.

Native servants looked after Mr Cain in the chalet where he was billeted at the Government Rest Camp. They cooked his food and washed his clothes and he found them quite reliable. "The food was differently served and differently cooked," added Mr Cain, "but I found it to be quite palatable - at any rate I thrived quite well upon it!"

Praise For Missionaries

Mr Cain paid a glowing tribute to the work of the English missionaries. "no praise can be too high," he said, "for the excellent way in which they are carrying out their difficult task. They are helping to build schools, small maternity hospitals and dispensaries, and even small shops. They are working happily in villages that are very primitive. District Officers appointed by the Government are also doing a tremendous job."

Ninety per cent of the miners, estimated Mr Cain, were very illiterate – they could neither read nor write. They worked at the coal-drifts in shifts of eight hours.

When Mr Cain flew to Enugu it was the first time he had been in the air. "And it was a thrilling experience," he said. It is a journey of about 4,000 miles. There's a small landing strip at Enugu, and on the return journey Mr Cain flew from there to Lagos – a three hour trip. He left Lagos at 1.40 pm and, after one hour stops at Kano and Tripoli, reached England at eight o'clock the next morning.

EJECTMENT ORDER AGAINST THORNELY WOMAN

Easington Rural Council successfully applies at Castle Eden magistrates' court on Saturday for an ejectment order against one of their Council house tenants, Mary Burke, 74 Thornlaw South, Thornley.. After hearing the evidence, the Magistrates' Clerk (Mr A J Finlay) told the Bench they had no other option but to issue an order for ejectment within 21 to 30 days.

Applying on behalf of the Council, Mr Ambrose Johnson said that notice to quit her house on 2 September because of arrears of rent had been served upon Mrs Burke on 22 August, but she had failed to leave. The weekly rent of her house was 12s.9d and her arrears totalled £5.16s.

"Mrs Burke has been a tenant since November, 1948," went on Mr Johnson, "and over the last 11 weeks, against £7.0s.3d rent due, only £2.11s has been paid – an average of only 4s.8d per week. During the last 17 months we have served notice to quit four times, and three times Mrs Burke was summoned to appear before this court. Mutual arrangements were made, however, each time and the notices and summonses cancelled."

Numerous letters had been sent to Mrs Burke about the arrears, said Mr Johnson, who added that he had also personally interviewed the tenant. "Promises have been made," continues, Mr Johnson, "but it seems that this tenant will not pay except under constant pressure."

22 September 1950

MET IN HONG KONG

Mrs John Piercey, Nelson Street, Thornley, told our representative how her two younger sons, Gilbert and Douglas Armstrong, serving in the Middlesex Regiment, now in Korea, met their elder brother, Gordon Piercey, her stepson.

Gordon (30), has been in the Royal Navy since he was 15. He is a Petty Officer on the aircraft carrier "Unicorn," and it was this ship which picked up the younger boys, Corporal Gilbert (23) and Private Douglas (19), at Hong Kong, ultimately landing them at Pusan on the east coast of Korea.

Mrs Piercey is naturally very anxious to have more news of the three boys. "It takes a long time for a letter to come all the way from Korea," she said,

She has taken a close interest in the campaign, following it by the maps in the newspapers.

Gordon served on the famous aircraft carrier "Illustrious" when it was badly treated by German bombers in the Mediterranean. He escaped injury, but one of his chums was killed. He is married and his wife resides at Plymouth.

Gilbert and Douglas both worked at Thornley Colliery before joining up. Recently, Gilbert wrote that he regretted Douglas was with him because it made him feel responsible for him.

WHEATLEY HILL WI - Mrs R H Hutchinson presided and Mrs Atkinson and Mrs Horn were chosen to attend "Canada Day." Mrs P Wharrior was elected delegate to the autumn council on 31 October, and several members are also to attend as visitors. An account of her visit to Denman College was given by Mrs Atkinson who was thanked by the president. Miss Mary Chisholm, a missionary in Nigeria who is home on furlough, spoke on missionary work and the women of Nigeria. She was thanked by Mrs English. During the social half hour Mrs White and her pupils entertained with folk and old-time dancing, the pianist being Mrs Harrison. Winner of the competition for the best knitted socks was Mrs Snowdon.

OCTOGENARIAN'S DEATH - One of Wheatley Hill's oldest residents, Mr Frederick Bromilow (81), 7 Seventh Street, Wheatley Hill , died on Sunday in Leeholm Hospital, Easington, where he had been 4½ years. He lived with his son-in-law and daughter (Mr and Mrs John Peters, Wheatley Hill). Mr Bromilow, a native of Hindley, Lancashire, lived in Wheatley Hill for half a century. He was employed at the colliery until his retirement more than 20 years ago, and was a member of the Workmen's Club. Mr Bromilow's wife died 27 years ago and he is survived by four sons and four daughters. Funeral took place at Wheatley Hill yesterday following a service in All Saints' Church.

THORNLEY PARISH COUNCIL
The "Hilly" and Pit Refuse

When Mrs Roper suggested at Meeting of Thornley Parish Council that there should be a special meeting to go fully into the proposal of the National Coal Board to fill up the "Hilly," a local beauty spot, with pit refuse, Coun J Williams, a member of Easington Rural Council, advised that it would be better to await the result of another meeting of the District Council with representatives of the NCB.

Coun Williams gave the Council some information about the proposals of the Board. The old Trimdon Quarry, for example, would probably be used for refuse from Deaf Hill and Wingate pits. The low-lying land between Thornley and Wheatley Hill would be reserved for emergency tipping, and the "Hilly" was estimated to serve as Thornley's tip for 30 years. The alternative to the "Hilly" would be a number of conical heaps like the one they already had. He advised the Council, if they were represented at the next meeting, to put forward their ideas.

Coun F Walker, who works underground at Thornley pit, told members in reply to a question that even if Thornley pit worked another 60 years, the seams to be worked would always be thin and always contain a good deal of refuse. In such seams it would not be possible to "stow" the refuse underground.

Coun J H C Scott thanked Couns Williams and Walker for the information they had given. As far as cost was concerned, he suggested that if this was spread over 60 years it would not be unreasonable.

6 October 1950

THORNLEY'S WELFARE CENTRE

It was stated at a meeting of No 8 area Health Sub-committee at Easington on Tuesday that the County Health Committee would consider renovating the old Literary Institute at Thornley to serve as a welfare centre. Subject to securing a long lease of the premises or the acquisition of the Institute by the County Authority, it was decided that the county architect should make an examination of the premises and submit a report. Estimated cost of renovation would be about £620.

A suggestion from the voluntary committee that one or two houses in the village, which would soon become available, should be bought for conversion into a welfare centre was considered. It was decided that the houses be inspected by the county architect.

20 October 1950

THORNLEY FOOTBALL

Dickie Dunn, Wingate CW's new centre forward and an experienced player, has agreed to give Thornley CW players expert tactical tuition. This effort, together with some practice games, should uncover new talent and should assist Thornley in their quest for honours.

Thornley CW entertained Station Town in a Wingate League game. The home side pressed from the start, but no goals arrived until after 25 minutes. Then R Potts, making a promising debut as left winger, crossed the ball over the goalmouth and W Wilson, right winger, touched it into the net. The goal was disallowed for the whistle had sounded apparently for a penalty for hands. A Abbs made no mistake with the kick. Five minutes later Blakemore, centre forward, ran in and gave the unsighted Station Town keeper no chance.

Station Town forwards raided three times after that, but Thornley full backs A Abbs and L Williamson, with Bob Miles, centre half, and Jim Nicholson, keeper, nullified their efforts. Just before the interval W Wilson bustled between the Station Town backs but shot wide.

Soon after the restart Blakemore put Thornley three up. After this Thornley seemed to take a breather, for Station Town were given more scope and J Watson, their left winger, reduced the arrears with a good goal.

Score stood at 3-1 for a long time until R Potts placed in the net a rebound from a powerful drive by R Parker. Just before the end Potts and Blakemore combined well for the latter to score and complete his hat-trick.

All Thornley players did well with some entertaining football. Smith, Parker and Niles made a splendid half-back line. On this form Thornley forwards should get many goals. Watson, on the left, impressed for the losers while Carter, keeper, could not be blamed for the defeat in any way.

LUDWORTH WERE UNLUCKY

Cup fever seemed to grip spectators and players alike at Chester Moor when Chester Osborne entered the semi-final of the Lumley Nursing Cup by their 4-1 victory over Ludworth Rising Star. The visiting supporters were far from satisfied with the result.

Many spectators claimed that Ludworth seemed to have scored a good goal ten minutes from time. This effort, which would have been the equaliser, was disallowed for offside amid protests. Ludworth Rising Star have not been doing so well this season as in the past, but they are pleased with two recent signings. The "Napoleon of Soccer," Tommy Usher, the evergreen Sherburn Hill veteran, has thrown in his lot with them, while Rennie Martin, wing-half from Sherburn, has also joined.

Chester Osborne have changed their name from Cestrians, but still have most of last season's players, and are under the same management. Reason for the change, I understand, is the help given by Chester Osborne Workmen's Club to the team. Having sampled Fence Houses and District fare last season, they are now in the Washington and District League and have found recent performances have attracted a few more spectators.

There was some argument before the match as to whether Ludworth should have asked for the match to be played somewhere else other than the Greens, Chester-le-Street. It was only through the Chester Moor Club's generosity that Osborne were able to take advantage of a "home" fixture.

Many Free Kicks

Seldom have I seen so many petty infringements with resulting free kicks. Ludworth were disallowed their "equaliser" on several occasions in the second period, and it seemed as if the players were "playing the man" instead of the ball.

Heavy rain at the start, and a cold wind did not help, and the few supporters left at the finish were rather glad – as must have been the players – when the full time whistle sounded.

Ludworth had first half advantage of slope and wind. Both teams, using swinging passes to the wings, kept defences at full stretch. Osborne went nearest to scoring when Van Hoof shot quickly only for Hutchinson to punch the ball over the bar for a good save.

Osborne went into the lead in 15 minutes when centre-forward flicked the ball neatly into the net. This encouraged Ludworth and centre-forward Ferguson should have levelled matters, only for Campbell to make a fine save. Equaliser arrived in 22 minutes when Slack sent Ferguson through to head in.

Ludworth might have gone into the lead a minute later when full back McGahan, attempting a back pass, sent wide of the keeper only for the ball to hit the upright. Ludworth were now pressing and the Osborne keeper was the busier of the two.

Compact Defence

Ludworth defence seemed more compact and steadier under pressure. Usher kept a tight grip on Middlemas. After a spell of pressure by Ludworth, Osborne rallied and in the five minutes before the interval produced the best football of the match.

Against wind and slope in the second period, Ludworth won "on points" but not "on goals." They seemed to have more method in their forward play and their "insides" were clever schemers. Nevertheless Osborne had two grand defenders in McGahan and Austin.

Sharp, at centre-half for the home side, also showed up well with neat interceptions. With Ludworth doing the pressing, Osborne broke away for a lucky goal. A corner was forced on the right. Dawson placed the kick perfectly, but the ball was cleared. It was returned and Gardner tried a header from 15 yards for the ball to bounce over Hutchinson's body into the net.

This acted as a spur to Ludworth, and Ushaw moved up into the inside berth, Martin also acting as an extra forward. Osborne packed their goal, Campbell did well to punch a fierce drive from Usher over the bar, and left-back Austin headed out a full-blooded drive from Brown, being injured in so doing.

In the last 15 minutes Ludworth produced their best football. When they had the ball into the net there was uproar when the referee disallowed the goal. Several Ludworth players were cautioned. In the final few minutes Ludworth seemed to go to pieces, and Middlemas and Dawson added two quick goals for Osborne.

Comments

Osborne finished well, but did not deserve to win by four goals to one. Ludworth were superior in the second period and should have earned a replay.

Middlemas, with few opportunities, did well for Osborne and kept his line well together. Full backs McGahan and Austin were sound and left-half Birkett produced some grand defensive work.

For Ludworth, Usher and Martin did their share and left-back Youll made fine clearances, Ferguson was perhaps most thrustful in the visiting attack, but their weakness seems to be at inside-forward, where more punch is needed.

Teams – Chester Osborne: Campbell, McGahan, Austin, Gardner, Sharp, Birkett, Thompson, Van Hoof, Middlemas, Stevenson and Dawson.

Ludworth RS: Hutchinson, Levitt, Youll, Slack, Usher, Martin, Stones, Brown, Ferguson, Jones and Carr.

3 November 1950
DEATH OF MR A BALDASERA, THORNLEY

The respect in which the late Mr Angelo Baldasera (72), was held in Thornley district was shown by the large congregation at Requiem Mass on Wednesday at Thornley RC Church preceding the interment in the family grave at Wheatley Hill cemetery.

Mr Baldasera died in hospital at Newcastle following an operation. He had been in failing health for some months but had carried on his business activities. He went to Thornley from West Hartlepool 40 years ago and set up ice-cream and confectionery bars at Thornley,

Wheatley Hill and Shotton. He frequently altered and improved these premises to bring them up-to-date.

Of his eight sons, some joined him in the business and will now carry on themselves. The youngest son, Joseph, is a medical student. Of his two daughters, the younger one, Rosaline, is now serving her novitiate at Sunderland as a nun.

Mrs Baldasera, who is his second wife, was on a pilgrimage to Italy when her husband died, and had not returned for the funeral.

The death of Mr Baldasera has removed from the district a kindly man who was always ready to help worthy causes.

THORNLEY PARISH COUNCIL
Gas Supply to be Discussed

Coun JHC Scott raised the question of whether Thornley should join in seeking to have the domestic gas supply which is now being discussed in the Horden area. He said the present electricity supply was bad and that a supply of gas would be of great value to the people of Thornley.

Coun M Fleming said it would certainly ease the tension on the present electricity supply. He suggested that the question be referred to the Easington Area Committee of the Durham County Parish Councils' Association with a request that they discuss it with the Easington Rural District Council. This was agreed.

Recreation Ground

Reporting on an inspection of the recreation ground at Percy Street, Coun Scott took the strong line of suggesting that as the ground was in a bad condition the amenities it contained should be shifted to other parts of the parish.

Mrs Roper disagreed. "I move that the recreation ground be not moved," she said.

Mrs Brewster and Mrs Anderson, joining in the discussion, said that repairs to the swings and concreting the bases were necessary. The closing of a large gap in the wall near Ludworth street and renewals of fencing on the allotments side of the ground were also necessary.

The discussion closed with the passing of a resolution that the question be fully considered at a meeting immediately after the winter. In the meantime a notice is to be erected giving warning against the running of pigs and other animals in the ground without the permission of the council.

Public Footpaths

Members of the council reported on the final walk-over of the public paths with surveyors of Durham County Council. It was agreed to hold a parish meeting on the first Tuesday in December when the marked map will be exhibited so that members of the public may approve or disapprove of any paths included in the survey. Clerk said the survey had shown that no paths had been lost to the parish since 1887.

The County Librarian wrote regretting the delay in opening the proposed branch of the library at the Waterloo Street Chapel. He said that so far as he could judge it would be the middle of November before the library would be in operation.

In a letter on the tipping of pit refuse in the "Hilly," the Clerk of the Easington RDC said his Council had agreed to the Thornley Parish Council being represented at any further meeting with representatives of the National Coal Board.

10 November 1950

FATAL COLLAPSE:- While waiting for a shave in a hairdressers shop at Wheatley Hill on Friday morning, shortly after he had drawn his week's pension, Mr William Kears (78), 8 Smith Street, Wheatley Hill, collapsed and died. The day was the 13th anniversary of his second marriage. He is survived by his second wife and a family of six daughters and two sons. Mr Kears was employed as a miner at Wheatley Hill Colliery until his retirement at the age of 65. Funeral took place at Wheatley Hill Cemetery on Tuesday following a service in Patton Street Methodist Church, Wheatley Hill, conducted by Rev Noel Catherall.

REMEMBRANCE:- All Saints' Church, Wheatley Hill, was filled to capacity on Sunday afternoon for the annual service. Before the service a parade, consisting of representatives of Wheatley Hill branch of the British Legion (both sections), Wheatley Hill Boy Scouts and Wolf Cubs, Wheatley Hill WI and the local Co-operative Society, was headed from Patton Street to the Welfare Hall by Wheatley Hill Silver Prize Band, conducted by Mr W Forrest. Wreaths were laid on the war memorial at the Welfare Hall, and silent tribute was in charge of the chairman of the men's section of the Legion, Mr William Poole. Afterwards the "Last Post" and "Reveille" were sounded. Service in church was conducted jointly by Rev Arthur Preston (Vicar) and Rev Noel Catherall (resident

Methodist minister) and the band accompanied the hymn-singing. A collection in aid of Earl Haig's Fund realised £3.18s.

WHEATLEY HILL MINERS DISCUSS PAY AWARD

Members of Wheatley Hill miners' lodge turned up in full force at a special lodge meeting on Sunday to hear the report of their delegate, Mr J W Burrell, about the recent wage award made to the lower-paid mineworkers and though, after a long discussion, the award was accepted, strong disapproval was expressed at what was termed "a meagre increase."

After the meeting, which was presided over by Mr J Frost, lodge secretary, Mr E Cain told our reporter that the members were disappointed that the National Executive, NUM, had accepted such a poor offer and it was decided to urge the Executive to persevere with their original decision to seek an increase of half-a-crown a day.

"In view of the fact that wage increases have been granted to other industries dependent upon the coal industry," said Mr Cain, "the meeting felt that the recent award to lower-paid miners was very poor. Some of the lodge members made reference to the recent increases granted to school-teachers who, they declared, worked only 27½ hours a week. The Coal Board, they felt, should realise that the miner in his dangerous calling should at least have had the same weekly rise of 30s as the teaching profession. Whilst we are not declaiming the teachers – let them get as much as they can – we certainly feel that the miner, faced with a much more arduous task, should at least have been treated equally as well in the matter of pay increase.

VIEWS EXPRESSED BY WINGATE MEMBERS

Several members of Wingate Parish Council, at their meeting at Wheatley Hill on Monday, criticised their Member of Parliament, Mr Emanuel Shinwell, following correspondence received from him relating to a conference the Council propose holding to discuss further the question of establishing new industries in the western part of the Easington Rural Council area.

Mr Shinwell and the RDC

The neighbouring parish councils of Thornley, Shotton, Haswell and Hutton Henry were to be invited to the conference, together with the parish representatives on Easington Rural and Durham County Councils and Mr Shinwell and representatives of the Town and Country Planning and the Board of Trade.

Mr Shinwell was asked for a date most suitable for him to attend the conference. In reply he wrote he would be quite willing to attend in December but he felt it "desirable" to bring in Easington Rural Council and the other parish councils in the Easington Rural area into the conference and had written Mr Gray (clerk to Easington Rural Council) accordingly.

A second letter from the Minister said that he would be attending a divisional conference in the Easington area on 9 December and it would suit him, therefore, if the conference could be held either in the morning or evening of that day.

Coun S Hughes declared that Mr Shinwell should have written to the council first "before giving an invitation" to other parish councils to attend the conference.

Was Invited As Guest

"It was bad form for Mr Shinwell to take it upon himself to invite the rest of the Rural Council," continued Coun Hughes. "We were the instigators of the conference and the problem of new industries concerns mainly the parish councils in the western area. The problem does not exist in the coastal areas because the people there will be catered for by the new town of Peterlee. Mr Shinwell was only invited as a guest to the conference, yet he himself invites the rest of the Rural Council!"

Coun J L Bell said he did not think they would get "very much backing" from Mr Shinwell, for his chief support seemed to be for the new town of Peterlee. The morning or evening of 9 December would not be very convenient for a conference, added Coun Bell, the following Saturday, 16 December, would be more suitable.

"I am quite in agreement with the 16th," declared Coun Hughes, "irrespective of whether Mr Shinwell comes or not. The Board of Trade representative can attend on that date, so we will be able to put up a case to him for new industries. He is the main man we want at the conference and not Mr Shinwell, for Mr Shinwell is not helping us very much with regard to new industries."

On the motion of Coun Bell it was agreed to hold the conference on 16 December and to inform Mr Shinwell and the four neighbouring parish councils of the date. At the same time the Clerk (Mr William

Stoker) was instructed to point out to Mr Shinwell that only the parish councils and local rural and county councillors in the western part of the area would be invited.

Wheatley Hill Project

The draft plan and estimates for new playing fields at Wheatley Hill were submitted by Easington RDC. Included in the plan were a football pitch, concrete cricket pitch, facilities for net-ball and a children's playground and the estimated cost was £3,000.

"It is an ideal plan," commented Coun J W Moore, "and would be much appreciated by the people of Wheatley Hill, but the Education Authority would not look at anything costing more than £1,000. If we want help we will have to reduce the estimate to this figure. The village is short of football pitches. I don't see why we should not get the figure down to £1,000 and go forward with a scheme for two football pitches and a concrete cricket pitch."

For the present, continued Coun Moore, they could cut out the other amenities mentioned.

REMEMBRANCE:- It was the turn this year for the Thornley Service of Remembrance to be held in the Bow Street Methodist Church. There was again a large attendance. Rev W T Rose (superintendent Methodist minister), Captain Taylor (Salvation Army) and Rev J M How (Vicar of Thornley) all took part. Wreaths were laid on behalf of the British Legion men and women, the Thornley Miners' Lodge, the Workmen's Club, Girl Guides and the Parish Council. The Legion women's wreath was placed by Mrs Bovill, 80 years old president of the branch. Service was arranged by the British Legion branch, Messrs W Bovill and J W Waite being the organising officials. Singing of the hymns was led by Thornley Colliery band, who also led the procession from the Legion headquarters to the church.

17 November 1950

TO WORK SATURDAY SHIFT:- At a special "all-sections" meeting in Thornley on Sunday morning Mr A Welsh (manager), presided. Purpose of the meeting was to seek the approval, of the workers, on the colliery consultative committee's recommendation "that the Saturday shift be worked." Mr Fry (Area General Manager) and Mr W Dowding (miner's secretary), addressed the gathering. By a majority vote the recommendation was approved.

BALL:- The second annual old-time ball of Wheatley Hill Embassy "Old-Tyme" Dance Club, was held in the Embassy Ballroom, Wheatley Hill. A large company thoroughly enjoyed themselves to the music of Don Troando's Old-Tyme Band. A large party of visitors from the Ferryhill and District Old-Tyme Club were welcomed. Two of their members, Mr and Mrs McAdam, giving a demonstration dance. Various prizes were given, the judges being Coun E Cain, Dr J Grey and Mrs Grey. Mrs Grey also presented the prizes, and was in turn presented with a bouquet by Miss Joyce Marsden, one of the Club's youngest members. Prizewinners were: Misses K Stephenson, F Cain, M Graney and V Loftus; Messrs E Kears, R Cook, G Coxon, A Forster and B White. MC's were Messrs Wilson, Barnes and Brydon. Secretarial duties were by Miss D Williams.

1 December 1950

WHEATLEY HILL PIT TO WORK ON SATURDAYS

Wheatley Hill miners' lodge, at a special meeting on Sunday, rescinded a resolution of a fortnight previous not to work on Saturdays. From now on the miners will work the Saturday shift in an effort to increase production. For nearly two years neither the extra half-hour on the daily shift nor the Saturday shift has been worked at Wheatley Hill.

Sunday's meeting was called at the request of the pit consultative committee, and was addressed by Mr F W Fry, No 3 Area general manager, Durham Division, NCB; Coun Jack Joyce, Durham miners' agent; and Mr E Cain, secretary, Wheatley Hill miners' lodge. Coun T Knowles presided over a large gathering and a long discussion took place on the question of working extra hours.

A request from the lodge that the Saturday shift should start at midnight on Friday instead of 3am on Saturday was granted by the management.

Wheatley Hill miners formerly worked the Saturday shift but nearly two years ago it was stopped by the Coal Board as it was not considered an economical proposition.

15 December 1950

WHEATLEY HILL NUT-CRACKER CLUB

A supper-dance in the Embassy Ballroom, Wheatley Hill, organised by Wheatley Hill Nut-cracker Club attracted a gathering of 120 members and friends. Supper was served and a table competition testing the general knowledge of the guests, which was organised by Mr R Crosby, was won by the guests at the two tables in charge of Miss E Fenwick. Dance music was played by Norman Richardson and his orchestra, Easington, and during an interval Mr E Cain, JP, on behalf of the club, presented a small wedding present to the band leader, who was to be married a few days later.

22 December 1950

MINERS' ROAD RACE

The second annual road race on Christmas Day, organised by No 3 Area Welfare Committee of the Durham Divisional Coal Board for miners employed at the eight collieries in the area, attracted 18 entries in the senior section. The route, covering a distance of nearly four miles, started at Wheatley Hill and finished there after a circular course via the Fir Tree, Wingate. In the junior section, which covered a route of nearly two miles, Kenneth Robinson, of Easington, was the only entrant and thus had a "walk-over."

Winner of the senior section, R Jewson, a 23 year old Easington miner, carried off the trophy for the second year running. He was presented with the Seymour Challenge Cup and a canteen of cutlery by Mr E Cain, JP, secretary of Wheatley Hill Miners' Lodge, who also made the following awards: 2, R Nattrass (Wheatley Hill); 3, D Pearn (Shotton Colliery); 4, T Harrison (Shotton Colliery).

WHEATLEY HILL WIN 6-0 - Wheatley Hill SC had one of their easiest games of the season on Christmas Day when, visiting Coxhoe in the Durham Central League, they won by six clear goals. "Star" of their attack was young Lofthouse, their centre forward, who netted no fewer than five of their goals, one in the first half and four in the second. He received excellent support from inside forwards Jackie Duffy and Stubbs.

The "Hill" played as a combination throughout, with the result that Coxhoe were on the defensive for the greater part of the game. First goal for Wheatley Hill was netted by their left winger, Hold.

Because of the state of the ground the "Hill's" away game with Deaf Hill United last Saturday was cancelled.

To-morrow Wheatley Hill entertain Deaf Hill United with the following team in a league game: Nicholson, Lumley, Scott, Slack, Robinson, Gittens, Huntingdon, Duffy, Lofthouse, Stubbs, Hold.

29 December 1950

189

1951

CONSULTATIVE COMMITTEE – As a result of a ballot Mr T Buxton has been re-elected to represent the surface workers at Wheatley Hill colliery on the local consultative committee, and Mr J Hedley has been elected to represent the contract workers.

RELIEF FUND OFFICERS – Officers elected at the annual meeting of Wheatley Hill branch, Northumberland and Durham Miners' Permanent Relief Fund were: Chairman, Mr J Frost; Secretary, Mr J Hedley; Treasurer, Mr W Dixon (for the 18th successive year); Delegate, Mr T Harper, Committee: Messrs T Harper, W Hill, J Fishwick and A Wylie.

GIRLS' CLUB PARTY – The annual party of the Girls' Club of Church Street Methodist Church, Wheatley Hill, in the Welfare Hall was attended by about 60. Supper was served and a programme of games and dancing was in charge of Messrs Ron Brown and Edward Harrison. Pianist was the club leader, Mrs J Harrison, who was assisted by Mrs M Nixon in making the arrangements for the function.

POPPY DAY – Thornley British Legion's Poppy Day collection was £127.10s.11d, an increase of £18 over last year. It included a donation of £50 from Thornley Women's Section.

MECHANICS LODGE – Officials and committee of Thornley Mechanics Lodge have been elected as follows: Chairman, Mr A Bushby; Secretary, Mr W Straughan; Treasurer, Mr J Ullatt; Delegate. Mr A Bushby; Committee, Messrs N Fort, J Abbs, T Henderson, T Kirk and J Troup; Death Fund Representative, Mr J Troup; Hospital Fund, Mr G Ashford; Aged Miners Homes Committee, Messrs G Ashford and S Dower; Colliery Band, Mr J Adamson; Auditors, Messrs W Hope and N Fort; Superannuation Committee, Messrs Bushy, Ulatt, Straughan, Ashford, Barker with J Abbs as Financial Secretary.

5 January 1951

MOTOR CLUB FOR WHEATLEY HILL

Motor cycling enthusiasts in the Wheatley Hill area have formed a club named the Wheatley Hill and District Motor Club with the aim of becoming affiliated to the ACU so that they can enter sporting events in the county.

"Already we have a membership of 23", the newly-elected chairman of the club, Mr S Poulson of Wheatley Hill told me this week, "and about half of them are under 20 years of age. We hope to instruct these younger members in the art of correct riding and another of our aims is to instil road safety into the minds of all motor cyclists. Later we hope to enter competitions and map out week-end tours".

The club members meet every Wednesday night at 7.15 in the Nimmo Hotel, Wheatley Hill. Discussions take place and problems affecting the motor cyclist are fully thrashed out. There is plenty of room for more members and those wishing to join the club are asked to contact any of the officials or attend any of the meetings.

Officials in addition to Mr Poulson are: Secretary, Mr C Kellett (Wheatley Hill); Treasurer, Mr J Starkie (Shotton Colliery), Committee, Messrs T Fox, A Edwards (Shadforth) and B Henderson.

"NEW LOOK" AT WHEATLEY HILL
Fine Voluntary Labour

Through the voluntary efforts of its members, who have worked assiduously during their spare time, Wheatley Hill Church Street Methodist Church has undergone a complete transformation. The interior has been re-decorated with the walls panelled in two shades of brown, and structural alterations include erection of a new pulpit adjoining a newly-built vestry, re-modelling of the choir stalls and renovation of pews.

The only work done by contract has been the dismantling of the organ and its complete overhaul and the re-decoration of the ceiling.

When the special services were held in the church to mark the completion of this "labour of love" on the part of the members, the trustees treasurer (Mr Maurice Nixon), revealed that the voluntary work carried out had resulted in a saving to the church of some £700. Cost of materials and contract work was estimated at £350 and towards this £100 had been donated.

Dedication Service

The dedication service on Saturday was conducted by Rev Noel Catherall, and an address was by Rev Douglas Hubery, Sans Street Mission, Sunderland. Rev W T Rose was also present.

During the service a Remembrance Book containing the names of past and present members of the church, which had been designed and compiled by a member of the church, Mr Jack Harrison, JP, was dedicated. Three collection plates given by the trust, Mrs J Harrison and Mrs J Brown, were also dedicated.

Tea followed and at night Mr G W Morris (West Hartlepool) presided at a public meeting addressed by Mr Hubery. Soloist was Miss Bessie Galley and duet was by Mr and Mrs H Lang. Men members of the choir gave a part song, "Bless this House". Organist was Mr T McCartney. Supper was served.

12 January 1951

THORNLEY'S OLDEST RESIDENT DIES

Mr William Bulmer, Thornley's oldest resident, has died in his 91st year. He started his pit career at Trimdon colliery when he was 10½ years old and his wage for a shift of 12 hours was 10d a day. His pit career ended when he was 75 years old, and he was then hewing at Thornley Colliery. In his working life he was miner, handyman, musician, village carrier and general dealer. As an amateur tinsmith, he made some hundreds of miners' tin drinking bottles and 'bait' tins.

He was working at Thornley Colliery when the historic "putt pay" took place in the 1880's. Through financial difficulty the colliery owners were unable to pay the wages and the pit was temporarily closed. Eventually the wages were paid in instalments but Mr Bulmer declared he did not get his £1.14s for the fortnight he had worked. He did not, however blame the owners for this. He said his father, a man of short temper threw the pay notes in the fire.

Mr Bulmer resided with his daughter, Mrs Ramshaw, in Hartlepool Street, Thornley.

KEEP IT UP LUDWORTH!

The village of Ludworth has no village hall. It has no miners' welfare hall; no community centre; no place for its youth to meet; no facilities for social functions.

So, under the leadership of the Rev Canon R H Tillard MA (Rector of Shadforth) and Coun D Thornton, the people have taken matters into their own hands. They have decided to renovate the old Church Hall which, subject to the agreement of the Board of Education, is to be given by its present trustees to become the first Ludworth Village Institute. When finally conveyed for this purpose, the hall will become the property of the local inhabitants and will be so held by chosen trustees.

Will Be Shared

The institute will then be managed by a committee composed partly of representatives of the various Ludworth organisations wishing to use the hall and partly of the members of the public to be elected at an annual general meeting. The committee so constituted, shall have absolute power to ensure that each organisation has its full share of the use of the premises; it will also arrange the hiring out of the institute for dances, parties and other functions.

The underlying aim is that the Institute shall be managed by people of Ludworth for the benefit of the whole village – never to be monopolised by any one section of the community to the disadvantage of the remainder.

However the way will be hard. Much money will have to be raised. Much labour will have to be undertaken. We, therefore wish the working committee success in its endeavours. Keep it up Ludworth!

19 January 1951

MISSIONARY RETURNS
From Wheatley Hill to Nigeria

After a four-month furlough at home, Miss Mary Chisholm, only daughter of Mr and Mrs R S Chisholm of 1 Office Street, Wheatley Hill, this week returned to Western Nigeria, where she has worked as a Methodist missionary since September 1947. It was Miss Chisholm's second furlough – the first time she returned home was in December 1948 after 15 months in the mission field.

Miss Chisholm, who was formerly on the teaching staff of Wheatley Hill Girls' Modern School, has addressed many meetings on her missionary experiences while she has been at home, and for ten days was on a mission "deputation" in Cumberland.

"Quite Ready"

When our reporter met Miss Chisholm on Tuesday – the day before she left home for Liverpool on the first stage of her long trip back – she said she was "quite ready" to return to work again among the natives of Nigeria. She is one of three European missionaries who teach in a girls' boarding school on the boundary of the town of Shagamu, which has a population of 25,000. About 130 girls from eight years upwards attend the school and a training college is attached with a roll of about 24 students.

"There is a certain amount of prejudice against sending girls to school", said Miss Chisholm, "The natives or at any rate some of them can see the advantages a boy can gain by a good education, but with girls they think it is different. Girls, they think do not have to be educated – jobs are not necessary for them because they will be getting married!"

Marriage Dowry

"But a girl who had been properly educated", went on Miss Chisholm, "cost a higher dowry when she married. Her future husband had to pay her parents a much bigger dowry than if she had not been at school. Usually the dowry was £8 or £10 but it varied considerably".

"The Nigerians", said Miss Chisholm, "mostly lived on yams – these look like mouldy turnips on the outside", she said, "but when cooked are rather like potatoes – and Indian corn". All the vegetables she had ever tasted, went on Miss Chisholm, were tinned ones.

"There's a lot of malnutrition" added Miss Chisholm, "because the people do not get sufficient meat and fish".

Buried At Home

"When non-Christians died", said Miss Chisholm, "their relatives buried them close to their dwellings or underneath the floor of their homes. There was a cemetery however for the burial of Christians. It is far from a mournful occasion when an old person dies", continued Miss Chisholm, "rather is it an occasion for dancing, singing and feasting and sometimes this goes on for days. They take the attitude that the old person has lived a full life and therefore there is nothing to be sorry about. But they go into mourning for younger persons".

"On the whole", concluded Miss Chisholm, she had found the natives to be very friendly and hospitable. She had visited some of them in their primitive homes and found conditions very poor, but she had always been made welcome. Many of them are eager to learn, she added, "but not all can afford to pay the school fees".

Miss Chisholm's many friends in the Wheatley Hill area wish her continued success and good health in the excellent work she is doing and are looking forward to renewing acquaintance with her when after another spell in the mission field, she returns home again

GFS VISIT – At their opening meeting of the year in the Church Hall, Wheatley Hill on Monday night, the Girls' Friendly Society of All Saints' Church were visited by Miss Pamela Lucas, Durham Diocesan organiser for GFS activities. Society now has a membership of more than 70 and 40 attended Monday's meeting.

SUNDAY SCHOOL TABLEAUX – Sunday School scholars of the Infants' Department of All Saints' Church, Wheatley Hill took part in a series of tableaux illustrating the boyhood days of Christ, before a large company of their parents and friends in the church. The tableaux were accompanied by appropriate hymn-singing and Mrs A Preston (wife of the Vicar) and the Sunday School teachers were in charge.

MOTHERS UNION PARTY – The annual party of the Mothers' Union of All Saints Church, Wheatley Hill, held in the Church Hall on Saturday night, attracted about 150 members with their husbands and friends. After a short whilst drive at which Mr T Simpson officiated as MC, an excellent supper was served by the Mothers Union committee. A sketch was given by Mesdames Kelly, Orton, Woodward, Gregory, Ayre, Purvis and Miss Cowell. Games and dancing followed to radiogram music supplied by Mr F Orton.

26 January 1951

THORNLEY FOOTBALL

Thornley CW consolidated their position at the top of the Wingate League when they visited Shotton YMC. The home side more than held their own in the first 25 minutes but could not get near goal. In the next 20 minutes, however, Thornley put on pressure and recorded goals by J Laverick and Ken Orton, direct from a corner.

Shotton tried hard in the second period, but Thornley, superior in all departments, added another goal through J Laverick. The last eight matches have earned Thornley 16 points, 41 goals for and six against.

9 February 1951

INQUEST ON MAN WITH FAILING MEMORY

Robert Thomas, a 69 year-old retired miner of 13 Smith Street, Wheatley Hill, was a man with a failing memory and an inclination to wander and lose his whereabouts. He left his home on the afternoon of Saturday 10 February and did not return. When his son reported his disappearance to the Police the next day they told him of a man who had died in hospital after being knocked down by a 'bus at Thornley. At the County Hospital, Durham, he identified the man as his father.

The inquest was held on Wednesday at the hospital, where a jury returned a verdict of "Accidental Death". Mr W Carr was Coroner.

The son, Norman Thomas, of 1 Patton Terrace, Wheatley Hill, told how his father was subject to lapses of memory, and used to wander about until he found his bearings and went back home. His son-in-law, John Watson of 13 Smith Street confirmed this.

Ralph Coxon, a 'bus driver employed by the United Automobile Co of Sunderland Bridge, Durham, said he left Thornley at 7.15 in the evening for Wheatley Hill. It was a foggy night and he was using only his fog lamps, using the nearside kerb as a guide. He was travelling slowly, when he saw a huddled figure about a yard ahead, moving slightly from side to side. He braked immediately, but was unable to avoid the accident. He pulled up in a short distance, and climbed out of the 'bus to find an old man lying with his head in the gutter, his legs on the road, and his coat over his face. An ambulance was sent for and appeared 15 minutes after the accident. Coxon added that he had been a driver for 30 years.

Dr J E Robson of the County Hospital said that in his opinion death was due to injuries to the forearm, abdomen, cold and shock.

LUDWORTH VILLAGE INSTITUTE MEETING

Owing to the delayed arrival of Coun D Thornton, Mr Sanger, vice-chairman, presided over the meeting of Ludworth Village Institute Committee, when Mr Scollen, Welfare Officer for No 3 Area, NCB, attended.

Mr Sanger explained to the Welfare Officer how the committee had been exploring all possible ways to raise funds for the restoration of the building. Most of the male inhabitants of the village were miners, about 95 to 98 per cent, and they had contributed to the Miners' Welfare Scheme. He thought they were justified in asking for financial help.

Miners and their families in Ludworth had no place where they could meet for recreational or social activity as the nearest miners' welfare was too far from the village.

Mr Scollen said he appreciated the difficulties and sympathised wholeheartedly with the scheme. He wanted to encourage all such schemes, but a communal hall of this type did not come within the framework of the Miners' Welfare scheme. In his opinion. it could not qualify for financial assistance, but it would be submitted to a meeting he was to attend in the near future. Canon R H Tillard, seconded by Coun Thornton, moved vote of thanks.

Mr R Champley, treasurer, submitted a satisfactory report. Sub-committee was elected to go into the question of gaming rules. Members are: Canon Tillard, Miss Davison (secretary), Coun Thornton (chairman), Mr Sander, Mr A Winter and Mr R Champley.

WHEATLEY HILL'S SMART FEAT

Sherburn Hill U have been going great guns this season and their supporters fully expected that they would have a long run in the Durham Amateur Cup. It was not to be however, and the Hill supporters will be the first to admit that their defeat at the hands of the Wheatley Hill visitors was in keeping with the play.

Sherburn had expected a hard tussle with a team that had beaten Trimdon Grange in the previous round, but they did not expect to lose by 5-1. A feature of the game was the blotting out of Blacklock the home team's inside forward, by skipper Sid Slack, at right-half. Usually the schemer of the attack, Blacklock was subdued by this non-stop, quick-tackling half-back.

Wheatley Hill had first use of the strong wind. They had a defence that gave little away, a half-back line that was able to switch quickly from defence to attack and a forward line which swung the ball from wing to wing with accuracy.

Wheatley Hill were two up in seven minutes. The first followed a grand 18-yard lob by Cliff Stubbs after a goalmouth scramble, and two minutes after George ("Nat") Lofthouse converted a penalty award. Within another three minutes Hill had found the net and an even game looked likely.

It became 3-1 after 20 minutes when a strong shot by Stubbs entered the net via the crossbar. From then till the end Wheatley Hill had command and goals by Hold and Stubbs in the second period completed the home rout.

Wheatley Hill team which did not show a single weakness, was Turnbull, Ball, Lumley, Slack, Robinson, Gittens, Fishwick, Goyns, Lofthouse, Stubbs, Hold.

23 February 1951

LIBRARY FACILITIES

At Wingate, Thornley and Wheatley Hill

The first paragraph of this article relates to library facilities at Wingate which we feel are outside of the remit of this book. The following is the second and third paragraphs of the article:

Thornley people also have library facilities now with the opening last week of a part-time branch of the County Library. It is open from 9.30am to 6.30pm on Wednesdays and Fridays and from 9.30am to 1.00pm on Thursdays.

Mr G Jefferson, librarian said: "The library is proving its worth. Many children are taking advantage of it and we are hoping to enrol many more adult readers once they know that the facilities are there". Headquarters are in Waterloo Street Methodist Church.

Mr Jefferson is the librarian at Wheatley Hill part-time library (open from 9.30am to 6.30pm on Tuesdays and Saturdays and from 2.00pm to 6.30pm on Thursdays). This service, in the Welfare Hall, Wheatley Hill, has been in operation for some moths.

2 March 1951

THORNLEY CHILD WELFARE CENTRE
Opened by Mr E Shinwell, MP

Opening Knayton House, Thornley as the new headquarters of Thornley Child Welfare Centre on Saturday, Mr E Shinwell, MP for Easington, said that although the country was passing through an economic crisis the one thing we could not afford to dispense with was the care that was bestowed upon our young children.

Commenting on the progress made during recent years in children's welfare, Mr Shinwell said that in 1938 only five per cent of children in this country had perfect teeth, but last year that figure had increased to 37.5 per cent. This was indeed a "vast improvement". Our children were our greatest national asset and if we were to maintain our position as a power everything depended upon how we looked after them.

Debt To Womenfolk

Referring to the voluntary work done by committees of Welfare Centres, Mr Shinwell declared it would be a "bad thing" for the country if the "well of voluntary action" ever dried up. It was one of the principal characteristics of the British people to respond to the needs of their fellow-men without accepting any sort of fee. In this voluntary work we were indebted a great deal to the women-folk. Mrs E Clark, Chairman of the Voluntary Committee at Thornley presided at the opening ceremony and extended a warm welcome to Mr Shinwell and thanks to the former Minister of Defence were expressed by Dr A P Gray and Mrs B Bosomworth.

Despite the fact that they had been working under bad conditions in dilapidated premises at Thornley, Dr Williamson, the child Welfare Medical Officer said it spoke well not only for the work of the committee but also for the co-operation of the mothers that the Centre had made considerable progress year after year. With new premises and better conditions even greater progress could be expected in the future.

To mark the opening of the new Centre the Mothers' Club presented half a tea-set for the use of the committee. Among the large representative gathering present were Dr R D Greenslade, Miss Frazer (superintendent Health Visitor), Nurses Brewster and Gutteridge and Mrs D Roper and Mrs Anderson (secretary and treasurer, respectively of the Centre).

7 March 1951
THORNLEY STILL "GOING STRONG"
Thornley CW continue to do well in their bid for the Wingate and District League title. Playing away to Black Boy (Quarrington Hill) last week, they recorded a grand 4-0 victory in spite of the fact they had four reserves in place of regulars who are injured. With the advantage of the wind in the first half, they opened the scoring in the fifth minute through centre-forward Kent, who outran two players before shooting a good goal from 10 yards. Fifteen minutes later Border (outside-right) increased the lead with a great shot from six yards. Black Boy attacks were few and far between, but they were rarely dangerous due to the sound Thornley defence. The game was stopped for 10 minutes as a result of both balls bursting.

Shortly after the interval, Thornley centre-half had to retire injured, but in spite of this depletion they continued to have command. A long lob by Williams placed Kent in possession, who passed to Border, who went on to score. Border scored the fourth to complete his hat-trick – it was a well-placed penalty kick.

Tomorrow Thornley entertain Shotton CW in a league game. Selection of team has been deferred.

DIED AFTER WAR SERVICE – Evidence that he had frequently received medical treatment since his discharge from the army during the first World War, suffering from nephritis contracted through malaria, was heard by the Coroner, Mr T V Devey, at the Inquest at Thornley on

Friday night on William John Pyle (58) of 15 Hillside Crescent, Thornley, who was found dead in bed on 4 March. The Coroner, after hearing a report from Dr Gray, recorded a verdict that death was due to heart failure and that Pyle's war illness had been a contributing factor. Mrs Margaret Pyle, the widow, said her husband was discharged from the army in 1917. He had been employed on light work at Thornley colliery, but had often been treated for nephritis and several times had been into the Ministry of Pensions Hospital. He was in receipt of a disability pension from the military authorities.

APPOINTMENT of Mr H L Rees (West Hartlepool) as head teacher of Wheatley Hill County Senior Boys' School has been confirmed by Durham County Education Committee. Six selected candidates were interviewed for the post.

NEW HEADMASTER – a member of the staff of the Henry Smith Grammar School, Hartlepool, for the past 22 years, Mr H L Rees has been appointed headmaster of Wheatley Hill Senior Boys' School. Mr Rees, who has been senior history master at the Grammar School, takes up his new appointment on 1 April. He succeeds Mr J Andrews, who was appointed County Inspector of school meals during the latter part of last year.

4 March 1951

DURHAM CHRONICLE IN PITTSBURG

Mr W M Tunney, 841 Glenwood Avenue, Ambridge, Pa, USA, who emigrated from South-East Durham many years ago, has addressed to the editor a cutting from a Pittsburg paper containing pictureS of George Washington and the old Hall at Washington, County Durham, and an interesting article.

He says he is glad to know that "the old country is getting a little publicity out here". He receives regularly from his brother, at Wheatley Hill, a copy of the Durham Chronicle and is still greatly interested in the "Doings" at Kelloe, Thornley and Wheatley Hill and that area. He likes the Corner End stories and all the interesting football news.

His many friends send Mr Tunney their best wishes.

9 March 1951

POETIC TRIBUTE TO PETER LEE

Official opening of the first houses in the new town of Peterlee brought vividly to the mind of Mr R Straughan, of 23 Ridsdale Avenyue, Ashington, the biography of Mr Lee by Lord Lawson of Beamish. Mr Straughan had never seen Peter Lee but from the biography "always likened him to St Peter of the Gospels". Mr Straughan wrote these lines about Mr Lee and sent them to Lord Lawson:

Who can explain this mystery?
Why a hulking lad like Peter Lee,
Half gipsy – with flashing eyes,
Handsome, strong, of giant size.
Man at seventeen, couldn't write,
Knew hard work and how to fight
And drink – became a slave
Like all m en do who so behave –
Then suddenly, seeing himself apart,
Turned about, What changed his heart?
What drove this man to school at night
To learn to read and learn to write?
Avoid the brawls that led to blows –
Black eyes, cuts and bloody nose.
How could he learn so very quick?
And still be expert with a pick?
Was it he'd visions of a bride
He'd walk beside with kingly pride?
Or was it thinking of his mother?
Methinks it could have been another –
Jesus. Perhaps He said "Come follow Me",
Like He said to Peter of Galilee;
And with his gipsy blood of wandering purged,
Returned, fulfilled the mission Jesus urged.
Monuments to these Peter's stand:
One far off from his native land –
Peter the Fisherman's in Rome
Peter the Miner's near his home.

NEW SECRETARY - Mr E Carter a member of Thornley Aged Miners' Homes Committee, has been elected secretary of the committee in succession to Mr Matthew Lonsdale, resigned. Mr Carter is chairman of the Thornley Miners' Lodge.

PRESENTATION - A timepiece and a pipe, subscribed for by fellow officials and workmen, were presented on Monday to Mr Herbert Walton of Haswell, who recently retired from the post of foreman mason at Thornley Colliery. The gifts were handed to him by Mr William Atkin, engineer, who spoke of the excellent service of Mr Walton during his many years as an official and workman at the colliery.

THORNLEY WI – Mrs J H C Scot presided and welcomed new members. Mrs Miller was appointed delegate to the County meeting at Darlington. A talk on "Wild Birds and Animals" was given by Mr Walton who was thanked by Mrs Straughan. Mrs Sudders gave the "Item of Interest". Winner of the dyed egg competition judged by Mrs Walton, was Mrs Fletcher. The eggs entered by members are to be sent to Winterton Hospital. Taking part in the social half-hour organised by Mrs Winter were Mesdames Miller, Sudders, Horn, Smith, Fleming, Luke, Carlson, Parker, Abbs, Henderson and Bradley.

FIRST AID – 34 of the 36 members of Thornley Colliery Ambulance Class passed the recent examination. They were: Certificates - B B Foster, F Bromilow, W Carter, J R Gill, L Slater, H Mills, t f Lackenby, T Harrison, T F Brandling; Preliminary, R Youll; Re-examination – F W Woodhead, W Chaytor, M Commons, Jos Lark, G M Peel, J Campbell, C Woodward, J Orange, W Armstrong, T D Hardy, R W Conway, J Troup, E Monaghan, J H Lewis, J Storey, J Wrightson, J Gowland, Jas Nicholson, P Wilson, J W Turner, J Champley, R Orange, J R Greener and J Sims.

WHEATLEY HILL'S LONG-SERVICE MINERS

Wheatley Hill veteran miners who, at a presentation tea and concert in the Welfare Hall last Thursday, received certificates from Wilfred Pickles of BBC fame, for 50 or more years' membership of the Durham Miners' Association were:

T Simpson, W Luke, C Local, H Lowe, W R Hird, L Jones, T Clish, W Brown, T Cutty, T Dunn, J Waistell, J Snowdon, B Bowes, J Cairns, J R Walton, R Lord, Robert Bowes, J Bartley, R Jameson, B Miller, J Hoban, M Metcalfe, T Robson, W Snowdon, J Luke, G

Charlton, J Routledge, R Anson, R Facey, F Burrell, J Martin, W Burdett, G P Brown, J Robson, J Waugh, J Bell, J Scott, E Wharrier, G Poulson, R Marley, J Fletcher, G Wilson, P Smallwood, R Johnson, E Dowsey, W Stannard, W Clarkson, G R Buxton, W Kipling, D Simms, J Jordan, S Charlton, S Kellett, T Thompson, G Scrafton, A W Havelock, J Doyle, G Muster, J Davies, R W Forster, W Turnbull, W Poulson and J Turton.

The tea was provided by Wheatley Hill miners' lodge and the concert was given by Johnny Quinn's party.

COAL PROPOSAL ACCEPTED – At a special meeting on Sunday, presided over by Coun T Knowles, members of Wheatley Hill miners' lodge accepted a proposal by the Coal Board that their yearly coal allowance should be reduced by eight cwts. The Lodge Secretary, Mr E Cain, explained that by consenting to this reduction the lower-paid miner, who at present has 4s.6d deducted from his pay for his periodical load of coal, would get his coals free. Durham headquarters of the NUM had recommended acceptance of the Coal Board proposal. Miners at Wheatley Hill already voluntarily give up 15cwt load of their coal every year to enable all retired miners to receive a free load every 5½weeks. The yearly allowance of coal for each workman is approximately 12 ton.

WILFRED PICKLES WITH THE MINERS
Three-day Tour in East Durham
CHEERY SMILE FOR EVERYONE

Wilfred Pickles three-day tour of East Durham mining villages last week was an unqualified success (writes Norman Passfield).

His warm handshake and familiar "How are yer"? greeting were repeated thousands of times and he left behind a picture of friendliness, good humour and sincerity that will be difficult to eradicate from the memories of the many people who shares his company.

Wilfred had a word for everyone, from the youngest baby-in-arms to the oldest pensioner, and throughout his exhausting tour he managed to retain his cheery smile and joke and quip with the miners and their families both at their work and play.

Wilfred and his wife sat down to an excellent tea provided for the aged miners of Blackhall and their wives' then after more smiles and handshakes they left amidst tumultuous cheering. Outside the hall, waiting to give them a farewell greeting was 59-year-old William Horn of 5 South View, Wheatley Hill, who has been unable to walk since a pit accident 15 years ago. Mr Horn was in his self-propelled chair. He had waited patiently outside just to "have a word" with Wilfred. He told the radio star he had fractured his spine while employed as a deputy-overman. For two years he was bedfast and since then had only been able to get about in his chair. "But I cannot really grumble", he smiled at Wilfred, "I am well looked after".

16 March 1951

The above article is only part of a much larger article dealing with the visit of Wilfred Pickles to other East Durham villages, we have only produced the part of the article which mentions Wheatley Hill.

WHEATLEY HILL SCHOOL'S FIRST SPEECH DAY

So many parents arrived for the first annual Speech Day of the Wheatley Hill Senior Boys' School that there was insufficient accommodation and some of them had, unfortunately to be turned away. The headmaster, Mr J Andrews, expressed his apologies for this and hoped that next year there would be room for everybody.

The Speech Day was held in the Girl's Modern School by permission of the headmistress, Miss Alderslade, and Mr F B Smith, divisional education officer.

Mr Andrews presented an excellent report of the past year's work. Activities both during and outside school hours had flourished and as far as possible every taste was catered for. Indoors there were classes in woodwork, metalwork, drama and singing, while outdoors a successful junior football team was already running. This team had already won sufficient points to be sure of ending the season as champions of the East Durham Youth League.

During the coming cricket season, went on Mr Andrews, two cricket teams were being formed among Wheatley Hill and Thornley pupils. They will function in the Wingate Schools' Cricket Association. An attraction this summer will be an inter-county school cricket match, to be played on the Wheatley Hill pitch. Last season Eric Barker brought honour to the school and village by gaining his county cricket "cap". It was the first honour of its kind to come to the village.

The school, said Mr Andrews, had an enthusiastic cycling club and one of the places to be visited this Easter was the Roman Wall. A hiking club was also being formed. Arrangements were being made for an

"Open Day" and a sports day and some of the pupils would be going to camp during the first week of the summer holidays. A trip to the Festival of Britain was also being planned.

Mr Andrews stated that although each boy received a written report about his work, his character, his effort and his aptitude could not be summarised in so many words. "Parents are welcome to come and see me at any time to discuss their boys' reports", he added.

Pupils' Programme

Pupils gave an enjoyable two hours programme of their activities. An excerpt from Julius Caesar by the Drama class was well presented, the introduction having been written by the producer, Mr J E Etherington, a member of the staff. Under Mr E Ward, a display of Indian club work was given and the PT team, led by Mr V Brown successfully went through their paces. Recitations were given by H Copnall and B Hindle.

Under the able conductorship of Mr T Francis, the school choir gave a programme of songs and descants including "John Peel", "All Through the Night", "Early in the Morning" and "Cradle Song". Part-songs were also contributed and the soloist was Stanley Bramfitt.

Coun E D Wharrier, Chairman of the school managers presided and presented the year's prizes as follows: Form 4a – G Blackett (form prize), N Watson (endeavour) and F Mullen (progress). 4b – Sidney S Humes, R Hedley and J Lee (form prizes). 3a - W Broomfield and A Miullington (form prizes), M Turner (progress); 3b – W Wetherell and S Carr (form prizes), A Forbes (progress) and N Ramsey (art); 2a – W Shutt, G Mason and M Almond (form prizes), A Muir (physical education); 2b – W Stephen and K Butler (form prizes), E Lowes and G Wilson (neatness). 1a – E Cockburn and W Walker (form prizes), B Hindle (drama), A Parsons (progress). 1b – J Rutherford, K Harvey and J Robson (form prizes), R Worthington (progress).

Thanks to the chairman and to the parents, for their support, were expressed by Mr Andrews who also said he was indebted to several parents from Thornley who had assisted in the running of the school's successful football team.

23 March 1951

THORNLEY COUNTY COUNCIL CANDIDATE

There is an echo of the turbulent past of the women's suffrage movement in the nomination of Mrs Doris Adelaide Newton Roper, farmer's wife, of Thornley as Independent candidate for the Thornley division of the Durham County Council at the election on 8 April. She makes a worthy opponent for Coun Emmerson Featherstone Peart, the sitting member, who, of course has become known throughout the county as a tough fighter for the Council's "closed shop" policy.

Two of Mrs Roper's maternal aunts were in the front line of Mrs Pankhurst's women's suffrage army, and both were imprisoned. In a broadcast talk some years ago, Mrs Roper told the story of her aunts and it was very evident from the talk that she had a great admiration for them. In her public work at Thornley she has often shown herself to be of the same fighting quality. This was so in Thornley Parish Council meetings in recent months when she was very forcible on the question of a new child welfare centre. For six years she has been a JP and is a member of two committees appointed by Quarter Session. Locally she is the representative of SAAFA and the Society for the Prevention of Cruelty to Children.

DURHAM CHRONICLE IN MIDDLE EAST

Two Thornley men are interested in the back page of "The Durham Chronicle". They are LAC Abraham Walls (19), son of Mr and Mrs John Walls of 9 Thornlaw South and ACI A Jobes, son of Mr and Mrs Wm Jobes of Thornley. They met in Aden in the Middle East. Jobes has been in the RAF since November last year. Walls joined up for five years. He worked in Thornley pit but his father says "he always had a fancy for joining the services".

28 March 1951

LEGION'S "COMING OF AGE" – The 21st birthday party of Wheatley Hill British Legion (Women) was a huge success. During supper a large birthday cake, made by the Chairman (Mrs M Brain) from ingredients given by members, and iced by Mr G Heal, a members' husband, was cut by the president (Mrs P H Galley), who wished the section continued success. The vice-president (Mrs Dr Maclean) was present. Members of Thornley women's' section concert party, under the leadership of Mrs Bessie Bosomworth, gave an excellent programme of songs and dances. Music was by Mr Jack Toye, Thornley's blind piano-accordionist. Thanks to the entertainers were expressed by Mrs Brain. Prizes given by members were won by Mesdames Frampton, J Forster, Atherton sen and jun, Higham and F Straughan (Wheatley Hill) and Mes-

206

dames Mitchell, Herd and Archer (Thornley). At the meeting of the section a talk on his visit to Nigeria last year was given by Mr E Cain JP. **OCW CAMPAIGN** – United Services of Christian witness were organised by members of the Order of Christian Witness Campaign of Church Street and Patton Street Methodist Churches, Wheatley Hill. Services at the weekend were conducted by Rev A Kingsley Turner, MA and Mr Colin Barnett, London and local Methodists also took part. On Tuesday in Patton Street Church, a team of campaigners took the service and on Wednesday, in the same church, the speakers were sisters Marjorie Lewis and Beth Bridges, Newcastle. Speaker tomorrow night will be Mr Allan Radcliffe, MA, ex-Middlesex and England cricketer. Arrangements were made by Mr Jack Harrison JP.

6 April 1951

PLAY AT INSTITUTE – Shotton Players skilfully presented four one-act plays in Ludworth Village Institute. Considering the high standard of the presentation it was disappointing that the attendance was so small. Coun Thornton thanked the players and producer for their efforts. Proceeds were for Institute repair funds.

LEGION MEETING – Mr W Winter presided over Ludworth British Legion branch's annual meeting. Owing to the cost it was decided not to send the standard to the Festival of Britain parade in London. Mr Egdell thanked members for the county certificate presented to him for his long service in the organisation.

WOMEN'S LEGION – Mrs Shepherd presided over Ludworth women's section of the British Legion when the delegate Mrs M Morgan was instructed on members views for the ground meeting at Dubmire on Wednesday. Tea was provided by the "under 40's" who also provided a variety concert. They were thanked by Mrs Bell. Prizewinners were Mesdames V Smith, Harper, M Morgan and Ingram.

SIXTY YEARS A PREACHER
Wheatley Hill Man's Grand Record

A 76-year-old Wheatley Hill Methodist who, in his younger days, thought nothing of walking as far as eight and nine miles on a Sunday to fulfil a preaching appointment, was the guest of honour at a supper and concert in Thornley Bow Street Methodist Church on Saturday night to mark his completion of 60 years' service as a fully-accredited Methodist local preacher.

He is Mr Matthew F Stephenson, Eastfield, Cemetery Road, Wheatley Hill, who still enjoys the best of health and is as active a preacher as ever. "I have fulfilled appointments on each of the past four Sundays", he told our reporter this week, "and am booked for the next three Sundays, making seven Sunday appointments in a row!"

Mr Stephenson was not quite 16 when he preached his first sermon in Haswell Moor Methodist Church. He was "on trial" then, but before a year had passed he had been accepted onto the full "plan" of the former Thornley Primitive Methodist Circuit. He is now the longest-serving preacher on the present Thornley Methodist Circuit "plan".

Born at Haswell, Mr Stephenson lived there until moving to Wheatley Hill some 40 years ago.

13 April 1951

LABOUR PARTY – Mr James Nicholson has succeeded Mr W F Whitehead as secretary of the Thornley Local Labour Party. Coun E F Peart will again be chairman and Mr F Walker treasurer.

FOR LONG SERVICE – Four Thornley Colliery underground officials have been awarded NCB certificates and medals for long service as rescue workers. They are Messrs James Orange (with 27 years service), Leonard Ellwood, Gordon Brownless and Robert White.

AGAINST EXTRA HOURS – Despite a recommendation from their national and area officials that they should agree to a renewal of the overtime agreement between the NUM and the NCB, introduced four years ago, Wheatley Hill Miners' Lodge on Sunday voted against extra hours being worked. Their decision will be sent to headquarters at Durham. Coun T Knowles presided and the members heard a report from their delegate, Mr J W Burrell, about the area and national union recommendations. Mr E Cain, Lodge Secretary, told our reporter that the members felt that "no useful purpose" could be served by continuing to work the Saturday shift at Wheatley Hill. "Machine mining", he added "does not lend itself to only one shift being worked". During recent months, Wheatley Hill colliery has been open for Saturday working.

20 April 1951

DIED IN THE LAMP CABIN – "Death from natural causes" was the verdict recorded by the Coroner, Mr T V Devey at a Thornley inquest on Tuesday on a 64-year-old bachelor, Thomas Grosvenor, of 8 Galt Street, Thornley, who was found dying in the lamp cabin at Thornley colliery early on 9 April. Grosvenor who was employed as a colliery caller, had, it was stated, been visiting his doctor for the past 12 months for minor rheumatic complaints. His sister, Mrs Mary Thompson, with whom he had lived for the past 45 years, said that when he left home for work at 9.45pm on 8 April he complained of pains in his head. He had been suffering from these pains for some time and had been taking tablets from his doctor. Apart from an odd day off work because of a cold, Grosvenor, however had never lost much work. Medical aid was summoned when he was found lying unconscious in the lamp cabin at 5.55am on 9 April but Grosvenor died before the arrival of the doctor.

25 April 1951

THORNLEY PARISH COUNCIL

Thornley Parish Council, at their meeting on Tuesday, decided to lodge a protest against Easington Rural Council charging threepence a week on the rates for sweeping the chimneys of council houses.

"They have had the houses for 25 years and haven't done anything about it until now", remarked Mr M Fleming. "I am disgusted with the attitude of the Rural Council. I want this Council to protest against the Council doing what an ordinary landlord dare not do. My advice to the Council is not to pay the extra rent".

Advocating that the Council do everything in their power to assist in getting the Ritz Cinema, which was destroyed by fire in 1944, re-opened, several members agreed that because of lack of competition Thornley people were being served with 'tripe' at their only remaining cinema. "While millions of pounds are being spent on the Festival of Britain, we in our mining village cannot get anything done towards the re-opening of this cinema", said Mr Fleming. "There is no cinema entertainment at all for children because of the lack of competition".

LUDWORTH – Pigeon Club members opened the season with a race from Selby on Saturday. Prize winners were Messrs S Davie, Dixon and Raine. It is hoped to increase the strength of the Club to ten lofts.

4 May 1951

WHEATLEY HILL FUNERAL OF MRS VINCENT

Following a service in All Saints' Church, Wheatley Hil,l on Saturday, Mrs Jane Annie Vincent, Lambourne House, Wheatley Hill, whose death occurred under tragic circumstances last week while she was spring-cleaning, was cremated at Darlington.

Mrs Vincent, who was 64 years of age was on top of a pair of step-ladders white-washing the ceiling of her back kitchen when, while stretching with her brush to reach the corner of the ceiling she overbalanced and crashed to the floor. She died almost immediately. At the inquest, medical evidence revealed Mrs Vincent died from a fracture of the cervical vertebrae and a verdict of "Accidentally killed" was returned by the Coroner, Mr T V Devey.

Mrs Vincent moved from East Rainton to Wheatley Hill, as a girl of 12 and had since lived in the village. Well-known and esteemed, she was formerly associated with the Patton Street Methodist Church, Wheatley Hill and the Sisterhood, and attended a Sisterhood meeting only the day before her death. Her husband, Mr Thomas Henry Vincent, has been in business as a general dealer at Wheatley Hill for the past 12 years, the business having been in the family for more than 50 years.

Mrs Vincent, who formerly lived with her husband in South View, Wheatley Hill, had been married 43 years. She is survived by her husband and an only married daughter.

Rev Arthur Preston (Vicar of Wheatley Hill) conducted the funeral service.

18 May 1951

WHEATLEY HILL EXHUMATION

The Clerk (Mr William Stoker) at a meeting of Wingate Parish Council on Monday night, revealed that in "strict accordance with instructions from the Secretary of State", an exhumation took place at Wheatley Hill Cemetery at dawn on 2 May.

The body exhumed was that of Mr John William Barron, 75 years of Wheatley Hill, whose widow had applied for the exhumation order from the Home Secretary. When Mr Barron was buried on 17 March, Mrs Barron had expected the burial to take place at the family burial ground. By an unfortunate error, however, he was buried in another part of the cemetery.

"This Council was in no way implicated in this unfortunate mistake", said the Clerk on Monday night, adding that the body of Mr Barron had been exhumed and re-interred in the correct grave space "with all due reverence". Mrs Barron said the Clerk had had a fee to pay to the Home Secretary for the exhumation order, but the Council had provided the labour for the exhumation. It was decided to waive the cost of the labour to the widow. Mr Stoker mentioned that it was the second exhumation that had taken place in the parish during his term of office as Clerk.

COAL ALLOWANCE FOR RETIRED MINERS

Retired Miners throughout the county, who are at present dependent upon the generosity of miners at individual pits for coal supplies, are likely to have some of their future fuel problems solved if agreement to a new county coal scheme advocating an annual coal allowance for them is forthcoming between the Durham Area of the National Union of Mineworkers and Durham Division of the National Coal Board.

Durham Area Council heard on Saturday, at Durham, that the scheme might possibly come into force before the end of the year if the Board and the Union agreed as to the contribution each should make towards it and provided it was accepted by miners' lodges.

At present each miner allows a certain percentage of his household coal to be pooled, and from this pool each retired miner is supplied. Amounts are governed by the size of each pit and the number of retired miners on its roll. Under the new scheme every retired miner will be assured of receiving the same allowance of coal.

25 May 1951

GUESTS OF DARTFORD
Wheatley Hill Boys' Interesting Experience

Thirty-two little boys boarded a coach to begin their journey home to Wheatley Hill. They had been the guests of Dartford (Kent) for the previous three days.

Mr William Fenwick who lives not far from the Wheatley Hill School, happened a few weeks ago to be talking to the Headmaster, Mr J T Andrews. Mr Andrews told him that he would like to take some of the boys to see the various exhibitions in London during the Festival period. There was however, one big obstacle – the difficulty of obtaining accommodation. Could Mr Fenwick help?

Mayor Organised

Mr Fenwick said he could. He wrote to his daughter and her husband, Mr and Mrs Leslie Light, the Bull and George Hotel, Dartford. Mr Light got into touch with the Mayor of Dartford and things began to move. The Mayor made the arrangements and the Kent Education Committee provided a hall at West-hill schools. The canteen authorities agreed to give the boys breakfast every morning during their stay.

211

They arrived last week and went to the hotel for a supper of fish and chips and ice cream. The Mayor spoke to them ("Not at great length, because you must be very, very tired after your long journey") and told them of their debt to Mr Fenwick and Mr and Mrs Light. In true Durham fashion the boys cheered the principals in their Festival cause.

The following morning there began for the lads "a ripsnorting time" (as one put it). They went to the South Bank Exhibition, House of Commons, the Zoo, Westminster Abbey, Madame Tussauds, The Science Museum and of course the Battersea Funfair.

1 June 1951

EXPLOSION BLAST AT EASINGTCON COLLIERY
81 Men were Trapped in the Workings

Not for a long time in the history of coal-mining in Durham County has the price of coal – in men's lives – been so poignantly illustrated as at Easington Colliery on Tuesday when a terrific explosion shortly before five o'clock in the morning was followed by an official announcement that 81 miners were missing. Later is was stated that one of these, Matthew (Mattie) Williams (19), Ashton Street, Easington Colliery, who was rescued seriously injured, had died a few hours afterwards in Ryhope Hospital, and in a statement to reporters at three o'clock in the afternoon, Mr S H D Skinner, Chairman of the Durham Divisional Coal Board, said that seven bodies had been recovered.

The official list of 83 iners killed in the explosion at Eashington Colliery on 29 May included Stanley Peaceful (37), stoneman of 6 South Street, Thornley, buried at Thornley Cemetery. Herbert Goyns (56), stoneman of 1 Fifteenth Street, Wheatley Hill, buried at Thornley Cemetery. Ernest Goyns (60), stoneman of 20 Stokoe Crescent, Wheatley Hill, buried at Wheatley Hill Cemetery

8 June 1951

GIRLS' SPORT AT WHEATLEY HILL

Staff and pupils of the Wheatley Hill Girls' Modern School held their annual sports day in Wheatley Hill CC's grounds, when a silver challenge cup was won by Stuart House with 78 points. Results:

Short Sprint 1st year – Joyce Iddon; 2nd Year, Betty Laverick; 3rd Year Joan Gallon. **100 yards** 1st year - Dorothy Powell; **150 yards** – 2nd year,

Margaret Jones; 3rd year, Margaret Soppitt. **Throwing the ball** 1st Anne Burnip; 2nd Margaret Fishwick; 3rd June Armstrong.

Long Jump, Senior, Joyce Milburn; junior, Dorothy Powell. **High jump,** senior, Joan Gallon; junior Joan Foster. **Potato Race**, 1st year Anne Burnip; 2nd, Maureen Barker; 3rd June Williams. **Sack**, 1st Anne Edwards'; 2nd Maureen Barker; 3rd Jessie Piercey. Games captain for 1951-52 is Joan Gallon and Vice-Captain Dorothy Powell.

15 June 1951

WHEATLEY HILL "CO-OP CHIEF'S" HONOUR

Not only was Tuesday the 65th birthday of Mr Anthony Cairns, Vernon House, Wheatley Hill, general manager of the Sherburn Hill Co-operative Society, but it also marked his retirement after 50 years service with the Society. A crowd of more than 600 employees of the Society gathered in Easington Welfare Hall on Tuesday to wish Mr Cairns a long and happy retirement and on their behalf, Mr J Brady presented him with a television set.

Mr Cairns, whose first job when he left school was as a pit boy, expressed appreciation to the employees for their valuable gift. He was genuinely sorry, he said, to sever such a long association with such a fine team of work-people. Outlining his successful career he rose to be general manger from an apprentice – Mr Cairns paid a glowing tribute to the help he had received from his wife. "Without her behind me I would never have succeeded", he declared.

Mr J Shutt, the new general manager, and Mr J Coker, Northern Divisional Officer, USDAW, both eulogised Mr Cairn's devoted service to the Society and Miss Allison presented a bouquet to Mrs Cairns.

Before the presentation, which was presided over by Mr H Sangster, the employees were entertained to a "Road Show" in Easington Workmen's Club. Entertainment was also provided by Mr R Welsh, the Easington hypnotist.

Mr Cairns was one of a family of eight born at Sherburn Hill. After gaining a "Labour Certificate" at the Bluecoat School, Durham, he started work at the local colliery when only 12. He was then employed at Chopwell colliery, but when he was 15 became the first apprentice at the first branch of Sherburn Hill Co-operative Society opened at Shotton Colliery. The branch consisted of a single house.

Mr Cairns became one of the Society's 'pioneers' at Wheatley Hill and 41 years ago, was appointed foreman at Sherburn Hill. He rose to be branch manager at Sherburn Hill, and then occupied a similar position at Wheatley Hill before his appointment as general manager 13 years ago. **EASINGTON COLLIERY DISASTER RELIEF FUND** – reached £41,267 on Wednesday

22 June 1951

SUNDAY SCHOOL ANNIVERSARY – During the past two Sundays successful Sunday school anniversary services have been conducted in the Patton Street Methodist Church, Wheatley Hill, by the Sunday school superintendents, Messrs W Dowding and J Scrafton. Each Sunday morning the scholars, teachers and friends sang in the streets of the village and programmes of singing and reciting were given by the scholars afternoon and evening. The singing was conducted by Mr J Mann and Mrs T Venables was organist.

LATE MR J H MARTIN – One of Wheatley Hill's oldest standards, Mr James Henry Martin, 70, of 96 Wordsworth Avenue, who died suddenly on Saturday, was buried at Wheatley Hill cemetery on Tuesday, following a Salvation Army service at "The Rest". Mr Martin had lived in the village practically all his life and was employed as a wagonwayman at Wheatley Hill colliery until 14 years ago when ill health compelled him to cease work. He is survived by his wife, two sons and two daughters.

GIFTS DEDICATED – Gifts to the church in memory of three members, who had had an active association with it, were dedicated at a special service in Church Street Methodist Church, Wheatley Hill, on Saturday night. Mr James Fairless presented a new altar table and flower vase in memory of his wife and the gifts were handed over for dedication by Mr Fairless's only daughter. Another gift of a pair of oak altar chairs was made by one of the church's oldest members, Mrs Rose E Nixon, in memory of her husband John and son James. On behalf of Mrs Nixon the chairs were presented for dedication by her son, Mr Maurice Nixon. The gifts were accepted on behalf of the trustees of the Church by the Resident Minister, Rev Noel Catherall, and were dedicated by Rev W T Rose, Thornley (Superintendent Minister, Thornley Methodist Circuit). After the dedication, Holy Communion was administered.

DISASTER FUND - Although minus one of their brightest stars (Johnny Quinn), Thornley St Godric's Choral Society gave a variety show in the Welfare Hall, Wheatley Hill, on Tuesday, on behalf of the Church of English Martyrs, Thornley and in aid of Easington Disaster Fund. It was a non-stop programme of music, lively patter and an amazing novelty act by lightning cartoonist, Phil Terry. Other guest artistes were Jack Toye, Thornley's well-known blind accordionist; Jack Cain (sons at the piano), and Pat Brennan (character comedienne), Sunderland. Principal singers in the musical scenes were Doris Surman, Ann McCoy, James Wilson, Angela Ellwood, Joan Wilson and Marie Mitchell. Others taking part were Teresa Morton, Agnes Fleming, Mary Wilson, Betty Maddison, Betty Robinson, Pat Hoban, Isabel Luke, Marie Graney, Mary Garrigan, Bob Trisnan, Bernard Hodgson, Fred Graney, Pat Lenehan and Gerard Flanagan. Mr John Tunney was an excellent compere and Miss M Scully was producer and accompanist.

Mrs B Bosomworth, Chairman of Thornley Parish Council, expressed thanks to the artistes and congratulated them on a fine talent display.

CYCLIST INJURED – In an accident at Wheatley Hill on Friday, a 15 year-old cyclist, Kevin Hunt, of 8 Thornlaw South, Thornley, received facial injuries, suffered shock and was taken to Sedgefield Hospital. It appears he crashed into a farm tractor which was turning off the main road near the Royalty Cinema into the farm entrance. The cycle was badly damaged.

29 June 1951

MARRIED FIFTY YEARS
MR & MRS J GIBSON, WHEATLEY HILL

Miner, soldier, "caller-up", labourer, factory worker – a 72 year old Wheatley Hill man, Mr James Gibson, 40 Quetlaw Road, who celebrated his golden wedding on Friday, has been all these, in turn, during a working career of 52 years. Ill health, the result of being twice wounded during the first world war, caused Mr Gibson to finish work altogether at the age of 64.

The first time he was wounded - in 1916 – Mr Gibson was reported missing. It was shortly after his company went "over the top" on a Monday night that Mr Gibson was severely wounded in the head. He managed to crawl over some dead comrades into a shell hole and lay there, until the Friday, before he was discovered. His head was badly cut and it is believed that the dirt which clogged the wound prevented him from bleeding to death.

Mr Gibson's wife, Mrs Ellen Sparks Gibson, who will be 67 in October, was unfortunately unable to be with her husband on their golden wedding day. The previous Monday she was taken to Durham County Hospital suffering from pneumonia, but her condition is now steadily improving. It is the first time she has been in Hospital. She has led a very active life and during the 1939-45 war, the beginning of which she lost her second youngest son, she worked at Aycliffe factory, rarely missing a shift. Her son, Gordon was only 17 when he was lost at sea in the "Royal Oak".

Shilling A Day

Born at East Murton, Mr Gibson started work at Wingate colliery when he was on 12 as a trapper-boy. He received 1s a day wages. Shortly afterwards he went Sherburn House colliery to work on the screens, then at the age of 15 transferred to Lady Durham pit, near Sherburn. He remained there until after his marriage, then went to Sherburn Hill colliery.

"I was there for five years," Mr Gibson told our reporter, "but when work got slack – we were working only one day a week – by brother-in-law and I left to start work at East Howle Colliery!.

Mr Gibson was at East Howle for only 13 weeks but he was not sorry to leave! He had only been there a short time when he had a providential escape from being involved in an accident. "After taking me to the shaft bottom," he said, "the cage went back for another load of men. This cage crashed to the bottom and 16 men were injured. I had just gone in-bye and was waiting with the deputy at the kist for the men to come along when we were told of the accident".

Not long after this incident, at the same colliery, a fall in the shaft burst some steam pipes and severely scalded about 50 ponies, not one of which survived. "After that the pit was idle for four days", said Mr Gibson.

"Believe me," added Mr Gibson, "I was glad when I said goodbye to that pit! Not long after I left, the pit-heap caught fire and that laid the pit idle for good!"

"Caller Up"

Mr Gibson returned to work at Sherburn Hill colliery and moved to Ludworth, where he lived for 20 years. Later he was employed at Wheatley Hill colliery until 1914, when he joined-up in the Northumberland Fusiliers (Tyneside Scottish). He was invalided out in 1917 and worked no more until 1924 when he started light duties at Wheatley Hill Colliery.

Later Mr Gibson was "caller up" for 4½ years at Shotton Colliery – he called up the men there who were employed at Wheatley Hill colliery. After a few months labouring he went to work in a factory at Coventry, where he was employed at the same time as his wife was in the Aycliffe factory.

Mr and Mrs Gibson who have lived at Wheatley Hill for the past 27 years, were married at the Jubilee Methodist Church, Durham, on 29 June 1901. They have living, three daughters and three sons, 17 grand-children and three great-grandchildren.

A churchwoman all her life, Mrs Gibson is associated with All Saints Church, Wheatley Hill, and a member of the Mothers Union there. That she may soon be restored to good health and enjoy many more years of happiness with her husband, is the sincere wish of her many friends in the District.

THORNLEY PARISH COUNCIL
Welfare Centre and Housing Position

Exception was taken at a meeting of Thornley Parish Council on Tuesday to statements contained in a letter written by the Clerk of Durham County Council to Mr E Shinwell, MP, on the question of Thornley Child Welfare Centre.

The letter said the County Council had considered the acquisition of a house for the purpose of holding the maternity and child welfare centre, although the suggestion encountered considerable opposition locally in view of the shortage of housing accommodation.,

To this Mrs D Roper, who is hon secretary of the centre, said that such a statement might give the impression that half the village was against the proposal to acquire a house. They of the centre felt sure there was no considerable opinion against the proposal.

Opposition To Wheatley Hill Move

Mrs Todd said that if a house was used as the centre it would not affect the housing position as the upstairs rooms could be occupied by the caretaker.

Objection in the letter to the suggestion of considering the transferring of the centre from Thornley to the centre at Wheatley Hill was made by Mrs E Bosomworth (chairman). She said that would be putting the clock back fifteen years to the time when Thornley mothers had to take their children to Wheatley Hill. She believed Thornley mothers would not go to Wheatley Hill. "To lose our centre and have to go to Wheatley Hill would be disgraceful" she said.

Mr M Fleming said he was in favour of a prefabricated building and thus keep clear of the housing question.

Mrs Todd said that the taking of Knayton House, which the County Council had been informed would be available, need not necessarily be a permanent arrangement. "We ought to have it until the County Council can provide a building which is fully suitable", she said. The present building was not clean and the roof was not safe.

Mrs Anderson said the County Council had in other places taken houses for child centres.

In the end it was decided to ask the County Council to receive a deputation from the Parish Council along with the chairman of the centre.

Other Matters

Easington Rural Council informed the parish council they could not entertain the request to give three seats for the recreation ground.

When Mr J H C Scott suggested asking the Playing Fields Association to make the gift he was told that the association had practically no money of its own.

The District Council are to be asked to erect the seats and charge them to the parish council. An effort is also to be made to fence in a large gap on the recreation ground boundary with old railway sleepers.

It was reported that a children's sand pool had been laid at the South Thornlaw recreation ground and two of the swings at Percy Street recreation ground had been provided with new concrete platforms.

6 July 195

DEATH OF WHEATLEY HILL JP

Wheatley Hill said farewell to one of its most prominent and best loved inhabitants when the funeral took pace of Mr William Snaith, JP, 82, of 11 Gowland Terrace, Wheatley Hill. Mr Snaith had lived in the village since 1889 and was connected with almost every aspect of is daily life.

A native of Trimdon, Mr Snaith started work at Wheatley Hill Colliery as a blacksmith and retired at the age of 79. He was presented with a diploma by the Durham Miners' Association for 50 years membership.

Always prominent in Methodist circles, Mr Snaith was superintendent of Patton Street Methodist Church Sunday School for 53 years, secretary of the Trust for 48 years, circuit steward for 34 years and society steward for 31 years. He was always prominent in local government activities and was a member of the first Wingate Parish Council serving at the same time as the late Peter Lee.

Mr Snaith represented the Wheatley Hill Ward for 22 years and was a member of Easington RDC for a further 15 years. He was also chairman of the Easington Education Committee for a number of years. Much of his time was also given up to Co-operative Society work and he was an active member of Haswell Co-op for many years.

One of the most important events of his life came in 1926 when he was made a Justice of the Peace for the County. In 1929, Mr Snaith performed the opening ceremony at Blackhall Council Schools and possessed a silver salver which was handed to him to mark the occasion.

Good Templars throughout the county benefited from Mr Snaith's work for them and he was one of the founders of Trimdon and Wheatley Hill Temperance Halls. As the oldest member of Wheatley Hill Miners' Lodge, Mr Snaith had the honour to unfurl the first NCB banner for Wheatley Hill.

He was first married in 1890 but his first wife died in 1918. Two years later he married the present Mrs Snaith. He is survived by a widow and three sons.

SPORTS DAY AT LUDWORTH SCHOOL

Ludworth School held its second annual sports day last week on a field loaned by Mr Davison, of Tower Farm. In perfect weather a large number of parents and friends were present to witness many keenly contested events. Ellemore House won the house shield with 146 points followed by Dene House (130), Tower House (121) and Peel House (66). Shield was presented by Coun D Thornton and the results are as follows:

Infants Section: 40 yards flat six years old: G Cairns (T), J Morgan (E), M Thornton (E) and J Davis (E); **Seven years old:** W Stones (T), K Langland (T), W Kelly (T), J Hodgson (T); **Five years old:** K Hay (T), B Dixon (E), S Hughff (P), D Elcoat (T). **Potato Race – five years:** K Harp (T), A Appleby (E), S Hughff (P), B Dixon (P); **Six years old** J White (D), G Cairns (T), A Leathers (E), B Armstrong (P); **Seven years old:** M Hogg (D), G Wade (T), A Stoker (T), J Hodgson (T). **Egg and spoon – five years old –** L Morgan (D), A Appleby (E), B Davis (P), N Surtees (E); **Six years old -** A Hammond (T), J Milburn (D), A St Julien (D), J Morgan (E); **Seven years old –** W Stone (T), J Hodgson (T), W Kelly (T), P Turnbull (P).

Junior Section boys – 60 yards E Bryce (E), A Lowther (E), W Kipling (D), R Bellingham (E). **Three-legged race**: Bryce and Lowther (E), Hartley and Mowatt (E), Hall and Stamfield (D), Leathers and Bellingham (E). **Sack Race**: E Bryce (E), J Mowatt (E), F Blanch (T), A Lowther (E). **Mixed Shoe:** E Bryce (E), W Hartley (E), A Grainger (E), R Bellingham (E). **Obstacle:** F Blanch (T), M Hammond (T), F Blanch (T), G Youll (D)

Junior Section Girls – 60 yards: V Maitland (D), M Sample (T), J Bellingham (P); **Three-legged race:** M Barrasford and J Bellingham (D), V Stones and E Stannard (T), M Morgan and H Sample (T), S Osbaldestin and G Robinson (E). **Sack**: E Stannard (T), M Barrasford (P), S White (D), B Hughff (P); **Egg and Spoon**: V Stones (T), J Dixon (E), S Osbaldestin (E), V Maitland (D). **Skipping:** J Dixon (E), C Hogg (E), S White (D), M Barrasford (P).

Senior Section Boys – 100 yards: L Kennedy (D), G Greene (T), G Kilbourn (E), D Champley (T); **Wheelbarrow:** A Stannard and L Raine (D), R Green and J Crisp (P), M Osbaldestin and D Thompson (D); **High Jump:** M Gibbons (D), G Greene (T), E Hammond (E), A Stannard (D); **Obstacle:** A Stannard (D), W Simpson (P), G Kilbourn (E), J Grainger (D); **Slow Cycle:** N Davis (E), E Hutchinson (E), M Gibbons (D), D Thompson (D); **Relay** – Peel, Dene Tower, Ellemore.

Senior Section Girls – 80 yards: J Kipling (T), S Barrasford (D), V White (D), E Miller (D); **Mixed Shoe:** R Summerill (E), L Winter (E), V White (D), V Dixon (P); **Goal Shoot:** S Barrasford (D), J Wears (D), R

Summerill (E), F Hammond (T). **Sack -** S Barrasford (D), E Bott (E), V Dixon (P), V White (D). **High Jump|:** S Barrasford (D), O Stones (P), V White (D), N Gradon (T); **Relay**: Dene, Elemore, Peel and Tower.
13 July 1951

ACCEPTED FOR THE MINISTRY

Two young Wheatley Hill clerks, both actively associated with Church Street Methodist Church, have been accepted by the Methodist Conference as candidates for the Methodist ministry. They are Mr Ronald Brown, 24, youngest son of Mr and Mrs J Brown of 1 Stockton Street, Wheatley Hill, and Mr Edward Harrison, 23 only son of Mr and Mrs Jack Harrison of 12 Burns Street, Wheatley Hill. Mr Brown is employed as a finance clerk at No 3 Area Headquarters of the Durham Divisional Coal Board, The Castle, Castle Eden, while Mr Harrison is an insurance clerk at Newcastle.

Both candidates are on the "plan" of Thornley Methodist Circuit and prominent members of Wheatley Hill Youth Fellowship which Mr Harrison's father, a magistrate on Castle Eden Bench, founded. Best wishes for their future success are extended by their many friends in East Durham.

WHEATLEY HILL
FORMER HARRIER'S DEATH

Formerly actively associated with West Hartlepool Burn Road Harriers and winner of many road races, Mr William Middleton, 41, of 4 Luke Terrace, Wheatley Hill, who died last week, was buried at Wheatley Hill cemetery on Tuesday 24 July. Mr Middleton won many trophies and prizes for running, his most outstanding achievement being on 1 January 1938 when he won the Morpeth Road Race in 1hour:13m:16seconds, an arduous 13 miles five furlongs from Morpeth to Newcastle. Not only did he win the "Sunday Sun" handicap award, three guineas handicap first, but a record "Double", a cup replica and a three guineas gold medal. There were 58 starters in the race, seven failing to finish the course.

Since leaving school, he had been in the bricklaying trade, having worked for various firms in East Durham, but had not worked for the past 2½years through ill-health following a wrist injury. In his younger days he played the piano in a number of local dance bands. During the war Mr Middleton served for three years, principally abroad, in the Royal Corps of Signals. The son of Mrs Mary Ann Middleton of 6 No

Mr William Middleton

Road, Wingate, he lived at Wingate until moving to Wheatley Hill 17 years ago. He leaves a widow, one son and three daughters. Funeral service at The Rest was conducted by Rev Noel Catherall.

Medals Won by Mr W Middleton

LATE MR W DEAN – One of Wheatley Hill's oldest residents, Mr William Dean, 78 of 1 Arne Street, who died in Sedgefield General Hospital, was cremated at Newcastle on Wednesday, following a service in All Saints' Church, Wheatley Hill, conducted by Rev G Beckwith (Vicar of Shotton). Mr Dean, who had lain in hospital seven weeks following a stroke, had lived at Wheatley Hill for 33 years, moving there from Shotton. A native of Lancashire he started work as a mill boy there, but later began work as a miner, and for 50 years was employed at Wheatley Hill colliery until his retirement at the age of 72. His death breaks a married partnership of 56 years and he is survived by his wife, who has had a long association with All Saints' Church, three sons and three daughters.

MR KITTO MISSED THE GALA

Mr Edward Kitto, 28 Hederson Avenue, Wheatley Hill, missed his first Miners' Gala due to a fall of stone when coming out-bye after completing his shift. He was removed to the County Hospital, where in an X-ray, it was discovered that his spine was injured.

Mr Kitto is in a plaster cast and can walk a little. Thornley Colliery Band, for which he has been bandmaster for many years, came up to his home on Saturday morning before starting for the gala, and played a few tunes. It was a gesture that touched him greatly. In the evening, Wheatley Hill band and banner paraded outside the house, and when he heard their gay laughter and calls to "make sharp and get well" he felt he had been given a little of the gala spirit.

"Everyone has been very kind to me", said Mr Kitto. "I am sorry I missed the Cathedral Service".

All bandsmen will wish for Mr Kitto a speedy recovery and a resumption of his many activities.

DURHAM DIALECT

DIALECT	MEANING
Had thi 'ogger or Get thi pipe	Wait awhile
Stick thi toes in	Got off to a good start at work
Howld	Stop!
Marra	Colleague
Aa see thoo's makkin in	Miners going to work
Hoo's tha makkin out?	How are you getting on?
Ower much cloth and too little pudden	Too much cloth that the pudding is cooking in and not enough of the pudding itself
What fettle?	How are you?
Thoo's makken gam	You are pretending

27 July 1951

WHEATLEY HILL SCHOOL CAMP

Shortly after they "broke up" for their summer holidays on Friday, forty pupils of Wheatley Hill Senior Boys' School, in charge of their headmaster, Mr J Andrews, and a number of teachers, left for a week's camp at Wolsingham. A similar camp last year proved an outstanding success and the boys have been eagerly looking forward to this years.

A party of other pupils – members of the school's cycling club – are leaving this weekend for a tour of the Lake District. They will be in charge of Mr Victor Brown, a member of the staff, and expect to be away five days.

3 August 1951

ON HOLIDAY – Thornley and Wheatley Hill Collieries are on holiday this week and will resume work on Tuesday.

BABY'S ESCAPE AT WHEATLEY HILL

A YEAR-OLD BABY BOY, John Snowdon, Church Street, Wheatley Hill, son of a Wheatley Hill cricketer, had a miraculous escape from being hit by a cricket ball on Wednesday afternoon.

He was seated on the knee of a nine-year-old girl, Margaret Thompson of Granby Terrace, Wingate, at Wheatley Hill cricket ground where a match was in progress between a Durham County side and the Durham Coast League, when the girl was struck by the ball. The baby was untouched but the girl's brow was bruised and she suffered from shock.

10 August 1951

CLUB COMMITTEE - From 39 nominations the following have been elected to the committee of Wheatley Hill Workmen's Social Club and Institute for the ensuing year: Messrs J Bromilow, R Cook, T Harper jnr, G Hedley, M O'Connor and R Trotter.

WHEATLEY HILL WI – Mrs Hutchinson presided when a demonstration "Tea time Tasties", was given by Mrs Raine (Durham), who was thanked by Mrs P H Galley. Winners of the samples made by Mrs Raine were Mesdames Robinson, Harker, Snowdon and Brown. Competition for the best home-made ginger snaps, judged by Mrs Hedley, was won by Mrs Brown. Tea hostesses were Mesdames Inchcliffe, Tunstall, Armstrong and Lee.

TWENTY-FIVE 'BUSES ON TRIP – Biggest fleet of 'buses to leave Wheatley Hill on a seaside trip was seen on Saturday when no fewer than 25 took more than 500 children of the members of Wheatley Hill Workmen's Club on their first annual outing to Seaburn. Many of the children were accompanied by their parents or friends, and the 'buses were supervised by officials and committee of the club. In addition to the free trip, the children received 5s pocket money each. Arrangements were made by the club secretary, Mr T Storey.

17 August 1951

GOLDEN WEDDING AT WHEATLEY HILL

A Wheatley Hill couple, who celebrated their golden wedding on Tuesday, were unfortunately, unable to be together for the occasion. The couple, Mr and Mrs Samuel Routledge, of 10 Third Street, Wheatley Hill, have lived in the village practically the whole of their married life, but a fortnight ago Mrs Routledge was taken to Dryburn Hospital where she is still a patient.

Aged 71, Mrs Routledge has not enjoyed the best of health during recent years. Not long after he finished work at Thornley colliery 2½ years ago, as a redundant worker, Mr Routledge was taken ill for about four months, but he is now in improved health.

Mr Routledge, who is 72, started work at Castle Eden Colliery at the age of 12, but three years later transferred to Haswell colliery. When Haswell closed down in 1896, he went to work at Thornley colliery where he remained until his retirement.

Gardening and pigeon keeping are now Mr Routledge's main hobbies. It is his proud boast that he was the owner of the first pigeon to fly in a registered club race from Troyes, in France, to Wheatley Hill. "Only a fortnight after that achievement", Mr Routledge told our reporter, "someone killed the pigeon in its loft. I had it stuffed and still have it today!"

Mr and Mrs Routledge, who were married at Thornley Parish Church by the late Rev E C Briggs, have a family of six sons and two daughters, 27 grand children and four great-grandchildren. Mr Routledge himself was one of a family of eleven. His brother, Alex who lives at Blackhall, celebrated his golden wedding about a year ago.

"GOLDEN DAY" AT WHEATLEY HILL
Memories of Unmade Roads in the Village

The days when there were no roads, lights or 'buses at Wheatley Hill are recalled by Mr and Mrs William Robert Hird, 26 Aged Miners' Homes, Wheatley Hill, who today celebrate their golden wedding. Apart from about two years he spent at Castle Eden colliery, Mr Hird has lived at Wheatley Hill all his life and his wife came to the village from Spennymoor as a schoolgirl.

"How well I remember the day we moved to Wheatley Hill!" Mrs Hird told our reporter. "There was no proper road into the village and we had a terrible time coming from Spennymoor with a cart-load of furniture. Often the wheels of the cart sank into a deep rut and we seemed to trudge along uneven ground for ages before finally we reached our new home".

Grass in The Kitchen

Mrs Hird's new home near the railway had grass growing in the kitchen, doors which did not lock and windows with no panes in. The house, she explained was one of a number which had remained untenanted for a long time. They were opened up again with the re-opening of Wheatley Hill colliery which brought more miners back to the village.

"Believe me", said Mrs Hird, "we had a lot of inconvenience to put up with when we first moved in, but gradually a brick floor was built in the kitchen and the doors and windows were repaired. Eventually, by the standards of those days, we were reasonably comfortable". The house and the street have long since been demolished".

Until two years ago Mr Hird, who is 74, served on Wingate Parish Council for "more years than he can remember". When he first became a councillor the meetings were held alternately at Wheatley Hill, Wingate and Deaf Hill. "There was just a path over the quarry from Wheatley Hill to Wingate and Deaf Hill", he said, "and when we went to the meetings during the winter I always took a hurricane lamp to light our way. If no lamp was available then there were no Wheatley Hill councillors at the meetings!"

Worked at 12 for 10d per day

Mr Hird was born at Wheatley Hill and started work at Castle Eden colliery at the age of 12 for tenpence a day. When part of the pit was flooded in 1892 he and his parents returned to Wheatley Hill where he continued to work as a miner until he was 58. "I had to give up then", he said, "when 400 of us were given our notices through part of the colliery being closed down". Since then Mr Hird has had several periods of employment as a casual labourer, but now he is retired.

During the early part of his mining career, Mr Hird had a lucky escape at Wheatley Hill colliery when the cage carrying him and 23 other miners crashed to the bottom in 1902. "We were all shot out of the cage at the bottom", he recalled, "but fortunately no one was killed. Only two escaped injury". Mr Hird lost six weeks' work as a result of his injuries. The worst injured man – a miner called Herbert Broughton

– had both legs broken. He recovered, but later was killed in another pit accident.

Though no longer on the parish council, Mr Hird still takes an active interest in local affairs. He is chairman of Wheatley Hill Hospital Committee and vice-chairman of Wheatley Hill Welfare Bowls Club and a loyal Methodist, is a society steward at Patton Street Methodist Church. He plays bowls for the local Welfare team.

No Retirement For Women

Mrs Hird, who will be 71 next month, is also associated with Patton Street Church. Quite active for her age, she does all her own housework. "There's no retirement for womenfolk", she declared. The couple have one daughter and one granddaughter. At a celebration party on Sunday a golden wedding cake presented to Mr and Mrs Hird by Shotton Colliery friends, Mr and Mrs Norman Jameson, will be cut.

24 August 1951

DIAMOND WEDDING
Contented Couple at Wheatley Hill

The post-woman carrying a bundle of greetings cards, and our reporter, who arrived simultaneously at 8 Aged Miners Homes, Wheatley Hill, on Wednesday morning, were the first to offer congratulations to Mr and Mrs John Hogg, on the celebration of their diamond wedding.

Both in excellent health, Mr and Mrs Hogg were married at St Andrew's Church, Spennymoor. "The sun shone beautifully all morning that day", reminisced Mrs Hogg, "but on our way to the church it suddenly changed to heavy rain and hail stones. It was a very happy day for all that. We've had a happily married life together – of course we've had our squabbles, who hasn't? but we think just as much about each other today as we did then!"

Mr Hogg, who is 81 in March, is up first every morning to light the fire, often as early as half past six, and he 'potters around' all day, either helping his wife a little with the housework, doing a "spot of gardening" or enjoying a pipe of tobacco and the wireless. He also does a little reading. "I like a good cowboy story now and again" he smiled.

Worked At Croxdale

Born at West Cornforth, Mr Hogg started work at Croxdale as a trapper-boy at the age of 12. His first wage was at the rate of 11½d per day. Later he worked at Pelton Fell, then started pony putting at Kibblesworth and hand-putting at Craghead. Before moving to Wheatley Hill 43 years ago, Mr Hogg worked at quite a number of collieries in North-West Durham.

"In those days", he reflected, "if we didn't like our job or conditions we soon moved off to another colliery".

Mr Hogg and his wife settled in Wheatley Hill, Mr Hogg working at the colliery until he was 64. "I was forced to retired then", he said, "for with many more miners I was given my notice when they decided to close part of the pit". Mr Hogg was a deputy at the colliery for 20 years.

"Good Old Days"

Though the conditions have improved in the mining industry, said Mr Hogg, he still preferred the "good old days"!. The country was in a far more settled state in the early part of his married life, he said, and there wasn't so much "squabbling" throughout the world. "Then look at the value of money now compared with the good old days!" exclaimed Mr Hogg. "When we were first married you could cover a kitchen table with groceries for 10s".

Mrs Hogg was born at South Shields, will be 79 in November. She does all her own housework and has few grumbles. "We have what does our turn", she said, "and we both keep good health so that's all that matters".

Mr and Mrs Hogg have a family of two sons and two daughters, and 16 grandchildren. Their elder son, William, who used to work at Shotton Colliery emigrated to America during the 1926 strike and has never been back home since. He is employed in a gramophone record factory at Bridgeport. "If he was to walk through our front door it would be the best diamond wedding gift we could wish for", said Mrs Hogg.

At a small family celebration party at the couple's home on Wednesday, a birthday cake, which Mrs Hogg had made and iced herself, was cut and heart-felt wishes were expressed for the future good health and happiness of the aged couple.

RETIREMENT OF MR T H HOLDER
Fifty-two years in Mining Industry

Mr T H Holder is retiring on 31 August from the post of cashier at Thornley colliery after nearly 52 years service in the mining industry. He has been actively engaged in colliery village welfare work since 1913, when he became the first secretary of the Thornley Aged Miners' Homes

Committee. With the late Mr G A Curry, then manager of Thornley Colliery, and chairman of the committee, he organised the foundation stone-laying ceremony of the first 12 cottages and the single men's home in 1914. In 1926 he became honorary treasurer and trustee, and has held that office ever since. The committee own 37 cottages and the single men's quarters, an unusually large number for a colliery the size of Thornley. He is also a trustee and treasurer of the Miners' Welfare Committee and treasurer of the pithead baths and canteen committee.

As clerk to the parish council since 1918, he has been secretary to many public committees which have organised successful peace celebrations, soldiers' gifts and Coronation and Royal Jubilee events. He is honorary secretary of the war memorial committee, whose work is not yet completed. Past and present members of the council recognised his services when he completed 25 years as clerk to the council.

Attached to Thornley parish church for the past 40 years, he has been a member of the church council since its formation, and was people's warden for 16 years. He is now vice-chairman of the church council and a member of the diocesan conference and the ruri-decanal conference.

Mr Holder has contributed numerous articles to national daily and weekly journals, and to the North County press, on colliery life.

He is being succeeded as cashier at Thornley, by Mr R Brandling, cashier at Deaf Hill Colliery, who is vicar's warden, and treasurer of the Thornley parochial church council. His successor at Deaf Hill is Mr W Turnbull of the Thornley office staff.

31 August 1951

FELLOWSHIP PRESENTATION – Two members of Wheatley Hill Young People's Fellowship, Nurse Patricia McAloon and Mr Fred Hobbs, who are being married later this month before going to work in a leper colony in South Africa, were presented with a gift of bed linen by the Fellowship at its weekly meeting on Sunday night. The presentation was made by Mr Maurice Nixon.

RESOLUTION RESCINDED – Wheatley Hill miners' lodge, which a week past Sunday, decided, by a small majority, not to work the Saturday shift despite an appeal from county headquarters to carry out the extra hours agreement, rescinded the resolution on Sunday. It is understood that the resolution was rescinded on the casting vote of the chairman and that the pit will be working tomorrow (Saturday).

SUNDAY SCHOOL PRESENTATIONS – At the Sunday School service in Church Street Methodist Church, Wheatley Hill, on Sunday, two former Sunday School scholars who have been accepted as candidates for the Methodist ministry, Messrs Ron Brown and Ted Harrison, were presented with gifts of two books each to assist them in their studies. The presentations were made on behalf of the Sunday School by Mr George Poulson (Sunday School Superintendent). Mr Brown is entering college this month and Mr Harrison is going straight into circuit work at Basingstoke.

7 September 1951

WHEATLEY HILL BOY'S 40FT FALL

Climbing up the almost perpendicular face of Wingate Quarry, near Deaf Hill, on Sunday afternoon, a 15-year-old boy, Ronald Young of 17 Shop Street, Wheatley Hill, fell about 40ft to the bottom when he lost his foothold.

For part of the way up the quarry, which is now in disuse, the side is covered with grass but nearer the top it is solid rock. Two 16-year-old youths, Thomas Wilson of 11 Darlington Street, and Brian Morgan of 2 North View, both Wheatley Hill, were nearby when Young attempted his upward climb.

Wilson had himself climbed to the top of the 90ft deep quarry when the accident occurred and Morgan was watching down below. They summoned help and after medical attention by Dr Gallagher (Wheatley Hill), Young was rushed unconscious to Durham County Hospital, where later his condition was described as "still poorly".

PRIZE PRODUCE AT THORNLEY

There were 191 entries at Thornley Allotments Society Show on Saturday. Mr J Grainger (Leamside), was judge and the official duties were carried out by Mr T Ridley (chairman), Mr J Garbutt (Secretary) and Mr J Thompson (treasurer).

A notable success was that of Mr Alan Hutchinson who took 12 firsts, 12 seconds and three thirds.

Results

Vegetables: Beet (Round): A Hutchinson, G Harris, S Wilson. **Beans (Broad):** W Shepherd, A Hutchinson, J Abbs. **Celery (White):** R Barker, D Baker, W Shepherd. **(Pink)** A Hutchinson, W Shepherd, D Baker. **Cabbage:** S Wilson, H Mills, G Hutchinson. **Carrots (Long):**

A Hutchinson, G Hutchinson, R Lewis. **(Stump)** A Hutchinson, D Baker, A Charlton. **Cauliflower:** W Shepherd, A Charlton, S Wilson. **Cucumber:** R Lewis, A Charlton, M Charlton. **Leeks (Pot):** A Hutchinson, M Charlton. **Trench:** A Hutchinson, R Baker, A Charlton. **Onions:** J Abbs, A Hutchinson, R Lewis. **Parsnips:** G Atkin, A Hutchinson, R Lewis. **Potatoes (Kidney White):** A Hutchinson, G Hutchinson, S Wilson. **(Round White):** W Shepherd, A Hutchinson, G Hutchinson. **(Kidney Coloured):** R Forster, W Shepherd, D Baker. **(Round Coloured):** A Hutchinson, G Hutchinson. **Peas:** W Shepherd, A Hutchinson, D Baker. **Shallots:** W Shepherd, S Wilson, A Hutchinson. **Tomatoes:** W Shepherd, J Abbs, R Forster. **Tray of vegetables:** A Hutchinson, G Hutchinson, R Lewis.

Flowers

Asters: H Hood, A Hutchinson, R Forster. **Chrysanthemums:** A Charlton, A Hutchinson, W Shepherd. **Dahlias (pom pom):** A Charlton, A Hutchinson, M Charlton. **(decorative):** A Charlton, R Baker, J Harris. **Buttonhole:** W Shepherd, A Gulliver, R Baker. **Gladioli:** R Forster, J R Blair, W Shepherd. **Spray:** W Shepherd, D Baker, A Charlton. **Bouquet:** A Hutchinson, A Charlton, D Baker. **Cut flowers:** A Hutchinson, W Shepherd, D Baker.

14 September 1951

THORNLEY ROAD SAFETY WEEK
Parade of Decorated Lorries

Thornley Road Safety Committee completed a very successful Road Safety Week with a parade of decorated lorries on Saturday afternoon. It began at Dunelm Road and headed by Thornley Colliery Prize Band, proceeded down the Main Street to the entrance to the Welfare Football Club field, where Miss Enid Kell, the village Road Safety Queen, kicked off in the Thornley Aged Miners' Cup-tie between the Welfare and Deaf Hill United. Miss Kell had been specially invited to do this in celebration of the opening of the ground. She was given a splendid ovation by a large crowd.

The motor-lorry on which Miss Kell rode with her attendants, Margaret Charlton, Mary Oswald, Mary Bellwood and Kathleen Rutter was in the charge of PC J L Jackson, Accident Prevention Officer of the Castle Eden Area. There were also on the lorry a number of children who held up copies of road signs and slogans.

Another lorry, entered by the Thornley Mothers' Club, carried children. Two were in a crib, and apparently were suffering from the results of accidents. A little nurse sat alongside. A lorry put in by the Thornley Scouts showed a boy in bed with a bandage round his head. His anxious "mother" sat at the bedside.

A novel contribution was that of Mr J Burgin. It was an imitation of a pit tub drawn by a pony, and carrying black-faced boys wearing pit safety hats. A placard at the rear of the tub enjoined all miners to always wear their helmets. This effort was a useful reminder of the need for Safety First on the roads underground.

During the afternoon there was a Mr Road Safety challenge competition and Miss Isabel Watson, of Hartlepool Street, successfully challenged Mr Bert Winter, the mystery man.

5 October 1951

CAR FOR "MR SUNSHINE"
Presentation at Wheatley Hill

The presentation of a £600 specially adapted 8 hp car to Arthur Bonar, aged 21 of 40 Hillsyde Crescent, Thornley, on Friday was a big event in his life.

Known as "Mr Sunshine" when he was an inmate of Dryburn Hospital, Arthur has remained cheerful and bright for the whole 18 months since he had the great misfortune to lose both legs following an accident in Thornley pit when he became entangled in a coal-cutting machine which he and another young fitter were repairing. It was some time before Arthur could be released, and his courage then was described by eye-witnesses as wonderful.

The presentation was made at dance at the Embassy, Wheatley Hill by Mr J Callighan, chairman of the small committee which was immediately set up to assist Arthur. The other members of the committee were Mr James Hobson (vice-chairman), Mr J C Kirk (secretary), Mr John Tunney (treasurer) and Mr Leo Tunney (assistant secretary).

Arthur was accompanied by his fiancée, Miss Gwendoline Turnbull of Thornley, to whom he has become engaged since his accident. He told our reporter that he is not intending to get married immediately. He says he is quite happy and "without a care in the world" but is anxious to bet back to work.

£50 From Lord Nuffield

He hopes to start training soon as a tracer in a drawing office and is hoping that the Coal Board will find him a job. He will be able to get about an office all right because he has a pair of the latest type of artificial legs, supplied by the Ministry of Insurance. He wore them throughout the presentation ceremony.

Great credit is due to the committee for the energy they put into reaching their target. Mr Kirk, the secretary, said there were times when they had doubts about collecting sufficient money to acquire a car. He said the public had given great help in patronising concerts, dances and football matches, but the majority of donations had come from outside Thornley and Wheatley Hill, ranging from anonymous half crowns to a £50 cheque from Lord Nuffield. Mr Kirk said that raising the money was one thing and obtaining priority was another. Success in priority was due to the combined efforts of Lord Hyndley, late chairman of the NCB, Mr Churchill and Lord Nuffield.

THORNLEY BEAT TRIMDON MECHANICS

A large crowd saw a thrilling duel between Thornley CW and Trimdon Grange Mechanics in a Wingate and District League Cup game at Thornley. The score was 1-0 in favour of Thornley. After 30 minutes Blakemore scored the only goal with a great cross-shot from about 15 yards. Then Trimdon were awarded a penalty for a handling offence and Nicholson did well to save Ford's shot.

12 October 1951

THORNLEY CUP HOPES

Has any local football supporter in the Thornley area picked the winners yet of the Thornley Aged Miners' Cup. If not, what are the chances of Thornley St Godric's winning the cup? They have some stout hearted supporters and some confidence of carrying off the trophy.

Much can be said of the claim that St Godric's are one of the strongest yet least known clubs in the district. They have a liking for cup ties, and to date are unbeaten in cup competitions. By beating the strong Murton Knaresboro team on Saturday to the tune of six goals to two, they appear to have established themselves favourites for the Aged Miners' Cup.

Stars in the side are McGee (goalkeeper), who has assisted Murton CW; 18 year-old Slack, an outside left who hails from Wingate. Both

233

these players have refused offers to play in the Wearside League. Already on the trail of Slack is a Third Division club. Other players who impress are Taylor, long service full back, Rhodes at centre-half and Connor ex-Stockton and Hartlepools centre-forward.

2 November 1951

WHEATLEY HILL DOG-OWNER'S SUCCESS

Mrs K Million, wife of the owner of the Black Lane Greyhound Stadium at Wheatley Hill, achieved a wonderful run of successes on Saturday at the Cleveland Dog Society Show at Redcar. Her one-year-old Borzio, "Quiz of Rydens", in addition to winning the Charles Dorman Cup for the best dog in the show and the Sir Park Goss Cup for the best sporting exhibit, also took first prize in all of the seven classes in which he was entered. Mr C Smith (Colne) was judge and the prizes were presented by the Mayor and Mayoress of Redcar.

This sporting dog, which is already gaining the reputation of being one of the best in the North of England, also won the Bell Trophy for being the best dog in the show at East Herrington recently.

NEW VICAR OF THORNLEY

Thornley's new Vicar to succeed Rev J M How, is Rev Hilary Walton Jackson, 34-year-old son of the late Canon Edgar Jackson, formerly of Sunderland and Frosterley. From Durham School he went to St Chad's College, Durham, and took a degree of BA in 1940. Joining the Royal Artillery in 1940, he served with the Eighth Army in the Mediterranean and later in Europe, being commissioned as a lieutenant in 1942.

Ordained deacon at Selby Abbey and priest at York Minster, Mr Jackson was assistant priest at Selby Abbey from 1946 to 1949. He took up his present appointment as assistant priest at All Saints' Church, Middlesbrough. He obtained the degree MA in 1948. He has been married eight years and has a son and daughter. His wife is the daughter of Mr John Daintith, Warrington.

The new Vicar's arrival at Thornley may be somewhat delayed because of the need for urgent repairs to the Vicarage, towards the cost of which Thornley churchpeople have set themselves the task of raising £200.

9 November 1951

DIAMOND WEDDING
"I Would Choose the Same Man", says Mrs Peacock

"If I had my life to live over again I should certainly choose the same man for my husband", declared Mrs Peacock of 19 Gowland Terrace, Wheatley Hill, who, with her husband, Mr Harry Peacock, celebrated her diamond wedding on Wednesday.

"We've always looked well after each other", chimed in Mr Peacock "and hope to spend more happy years together".

Though both are well past the eighty mark, they enjoy reasonably good health. Mr Peacock who will be 85 in January, only recently recovered from a six weeks illness. His wife, who is in her 82nd year, does all her own housework, including the baking, and certainly looks much younger than her years.

Bound Apprentice

Mr Peacock has a wonderful memory. Recalling the early days of his working career, he said that at the age of 15 he became a "bound apprentice" to a blacksmith, called William Dalkin, at Old Trimdon. He was "bound" for six years and throughout this time received no money, only his food, lodging and clothes. "The only way I was able to get some pocket money for myself", smiled Mr Peacock, "was to make odd things such as pokers and coal rakes – but I hadn't to let the gaffer see me!"

Mr Peacock still has the faded parchment indenture stating the terms under which he became an apprentice.

"Those were certainly the days", he said. "During the busy summer months we often worked from five o'clock in the morning until nine at night although our day's work was supposed to be from seven in the morning till seven at night. On Saturdays we worked from seven to four, but often it was much later than four when we finished. It was all solid hard work with a big hammer – there were no steam hammers or any of the contrivances used today in a blacksmith's – it was muscle and brawn all the time!"

Worked At Fishburn

At the end of his apprenticeship in 1888, Mr Peacock took over the management of a blacksmith's shop at Fishburn when the owner was taken ill. Later he worked at Trimdon Grange and Stanhope, then at Esh Village near Durham where he met his wife. Before going to Wheatley

Hill colliery as foreman blacksmith in 1914, Mr Peacock worked at West Stanley and Thornley collieries.

He was at West Stanley during the big explosion of 1909 which killed 168 miners – he missed being among the victims by a few minutes! "I was at the pit head waiting for the cage to go down to start my shift", he said, "when the explosion occurred. I certainly thought I was under a lucky star that day!" Shortly before he started his apprenticeship, Mr Peacock was living at Trimdon Grange when an explosion there in 1882 resulted in the loss of 75 miners. The last to be brought out alive, he recalled, was Mr Harry Neasham.

Champion Quoits Player

Mr Peacock remained at Wheatley Hill Colliery as foreman blacksmith until his retirement on his 80th birthday. He is well known throughout the county as a champion quoits player. For many years he held the title of champion three-step quoits player and even at the age of 75 was still winning matches. It was when he was this old that he played three matches at Easington. He won two of them but lost the third by only one "chalk" after giving his opponent five start. He made all his own quoits.

Mr and Mrs Peacock, who were married at Esh Parish Church, have had a family of ten. There are now living four daughters and three sons, 24 grandchildren and four great-grandchildren. Their second daughter, Mrs Violet Banks, emigrated to Canada 25 years ago. The other three daughters, Mrs Elsie Husband (Richmond), Mrs R Dickinson (Thornley) and Mrs Gladys Scott (Easington) are providing the "eats" for a family celebration party to be held at the home of the couple tomorrow.

That the couple may be blessed with good health and happiness for the remainder of their married life is the sincere wish of their many friends in the area.

23 November 1951

WHEATLEY HILL APATHY

They seem to have considerable difficulty in keeping the British Legion flag flying among men legionnaires at Wheatley Hill. The women have a flourishing section, but the men's section is almost defunct. For the annual meeting recently only four members turned up and it was impossible to carry on with any business. It is only four years ago that the men's section was re-formed after a considerable lapse of years. It made sound progress in the early months of its re-birth, but gradually interest waned and during the past year, although there were 40 paid-up members on the books, only a handful attended the meetings.

"There has been considerable apathy among local ex-Servicemen, especially among those who served in the last war", Mr James Robinson, secretary of the branch, told me this week. "One of the main reasons for the decline in enthusiasm and membership has been the lack of a building of our own. We had high hopes of putting up a new building, with both men and women members co-operating in the venture, but lack of finance is holding us up".

Permanent Headquarters Needed

The Legion already owns a site at Wheatley Hill and has the foundations of a building, complete with drainage and water supply, built up to ground level. More than £200 has been spent on the project, but now, though the necessary permit has been obtained to build, there is no money in the building fund. The present headquarters of the Wheatley Hill branch is in the old Home Guard building.

"If we had a place of our own, interest, I am certain, would be re-kindled in the work of the Legion for we would be able to organise many social events and this would help to attract the younger ex-servicemen," said Mr Robinson. "At the moment, however there seems little hope of continuing with our building scheme and the men's section is almost defunct". Only one other official still retains an interest in the section – he is the chairman, Mr W Poole.

7 December 1951

WHEATLEY HILL COLLIERY ACCIDENT
Electrician Fatally Injured

Well-known throughout East Durham as a bass singer – he had taken part in many concerts at Methodist Churches in the Wheatley Hill area – Mr Norman Lowes (51) of 26 Henderson Avenue, Wheatley Hill, was fatally injured in an accident at Wheatley Hill Colliery on Friday morning only a few minutes after the start of his shift.

Mr Lowes, who was employed as a colliery electrician, had just descended the pit shaft and was on his way in-by, to the place where he worked, when he was knocked down by a set of empty tubs travelling in his direction. He received serious injuries from which he died almost immediately. The colliery was laid idle for the rest of the day in accordance with local pit custom.

Keen Methodist

Mr Lowes, who is survived by his wife and a family of two daughters and one son, had been a member of the choir of Wheatley Hill Church Street Methodist Church for many years. On the night after the accident he was to have taken the bass part in a cantata, "The Conqueror's Crown", which the choir gave in connection with their anniversary celebrations. The cantata was still given, but the principal solo Mr Lowes was to have sung, was omitted.

Mr Lowes was also actively interested in other departments of church life. He was treasurer of the Methodist Guild and a regular attender at Sunday worship and in his younger days was a member of the Wheatley Hill Male Voice Choir. Mr Lowes had lived in the village all his life and been employed at the local colliery since leaving school. He was held in the highest esteem by a wide circle of friends and the deepest sympathy is extended to his wife and family in their tragic bereavement.
14 December 1951

1952

WHEATLEY HILL GOLDEN WEDDING
Mr and Mrs J Atkinson

A busy man is Mr John Atkinson, 2 Aged Miners' Homes, Wheatley Hill, who, although he retired from work at Wheatley Hill colliery ten years ago after a mining career of 54 years, has plenty to do each day and never finds time hanging on his hands. With his wife, Mr Atkinson celebrated his golden wedding on Monday and when our reporter called at their home to offer his congratulations he found Mr Atkinson busy chopping sticks.

"I haven't much time to talk to you," he said with a twinkle in his eye, "for I've all sorts of jobs to do"!

Though 76, Mr Atkinson enjoys remarkable good health. His wife, who is 72, is not so fortunate, however. She has been an invalid for some 15 years and Mr Atkinson does most of the housework. "I've never ailed a minute of my life," declared Mr Atkinson. "I'm first up every day to light the fire and am always last to bed".

Ten Pence a Shift

Three months before his 12th birthday Mr Atkinson started work at Kelloe colliery as a trapper-boy. He was paid tenpence per ten-hour shift. Later he started driving. "And for that," he said, "my wage rose to fifteen pence per shift". When he was 18 Mr Atkinson went to Wheatley Hill colliery, where he remained until his retirement at the age of 66.

Mr Atkinson is fond of gardening and in his younger days was interested in "pigeon-flying, dog running and birds". His chief hobby was training birds to sing. "Often," he recalled, "I had as many as 15 linnets in the house at the same time – and they could all sing". People came from many villages round about to hear his famous birds.

Mrs Atkinson – maiden name, Jemina Scott – was born at Hesleden and lived at Wingate before her marriage. She and her husband have lived in Wheatley Hill all their married life. When she enjoyed better health Mrs Atkinson was a regular attender at the Patton Street Methodist Church, Wheatley Hill.

The couple, who were married at Holy Trinity Church, Wingate, have living two daughters, one son and two grandchildren. Best wishes are extended to them for many more happy years together.

CASSOP AND THORNLEY IN "DERBY" GAME

"Derby" game between Cassop Victoria and Thornley CW attracted a good gate when these two Wingate League clubs met for the first time this season. Thornley had lost but one league game, while Cassop had won their last six in this competition. It proved an exciting struggle with Cassop victors by 4-3.

In the opening stages, play was even. When Thornley attacked, Ward made grand saves from Border and Laverick. At the other end Carr was just wide. For a time Cassop kept up the pressure and it came as a surprise when the visitors broke away, and, from a pass by Border, Laverick placed them in the lead.

The next three minutes were well appreciated by the crowd. Cassop went straight up and equalised through Dick Soppitt, who received a fine pass from Lawson. Immediately after Thornley again attacked and Laverick regained their advantage, only for Cassop to equalise again within seconds after Dick Soppitt converted a headed pass from Smith. Soon after, Dick Soppitt completed his hat-trick and placed Cassop ahead for the first time.

Cassop were now on top and only good goalkeeping kept them at bay. Smith was particularly unlucky with three grand headers, one hitting the bar and the other two being brilliantly saved.

Thornley had the initiative at the start of the second period but good defensive work by Fox and Walton kept them at bay until a slip by Wilkinson allowed Border to nip in and net for them. Afterwards there was a real ding-dong battle with both teams all out for the winner. Within ten minutes of the finish, Dick Soppitt recorded his fourth goal to collect the points for Cassop.

It was always a good, fast and clean game. If Cassop play like this against Bearpark CW in the semi-final of the Thornley AM Cup, the Central League team might well receive a shock.

Cassop visit Wheatley Hill Mechanics tomorrow and will field: Ward, Wilkinson, Fox, Foster, Walton, Lawson, T Scott, J Scott, R Soppitt, Smith, W Soppitt. Res: Carr, Hewitson, Holden, Horner.

18 January 1952

LUDWORTH

BRITISH LEGION – Mr Winter presided at monthly meeting. Thanks were expressed to Mr J Gibson, landlord of the Standish Arms, for the use of a room for headquarters. Members expressed sympathy with the vice-chairman (Mr M Morgan, DCM) on the injuries he received in a pit accident. Arrangements were completed for the old people's treat at a joint meeting.

VILLAGE INSTITUTE DANCE – Residents of Ludworth, who have put in so much work to raise money for necessary repairs at the Institute, were disappointed at the lack of support at the weekly dance. Success can only be attained if the people of Ludworth support functions organised in the hall, which is the only place of entertainment in the village. The old people have a cosy club in the building and, if only for their sakes, it is hoped the people will rally round. Dance is to take place on Monday (7.30 to 11.30).

FUNERAL OF THORNLEY BOER WAR VETERAN

Funeral of a South African War veteran, Mr Henry Palmer (75), who lived with his son-in-law and daughter, Mr and Mrs Charlton, 6 Passfield Square, Thornley, took place on Saturday. The service in Thornley Parish Church was conducted by the Rev H W Jackson (Vicar) and interment was at Thornley Cemetery. Mr Palmer, who worked at Thornley as a slater in his youth, served in the Grenadier Guards in the Boer War and throughout the first World War in the RG Artillery. He leaves a son and two daughters. His wife died eight months ago.

Chief mourners were: Mr Fred H Palmer (son), Mr and Mrs W Plant (son-in-law and daughter), Mr and Mrs M Charlton (son-in-law and daughter) and Misses Ann and Margaret Charlton (granddaughters).

WHEATLEY HILL CHURCH EXTENSIONS

Preliminary work was begun this week on extensions and improvements to All Saints' Church, Wheatley Hill, costing in the region of £2,000. A 14-feet extension is to be built on to the chancel, which will have a three-light lancet window on the east side in place of the present four-light window and a new entrance porch is to be built on the north side.

A new system of concealed electric lighting is to be installed in the church itself and the exterior is to be re-pointed. The extension to the chancel is the most costly item – it is expected to cost about £1,500 – but when the extensions and improvements are completed the church is not expected to be in debt as there is now more than £2,000 in a special building fund.

£1,200 Needed

"But," Rev Arthur Preston, Vicar of Wheatley Hill, told me this week, "we hope later to build a new south aisle and for this we need a further £1,200. We are making an all-out effort to raise this sum and we would be grateful for any contribution, large or small, from parishioners and others interested in this project".

All Saints' Church was built as a mission church in the parish of Thornley in 1873 and it was not until 1914 that it was consecrated as a parish church. The present extensions are being undertaken to make the building "more suitable to the needs of the large community that it serves" said Mr Preston.

WHEATLEY HILL

CHOIR ELECTIONS – Mr R Nixon presided at the annual choir meeting of Wheatley Hill Church Street Methodist Church, when the financial statement showed a credit balance of £18.9s. It was decided to donate £10 to trust funds and £1 to the church's Gift Fund. Officers elected for the ensuing year were: President, Mr R Nixon; vice-president, Mr H Lang; secretary, Miss M Harrison; treasurer, Mr G Mason; librarian, Miss Jean Henderson; sick visitors, Mr A Straughan and Mrs E Parnham; auditors, Miss M Kent and Mrs P H Galley sen.

LABOUR NOMINATIONS – From six nominations already put forward, Wheatley Hill Local Labour Party will make their final choice for three candidates to represent Wheatley Hill Parish in the forthcoming Easington Rural Council elections at a meeting to be held on 6 February. The nominations are: Messrs E Cain, E Wharrier and J Andrews (nominated by Wheatley Hill miners' lodge) and Messrs W Dowding and J Johnson and Miss E Bellinger (nominated by the Labour Party). Messrs J Johnson and E Wharrier and Miss Bellinger are the retiring members.

OCTOGENARIAN'S SUDDEN DEATH – One of Wheatley Hill's oldest standards, Mr Mark Thornton, who lived by himself at 9 Aged Miners' Homes, was found dead on his bedroom floor on Wednesday morning, having apparently fallen from his bed. The discovery was made by an 85-year-old neighbour, Mrs Furnevel, when she went to take him a cup of tea. Mr Thornton, who would have been 83 next month, had been bedfast for two days and death, it is understood, was due to natural causes. He had lived by himself since the death of his wife some four years ago, and is survived by a son and a daughter, who live at Grimethorpe, Yorkshire. Mr Thornton had lived at Wheatley Hill for more than half a century, and for many years was employed as a wagonwayman at Wheatley Hill colliery until his retirement.

PULPIT DEDICATED – Tribute to the work and sterling character of the first Vicar of Wheatley Hill, Rev Philip T Casey, who held the living from 1914 until his death in 1949, was paid by the Archdeacon of Durham, the Venerable E de Gray Lucas. At a special service in All Saints' Church, Wheatley Hill, on Wednesday night, he dedicated a new oak pulpit to the memory of Mr Casey. The pulpit, bearing a suitable inscription recording Mr Casey's long service as Vicar, was subscribed for by parishioners and friends. Also taking part in the service were Mr Casey's son, Rev Ernest Casey (Vicar of Chilton Moor), Canon R H Tillard (Rural Dean of Easington) and Rev Arthur Preston (present Vicar of Wheatley Hill). There was a packed congregation

25 January 1952

PRISONER OF WAR – A handmade Christmas card showing the winding road home, received from her husband on Saturday by Mrs Isabella Matthews, 188 Thornlaw South, Thornley, was the first news she has had that he is a prisoner of war in Korea. Serving in the 1st Battalion of the Gloucester Regiment, Pte R C Matthews had been missing since 26 April 1951. Serving his year "for the King" , as a long-service man, he had expected to be discharged last October. Mrs Matthews, who lives with her mother, Mrs Hannah Walls, has three children, aged five, three and two.

PANTOMIME given by Thornley British Legion Women's Concert Party was a great success. Over 200 people attended. Proceeds were for branch funds. The pantomime, "Cinderella", was presented in Thornley Workmen's Club Hall. Taking part were Miss Readshaw, Mrs Gordon, Mrs Bartram, Mrs H Slater, Mrs Barrass, Mrs M Mitchell, Mrs Middleton, Mrs Convery and the "Sunshine Girls".

Guest artistes were Misses McCoy, Mitchell, Wilson and Ellward, Mesdames Williams, Hobbs and Chapman. Producer was Mrs Bessie Bosomworth and at the piano was Mr Jackie Toye, who is blind.

ELECTED TO WHEATLEY HILL CO-OP COMMITTEE – As a result of a ballot, Mr W Smart (Kelloe) and Mr W Dowding (Wheatley Hill) have been elected from four nominations to represent the Wheatley Hill district on the committee of Sherburn Hill Co-operative Society for the ensuing year.

1 February 1952

THE "LAKE" AT THORNLEY

Thornley's "lake" has had skaters upon it for the first time. The "lake", situated on the east side of the highway from Thornley to Ludworth, formed about two years ago, and has gradually become larger. During the year swans increased in number until there were 27 of them, and a local poet wrote a poem about their reflections in the water.

Local residents are rather puzzled as to how the "lake" has formed, but some are of the opinion that the fields have been settling for some years owing to pit workings. There is a way out for some of the water through the railway embankment and into the concreted Wheatley Hill beck which finds its way eastwards to the sea, but the "lake" appears to be at a higher level than the old outlet. There is local talk about a drainage scheme being undertaken by the National Coal Board, the owners of the land, but pumping alone would be an expensive job.

Local ornithologists identified many kinds of water birds during the past year, and they would be sorry to lose the swans.

8 February 1952

ELIZABETH PROCLAIMED QUEEN OF THE COMMONWEALTH

"A New Sense Of Values" – Says The Prime Minister

His Majesty King George VI, who died in his sleep at Sandringham, last week, will be interred at Windsor today. Her Majesty's Ministers have advised that there should be no general suspension of work on the day of the funeral. The Queen knows well that her father will be constantly in the thoughts of her people on that day and it is her wish that as a mark of respect for his memory a two-minutes silence should be observed during the period of the service at Windsor. Cinemas and theatres will not open until 6 pm on that day.

The advice of the Minister of Education is that schools should not be closed, but that all pupils should observe the two-minutes silence.

The Queen, in her Accession declaration, used these words: "I pray that God will help me to discharge worthily this heavy task that has been laid upon me so early in my life".

SERVED WITH THE KING – Mr John Burnside, 18 Wordsworth Avenue, Wheatley Hill, who served as a stoker in the Royal Navy during both world wars, was with the cruiser Cumberland when King George VI was a midshipman on that ship.

15 February 1952

MR E LENNOX – MR H TRISNAN – Miss Hilda Trisnan, only daughter of Mr and Mrs T W Trisnan of 8 Gowland Terrace, Wheatley Hill, was married in Thornley RC Church on Saturday, to Mr Edward Lennox, youngest son of the late Mr and Mrs T Lennox, 3 Park Street, Thornley. Rev Father Magin officiated. Given away by her father, the bride was in white crepe, with a veil and coronet of camellias. She was attended by her sister-in-law, Mrs Doris Trisnan, wearing pink silk with coronet head-dress to match, and Miss Mary Trisnan (niece), wearing blue taffeta with head-dress to match. Best man was Mr Robert Trisnan (bride's brother). Reception was in the Welfare Hall.

MR W TAYLOR – MISS S SIMPSON – Rev Arthur Preston, assisted by Rev A C Robertson (Easington Colliery) officiated at the wedding in All Saints' Church, Wheatley Hill, on Saturday, of Miss Sheila Simpson, second daughter of Mr and Mrs W Simpson, 9 Fifteenth Street, Wheatley Hill, and Mr William Taylor, 46 Hopper Terrace, Shotton Colliery. Given away by her father, the brige wore a gown of broderie anglaise, with a tulle veil and head-dress of white freesia. She was attended by her sisters, Miss Patricia Simpson and Mrs Doreen Owen, wearing shaded cyclamen tulle with head-dresses to match. Best man was Mr Kent and groomsman Mr John Hickman. On leaving church the bride was presented with a silver horse-shoe by her cousin, Michael James. A congratulatory cablegram was received from the bride's brother-in-law, Mr Roland Owen, now working near the Niagra Falls in Canada. Reception in the Welfare Hall, Wheatley Hill was attended by 300 guests. Later the happy couple left for their honeymoon, which is to be spent touring London and Kent. The bride has been employed as manageress of Moore's Stores, Easington Colliery.

WHEATLEY HILL AIRMAN HONOURED

Representing his RAF Station at Waterbeach in the Guard of Honour at the King's funeral on Friday was Sgt Pilot John Atkinson (25), son of Mr and Mrs John Atkinson, well known local business people, of Front Street, Wheatley Hill.

Sgt Atkinson, who is married and has served in the Royal Air Force since he was 16, had a narrow escape only last November while flying a jet aircraft. When engine trouble developed he was compelled to make a forced landing. He was near a village at the time and just managed to keep his machine above the houses before hitting a tree. He escaped with only slight injuries.

Sgt Atkinson's elder brother, George, who was a Flight Sgt Pilot in the RAF, lost his life in 1943 while on a bombing raid in Germany.

DAMAGES FOR THORNLEY YOUTH

An accident at Wheatley Hill in June of last year had its sequel at Durham County Court on Monday when Judge H R P Gamon approved settlement of £75 damages for a 16-year-old Thornley youth, Kevin Hunt, bank hand, 8 Thornlaw South. The accident occurred when the plaintiff was riding his bicycle along Church Street, Wheatley Hill, and came into collision with a tractor owned by Mrs Ruth Mary Gregory, Rock Farm, Wheatley Hill, as the tractor turned into the farm entrance.

The youth was said to have made a good recovery from injuries he had received in the accident. His father, who accompanied him to court, corroborated. "He is all right now except for a pain in the back," he said. After the father had said that his son was allowed to look after his own money, Judge Gamon consented to £30 being paid over in court, the balance to be held by the court until the youth reached the age of 21, or unless the money was needed for a special purpose, in which case it could be drawn with the court's approval.

22 February 1952

MINERS' PENSION SCHEME TO BE COMPULSORY?

A resolution to make membership of the mineworkers' pension scheme a condition of employment was unanimously accepted by Durham Miners' Council when they met at Durham on Saturday. The resolution, from Eppleton Miners' Lodge, is to be forwarded to NUM headquarters asking for implementation.

About 89,000 are paying to the scheme, but a few thousand of these men have not signed the official pension form. They are warned that unless they do so before 1 June next they will lose all their back service credits. Meanwhile every effort is to be made to try and persuade those who have not officially joined to do so immediately. It was stated that Durham with a membership of 64 per cent had the second highest number of voluntary entrants in the scheme.

A progress report was given to the council on negotiations which have taken place with the Divisional Coal Board to inaugurate a county coal pool scheme in place of the present individual pit scheme. If an agreement can be reached with workers to give up part of their allowance, retired miners who are not already getting free coal will receive an allowance.

It was stated that progress had been made in the request by the Durham Area Union for a research and treatment centre for miners suffering from pneumoconiosis. The matter had been taken up with the Divisional Coal Board and it was understood that Dr Rogan, of the Manpower and Welfare Department of the Board, had arranged a meeting at Durham to discuss the request.

WEDDING – A Couple married at the Church of the English Martyrs, Thornley, on Saturday, received the Papal Blessing during Nuptial Mass, administered by Fathers Magin and Murray. They were Police Constable Joseph Carr, Batley, only son of Mr and Mrs T Carr, Front Street, Trimdon, and Miss Elizabeth Wilson, third daughter of Mr and the late Mrs M J Wilson, Nelson Street, Thornley. Miss M Scully was at the organ. Bride, given away by her father, wore a beige suit with blue and gold feathered hat, and was attended by her sister, Mrs Catherine Bruce, as matron of honour. Mr T Fleming was best man. The honeymoon is being spent at Harrogate.

INQUEST VERDICT – A Thornley retired miner, who was found dead in bed at 8 am on 19 February, was stated at the inquest at Thornley Police Station on Monday to have been partially disabled since he was wounded in the first World War while serving with the Lancashire Fusiliers. The inquest was on Henry Houghton Leigh (76), 21 Aged Miners' Homes. Leigh, it was stated, was shot in the left leg and was discharged from the Army in September 1916. He had been in receipt of an army pension. Medical evidence revealed that death was due to cardiac failure and the Coroner, Mr T V Devey, returned a verdict in accordance with this evidence, adding that Leigh's war wounds had been a contributing factor.

29 February 1952

MR RICHARD GIBSON – of Ludworth, at 35, is one of the youngest holders of the office of vice-chairman, Northern Area British Legion, which comprises 600 branches. While serving in the war in tanks he was awarded the MM and was Mentioned in Despatches for gallantry. Afterwards he volunteered for the mines and works at the coal face at Thornley. Married, with two young children, nearly all his spare time is devoted to Legion work.

He regards this work so well worth doing as so many grand fellows in the Services have, because of broken health, fallen on hard times. He feels that all, like himself, who are sound in wind and limb, should do their best to make life easier for their less fortunate comrades.

THORNLEY CHILD WELFARE CENTRE
Opened by Mr E Shinwell, MP

Opening Knayton House, Thornley, as the new headquarters of Thornley Child Welfare Centre, on Saturday, Mr E Shinwell MP for Easington, said that although the country was passing through an economic crisis the one thing we could not afford to dispense with was the care that was bestowed upon our young children.

Commenting on the progress made during recent years in children's welfare, Mr Shinwell said that in 1938 only five per cent of the children in this country had perfect teeth, but last year that figure had increased to 37.5 per cent. This was indeed a "vast improvement". Our children were our greatest national asset and if we were to maintain our position as a power everything depended upon how we looked after them.

Debt To Womenfolk

Referring to the voluntary work done by committees of Welfare Centres, Mr Shinwell declared it would be a "bad thing" for the country if the "well of voluntary action" ever dried up. It was one of the principal characteristics of the British people to respond to the needs of their fellow-men without accepting any sort of fee. In this voluntary work we were indebted a great deal to the women-folk.

Mrs E Clark, chairman of the voluntary committee at Thornley, presided at the opening ceremony and extended a warm welcome to Mr

Shinwell, and thanks to the former Minister of Defence were expressed by Dr A P Gray and Mrs B Bosomworth.

Despite the fact that they had been working under bad conditions in dilapidated premises at Thornley, Dr Williamson, the Child Welfare Medical Officer, said it spoke well not only for the work of the committee, but also for the co-operation of the mothers that the Centre had made considerable progress year after year. With new premises and better conditions even greater progress could be expected in the future.

To mark the opening of the new Centre the Mothers' Club presented half a tea-set for the use of the committee. Among the large representative gathering present were Dr R D Greenslade, Miss Frazer (Superintendent Health Visitor), Nurses Brewster and Gutteridge and Mrs D Roper and Mrs Anderson (secretary and treasurer, respectively, of the Centre).

7 March 1952

THORNLEY STILL "GOING STRONG"

Thornley CW continue to do well in their bid for the Wingate and District League title. Playing away to Black Boy (Quarrington Hill) last week, they recorded a grand 4-0 victory in spite of the fact they had four reserves in place of regulars who are injured. With the advantage of the wind in the first half, they opened the scoring in the fifth minute through centre-forward Kent, who outran two players before shooting a good goal from 10 yards. Fifteen minutes later Border (outside-right) increased the lead with a great shot from six yards. Black Boy attacks were few and far between, but they were rarely dangerous due to the sound Thornley defence. The game was stopped for 10 minutes as a result of both balls bursting.

Shortly after the interval Thornley centre-half had to retire injured, but in spite of this depletion they continued to have command. A long lob by Williams placed Kent in possession, who passed to Border, who went on to score No 3. Just before the end Border scored the fourth to complete his hat-trick – it was a well-placed penalty-kick.

Tomorrow, Thornley entertain Shotton CW in a league game. Selection of team has been deferred.

DIED AFTER WAR SERVICE

Evidence that he had frequently received medical treatment since his discharge from the army during first world war, suffering from nephritis contracted through malaria, was heard by the Coroner, Mr T V Devey, at the inquest at Thornley on Friday night, on William John Pyle (58), 15 Hillsyde Crescent, Thornley, who was found dead in bed on 4 March. The Coroner, after hearing a report from Dr Gray, recorded a verdict that death was due to heart failure and that Pyle's war illness had been a contributing factor. Mrs Margaret Pyle, the widow, said her husband was discharged from the army in 1917. He had been employed on light work at Thornley colliery, but had often been treated for nephritis and several times had been into the Ministry of Pensions Hospital. He was in receipt of a disability pension from the military authorities.

APPOINTMENT of Mr H L Rees (West Hartlepool) as head teacher of Wheatley Hill County Senior Boys' School has been confirmed by Durham County Education Committee. Six selected candidates were interviewed for the post. Mr Rees has been a member of the staff of the Henry Smith Grammar School, Hartlepool, for the past 22 years. Mr Rees, who has been senior history Master at the Grammar School, takes up his new appointment on 1 April. He succeeds Mr J Andrews, who was appointed county inspector of school meals during the latter part of last year.

14 March 1952

THORNLEY COUNTY COUNCIL CANDIDATE

There is an echo of the turbulent past of the women's suffrage movement in the nomination of Mrs Doris Adelaide Newton Roper, farmer's wife, of Thornley, as Independent candidate for the Thornley division of the Durham County Council at the election on 8 April. She makes a worthy opponent for Coun Emmerson Featherstone Peart, the sitting member, who, of course, has become known throughout the country as a tough fighter for the Council's "closed shop" policy.

Two of Mrs Roper's maternal aunts were in the front line of Mrs Pankhurst's women's suffrage army, and both were imprisoned. In a broadcast talk some years ago, Mrs Roper told the story of her aunts, and it was very evident from the talk that she had a great admiration for them. In her public work at Thornley she has often shown herself to be of the same fighting quality. This was so in Thornley Parish Council meetings

250

in recent months when she was very forceful on the question of a new child welfare centre. For six years she has been a JP and is a member of two committees appointed by Quarter Sessions. Locally she is the representative of SAAFA and the Society for the Prevention of Cruelty to Children.

DURHAM CHRONICLE IN MIDDLE EAST

Two Thornley men are interested in the back page of "The Durham Chronicle". They are LAC Abraham Walls (19) son of Mr and Mrs John Walls, 9 Thornlaw South, and AC1 A Jobes, son of Mr and Mrs Wm Jobes, Thornlaw. They met in Aden in the Middle East. Jobes has been in the RAF since November last year. Walls joined up for five years. He worked in Thornley pit, but his father says, "he always had a fancy for joining the services".

28 March 1952

THREE EAST-DURHAM PITS PASS TARGETS

Only three of the eight collieries in the No 3 Area (East Durham), Durham Division, NCB – Shotton, Thornley and Wheatley Hill – passed their targets last week, when the area's total output of 84,953 tons represented 98.61 per cent of the combined target of 86,150 tons.

Wheatley Hill had the best achievement, beating its target by nearly 6 per cent. Thornley passed its target by 4.26 per cent and Shotton by .93 per cent.

Individual outputs, with the targets in brackets, were: Horden 22,002 (22,750), Easington 16,499 (17,000), Blackhall 14,705 (15,000), Shotton 9,690 (9,600), Thornley 7,820 (7,500), Wheatley Hill 6,353 (6,000), Wingate 4,491 (4,800), Deaf Hill 3,390 (3,500).

4 April 1952

DIED IN LAMP CABIN - "Death from natural causes" was the verdict recorded by the Coroner, Mr T V Devey, at a Thornley inquest on Tuesday, on a 64-year-old bachelor, Thomas Grosvenor, 8 Galt Street, Thornley, who was found dying in the lamp cabin at Thornley colliery early on 9 April. Grosvenor, who was employed as a colliery caller, had, it was stated, been visiting his doctor for the past 12 months for minor rheumatic complaints. His sister, Mrs Mary Thompson, with whom he had lived for the past 45 years, said that when he left home for work at 9.45 pm on 8 April he complained of pains in his head. He had been suffering from these pains for some time and been taking tablets from his doctor. Apart from an odd day off work because of a cold, Grosvenor however, had never lost much work. Medical aid was summoned when he was found lying unconscious in the lamp cabin at 5.55 am on 9 April, but Grosvenor died before the arrival of the doctor.

MINEWORKERS' PENSIONS
Durham Coalfield Drive Planned

Arrangements are being made between Durham National Union of Mineworkers and Durham Divisional Coal Board for an all-out drive in the first week of June to secure 100 per cent membership of the new mineworkers' pension scheme. This, it is understood, was one of the decisions taken at a Durham Area Council, NUM, meeting in Durham. So far, 66 per cent of the miners in the county have voluntarily joined the scheme.

Personal interviews with every miner who has not yet "signed up" will be sought and arrangements made to assist them to complete the pension forms. The forms will be filled in for them and only the signature of the proposed members will be needed. This step is being taken because union leaders believe that many miners have not yet joined the scheme because of the form-filling it entails. Durham County has the fourth largest membership of the scheme in the country.

Holiday Payments

It was learnt after the council meeting that negotiations were scheduled to take place this week in London to decide how the second week's holiday payments for this year are to be made. There is much support for a proposal that payment for both weeks should be made at the same time. Durham County miners gave up their second week's holiday this year although they will still be paid for two weeks.

25 April 1952
LUDWORTH

Homing – Members of Ludworth Society sent 86 birds to Selby on Saturday. Prizewinners were B Vasey, and S Davis and partners.

Whist and Dominoes – For the first time for a number of years a whist and domino drive was held in the Village Hall, Ludworth, in aid of the hall renovation fund. Mr A Winter, on behalf of the committee, thanked the hostesses and helpers.

Legion Group Meeting – Mr A Winter (chairman of Ludworth British Legion) welcomed 19 delegates and 40 members at the group meeting at Ludworth on Saturday. Mr T Shaw (Seaham Harbour) presided. The arrangements were made for the group rally at Dubmire. Mr Richardson (Houghton) spoke on the pension scheme. The Northern Area vice-chairman (Mr R Gibson, MM), in moving a vote of thanks, requested members to keep up the campaign for higher disablement pensions. The Ludworth Women's Section served tea.

NATIONAL UNION OF MINEWORKERS
Holidays with Pay

Durham Area, National Union of Mineworkers, have been notified, from the NUM headquarters, to holidays with pay between May this year and April next year will be as follows:-

Annual Holiday – Males and females: 21 years of age and over, £9; 18 to 20 years inclusive, £7.4s; under 18, £5.8s.

Statutory Holidays – 21 years of age and over, 30s; 18 to 20 years inclusive, 24s; under 18, 18s.

The conditions in connection with these payments will be those which were in operation during the year May 1951 to April 1952. With regard to payment in lieu of the additional week of holiday in 1952, the Joint National Negotiating Committee have agreed that payment shall be made on the pay day preceding the taking of the holiday at the colliery concerned.

2 May 1952

MAY DAY DEMONSTRATION
Big Parade at Wheatley Hill

A procession nearly a mile in length, which included officials and members of eight miners' lodges in the Division and a number of women's sections of the Labour Party, preceded the speeches in the Welfare Hall, Wheatley Hill, at the May Day demonstration of Easington Divisional Labour Party on Saturday.

Headed by Wheatley Hill Colliery Band and officials of the party, with Mr E Shinwell, MP, the parade marched nearly two miles from the Ritz Cinema, Thornley, to Wheatley Hill.   ,

The miners' lodges represented, with their bands and banners, were Wheatley Hill, Thornley, Blackhall, Murton, Horden, Easington, Wingate and Shotton. Earlier, Wingate lodge had threatened to withdraw from the parade if their chairman marched alongside them under the banner. Their threat followed the action of their chairman, Mr William H Taylor, in opposing, as an Independent, the three official Labour candidates in this week's Wingate Ward elections for Easington Rural Council.

Not on Parade

Mr Taylor, however, was not in the parade, and so the threat did not materialise. Each lodge was strongly represented by members and supporters, and also present with their green and white banners were Wheatley Hill, Thornley, Blackhall, Murton, Horden and Shotton women's sections of the Labour Party.

The meeting in the Welfare Hall, presided over by Mr C St Julien, High Hesleden, newly-appointed chairman, was addressed by Mr Shinwell and Mrs D Turner (Sedgefield).

Dealing with the international situation, Mr Shinwell declared he believed that this country was united in the desire for peace. "It is unfortunate," he said, "that the Korean armistice talks should have been prolonged and so far produced no useful results. Now the Western nations are faced with a Russian Note which is of the utmost importance because it concerns Germany, the most likely danger spot in Europe. We may be suspicious about Russia, and there is some reason for our suspicions, but it would be very foolish indeed to reject the Russian Note without the most careful consideration".

If, went on Mr Shinwell, the Russians were seeking to promote negotiations which may last a long time, this should not prevent us from building up a defence organisation in the West.

Foresees "A Great Danger"

"I see a great danger in what is happening," said the speaker. "We may fail to produce peace in Europe and at the same time leave ourselves without adequate means of defence. That would mean complete victory for Communism.

"I warn the Government," he added, "that if they muck about with the nationalised industries it will only produce a further mess. I suppose we shall have to put up with the Tory Government a bit longer, but there is nothing more certain than that at the next election the Tories will not only be defeated, but will be almost swept out of existence".

Arrangements for the demonstration were in the hands of the divisional secretary (Mr T Toft, South Hetton), who, with County Coun E F Peart, walked alongside Mr Shinwell at the head of the winding procession.

9 May 1952

FOOTBALLERS' PRESENTATIONS

About 120 members and friends of Wheatley Hill Mechanics' Football Club (Wingate and District League) attended the club's annual supper in the Colliery Inn, Wheatley Hill, on Saturday night. The supper was served by wives of the committee members and entertainment was provided by the "Four Trumps" Concert Party, of Framwellgate Moor, under the leadership of Mr J Wright. Mr J L Snaith, manager of Wheatley Hill Colliery, and Mr R Darby, secretary of the Wingate and District League, were among the guests, and during an interval Mr Snaith presented miniature cups to the team successful in reaching the final of the Ferryhill Nursing Cup. The recipients were: Stanley Turnbull, Jonathon Sanderson, George Bean (capt), William Banks, Robert Williams, Eric Kirby, Norman Price, Raymond Carr, Robert Patterson, Wilfred Goyns and Leslie Lee, and reserves John Nicholson and Lawrence Blakemore. Mr W Ruth, chairman of the club, presided, and congratulated the team not only in ending as runners-up in the cup, but in finishing third off top in the league.

FIREMEN'S EFFORT

The Fire Services' National Benevolent Fund is expected to benefit by a handsome donation as a result of a successful concert in the Regal Cinema, Wheatley Hill, on Sunday afternoon, organised by Wheatley Hill Unit of the Durham County Fire Brigade. Principal artiste contributing to an excellent programme of vocal and musical items was Bobby Thompson, of "Wot Cheor, Geordie" fame, who was given a cordial reception by the large audience. Items were also given by Frank Derrick (Newcastle) on his piano-accordion, and Will Cowling (ventriloquist), Fence Houses. Other local artistes taking part were: Mr John Quin (baritone), Thornley; Dorothy Turner (soprano), Easington; Miss Anne McCoy (soprano), Thornley; Mr James Pyle, Wheatley Hill; Mr J Dodds, Mr R Harrison and Mr L Arnell, Deaf Hill; and Mr J Bell and Miss Bell, Easington. Mr John Tunney (Thornley) was compere and the accompanist was Mr J Cain. Thanks to all who had helped to make the effort such an outstanding success were expressed by the Chief Fire Officer for Durham County, Mr C V Hall. Arrangements were in the hands of Sub-Officer Stan Poulson, assisted by Leading Fireman F Horner and other Wheatley Hill firemen.

16 May 1952

THORNLEY CINEMA TO RE-OPEN

The Ritz Cinema, Thornley, which has been closed since it was severely damaged by fire in 1944, is expected to be re-opened in about a month's time.

This was revealed at Castle Eden court on Tuesday when Mr L A Hope, on behalf of Mr George Wheatley, Houghton-le-Spring, successfully applied for a licence for the cinema.

Difficulty in obtaining building materials during and shortly after the war had held up the work of re-building the cinema but, said Mr Hope, it had now been fully restored and would soon be ready for opening.

Supt A S Thornton, offering no objection to the licence, said that the cinema has been inspected by both the fire authorities and the police and a "very favourable" report had been presented. "Mr Wheatley has done everything possible to make the premises as safe as possible for use by the public," added the superintendent.

THORNLEY'S SUCCESS AT BELLE VUE - Competing in the senior cup section of the Spring Brass Band Festival at Belle Vue, Manchester, on Saturday, the Thornley Colliery Band (conductor, Mr E G T Kitto) was awarded second prize and the Belle Vue 50 guinea challenge cup, and a specially engraved illuminated certificate to mark the occasion, also a set of march-card covers presented by Messrs Quickfit Publishing Co, Rochdale. The test piece, "A Tone Poem" composed by Drake Rimmer, is based on incidents and personalities in the play by Shakespeare, "Othello".

HOMING – J Hartley filled the first three positions in the Ludworth Homing Club race from Peterborough on Saturday.

INSTITUTE COMMITTEE are making great efforts to raise funds for the hall. Recent activities have included a hostess whist and domino drive. On Monday the Shotton Players presented four one-act plays. Mr A Winter moved a vote of thanks.

CHALLENGE TO MINERS' LEADERS

Speaking at a social gathering at Thornley to celebrate the election of a full complement of Labour candidates at the recent local government elections at Thornley and Wheatley Hill, Ald Louis Martin (Wingate) offered a challenge to miners' leaders in the county of Durham to come forward and tell the miners where they stood in regard to the County Council's 'closed shop' policy. Ald Martin said it was evident that the miners were fully behind the County Council, but their leaders in Durham were very quiet on the matter. "This is a serious position," declared Ald Martin.

County Coun Peart, who presided at the gathering, said the successes of Labour in the elections was a magnificent victory. "This is the first time we can say that we have had a full complement of Labour Party representatives at Thornley and Wheatley Hill. The 'closed shop' must have put new life into the Party".

Those present included Councillors Miss E Bellinger, J J Johnson, Mrs F M Peart, J Williams, J Moore, Mesdames Harker, M Fleming, E Bosomworth, H Brewster, S Gott, H Slater, J Anderson, M Murray, J Nicholson, J Hoban, J McGregor, W Thompson, Mr T Toft (agent for Easington Divisional Labour Party), Mr J Harper (County Council Area agent) and Mr E Carter (Chairman of Thornley Miners' Lodge).

Speakers included Couns Mrs F M Peart, J Williams, M Fleming, J Nicholson. Entertainment was provided by the Thornley British Legion's women's section.

WORKMEN'S ESCAPE AT WHEATLEY HILL

Thirteen men on their way to work in a five-ton lorry from the Houghton area had a miraculous escape yesterday when the lorry collided with a fish wagon, and crashed on to its side near a zebra crossing at Vincent's Corner, Wheatley Hill. The lorry belonging to G M Pearson and Son, Hetton, was travelling up the bank from Thornley on its way to Sedgefield and the fish wagon was approaching it at right angles along Front Street, Wheatley Hill.

One of the workmen, John Applegarth (45), of 78 Fletcher Crescent, New Herrington, was taken to Dryburn Hospital with a suspected fracture above the left eye. Most of the others were treated for shock and slight injuries and some were taken home by ambulance.

Among them were Herbert Hill (33), 9 Mount Peasant, Houghton (shock and bruises); and William Sill (36), 4 Mildred Street, Houghton-le-Spring (head injuries and bruised eye). The driver of the lorry, Robert Robson (39), of 15 Ulswater Avenue, Easington Lane, was pinned in his cab as the vehicle overturned and his right elbow went through the side window.

Apart from a cut elbow and shock, he was uninjured. He was quickly freed from the cab by other workmen.

Considerable damage was done to the vehicle. The radiator and the cab of the fish wagon, driven by Robert Starling (33), of Rockside, 12 Pesspool Terrace, Haswell, were extensively damaged. Boxes of fish were strewn all over the road. Police controlled traffic for about three hours until the vehicle was removed.

WHEATLEY HILL AMBULANCE FUND TO CONTINUE

At a special meeting of subscribers to the Wheatley Hill Colliery Hospital and Ambulance Fund, presided over by Mr R Hird on Sunday, it was agreed to continue to operate a local ambulance service in the village and to end the "agency" with the Durham County Ambulance Service which has been in existence since 1948. So that there would be sufficient funds to run the service without aid from the county, it was agreed to double the present weekly levy of three pence.

Officials and members of the Fund felt that the ambulance service could be run more efficiently locally than if they were associated with the county service. A letter from the County Ambulance Officer stated that as the County Council now had its full establishment of ambulances the question of ending the Wheatley Hill "agency" service would have to be considered. The Wheatley Hill Fund, said the County Officer, was now the last agency in operation in the county. "We would like to say," ran the letter "that your assistance since the beginning of the scheme has been invaluable". A special tribute was paid to the Wheatley Hill ambulance driver, Mr Mullen, who "had done so much to establish good relations and given good service throughout".

The treasurer of the Fund, Mr H Bradshaw, reported that since 1948 a total of £2,931 had been received from the county authority for the "agency" ambulance service at Wheatley Hill, and the workmen at the colliery had contributed £2,359 by levy. Each year train fares for patients going for treatment and totalled £120 and the running costs were

approximately £330 a year. Subscribers to the Fund going to Conishead Convalescent Homes had received £2 each from the Fund, which had also met three-quarters of the cost of surgical appliances.
30 May 1952

Road Traffic Accident at Vincents Corner, May 1952

THORNLEY FOOTBALL CLUB CELEBRATE

There was a good gathering of players and supporters at Thornley CW Football Club's "social" in the local Club Hall, to celebrate a successful season. Mr Charles Lamb (president) said the team had done very well to finish runners-up in the Wingate and District League.

"But the mere winning of medals is not the most important thing," went on Mr Lamb. "It is how the players conduct themselves on the field that matters most. In all the games I saw in which Thornley were participants our lads showed fine sportsmanship. What also impressed was the excellent team spirit.

"Behind the team was the inspiration of a good committee," continued Mr Lamb. "We had a fine chairman in Mr Armstrong, a good secretary in Mr Bob Bullock, a grand treasurer in Mr Bosomworth, and a fine trainer in Mr Bullock. We were also fortunate in having the backing of a small band of women in the Ladies' Supporters' Club".

Mr Lamb presented medals to A Abbs, J Nicholson, A Smith, H Carr, L Williamson, G Armstrong, W Luke, W Border, J Kent, J Laverick and G Brownless. Following members of the Ladies' Supporters' Club served at the tea tables – Mesdames E Williamson, M Bullock, C Bosomworth, P Cook, R Bullock and N Fleecher. Entertainment was provided by Tom and Joe Kent, Jim Cookson, Bill Taylor, E Davis, D Docherty, R Cockburn, P Gallagher and Peggy Hopps. Mr R Bullock (secretary) gave a vote of thanks, and Mr R Darby (secretary of the Wingate League) also paid tribute to the sportsmanship of the Thornley players.

1 June 1952

MR E F PEART REBUKED
Protest by Thornley Miners

We have been asked by Mr W Dowding, 15 Burn Street, Wheatley Hill, correspondence secretary to Thornley Miners' Lodge, to print the following:

"It was said at our last lodge meeting that County Coun Peart had been reported as saying 'I could have a strike at Thornley Colliery tomorrow over the colour of the wagons if I could guarantee them full pay. This comment followed his statement that the teachers were being assured of full pay for their 'strike de luxe.

Our members object to the irrational and irresponsible statement made concerning Thornley Colliery and its workers and protest against the implications it contains, namely, that if full pay were guaranteed to them they would come out on strike for any reason, just or otherwise".

WEST CORNFORTH MAN MARRIED AT WHEATLEY HILL

Professional footballer Walter Miller, son of Mr and Mrs J Miller, 27 Poplar Terrace, West Cornforth, was married in Patton Street Methodist Church, Wheatley Hill, on Saturday to Miss Eileen Kirby, elder daughter of Mr and Mrs T Kirby, 16 Shinwell Terrace, Wheatley Hill. The bridegroom, who is at present serving in the RAF equipment section stationed at Gainsborough, plays for Luton Town and was previously with Hartlepool and Spennymoor clubs. His twin brother Wilfred, who is also serving in the RAF at the same station, was best man. Rev N Catherall officiated and Mr W Luke, jun, was organist.

The bride, who is a cashier with Messrs Doggarts at Wingate, wore a white cloche gown with veil and orange blossom headdress. She carried pink carnations and was given away by her uncle, Mr J Bedford. Her brother, Mr E Kirby, was groomsman. Bridesmaids, in turquoise dresses, were Misses Kathleen Kirby (bride's sister) and P Marrin. After a reception at the home of the bride's parents, Mr and Mrs Miller left for their honeymoon at Scarborough, the bride travelling in a blue costume.

6 June 1952

TO SEABURN – Wheatley Hill Workmen's Club and Institute held annual trip for members' children on Saturday. Two special trains conveyed nearly 1,000 children and their parents to Seaburn. Although the weather was not good, the children had an enjoyable time. Each child received 5s from the club and there were competitions of various descriptions on the sands. Mr John Gibson, chairman of the club, was handicapper, and cash prizes amounting to nearly £10 were distributed. Arrangements were made by Mr T Storey (secretary).

LATE MR H E FROST – After a service in Church Street Methodist Church, conducted by the Rev W T Rose (Thornley), the funeral took place on Saturday of Mr Henry Ernest Frost (67), 10 Jack Lawson Terrace, Wheatley Hill. Mr Frost left Yorkshire to work at Ryhope Colliery in 1908, and a few years later went to Shotton Colliery and then on to Wheatley Hill Colliery, where he retired a year ago. He was presented with a certificate for 50 years' membership of the DMA. During the 1914-18 war Mr Frost served in the DLI as a sergeant-major and was gassed after going to France. He was a former secretary of Wheatley Hill Soldiers' and Sailors' Club, and leaves a widow, three daughters and a son.

27 June 1952

THORNLEY PITHEAD BATHS AND CANTEEN

At midnight on Monday representatives of the National Coal Board took over from representatives of the pithead baths and canteen trustees, all their buildings, stocks and plant. This comes about owing to the recent passing of the Miners' Welfare Act. The sole management of the baths and canteens will now rest with the Coal Board. Baths and canteen trustees and committees will go out of office as soon as the assets and liabilities are finally agreed. In the future questions arising between workmen and the management of the baths and canteens will be dealt with by the existing consultative committees.

The Board has agreed that credit balances existing after all liabilities have been met can be used for local miners' welfare purposes.

The Act provides that disputes in arriving at the final figures - which, of course, might affect the balance to be turned over to local welfare schemes – can be referred to arbitration.

Miners' welfare institutes and outdoor schemes will not be affected by the above mentioned transfer. The committees jointly representing the Board and the workmen will continue in office and will continue to manage as formerly.

4 July 1952

GARDEN PARTY AT THORNLEY

There was a large attendance at the second annual garden party of the Church of the Sacred Heart and English Martyrs in the St Godric's football field, Thornley, on Saturday. Items were given by Wheatley Hill Colliery Prize Band and refreshments were served in a marquee by members of the Catholic Women's League.

Tug-o'-war contest results were: Men, M Connell's team; Women, McCoy's team. PC Jackson supervised a road safety competition and made the following awards: Best rider: under 11, girls, P Burke; boys, T Hoban; 11 to 15, girls, M Durkin; boys, T Ashford; roadworthy machine: under 11, girls, P Burke; boys, T Hoban; over 11, girls, M Walls; boys, B Bell; road signs: under 11, J Regan; 11 to 15, J Mangles, M Walls.

Sports: Baby boys: T Barlow; girls, D English; second class: boys, J Cairns; girls, C Davis; bunny race: boys, D McCoy; girls, M Armstrong; second class: boys, J Cairns; girls, J Stoll; 7 years: boys, P Luke; 6 years: boys, R Ewens; girls, J Swann; potato race: P Luke; hoop race: K Boulger; skipping race: M Connelly; obstacle race: E Lennox; egg and spoon: J Poulson; flat races: 8 years, J Ridley (girls); M Tinkler (boys); 11 to 15, F Ashford (boys); V McCoy (girls); 7 to 11, H Morton (boys); P Burke (girls); three-legged race: Smyth and Hoban (boys); Ramshaw and Ellis (girls); relay race: P Bonar's team (boys); V Connelly's team (girls).

11 July 1952

WHEATLEY HILL STUDENT'S SUCCESS – After five years at Edinburgh University, Mr John Patrickson Shutt (22), second son of Mr and Mrs J F Shutt, Thornley Road, Wheatley Hill, has qualified as a doctor, winning the degrees of MB (Bachelor of Medicine) and ChB (Bachelor of Surgery). With his parents he attended the convocation at the university on Wednesday.

Mr Shutt, whose father is general manager of Sherburn Hill Co-operative Society, is a former pupil of Henry Smith Grammar School, Hartlepool. Next week he sets sail for New York, USA, to take up his first appointment as a member of the medical staff of a hospital on the outskirts of the city.

LUDWORTH – Welcome Home – After eight years in Canada, Mrs Tetro, daughter of Mr and Mrs Yule, Barnard Avenue, Ludworth, has returned home for three months' holiday to recuperate after a serious operation. Over 100 people attended a "Welcome Home" tea given by the British Legion Women's Section. Mrs Tetro was presented with a necklace by Mrs Shepherd (chairman). Mrs Tetro said she felt over-whelmed at the warmth of her welcome. After tea (cake was presented by Mrs Yule) a happy evening followed and many prizes were won. Mrs Tetro married a Canadian and has two children. Twice she and her family have been flooded out of their homes, but now live on higher ground.

WINGATE PARISH COUNCIL

When the Clerk announced that 25 new 80-watt street lamps had been received for distribution in the parish, it was agreed to allocate ten each to Wheatley Hill and Wingate and five to Deaf Hill. Now that the roads were "well-lighted", said the Clerk, the council had agreed to concentrate on better lighting for the back streets. The new lamps will be used for such a purpose and it was left with the councillors in each parish to decide where they should be erected.

Other Matters

It was decided to apply to the Easington Rural Council for five new road-side seats for Wingate, three for Wheatley Hill and two for Deaf Hill. "These seats are especially appreciated by the old men of the village," commented Coun J T Gilchrist.

After a discussion lasting three-quarters of an hour on the question of raising the wages of the Wheatley Hill cemetery superintendent, Mr J C Stott, it was decided to give him an increase of 2s.6d weekly. Mr Stott wrote saying that at present he received 7s.6d more than the superintendent at Deaf Hill cemetery, which was also in Wingate Parish. In the past, however, there had always been a 10s difference between their wages – he would like this difference restored.

Before the Council agreed to the half-crown increase so that Mr Stott would continue to be paid 10s more than the Deaf Hill superintendent, two other motions were defeated. One of these sought to give the Wheatley Hill superintendent an increase of 12s.6d and the other to give him an increase of 8s.6d and the Deaf Hill superintendent an increase of 6s.

A report of the Parish Councils' Association Conference held at Blackpool last month was given by the Clerk, who attended with Coun G B Hobbs.

The meeting was presided over by Coun J Carter, Deaf Hill.

WHEATLEY HILL AMBULANCE SUCCESSES

In their recent first aid examination the following members of Wheatley Hill Ambulance Class were successful:-

Preliminary certificates: D Herring, D Alderton, A White. First year certificates: J Hodson, J Carr, H Carr, W Vincent, R Maughan, H Poole, W Poole, F Martin, W Warnes, W Forrest, J Lewis, T Chapman, A Alderton, J Alderton, A Martin, J Amies, J Graham, J Sunley, T Todd, C V Brown, J Gair, J Pringle, T Harper, M Foster, J Johnson, J Cook, J Scrafton, M Simons, T Smyth, F Winnard, H Wilson, R Hodgson, J Coates, Miss Rita Banks and Miss Jean Hughes. Vouchers: J Sims and W Hicks. Medallion: J Pratt. Labels: T W Ayre, A Thomas, R Wilson, R Walton, E Dawes, R Watson, J Booth, A Watson, J Jones, O Warnes, P Leck, O Rowlands, S Poulson, I Hughes and G Armstrong.

Examiner was Dr Barrie Scott (Shotton Colliery). Dr A P Gray (Wheatley Hill) was surgeon instructor; Mr G Buxton, class instructor, and Mr Richard W Storey, class secretary.

18 July 1952

WHEATLEY HILL VICTORIES

Two cousins, both named Bobby Patterson, took the batting honours when Wheatley Hill recorded a dual success in the Durham Coast League on Saturday. Bobby, jun, carried his bat for 60 in the first eleven's four wicket victory over Boldon, while Bobby, sen, secretary of the club, was also undefeated for 29 in the second team win by 47 runs over Boldon seconds.

Playing at Wheatley Hill, Boldon were dismissed for 97, T Robson being their top scorer with 34. George Lumley took three wickets for 22, W Marshall two for 16 and E Lambton two for 18.

The "Hill's" first four wickets produced only 22 runs but thanks to a faultless fifth wicket partnership between Patterson and T Hall (23 not out), the visitors' score was wiped off without further loss. No fewer than 50 of Patterson's 60 runs were made up of boundary hits – 11 fours and one six. Gilbert took three wickets for 30. Scores:

Boldon: 97

Wheatley Hill: G Allison c Noble b Gilbert 0, J Charlton c Humphries b Gilbert 8, R Patterson jun not out 60, G Gribbens b Gilbert 4, D Alderton b Humphries 2, T Hall not out 23, extras 5, total (for four wickets) 102.

Visiting Boldon II, in Division II of the Coast League, Wheatley Hill scored 102 then quickly sent the home team back for 55. Other "double-figure" batsmen, besides Patterson, were G Carr (13), T Shearsmith (11) and A Fishwick (10).

Four Wheatley Hill wickets were taken by B Johnson for only 16 runs and B Poulson had four for 47. Chiefly responsible for Boldon's dismissal were George Carr with five wickets for 20 and W Turnbull with four for 20.

CHARMIAN'S GALLANT DISPLAY
In Olympics Swimming Test

The outstanding performance of 15-year-old Charmian Welsh, of Thornley, Durham High School girl and "baby" of the British Olympics team, has warmed the hearts of sports enthusiasts throughout the county and particularly her fellow members of Durham City ASC, who have closely followed her progress in the Games at Helsinki.

In nerve-testing competition against the cream of the world's aquatic talent, Charmian was placed fifth in the three-metre springboard finals on Wednesday. Now she is one of the great, and by the time the next Olympics come round, she will undoubtedly be one of Britain's biggest hopes for a gold medal.

While she was well behind the more experienced American who led the placings, Charmian declared after the events that she could have done better. Her best dive of the day was a backward spring, one and a half somersault with forward tuck, which scored 14.44 marks, bringing her total to 116.38 points.

Coached By Norman Sarsfield

Two weeks before her 11th birthday, Charmian could not swim a stroke, and it was only two years ago that she started diving. Much has been made of the alleged fact that she learnt her diving from text-books. Nothing could be further from the truth. The real fact is that for the past two years she has been carefully and systematically coached by one of the most competent instructors in Durham County, and possibly in the country – Mr Norman Sarsfield, captain of Durham City AFC.

Charmian won her first award for diving at the City Baths shortly after she started – a small St Christopher medallion. She considers it her lucky talisman and wherever Charmian goes, so does "St Christopher".

The competitions at Helsinki are only the third three-metre springboard competitive events she has taken part in. Asked if she had anything to say about her daughter's remarkable performance, Mrs Welsh said: "There is nothing I can say that hasn't already been said. I think she did wonderfully well".

Charmian's performance will be of particular satisfaction to Ald H C Ferens (president), who gave a new three-metre springboard to Durham City Club in time for her to get in some practice before the Games.

On 18 August Charmian goes to New Brighton to compete in the ASA diving championships.

1 August 1952

THORNLEY IS FAMOUS
In Industry As Well As In Sport

The return home of 15-year-old Charmian Welsh, Durham High School girl, who, by her remarkable performance in the Olympic diving championships, spotlighted her native village of Thornley, recalls to many of its older inhabitants previous occasions when the village has hit the sports headlines.

At one period in its history, Thornley turned out champions in almost mass-production. The years leading up to the end of the last century and the first few years of the present century saw men from the Durham mining village smashing records in almost every field of sporting endeavour.

Those were the halcyon years when men like Jack Kitto, Jackie Shaw and Jack Beresford reigned supreme in their particular fields. It was also at this time that Thornley mourned the death of one of the greatest athletes of his day. Who in Thornley even today has never heard of the great George Wallace, who, round about the 1860s, knocked the bottom out of many of the national sprint records. Perhaps his greatest performance was when he won the national 220 yards Sheffield Handicap in even time. George died at the early age of 43, a pauper in a Newcastle public house. The landlord bore the expense of his funeral.

Fives Champion

In the early '90s Jack Beresford became the unofficial "fives" champion of the world when he took on and beat all-comers at Tudhoe Park. A few years later Tom Nicholson took the unofficial championship of potshare bowling and retired unbeaten. He did most of his bowling on the sands at Seaton Carew.

During those years Jack Kitto floored the best of the country's light-weight wrestling (Cumberland style) exponents and the word Thornley was whispered with reverence in wrestling circles throughout the country. Jack Kitto's son, Mr "Teddy" Kitto lives today in the neighbouring village of Wheatley Hill. He also is a champion. But his talents are directed in the field of music. He is leader of Thornley Colliery Prize Band and holds numerous awards.

And In Quoits

It would be strange indeed if Thornley could not also boast a quoits champion. Well, who was there in all England to touch Jackie Shaw for almost ten years?

When the 19th century Thornley man could not get in enough sport in his leisure hours, he squeezed it from his work. Take this cutting from "Surtees' Local Records" for example: "Two miners of Thornley Colliery, Co Durham – Storey and Surtees – agreed to hew coal against each other for five guineas a side. The wager was won by Storey who hewed 33½ tubs of 20 pecks each. Surtees hewed 30 tubs. The former weight was 10 tons 1 cwt and the latter nine tons. The man Storey earned 11s.2d and Surtees 10s. The time taken was eight hours and owing to the extreme hardness of the seam the performance can be considered unprecedented".

In later years, Thornley has also been the breeding ground of many first-class footballers including English schoolboy international Stan Lloyd.

CINEMA RE-OPENED – The Ritz Cinema, Thornley, which suffered serious damage by fire during the last war, was re-opened by its proprietor, Mr George Wheatley, of Houghton, on Friday night. A complete new roof was given to the building five years ago, but since then Mr Wheatley has had considerable difficulty, owing to the national stringencies, in getting the necessary material to enable him to carry out his desire to re-open the cinema. He has, however, managed to effect the work necessary to re-open. Some time ago Thornley Parish Council used their endeavours to assist, asking Mr Shinwell, the MP for the Easington Division, to impress upon the various Government departments the need for the cinema to be refitted.

MISS THORNLEY – MISS CRIMDON
Mr Shinwell Chooses Beauty Queen

Mr Gilbert Oliver, entertainments manager at Easington Rural Council's holiday lido at Crimdon, took a gamble on Monday – and it came off!

All morning he had looked anxiously at the skies and his face grew gloomier as heavy showers fell with monotonous regularity. It was Crimdon's "Big Day" of the year – the choosing of "The Beauty Queen", and the problem facing Mr Oliver was should he take the risk that the weather would clear up and hold the contest in the open-air in the Dene, where he knew thousands could be comfortably accommodated? Or should he cancel all arrangements for the judging out-of-doors and hold the contest in the Pavilion, where he knew everybody would be uncomfortably packed tighter than the proverbial sardine?

The problem still faced Mr Oliver after lunch for still the rain fell and there was only a faint glimmer of blue sky in the far distance. Mr Oliver looked at that "bit of blue" and decided to take a gamble! The contest would take place in the Dene! And, before a holiday crowd of many thousands, the contest did take place in the natural amphitheatre of the picturesque Dene with old King Sol beaming down and chasing the clouds and the gloom away.

Mr Oliver's gamble had come off. Shortly before the "beauty parade" began, as if a magic wand had been waved, the sun shone with all its power and its smiling face was reflected in the happy countenances of the men, women and children who flocked into the Dene from all directions.

Their Big Moment

Mr E Shinwell, MP for Easington Division and former Defence Minister – "Manny" to his many friends among the pit-folk – was there with his wife to judge the contest. The 12 finalists, all of them chosen at dances held throughout the Easington Rural Area during recent months, put the "final touches" to their make-up in the large marquee adjoining the band-stand. Then, accompanied by suitable music relayed over the loud-speaker system, they walked gracefully towards the band-stand, up the steps, then lined up, somewhat nervously, before Mr and Mrs Shin-well.

Then it came the turn of the crowd. One by one the village "queens" mounted several steps to reach a small platform where for a few brief seconds, they smilingly posed before the vast sea of faces and were cheered loud and long. It was their "big moment" of the "Big Day".

Again they lined up before the former Defence Minister and his wife and it was evident that the task of choosing the winner was proving extremely difficult. For they all were "bonnie lasses" and "dressed for the occasion"; formed a line of beauty that would have compared favourably with any in the British Isles.

Mr Shinwell had to confess that his task was difficult. "The girls are all good-looking," he told the crowd – as if they needed to be told that! "But," he added, "we have got to select the three best – I only wish we could select the lot"! Then, after Mr Shinwell had whispered the name of the winner to Mr Oliver, he smiled to the holiday-makers, "I hope this is not going to lose me the next election"!

Daughter of Thornley Miner

As Mr Oliver walked towards the microphone to announce the winner there was a sudden hush – and the hearts of all the finalists themselves must have beaten just a little faster! Then the name of the winner was announced – Miss Elizabeth Peacock, the 17-year-old daughter of a Thornley miner. Cheer after cheer filled the air as Miss Peacock stepped forward to receive the "Miss Crimdon 1952" silken sash, a beautiful bouquet and the first prize of £5 from Mrs Shinwell. An attractive brunette, with an infectious smile, Miss Peacock is the only daughter of

Mr and Mrs G Peacock, 6 High Street, Thornley. She is on the nursing staff of Shotley Bridge Hospital.

The runner-up was Miss Joan Glaister of Deaf Hill. Joan, who reaches her 16th birthday this month, is the younger daughter of Mr and Mrs W Glaister, 16 May Crescent, Deaf Hill, and is employed as a shop assistant in her village. Her father is a miner at Trimdon Grange colliery. The third prize went to Miss Muriel Elwell (19), daughter of Mr and Mrs N S Elwell, 12 Sycamore Terrace, Haswell. Miss Elwell was actually the "stand-in" for the girl originally chosen to be "Miss Haswell", namely, Miss Hilda Turner, 15 Windsor Terrace, Haswell, who withdrew from the competition because of a family bereavement.

Bouquets were presented both to Miss Glaister and Miss Elwell as well as cash prizes and, with the winner, they smilingly posed for photographs with Mr Shinwell's arms around them. All the finalists were then entertained to tea with Mr and Mrs Shinwell and officials of Easington Rural Council, including the Clerk, Mr J W Gray.

For half an hour before the judging took place excellent entertainment was provided by Bobby Thompson, the well-known Tyneside comedian, of "Wot Cheor, Geordie" fame, Jimmy Elliott, Hetton-le-Hole's "own" comedian, and Miss Lorna Dean of Newcastle, who gave a lively "song and dance" turn. The accompanist was Mr Michael Hill, Newcastle. A Civil Defence display, arranged by Easington Rural Council, also thrilled the crowd.

Mr Shinwell congratulated Easington Rural Council on their efforts to popularise Crimdon and paid a warm tribute to the work of the entertainments manager, Mr Oliver. "I think Mr Oliver deserves a special word for the part he is playing in the remarkable progress which is being made at the lido," added Mr Shinwell. "I haven't the least doubt but that in the coming years Crimdon will be the greatest and finest and most extensive and enjoyable workers' playground in the United Kingdom".

Mr Shinwell was introduced to the holiday crowd by Coun T Akenhead, chairman of Easington Rural Council, who, in turn, was introduced by Coun R W Rowe, chairman of the Parks Committee. A warm welcome was also extended to Mrs Shinwell, who was charmingly presented with a bouquet by six-year-old Jean Rowe, daughter of Coun Rowe.

Many Visitors

The weather remained warm and sunny for the remainder of the Bank Holiday and Crimdon was thronged with visitors until late evening. One of the main attractions was an old-time dance in the Pavilion, where music was supplied by Norman Richardson and his Band.

Considering the bad start to the day, Mr Oliver told our reporter, he was well satisfied with the day's receipts. "The week-end's takings were an increase on last August Bank Holiday," he said. "The heavy morning rain undoubtedly stopped a lot of people from venturing out".

FAMILY HOLIDAY CUT SHORT
Tragic Death of Miss D Briggs, Ludworth

The lamentable death of Miss Dorothy Briggs while on holiday at Douglas, Isle of Man, plunged the whole of the village of Ludworth into sorrow. She was aged 37. The sorrow was heightened by the fact that the holiday was organised by Miss Briggs on behalf of the family to celebrate the golden wedding of their parents, Mr and Mrs Thomas Briggs. The actual date of the golden wedding was 28 June.

The happy family party, which left Greatham airport for Douglas on 26 July, consisted of Mr and Mrs Briggs, Dorothy, her sister Ella, Mr and Mrs J Charlton (her sister and brother-in-law) of Wheatley Hill, and her niece, 11-year-old Ella Sunley of Wheatley Hill. An hour and a half after leaving Greatham, the plane landed near Douglas. A programme of sightseeing, supervised by Miss Briggs, was gone through on Saturday and Sunday, but on Monday morning, after breakfast, she complained of a pain in her chest. A doctor was soon in attendance, but Miss Briggs, who had been taken upstairs because she felt sick, died immediately.

The Funeral

Mr Briggs informed our representative that the authorities in Douglas extended to the family every kindness and assistance in their serious predicament. The parents returned on Monday in the same aeroplane to Greatham, but the others travelled by steamer from Douglas to Liverpool with Miss Briggs' coffin.

Many villagers attended the funeral on Saturday afternoon. Interment was at Shadforth cemetery following a service conducted by Canon T Tillard (Rector). Among many floral tributes were wreaths from the management, foremen, staff, workmates and the General Work-

271

ers' trade union branch at the ICI explosives factory at Tuthill, near Haswell, where Miss Briggs had worked for nearly 13 years. She was on the graded staff at the factory, and in a letter of condolence to her parents the firm said they had come to regard her as one of their best workers. Interested in church work and the social work of the village, Miss Briggs was a regular communicant at Ludworth (St Andrew's) Mission Church.

CHARMIAN WELSH

The fine performance of the Olympics diver, Charmian Welsh, the 15-year-old Thornley girl, was the subject of comment at Durham County Council's meeting on Wedneday. "This girl as been a credit to the county," stated Coun W Baines, Education Committee chairman, who asked that a letter of congratulations should be sent to her.

Coun Peart, who lives at Thornley, said that Charmian had brought honour to the county, and Thornley Parish Council had decided to circulate organisations for contributions towards a fund with a view to giving her some tangible recognition of her accomplishment.

City's Congratulations

The Mayor of Durham (Coun G McIntyre) has sent a letter to Charmian congratulating her on her fine performance at Helsinki. The letter states: "We in the City of Durham are very proud of your wonderful diving display and you, I am sure, realise that you went to the Olympic Games with all the good wishes from we people in Durham City. Please accept my personal good wishes and congratulations".

Commenting on Charmian's feat, at the meeting of Durham City Council on Wednesday, the Mayor said they were particularly proud of her effort because she was trained in Durham swimming baths by Mr Norman Sarsfield, captain and coach of Durham City Amateur Swimming Club.

8 August 1952

THORNLEY'S PRIDE

Sir, Our Parish Council feel that the people of Thornley would like to make a gift in kind to Miss Charmian Welsh in recognition of the great honour she has earned for herself – and for Thornley and the County of Durham – in being chosen to represent Great Britain at the Olympic Games at Helsinki, in which seventy countries, includ-

ing all the great countries of the world and our own Commonwealth, were competing.

To get into the British team – after tough competition at Blackpool – was in itself proof that she is a fine young athlete; but her success in reaching the final against the best women divers (3-metre springboard) of all the other countries was indeed a performance which we think deserves to be marked in a tangible way.

This appeal for donations to the gift fund is primarily intended for Thornley people, but contributions from anyone residing outside Thornley who feels admiration for Miss Welsh's performance would be welcomed. Donations would be gladly welcomed by the treasurer, Mr T H Holder, Clerk to the Thornley Parish Council, Villas, Thornley, Durham. It is hoped to close the fund on 1 September.

E F Peart
Chairman of Thornley Parish Council

KILLED IN PIT – While employed as a conveyor man in the Busty seam at Wheatley Hill colliery on Tuesday afternoon, Thomas William Piercy (43), 41 Wheatley Terrace, Wheatley Hill, was killed out-right by a fall of stone. In accordance with local custom the pit was laid idle for the rest of the day. Mr Piercy, who had been back at work only a week after his annual holiday, had been employed at the colliery since leaving school. He had lived in the village all his life and was held in high esteem throughout the area. He was secretary of the Darts Club at the Tavern Inn, Wingate Lane. Mr Piercy is survived by his wife, three sons and a daughter. His eldest son, Edwin, has been serving in the RASC in Egypt for nearly three years. Mr Piercy is to be buried at Wheatley Hill cemetery tomorrow (Saturday 16th) following a service in All Saints' Church.

NARROW ESCAPE – A 20-year-old colliery apprentice electrician, William Chisholm Warnes, elder son of Mr and Mrs O Warnes, 12 Thirteenth Street, Wheatley Hill, had a narrow escape from being electrocuted at Wheatley Hill on Tuesday afternoon. While linking up a new service line with the main electricity cable at the top of an electric light standard near Peterlee Cottages he received a severe shock. The safety belt by which he was held to the standard prevented him from falling and for a short spell he was unable to free his hands from the electrically

273

charged cable. Charles Thompson, another electrician working with him, rushed to cut off the current, then he and Cyril Raffell, who was also working on the job, got Warnes safely to the ground. He was taken to Dryburn Hospital, where later his condition was stated to be satisfactory. Warnes started work only on Monday after a hitch-hiking holiday in France.

15 August 1952
COUNTY PRESS COMPETITION ATTRACTS LARGE ENTRY
Football for Wheatley Hill

Already the weekly Durham County Press competition for the most meritorious performance by a football club in Durham county has attracted considerable interest and there were many entries as a result of last Saturday's games. It will be recalled that entries for this competition should be in the hands of the Sports Editor, Newspaper House, Durham, by first post each Tuesday and that a small committee will award a football weekly to the club producing the most meritorious performance.

High scoring feats will not always win the competition, and the best quality football will on occasions go to a team which has ended on the losing side. It may be that an individual performance of especial merit will capture the ball for the club concerned, but team work will generally hold sway.

Great Revival Earns Success

The first competition of this campaign has been won by a team which had a poor season in the Central league last year and have now started off this campaign by beating the runners-up, Craghead CW, on their own ground. The team concerned is that from Wheatley Hill Sports Club, secretary, Mr Frederick Smith, 11 Cooper's Terrace, Thornley.

In his claim on behalf of the club Mr Smith points out that last season they finished second from the foot of the table and did not gain one single point away from home. Their eight points were all secured from home matches.

Their first attempt this season has brought two points away from no less a team than Craghead CW. Craghead were the runners-up last season, and are turning out nearly the same side as performed so well then.

Ludworth's Feat

Others "knocking at the door" for this week's award were such clubs as Ludworth Juniors, who had a poor season during last campaign but who, now in the Durham and District Junior League, visited strong Pittington Juniors and won by 4-2. In an ordinary week this achievement by Ludworth may well have won the award for no doubt great improvement is meritorious.

Feature of the Ludworth victory was that three of their goals were recorded by an ex-schoolboy player who was chosen to play for Stanley United in the Northern League.

LATE MRS I MIDDLETON

A large cortege, including many of her friends in the Methodist Church, attended the funeral at Wheatley Hill cemetery on Monday of Mrs Isabella Middeleton (42), 4 Luke Terrace, Wheatley Hill, who died in Winterton Hospital, where she had been a patient for five weeks. It is only 13 months ago that Mrs Middleton's husband, William, died. Three daughters and one son, ranging in age from eight to 17, are left orphans. A life-long Methodist, Mrs Middleton was a member of the Patton Street Methodist Church, Wheatley Hill, and was also actively associated with the Sisterhood and, some years ago, with the choir. She was also a member of Wheatley Hill Mothers' Club. For some time she worked as a "nanny" at Wheatley Hill Infants' School. Mrs Middleton, who was the youngest daughter of Mrs Isabella Burrell, 3 Stephen's Terrace, Wheatley Hill, was buried following a service in the Patton Street Church conducted by the Rev Noel Catherall. Sisterhood members of both Wheatley Hill Methodist Churches together with members of the Mothers' Club preceded the cortege and there were many beautiful floral tributes.

29 August 1952

SHE DOES IT AGAIN!
Charmian "Stars" In Swimming Gala

You just can't keep Charmian Welsh out of a swimming story. This 15-year-old Thornley Miss with the golden Helsinki tan collected yet another title when she eclipsed five other competitors to retain the North-Eastern Counties Ladies' one-metre springboard championship at Durham on Friday. Her superb performance was one of the highlights of Durham City Amateur Swimming Club's gala in aid of the Mayor of Durham's Korea Comforts Fund.

The gala was a family affair for the Welsh's. Grandfather Mr Arthur Welsh was there to see Charmian show the form that won her two national championships at New Brighton a fortnight ago. Her father and mother, Mr and Mrs Arthur Welsh jun, were among the on-lookers – and twin brothers Peter and Anthony, aged 14, and 12-year-old sister Hilary were prominent competitors. Anthony earned further honours by carrying off the schoolboys' 50 yards breaststroke event.

Jimmy Also "Shone"

But Charmain's success did not overshadow the grand performance of her young clubmate Jimmy Harris. Competing against the cream of Yorkshire talent, he was a worthy runner-up in the NE Counties men's one metre springboard championship with 36.67 points. The holder, J Dickinson of Thornaby Shiverers, retained his title by gaining 42.04 points. Little Jimmy, by far the youngest entrant, looked almost puny alongside his burly opponents – one of whom, H Belay (Bradford), had a tan that would have done credit to Tarzan.

The large crowd that packed the bathside and galleries obviously thoroughly enjoyed themselves and they gave freely for the novel under-water collection in aid of the comforts fund. As the 24 young swimmers waited on the side of the baths, the spectators threw handfuls of money into the water. When the silver and copper settled in a layer on the bottom, the swimmers dived in – and within a matter of minutes had collected over £3.18s! "I am sure that the fellows from Durham County who are in Korea will be cheered by the fact that we have held a gala in the City for funds to send them comforts".

5 September 1952

COUPLE FOUND IN POOL OF BLOOD
Thornley Licensee Dies From Throat Wounds

Shortly before midnight on Saturday, Matthew Youll, 47-year-old licensee of the Queen's Head Hotel in Hartlepool Street, Thornley, and his wife, Mary Anne Youll (48), both of whom had been serving drinks in the bar less than two hours before, were found lying in a pool of blood in the passage-way at the foot of the stairs in the hotel.

Mr Youll, who had been licensee for a good number of years, was dead from throat wounds. His wife was lying seriously injured, suffering from wounds to the throat. She was rushed to Dryburn Hospital, Durham, and shortly after being admitted underwent an operation. Later her condition was stated to be "slightly improved".

Son made discovery

The tragic discovery was made by a 19-year-old son of the licensee, Jack Youll, when he entered the house about 11.30 pm. Police and doctors were quickly summoned to the scene and on Sunday, Supt A S Thornton of Castle Eden Divisional Police, told our reporter that enquiries had revealed that "no outside agency" was involved in the incident.

Mr Youll, who had a grown-up family, was the second husband of Mrs Youll and she was his second wife. The couple had both been serving in the bar of the public house until closing-time at 10 o'clock on Saturday night. "They seemed to be in quite good spirits and in good humour – Mr Youll, in fact, was entertaining the customers with a few parlour tricks," a customer who was there until closing-time told our reporter on Sunday.

Police Investigations

The public house was closed all day on Sunday, while police continued their investigations. They took statements from the son who found his father dead, and from others.

SIX FOR THORNLEY

The effort of Thornley CW, in winning 6-0 at Cassop, was near the mark, both teams having unbeaten records. Thornley faced this match with the knowledge that never previously had they won a game on the Cassop Victoria ground.

Cassop kicked with a slight breeze and their early attacks were so strong that it seemed they must score eventually. Thornley defence, under the able leadership of centre half and captain, John Levitt, withstood all attacks and J Nicholson brought off some brilliant saves. Thornley had an escape when outside right Taylor missed an open goal.

After this Thornley got into their stride and took the lead through Kent, after inside-right Waller had seen that the former was the better placed. The second half saw a change with Thornley doing most of the attacking, and Barrass soon placed them two up. This gave inspiration to them and the play had swung round so much that Nicholson, in the visiting goal, had to deal with isolated raids only.

Waller recorded the third goal and then Luke, with a grand left-foot drive, made it four. Kent made it five and Barrass collected the sixth. Kent scored a personal triumph with four goals while Thornley laid the Cassop bogey with a vengeance.

SHOTFIRERS' WAGE SETTLEMENT

Durham Area Council of the National Union of Mineworkers on Saturday confirmed a settlement reached with the Coal Board to pay shotfirers a weekly upstanding wage of £13.14s. Under the agreement, back money will be paid from the first full pay week after 20 November last year.

Wheatley Hill Resolution

The Council unanimously supported a resolution from Wheatley Hill Lodge that when pits are on summer holiday next year the whole of the ponies should be brought to the surface so that they may also "enjoy the fresh air and sunshine". Mr Sam Watson (secretary, Durham Area NUM) said after the meeting that there were more ponies employed in Durham coalfield than anywhere else in the country.

The meeting unanimously agreed to an increase of 2d in the union contribution, making the new figure 11d a week.

LUDWORTH

HOMING – By gaining first and second places in the last race of the season from Welwyn Garden City, S Davies and Partner also topped the young bird averages for the club. J Hartley, who was third, tied for second place with Cordnes and Son.

MEMORIAL PLAQUE – British Legion Women's Section will be making a house-to-house collection as part of their efforts to raise the £52 required for the 1939-45 plaque to added to the existing memorial in the Parish Church, which it is hoped to unveil on 2 November. All parishioners are urged to give generously. Both Sherburn Hill and Ludworth Women's Sections are making efforts to raise the sum as quickly as possible. Canon H Tillard, Rector of Shadforth, has been helpful in putting the project into operation.

WON 14 FIRSTS AT THORNLEY SHOW

At Thornley Allotments Society's 11th annual show on Saturday, Mr Alan Hutchinson won 14 firsts, 11 second and three thirds. Mr G Poulson (Wheatley Hill) was judge, and the show officials were: Messrs T T Ridley, chairman; J Garbutt, secretary; and J Thompson, treasurer.

Awards – Tray of vegetables, A Hutchinson, J Abbs, A Hutchinson; pot leeks, G Atkin, J Abbs, A Charlton; trench leeks, A Hutchinson, G Atkin, J Abbs; onions, W Shepherd, G Atkin, A Hutchinson; celery (white), A Hutchinson, M Charlton, R Barker; (pink), 1 and 2 A Hutchinson, 3 M Charlton; (bulk), G Atkin, J Abbs, A Charlton; parsnips, A Hutchinson, A Charlton, R Barker; carrots (long), A Hutchinson, G Atkin, R Barker; (short), J Moor, A Hutchinson, R Dunn; potatoes (white kidney), 1 and 2 A Hutchinson, 3 J Garbutt; (round white) W Shepherd, A Hutchinson; (coloured kidney), 1 and 2 A Hutchinson, 3 G Atkin; (round coloured), 1 and 3 A Hutchinson, 2 J Robinson; peas, 1 and 3 A Hutchinson, 2 R Barker; shallots, L Mitchell, A Charlton, J Mole; cauliflower, R Barker, G Atkin, J Abbs; cabbage, 1 and 2 A Hutchinson, 3 G Atkin; beans, G Atkin, A Hutchinson, J Abbs; beet (round), A Hutchinson, J Thompson, W Shepherd; tomatoes, G Atkin, W Shepherd, J Abbs; cucumber, G Atkin.
Flowers – Lady's spray, R Baker, W Shepherd, A Charlton; gent's buttonhole, R Baker, A Charlton, M Charlton; asters, G Atkin, A Hutchinson, L Mitchell; dahlias (decorative), 1 and 2 A Charlton, 3 L Mitchell; (pom-pom), 1 and 2 A Hutchinson, 3 M Convery; gladioli, J Abbs, G Atkin, S Brentley; bouquet, 1 and 2 A Hutchinson, 3 W Shepherd; vase of flowers, L Mitchell, W Shepherd, G Atkin; chrysanthemum, 1 A Hutchinson, 2 and 3 L Mitchell.

THREE EAST DURHAM PITS BAN SATURDAY WORK

With miners at Thornley colliery having unanimously decided at a special lodge meeting not to work the Saturday shift in regard to the county extended hours agreement, three of the eight collieries in No 3 Area (SE Durham), Durham Division, NCB, are now not working the shift. The other two collieries are Horden, the biggest in the area, with a weekly target of 22,750 tons, and Wheatley Hill. Thornley miners had rejected the Saturday shift, though hitherto they have worked it, because, Mr E Carter, chairman of the miners' lodge, told our reporter, they felt they now "deserved the pleasures of a five-day week".

Though the industry had been granted a five-day week in May 1947, said Mr Carter, only a few months later the extended hours agreement was drawn up. Since then they had been "more or less" back again to the six-day week. "If they don't make a stand on the matter now," added Mr Carter, "the men feel they may eventually lose the five-day week altogether. There would be no need for extended hours if every miner in the industry worked his full quota of shifts in the five-day week".

Wheatley Hill Decision

Coun E Cain, secretary of the Wheatley Hill miners' lodge, told our reporter this week there was "little likelihood" of miners at Wheatley Hill reconsidering their decision not to work extra hours. There is a possibility, however, that Horden may resume working the Saturday shift this week as differences between the miners' lodge and the Coal Board over "waiting on" time, are understood to have been settled.

12 September 1952

WHEATLEY HILL ROAD SAFETY WEEK

To bring the urgent need for road safety precautions before the public eye, Wheatley Hill Road Safety Committee this week organised a series of lectures, entertainments and displays in the village. The programme opened on Sunday night with a concert in the Welfare Hall by Wheatley Hill Colliery Band, under the conductorship of Mr Buckley. Solos were contributed by a well-known local tenor, Mr James Pyle, and the sisters Joan and Irene Lewis gave pianoforte solos and duets. Coun J W Moore presided and during an interval PC J L Jackson, Accidents Prevention Officer for the Castle Eden Division, spoke on road safety.

A demonstration of "Kerb Drill" for the special benefit of schoolchildren was organised in Front Street, Wheatley Hill, after school hours on Monday. Later, in Wheatley Hill cricket field, a police team and specialty-trained dogs gave a display of accident prevention. Mr J W Willan, a local schoolmaster, was chairman.

Entertainment

Entertainment in the Welfare Hall on Tuesday was provided by Thornley St Godric's Choral Society. Mr John Tunney was compere and principal artistes were John Quin, Doris Surman, Ann McCoy, Angela Ellwood, Teresa Morton and Jacky Toye (Thornley's blind accordionist). The accompanist was Miss M Scully. Coun E Cain JP, presided and Sgt Hedley, of the Durham County Constabulary Accidents Prevention Department, gave a helpful talk on road safety measures, stressing that the utmost vigilance should be observed at all times by all road-users, whether motorists, cyclists or pedestrians.

FELL FROM LADDER
Inquest on Thornley Man

While white-washing the shaft sidings in the Busty Seam of Thornley Colliery, 61-year-old John Smith Hall, 75 Dunelm Road, Thornley, slipped from a ladder. He as given first-aid treatment, and next day admitted to Durham County Hospital suffering from a fractured pelvis and an injury to his right arm. He died in the hospital nine days later.

At the inquest held at Durham on Tuesday, the jury returned a verdict of "Accidental Death" in accordance with medical evidence given by Dr J E Ennis.

Mrs Miranda Hall said her husband left for work at the colliery on 3 September in his usual state of health. At 1.30 the next morning he was brought home by Mr Woodward, the colliery first-aid man, who told her that her husband was badly bruised.

Third Accident

Mrs Hall said, "When I asked my husband what had happened, he told me that the ladder he had been working on had slipped and that he had fallen with it". She said that this was the third accident her husband had sustained at the colliery. In 1943 he had fractured his collar bone and was awarded £1.4s.11d per week as compensation. In 1944, as a result of another accident, he had had several stitches inserted into a wound in his head.

David Kilbourne, 4 Seventh Street, Wheatley Hill, said that he did not see the accident, but heard Hall call to him for assistance. He continued, "I found Hall lying on the concrete floor. His brush and pail were upset. He was conscious, but complained of a pain in his right hip. I helped all I could, and then some other men came to my assistance".

Christopher Woodward, 100 Dunelm Road, Thornley, senior first-aid attendant at Thornley Colliery, said that when he found the injured man there were no signs of bleeding. "He complained of pains in his right thigh," he said.

19 September 1952

WHEATLEY HILL MECHANICS – Wheatley Hill Mechanics have chosen the following side to entertain Shotton Mechanics tomorrow in the first round of Thornley Aged Miners' Cup: Errington, Sanderson, Bean, Blakemore, Williams, Goyns, Rigby, Laverick, Patterson, Kirby, Lee. Reserve: R Bean.

THORNLEY WOMAN LEGIONAIRE'S FUNERAL – Funeral of Mrs Mary Bovill, well-known in Thornley for her long and faithful connection with the women's section of the Thornley branch of the British Legion, took place on Saturday, the men and women's sections of the Legion being well represented. The service at Thornley Parish Church, conducted by the Rev H W Jackson (vicar), was followed by interment at Thornley cemetery. Women legionnaires walked in front of the cortege in memory of their 82-year-old founder member and president.

GIFTS FOR CHARMIAN WELSH

Gifts to Miss Charmian Welsh of Thornley, who gained fifth place in three-metre springboard diving at the Olympic Games at Helsinki, are to be made on Tuesday night in the Thornley Workmen's Club Hall.

The gifts will be handed over by County Coun E F Peart, chairman of Thornley Parish Council, the organisers of the presentation. It is expected that the Chairman of the Durham County Council (Coun M Tate), chairman of Easington Rural District Council (Coun T Akenhead), and representatives of the Northumberland and Durham Counties Amateur Swimming Association, will attend.

One of the gifts is a silver trophy which will be inscribed as a gift from the residents of Thornley and the officials and workmen of Thornley Colliery. Miss Welsh intends this trophy to be competed for annually in women's three-metre springboard diving by members of the Northumberland and Durham Association.

All residents of Thornley, including all colliery officials and workmen, and other contributing organisations, are being invited to attend the presentation, which will be made in the interval of a free musical programme by local artistes.

26 September 1952

THORNLEY PARISH COUNCIL

Further legal advice is to be sought by the County Council on the question of whether the proposal of the National Coal Board to use the "Hilly" as a refuse tip was permitted development. This information was given to members of Thornley Parish Council on Tuesday. Representatives were chosen to attend on behalf of the Parish Council at any future meeting between the County Planning Officer, Easington Rural Council and the NCB.

Letters were received from bus operators, the police and the County Surveyor agreeing to bus stops at each side of the east end of Hartlepool Street being moved westwards in the interests of road safety. The County Surveyor raised the question of whether any agreement had been made as to who would bear the cost of moving the signs to their new places. It was agreed to ask the County Surveyor to give assistance.

10 October 1952

SATURDAY SHIFT AT THORNLEY

A resolution not to work a Saturday shift has been rescinded by Thornley miners' lodge. As a result the pit was open on Saturday for this extra shift for the first time since the extended hours agreement was resumed by Durham County pits at the beginning of September.

Thornley miners' original decision not to work on Saturdays was made because, according to one of their officials, the men felt they should enjoy the hard-earned privilege of a five-day week. The Saturday shift will be worked on a purely voluntary basis.

Only two pits are now not working the Saturday shift in the No 3 Area (South-East Durham), Durham Division, NCB. They are Horden and Wheatley Hill.

There is no likelihood of the shift being resumed at Wheatley Hill colliery, a miners' lodge official told me. At Horden the shift has been banned because of a lodge grievance regarding the difficulty of compensation men getting employment.

THORNLEY WOMAN'S TRAGIC DEATH

Returning home after spending the evening out with her husband and two friends a Thornley woman was carrying one of her year-old twins to bed when she fell from nearly the top of the stairs to the bottom. She fractured her skull and died shortly afterwards.

This was revealed at the inquest in Thornley Police Office on Monday night on Mrs Eva Gaskell (32), 3 Thornlaw South, Thornley, when the Coroner, Mr T V Devey, returned a verdict of "Accidental death".

Jean Kay, the 17-year-old sister of the dead woman, told the Coroner that for the past six months she had been in the habit of going to look after the twins, John and

Richard, on a Saturday night while their parents went out together. As usual she went about 6.30 pm on 27 September and found that the children were ready for bed. Her sister went out shortly after seven o'clock with a Mrs Laverick and both women later joined their husbands.

About 10.15 pm, continued Miss Kay, she put both children on the settee and was trying to "pat them to sleep" when her sister returned. Mrs Gaskell took off her coat and took hold of John to carry him upstairs to bed.

"She was nearly at the top," said witness, "when I heard a rumbling noise and John crying. I rushed to the bottom of the staircase and saw my sister and John lying there beside the door. John was lying over the arm of my sister who was bleeding from the nose and ear. She didn't answer me and so I took the baby off her and ran for help". At the top of the stairs, said Miss Kay, a piece of carpet was "ruffled".

Dr Gallagher arrived at 10.45 pm but within quarter of an hour Mrs Gaskell was dead.

17 October 1952

LUDWORTH AGAIN

Ludworth Juniors again came into the picture with a fine seven clear goals when visiting Hamsteels Boys' Club, but the claimant points out that the home side deserved a ball for their plucky display. Although outclassed Hamsteels never gave up and kept on fighting back. Their goalkeeper Donnelly and full-backs, Bussey and Waller, put up a grand defence.

After five minutes Fishwick scored for Ludworth and he and Scullion continued to put in grand shots only to find Donnelly in magnificent form. Thompson made it two and a corner by the same player led to the third, from Fishwick. Ludworth were doing all the attacking and in eight corners Fishwick netted once to make it four.

It was again all Ludworth in the second period and corner after corner was conceded by Hamsteels. Scullion scored two more and Fishwick one. Ludworth's best players were P Carr, Elcoat, Fishwick and Scullion. Donnelly, Waller, Bussey, Richardson and Stephens were good for the losers.

31 October 1952

THORNLEY PARISH COUNCIL

Filling up the "Hilly" – Details of the National Coal Board's scheme for filling up the "Hilly" beauty spot with pit refuse were received at Wednesday's meeting of Thornley Parish Council, presided over by

County Coun E F Peart. The letter was from the County Planning Officer (Mr W A Geenty), who said that the most important point that had to be settled at the recent meeting of representatives of the Coal Board, Easington RDC, the County Planning Department and the Parish Council, was whether the site had been used before the coming into force of the Town and Country Planning Act 1947.

"It was generally accepted by all present," wrote the County Planning Officer, "that the original fence had been tipped over as far back as eight or nine years, and therefore it appeared that the National Coal Board had established a right to continue tipping into the "Hilly" without seeking planning permission".

Mr M Fleming and Mr W E Thompson said the members of the Parish Council who were present had no other option than to agree with this, and Mr Thompson said he hoped the Press would make it clear to the public that the tipping on the site before 1 July 1948 gave the Coal Board the right to continue tipping.

Prepared To Level The Ground

The Planning Officer said the National Coal Board were prepared to level the ground by means of a mechanical scraper so as to practically eliminate subsequent firing. They would use waste material from the washery which, being wet when deposited, would not cause dust to blow about, and they would confine their activities for many years to existing ground levels at the highest points of the embankments on either side of the "Hilly". They would consider any reasonable suggestions regarding tree planting at the "Hilly".

The Council unanimously decided that they had no alternative than to agree to the Board continuing to tip at the "Hilly".

Coronation Celebrations

All organisations in Thornley are to be invited to attend a meeting on the second Tuesday in December for the purpose of considering arrangements for celebrating the Coronation. The Clerk said that information he had collected showed that there were about 900 school pupils and 430 children under school age in the parish. The meeting will be open to members of the public.

Mr N Sarsfield (Durham) who coached Miss Charmian Welsh, the Thornley girl who took part at the Olympic Games, wrote that he was preparing film scripts of Charmian diving and would be glad to show them to the people of Thornley when they were completed. Mr Sarsfield's offer was accepted.

It was reported that 70 drivers of motor vehicles residing in Thornley had been invited to attend three road safety lectures starting next Tuesday. Couns Mrs Anderson, M Fleming and J Nicholson were appointed to preside at the lectures.

When Mr J Nicholson complained of inferior street lighting in Wood Street and Henry Street he was informed that the matter was receiving attention. It had been on the schedule of lighting improvements for some time.

EARLY DASH FROM FIRE – A Thornley family, residing at 101 Thornlaw South, had to make an early morning dash from their bedrooms on Wednesday when fire broke out in the kitchen below. The householder, John Lumsden, woke at 2 am and smelt dense smoke coming up the stairs. He called his family together and they managed to reach the front door and escape to safety. When they got outside they broke a kitchen window and neighbours, who quickly came on the scene, helped them to pour buckets of water on to the flames which were kept under control until the arrival of Horden Unit of Durham County Fire Brigade. The firemen soon put out the blaze. "If Mr Lumsden had not awakened when he did the whole house might easily have been burned down," said a Brigade officer. The fire was caused by spark from the kitchen range setting alight an easy chair. The chair was badly damaged, together with the wireless, furnishings and floorboards.

7 November 1952

EASINGTON RESCUE WORKERS
Presentations to Wheatley Hill Men

In recognition of their valuable services during the rescue operations which followed the pit disaster at Easington last year, the manager of Wheatley Hill colliery and four of his workmen were each presented with a Westminster chiming clock during an interval in a concert at Wheatley Hill Welfare Hall on Saturday night.

Each time-piece bore the inscription, "Presented by the mine-workers and friends of Wheatley Hill Colliery in recognition of valuable services during the rescue operations at the Easington Colliery disaster, 29 May 1951".

The recipients were Mr J L Snaith (colliery manager), Mr Arthur Gill Brown Hardy (head ambulance attendant at the colliery), Messrs Stanley Poulson and Alfred Cook Watson (deputies), and Mr Robert Gordon Horner (underground fitter). The last three are all members of Wheatley Hill Rescue Brigade, Mr Poulson part-time retained sub-officer of the local unit of the Durham County Fire Brigade, being captain of the team. Mr Horner, too, is a member of the Fire Brigade.

"Their Sole Thought"

When the disaster shook the pit village of Easington, said Coun E Cain, JP, secretary of Wheatley Hill Miners' Lodge, who made the presentations, everybody that was available and qualified rushed to take part in the rescue operation. "No matter whether one was a colliery manager, a deputy or an ordinary workman, these men went hand in hand and wherever there was danger they were to be found," went on Coun Cain. "Suffering humanity was their only thought – it mattered little what their religious, political or other convictions were. Their sole thought was to

Wheatley Hill Rescuers & Ambulancemen - Easington Disaster. 1951
Bob Horner, Alf Watson, Mr Snaithe, Mr Hardy, Stan Poulson

287

help their comrades in distress as quickly as possible and we are proud tonight to honour these five men from Wheatley Hill Colliery who played their part – and played it well – in the heroic rescue work that followed the terrible catastrophe at Easington".

It was the tradition of the Durham miner, said Coun Cain, that nothing else mattered with him when danger threatened. He was ever ready to help others, without a thought for himself and under perilous conditions. "These men went to Easington without any thought of reward," he added, "and I am certain they would do the same again if ever their services were needed. In the days that lie ahead, as they look at these clocks, they will remember the perils they faced together at Easington. And as their friends look at the clocks and the inscriptions upon them they will not only see something that was given as a reward for services nobly given but something that was presented to men who were brave and who were prepared to sacrifice themselves to aid their comrades".

Voluntary Levies

Mr H Bradshaw, who presided, told the audience that the local Workmen's Federation Board felt that it was the least they could do to make some tangible recognition to the men at the colliery who had taken part in the rescue operations. Without exception every workman at the colliery had paid two voluntary levies amounting to a shilling to make the presentations possible. This levy had realised £47.1s. Generous donations had also been received from the managements of the Regal and Royalty cinemas at Wheatley Hill, Wheatley Hill Workmen's Club, Wheatley Hill Soldiers' and Sailors' Club, Mr R Crosby, Dr and Mrs McLean and Dr A Gray.

"We are grateful to all who have contributed to the presentations," added Mr Bradshaw. "At the same time we fully realise – and so do the contributors – that we cannot measure the value of these gallant men's rescue work in terms of money. Nobody, except the men themselves, will ever realise what they went through".

An excellent concert was given by Wheatley Hill Colliery Band, under the conductorship of Mr W F Buckley, supported by two well-known local vocalists, Mr "Johnny" Quin (baritone), and Mr James Pyle (tenor). Mr Quin was accompanied at the piano by Miss M Scully and Mr Pyle by Miss J Buckley.

Among the guests present at the function, which was arranged by Wheatley Hill Workmen's Federation Board, with Mr Jack Harrison, JP, as secretary, were Supt and Mrs A S Thornton (Castle Eden Police Division), Dr and Mrs McLean (Wheatley Hill), and Miss Balmforth (Matron of West Hartlepool General Hospital).

FORTNIGHT'S HOLIDAY FOR MINERS
Output Will Not Be Affected

A Council meeting of the Durham County Mining Federation Board – which represents every worker in the Durham coalfield – agreed, subject to approval from lodges and branches, with the settlement reached with the Durham Area of the NCB, fixing the two weeks' annual holiday for the next six years.

Every workman will know for the next six years exactly which fortnight he will be on holiday. The proposals are on the caveling principle and will ensure that the flow of coal is maintained.

The council meeting in Durham on Saturday also expressed the hope that speedy negotiations would begin with the Coal Board to set up a new wage structure whereby some improvement can take place in the wages of day wagemen.

Bonus Qualifications

An offer by the Coal Board relating to bonus qualifications was accepted. This means that any shift lost which is covered by a medical certificate will safeguard other shifts worked in the pay week for payment of proportionate bonus, provided the member is not otherwise disqualified.

Shifts lost through the death or sudden sickness of a near relative will be safeguarded in the same way as long as the member can prove to the management that it was not reasonably possible for him to attend work. Any shift lost by representatives on local government work will be safeguarded, provided the councillor has given reasonable notice beforehand to the management.

In all these concessions, the overriding reservation is that the member must prove he is not otherwise disqualified, a spokesman said after the meeting.

14 November 1952

THORNLEY WELFARE HALL WILL OPEN –
DESPITE DAMAGE

Although a crack appeared in the wall of the new Thornley Miners' Welfare Institute some time ago, the committee is going ahead with arrangements for the opening on 27 December. The crack is also visible in the floor, and the subsidence which has apparently caused the trouble has also affected houses in the vicinity.

Not Dangerous

The National Coal Board and the architectural department of the miners' welfare organisation have gone into the matter, and have expressed the opinion that the damage is not dangerous. The old institute, once the centre of village activities, was destroyed by fire on the night of 11-12 November 1944. The new building covers the same site as the old. The large public hall is on the ground floor and the billiards room has five tables. There is also a supper room, reading room, kitchen and secretary's room.

COUNCILLOR E F PEART
Dies After A Week's Illness

While at the Shire Hall, Durham, on 14 November, Councillor Emmerson F Peart became ill and was removed to his home at Thornlaw, Thornley, and later to Dryburn Hospital, Durham, where, we regret to say, he died on Friday at the age of 61.

Much sympathy will be felt for his widow, who is a school teacher at Wheatley Hill, and his two sons, Mr T F Peart, MP for Workington and Mr Henry Peart, a sports master at Ryhope School. At the time of his death, Coun Peart was employed as a clerk of the Durham No 2 (Central Valuation Panel) and was chairman of Thornley Parish Council. In both world wars he served in the Royal Artillery and in the last war attained the rank of Major. He saw service in Germany.

Coun Peart was returned as the County Council representative for Thornley in 1949 and was a member of the County Education and other committees. He was a deeply sincere man who had the courage of his convictions.

He came into prominence during the campaign that the County Council's Labour Party waged for the "closed shop", and was a member of the emergency committee set up by the Council to implement that policy.

He served on all deputations which interviewed Ministers in London, and when the dispute was at its height broadcast a message to the nation. He was expelled in July last year from the National Union of Teachers because of the part he had played in the campaign.

Chairman's Tribute

The Chairman of the County Council, Coun M Tate, when notified of Coun Peart's death, said: "Although some people disagreed with certain of his views in the past few years, no one doubted his ability and his sincerity. Being a loyal trade unionist, he always had the interests of the workers at heart. I am shocked at the loss of a close personal friend and the Council has lost a man of outstanding merit".

Among those who attended the funeral service at St Bartholomew's Church, Thornley, on Tuesday, were representatives of Durham County Council, Easington RDC, Thornley Parish Council and Local Labour Party organisations. As the coffin, draped with the Union Jack, was carried through the gateway of the church, standard-bearers of Thornley British Legion formed a guard of honour.

During the service, conducted by the Rev H W Jackson, Coun Peart's favourite hymn, "Jerusalem" was sung. The organist was Mrs G Armstrong. Cremation took place at Sunderland.

The underbearers, members of Wheatley Hill and Thornley Labour Parties, were Messrs J Harper, S Hughes, J Johnson, T Williams, J McGregor and J Nicholson. British Legion standards were carried by Mr and Mrs R Slater.

28 November 1952
THORNLEY AGED MINERS' HOMES

Mr E Carter, secretary of Thornley Aged Miners' Homes Committee, on Saturday told how in the bitter stoppages of 1921 and 1926 the homes were mortgaged for £3,000 in the first case and £3,700 in the second. The money was used as relief to the miners, but was paid back expeditiously at the rate of a shilling per man per week in the first case. Easier terms – sixpence a week – were allowed for refunding the second advance.

In December 1918 the balance at the bank was £9.3s.2d, but as Mr Carter said, powers of recovery were "second to none", for in March 1919 the fund lent £100 to the colliery band on the guarantee of the miners' lodge. Again, in 1920, £100 was lent to the parish council to purchase land for what is now a children's recreation ground.

The cost of building the first 12 cottages, opened on 14 November 1914, was £166 each. Nine cottages opened on 1 December 1923, cost £270 each. Mr Carter contrasted these costs with £2,400 spent during the past year on repairs and renewals. The Thornley Colliery workmen own 37 cottages, a caretaker's cottage and a single men's hostel – certainly a record number for a colliery employing about 1,500 people.

PRESENTATIONS AT THORNLEY
Aged Miners' Homes Officials Honoured

At a social gathering on Saturday of representatives of the sections making up the Thornley Colliery Workmen's Federation, two retiring honorary officers of the Aged Miners' Homes Committee – Messrs A Welsh jun, manager of Thornley Colliery and chairman of the Homes Committee, and Mr T H Holder, treasurer of the Homes Committee – were honoured with gifts to mark their services on behalf of the aged miners' homes.

Mr A Bushby, chairman of the Federation, who presided, said Mr Holder was elected secretary of the Homes Committee in 1913, a post he held until he was appointed co-treasurer until 1927. He continued as treasurer until 1951, when the Federation took over the management of the homes. He was the only person who had served on the Homes Committee throughout the whole of its existence. On behalf of the Federation he thanked him for his excellent service extending over 38 years. In making the presentation of a typewriter to Mr Holder, Mr Welsh joined in the appreciation expressed by the chairman.

Tributes

The chairman then remarked on the excellent three years' service as chairman of the Homes Committee, so willingly given by Mr Welsh after being appointed chairman in succession to his father in 1948. They all knew, said the chairman, that Mr Welsh had always had a deeply sympathetic interest in the aged people's homes.

Mr T H Holder then handed to Mr Welsh a framed enlargement of his own portrait, which is to be hung in the single men's reading room, alongside the photographs of previous chairmen.

Both recipients made suitable replies of thanks for the gifts, and appreciatory remarks were then made of Mr Welsh and Mr Holder by Messrs E Carter (homes secretary), W Dowding (Federation secretary), E Green (Officials' secretary), G Johnson (deputies' chairman), W

Straughan (mechanics' secretary), W Henderson (enginemen's treasurer), W Walls (oldest committee member) and D Dempsey (youngest committee member).

Excellent entertainment was provided by Peggy Lawrence and Messrs R Oswald, W Parker, G Wigham, J Webb, W Henderson, E Carter and F Walker.

5 December 1952

PRESENTATION – At the Christmas party of Wheatley Hill County Infants' School Parent-Teacher Association on Tuesday, Miss Edith Bellinger, former headmistress at the school and one of the founders of the Association, was presented with a pearl necklace as a token of appreciation of her services. Miss Bellinger is leaving Wheatley Hill to take up a new post as County Women's Inspector of Infants' and Nursery Schools. The presentation was made on behalf of the Association by the vice-chairman, Mrs Taylor, and best wishes were expressed for Miss Bellinger's future success. Supper was served during the evening and Mrs Charlton (secretary), was MC for an enjoyable programme of games, competitions and dancing.

OLD FOLK ENTERTAINED – Retired members of Wheatley Hill Discharged and Demobilised Soldiers' and Sailors' Club, and their wives, and widows of retired members, were entertained to their third annual Christmas treat in the club on Wednesday night. There were more than 100 guests and an excellent knife-and-fork tea was provided. Each retired member was presented with a gift of £1 while the women-folk received 10s each. Mr Charles Brady, Trimdon Grange, a member of the Durham County Club Union Executive, represented the Club Union, and also present were Mr T Storey, secretary of Wheatley Hill Workmen's Club, and Coun J Johnson, a member of Easington Rural Council. Eighty-two-year-old Mr John Wallace was the oldest guest present. After tea Mr Norman Carr presided at a concert given by local artistes, with Mr J Powell at the piano. Arrangements for the function were efficiently carried out by Messrs A Carr (club chairman), W Hackworth (secretary) and G Hargreaves (treasurer).

12 December 1952

POPPY DAY RECEIPTS – As a result of the annual Poppy Day effort at Wheatley Hill, organised by the local women's section of the British

Legion, the sum of £72.18s.9½d was raised for the Earl Haig Remembrance Fund.

LEGION PRESENTATIONS – Presentations to two former officials of the section were made at the party of Wheatley Hill women's section of the British Legion in the Church Hall on Monday. Mrs P H Galley, who recently retired as vice-president after 22 years' service, and Mrs Eve Richardson, who has been an official for 15 years, part of the time serving as vice-chairman, were the recipients. They were each presented with a pair of oak and chromium candlesticks by Mrs McLean (president). Tribute was paid to the long service of both officials. A social followed, vocal items being contributed by Mrs Mullen and Mrs Maughan. A fancy dress parade was won by Mrs M Saxby, and Mrs Brain won the comic costume competition. Pianists were Mrs Eddy and Mrs Henderson.

DIED IN BARBER'S SHOP – While having a shave in a barber's shop at Wheatley Hill on Friday night, a well known figure in the village, Mr William Carter (53), 24 Wordsworth Avenue, Wheatley Hill, collapsed and died. Mr Carter had been in ill-health for four years, and for the past two had only been able to get about in an invalid chair pushed by his wife. His wife had taken him to the barber's for a shave and it was while she was outside that her husband was taken suddenly ill. Mr Carter had lived at Wheatley Hill for 35 years and was employed at Thornley Colliery until his illness. Before that he worked at Ludworth, Horden and Easington collieries. He is survived by his wife, an official of Wheatley Hill Women's Section of the British Legion, and two sons. Funeral took place at Wheatley Hill cemetery on Tuesday following a service in All Saints' Church conducted by the Rev Arthur Preston (Vicar of Wheatley Hill).

PRESENTATIONS TO HEADMISTRESS – During the Christmas parties in Wheatley Hill County Infants' School on Wednesday presentations were made to Miss Edith Bellinger, headmistress for nine years, who left at the beginning of the month to take up a new appointment as County Women's Inspector of Infants' and Nursery Schools. On behalf of the teaching staff Miss Cruttenden presented Miss Bellinger with a brief case, while seven-year-old Christine Hedley, on behalf of the pupils, presented her with a navy handbag. A diamante lapel brooch was also presented to the former headmistress by Mrs M Shevels (caretaker), on behalf of the domestic staff. Tribute was paid to the valuable services of Miss Bellinger while headmistress at the school, and best wishes were extended for her future success. Miss Bellinger suitably acknowledged the gifts and spoke of the happy years she had spent at the school with both the staff and the pupils.

RISING STAR'S FOOTBALL
Ludworth Can Say "At Last" In Our Contest

At last! Ludworth Rising Star Juniors, who have made the most claims for the Durham County Press football for the weekly meritorious performance, have at last secured the award after appearing in the honours list time and time again. It should be noted that those officials sending entries for their clubs next week should send off their letters as soon as possible owing to possible delays in postal delivery. No entry received after first post on Tuesday can be considered.

Ludworth's feat that earned them the award was the infliction on Bowburn CW Juniors of the heaviest defeat on that club for over seven years, by ten clear goals. In fact supporters of Ludworth say that had it not been for the brilliant goalkeeping of Halpin, the score would easily have been doubled.

Mr C Campbell, Ludworth treasurer, making the claim, comments: "If you do not think that Ludworth are worthy of the ball of the week, then I ask you to give it to Halpin, the Bowburn goalkeeper". Halpin on this showing must be the best junior goalkeeper in the county.

Every member of the winning side was on top form, but even so, Bowburn, at full strength, had their turns of attacking. Bower, Fishwick and Scullion netted for Ludworth in the first half and second period scorers were Bower (3), Scullion (2), Barker and Hammond.

Bower, who scored four times, was far the best of the home forwards, and half-backs Thompson, Barker and S Carr must have praise for their fine displays. Ludworth have had many fine displays this season, but this must beat the lot, for probably no other junior side could have accounted for Bowburn by such a margin.

19 December 1952

CHRISTMAS GIFTS – Retired miners, at Wheatley Hill Colliery, over 65 and their wives, and widows over 55 whose husbands had worked at the colliery, received Christmas gifts of 7s.6d each on Saturday from the Wheatley Hill Aged Miners' Christmas Treat Fund. Arrangements for the distribution were made by Mr T Allan (chairman of the Fund), Coun E Cain (secretary) and Mr J Hedley (treasurer).

MINERS' DECISION – Wheatley Hill Miners' Lodge, at a special meeting on Sunday, decided, after hearing a report from their delegate, Mr J W Burrell, to support the Durham County Mining Federation Board's decision to uphold the national miners' delegates' rejection of the recent Coal Board wages offer. Mr H Bradshaw presided at the meeting.

NOMINATIONS FOR COUNCILLORS – Mr John Andrews has been nominated as a candidate by Wheatley Hill Miners' Lodge to represent the Thornley Electoral Area on Durham County Council. The vacancy has been created by the death recently of County Coun E F Peart. The lodge has also nominated Mr Anthony Wharrier as a candidate for the Wheatley Hill ward of Easington Rural Council in succession to Miss Edith Bellinger, who has resigned from the Council owing to leaving the district. Both nominations will be forwarded to the local and area Labour Party for their consideration.

WELFARE CENTRE PARTY – About 160 children attended the annual party of Wheatley Hill Child Welfare Centre. Tea was provided and each child was presented with a gift and a bar of chocolate from Santa Claus. Ice-cream was given to the children and Dr Anderson, Nurse Boyes, Nurse Sawdon and Mrs Hindson (county clerk) were in charge of the entertainment. The committee presented a bouquet to Nurse Boyes as a token of appreciation of her services.

CLUB BALLOT – Twenty-nine nominations have been received for six vacancies on the committee of Wheatley Hill Workmen's Club and the ballot will take place on Saturday, 10 January. Mr T Storey has been re-elected secretary, unopposed, for the 28th successive year, and Mr J Dunn treasurer for the 18th year. The chairman, Mr John Gibson, is opposed by a former chairman, Mr T Cowie, and the present librarian, Mr J Walton, is opposed by Mr W Heard. Mr W Rankin has been re-elected doorman, unopposed.

OLD FOLK ENTERTAINED – More than 200 old folk were entertained in Wheatley Hill Welfare Hall at the treat organised by Wheatley Hill Workmen's Club for retired members over 65 and their wives and widows over 60. An excellent knife-and-fork tea was served and each retired member was presented with £1. A welcome to the old folk was extended by Mr John Gibson, chairman, and among the guests were Mr Stan Hall, secretary, Durham County branch of the Club and Institute Union, Mr C Brady (Trimdon), area representative on the County Club Union Executive, Coun and Mrs E Cain and Coun and Mrs J Johnson. Officials and committee of the Wheatley Hill Constitutional Club and the Soldiers' Club were also present with their wives, together with Mrs Williams, stewardess of the Workmen's Club, and her staff. Entertainment was provided by Messrs Bob Armstrong, Tom Christopher, Michael Cain and Johnny Quinn, with Mr Ernest Evans accompanist. Thanks to the club management for the practical interest they showed every year in their old members was expressed by Mr Hall and others. The club secretary, Mr T Storey, who was responsible for the arrangements, replied on behalf of the club and said it was a pleasure to bring a little happiness into the lives of the old folk.

26 December 1952

Wheatley Hill Coronation Committee 1952
B Richardson, G Wharrior, Mrs Harper, A Lowther, M Alderton, J Steel,
W Warnes, E Bradley, J S Burnett, Mrs Storey, E Shinwell, Mrs Topham, W Bowes,
T Caine, J Johnson, Ralph Watson, B Hedley
Children at front: G Wharrior, J Harper

1953

MRS PIERCEY'S THREE SONS

Private Douglas Piercey (21), son of Mr and Mrs John Piercey, of Nelson Street, Thornley, is home on leave from Korea. Fit and well he expects to be at home for two months, after which he will go with his regiment, the famous Middlesex Regiment, to Austria. He is looking forward to this as a welcome change from the rough and ready life in the wild mountainous country of Korea.

Douglas is one of three brothers who have been in the services during the past few years. He is due to finish in 14 months' time after having served over five years. He was working in Thornley pit when he joined up, but is not at all sure that he will return to the pit, though at the moment, he thinks that he will not re-sign for the Army.

Gilbert (25), left the Army in August. He served close to Douglas in Korea. Douglas was told by friends of Gilbert that on one occasion when the "Chinks" were putting on heavy pressure Gilbert found his machine gun had stuck. With the enemy coming closer and closer he changed the barrel of the gun, got it going again, and did fine work in helping to check the enemy's advance. Gilbert is settling in London, but may visit Thornley while Douglas is on leave.

Met Brothers In Far East

The other brother is Gordon Piercey, 32, a petty officer in the Royal Navy. He is married and his home is in Plymouth. He has been in the Navy since he was 15. In the Far East he met his two brothers, who happened to be travelling in his ship.

Gordon says the North Koreans and Chinese are pretty accurate with their artillery and mortar fire, but they do not care to face any hand to hand fighting. He says that the fighting is desultory and gives the impression that it is leading nowhere. He feels sure that the North Koreans and Chinese have no chance of winning the war.

Mrs Piercey is naturally delighted that her three sons are all safe and sound. She herself has made a close study of the Korean conflict ever since it started and is as familiar with the map of Korea and the strange names on it as Douglas, whose travels have taken him to Japan as well as Korea.

MIDNIGHT COMMUNION – All Saints' Church, Wheatley Hill, was filled on Christmas Eve for a midnight Holy Communion service conducted by the vicar (the Rev Arthur Preston). Another celebration was held on Christmas morning. On Sunday evening a service of the nine lessons and carols was conducted by the vicar. The lessons were read by choir boys, choir-men and servers.

PERMANENT RELIEF FUND – Mr G W Dixon was re-elected treasurer for the 20th successive year at the annual meeting of Wheatley Hill branch of the Northumberland and Durham Miners' Permanent Relief Fund. Mr A Wyle was also re-elected chairman, and Mr J Hedley secretary, and the following were elected to the committee; Messrs F Carr, W Hills, W Soulsby and J R Fishwick.

NEW WELFARE INSTITUTE – The opening of Thornley's new miners' Welfare Institute is being eagerly anticipated. It was to have been opened on December 27, but had to be postponed to give the building contractor more time to finish a number of jobs. The benefit of this will be seen when the opening takes place this month. Several organisations have already made bookings of the large hall for drives.

CHRISTMAS - The day school children and the children connected with the Sunday Schools and various organisations had their usual parties. Carol singers from the churches and the Boy Scouts did their rounds. There was a large congregation at a midnight Communion service at Thornley Parish Church. Midnight Mass at the Church of the English Martyrs was also well attended.

GIFTS - A Christmas gift of 5s was made to each aged person at Thornley, and to those at Wheatley Hill and Ludworth who were formerly associated with Thornley Colliery. The pay-out was made by Mr Joseph Cherry and Mr E Carter, officials of the Thornley Colliery Federation Committee. Part of the fund was raised from donations, but the larger part was, as usual, from the aged miners' homes fund.

MINERS AND THE CORONATION
To Seek Day's Holiday With Pay

Holiday with pay on Coronation Day is to be sought by miners. At Saturday's meeting of Durham Miners' Council the following resolution was unanimously carried: "That the National Union of Mineworkers seek to have a day's holiday with pay on the occasion of the Coronation."

Protective Equipment

Concerned at the number of complaints from all parts of the coalfield regarding alkaline burns, the Council is to try and have introduced on the schedule of protective equipment, leather holders for cap-lamp batteries.

Free Coal For Retired Miners

When the question of supplying free coal to retired miners was raised, it was reported that agreement had now been reached with the Divisional Coal Board to form a county coal pool scheme. Under the scheme which was to go into operation yesterday, employed men will give up a portion of their free coal allowance to enable retired men to be given four and a half tons a year.

LUDWORTH

PARTY - The committee of Ludworth Rising Star Juniors F.C. gave a party for players, parents and friends to celebrate the winning of the Durham County Press football. After tea, Mr A Welsh, manager of Thornley Colliery, presented the ball to Mr Eric Barker, captain of the team. Dancing followed to music from an amplifier loaned by Ludworth British Legion, with Mr A Winter in charge.

DANCE – A large crowd attended the annual dance of the Ludworth Rising Star Junior's Football Club. Music was provided by the Gleneagles Band. M.C. was Mr C Campbell. Prize winners were: Lucky numbers: Messrs R Langlands and N Croft; card dance: Misses Peggy Greener and Betty Longstaffe; spot dance : Miss Enid Wade and Mr R Langlands: statue dance: Misses Kitty Hall and Marjorie Hammond. Over £14 was added to the club's funds. The prizes were given by Messrs T Cowan, J Foster, T Stephenson, C Robinson, J Wood and C Campbell.

2 January 1953

THORNLEY GOLDEN WEDDING

Mr and Mrs John James Robson, 105 Thornlaw South, Thornley, who celebrated their golden wedding on Saturday, have had seven daughters but no sons. All the six surviving daughters are married. There are 11 grandchildren.

Their wedding was the second in the Church of the English Martyrs, Thornley. The late Father M J Haggerty officiated. Mrs Robson was 17 and her husband 25. Both are in fairly good health.

Mrs Robson, born at Thornley, says it was a tough job bringing up six daughters on the wages of those days. Mr Robson was born at Cassop and started work at Ludworth Colliery at 10d a day when he was 14. Apart from a short period at Leasingthorne pit, the greater part of his working life was spent as a miner at Wheatley Hill and Thornley pits.

9 January 1953

MINER INJURED – Following a fall of stone at Thornley Colliery, 60-year-old Michael Phenney, 105 Barnard Avenue, Ludworth, was admitted to Durham County Hospital suffering from spinal injuries. His condition is stated to be improving.

LUDWORTH WI – Miss Davison presided at the January meeting. Mrs Bewick is to attend the county meeting at Darlington. The president welcomed four new members. Mr Gibbons gave a talk and film show on Australia and New Zealand, and was thanked by Mrs Winter. The competition, the best homemade chutney, was won by Miss Davison. Social half-hour took the form of a household "quiz". Taking part were Mesdames Forster, R White, Summerill and Bewick. Quiz-master was Miss Davison. Door prize was won by Miss Kilburn.

WHEATLEY HILL CORONATION PLANS

An order for 2,100 souvenir mugs to be presented to all children under school-leaving age on Coronation Day is to be placed by Wheatley Hill Coronation Celebrations Committee. This was decided at a meeting of the committee, presided over by Coun J W Moore, in Wheatley Hill Senior Boys' School on Tuesday. The mugs will cost 1s 5½d each.

Nineteen organisations were represented at the meeting as well as many individuals and it was agreed that each organisation should draw up plans for raising money and make suggestions for the celebrations. Many sporting organisations were represented and after tentative proposals had been discussed, it was agreed that delegates should report back from their organisations at the next full meeting of the committee on February 10, at 7.15pm. A banking account is to be opened and the treasurer, Mr A D Wharrier, announced that the first donation of £5 had been received from Wheatley Hill Soldiers' Club and £1 from a retired miner, Mr Tom Simpson.

Messrs P Galley, senior, and J Waite and the Rev. Noel Catherall were appointed auditors. Thirty collecting-boxes were issued for a house-to-house collection to be held in the village on Friday and Saturday, January 30 and 31. The emptying of the boxes and counting of the money will be supervised by a special sub-committee and a receipt issued to every collector.

16 January 1953

IGNORED SAFETY DEVICE
Fatal Accident At Thornley Colliery

"I take it the workmen know that they should stop the machine before they tinker with it," commented the Coroner (Mr W Carr) at the inquest on a 22-year-old waggonwayman, James William Kidd, 26 Front Street, Haswell, who died on his way to Durham County Hospital on Monday after being involved in an accident at Thornley Colliery.

The jury returned a verdict in accordance with the medical evidence that death was caused by a severe crush injury to the right side of the chest and loss of blood from a large wound in the armpit, accidentally sustained as a result of being involved in a conveyor belt while it was running.

Giving evidence, Clifford Miller (21), 1 Barnard Avenue, Ludworth, said he was employed as a datal hand at Thornley Colliery. He started work at about 1.30p.m. on Monday in the South Busty where the conveyor belt was carrying coals from the face.

"About five minutes after we had started work," he continued, "I heard a scraping noise while the belt was running. I noticed Kidd take off the guard in order to see what was wrong. I saw him put his arm underneath the belt and on top of the trays.

Had Only To Press Button

"The next thing I knew, he was coming over the belt and was then dropped into the tub. He was conscious and I told him to stay where he was while I went for the deputy. I noticed that his right shoulder was bleeding. When I returned with the deputy he was unconscious, He was taken out on a stretcher."

Asked by the Coroner if there was a device to stop the belt, Miller replied in the affirmative, adding that deputies frequently advised them to apply the device should the need arise. He admitted that this safety measure should have been adopted by Kidd at the time, and believed that if he had done so, the accident could have been prevented. To stop the belt, Kidd had only to press a button which was within easy reach.

In summing up, the Coroner remarked, "It was very unfortunate that when the means of stopping the belt was handy, the man did not do so before removing the guard."

Returning the verdict, the foreman of the jury said that he believed the accident could have been avoided if only the conveyor belt had been stopped.

23 January 1953

SAD DEATH OF MR JAMES W KIDD
Funeral At Haswell

The funeral has taken place at Haswell of Mr James W Kidd (22), husband of Mrs E Kidd, 79 Front Street, Haswell. He was the victim of a fatal accident which took place at Thornley Colliery. The cortege was headed by Thornley Colliery Silver Prize Band with the lodge banner under which walked officials and fellow members. At last Durham Miners' Gala (1952) Mr Kidd proudly helped to carry the banner, which this year will be draped to mourn his death

Mr Kidd was connected with Haswell Church Street Methodist Church and only recently he and his wife celebrated their first wedding anniversary. Seven weeks ago his mother collapsed and died.

Methodist Church Service

A service took place in Haswell Plough Methodist Church when the Rev W T Rose (superintendent minister of Thornley Circuit) officiated and the burial was at South Hetton Churchyard on Thursday 22 January. Four of his friends were underbearers, viz. Messrs J Hughes, R Hughes, L Surtees and T Betts. Many representatives from various organisations were present including Mr Hesler (under manager Thornley Colliery) and among the many floral tributes were those from N C B No 3 area and fellow workers. Organist at the church service was Mrs R W Egdell and the hymns sung were "The Lord's My Shepherd" and "In Heavenly Love Abiding.

GREAT DAY FOR THORNLEY RESIDENTS
New Institute Opened

What a Coal Board official confessed he had already dubbed "Henderson's Hall" was opened at Thornley on Saturday afternoon as the new Miners' Welfare Institute for the village. The building - roomy, two-storied, and with a warm interior colour scheme- has cost in the region of £28,000. It stands at the entrance to Thornley from Wheatley

Hill and Ludworth on the same site as the old Institute which put an abrupt end to social life in the village when it was burned to the ground during the night following Remembrance Day, 1944.

It was Mr F W Fry, formerly No.3 Area General Manager for the Durham Divisional Coal Board and now at Divisional Headquarters, who, paying a tribute to the work of Mr W Henderson, the Institute secretary, called the new Institute "Henderson's Hall."

"Perhaps it is invidious to mention any one individual who has worked for this new building," said Mr Fry, "but I must mention Billy Henderson, your very active secretary. He never failed at every Area Welfare committee meeting to mention the new Institute - so much so that I came to give it the nick-name, Henderson's Hall." (Laughter).

Eight Years' Wait

Since that disastrous fire over eight years ago Thornley people have had to depend upon the hospitality of neighbouring villages to hold their concerts, dramas and social functions. Without a sizeable hall of its own the village has seemed "almost lost."

But Saturday saw a re-awakening of all the local organisations- their representatives, a fair mixture of men and women, packed the spacious concert hall at the opening ceremony and their eyes lit up as they explored the whole of "their very own" Institute after the speech-making.

"Isn't everything beautiful?" declared one young woman, the wife of a miner, as she sauntered through the recreation rooms upstairs. "What good times there are in store for us now!"

"This is the happiest day for the people of Thornley since that November night when we saw our old Welfare Hall go up in smoke," declared Mr A Welsh, manager of Thornley colliery, who presided at the opening ceremony. "Today ends eight years of waiting and frustration. During this time we have had to take our recreation, our dances, and even our billiards, outside the village. But during the last year we have watched this new hall taking shape, brick by brick, until now we have a really fine Institute."

Opened By Mr Tunney

Outside the main entrance of the imposing building Mr Welsh handed a small chromium key to the first secretary of the original Institute, Mr Hubert Tunney, of Thornley, now deputy Labour Director for the Durham Divisional Coal Board, who, because of his long and active association with Thornley, had been chosen to perform the opening ceremony. After opening the large doors, Mr Tunney was presented with the key as a memento of the occasion.

Crowds filed into the concert hall which has a seating capacity of 400, and the speech-making took place after the new building had been blessed in a short prayer by the Rev W H Jackson (Vicar of Thornley).

Mr Tunney said he considered it "a very great honour" to have been invited to open the Institute.

"My mind goes back," he said, "to the opening ceremony of the original Welfare Hall in 1925 – that was a real red letter day in Thornley for it was a dream that had come true. When I first took an interest in Thornley miners' lodge we held our meetings in a long room over a stable owned by a publican and not one headquarters of the lodge were in the public-house. Some of us then decided that what we required in Thornley was a hall that could be used not only as the headquarters of the miners' but by the com-

A TURN OF THE KEY

—and Mr Hubert Tunney declares open Thornley's new Miners' Welfare Institute.

munity in general. We accumulated money and the Miners' Welfare Fund enabled us eventually to build a hall."

Though the period 1921 to 1931 was the darkest in the history of the miners of this country, went on Mr Tunney, there was never more social work done in this county than during those years, thanks to progressive local authorities and the Miners' Welfare Fund. In Thornley itself immense improvements were seen. "When I was elected to the Rural District Council in 1919," said Mr Tunney, "there was only one street made up in the village. We had no electric light, no water in our houses, no council houses and no scheme houses. Even when we built some council houses, we found there was an inadequate water supply and we had to build a reservoir at Halfway House. We had only 12 aged miners' homes – now we have 36. We had no pit-head baths or Welfare Hall. Now we have all these amenities – that is the measure of the work that was done in Thornley alone and I am proud I was privileged to take an active and leading part in it."

As he was no longer in public work or likely to be, concluded Mr Tunney, opening the hall that day would probably be his last public function in Thornley. "I would ask to go out on no better ending than to open this magnificent Welfare Hall," he added. "I am glad to be able to say that my last public function has not only been the opening of this hall, but a manifestation of the confidence of the people of Thornley."

MP'S Congratulations

Congratulating the local Welfare Committee on their remarkable achievement, Mr E Shinwell, M P for Easington and former Defence Minister, said that after the last hall had been burned down the committee wrote to him on many occasions to support their efforts for a new place. "For a long time," he went on, " we maintained an almost perpetual correspondence. They kept pressing me to press members of Parliament to get the licences to build and extend. Now at last the job has been done and I am satisfied. It is a great tribute to the patient efforts of the Thornley committee and at the same time a great tribute to the patience which is characteristic of all sections of the mining community in this country."

Mr Shinwell said he was proud of his long association with miners' welfare. There were few mining communities today without some form of miners' welfare such as pit-head baths, canteens and welfare halls.

Recently, said Mr Shinwell, he had made a speech in the south which had apparently offended quite a number of people, mostly those living in the coastal resorts, as he had received many letters of " the most offensive and filthy character."

"I described certain people in the country – scientists, teachers and also miners and farmworkers - as the salt of the earth," went on the speaker. "These letters have condemned me because I praised the miner - the senders talk about highly-paid miners and particularly miners who do not pull their weight and produce enough coal. I have always felt there was an easy answer to this criticism. The people from these resorts can come up here and produce coal for a change, I would not withdraw a single word I have said for 40 years about the people in a mining community."

They were meeting that afternoon, said Mr Shinwell, "almost in the shadow of a harsh industrial atmosphere." " I hope," he added, " for the sake of our country, the mining community, the coal industry and the export trade and for the purpose of our survival as a great nation, that there may be promoted peace in the mining industry at the earliest moment. We cannot afford trouble in any of our great industries at the present time. This country, whether we like it or not, is on the verge of either disaster or progress. We have to make ourselves independent. We have to shake off the shackles and our industries must throb and prosper and be maintained at the highest possible strength. I hope most fervently that there may be peace in the mining industry, peace with justice and honour all round."

More and more culture – art, science, music and the drama - will have to be injected into mining villages and townships, said Mr Shinwell. After all, it was culture which led to a higher and better civilisation. "There exists among the mine-workers and their wives and families and, indeed, among all sections of the community high talent, which ought to be used to promote a higher civilisation and the sooner we understand that the better," concluded Mr Shinwell.

Continued to Pay Levy

The first application for the new Institute, Mr Norman Nattrass, Labour Director, Durham Division , NCB told the audience, was made in 1945, but the scheme was turned down. The plans, specifications and estimates then had to be revised, and after much delay, due to licences, permits and shortages of materials, they had finally been able to go ahead.

Paying a tribute to the miners at Thornley, Mr Nattrass said that after the destruction of their old Institute they could "quite easily" have discontinued paying their levy. "But," he added, "they didn't. They had a vision that some day that money would be needed for welfare purposes and they very generously continued to subscribe their levy. They now see the marvellous results today."

Endorsing Mr Shinwell's remarks on the present situation in the coal industry, Mr Nattrass said he sincerely hoped that any delay in present wage negotiations would not upset the " amicable arrangements" they had for co-operation in the Durham Division. Negotiations are taking place at a higher level," continued Mr Nattrass, "and I hope that wise counsel will prevail and a settlement soon be reached. There have been wonderful improvements in the standard of the miner. Do not let us do anything that will impair the progress that has been made. Any interruption in our industrial life, particularly in the mining industry, will impair all those facilities we have won."

Adding their congratulations to the Thornley Welfare Committee for their hard work over so many years in seeking to build a new Institute, were Mr F W Fry, Mr R S MacLaren, the present No 3 area general manager, NCB, and Mr Tom Scollen, No 3 Area Welfare Officer, who recently took up a higher post at Divisional Headquarters.

"I hope you feel ," said Mr Fry, "that this Institute has been well worth waiting for and that it will become the cultural centre of Thornley. I hope, to, there will be something to interest the young people of the village and, in fact, that there will be all kinds of activity for all ages."

"Not Finished Yet!"

Proposing a vote of thanks to all who had taken part in the opening ceremony, Mr T H Holder, treasurer of the Institute, and one of the oldest members of the Welfare Committee, declared that "they were not finished with the welfare yet!"

"Behind this building," added Mr Holder, "we want a football and cricket ground – only today I received a letter which seems to point the way to a move in that direction. We will be patient in this matter – but we don't want to have to be too patient!" Seconding the vote of thanks was another long-serving member of the committee, Mr W Atkin.

The contractor, Mr C Hewitt, presented Mr Tunney with a barometer, suitably inscribed, as a permanent reminder of the part he had played that day in the opening of the Institute.

After the speeches tea was provided for the guests, and at night a concert – the first public function to be held in the new hall – was given by a Murton concert party, with Coun J Williams presiding. A collection was taken in aid of Thornley Aged Miners' Homes.

Crowds of villagers were given the opportunity to inspect the Institute, and soon the billiards and recreation rooms were in full swing. The large billiards hall, adjoining the concert hall on the ground floor, has five tables, and also on this floor are a supper room and kitchen, with all the latest equipment.

The concert hall, with a spring dance floor, is beautifully furnished with new red and gold chairs, the general colour scheme harmonising with the cream coloured walls, pale salmon ceiling and the heavy blue velvet curtains at the windows. The stage goes a good distance back and beneath are well laid out dressing–rooms. Cloakrooms are in the foyer near the main entrance.

On the upper floor women are especially catered for with a room of their own for various activities, and there are several recreation rooms, a reading–room, table tennis room (with a full size board) and a committee room. The rooms are all partitioned so that, if necessary, they can be converted into a long narrow hall running the length of the building. Electric light fittings and heating installations are of the latest type throughout.

Before the opening on Saturday, Thornley Colliery Silver Prize Band, under the conductorship of Mr E Kitto, together with Thornley Miners' Lodge banner and officials, headed a parade through the village from Dunelm Road.

Mr Nattrass, who apologised for the absence of the chairman of the Durham Divisional Coal Board, Mr E H D Skinner, due to another engagement, marched with the lodge and band. Later, in the new hall, he complimented the band upon the high standard of its playing. "I have always been a band enthusiast," he confessed, "and it always gives me great pleasure to march behind a band in a parade.

30 January 1953

CORONATION COMMITTEE – Considerable satisfaction was expressed at a meeting of Thornley Coronation Committee when Mr E Carter said that the Thornley Colliery Federation were prepared to undertake full responsibility for providing the tea for the aged people. Mr C Lamb (treasurer) reported that sums, received and promised, amounted to £55. Sub-committees were formed to deal with decoration of houses and shop property, children's events and souvenirs, and a dance to raise funds. A united religious service is also to be arranged. It was reported that orders for children's beakers had already been placed, and a quotation for children's bags of cakes and tea was accepted.

PRESENTATION TO THE REV J M HOW – At a social gathering in Thornley Church Hall on Saturday night a set of volumes of the Everyman Enclyclopaedia were presented to the Rev. J M How, who left

Thornley in the latter part of 1951 to become Vicar of St Andrew's, Roker. The Rev W H Jackson presided and the presentation was made by Mr H Hetherington (Vicar's warden), supported by Mr R Brandling (People's warden). Both spoke highly of the work done by Mr How in the period when he was at Thornley. In the night's entertainment, following supper, an amusing "turn" was given by Messrs F Bradley and W Hetherington. Songs by Mr H Hetherington and Miss Anne Hetherington, and country dancing by pupils of Mrs Swinburne, were excellent contributions towards a happy evening. Difficulties caused by the breakdown of the lighting owing to the gale were overcome by Mr W Hetherington.

6 February 1953

DEATH OF MR M LONSDALE
Married For Over 67 Years

A married partnership of nearly 68 years was broken by the death at Wheatley Hill last week of one of the village's oldest residents, Mr Matthew Lonsdale, 28 Luke Terrace, who would have celebrated his 90th birthday in April. His wife, who survives him with four sons and a daughter, will also be 90 in April – she was born five days after her husband. The couple would have celebrated their 68th wedding anniversary on May 3. They were one of Durham County's oldest married couples.

Mrs Lonsdale has been bedfast for the past three years, but her husband, though he had been in failing health, was bedfast only a few days before he died. The couple's second son, Jack, lives at Bridgeport, Connecticut, USA, and their two youngest sons, Robert and Matthew, at Slough, Bucks. Their eldest son, William, lives at Station Town, and their only daughter, who is unmarried, has been at home looking after the couple.

Started Work At 11

Mr Lonsdale retired from work at Wheatley Hill Colliery at the age of 73 after a mining career of 62 years. He began work as a trapper boy at the neighbouring colliery of Thornley when he was only 11 and the following year he was driving. He remembered when the pit-heapstead was totally destroyed by fire at the colliery.

In the early part of his career Mr Lonsdale had a lucky escape at Thornley. He was working in the Low Main seam when the boiler burst near the shaft bottom. He was blown into a tub, but escaped serious injury, though a number of lives were lost in the accident.

Mr Lonsdale had a life-long love of good music, He was a well-known tenor in his younger days and was a member of Wheatley Hill Choral Society until it disbanded. He took part in many concerts in the area. Until four years ago he could read without the aid of spectacles but latterly his eyesight had failed.

Following a service at "The Rest," conducted by Rev Arthur Preston (Vicar of Wheatley Hill), Mr Lonsdale was buried at Wheatley Hill cemetery on Saturday.

13 February 1953

THORNLEY BONFIRE ON CORONATION EVE

Thornley Coronation Celebrations Committee have decided to have a bonfire, but it will be lit on the eve of Coronation Day so as not to interfere with the attraction of the beacon on Coronation night at the Witch Hill near Signing Bank, about two miles from Thornley. Scouts of Wheatley Hill and Thornley will be in charge of the beacon, one of the national chain of beacons. The bonfire at Thornley will be on the high point near Gore Hall farm or on American Hill.

It was reported to the meeting of the Committee that orders had been placed and accepted for beakers, children's teas and chocolate for children under three. There are to be gifts for children from 11 to 15 years old, and it is expected that arrangements will soon be completed to provide high tea for aged people.

The decorations committee's plans and proposed prize money for decorated houses, business premises, and gardens were approved. Prize money and classes for a procession starting from Dunelm Road were also approved. Other attractions are a dance on May 1 and a display of fireworks on a date not yet fixed.

27 February 1953

ROAD SAFETY QUIZ
Won By Thornley St Godric's

The Vicar of Thornley (the Rev H W Jackson) was quiz master and Parish Councillors Mrs Anderson, J Nicholson and M Murray were judges at a road safety quiz in Thornley Welfare Hall. The winning junior team was Thornley St Godric's School (Sarah Fleetham, Patricia Ridley, Patricia Burke and Ruth Hoban), and the winning senior team

Wheatley Hill boys (J Noble, K Hall, J Taylor and D Caster). The competitors were Thornley boys and girls attending schools at Thornley, Wheatley Hill and Wellfield.

This was a preliminary round in the Easington Rural District Road Safety Committee competition. The villages are all expected to enter teams. They will be eliminated round by round, and the finals will take place at the special road safety day at Crimdon in July. There will be senior and junior shields for the winners.

The same conditions applied to a "Top of the Town" talent spotting competition. Out of 55 competitors Thornley's winning team was Derek Caster (singer), Malcolm Galloway (pianist), Ernest Grutton (elocutionist), Irene Horner (singer), Doreen Caster and Lorna Rutter (duettists) and James Rutter (cornettist). P C John L Jackson was compere. The large audience was comprised mainly of mothers and children. Judges were Miss Scully, Messrs I P Martin, J Tunney, E Kitto and W Henderson.

LUDWORTH

Fire broke out on Wednesday at 6 Moore Crescent, tenanted by Mr Deluce. Damage was considerable, but no one was hurt.

FUNERAL – Full Legion honours were paid at the funeral of Mr John Miller, (62), 53, Barnard Avenue. Service was conducted by the Rector (Canon H Tillard) at St. Cuthbert's Church. A cross of Flanders' poppies was laid by Mr R C Gibson M M who Recited Binyon's words. Survived by his widow. Mr Miller was employed at Thornley Colliery, and served with the DLI in the First World War.

6 March 1953

QUIZ FOR FIREMEN
Wheatley Hill Beaten In District Final

Part-time firemen were told at Durham on Saturday that their technical knowledge of their job was as high as that of full-time firemen. The tribute came from Mr C V Hall, Chief Fire Officer of Durham County, who acted as quiz master in the district final of the Fire Service technical quiz held in the Shire Hall.

The winning team, who received a prize of £15, was Alnwick (46points), Wheatley Hill, with 42 points, finished second and Kirby Moorside (35 points) third.

At the end of three rounds, Alnwick and Wheatley Hill were on level terms, each with 31 points, and an extra round was ordered. In this Alnwick obtained the possible number of points and dashed Wheatley Hill's hopes of going to Leeds to compete in the group final on March 21 when brigades from all parts of the North will take part.

Wheatley Hill Team

The Wheatley Hill team, composed of Sub-Officer S Poulson, Leading Fireman H F Horner and Firemen T W Ayre, J Goyns and P E Whinn, received a prize of £8. Kirby Moorside's third prize was £5.

Prizes were presented by Coun E Leggett, Chairman of Durham County Fire Brigade Committee, who had previously welcomed a large audience which included seven Chief Fire Officers from various parts of the North.

Mr J McKenzie, Chief Fire Officer for Newcastle, who was in charge of arrangements, said the quiz had met with great success in the North. He thanked all Chief Fire Officers for their co-operation.

WHEATLEY HILL TRAGEDY
Young Mother's Sudden Death

Only a week after coming out of hospital, where she had spent three weeks shortly after giving birth to a baby boy, Mrs Mary Ellen Dobson, (31), 29 Luke Terrace, Wheatley Hill, fell down a few stairs at her home on Friday and died within half an hour.

Mrs Dobson's baby – her second child – was born on January 18. She had not enjoyed good health after this birth and after about a month was taken to Sunderland Isolation Hospital. After her return home she had been compelled to rest in bed most of the day. Last Friday afternoon, with her baby, Michael, in her arms, she was on her way downstairs when, only a few steps off the bottom, she apparently had a dizzy bout and fell. The baby was unharmed.

Fell Downstairs

Her husband, Mr Thomas William Dobson, was alone in the kitchen at the time. He had also just come out of hospital the previous Friday after having been laid up for six weeks with a broken ankle and injuries to his left hand, following a fall at his work as a joiner. He can only get about with the aid of crutches.

"I heard my wife shout near the bottom of the stairs," Mr Dobson told our reporter, "but before I could reach her, after hobbling across by holding the furniture, she had fallen." Mr Dobson quickly summoned help and Dr Gray was called, but Mrs Dobson died shortly after the doctor's arrival.

Mrs Dobson, who was the only daughter of Mrs Isobel Hall and the late Mr E Hall, was born at Thornley but had lived at Wheatley Hill most of her life. She was held in high esteem by a wide circle of friends. She is survived by her husband, the baby, and a nine-year-old son, Edward Barry.

The funeral took place at Wheatley Hill cemetery on Tuesday, following a service in All Saint's Church, Wheatley Hill, conducted by the Vicar, the Rev Arthur Preston.

13 March 1953

AWARDED SCHOLARSHIP – A student at West Hartlepool Art College for five years, Miss Elsie Bradley, younger daughter of Mr and Mrs Benjamin Bradley, of Haswell, and formerly of Thornley, has been awarded a scholarship entitling her to a further course of study at the Royal College of Art in London. Her etching and engravings of industrial scenes in Durham County have carried considerable weight in gaining for her admission to the engraving school of the Royal College. Her ambition at the moment is to work on book illustration when she comes out of college.

CORONATION CELEBRATIONS - "Keep the Coronation in mind" is advice given by Thornley Coronation Committee to competitors who enter the parade and the decorated premises competitions to be held at Thornley on Coronation Eve. The Miners' Welfare Committee is to be asked to grant the use of the Welfare Hall for a commemoration service on Sunday, May 31. The Vicar of Thornley (the Rev H W Jackson) and the Rev W T Rose (Methodist minister) are making the arrangements. On the afternoon of Coronation Day about 440 aged people will be entertained to tea. The fund amounts to £131.1s.7d, but this will be considerably increased by a grant from the rates and by further social efforts and donations.

20 March 1953

EXCITEMENT AT WHEATLEY HILL

All the thrills in the semi-final of the Durham Central League Cup between Wheatley Hill S C and their neighbours Thornley St Godric's at Wheatley Hill, on Saturday, came in the second half. The result - a 1–1 draw – was perhaps a fair reflex of the play.

The first half was a drab affair and the closest effort at scoring came from a goalkeeper! He was Charlie Hesp, normally regular keeper for the "Hill," who was playing at outside right. Newly returned from a trial at Everton Hesp had not expected to play but was included in the side when the "Hill" found themselves short. Just before half-time he sent in a beautiful cross-shot which Magee just managed to tip over the bar.

The game livened up considerably after the change of ends. After 22 minutes, in a desperate effort to save a goal Chaytor, one of Thornley's backs, fisted out a header from Hold which had beaten Magee. From the resultant penalty Robinson made no mistake to put Wheatley Hill ahead. Exchanges were keen and fast after this with both goalkeepers, Clish and Magee, coming into the picture with some great saves.

Seven minutes from time Price had a good chance to increase the "Hill's" lead when he was clean through but he fired straight into Magee's hands. A minute later, in a storming attack, Thornley equalised when Clish dived at G Wilson's feet to try and stop the centre-forward's shot but the ball rolled into the net.

The closing minutes were packed with excitement. Brian Wilson, the visitors' left winger, and Clish were involved in a clash resulting in the goalkeeper being taken off with an injured arm. Hesp took his place between the sticks and in the last few seconds kept the "Hill" in the competition with a spectacular save on the goal-line. The replay resulted in a victory for Wheatley Hill by 3 goals to 2.

ALLOTMENT HUT FIRE – A number of young chickens perished when fire destroyed a wooden hut belonging to Mr John Bellwood, Moor View, Thornley, on the Wheatley Hill allotments last Thursday. Horden Unit of the Durham County Fire Brigade quickly reached the scene, but found the hut well ablaze and they were unable to save it or the chickens inside. The fire is believed to have been caused by the over-heating of an oil-lamp.

£500 CELEBRATIONS – After considering estimates from the various sub-committees responsible for the celebrations, the Finance Committee of the Wheatley Hill Coronation Celebrations Fund decided, at a special meeting, to sanction the spending of £500 on the local festivities. Mr Mark Alderton presided, and the financial statement, presented by Mr A

D Wharrier, revealed that the Fund had now reached £370. Included in this sum was £170, as Wheatley Hill's share of a rate levied by Wingate Parish Council – the rest of the money has been raised by donations and special efforts. Further efforts, including a supper and social evening in the Welfare Hall tomorrow, and a pantomime, "Cinderella," by Thornley "Imps" on Monday, are being arranged to raise the balance of the money required. Confidence was expressed that the £500 "target" will be reached.

CORONATION "QUEEN" - Twenty-seven entrants were reduced to six finalists in a "Coronation Queen" contest organised by Mr R Crosby, manager of the Embassy Ballroom, Wheatley Hill, at a dance in the Ballroom on Saturday. The young lady chosen as "Coronation Queen" for Wheatley Hill at a further dance to held on April 25 will be presented with a prize of £5. The six finalists are: Miss E Cummings, 12 Kingston Crescent, Haswell; Miss Mary Barnett, 22 Donald Avenue, South Hetton; Miss Elizabeth Cowie, 19 Barnard Avenue, Ludworth; Miss June Booth, 9 Luke Terrace, Wheatley Hill; Miss Margaret Soppitt, 7 Fifth Street, Wheatley Hill; and Miss C M Delwood, Quilstile Road, Wheatley Hill. They will take part in a mannequin parade in the final, and the winner will be decided by ballot among the dancers. The chosen "Queen" will be crowned at a Coronation Eve dance and will take part in a tableau.

THORNLEY

PANTOMIME – Two performances of a pantomime, "Jack and the Beanstalk," given in Thornley Welfare Hall by children trained by Mrs Caster (Thornley) raised £25 for Thornley Coronation Celebrations fund. Mrs Walton was pianist and Mr B Pattison was in charge of lighting. Mrs J Anderson, chairman of the Coronation Committee, thanked Mrs Caster and all who had assisted in making the effort so successful.

27 March 1953

SERVING IN KOREA

The country may be new, but the inhabitants are familiar to Sgt J Clem Franks (26), Royal Army Service Corps, 182 Thornlaw South, Thornley, serving with the Motor Ambulance Platoon near the front line in Korea.

In 1945 and 1946 he was stationed at the thousand strong "Stanley Fort" POW Camp at Hong Kong where he guarded Korean and Japanese P O W's and civilian internees. A Commando at the time, he helped repatriate P O W's and internees early in 1946, paid his first visit to

Inchon, Korea, and Omuta, Japan, long before being posted to the Commonwealth Division.

His present work consists of administering the motor ambulance platoon of his company, which played a major part in evacuating Black Watch casualties during and after the "Hook Battle" of last November. Married, with one son, he looks forward to returning to his family in June. – Sgt. Mark Carson.

TWO PERFORMANCES OF FOUR PLAYS AT THORNLEY

Two performances of four one-act plays were given in Thornley Welfare Hall on Wednesday and Thursday of last week by Thornley Youth Drama Group, led by Mr John Tunney. The first was given free for the aged people. The second performance drew an excellent audience, who thoroughly enjoyed themselves, but not more that the young players themselves.

Miss Carr, the Durham County Drama Organiser, who attended on Thursday, said she was highly satisfied with the performances of the young players, most of whom are in their teens and drawn from Thornley and Wheatley Hill. She also said that she admired the way in which Mr Tunney kept his rather large group together.

The players were: first play, Maurice Hirst, Marie Mitchell, Millie Lowes, Alan Howe, Stanley Bramfitt, Margaret Hoban, Alan Lincoln; second play, Anne McCoy, Dorothy Burlison, Marjorie Gascoigne, Kitty Stephenson, Anne Connelly; third play, Marie Mitchell, Kathleen Regan, Millie Lowes, Margaret Hoban, Anne McCoy, Marjorie Gascoigne, Dorothy Burlison, Audrey Harrison, Kitty Stephenson, Veronica Connelly, Anne Connelly, Alan Howe, Joseph McCoy; fourth play, John Tunney, Maurice Hirst and Margaret Hoban.

3 April 1953

LONG SEARCH ENDED – A well known Wheatley Hill insurance agent, Mr Thomas Richardson (59), 10 Wordsworth Avenue, who had been missing from home since November 5 last year, was found dead on Thursday last week on waste land near the ICI Nylon Works, Billingham. His body, it is understood, had lain there for some considerable time, but foul play is not suspected. The last Mrs Richardson saw of her husband alive was when he left home at mid-day on November 5, to attend an insurance agents' meeting at Middlesbrough. It was learned that he had attended the meeting and was afterwards understood to have boarded a homeward bus. Nothing more, however, was heard of him, though several people had reported seeing a man answering to his description in the Stockton and Norton Area. Mr Richardson, who is survived by his wife and a married son and daughter, had lived at Wheatley Hill practically all his life. He formally worked at Wheatley Hill colliery, but later began work as an insurance agent for the United Friendly Insurance Company, which position he filled for 12 years. Mr Richardson was formerly librarian for Wheatley Hill Workmen's Club for many years, and for some time was secretary of Wheatley Hill Juniors' Football Club. He was buried at Wheatley Hill cemetery yesterday, following a service at "The Rest," conducted by the Rev W T Rose (Thornley).

10 April 1953

BOW STREET CHURCH
£240 Raised At Spring Fayre

The ample room in the new Welfare Hall at Thornley proved to be ideal for the holding of the Spring Fayre by Bow Street Methodist Church members on Saturday. Stalls were in the main hall, refreshments on the self-service style were served in the supper room, and a small curtained-off portion brought in a revenue as a museum.

Coun Mrs J J Rushford, of Durham, introduced by the Rev W T Rose, superintendent minister, opened the fayre. "I know a good deal about Thornley people," she said. "I know that Thornley people could always be relied upon to work hard to help to keep Durham County Hospital going.

"I felt that when Thornley Welfare Hall was burned down it was a disaster," said Mrs Rushford, "but I am glad that social life in Thornley can now take its normal course, and I hope the new hall will be used for much good work, as the old hall was used."

Church Work Vital

Now that the hospitals had been taken over by the State, Mrs Rushford said she felt that the great amount of time Thornley people used to devote to the hospital might now be given to their churches and for the Christian life which was going to play such a large part in the affairs of the world. "If we can only strengthen our Church, and strengthen it by ourselves, we will help to bring peace and prosperity in the world."

After declaring the sale open, Mrs Rushford was presented with a bouquet by Dorothy Gilding, one of the Sunday School children.

Enthusiastic Workers

Mrs A L Miller, Secretary of the Trust, after paying tribute to the church treasurer, Mr T T Ridley, and to the Fayre secretary, Mr Hedley Ridley, mentioned three lady workers – Mrs Jackson, aged 83, who had raised £6.7s.6d, Mrs Willey, who had handed in £27.12s.6d, and Mrs Palmer, Birmingham (a guest of Mrs Plant), who had supplied a large quantity of goods.

Mr T T Ridley, treasurer for 14 years, said it was taking more money than ever to keep the church going. The present boiler for example, installed forty years ago, needed to be replaced, and the cost would be £120. "Another thing," said Mr Ridley, "is that we must keep our members occupied – they cannot do anything better than work for their church."

At the stalls

The stalls included: Draperies (Sisterhood), cakes (choir), jellies and trifles (CE), woodwork (men and boys), Coronation souvenirs (general), groceries (church), comic photographs, handkerchiefs and soap (Sunday School), over 20 club (tea). Amongst the old members of the church in attendance at the Fayre were Mr George Archer, aged 88, a member for about 50 years; Mrs Fort (50 years), Mrs Davis (50 years), Mrs Archer (50 years in the choir), Mr J Farrell and Miss Kirk (christened in the church).

The event concluded with a social, for which Mr J Plant was M C. The day's proceeds amounted to £240.

THORNLEY

DRAMA GROUP – The first appearance of a local drama group on the stage of the new Welfare Hall at Thornley was made on Wednesday when the Thornley Group gave the first of three performances of "Arsenic and Old Lace." To make up the cast of 14, friends from the Wheatley Hill group were included. Mrs Vera Fairclough was again the producer, and the players were : Alice Winter, Olive Lincoln, Marjorie Swinburne, Frank Bowes, Vic Brown, Bert Martin, John Tunney, David Gott, Herbert Galley, Tom King, Jim Bewick, Bob Atkinson, William Dowson and Brian Askew. Back stage were Mrs Potts (manager), Arthur Clark (lighting), H Hetherington (scenery) and Rita Orange (wardrobe mistress).

17 April 1953

KNOCKED DOWN BY 'BUS - Knocked down by a bus on the main road through Thornley on Saturday, four-year-old Robert Gallon, Shinwell Crescent, Thornley, was taken to Durham County Hospital, suffering from a fractured skull and severe shock. Later at the hospital his condition was stated to be "a little improved."

CORONATION ARRANGEMENTS at Thornley are well in hand, and there is every prospect that funds will be available to carry out the whole programme. A donation has been given by the Thornley Colliery Federation, which will meet the larger part of the cost of high tea for about 440 aged people on June 1. Also on that day there will be an evening procession with prizes for tableaux and dresses, the judging being at St Godric's football field. On the same night there will be judging of decorated shops, houses and gardens, and a bonfire and fireworks. Children's sports, with tea, will be in the school sports field on Coronation Day. Souvenirs will be given out on the Wednesday before Coronation Day at Thornley school to all school children up to 15 years of age.

ROAD SAFETY AID – After hearing that a playing field project at Wheatley Hill was being held up because of Wingate Parish Council's refusal to pay the legal fees involved in the cost of conveyancing land from Easington Rural Council, Wheatley Hill Road Safety Committee, at their meeting on Tuesday, decided to give support to any local committee that may be formed to take over land for playing fields. Mr J W Willan presided and members expressed the opinion that playing fields in the village would lessen the risk of accidents to young people.

WI EFFORT – About £9.10s. was raised for their funds as a result of a whist and domino drive and dance in the Welfare Hall on Tuesday, organised by Wheatley Hill W I . The president, Mrs Thackeray, who was M C presented the prizes to the following: Whist, Mr & Mrs A Atkinson, Mrs Haddock and Miss Cowell; dominoes, Mrs Smart and Mrs Smith (consolation). Special competitions were won by Mesdames W Poulson, Clogg, Parnham, W Hedley, sen, H Poole and J Ord. Refreshments were served and music for the dance was by the Gleneagles Band, Wingate. Mrs E Parnham and Mrs R Ord won spot dance prizes.

SISTERHOOD – The Sisterhood of Church Street Methodist Church, Wheatley Hill, began anniversary celebrations on Monday with a concert in the Welfare Hall. Sisterhood members and young people took part in a musical play, "Mrs Winter's 'At Home'." Mrs P H Galley, sen, was producer and accompanist was Mrs A Kirk. Principal roles were filled by Mesdames C Venables, Ord, Milne, Carter, J Harrison, H Lang and Calvert, Miss M Kent and Mrs B Galley. Solos were by Miss J Calvert and Miss S Lowther, and the Lewis sisters gave pianoforte duets.

MINERS' DECISIONS – After a lengthy discussion, Wheatley Hill Miners' Lodge, at a meeting presided over by Mr H Bradshaw, decided to celebrate Whit Monday as a holiday as usual instead of working that day, and having the Monday before the Coronation as a holiday. A number of members expressed the view that had those responsible for fixing the date of the Coronation been interested in coal production they would not have chosen a Tuesday as this meant breaking up the week in the mining industry. The lodge has also decided not to work the Saturday shift during the summer months, despite a Coal Board appeal for Saturday working to increase production. Wheatley Hill colliery, in fact, does not work the Saturday shift during the rest of the year either.

24 April 1953

WHEATLEY HILL NONAGENARIAN

One of Wheatley Hill's oldest inhabitants, Mrs Mary Lonsdale, 28, Luke Terrace, celebrated her 90th birthday on Saturday, but her birthday passed quietly as she has been bedfast for the past four years. Living with her is her only daughter, Miss Lydia Lonsdale, who has cared for the old lady during her long period of illness.

Mrs Lonsdale's husband, Mr Matthew Lonsdale, died in February – his death broke a married partnership of more than 67 years. In addition to her daughter she has four sons, the second oldest, Jack, living at Connecticut, USA, where he emigrated during the 1926 strike.

Mrs Lonsdale has lived in Wheatley Hill for more than half a century. Previously she lived at Castle Eden. Though in full possession of all her faculties she has been in poor health for many years.

1 May 1953

CONGRATULATIONS, WHEATLEY HILL!

Congratulations to Wheatley Hill S C who, by defeating Shildon Reserves 6-0 in their last game of the season on Saturday, became champions of the Durham Central League. It was only by a narrow margin that the title came to the "Hill," they ended with 37 points from their 24 games – only one more than the runners-up, Cockfield.

Wheatley Hill's achievement is all the more meritorious when it is remembered that they had a packed end-of-the-season programme, playing nine games in a fortnight. Eight of these games were won, the one they lost – by 3-1 away to Bearpark last week – nearly lost them the league title as it meant they had to win their final game against Shildon.

The "Hill," however, made no mistake against Shildon. The game was played before one of their best "gates" of the season and was a personal triumph for their inside left, "Nat" Lofthouse, who got a second half "hat-trick." It was from a Lofthouse drive, which was deflected into the net by a visiting full-back, that Wheatley Hill opened their account shortly after the kick-off. Further goals before half-time came from Knapper and Smith.

Shildon were rarely in the picture after the change-over and Wheatley Hill left no doubts about their superiority when Lofthouse found the net with three beautiful efforts.

Wheatley Hill joined the Durham Central League only three seasons ago. In their first season they ended about midway in the league table, but last season finished third off bottom.

In their second last game on Friday night the "Hill" defeated Sacriston 6-1 at home. Lofthouse was again among the scorers, helping himself to two goals, and the other marksmen were Smith (2), Knapper and Hold.

LUDWORTH END WITH TWO TROPIES

Ludworth RS Juniors visited Bowburn in mid-week to beat Kelloe Juniors by 4-3, after extra time, to carry off the Durham and District League Knock-out Cup. Hammond (2), Scullion and Fishwick were the scorers.

On Friday evening, Ludworth went to Shotton and accounted for Boldon by 2-1 in the final of the divisional competition. Fishwick and Scullion netted.

On Saturday, Ludworth completed their league programme with a ten goals to nil win over Kelloe Juniors, and strengthened their hold on runners-up position in that competition. Hammond (4), Thompson (2), Fishwick (2), Scullion and Ainscough were the scorers.

In addition to the two trophies they won, Ludworth had won 19, drawn two and lost one league match for a grand season, collecting 39 points out of 44 possible for runners-up place.

They have secured 173 goals throughout the season, scorers being Scullion 50, Fishwick 44, Hammond 25, Elcoat 19, Bower 16, Stones 6, Thompson 5, S Carr 4, Barker 2, Greener 1 and Aincough 1.

8 May 1953

NEW HEADMASTER – The appointment of Mr Arthur Harris as headmaster of Wheatley Hill Boys' Modern School was confirmed by the County Education Committee on Wednesday.

FOOTBALLERS' PRESENTATIONS – Awards won by Wheatley Hill Mechanics' Football Club, as runners-up in the Hetton Charity and Thornley Aged Miners' Cups, were presented to the players at an enjoyable social evening in Wheatley Hill Welfare Hall on Saturday. Mr William Ruth, chairman of the club, presided and welcomed the club president, Mr J L Snaith (manager of Wheatley Hill colliery), who presented runners-up plaques (Hetton Charity Cup) and miniature cups (Thornley Aged Miners' Cup) to the following players: Eric Errington, Jonathan Sanderson, Robert Williams, Lawrence Blakemore, Terence Allison, Eric Kirby, Tom Nicholson, Wilf Goyns (captain), Hedley Rigby, John Molloy and Leslie Lee, and Ray Carr and George Bean (plaques only). Mr Snaith congratulated the club upon its successful season – they also won the Wingate and District League Cup and ended the season third off top in the league – and expressed the hope that even better progress would be made next year. Congratulations were also added by Mr C Scott (secretary, Hetton Charity Cup) and Mr C Campbell (secretary, Thornley Aged Miners' Cup). Supper was served and entertainment was provided by "The Cordells" concert party, Newcastle. Arrangements were made by the club secretary, Mr J G Davies.

PIT VICTIM'S FUNERAL – A large representative cortege attended the funeral, at Wheatley Hill Cemetery on Saturday the 9th of Mr John Lamb (59), 2 East View, Wheatley Hill, who was killed by a fall of stone while following his employment as a stoneman in the North-West Busty seam at Wheatley Hill colliery the previous Wednesday. Mr Lamb had lived in the village practically all his life, and except for two years at Deaf Hill colliery had been employed at the local colliery from leaving school. He served as a gunner in the Royal Artillery during the first world war, and soon after his demobilisation re-joined the Army for a further period of three years, serving for some time in Turkey. During the last war he was a sergeant in the Wheatley Hill Home Guard. Mr Lamb was a member of both the Workmen's and Constitutional Clubs at Wheatley Hill, and had recently served on the committee of the Workmen's Club. He was held in high esteem in the village and much sympathy is felt for his wife and only son, who survive him. The cortege on Saturday was headed by Wheatley Hill Colliery Band and officials of Wheatley Hill Miners' Lodge, bearing aloft their banner. Mr J L Snaith (manager) and Mr Simpson (under-manager) represented the colliery management, and there were many representatives of local organisations. Members of the committee of the Workmen's Club acted as under-bearers. The funeral service at "The Rest" was conducted by the Rev Noel Catherall.

15 May 1953

MARRIED FOR 50 YEARS
Mr and Mrs J R Scott, Wheatley Hill

Mr and Mrs John Robert Scott, 14 Wolmerhausen Street, Wheatley Hill, who last week celebrated their golden wedding with a party at their home, attended by all their family of four sons and five daughters, have lived in Wheatley Hill since 1916. Both enjoy good health and are quite active for their years.

Mr Scott, who will be 75 in October, often gives his wife "a hand" with the house-work and is always there to help on washing day. A retired miner Mr Scott began work at Rainton Colliery when he was 13 years of age for 10d a day. Four years later he transferred to Kelloe Colliery, where he was employed for 22 years before going to Wheatley Hill, where he retired eight years ago. Most of his mining career was spent as a coal-hewer.

For a number of years before his marriage Mr Scott played football for Kelloe St Helen's. "They had quite a good team in those days," he recalled, "and one of the best goal-keepers in the county - Tommy Fisher. He's still alive today and lives at Kelloe. There was none to beat him for miles around.

Footballer

Mr Scott, a right-half, was a member of the team which won the Mid-Durham League in 1901 and reached the semi-final of the Durham

Amateur Cup. They had to win all their last 11 games to end the season with the same points as Trimdon Grange. Both clubs then played a "decider" – the first meeting ended in a draw, but in the next encounter Kelloe St Helen's won and were presented with the league championship trophy.

Mr Scott won quite a number of medals – "real gold ones" – but later parted with them to his family and two of them were converted into brooches for his daughters. Two of his sons, Sammy and Jim, are well-known in football circles in East Durham. Sammy was a professional with Sunderland and Torquay after playing for Bishop Auckland, and, until he "hung up his boots" two years ago, played for Wingate Welfare, Murton C W and South Hetton, among other local clubs. Jim, who has also given up the game, has played for Wheatley Hill S C, Deaf Hill and Crook.

Mrs Scott, who is 68, looks after her own home. She had quite a struggle to bring up her big family. "But we pulled through together," she said, "and it's nice to have them all with us today." The couple, who were married at Durham Register Office, have 11 grandchildren.

At the celebration party the health of the old couple was toasted and best wishes extended to them for many years of good health and happiness together. The golden wedding cake was made by their second youngest daughter Mrs Joan Potts (Wheatley Hill).

22 May 1953

CERTIFICATES FOR C-DAY BABIES

Babies born at Thornley on Coronation Day will be presented with National Savings Certificates. A note in the programme says: "The committee will be disappointed if there are no claimants."

Wheatley Hill C – Plans

For months now a representative committee has been working at Wheatley Hill to make the Coronation a never-to-be-forgotten celebration in the village. Events have been organised to cater for all ages and to suit every taste, and with more than £500 having been raised to cover the cost of the festivities the committee have been able to "launch out" with prizes and mementoes.

The celebrations start on the Saturday before Coronation Day when the finals of children's sports will be staged in Wheatley Hill cricket field, by permission of the cricket club committee. The preliminary heats are being run off at the different schools in the village. Eight finalists will appear in each of the 33 events, which cover races for infants, juniors and seniors of both sexes. More than 200 prizes are to be awarded, and in charge will be Mr E Ward and his committee.

Refreshments both for the competitors and spectators are being organised by Wheatley Hill Cricket Club, the prizes will be presented by Coun J W Moore, chairman of the Celebrations Committee. If the weather is unfavourable on the Saturday the sports will take place the following Monday.

Afternoon Parade

A fancy and comic dress parade, including tableaux, decorated vehicles and decorated cycles, gives a send-off to celebrations on Coronation Day itself. The parade, headed by Wheatley Hill Colliery Prize Band, will start at the colliery offices at 2pm with Mr S Woodward as parade marshal. Miss Watson and her committee are in charge. The parade will follow a route through the council housing estate and on to Wingate Lane and will return via Front Street To Welfare Park, where judging will take place.

Prizes are to be awarded for the best decorated shop window, and decorations will be artistically arranged in the main thoroughfare by the Celebrations Committee, with the support of local tradespeople. House-holders are being invited to hang out streamers and flags to give the whole village a real Coronation atmosphere.

At 6pm a four-mile race for villagers over 15 is to be staged in the cricket field. Two cups will be presented to the winner – one to hold for a year and the other to keep – and other prizes will be awarded. The cups have been presented by Mr A Baldasera and Mr James Steel. A "sealed" handicap for "over-40's" is to follow.

One of the high-lights of the day will be the firework display and bonfire in the Welfare Park at 8.30pm. In charge will be Mr J L Snaith, manager of Wheatley Hill Colliery, and his committee. A "safety" area will be roped off and the display will last 45 minutes.

Old Folk's Tea

There will be no Coronation tea for the children, but the day before the Coronation, when they receive their gifts from the County Education Committee they will receive, at the same time, a souvenir mug from the

Wheatley Hill Committee and an sorted box of chocolates and sweets. Children under five will be given their gifts in the Welfare Hall.

On Thursday – two days after the Coronation – a knife-and-fork tea is being provided in the Welfare Hall for all aged people in the village, numbering about 400.

This will start at 3pm and in charge will be Mrs Bowes and her committee. Entertainment will be given by Mrs Richardson's party and the Wheatley Hill WI group. Those old folk unable to attend will have their teas taken to them – a fleet of cars has been loaned for this purpose.

A full-length film of the Coronation has been ordered and when it is delivered to the Committee it will be shown to all the schoolchildren and old people in the village.

A bowls tournament, open to all men and women in the village, is being organised, with the finals to be held some time during Coronation week. Medals for the winners are being provided by Mr Baldasera, and again, many prizes are to be awarded.

Programmes of the festivities are being printed – they are to be sold at threepence each. The holder of the programme with the "lucky" number – a sealed number sent by Mr E Shinwell, M P for the Division – will be presented with a special prize.

The committee has worked smoothly and efficiently throughout, with the object of providing a memorable time for both young and old, and it deserves the highest praise for organising such a varied and entertaining programme.

THORNLEY

Arrangements for celebrating the Coronation are complete at Thornley. On Sunday afternoon there will be a united service in the Welfare Hall, following a procession from the green at South Thornlaw. Organisations have been invited to send representatives. It is also expected that each of the schools attended by Thornley children will send pupils. The colliery band will be in the procession and at the service.

They will also lead a parade of tableaux and fancy dress from Dunelm Road to St Godric's football ground on Monday evening. On the afternoon of Monday, 440 aged people will be entertained to tea. At night there will be a bonfire and fireworks in the Welfare football field. The children's tea and sports will be on the afternoon on Coronation Day. Beakers and other souvenirs have already been given out to children.

FORMER MINER DIES – A resident at Thornley for the past 66 years, Mr Robert E Hoy (78), has died at his home in Chapel Street. He worked both underground and on the surface over a long period at Thornley Colliery. His wife died five months ago.

CONFIRMATION – The Bishop of Jarrow confirmed 18 Thornley candidates in Thornley Parish Church on Sunday morning. Assisted by the Rev H W Jackson, Vicar of Thornley, he also administered Holy Communion. The holding of a confirmation service on a Sunday morning was an innovation at Thornley.

OCTOGENARIAN – Thornley's "Grand Old Man," Mr William Thomas Roper (87), who's working life was probably the longest of any Thornley man, was interred in Thornley cemetery, the Rev Father Sharratt officiating. Starting his pit life as a boy he worked through all the stages, including those of the various official grades, until he became a fore over-man. In his later years he was transferred to the colliery office, continuing until he was 83. As the oldest worker at Thornley Colliery, he took a leading part in the vesting ceremony when the Coal Board took over the pits on 1 January 1947.

29 May 1953

AFTER THE CROWNING CEREMONY
HE KISSED HER LEFT CHEEK
Duke of Edinburgh's Homage to Her Majesty the Queen.

Deserted streets . . . . Flags, streamers and bunting battered about by blustery north-east winds and heavy continuous rain . . . .People wrapped up as though facing the rigours of a mid-December day. Men, women and children huddled together in their homes, huts and halls looking very cheerful and very happy on a day when history was being made at Westminster Abbey – the crowning of Her Majesty Queen Elizabeth 11.

That was the picture in our county that will always be in our minds when we look back upon Coronation Day, 2 June 1953, the day for which there had been weeks and months of careful and generous preparation. All out-door events were washed out, but the spirit of the people on such an occasion was not quenched even by the Arctic conditions, for they were able, through the magic of television and the radio to become part of the great London throng in the glorious pageantry that only London can produce at such a time.

5 June 1953

WHEATLEY HILL

GRANT TOWARDS SCHOOL CAMP - Subject to the approval of the Ministry of Education, a grant at the rate of 15s per head will be made towards the cost of Wheatley Hill Boys' Modern School camp, Durham County Education Committee decided on Wednesday. Forty pupils from the school will camp at Landieu Farm, Frosterley, from July 24 to 31.

CORONATION BONFIRE – The Coronation celebrations at Wheatley Hill ended on Saturday night when a bonfire in the Welfare ground, built under the supervision of Mr J L Snaith (colliery manager) and his committee, was lit and was followed by an hour's fireworks display. The brothers K and T Carr dead-heated for first place in a four-mile race earlier in the evening, and winners of the individual bowls tournaments were: Ladies, 1, Miss Todd; 2, Mrs G Wharrier; Men, 1, Mr J Watson; 2, Mr A Dobson.

SUNDAY SCHOOL ANNIVERSARY - In recognition of his 25 years service as secretary of the Sunday School, Mr Maurice Nixon was presented with a gift pen and pencil set at the Sunday School anniversary services in Wheatley Hill Church Street Methodist Church on Sunday. The presentation was made on behalf of the Sunday School by the superintendent, Mr J O Hughes. During the morning the scholars, teachers and friends paraded through the streets of the village, singing hymns and extending invitations to the services. Mr J W Willan (Wheatley Hill) presided afternoon and evening, and the organist was Miss Joan Lewis. In the afternoon the senior scholars, trained by Miss B Galley and Miss M Kent, gave a demonstration, entitled "The Meaning of the Coronation Service." The Primary Department gave a programme of recitations and singing at night, and in charge of their training were Miss J Calvert, Mr H Galley and Mr W Mowbray. The choir was conducted by Mrs R Ord. The services will be continued on Sunday.

FESTIVITIES AT THORNLEY
Many Prizes for Young and Old

The Thornley Coronation Committee, after nine meetings and quite a number of sub-committee meetings, which resulted in an excellent programme being drawn up, had to resort in the end to improvisation.

It began on Coronation Eve, when a motor coach was used to collect aged people for their knife-and-fork tea in the Welfare Hall. There were about 350 old people in the large dance hall. After tea, children from the junior school sang a number of songs, and Mrs Hopps also entertained. Coun Mrs Anderson gave out awards to some of the aged people with local records. Mr George Archer (88) was the oldest man and Mrs Hope (84) the oldest woman in the company. The couple married the longest were Mr & Mrs James Davies. Mr Robert West was born on Christmas Day, but there was nobody born on Coronation Day, nor was there any woman present born on the Queen's birthday. Mrs Million was the youngest to be married (under 17). Mrs John Shutt had been resident in Thornley for 83 years.

In spite of the weather there was a good turn-out for the parade from Dunelm Road to the St Godric's football ground on Monday evening. Thornley Colliery Band, led by Mr E G Kitto, led the procession which included single competitors and tableaux prepared by the Women's Institute, British Legion women, Mothers' Union Bow Street Sunday School, East Lea children and Labour Women.

Winners

Winners were: Not over 15, 1, Bow Street Sunday School, 2, British Legion Women; over 15, Women's Institute, British Legion Women; original dress, female over 15, Mrs Robinson; male, over15, A Dunnett; original dress not over 15, M Robinson, R Stephenson; boy not over 15, J Bennett, B Burnham; decorated house, Mrs M
Greener, 7 Shinwell Crescent; G A Foster, 117 Dunelm Road; shop window (interior) T H Hill, Baldasera and Sons (exterior) A Baldasera, G W Graymoore; decorated garden, Jonas Gott, 48 Hillsyde Crescent, James Plast, 141 Thornley South.

Judges were Mesdames Scott, Brandling, Todd, Potts, Jackson, Roper, Rose; Messrs Smart, H Ridley, W Lamb, R Robinson, W Potts, W Dowson, M Fleming, A Welsh, W Atkin and A Hesler, and Dr Todd.

A display of £25 worth of fireworks, lasting about 40 minutes was given in the Welfare football field, followed by the lighting of a large and well-built bonfire by Mrs Welsh in the presence of some hundreds of spectators.

Some of the children came to tea in the rain on Coronation Day and were served in a small room in the infants' school by Miss Berriman and lady members of the committee. Other children had their bags of cakes taken to them at their homes by owners of cars and vans.

In charge of sections were: - Aged people's tea, Mr E Carter; procession and decoration classes, Mr W Hetherington; bonfire and fireworks, Mr I P Martin, with Mr F Bradley as bonfire erector; children's tea and sports, Mr C Lamb, treasurer. Mrs J Anderson, as chairman of the general committee, is a great deal of useful work, and Mr T H Holder was secretary.

12 June 1953

SUNDAY SCHOOL PRESENTATION During the Sunday School anniversary services in Wheatley Hill Church Street Methodist Church on Sunday, the presentation of a book was made to one of the scholars, Stephen Walker, to mark his achievement in collecting £13.10s. for Overseas Missions during the past year. The presentation was made on behalf of the circuit by Mrs J L Snaith (wife of the manager of Wheatley Hill colliery), who presided at the services. In the afternoon a programme of recitations, solos and choruses was given by the Sunday School scholars, and at night the seniors took part in a demonstration entitled, "The Meaning of the Coronation Service." The singing was conducted by Mrs R Ord, and Miss Joan Lewis was organist. It was the concluding Sunday of the celebrations and collections taken both in the streets of the village and at the services totalled £35. The scholars, teachers and friends are to complete their tour of the streets, singing special hymns, on Sunday morning.

MINERS' LODGE BALLOT – Mr H Bradshaw, chairman of Wheatley Hill Miners' Lodge, who was the only official opposed in the annual ballot of the lodge, retained his position for the ensuing year, defeating Mr J Frost by 318 votes to 188. The other three principal officials were re-elected unopposed, namely, Correspondence secretary, Coun E Cain, J P ; financial secretary, Mr J Hedley; treasurer, Mr T Taylorson. Other officers elected by ballot were: Delegate, Mr J W Burrell; Auditors, Messrs T W Buxton and G R Buxton; Local Pit Inspector, Mr R Clish; Labour Party delegate, Mr A Wharrier (who defeated Mr J Andrews by two votes); Death Fund Committee, Messrs T W Buxton, H Bradshaw and J Brandling; Housing committee, Messrs E Jones and N Waugh; Aged Miners' Homes' Committee, Messrs M Alderton, J Bradley, H Bradshaw, J W Burrell, E Cain, N Cook, J Hedley and T Taylorson; Welfare Committee, Messrs M Alderton, T Buxton, R Clish, J Hedley and W Rotheray; Band Committee, Messrs M Cain, G Cook, H Peacock and R Teasdale; Lodge committee, Messrs J Bradley, J Brandling, R Clish, N Cook, J Hennessey, E Jones, H Peacock and N Waugh.

19 June 1953

FROM THORNLEY TO EVENWOOD

Mr William Dowson head costing clerk at Thornley Colliery has been appointed cashier for the Randolph Colliery at Evenwood, in the Sub-Group of the No 4 NCB Area. He takes up his duties on 1 July. A Methodist local preacher in the Thornley Circuit from the age of 21, Mr Dowson, is closely associated with the Thornley Waterloo Street Church as treasurer, vice-president of the Wesley Guild, and Sunday School teacher. Other offices he holds at Thornley are officials' representative on the Colliery Federation Board and treasurer of the drama group. In the recent war he served abroad in the Royal Artillery 7th Survey Regiment.

MR & MRS JOHN A WILLIAMS of 13 Stoker Crescent, Wheatley Hill have been informed of the death in action of their son Kenneth, aged 23 in Korea. 22283569 Gunner K Williams, Royal Artillery, died on 12 June and is buried in the United Nations Memorial Cemetery.

3 July 1953

Gnr Kenneth Williams,
Aged 23 years

United Nations Memorial Cemetery
Korea

THORNLEY PARISH COUNCIL
Entrance To The Parish Church

Members of Thornley Parish Council expressed themselves as highly satisfied when a letter was read stating that the No 3 Area General Manager (Mr R S McLaren) was arranging for the carrying out of the Council's request for the improvement of the entrance to the Parish Church and for the completion of the clearance of debris from Church Street.

The letter stated that is was realised that as the houses in Church Street were demolished before the war and the land handed back to the trustees, it was not really the Board's liability to undertake the work, but they were prepared to do so in order to improve the amenities of the district and in view of the Board's previous interest in the property.

Coun M Fleming (chairman) said the area had been inspected by the Board's property manager and the colliery engineer, and they hoped that the work would be carried out before the bad weather came.

Sanction Refused

In reply to the Council's request for authority to pay the expenses of a delegate or delegates to the Association of Public Lighting Engineers' Conference at Liverpool in September, a letter from the Ministry of Health and Local Government stated that the Minister did not feel justified in issuing a sanction. Coun Fleming remarked that this was a repetition of the refusal of last year's request, and he felt they could do little about it. It was agreed to accept the Minister's refusal of sanction.

WI Gesture

An offer by the Thornley Women's Institute to provide litter baskets was described by the chairman as a generous gesture and public-spirited action. On Mrs Bosomworth's motion it was agreed to accept the offer.

In their letter the Institute said the gift was being made as a memento of Coronation year. The Clerk is to make enquiries as to which authority – the County Council or the Easington Rural Council – will be responsible for the servicing of the baskets.

Damage To Roadside Seats

When considerable wanton damage of roadside seats, resulting in the putting out of use of several of the seats, was mentioned, the Clerk was instructed to make a second request to the Easington R D Council for repairs to be carried out. The Clerk said that in a number of cases all the wooden parts of the seats had been taken away. In at least one case a concrete seat end had been broken and was useless. It was decided to ask for a seat to be placed near the Manse at the Villas, the seat to face towards Dunelm Road.

Church Street Land

When Mrs Bosomworth asked if the promised gift of Church Street land had been carried through, the Clerk said he had made enquiries of the owners solicitors some time ago and was informed that it was expected the matter would be soon dealt with. It was decided to make another enquiry.

Payment Of Rates

Mrs Anderson was among those who made reference to the dissatisfaction caused by the Easington R D C's decision that ratepayers must take or send their rates to Easington, instead of paying them to an official of the Council sitting at certain periods in the parish. It was agreed the Clerk inform the District Council of the dissatisfaction, asking at the same time for the reasons for the change.

10 July 1953

CLUB COMMITTEE – From 23 nominations the following have been elected to the committee of Wheatley Hill Workmen's Club for the ensuing year: Messrs R Armstrong, C Hackworth, W Jones (Tich), W Jones (Trapper), G Henderson senior and G Aitken. The ballot was held at the weekend.

CHECKWEIGH FUND GIFT – From Wheatley Hill Colliery Checkweigh Fund, full members are to be presented with £1 each today, for the Durham Miners' Gala Day. The distribution, in charge of Mr E Jones (secretary), and the committee, is to be made from Wheatley Hill Welfare Hall.

SUNDAY SCHOOL OUTING – Ten buses took the Sunday School scholars, teachers and friends of Wheatley Hill Patton Street Methodist Church on their annual outing to Redcar on Saturday. Warm sunshine prevailed throughout the day and a happy time was spent by the sea. Arrangements were made by Mr W Luke, junior.

OLD PEOPLE'S TRIP – Through the generosity of all sections of workmen at Wheatley Hill colliery, who contribute a special levy during the year, retired miners at Wheatley Hill and their wives and widows over 55 were taken on their annual outing to Redcar on Saturday. The arrangements were made by the local Aged Miners' Homes Committee, with Coun E Cain secretary. To add to the enjoyment of the old folk they were each given 10s pocket money. Those qualifying for the outing but unable to make the journey, either because of their advanced years or indisposition, were given 5s each.

WHEATLEY HILL LODGE'S GUESTS

Accompanying Wheatley Hill miners' lodge when they march with their band and banner to Durham tomorrow for the "Big Meeting", will be a former official of the lodge who emigrated to Australia 27 years ago and is now back in England for his first return visit.

He is Mr Harold Taylor, whose widowed mother lives in Wheatley Hill Aged Miners' Homes. Mr Taylor, while in this country, is staying at his brother's home on Tyneside. Before emigrating he worked at Wheatley Hill colliery and was actively associated with the local Labour Party.

Three other "new faces" who will be seen marching alongside lodge officials are three German mining students who have arrived at Wheatley Hill to spend eight weeks studying mining methods at the colliery. All three came from the Ruhr district. They had several years mining experience before being given licences to train for managerial positions in the privately-owned German mines. The students are staying with a miner and his wife at Wheatley Hill. Three buses have been engaged by the Wheatley Hill lodge to take their officials, members and guests to the "Big Meeting."

THORNLEY

NEW LODGE BANNER – Mr E Shinwell, MP, Mr Arthur Greenwood, MP and Mr Sam Watson are to attend the unfurling on Friday of the new lodge banner acquired by Thornley miners. There will be a parade led by Thornley Colliery Silver Band from Dunelm Road to the Welfare Institute. The new banner is being unfurled in time for the miners' gala at Durham tomorrow. In the fire at the Welfare Institute in 1944 the lodge lost its banner, and the new one replaces another which has been repaired several times.

17 July 1953

EASINGTON RDC

The Clerk reported that the Ministry of Housing and Local Government approval had been received to the Council's estimate of £4,138.5s.4d for the erection of four bungalows at Wheatley Hill.

The Council is to utilise a site at Wheatley Hill previously reserved as a playing field, for future building. The Clerk reported that a deputation from the Housing Committee had met representatives of the N C B and Ministry of Agriculture and Fisheries, who were objecting to the original site selected by the Council for further building at Wheatley Hill.

The Ministry representative had stated that their objection was based on the fact that the proposed site was good agricultural land, while in their opinion there was in the vicinity inferior land from the point of view of agriculture, which could be utilised for housing.

NCB Objection

The Coal Board objected to building on this land because the Busty seam at Thornley was being worked towards the site and they would be working under the site in 1955 or 1956. A second seam would also be worked in the area and in the long term, probably a third seam. If building was to take place there would undoubtedly be considerable damage caused to the houses by these workings, while on the other hand, if the coal was left, it meant a loss of approximately 75,000 tons. The Coal Board contended that there was a site of some seven acres only about 700 yards away, which could be utilised for building, though it was understood that it had been reserved as a playing field. They suggested that if building was to take place on this site, another site could be found for a playing field, where any damage caused by subsidence would be comparatively inexpensive.

It was eventually agreed that the Council would utilise the playing field site for building and Area Planning Officer had said he would forward site clearance as soon as possible. He would obtain from the NCB their views on the density of building and consideration could then be given to building in blocks of four or six houses.

WHEATLEY HILL BAND APPEAL

Wheatley Hill Colliery Band, which shot into the limelight during recent months with some notable successes, is now appealing to local tradespeople and others interested in the Band's welfare for donations to buy a new set of uniforms.

"The present uniform has been in use for some 20 years," the secretary, Mr J Gair, tells me, "and we feel now we would like a new uniform in keeping with the Band's name."

Donations will be gratefully acknowledged either by Mr Gair, who lives at 58, Liddell Terrace, Wheatley Hill, or by the treasurer, Mr J Lewis, 78 Wordsworth Avenue, Wheatley Hill.

LODGE BANNER UNFURLED
By Mr Arthur Greenwood At Thornley

New Colliery Banner for Thornley
L-R G Soppit, J Morland, M Kirk, J Webb, e Carter, J William, D Gott, S Greener, L Williamson,
J Robson, J Joicey, D Swallow, W Dowden, J Cherry

On one side of Thornley Miners' Lodge's new banner is a painting of the village's row of Aged Miners' Homes called Greenwood Homes. It was a thoughtful gesture on the part of the lodge when they invited Mr Arthur Greenwood, M.P., Treasurer of the Labour Party, after whom the Homes were named, to unfurl the new banner on Friday night, the eve Durham's "Big Meeting." The banner, costing more

337

than £100, is an exact replica of the one it replaces, and it was proudly borne to the "Big Meeting" for the first time the following day.

Extending a warm welcome to Mr Greenwood, Mr Sam Watson, general secretary of the Durham Area, NUM, who presided at the unfurling ceremony in Thornley Welfare Hall, said that Thornley miners were well aware of the Parliamentarian's connection with the village. "In 1931, when Mr Greenwood was Minister of Health," said Mr Watson, "we opened the aged miners' homes in Thornley and named them after him. A subsidy of £100 was paid on each of the homes and, I am told, this money will have been paid off before the end of this year."

"Lodge's Important Part"

It was the men and women of Thornley in the year 1871 and the succeeding years who formed the back-bone of the present Durham Miners' Association, declared Mr Watson. Their banner was draped across the platform at the first Gala Day in Wharton Park. "The lodge," added Mr Watson, "has played a very important part in the history of the Durham Miners' Association and we gladly pay tribute to the work of those who have passed on."

It was on occasions like the present one," said Mr Greenwood after unfurling the new banner, that he was greatly impressed by the progress that had been made in the mining villages. "We have marched a very long way," he went on. "The lot of old people today is far better than ever they dreamed of in the days of their youth. I am glad to come back here to renew acquaintanceship with Thornley and thank the lodge deeply for this honour of unfurling their latest but, I hope, not their last banner."

On behalf of the lodge, Mr Watson presented Mr Greenwood with a framed oil painting of the Greenwood Homes – a miniature of the scene depicted on the banner. "With this gift," Mr Watson told Mr Greenwood, "go the appreciation and thanks of the people of Thornley and I hope that this will not be your last memory of Thornley."

Addressing the packed hall, Mr E Shinwell, MP for Easington, said he was delighted to be sharing in the unfurling ceremony with Mr Greenwood because much of the progress – particularly the social progress – that had been achieved through the years in this country had been due to the work of Mr Greenwood in the early days of the Labour Party.

Those "Silly Disputes"

The Labour Party had certainly made remarkable progress, said Mr Shinwell, especially during the last six years of Labour Government, but much of it was being frittered away by the present Conservative Government with the denationalisation of transport and the denationalisation of iron and steel. "But," declared Mr Shinwell, "they are not going to denationalise the mining industry because they know what would happen if they tried it out. The miners would not stand for that kind of trick!"

"I regret that this is happening," said Mr Shinwell. "One man attacks another and then he responds and so it goes on. When you come to examine them in detail these disputes are not worth talking about. It is not persons who matter, but this great Labour and Trade Union movement. On its progress depends the future of millions of men, women and children, not only in our own country, but throughout the world. We have to protect the Labour movement against either a Left Wing or a Right Wing or the centre. I wish somebody with greater influence than myself – I don't pretend to have much – had the courage to say to those people who are arguing among themselves about this, that and the other, "Shut up, we've had enough of it!"

Mr Shinwell's Prophecy

Shortly, declared Mr Shinwell, we would be having an election – he had already prophesied it would come in November: It was essential that the Labour Party won. "But we cannot win," he continued, "unless this Labour and Trade Union movement is completely united and unless we subordinate personal and private opinions for the good of the Party as a whole."

Turning to the mining industry, Mr Shinwell said there had been a lot of criticism about nationalisation of the mines. He did not pretend that things were good as they would have liked, but it had to be remembered there had been years and years of persistent neglect in the mining industry under private ownership. "It takes a long time to make up the lee-way," he added. "When I was responsible, for the Labour Government, for piloting the nationalisation of the mining industry through Parliament, I said it was a great experiment. The experiment is still proceeding. But the miners and the miners' officials are doing their bit. Let the Government stand aside and not interfere!"

DURHAM MINERS' GALA
TWO AMBASSADORS

A more peaceful demonstration than that which the Yugoslav and Israeli Ambassadors and many other foreign visitors to Durham saw on Saturday could not be imagined. Miners, their wives and families, started from their homes in the early morning and, with their bands and banners, travelled by bus and train and even on foot to the Cathedral City, and were free to do just what they liked within the limits of the law. There were no orders rapped out from the Miners' Hall. The people could sing, shout, dance and drink all day, and members of the Association were free to attend or to absent themselves from the gala as they chose. No thought of regimentation.

Cherished Freedom

They could criticise or even ridicule their leaders or the political speakers who address them. There were no secret police: indeed the Durham police, led by their Chief Constable (Mr A A Muir) seemed to be enjoying themselves just as much as the miners. That is our cherished freedom which is unknown in the country from which Mr Horner has just returned. The Soviet people, says Mr Horner, want peace.

Of course they do, now that the free nations, in self-protection, have been compelled to build up the greatest accumulation of armaments ever known in the history of the world.

Free and Unfettered Folk

Here in Durham on Saturday we saw democracy in action, the democracy of a free and unfettered people . . . canny folk, happy and law-abiding. They came into the city with a smile, a dance and a song, and after listening to the speeches and worshipping in the Mother Church – "that vast place which is timeless, and where men and women have prayed for centuries," says Lord Lawson of Beamish – they turned for home again in an orderly unorganised procession after yet another wonderful day in the company of their fellows from every part of the coalfield.

"Aa dinnat knaa what it is," said a middle-aged miner to his companion. "You come here and get pushed about and squeezed in the crowds, and yet Aa wadn't miss it for worlds." That typifies the spirit of these people who come to Durham year by year to claim, as one of them once said their "reets" (rights). "We dinnat knaa what they are," he said, "but we've come to get them".

Thousands stood around the gala platforms to hear the speeches of the political leaders, and thousands more packed the Cathedral for the Miners' Service at which the Bishop Designate of Birmingham, Dr. J L Wilson, who is at present Dean of Manchester, was the preacher.

A Startling Statement

We often hear the remark that the churches and chapels are empty, but this can never apply to the Miners' Service, and a pronouncement at the beginning of Saturday's worship within the Cathedral might well be historic. Miners, their wives and families had reverently passed within the North Door and occupied every seat. Thousands more followed them until the building was absolutely packed with a seething mass of humanity. Then we heard the voice of Mr E Clark through the loud-speakers – "There is a solid mass of people between the North and the South Doors, and the choir cannot get into the church. Will you please leave a way for them."

Just think of it, a church – not a circus nor a cinema – so crowded with people that the choir could not get in.

Familiar Hymns

The crowd of standing people divided as best they could and left a passage for the solemn procession of clergy and choir as they entered from the cloisters and moved along the Nave as thousands of voices were uplifted in the grand old hymn, "O Worship the King." The Bishop of Durham (Dr A M Ramsey), who is not unfamiliar with the Durham Miners Service, was a picturesque figure carrying the ancient crook and preceded by his Domestic Chaplain. We saw also the robust figure of the Dean of Manchester (Dr J L Wilson), who many remember in the early years of his career as Curate-in-charge of St John's Church, Neville's Cross. He is to be the new Bishop of Birmingham. The Dean (the Very Rev. J H S Wild) was also in the procession, as well as the Bishop of Jarrow (the Right Rev J A Ramsbotham) and Canon Richard-son, who is shortly to leave for his new appointment at Nottingham.

Bands Play in the Cathedral

Earlier, three bands – Thornley (led by Mr E G T Kitto), Craghead (Mr E W Cunningham) and Mainsforth (Mr R L Smith) – had marched slowly and reverently into the Cathedral each preceded by its silken banner borne along the full length of the Nave to a point near the Choir. The first band played "Onward Christian Soldiers," the second "Eternal

Father" and the third that glorious tune, "Deep Harmony." Would that Gala speakers and the visitors from European countries could have been present and heard that vast congregation singing such hymns as "All People that on Earth do Dwell," "O Happy Band of Pilgrims" and "Glorious Things of Thee are Spoken." This service provides a full and complete answer to the modern critics of the churches.

"How proud and happy I am as a Durham man," said the Dean of Manchester, "to have the privilege of speaking in this Cathedral Church." His theme was the place that the Kingdom of God ought to occupy in an individual and corporate life.

Many members of the congregation gathered round the memorial to the miners, who, through the centuries, have given their lives in the coal industry, and they admired the lovely array of lilies and carnations.

A Hundred Bands

There must have been nearly a hundred bands in the procession to and from the race-course. It was music all the way. A miners' gala without bands is unthinkable. They provide its colour and its charm, and also the lively airs that inspire the young folk to gaily dance and disport themselves in the streets which, for this one day of the year, are barred to motor and vehicular traffic.

And could anything be more impressive as massed bands assembled at No 1 platform just before speeches and play what has becomes the Durham miners' hymn, "Gresford," which was composed and for many years conducted by Bob Saint. The massed bands conducted by Mr George Jacobs, of Blackhall (bandmaster of the Brandon Silver Prize Band), who played the tune so impressively were Hetton-le-Hole, Ryhope, Pelton Fell, Deaf Hill and Eden Colliery.

24 July 1953

EX–THORNLEY MAN BECOMES SRN – AND TOP REFEREE

Mr John H Williamson, a Thornley man working as a male nurse in Mendip Hospital, near Wells, has qualified as a State Registered Nurse, following two years' training in Barnet General Hospital. He has also been appointed a first class referee with Somerset FA.

He was awarded the British Empire Medal for his work among British prisoners in Japan during the last war. After the war he returned to Japan to give evidence about the ill-treatment of British prisoners. He is a son of the late Mr and Mrs John Williamson, Thornley.

7 August 1953
LEGION PARADE AND RALLY AT THORNLEY
Five men's branches and five women's sections of the British Legion joined in a parade and rally of No 10 Group at Thornley on Saturday. The procession, headed by Thornley Prize Silver Band, marched from the west end of Thornley to the Welfare Hall, where a service was conducted by the Rev H W Jackson, ex-Serviceman and Vicar of Thornley.

Speakers were Mr W J Gibbon, of Sherburn (Durham County chairman) and Mrs A Armstrong (chairman of Trimdon Women's Section). Mr C E Hall (Coxhoe Group chairman) presided, and a vote of thanks was moved by Mr J Kennedy (secretary of Ferryhill Group). The parade marshal was Mr W L Jones (Thornley).

Sections represented were: Men – Ferryhill and Dean Bank, Blackhall, Trimdon, Coxhoe and Thornley; Women – Ferryhill and Dean Bank, Hesleden, Cassop, Wheatley Hill and Thornley.

WHEATLEY HILL BRIDE IN GERMANY
A war-time romance which began when the bride and 'groom were both stationed at Dover – the bride in the ATS and the 'groom in the Army – culminated in the wedding in Germany this month of Miss Marjorie Gradon, youngest daughter of Mr and Mrs G Gradon, 12 Gable Terrace, Wheatley Hill, and Major William Kerr Current, MC, of Edinburgh, who is serving in the Royal Horse Artillery near Munster.

The wedding took place at the Camp Church, Swinton Barracks, and two of the bride's sisters were present at the ceremony. They were Miss Winifred Gradon, a school teacher in London, who accompanied her sister on the trip to Germany for the wedding, and Miss Edna Gradon, who for the past two years has been stationed in Hamburg as a Nursing Sister for the Soldiers, Sailors and Airmen's Families Association.

The bride was given away by the Colonel of the bridegroom's regiment, and after a reception in the Officers' Mess the newly wedded couple left for their honeymoon at Bad Harzburg in the mountains. In October the 'groom is being posted to London, and there the couple will make their home. For the past five years the bride has been employed as a shorthand-typist at the East Durham Co-operative Dairies at Wellfield, Wingate.

ON WAY HOME FROM KOREA
Thornley Man Prisoner For Over Two Years

Mrs Isabella Matthews, 19, East Lea, Thornley, is eagerly looking forward to news that her husband, Private Robert Matthews, 1st Gloucesters, taken prisoner on the Imjun River in Korea on April 26, 1951, is on his way home.

"He won't know where we are," she said, with a smile, referring to the fact that since he was last home on leave, the family, comprising Mrs Matthews, her three children and her mother, Grandma Hannah Walls, have had two new addresses.

They were at 102, Thornlaw North, Thornley, when he left for Korea. Then they moved to 188, Thornlaw South, and a short time ago into Thornley's newest housing estate near the schools.

The three children are Margaret, aged six, Maureen, four, and Michael three. Michael was three weeks old when daddy was last home. All three were having a "rough - and-tumble" on the sitting room floor when a reporter called to ask Mrs Matthews if she had received any news of her husband's release.

Mrs Matthews said she regularly received letters from him about every three months, the last one being in the early part of July. They came from what is known as the "Big Camp," on the Yarlo river, where there were about 600 Gloucesters. He had never made any complaint of bad treatment.

Pte Matthews has neither father nor mother, but has two sisters, one residing at Newton- le-Willows and the other at Manchester.

Former Miner At Kelloe

He has been in the Army ever since he was a youth except for the five years following being demobbed in 1945, when he worked underground at Kelloe Colliery. His wartime service was with the Royal Berkshire Regiment in India. Recalled in August, 1950, his Army service now stands at nearly 15 years.

It was a war-time friendship between Mrs Matthew's sister's husband and Private Matthews that led to Mrs Matthews meeting her husband while he was spending part of a leave at the home of her sister at Haswell, three miles from Thornley.

Mrs Matthews believes that her husband will be finished with the Army soon after his release, and will then resume his underground work at

Kelloe pit. "We have been receiving free coal and rent allowance since he went away," she said.

21 August 1953

LEAVING THORNLEY
Presentation To District Nurse

Sister Elizabeth Gutteridge has been presented with a silver rose bowl in recognition of her ten years' service as district nurse at Thornley. For family reasons Miss Gutteridge is moving to Doncaster where she is to take up a post on September 1 as district nurse in the Cantley district.

Miss Gutteridge, a Queen's nurse, has wide experience as a hospital nurse at Sherburn and district nurse at Sheffield and Thornley.

In making the presentation, Mrs A Todd, president of the Association, said they had met to say goodbye to "our nurse." "We are all extremely sorry she is leaving us. We thank her for her service here in past years, and we want to say how much we esteem her."

Summarising the qualities of a good nurse, Mrs Todd said Miss Gutteridge possessed all those qualities in a marked degree. "I hope our gift will carry her mind back to Thornley and that she will have happy memories of us." Said Mrs Todd.

"Real Queen's Nurse"

Miss N Hawkins, superintendent of the Durham County Nursing Association, regretting that Miss Gutteridge was leaving the "county family" of nurses, described her as a "real Queen's nurse."

Miss Gutteridge said she was delighted with the gift. " I am sorry to leave my friends in Thornley, but I am going home."

Others who spoke were Mr T T Ridley (treasurer), Mr C Woodward (committee member), Mrs J H C Scott (past president), Mrs Willey (secretary) and Miss E M Kirk (past secretary).

Miss Gutteridge's mother and other members of the family are residing in the Doncaster area. When Miss Gutteridge takes up residence there her mother will reside with her.

Lady members of the committee were thanked for providing supper.

28 August 1953

BODY FOUND IN STREET
Early Morning Shock For Miner

Having apparently lain there all night the body of a 63 – year old Wheatley Hill miner, George Arthur Hargreaves, 8 Fifteenth Street, was found near the top of the street where he lived early on Tuesday morning.

The discovery was made by Mr John Simpson, who lives three doors away from Mr Hargreaves, while on his way to work at 6am. The police were notified and the facts have been reported to the Coroner. Mr Hargreaves had facial injuries but later, after enquiries, the police ruled out any suggestion of foul play.

Mr Hargreaves was in the nearby Wheatley Hill Discharged and Demobilised Soldiers and Sailors' Club until closing-time on Monday. It is thought that while on his way home he stumbled in the dark and fell, striking his face on the kerb.

Wife Was In Hospital

On Monday morning Mr Hargreaves's wife entered Sunderland Eye Infirmary to undergo an eye operation and as his house was unoccupied that night, there was no-one to raise the alarm when he did not return home. "I was in the club with my father from 7pm until closing-time on Monday," a son, Thomas Hargreaves, 100 Bruce Glazier Terrace, Shotton Colliery, told our reporter. "We had a few drinks but my father appeared to be quite all right when I left to catch the bus home."

This was the second week of Mr Hargreaves's fortnights holiday from Wheatley Hill colliery, where he was employed as a wagonwayman. He and his wife returned from a week's holiday at Blackpool only on Saturday night. "When they got back," Thomas said, "there was a note from the Eye Infirmary for my mother to go for her operation. She has been waiting for this for some time."

Mr Hargreaves is survived by his wife, four sons and three daughters. All his sons are employed at Wheatley Hill colliery. Two of them, Leslie, who is the only one unmarried, and George, have been on holiday at Crimdon Camp, and another son, Robert, lives at Thornley. The daughters, all married, live at Station Town, Shotton Colliery and Trimdon Village.

A native of Yorkshire, Mr Hargreaves had lived at Wheatley Hill for 33 years and formerly at Ryton and Shotton. For a few years he had been treasurer of Wheatley Hill Soldiers' and Sailors' Club and he was associated with the local Knights of the Golden Horn.

PLASTIC HELMETS FOR MINERS

Plastics are today being used in the manufacture of so very many different articles. They range from toothbrushes and sponges to complicated electrical equipment, car bodies and complete wings for large gliders. Latest development is the application of plastics to yet another field – the manufacture of safety helmets for miners.

A new helmet made from plastic foil sheets only half as thick as a postcard, yet as strong as armour plating, is now on the market. Known as the Oldham-Orbex Safety Helmet it is extremely light in weight, but is capable of standing up to the heaviest blow likely to be encountered under normal conditions. It has been designed to give the greatest possible protection to the miner under all circumstances.

This new helmet not only has great strength and lightness but has a further unique advantage. Moisture or water have absolutely no effect upon it. This is of vital importance because in the past most helmets were made of materials similar to vulcanised fibre, upon which in certain instances, water has a deleterious effect.

"Almost Indestuctable"

On the old type helmet it is necessary to coat the outside with a protective material. That was alright until the helmet received any damage in wear, when obviously the coating would suffer, allowing moisture to penetrate. When that occurred the strength of the helmet may have been reduced considerably.

The new plastic Oldham-Orbex helmet has been made with those points in view. It needs no protective coating and under normal conditions is almost indestructible. Not only does it give the miner better protection but it will last him far longer, thus saving money.

Provision has been made in the helmet for a cap lamp to be carried in a specially designed slot in the plastic shell which avoids the use of a metal clip, which often leads to corroding and further damage.

The new plastic helmet has been thoroughly tested and it is approved by the Ministry of Fuel and Power. It has been found to be unaffected by water, acid or oil; to be non-inflammable. It will not conduct electricity. It is very strong, but, being of plastic material, light in weight and therefore comfortable to wear. It is coloured white which is an important factor as regards safety when being worn in poor light.

4 September 1953

<h2 style="text-align:center">CHAMPIONS OF CHAMPIONS</h2>

Charmian's Treble At Blackpool

Charmian Welsh, Durham City Swimming Club's incomparable young diver, proved herself a champion of champions by taking three of the main events in the National Diving Championships at Blackpool last week, including the "Blue Riband" of the diving world, the Ladies' Springboard.

Charmian, who faced the toughest programme of any of the other competitors, emerged from six days of intensive and nerve-testing effort as Britain's best woman diver, and now holds more diving records than any other British woman has ever done before.

When the championships opened on Monday Charmian was faced with four days' gruelling effort and the problem of keeping "staleness" at bay before the Ladies Springboard event was held on the last two days, but when the critical time came on Saturday she not only proved what a great sportswoman she is but gave the crowds a glimpse of her magnificent fighting spirit when she came from behind to beat Ann Long, of Ilford, by half a point.

Was In Arrears

At the end of the qualifying rounds on Friday, Charmian was five points behind Ann Long and a fraction ahead of Dorothy Drew, her chief rivals. She was slightly below her best at this stage but after 1½ hours of intensive training on Friday evening she came up on Saturday afternoon determined to win, and by cool and concentrated effort pulled off the championship.

11 September 1953

THORNLEY MINERS have elected the following committees and officials for the ensuing 12 months: Lodge Committee: Messrs W Anderson, T Barron, D Dempsey, P Ellward, P Gott, W Heale, J Joicey, R Peters, J Walls, H Gill and W Williams; chairman, Mr E Carter; correspondence secretary, Mr W Dowding; finance secretary, Mr D Swallow; treasurer, Mr J Cherry; compensation secretary, Mr J Webb; delegate, Mr D Gott; auditors, Messrs W Quinn and T Luke; average taker, Mr H Gill; pit inspectors, Messrs E Christopher and R Hughes; Federation

Board representatives, Messrs E Carter, J Cherry, W Dowding, P Ellward, J Storey and J Webb; housing committee, Messrs E Carter and J Joicey; welfare committee, Messrs D Dempsey, W Dowding, W Heale, M Kell and D Swallow. Labour Party representatives, Messrs R Hughes, J Storey and J Webb.

MP HANDS OVER SET FOR THE AGED
AT WHEATLEY HILL

It was good to see "action for once instead of words," declared Mr E Shinwell, MP for Easington, when, at an informal ceremony in Wheatley Hill Aged Miners' Hostel on Saturday afternoon, he presented a 17-inch screen television set to the local Aged Miners' Homes Committee, on behalf of the Wheatley Hill Coronation Celebrations Committee. The set was bought by the Coronation Committee from the balance remaining in their funds after paying for the local celebrations, with the assistance of several outside donations. It was has been installed in the communal room of the hostel but is for the benefit of all the inhabitants of the adjoining 24 aged miners' homes.

Presiding at the handing-over ceremony, Mr J W Moore, chairman of the Coronation Committee, said it was a "happy and pleasurable" occasion both for the committee and the old people, and he hoped that the television set would bring great joy into the lives of the old folk. He thanked the people of Wheatley Hill for their loyal support of the Coronation Committee. It was through their generous help that it had been possible to buy the set.

"A Very Fine Effort "

Mr Shinwell congratulated the Coronation Committee on the success of their efforts, The greater part of the money to cover the cost of the celebrations locally had, he said, been raised by individual subscriptions – that was "a very fine effort indeed."

It was an excellent idea, continued Mr Shinwell, to buy a television set for the old folk. "If there is one thing on which we pride ourselves – and I am not speaking politically or, necessarily, on behalf of any particular Party – it is our concern for the welfare of the old folk," said Mr Shinwell. "Old people, who have had their vicissitudes, trials and tribulations, require a little comfort in the eventide of their lives. This gesture of the Coronation Committee is onE way of affording them a little comfort and contentment."

The set was accepted on behalf of the Aged Miners' Homes Committee by their secretary, Coun E Cain. Coun Cain said that he and Mr Shinwell had been "comrades in the Labour Party movement" for more years than they cared to talk about! The aged miners' movement in Wheatley Hill, he recalled, was started in 1913. The war years prevented any progress, but in 1923 the movement went ahead again, and in the years 1924-5 the present homes were officially opened. Television was a modern invention and the aged miners' homes committee highly appreciated the Coronation Committee's gift, which would bring the old folk "bang up-to-date."

Thanks to Mr Shinwell for so readily accepting the invitation to hand over the set were proposed by Coun Ralph Watson, secretary of the Coronation Committee, and seconded by Mr A Wharrier, treasurer of the committee.

RETIREMENT – Mrs Hannah Brewster, district nurse at Thornley for 27 years, has retired owing to ill-health. In many ways she has been a real friend of the village, notably when she took a leading part in the Working of Service People's Comforts Fund during the last war. In addition she has been a parish councillor for about 12 years and has held the office of chairman.

NO SATURDAY WORKING –Wheatley Hill Miners' Lodge, at a special meeting on Sunday, presided over by Mr H Bradshaw, rejected an appeal from the Durham County Mineworkers' Federation Board to work a Saturday shift in connection with the extended hours agreement. The matter was fully discussed and the decision not to work on Saturdays was almost unanimous. After the meeting the secretary, Coun E Cain, told our reporter that the lodge felt that it was in the best interests of production not to work on Saturdays. "This may sound ambiguous, but those conversant with work at the colliery will know it is not," added Coun Cain. "To work a Saturday shift would interfere with the three-shift cycle of work on the coal-filling faces and the men feel it would not improve output," Wheatley Hill Miners' Lodge has turned down the Saturday shift on many occasions during the past few years.

RECEPTION PARTY – Thornley War Committee, which acted as the Soldiers' Comforts Committee, are to hold a reception party for Private Robert Matthews, of the Gloucesters, to mark his return home to Thornley after being a prisoner of war in Korea. There will be a supper and an entertainment, and Private Matthews and his wife and children will be presented with gifts.

CRICKET CLUB – Officials elected at the annual meeting of Thornley Cricket Club are: President, Mr A Welsh; chairman, Mr E Green; vice-chairman, Mr C A Smith; secretary, Mr James Taylor; assistant secretary, Mr R Pattison; treasurer, Mr Brian Winter. It was reported that there was a credit balance of £8.10s. The knock-out competition had been a financial success and it was hoped to present the trophies next season. The first team, which played in the Coxhoe District League last season, are to seek admission to the North-East Durham League. The second team are already in their section of that League.

HILARY WINS CHARMIAN'S TROPHY

At Durham City ASC's Gala – Hilary Welsh, 13-year-old sister of Durham City Swimming Club's national diving champion Charmian, proved there is another champion in the family when she gave a superb exhibition of diving at the club's gala in the City Baths on Monday to win the ladies' diving event and become the first winner of the "Charmian Welsh" Bowl.

She was presented with the trophy by her sister, who donated it from subscriptions gathered by her townsfolk at Thornley to commemorate her performance in the Olympic Games. Earlier, Hilary had won the "Lewis Colin Isaacs" Shield for the club's 50-yards swimming championship for girls under 15 years. She won easily from Ann Short and covered the distance in 39 seconds. The trophy was won last year by her sister Charmian.

Hilary's success was the signal for a family attack which netted another three trophies for the well-stocked Welsh mantelpiece. Charmian retained the junior ladies' 50-yards club championship with a time of 34 seconds and went on to take the 50-yards backstroke championship, while 15-year-old twins, Peter and Anthony, finished first and second respectively in the junior 100-yards event for the "Coyne" Cup.

Medley Relay

The main event of the evening, a medley relay for the Durham County Challenge Cup, was won by Darlington ASC, with Stockton a close second and Arthurs Hill and Fenham third. Durham went out in their heat in a close finish.

During the evening, Charmian (holder of three national diving titles), gave a demonstration of some of the dives which brought her success in the National Championships at Blackpool.

Prizes were presented after each event by Mrs H E Ferens, mother of the club president, Ald. H C Ferens. Mrs Ferens accepted a bouquet from Miss Jill Perrin, a member of the club's ladies' section.

Moving a vote of thanks, Mr Norman W Sarsfield, the club's captain and coach, called for continued support to help maintain the enormous progress which had been made. The president, said Mr Sarsfield, was personally interested in all the club's swimmers and it was largely through the diving board presented by Ald. Ferens that the club had achieved so much success in diving.

Replying, Ald Ferens said it gave him the greatest possible pleasure to see such achievements by a club which was small in comparison to most others in the country. He paid tribute to the officials and echoed Mr Sarsfield's appeal for continued support.

18 September 1953

CORONATION "WIND-UP" - At a "wind-up" social evening organised by the Wheatley Hill Coronation Celebrations Committee, in the Welfare Hall on Saturday night, tribute was paid to the work done by the officials and committee by making the Coronation celebrations in the village among the best in the county. Members of the Wheatley Hill British Legion Concert party gave an excellent entertainment, following which supper was served and the committee members and their friends joined in dancing. Mr J W Moore presided.

"SAILOR JACK'S PAL
Daily Walks With Pet Monkey

A monkey may not be everybody's idea of a household pet – but in the home of a well-known Wheatley Hill personality, Mr John P Brown, 49 Liddell Terrace - for years familiarly known locally as "Sailor Jack" – a five-year-old monkey has been a popular "member of the family" for the past six months. And Mr Brown and the monkey, which readily responds to her name, "Jessie," have become firm friends.

"We walk miles every day," Mr Brown, who is 74 but does not look a day beyond 60, told our reporter this week. "People round the doors are quite used to Jessie now. She behaves herself quite well and there's nothing she likes better than our daily walk when I sometimes let her have her fling among the trees. She has never made any attempt to escape!"

Boer War Veteran

In his garden Mr Brown has built Jessie a special shed with a trapeze and "odds and ends" to amuse her. "She's quite content and has become a firm favourite," he said.

Mr Brown, who has nearly 18 years' active service in the Navy to his credit – he is a Boer War veteran – has always been fond of monkeys, but it is years since he possessed one. Knowing his fondness for them his 19 year-old grandson, Arthur Wilks, of Shotton Colliery, who is serving in the RAF gave him "the surprise of his life" by sending his grandfather a monkey all the way from the island of Mauritius, in the Indian Ocean, where he was stationed earlier this year. "He could not have sent me a more welcome gift!" declared Mr Brown.

Mr Brown, who has three daughters and one son, has many memories – happy and otherwise – of the sea. He joined the "Queen Victoria Navy" in 1896, and served throughout the Boer War. He then served in the "King Edward Navy" until 1908, when he left to return to his work as a miner at Wheatley Hill Colliery.

On the outbreak of the first world war, Mr Brown re-joined the Navy in the Royal Naval Division (Land forces), and in 1915 went to sea as chief engineer in a "mystery ship" – a vessel used to decoy enemy submarines. He served through-out the war and was eventually demobilised in 1920. Again he returned to Wheatley Hill Colliery where he retired at the age of 68. During the last war he served in the Home Guard.

"Victorian Navy"

Recalling the days when, as a youth of 17, he joined the "Queen Victoria Navy," Mr Brown declared "you could never get enough to eat!" "Breakfast at five o'clock in the morning consisted of a pint of cocoa and four slices of dry bread," he recalled, "and then at dinner-time we got half a pound of beef and a pound of vegetables. For supper at five o'clock in the evening we got a pint of tea without milk and four ounces of dry bread – and then we never had another bite until breakfast next morning! We were always hungry, but later the rations for the Services were improved and these made conditions a little better."

Mr Brown's first pay as a sailor was at the rate of half-a-crown a week. "And we had to work jolly hard for that!" he declared. "We knew we were in the Navy all right, but I always loved the sea!"

Mr Brown was the first chairman of the Wingate and District Royal Navy Old Comrades Association when it was formed in 1936, and still retains an active interest in it. Despite his age, he still "dresses-up" for local carnival processions – he was in the Coronation Day fancy-dress parade at Wheatley Hill.

He has appeared in carnivals throughout the North-East as "King Zulu" "And that costume has won me no fewer than 168 prizes," said Mr Brown with justifiable pride.

TEMPORARY FIRE STATION AT WHEATLEY HILL

The County Council propose this year to build a temporary station at Wheatley Hill in place of the present premises which, says Mr Hall, Chief Fire Officer of the Durham County Fire Brigade, "have almost fallen down". The cost of that scheme will be between £4,000 and £5,000.

25 September 1953

WELCOMED HOME
Thornley Reception for EX-POW

Pte Robert Matthews, recently re-turned to his home at Thornley, after being a prisoner-of-war in Korea for 2½ years, was given an enthusiastic reception by representatives of over 30 organisations in the Welfare Institute on Friday night. He was ac-companied by his wife, his three chil-dren – Margaret (six), Maureen (four) and Michael (three) - and his mother-in-law, Mrs Hannah Walls.

After supper, provided by lady workers headed by Mrs J Anderson, Pte Matthews was presented with a cheque for £5 from the Soldiers' Com-forts' Fund. The presentation was made by Mr T H Holder, who was secretary of the fund during the last

Robert Matthews (right)

war. He explained that he was deputising for Mr J H C Scott, chairman of the fund, who deeply regretted that he had been called away on business. He recalled the keen interest that Mr Scott took in the Comforts' Fund.

Mr Holder also said it was a joint pleasure to have with them some of the members of the old Comforts' Committee who had worked hard in raising the funds to serve 450 Thornley men and women who were in the Forces. He extended to Pte Matthews and his family the best possible good wishes of all those present.

Entertained

Mrs Jane Anderson then presented Mrs Matthews with chocolates, the children with sweets and Mrs Walls, their grandmother, with flowers. There was a separate round of applause for each member of the family as the gifts were presented.

Pte Matthews, in a brief reply, thanked the people of Thornley for their splendid welcome on the night he arrived home and kindness shown to him and his family at the reception.

The feeling of kindliness and goodwill towards Pte Matthews and his family was shown in short addresses by the Rev W T Rose, Senior Captain Margaret Kennedy, of Shotton (Salvation Army), Mr Jack Barker (prisoner-of-war for five years in the last war), Mrs H Brewster and Mr Jos Pattison.

Mrs Walls, a widow and mother of Mrs Matthews, feelingly expressed her thanks. "On our two pensions," she said, "we have had a hard time, but we have seen to it that the children have not taken any harm."

An excellent contribution to a very happy evening was made by the entertainers: Messrs N Strong, B Blenkinsopp, W Williams, Mrs Green, Horner Sisters, Jackie Toye, Mrs Hobbs and Mrs English. Apologies for absence were received from the Rev Dr McNeill, Father Sharratt and Mr M Lonsdale, an active member of the wartime Comforts' Committee.

2 October 1953

WORK HAS BEGUN on the building of a new south aisle in All Saints' Church, Wheatley Hill, and while this work is in progress, the Vicar (Rev Arthur Preston) tells me, Sunday services will be held in the Church Hall. Though the church will be closed for Sunday worship it will still be possible to hold funeral and wedding services there. It would, said the Vicar, be some weeks before the new aisle was completed and Sunday services could be resumed in the church. In the meantime the church hall is proving a suitable alternative - last Sunday it was packed for the harvest thanksgiving services.

The new aisle is costing in the region of £1,700. It is the concluding part of a scheme of additions and renovations which has been going on for some time. The chancel has already been extended and a new porch built, and after the aisle has been built a new system of lighting will be introduced into the church and redecoration will be carried out.

It speaks well for the Vicar and his parishioners, who have been working hard to raise money by special efforts, including one which meant systematic giving each week, that it has been possible to undertake such an ambitious scheme for the improvement of the church, whose "new look" is warmly welcomed locally.

FIRE-FIGHTING
Wheatley Hill's Success In NCB Contest

Fire-fighting teams from Wheatley Hill Colliery carried off the first and third prizes in the final of the first fire-fighting competition organised by No 3 Area (South-East Durham), Durham Division, NCB, in the grounds of The Castle, Castle Eden – the area's headquarters – on Saturday. Nine teams took part – three from each of the three groups in the area who the previous Saturday had won at group level. A team from Easington colliery was placed second.

Each competing team was required to carry out a series of three consecutive tests dealing with colliery fire-fighting on the surface and underground. The time taken to complete the tests was taken into account and time was added for faults committed.

In presenting the prizes, Mr E W Potts, area production manager, who was introduced by the area safety engineer, Mr E Gasgoigne, stressed the need of "quick organised action" should fire break out either on the surface or underground at any pit, The motto must always be the same as that of the Boy Scouts – "Be Prepared."

Prizewinners

From the display that afternoon, said Mr Potts, he was quite certain that the collieries in the No 3 Area were prepared for any emergency. The teams had shown keenness and intelligence and a sound knowledge of fire-fighting methods. The area competition was to become an annual event, Mr Potts revealed, and next year there may be a divisional contest. Prizes were presented to the winning teams as follows: 1. Wheatley Hill, Messrs B Nicholson (captain), J Dunn, W Gibson and G Robertson: 2. Easington, Messrs C Paley (capt), T Tully, C Nattrass and E Jones: 3.Wheatley Hill, Messrs T W Ayre (capt), L Barker, A Carr and J T Harker.

The contest was judged by Station Officer T Scott, of the Durham County Fire Service, assisted by Mr Gasgoigne and Mr W Roughley, the area Welfare Officer. The task of judging, said Station Officer Scott, though an enjoyable one, had been far from easy. A keen competitive spirit had been shown, he added, and there had been few mistakes.

Arrangements for the contest, which attracted visitors from other Coal Board areas as well as from Divisional Headquarters, were efficiently made by Messrs E Gascoigne and W Roughley, assisted by the group agents.

LUDWORTH BRITISH LEGION

Mr R Gibson presided at the monthly meeting. Arrangements for the local service of remembrance at the War Memorial on November 8 were discussed. Chairman appealed for generous support to the Earl Haig Fund

16 October 1953

JUMBLE SALE – Organised by the Mothers' Union of All Saints' Church, Wheatley Hill. A successful jumble sale was held in the Church Hall on Friday. The effort raised £20 for church funds.

SCHOOL SAVINGS – Through their local savings schemes the four schools in Wheatley Hill saved a total of £143.2s. during October. The Girls' Modern School topped the list with savings amounting to £53.1s.6d. and the totals at the other schools were: Junior Mixed School, £45.6s: Infants School, £34.16s.6d: Senior Boys' School, £9.18s.

NOMINATED AGENT – Wheatley Hill miners' lodge have nominated their chairman, Mr Horace Bradshaw, for the position of Durham Miners' Association agent, vacant through the recent retirement of Mr E Moore. Mr Bradhsaw has been actively associated with Wheatley Hill miners' lodge for years, formerly serving as its delegate. At present employed at Wheatley Hill colliery as a stone-man, he was formerly checkweighman there.

MISSIONARY PREACHER - At the evensong service of All Saints' Church, Wheatley Hill, in the Church Hall on Sunday, the special preacher was the Rev G W Hewitt, North of England area secretary for the Universities' Missions to Central Africa. The service was conducted by the Rev Arthur Preston (Vicar of Wheatley Hill), and at the close Mr Hewitt showed film strips depicting missionary work carried out by the church in Africa.

GUILD WEEK-END - Mr C Graham, Darlington, was the special speaker at the Guild anniversary celebrations in Church Street Methodist Church, Wheatley Hill, at the week-end. The Rev Noel Catherall (resident minister) presided at a rally on Saturday night, when Mr Graham gave an inspiring address and a duet was contributed by the Misses Joan and Irene Lewis, who were accompanied by Miss J Calvert. During an interval the roll call was responded to by kindred societies from the surrounding district. Mr Graham conducted the services on Sunday and at the evening service the soloist was Miss Joan Calvert.

A LUDWORTH MOTHER

Mrs E Thompson, 143, Barnard Avenue, is among the first who have received the practical gift offered by Lever Brothers Ltd to mothers of twins born in October. "A baby always means extra washing, but with two sets of nappies and baby clothes to deal with, this present will, we hope, be a great help to mothers" said a Lever Brothers representative. Mrs Thompson, whose twins were born on 2 October, has received a book of vouchers entitling her to six months free supply of the new washing powder – Surf.

30 October 1953

WHEATLEY HILL BOWLS CLUB
Trophies Presented At Annual Social Function

Trophies won by members of Wheatley Hill Welfare Bowls Club last season were presented at the annual supper and social evening organised by the club in the Welfare Hall, Wheatley Hill, on Saturday night. A good company of members and friends attended and an enjoyable programme, including whist, dancing and entertainment, was carried out.

Mr J Burrell was not present to receive either the Club Cup or the Moore Cup, both of which he won last season, but the runner-up cups were presented by Coun E Cain, JP, to the following: Club Cup, Mr J

Storey: Moore Cup, Mr A Dobson. Coun Cain wished the club continued success both in their local and league competitions.

Mr R Taylor was MC for the whist, prizes for which were won by the following: Mr T Robinson and Mrs E Hall, and Mr T Simpson (consolation); Mrs W Snowdon and Mrs R Taylor, and Mrs Raffell (consolation). Winners of the domino drive, for which Mr W Randall was MC, were Mrs Presho and Mr W Ponting.

After an excellent supper, entertainment was provided by Mrs Peggy Hairsing (accordionist), Mrs F Carr (pianist) and the Wilson Sisters and Mr W Williams (vocal items). Old-fashioned dancing followed and winners of the spot dances were Mrs E Richardson and Mr Jack Dobson.

Winners of the "lucky chair" prizes were Mr Hummerston, Mrs Taylor, Mrs Wilson and Mrs Parnham and special competitions were won by Mr W Craggs, Mrs Shutt and Mr Ferguson.

Secretarial duties were efficiently carried out by Mr Alf Todd.

VARIETY CONCERT

Thornley's week of road safety propaganda concluded on Thursday with an excellent variety concert by the Mothers' Club and British Legion Women. Items of every type, serious and humorous, Coronation and road safety, were included, much to the satisfaction of the large audience. Mr Jackie Toye, Thornley's blind accordionist, was the sole accompanist for this two hours' entertainment. P C John L Jackson as well as being compere, gave an address on road safety in which he mentioned that so far this year there had been seven fatal accidents in the Castle Eden Division, this being the highest for a similar period.

6 November 1953

THORNLEY AGED MINER'S FUNERAL

The funeral of Mr John Amos, almost 78 years old, and well-known for many years amongst Thornley miners, took place on Wednesday, cremation at Sunderland following a service in the Thornley Waterloo Street Methodist Church, the Rev W T Rose officiating. He died at his home in the Aged Miners' cottages after being ill in bed a fortnight. Mr Amos retired when he was about 72. He was then working on the surface at Thornley Colliery, but before that he worked underground for a long period. He was secretary of Thornley Miners' Lodge for about 20 years, a member of Thornley Parish Council for 15 years. Among other committees he served upon were the aged miners' homes and the nursing association.

BANDSMAN'S SUCCESS – At a slow melody contest at Durham on Saturday, Frederick Buckley, the assistant euphonium player in Wheatley Hill Colliery Band, won first prize out of 45 competitiors in the solo section. His father, Mr William Buckley, is conductor of the band, which has had numerous successes in various parts of the county this year. In aid of the ban's new uniform fund a jumble sale organised recently by the women's committee raised £12.10s.

SURPLUS OF THORNLEY'S CORONATION FUND DIVIDED

After a good deal of discussion amongst about 30 representatives of Thornley organisations at a meeting of the Coronation committee on Tuesday, it was decided that the balance of about £100 be divided equally amongst the six places of worship in Thornley, the two schools in Thornley and the two Catholic schools on the Wheatley Hill road. Mrs J Anderson presided.

The decision was made after three motions were put to the vote. They were: "That the balance be handed over to the War Memorial Fund," moved by Mr JHC Scott, four votes; "that a bus shelter with Coronation commemorative plaque be provided through the Parish Council after the balance had been handed to the Council," moved by Rev HW Jackson, seven votes; "that the balance be divided equally amongst the places of worship and schools," moved by Mr E Carter, 17 votes.

The churches and schools are to be asked to select a gift and have it inscribed as a momento of the Coronation.

The committee hope to have a formal presentation at a public gathering when the various bodies have obtained the gifts.

The Rev J W Jackson moved a vote of thanks to the officials for the work they had done in connection with the Coronation celebrations.

THE REV ARTHUR PRESTON (Vicar of Wheatley Hill) commented upon the "low standards of sexual morality" in the country at the present day, when he addressed the Armistice service in All Saints' Church, Wheatley Hill, on Sunday.

If the day of remembrance had to mean anything at all said the Vicar, it must involve an act of dedication to God. Referring to the low moral state into which the country had declined and to the enormous amount of money that was squandered in various unproductive ways, such as on gambling and drinking, Mr Preston declared that it was not to perpetuate conditions such as these that our soldiers died on the field of battle. There should be a "big moral reawakening" and the sooner the better.

Most village organisations were represented in the parade which, headed by Wheatley Hill Colliery Band, formed up at Patton Street and proceeded through the streets of the village to the service in church, which was conducted by the Rev. Noel Catherall (resident Methodist minister).

After the service the parade continued to the Welfare Park, Wheatley Hill, stopping en route at the memorial clock in Front Street, where prayers were said. At the Cenotaph, where a short service was conducted by Mr Catherall, wreaths were laid by Mrs M Brain (on behalf of the women's section. British Legion), Mrs E Thackeray (on behalf of Wheatley Hill Women's Institute), Mr T Taylorson) on behalf of Wheatley Hill Miners Lodge), Mr A Atkinson (on behalf of Sherburn Hill Co-operative Society), Mr R Hutler (on behalf of the Wheatley Hill Soldiers' and Sailors' Club) and Cub Alf Watson (on behalf of the Boy Scouts and Wolf Cubs).

DIPLOMA OF MERIT – Well known in the Wheatley Hill area, where they have been in the ice-cream business since 1910, Messrs A Baldasera and Sons, who have shops at Thornley, Wheatley Hill and Shotton, have been awarded a Diploma of Merit in the national ice-cream competitions held recently at Olympia, London. It is the first time that they have entered the competition.

WHEATLEY HILL PRESENTATION – To mark his retirement from the position of door-keeper at Wheatley Hill Workmen's Club after ten years service – he was never once opposed for the position throughout this period – Mr William Rankin, of Peterlee Cottages, Wheatley Hill, was presented with a gold wrist watch, suitably inscribed, at a social function in the club on Saturday night. Mr T Cowey presided.

The presentation was made by the club secretary, Mr Thomas Storey, CMD, who spoke in appreciative terms of the efficient and faithful service rendered to the club by Mr Rankin. Mr Rankin, said Mr Storey, had also done valuable work in helping to raise funds for the aged members' trip fund. Mr Rankin suitably responded – he would treasure the gift, he said, for the rest of his life.

LUDWORTH

A large gathering assembled at the Memorial for the service conducted by Mr Dowding, accompanied by Thornley Colliery Band. Buglers sounded the "Last Post" and "Reveille", after the silence, wreaths were placed on behalf of the British Legion by Mr Gibson, M.M (chairman). Women's section by Mrs S Sanger (chairman), Women's Institute by Mrs Foster (secretary) and relatives of the fallen. Mr M Morgan, DCM, was Parade Marshal.

13 November 1953

NURSE'S RETIREMENT
Presentation At Thornley

Tribute was paid on Tuesday, at a gathering of representatives of Thornley organisations, to Mrs Hannah Brewster, who retired recently from the post of district nurse after serving for 27 years. Her retirement was due to ill-health.

In presenting her with a handbag and a cheque , subscribed for by the people of Thornley, Dr A P Gray, senior doctor in the area, said he was glad "we have seen fit to recognise Nurse Brewster's services in a tangible form because she was a good friend to Thornley".

Her retirement had come as a climax to a long period of ill-health, but she had carried on her duty as long as possible with the utmost courage and fortitude. She had gone about her work most cheerfully - "often when I certainly did not look as if I was radiating happiness" – and had lived a life of sacrifice and devotion to duty. "I hope she will have a long period of restful retirement – a rest she thoroughly deserves," said Dr Gray.

In returning thanks, Mrs Brewster said she would like the represent- atives of organisations to tell their people how much she appreciated their very kind act of thankfulness. In all her time at Thornley she had been very happy in her work, and one of the greatest helps had been the confidence of the people. She had also been very happy in working with all the doctors, and they had always helped each other.

"It is this thought of helping each other that has helped me the most." Said Mrs Brewster.

Other Tributes

In his short address Dr W G Maclean said he wished Mrs Brewster "a little bit of quiet for a change – and a whole night in bed!"

Dr A Todd said he had never known anyone who had been more anxious about the welfare of the patients, and Dr John Gray said she had always thought about the interests of the patient and never about her own.

Joining in the tributes were Mrs Roper (Child Welfare Committee), Coun Mrs Peart, Mr E Carter (Miners' Lodge), Mrs Scott (Women's Institute), Mrs Willey (Nursing Association), Mrs P Wilkinson (Mother's Club), Mrs Middleton (British Legion), and Mr T H Holder (Clerk to the Parish Council).

A touching little tribute was "by Bessie to Hannah" when Mrs Bessie Bosomworth handed Mrs Brewster a "small homely gift from a homely person – a token of appreciation with love from Bessie."

Mrs E Clark presided over a very happy gathering. She thanked Mr and Mrs Roper, their host and hostess for having the gathering at their home. Ladies of the organisations with which Mrs Brewster has been associated served refreshments. The organisations represented included the Nursing Association, British Legion women, Miners Lodge, Women's Institute, Women's Labour Party, Mothers' Club and Child Welfare Centre.

LEGION WOMEN – At the annual meeting of the Women's Section of Thornley branch of the British Legion, Mrs H Brewster presiding, the following officers were elected: President, Mrs H Brewster; chairman, Mrs E Clark; vice-chairman, Mrs H Slater; treasurer, Mrs J Anderson, secretary, Mrs M W Slater; committee, Mesdames Heard, S Parker, Swallow, D Parker, Mason, Walls, Allen and P Luke.

CIRCUIT YOUTH COUNCIL – The Rev W T Rose presided at the annual meeting of Thornley Methodist Circuit Youth Council in Bow Street Methodist Church. The financial statement, presented by Mr Maurice Nixon, Wheatley Hill, showed a balance in hand of £77, and from this it was decided to donate £60 towards the cost of a projector for the circuit. The projector has been bought for £100 and Sunday Schools are to be invited to make contributions towards the remaining £40. Mr Nixon was re-elected lay treasurer, and other elections were: Lay secretary, Mr Hedley Ridley (Thornley); asst Mr T Robinson (Thornley); representative to District Youth Council, Miss A Griffiths (Thornley); representative to Circuit Women's Fellowship, Mrs N Catherall (Wheatley Hill).

20 November 1953

ROAD SAFETY QUIZ WINNERS AT WHEATLEY HILL

Four Boy Scouts – David Herring, Arthur White, Robin Hughes and Lynn Cook – comprised the winning senior team at a children's Road Safety Quiz in Wheatley Hill Girls' Modern School on Tuesday, organised by the local Road Safety Committee. Altogether eight teams competed – three from the Senior Girls' School, one from Senior Boys' School, two from Wellfield A J Dawson Grammar School and two from the Boy Scouts.

The winning team will now represent Wheatley Hill in the annual Easington Rural Area quiz. A team from Wellfield Grammar School, comprising Ann Smith, Joyce Young, Gwennyth Brownless and Lucy Chaffer, was placed second, and third was a team from the Senior Girls' School, comprising Irene Dunn, Marlene Lee, Jean Reay and Myra Bean.

Prizes, in the form of savings stamps, were presented to the three winning teams by Mrs O Slater, secretary of the local committee. Only one team - from Wheatley Hill Junior mixed School – entered the junior quiz and they will therefore represent the village in the area junior quiz.

Mr J W Willan, headmaster of the Junior Mixed School, presided, and the quiz-master was PC J L Jackson, Accidents Prevention Officer for the Castle Eden Police Division. The adjudicators were County Coun J Andrew, Coun Mrs J Harper and Mrs Fox.

THORNLEY BUTCHER BUYS A HOSPITAL

" A very small price indeed!" said the auctioneer, Mr Joseph Valks, Bishop Auckland, when bidding, which had started at £2,000 reached £3,000 for Wheatley Hill Isolation Hospital, which was put up for public auction in Fir Tree Inn, Wingate, on Wednesday night. In £100 bids the offers steadily increased to £3,800 and then in two £50 bids to £3,900 at which figure the hospital, with its accompanying double-fronted ten-roomed dwelling-house, out offices and outbuilding and about three acres of excellent grass land, was knocked down to the man who had started the bidding – 61-year-old butcher, Mr John George Barnett, 20 Hartlepool Street, Thornley.

And what did Mr Barnett, who has three sons – Matthew (38), Edwin (32), and John (27) – in the butchering business with him at Thornley, have to say about his newly-acquired hospital? "I've had my eyes on it since it was advertised for sale," he told our reporter after the auction.

"We think it will make a good pig and poultry farm. We keep pigs and hens in a small way but now we will be able to extend considerably!"

Auctioneer's Unique Experience

The hospital – "the first I have auctioned in my 25 years' experience," said Mr Valks – is situated close to the main Castle Eden to Durham road, midway between Wheatley Hill and Thornley. Built in 1906, it was last used as a hospital for infectious diseases in 1932. Since then its two wards of 24 beds have always been "at the ready" for emergency use but they have never been needed. There has been no nursing staff and only the caretakers have been in charge.

About 40 interested people – mostly farmers and tradespeople – attended the auction. At the outset Mr Valks revealed that the rateable value of the hospital and buildings was £58, but reminded those present that buildings used for farm purposes would not be assessed, since farm buildings were not rateable.

£3,900

Mr Valks suggested a starting bid of £5,000 - but there were no takers! When the first bid of £2,000 had increased to £3,400, the auctioneer declared "It is now for open sale." And he added, "You are not only buying useful property in a good state of repair, but you are buying a living as well! Consider that angle!"

When the selling figure of £3,900 had been reached the auction had lasted exactly 12 minutes!

Mr R Dobbin, secretary of Newcastle Hospital Regional Board, said other arrangements had been made to deal with any possible epidemic of infectious disease in the area.

11 December 1953

WINGATE TABLERS' GESTURE

For the second successive year the old men living in Wheatley Hill, Thornley and Haswell Moor Aged Miners' Hostels are to be entertained to a Christmas dinner – with all the "trimmings" – by members of the Wingate and District Round Table.

The dinner, cooked and served by the Tablers, is to be held on Sunday, January 3 in the Haswell Moor Hostel, and that is not the end of it. The old men, some thirty in number, will each be given a suitable Christmas "box" and "refreshments" will be provided.

"We aim to give them equally as good a time as last year," Mr Ralph Bell, a Wheatley Hill newsagent who is secretary of the Round Table told me this week.

18 December 1953

NONAGENARIAN CUTS CAKE AT WHEATLEY HILL

Tribute to the practical interest shown in their old members by Wheatley Hill Workmen's Club was paid by Mr Stan Hall, secretary of the Durham County Club Union, when he attended the ninth Christmas treat organised by the club for its retired members and their wives, and widows of retired members over 60. The function was held in the Welfare Hall and about 200 old folk attended.

Among the guests were the officials, committee and staff not only of the Workmen's Club but also of Wheatley Hill Discharged and Demobilised Soldiers' and Sailors' Club and Wheatley Hill Constitutional Club. The local member of the Durham County Council, Coun J Andrews, and his wife were also present, together with the three Wheatley Hill representatives on Easington Rural Council, Councillors E Cain, J Cowie and J J Johnson, and their wives, and Mr H Nicholson (Shotton Colliery), area representative on the County Club Executive.

Tribute To The Club

Mr Hall said he admired very much the wonderful spirit shown by the Workmen's Club in providing year after year "such a wonderful spread" for the older members and their wives. Much work was done "behind the scenes" in raising money by various efforts so that the veterans could be assured of a good time. "When you realise," said Mr Hall, "that during the course of a year something like £800 is disbursed by this club for charitable purposes, then you will have an idea of the fine work the club is doing!"

Supporting Mr Hall in his warm welcome to the guests was the club secretary Mr Thomas Storey. "We are glad to have the old folk with us tonight and we hope we may be able to see their smiling faces for many more years yet," declared Mr Storey. The club, he added, would never forget the veterans of the movement, and it was a joy for them to organise this Christmas treat each year.

During an excellent knife-and-fork tea a huge Christmas cake, beautifully decorated, was cut the oldest guest, Mr James Schofield, who will be 92 in two months' time. Mrs Dorothy Coxton, and 81-year-old widow, was the oldest woman present, and Mr and Mrs Thomas Gustard, who have been married 54 years, the oldest married couple. Serving the tea were wives of committee memers of the club, namely, Mesdames T Jackson, W Maughan, M Brain, J Dunn, J Richardson, D Holland, J Parker, R Cowey, M O'Connor, E Fulcher, T Hall and L Harker.

Gift of £1

Each retired member of the club was presented with a gift of £1. Entertainment was provided by Messrs Robert Armstrong, George Hewitson and Dennie Burke, with Mr E Evans accompanist. Mr T Cowie, chairman of the club, presided.

Expressing thanks to the club on behalf of the guests, Coun E Cain said it was "nice to know" that the old people were not forgotten. On occasions like this the old folk loved to exchange memories of the olden days and this in itself was part of their enjoyment. "As I look around tonight," added Coun Cain, "I can see men I used to drive off, men I used to putt off and men that I hewed with as 'marras.' The years are creeping on but these veteran miners will never be forgotten!"

CLUB GENEROSITY – Towards the cost of school Christmas parties, Wheatley Hill Workmen's Club donated £2 to each of the five schools in the village.

MINERS' RELIEF FUND – At the annual meeting on Saturday of Wheatley Hill branch of the Northumberland and Durham Miners' Permanent Relief Fund, Mr G W Dixon was re-elected treasurer for the 20th successive year. Mr A Wylie was re-elected chairman and Mr J Hedley secretary. Mr A Poole was elected delegate and the following were elected to the committee. Messrs. D Carr, J R Fishwick, W Mills and W Poulson.

CHOIR OFFICERS – The Rev Noel Catherall presided at the choir meeting of Patton Street Methodist Church, Wheatley Hill, when the financial statement showed a total income of £88.1s.9d. and a balance in hand of £6.4s.5d. Choir week-end was arranged for November 6 and 7 next year, and it was decided to hold the annual outing on August 2. Officers elected: Chairman, Mr H Bowes; secretary, Mr W Warnes; assistant secretary, Mr T Venables; treasurer, Mr L Williams; recording secretary, Miss Beryl Baxter; music fund treasurer, Mrs T Venables; auditor, Mr A Burrows; committee, Messrs. T King, P Metcalfe and L Cowell, Miss J Burnett, Mrs Baxter and Mrs Mann.

25 December 1953

1954

Wheatley Hill Church Reopened

For the first time for three months, during which extensive alterations have been carried out, All Saints Church, Wheatley Hill, was open for worship at Christmas. The re-opening was marked by a midnight Communion service on Christmas Eve, conducted by the Vicar, the Rev Arthur Preston. A further Communion service was held on Christmas morning, followed by a special children's service. Altogether there were 250 communicants.

While the church has been closed the Sunday services have been held in the adjoining Church Hall. A new south aisle has been built at a cost of £1.700, new lighting has been installed, and a scheme of interior decoration has been carried out. "The whole scheme of renovations and alterations is now practically complete," the Vicar told me this week, "and we are hoping to arrange a special dedication ceremony in the near future."

On Sunday evening choir members, churchwardens, choirboys and servers read portions of Scripture at a service of the carols and Nine Lessons, conducted by the Vicar. Mr J Atkinson was organist and choir master and a large congregation joined in the singing of the carols.

1 January 1954

All Saints Church, Wheatley Hill after refurbishment

105 YEARS' SERVICE
TWO WHEATLEY HILL MINERS RETIRE

With a total of 105 years mining service between them, two miners at Wheatley Hill colliery, one of whom has been employed the whole of his career underground and the other on the surface, have retired from work. They are Mr William Poulson, 5, Thirteenth Street, Wheatley Hill, who has spent the whole of his 53 years' mining career at the colliery, and Mr john Nicholson, 16, Institute Street, Wheatley Hill, who, except for three years at the neighbouring colliery at Shotton, has been employed at the colliery throughout his mining career of 52 years. Both men recently celebrated their 65th birthday and they have retired of their own accord.

Mr Poulson was born at Marsden Colliery, but as a boy moved with his parents to Wheatley Hill, were he started work at the colliery when he left school at 12. His first job was a trapper-boy and in those days he worked a ten-hour shift for a shilling. He has been a coal-hewer, putter and stone-man.

"In fact," Mr Poulson told our reporter this week, "I have done practically every job in the mine and have been underground the whole time. When he retired Mr Poulson was on maintenance work.

There had certainly been a big improvement in the conditions of wages of the miners, declared Mr Poulson. "And" he added, "there is much more incentive for young men entering the industry to make headway. They are given every encouragement – a big difference from my young days!"

Mr Poulson's father was employed at the same colliery, and he has three brothers still working there, namely, Messrs Joseph Poulson (a stone-man), Thomas Poulson (back overman) and Stephen Poulson (underground worker). Another brother, Mr George Poulson, retired at the colliery two and a half years ago, and a nephew, Mr Stanley Poulson, is safety officer there. The nephew is also officer in charge of Wheatley Hill Unit of the Durham County Fire Brigade.

Holds Certificates

Mr Poulson is the proud possessor of certificates from both the N C B and Durham Miner's Association for 50 years service as a miner. For a few years he has served on the committees of Wheatley Hill branch, Northumberland and Durham Miners' Permanent Relief fund, and Wheatley Hill Hospital and Ambulance Fund.

During the first World War Mr Poulson served for two years in the 5th D L I and throughout the last war was an A R P warden. He is married with a family of three daughters and one son, all married.

Mr Nicholson was born at Wheatley Hill and except for a few years at Wingate and Haswell has lived in the village all his life. He began work on the belts at Wheatley Hill colliery at the age of 13 and, like Mr Poulson, was paid at the rate of a shilling per ten-hour shift.

Worked "On The Belts"

Mr Nicholson has held a number of different jobs on the surface – for many years he was a banksman and until he was taken ill about a year ago was head banksman for some time. When he recovered from his illness he returned to work "on the belts," "the same job as I started my career," smiled Mr Nicholson.

A keen supporter of local football throughout his life, Mr Nicholson has served on the committee of Wheatley Hill S C, Durham Central League club. In his younger days he played at outside-left for several local teams. He is married, but has no family. Mrs Nicholson has been a member of Church Street Methodist Church at Wheatley Hill for many year

MINERS' RESPONSE TO KOREAN FUND

A reference to the response that the miners made to the appeal on behalf of those serving in Korea is made by Mr Samuel Watson in his report just issued. He says that Durham County Mining federation was asked to assist in collecting funds in order to provide comforts for every Durham County man and woman serving with the Forces in Korea. During the war, the Union itself had a similar fund which we supplied cigarettes and books to our prisoners of war.

"The organisers of the fund hoped to raise £2,000 to purchase comforts for servicemen and women from the county in Korea, and it was felt that this worthy appeal would receive the support of lodges and branches, some members of which had sons and daughters serving in Korea.

Parcels of 30s Each

"The cost of the parcels was about 30s each, and lodges were to use this as a guide in making their contributions. With the usual friendliness and generosity manifest among our members, the appeal received magnificent support from the lodges and branches, who contributed the fine total of £540 8s 9d to the fund.

"We would like to express our appreciation of all who assisted this worthy cause, as well as hope that the lads in Korea would accept them with the best wishes for a speedy and safe return to the county and their families."

12 January 1954

WAR MEMORIAL AT THORNLEY

Meeting of Thornley War Memorial Committee was presided over by Mr E Green. It was decided to aim at providing a memorial cross and layout similar to that at Blackhall inspected by members of the committee. It was stated that the cost would probably be from £875 to £1.000, against which the War Comforts Committee were prepared to subscribe their balance of £275.

It was decided that all organisations be asked to make donations and to make what arrangements they could to raise money for the fund.

There was some discussion on the site. Two proposals were made. One was for the old Church Street land, in sight of the main highway, and the other for the site occupied by the old institute. Consideration of the proposals was held over until enquiries can be made as to whether the new miners' welfare institute can accommodate the organisations now using the old institute, which would have to be pulled down if full use of its site was to be made.

It is intended that the new memorial should cover both world wars. The first war memorial, an oak and brass tablet, was destroyed when the miners' welfare institute was burned down in1944.

PIGEON SHOW AT THORNLEY

About 100 pigeons, all of excellent quality, were exhibited at the second annual show held on Saturday in Thornley Miners' Welfare Institute under the auspices of the N C B No 3 Area Welfare Committee. Entries were from Thornley, Wheatley Hill, Ludworth, Shotton, Easington, Horden and Blackhall.

Mr Ivan Jones, of the N C B staff at Castle Eden, made the arrangements, with the assistance of Mr N Stokoe, secretary of Thornley Homing Club, and Mr W Henderson, secretary of Thornley Miners' Welfare Committee. Messrs T Bryson (West Hartlepool) and J W Towers (Billingham) were the judges.

The best bird in the show was a two-year-old cock from the lofts of Bradley and Partners, of Thornley. It had a similar success in the Club Union show last year. Mr A E Pye, an Easington enthusiast, won a £1 special given by himself.

Class Results

200-mile old hen: Bradley Partners, Gorton and Son (Blackhall), Storey and Son (Thornley), Richardson and Sons (Thornley). 200-miles old cock: Bradley Partners, Richardson and Sons, Foster (Wheatley Hill). Heale Brothers (Wheatley Hill). Likeliest hen, any age: 1 and special, Pye and Son (Easington), 2 Hutton and Miller (Horden), 3 and 4 Pye and Son. Likeliest cock, any age: Pye and Son, Bradley Partners, Richardson and Sons, Gorton and Son. 100-miles young cock: Bradley and Partners, Gorton and Son, Hutton and Miller, Gorton and Son. 100-miles young hen: Gorton and Son (special), Pye and Son, Bradley Partners, Gorton and Son. Channel cock (flown 1953): Levitt and Son (Thornley), Richardardson and Son, Pye and Son, Raffle Bros. (Wheatley Hill). Channel hen (flown 1953: 1 and 2 Richardson and Sons, 3 and 4 Levitt and Son.

15 January 1954

WERE FELLOW-PRISONERS
Judge And Colliery Blacksmith

When John Barker, 34-year-old Wheatley Hill Colliery blacksmith, appeared at Durham County Court in December, Judge Clifford Cohen told him he was sorry to have to order him to give up his house. The judge made his remark after hearing that Barker had been a prisoner of war for five years. Barker did not know it then, but the judge was also a war prisoner.

John Barker, who was told that he would have to vacate his National Coal Board house within three months, has moved his wife and two-year-old son, Ian, within one month. They have found a home at Kirk's Buildings, Thornley, in a four-roomed house without a water supply. The nearest tap is in the wash-house in the yard five yards from the back door.

Rent of this house, which stands at the end of a muddy track, is 11s 1d a week. As he is not now living in a colliery house, Mr Baker receives a weekly allowance of 5s.

"A Hard Case"

In the court hearing, the Judge told the Coal Board solicitor, who sought possession because Mr Barker's late father had been the tenant, "This is a hard case, I have no doubt you will allow a little latitude if you can. Because of what they have been through, people like Mr Barker worry more than others about this sort of thing."

Soon after the case, Mrs Vera Barker told our reporter, they received notice to vacate the house in Fourth Street, Wheatley Hill, by March 11. "The Judge was very kind and we appreciate his remarks," she said, "but if the committee which controls colliery houses took notice of what the Judge said they did not come to see us, or offer us any help to get another house. We are not complaining.

"We know there have to be rules for allocating these houses. But it was all a terribly worrying time. In the end, when we found another house, we were not sorry to leave Fourth Street. Our landlady has promised to have a water supply put into the house. Now, after months of anxiety, we feel secure.**A Worrying Experien**"Being ordered out of the house in Fourth Street last year was so worrying that we had not the heart to have a holiday. It was all the more worrying when we knew my husband had worked at the colliery since he was a boy and that his health had been affected by war service."

A member of the committee which allocates colliery houses said, "We sympathised, but were pressed for the house by men who had been married much longer than Mr Barker."

In the court hearing, Mr W Kinghorn, for the Coal Board, said that "the tragedy" was that Mr Barker's own workmen were urging that he should be ordered to give up the house.

Mr Barker, a private in the R A O C, was taken prisoner at St Valery in 1940. Judge Cohen, then a lieutenant in the Tyneside Scottish, a unit of the Black Watch, was taken prisoner at the same place.

SUDDEN TRAGIC DEATH

On Saturday, conducted by the Rev Noel Catherall, the funeral took place at Wheatley Hill cemetery of Mr William Delbridge (71), 29, Wordsworth Avenue, Wheatley Hill, whose death occurred with tragic suddenness the previous Wednesday. Mr Delbridge had left home in his normal health to visit a neighbour when he suddenly collapsed in the street and died in a nearby house. A native of Haswell, Mr Delbridge had lived in Wheatley Hill for 54 years, being employed at the local colliery for practically the whole of his mining career until his retirement six years ago. He started work at Haswell colliery but was only there a year before transferring to Wheatley Hill colliery, where he spent 52 years. Mr Delbridge is survived by his wife and two daughters, both of whom are married.

FORMER OFFICIAL BURIED

Confined to an invalid chair for the past 15 years, following an accident at Wheatley Hill Colliery in August 1936, when he fractured his spine. Mr William Horn (62), 5, South View, Wheatley Hill, who died last week, was cremated at Sunderland on Saturday. Mr Horn had been a member of the Caradoc Lodge of Freemasons for some 20 years, and a number of Freemasons were among the mourners at the funeral service in Thornley Bow Street Methodist Church conducted by the Rev W T Rose. At the age of 12 Mr Horn began work at Stoneygate Water Works, near Houghton-le-Spring, but two years later began his mining career at Thornley colliery. Later he was a deputy and then an official at Wheatley Hill colliery and was employed as a deputy overman when the accident occurred which ended his career. He spent more than two years in hospital before he was able to get about in an invalid chair. Throughout the first world war Mr Horn served in the Gloucestershire Regiment and received a fracture of the skull through a bullet. A lifelong Methodist, he regularly attended Thornley Bow Street Methodist Church, Mr Horn leaves a widow and two sons, Gordon and Billy.

22 January 1954

NEW YEAR'S EVE TRAGEDY
Sad Happenings at Wheatley Hill

Shortly after returning home late on New Year's Eve after visiting a local club, a Wheatley Hill miner, it was stated at an inquest at Thornley on Monday, fell down a few stairs and died in the early hours of New Year's Day.

The inquest was on Arthur Wylie (46), stoneman, 3, Fourteenth Street, Wheatley Hill, and after hearing from a post-mortem report by Dr G E Stephenson, that Wylie had fractured the base of his skull, the Coroner, Mr T V Devey, recorded a verdict of "Accidental death."

At 7.45 pm on New Year's Eve, said the widow, Mrs Ethel Wylie, her husband left home for the club. When he returned later that night she

374

went upstairs for his overcoat as they intended visiting his brother's house before midnight. Her husband, who had had some drink, followed her upstairs and then came down behind her. When she reached the foot of the stairs he was about three steps up. She went into an adjoining room and then heard a thud and found her husband lying behind a door with his head against a vacuum cleaner box.

With assistance she got her husband to bed and later he appeared to be sleeping. Later she found him lying on the floor beside the bed and when Dr Gray was called he was dead.

MR SAUNDERS WRITES FROM ILLINOIS
WAS BORN AT WHEATLEY HILL

Mr Thomas A Saunders, 1022, Raleigh Road, Glenview, Illinois, USA emigrated from Wheatley Hill 26 years ago, and during the whole of that time he has been receiving week by week, the Durham Chronicle from his sister, Mrs J W Wilson, 6, Moore Square, Wingate.

He has thus been able "to keep up with what goes on in Durham County," and especially enjoys the accounts and pictures of Durham Miners' Gala. "My mother, now dead," he writes, "took me to my first gala when I was nine, and I attended every one of them until I left England."

"In your issue of December 11, 1953, there was a very interesting article which I 'devoured'- 'History was made in County Durham.' It gave me a nostalgic sensation."

School at Ludworth

Mr Saunders says he was born at Wheatley Hill and when he was two the family moved to Ludworth. He went to the church school there, but for special services they seemed to be linked with Shadforth. They marched in a body from the school to the parish church there. The two villages were linked for concerts. Of those belonging to Shadforth he recalls Misses Winifred and Eva Whittingham, and a Miss Frieda Fiedler.

"Shadforth Village," he writes, "I always likened to a poem we learnt at school - 'Sweet Autumn, loveliest village of the plain,' and I often wonder if it has changed. At 14 we moved back to Wheatley Hill, and it was while living there I frequently visited Hallgarth Church. I remember Sherburn and Sherburn Hill; visited Bishop Auckland and Wolsingham several times, and at 16 I was confirmed by Bishop Hensley Henson.

"I often muse upon those happy days and that is why I always enjoy the Durham Chronicle. It keeps me in touch."

If Mr Saunders revisited the haunts of his boyhood days he would not see many changes apart from the very considerable housing estates that have been developed in many parts of the county.

GALLANT THORNLEY C W TEAM
Won Cup Tie In Extra Time

Gallant Thornley CW! This Durham Central League side won the admiration of their supporters by putting up a great fight against Herrington CW in a Thornley Aged Miners' Cup game at Thornley. After extra time they ran out victorious by 4-2. It was the best game seen at Thornley for many years.

Play moved quickly from end to end in the first half with both goals undergoing narrow escapes. Hanner, for Thornley, opened the scoring, but Herrington equalised to make the half-time score 1-1. Thornley with wind advantage in the second half, had most of the play, and Smith, after missing a golden opportunity, gave his side the lead in the 89th minute. Then Herrington got on level terms.

Thornley played like a team inspired during the extra time, thanks to a "pep" talk by secretary "Jonty" Bosomworth. In the third minute of this overtime, Lee, moving like a greyhound down the left wing and cleverly tricked three players before crashing the ball into the net. The applauding of the Thornley crowd echoed like thunder.

Then Smith was cheered to the echo when he increased the lead from close in. Now it was apparent that Thornley would emerge victorious, but great credit is also due to the losers who had the consolation of knowing they had played a major part in providing the spectators with almost a thrill a minute.

"If such a standard of football could be seen on local grounds more regularly, there would be very few going miles away to watch Football League fare," said Mr Bosomworth (secretary).

"It was certainly a 'classic' game, with both teams putting every ounce of energy into the game. Both teams were almost exhausted at the end. What a sight they were in! – mud decorating every player from head to feet.

29 January 1954

WHEATLEY HILL TEACHER
Speaks Of Experiences In America

Trimdon Station Methodist Men's Fellowship, which is in its ninth season, made history when they invited a lady speaker to address them. She was Miss Goynes, a Wheatley Hill schoolteacher, who visited America for a year under the teacher-exchange scheme. She was introduced by Mr S Hornsby, who presided.

The speaker said she taught in Minneapolis, Minnesota, "I found it easy to settle in America," said Miss Goynes, "because I found so much that was familiar in their way of life. The similarity in language and outlook makes one feel at home. We must not take the cinema views of American life too seriously. In fact so far as I could judge, that view is quite false."

More comfortable Travel

The speaker went on to say that travel in the U S A was more comfortable than in England. Their roads were wide and spacious, and allowed for six lanes of traffic. Referring to housing, Miss Goynes said that many were built of wood and stucco. They were not laid out in rows, or even arranged as semi-detached residences. Many houses were detached, standing in their own spacious grounds.

"The tempo of life is much swifter out there," said Miss Goynes, "but that is not the same as saying that the Americans are quicker than we are. The action and movement of people is slower than in Britain. The quick tempo is due entirely to the higher degree of mechanisation: the car, the phone and labour-saving devices."

Self- Service

The speaker paid tribute to America's self-service establishments and the care that was taken to protect all food, which was sold in cellophane wrappers, "One thing that the self-service store has done was to encourage men to do the shopping," said the speaker "and men in America thought nothing of it."

"American women," went on Miss Goynes, "are the most emancipated in the world. They are no longer enslaved by the kitchen-sink. Their homes are stream-lined, and they enjoy far more leisure than their English sisters."

High Pressure Of Life

Commenting on American education, the speaker said that the system was not unified under one central administration. Each state made its own arrangements.

"I found," she said "that there was a tenseness and restlessness about American students that may be attributed to the high pressure of life. There is no economic pressure to cause Americans to hurry with their education, and I would say that may be the cause of British children being at least a year ahead of their American cousins educationally.

In answer to a question as to whether there was any friction or mistrust of Britain, in the States, Miss Goynes replied, "No. There is criticism of our way of life as there is criticism of America here. But it is the type of bickering which goes on between people of the same close family ties. I feel sure that from what I saw, America is firmly behind Britain."

BEAUTIFYING THE CHURCH
Wheatley Hill Vicar's Comments

Despite the fact that church services had to be transferred to the Church Hall for a period of nearly three months, All Saints' Church, Wheatley Hill, had not "lost any ground," writes the Vicar, the Rev Arthur Preston, in the February issue of his parish magazine. "Indeed," he adds, "the number of communicants in 1953 amounted to 7.799, the highest figure since pre-war years. We have a body of people who are prepared to support the church loyally and faithfully in spite of temporary difficulties."

The church was re-opened at the beginning of the year after been closed for the building of the new south aisle and for renovation and re-decoration.

"Like Coming Into Heaven"

"The first service to be held in the newly-restored church," writes Mr Preston, "was Midnight mass. With the new lighting system and the re-decorated walls, the altar shone forth in splendour. The happiest description of the scene was that given by one of our members who described it as 'like coming into heaven.'"

The extensive scheme of repairs and restoration begun a year or so ago was now almost complete, reports the Vicar. "When one bears in mind that the original building was a cheaply erected mission hall, the architect is to be congratulated on his plans," he adds.

"He has given to the church a sense of dignity and spaciousness which was completely lacking before and he has done this without destroying that feeling of homeliness which was the one redeeming feature of the old building. Whereas the church was gloomy and sombre it is now light and colourful. It will compare favourably with any of the surrounding colliery churches and this splendid result has been attained through the eager willingness and ready co-operation of our church people here and of members of our own community generally."

Holding the services in the Church Hall had involved a good deal of extra work and thanks were especially due to Mr and Mrs Ayre "for coping uncomplainingly" with this extra work, to the band of ladies who helped to clean the church from time to time, and to Mr Woodward and the band of men who cleaned and varnished the pews.

The Greater Privilege

"Much yet remains to be done," continued Mr Preston, "but it can be done gradually. There is wide scope for gifts to the church. High on the list of priorities are green vestments –the present vestments are shabby and worn – and hassocks. Only a small percentage of the congregation can devoutly kneel because of lack of hassocks. There is no magic wand to miraculously produce these things but it is wonderful what can be achieved by willing hearts!"

In his address at the licensing of the new curate-in-charge at Peterlee, the Bishop of Durham, recalls Mr Preston, said it was "a great privilege to worship in an ancient and beautiful church which has stood through the centuries, but there is a greater privilege and that is to build a church."

"That, in a sense, has been your privilege in Wheatley Hill," concludes the Vicar. "You can feel that you have played a part in the restoration and the beautifying of your church. You can feel that it is indeed Your church.

12 February 1954

HOSTESS EFFORT

As a result of a successful hostess whist drive and social evening in the Church Hall on Saturday, organised by women members of All Saints' Church, Wheatley Hill, the sum of £17 14s was raised towards the cost of buying new carpets for the church. Mt T Simpson was M C for the whist, and music for dancing was supplied by Messrs F Orton and H

Bellas. The prizes were presented by Mrs A Preston, wife of the Vicar of Wheatley Hill.

NURSES' HOME SOLD

Sold by auction by Messrs Pigg and Son, of Bishop Auckland, the nurses' home in Cemetery Road, Wheatley Hill, which belonged to the local District Nursing Association, realised £2,300 on Friday night. The home, which has been tenanted by district nurses since it was built by the Nursing Association in 1926, is, it is understood, to be used as a residence for the local Roman Catholic priest. The trustees have agreed to donate the proceeds of the sale to the local Aged Miners' Homes' Association. "The money will be spent principally on improvements to the aged miners' homes in the village," Mr E Wharrier, secretary of the trustees, told our reporter this week.

19 February 1954

WHEATLEY HIL WI EFFORT

As a result of a whist drive and dance in the Welfare Hall, Wheatley Hill, organised by Wheatley Hill W I , £11 11s was raised for the Westminster Abbey Restoration Fund. The president, Mrs E Thackeray was M C , and presented prizes to Mesdames A Bramfitt, H Sangster, Cook, R Walker, Clayton, Charlton, Thompson and Holder. Spot dance prizes were won by Mrs Richardson and Mrs Trees (Wheatley Hill) and Mrs Carr and Mrs Ayre (Shotton Colliery).

TRUCKS DERAILED

About 80 yards of the railway track were torn up and wooden sleepers were smashed when seven 20-ton trucks of coal were derailed on the mineral goods line near Thornley railway crossing on Tuesday. The trucks, in the middle of a set of 21 full trucks which had just left the colliery sidings at Wheatley Hill, left the rails only a few yards from the road that passes over the railway between Fir Tree, Wingate, and Shotton Colliery. Because of their weight none of the trucks overturned, but they sank some distance into the earth and a breakdown gang was busy the remainder of the day and all Wednesday lifting the trucks back onto the rails and repairing the damage.

26 February 1954

THORNLEY BILLIARDS TEAM WINS TITLE

Thornley Miners' Welfare Institute's billiards team, having won all their 14 league games, have become champions of the Northern Amateur

Billiards League. Their success is the more striking because the team was only formed after the new institute was opened 13 months ago.

Between 1944, when the old institute was burned down and 1953, there was no team. The Thornley league players have been John Watson, James Lennox, J J McCoy, Les Williamson and George Wake.

In addition to the backing of the Miners' Welfare Committee, the team has had the support of a bus load of enthusiasts at all their away matches. Teams in the League are Shotton (two), Easington C W, Deaf Hill Holt's (Houghton), Haswell and Philadelphia.

By defeating Easington C W in a semi-final, Thornley are finalists in the NCB No 3 Area billiards competition, and will play the winners of Blackhall v Horden in the final.

5 March 1954

Mr J WHITE'S RETIREMENT

Many tributes to his long service in the colliery offices at Wheatley Hill were paid to the colliery cashier, Mr John White, when he was guest of honour at the annual dinner of Wheatley Hill branch of the NUM Colliery Officials' and Staffs' Association in the Marine Hotel, Seaton Carew, on Saturday night.

Mr White, who is retiring at the end of the month, has been employed at the colliery for the whole of his 51 years' career, starting there when he left school at the age of 14. On behalf of the management and officials, Mr J L Snaith, colliery manager, presented Mr White

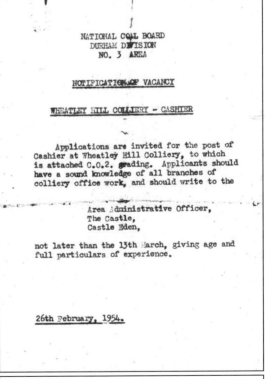

NATIONAL COAL BOARD
DURHAM DIVISION
NO. 3 AREA

NOTIFICATION OF VACANCY

WHEATLEY HILL COLLIERY – CASHIER

Applications are invited for the post of Cashier at Wheatley Hill Colliery, to which is attached C.O.2. grading. Applicants should have a sound knowledge of all branches of colliery office work, and should write to the

Area Administrative Officer,
The Castle,
Castle Eden,

not later than the 13th March, giving age and full particulars of experience.

26th February, 1954.

Advertisement for a Colliery Cashier
at Wheatley Hill after the death of Mr J White

with a standard reading-lamp and wished him many years of happiness and good health in his well-earned retirement.

Mr R Chisholm presided and others paying tribute to Mr White's service included Mr F Simpson (under-manager), Mr P H Galley (head clerk), and Mr G P Shaw, chief accountant, No 3 Area, Durham Division, N C B . Though Mr White had been employed in the office he had good knowledge of underground pit work, said Mr Simpson, but perhaps this was not so surprising when it was realised that his father had been under-manager at the colliery and a brother was a colliery manager.

After the presentation vocal items were contributed by Mr B Blenkinsopp (tenor) and Miss B Galley (soprano) with Mrs C English accompanist and Mt T King was elocutionist. Mr J J Harrison, J P arranged the function.

Under Five Managers

Mr White has served at Wheatley Hill Colliery under five colliery managers- Messrs J Laverick, M Barrass, J A Simpson, T H Dobson and J L Snaith. He has been cashier since the mines were nationalised, and before that was head clerk. He has done much good work in a quiet way-he certainly does not seek the limelight. He has been a trustee of the local miners' welfare scheme since its inception and until, they were taken over by the Coal Board, was secretary of Wheatley Hill pit canteen and baths from their inception. For many years also he has been secretary of Wheatley Hill Colliey Housing Committee.

Mr White has always been keenly interested in ambulance work and in his younger days was a member of the Wheatley Hill team which was successful in winning many contests. A life-long churchman, he is actively associated with All Saints' Church, Wheatley Hill, where he has been treasurer of the Parochial Church Council for the past 29 years and Vicar's warden for almost the same period.

LUDWORTH
Inquest on Ex-Soldier

Evidence that he had received frequent medical attention since his discharge from the Army with a 60 per cent pension in July, 1918, was heard at an inquest at Ludworth, on Saturday, on William Coxford (65), 41, Moor Lane, Ludworth, who died on March 11. Dr John Gray (Wheatley Hill) said that death was due to chronic bronchitis and was directly attributable to Coxford's war wounds, and the Coroner, Mr T V

Devey, returned a verdict in accordance with this evidence. Mrs Cox-ford said that her husband served in the Northumberland Fusiliers during the First World War and in 1915 received gunshot wounds in the lung. He had been in poor health and had not been able to work for the past 20 years.

FIRE BRIGADE QUIZ COMPETITION

Wheatley Hill Fire Station, representing the County Fire brigade, gained second place in a technical quiz competition, sponsored by the Fire Services Research and Training Trust in Shire Hall, Durham, on Saturday. Northumberland, represented by Alnwick, gained first place with 22½ points from a possible 45, and go forward to the Northern semi-final at Sheffield next month.

The Durham team first tied with Yarm (Yorkshire), for second place, with 21½, but a deciding round gave Wheatley Hill victory by 9½ points. They were represented by Sub-officer S Poulson, Leading-Fireman F Horner, Fireman J Goynes, Fireman P Winn, and Fireman Ayre.

Prizes were Presented by Coun E Leggett, chairman of the Durham County Fire Brigade Committee.

PIT VICTIM

Funeral took place at Shadforth Cemetery on Saturday of Mr Kenneth Bradshaw (28), husband of Mrs Lily Bradshaw, 67, Moor Crescent, Ludworth. Mr Bradshaw was fatally injured in an accident at Thornley Colliery on Tuesday 9th. Service at St Cuthbert's Church, Shadforth, was conducted by Canon R H Tillard. Cortege was headed by Thornley Colliery Silver Band and Thornley Lodge officials, with the banner, followed by a large number of workmates and friends.

BOB, NOW RETIRED, SLEEPS IN HIS MUSEUM
AT LUDWORTH
Mastered Art of Living

This is what Bob is: taxidermist, ornithologist, entomologist, botanist, coleopterist, naturalist, artist, and (perhaps it should come first), a humorist. Bob is a retired pit banksman, a bachelor, of middle height and broadish, and has only one eye (the other was lost in the first world war). He is full of sparkling life, though "seventy-three come his birthday."

I spent three bright hours with him recently in his museum-bedroom and two similar hours over and after tea in the living-room of his council house in the little colliery village of Ludworth, which (it may be necessary to say) is in East Durham. (writes Mr T H Holder,Thornley).

Robert Henry Lofthouse is the man I'm writing about - known to everybody for miles around as "Bob" Lofthouse.

"Bob," I said "Hez tha ivvor been bored?"

We used the vernacular frequently. Bob is such an integral part of this old colliery district that he cannot help "hissel," and doesn't want to. He hopes the dialect "nivvor gans oot."

"Bored!" he said, "Nivvor. Aa could live mi life aal ower agyen… and agyen…and agyen. It's been one grand song."

No Need For Parrot To Talk

He had me laughing a good part of the time I was with him. The parrot kept squawking, "Does it talk?" I asked, "Naw," he said. And I wasn't surprised. It wouldn't have been able to get a word in edgeways, Bob confirmed this.

"There's plenty taakin here when Aa's taakin'" he said.

He's had the parrot 30 years, but you can be sure that if it dies before him he will "stuff" it.

As an amateur taxidermist he has "stuffed" all sorts of birds and animals. The family's black retriever dog, for example. It had been a terror to small boys of the village. When it died Bob "stuffed" it and arranged it (duly tethered) in the kennel just over the low wooden fence of the backyard, it looked out of the kennel door savagely.

The small boys were awed. They still keep clear of the Loft-house premises. Then they became mystified. A queer dog - a savage dog that had lost its old bark.

Mystery Dog In Kennel

They began to apply tests. By throwing big stones at the dog, with the dog making no reply, they gradually reached the conclusion that this was another of Bob's funny ideas. They continued their tests (and getting their own back) with half bricks, until the Lofthouse family could stand it no longer. "Bob," said his father, "Get that dog oot 'o' the kennel – the joke's finished." Bob admits that the boys won.

Laughing at this story as I reached the top of the stairs and entered Bob's bedroom, I stopped suddenly. Two feet from the glowing fire there lay a fully grown fox – curled up and content, as though it owned the place. It looked straight at me. At any rate, there was a light in its eye. Bob bent down and stroked it. That gave me confidence, and I did the same.

Amazing Assortment

Though somewhat startled, I wasn't so taken aback as another visitor. He saw the fox, declared it had winked at him, retreated, and never came back again.

A yard away was another fox – looking out of its realistic hole. "It isn't a whole fox," said Bob. "Just a head. Some fellows were digging a ferret out, and one of them chopped the fox's head of with a spade without knowing it was in the hole waiting to come out."

The larger part of the wall is covered with cases of "stuffed" animals and birds-badgers, an ermine stoat, a wild cat from Perth, owls, sparrow-hawks, a bittern, and - yes- a tiny duckling, in, that fluffy yellow covering we all know. I asked Bob why he had "stuffed" it. He said he didn't quite know, but I knew that it was Bob expressing himself as an artist of great tenderness.

Birds, Moths And a Colorado Beetle!

Out of the cupboards Bob brought his beetles, his moths, and birds' eggs and spread them out on his double-size bed – not all at once, but in relays of closed cases. For the first time I saw a real Colorado beetle – bought by Bob in London for sixpence. And there were tit-larks' nests, collected locally, containing the egg of an intruding cuckoo.

All the hundreds of samples are labelled and marked in Bobs beautiful microscopic handwriting.

Part of one of the walls bears coloured pen-and-ink drawings. And this reminds me that Bob sends his close friends pen-and-ink Christmas cards, including the robin (of course) and other birds in their natural colours. He told me that he spends as much as eight hours in drawing a single Christmas card. What goodwill.

Comic Figures

In one little section of his museum his imagination and humour are blended in comic figures he has contrived out of pieces of twig. You imagine him picking up a twig in the hedgerow, looking at it, and seeing humorous possibilities in it. At home he fixes eyes and mouth to it, and then you have (say) a still more grotesque giraffe or a monkey funnier than any monkey you have seen.

All over the house there are colour and good cheer – all Bob's. On the kitchen wall to amuse the children who wander into the Lofthouse home – are Snowwhite and the Seven Dwarfs, Golly is having his hair cut – and half of it is gone already. Strung on the wall is Bob's lovely bunch of coconuts, all with expressive faces and pipes in their mouths. In the bathroom a beautiful life-size heron is poised ready to dive into the bath two feet below.

No Thought Of Money

Bob is a retired workingman with no more than the ordinary retired workingman income, but money is the thing furthest from his thoughts. He is rich in another way- in having mastered, much more than most of us, the art of living. His skill as a craftsman in taxidermy, learnt from books since he was a boy; his great knowledge and love of wild birds and plants; his facility in pen-and-ink sketching- all these have been his serious spare-time study.

In the past 12 months his visitors' book has been signed by 160 folk. In 40 years 6.000 have signed. I am sure that many of us have learned something from this happy philosopher, who sums up his life as having been "one grand, sweet song."

19 March 1954

WHEATLEY HILL CLUB
Long Service Recognised

During his 20 years' unbroken service as treasurer of Wheatley Hill Workmen's Club, Mr Joseph Dunn has seen the average weekly takings increase tenfold – from an average of £50 a week in 1934 to the present weekly average of £500.

"And during that time," the club secretary, Mr Thomas Storey, C M D, told club members on Saturday "he has handled into hundreds of thousands of pounds without a halfpenny deficiency in any respect whatever!"

Before a packed audience in the main bar Mr Storey, on behalf of the club, was making a presentation of a cheque for £75 to Mr Dunn in recognition of his long service. He presented a certificate of merit from the Club and Institute Union and a club badge to Mr Dunn.

Trustworthy Official

"Mr Dunn's 20 years' service is something worth thinking about!" declared Mr Storey. "Joseph Dunn has been a friend of mine for more than 40 years. We were young men together, and we worked down the pit together and then 20 years ago he was appointed treasurer of the club. When he began his duties I gave him a few words of advice on how to handle the club money - he then accepted them in the same spirit in which they were given but within a few months of him taking over I found that my words had scarcely been necessary:! He had been a most trustworthy treasurer and given 20 years' valuable service. He is a man of high character – unassuming and quiet in his manner – and without a doubt is the genuine article!"

In accepting the gift, Mr Dunn recalled that before taking over the treasurership he had served on the finance committee for 14 years. "This is one of the happiest and proudest days of my life," he added, "and I want to thank officers, committees and members wholeheartedly for this grand testimonial. I have always tried to do my best for the club and the members, I know, have appreciated my work."

Tribute To Stewardess

A warm tribute to the work of the stewardess, Mrs Florence Williams, was also paid by Mr Storey when he presented her with a cheque for £100 on her retirement after 20 years' service. Mrs Williams and her husband, Mr Edward Williams, were appointed steward and stewardess in 1934. Five years later Mr Williams died, but Mrs Williams was allowed to continue as stewardess – "and throughout the years," said Mr Storey, "she has given yeoman service!"

The club was in a poor state, financially, when Mrs Williams and her husband first took up their duties, said Mr Storey. "And for some time things got even worse and we had to make drastic cuts," continued Mr Storey. "But we were able to obtain a mortgage for £3,000 and build a new club. Our position then began to improve and takings increased. There is no doubt that Mrs William's devotion to duty has in no small way been responsible for the club's present sound financial position!"

It would be difficult to fill the position Mrs Williams was vacating in a fortnight's time. "When she leaves this club she is leaving behind evidence of one of the best characters obtainable," he said.

Mrs Williams Recalls

Expressing thanks Mrs Williams recalled the "ups and downs" experienced during the early days of her stewardship. "But we hadn't long been in this new club," she added, "when we were up on our feet again. I have always done my best to help the different committees who have served here and I received the same support from them."

On behalf of the bar staff, Mrs W Carr presented Mrs Williams with a bouquet.

Mr T Cowie, chairman of the club, who presided, added his tribute to the loyal service of both Mrs Williams and Mr Dunn. Sandwiches and biscuits were served free to the club members.

Mrs Williams is leaving the district early next month for Blackpool to make her home with her son, Stanley, who took over a boardinghouse, two years ago. In addition to her son she has two daughters at Wingate and Thornley.

Mrs Williams and her late husband first took up duties as publicans in 1929 as tenants of the Shoulder of Mutton Inn, West Herrington. After three years there they spent two years as managers of the Seven Stars Inn, Sherburn Hill before their appointment at Wheatley Hill.

LUDWORTH

MRS S SANGER presided at the meeting of Ludworth British Legion (women). Members agreed to entertain the Over-60 Club at Wheatley Hill on Tuesday. A pie and peas supper ended the evening.

FOOTBALL CLUB – By its fine performances Ludworth Junior Football Club has attracted scouts to the village from leading amateur and professional clubs. An invitation has come from Chelsea for 18-year-old Jacky Elcoat, a member of a well-known Ludworth family, to sign amateur forms and to go for a month's trial with this club. Jacky gives consistently level headed and outstanding performances and his unassuming good nature in the village has made him quite popular. The villagers send this boy, who may easily become a star, best wishes.

WHEATLEY HILL APPOINTMENT

The first wages bill clerk to be appointed at Wheatley Hill colliery when the weekly pay day was instituted in place of the fortnightly pay, has been appointed cashier at the colliery, to succeed Mr John White, who retires at the end of this month.

He is Mr Peter H Galley, of Front Street, Wheatley Hill, who has been employed in the colliery office since leaving school 48 years ago. For many years Mr Galley, who has lived in the village practically the whole of his life, was head wages clerk, and when the mines became nationalised he was appointed assistant cashier to Mr White.

26 March 1954

Mr Galley's successful letter of application

WHEATLEY HILL CHURCH JUBILEE

On Saturday 150 members and friends of Wheatley Hill Church Street Methodist Church assembled in the Miners' Welfare Hall for a banquet which was organised as the final function in the church's golden jubilee celebrations. Among the guests were a few who had left the village including Mr Ben Elliott (Bowburn), Mr and Mrs Tom McCartney (West Hartlepool) and Miss Carol Nixon, an assistant matron at a hospital in the Midlands. Thornley Circuit representatives were the Rev W T Rose and Mrs Rose; Mr T A Walker (circuit steward) and Mrs Walker. The Rev and Mrs Noel Catherall were host and hostess and Mr A Kirk was M C Mr J J Harrison, J P , welcomed the circuit ministers and officials. Mr G Poulson (society steward) welcomed the guests on behalf of the church. Mr B Elliott responded.

Mr Joseph Howarth paid a tribute to the early founders who had the courage to venture their all in building their church in Church Street. He said, "These pioneer Methodists did more than put up a building of bricks and mortar. They influenced men's lives."

Since 1897

Mrs Elizabeth Turnbull responding said she had attended services since they were held in a house in Ford Street in 1897. She remarked that while the early days were days of struggle they were marked by close personal fellowship.

Mr Maurice Nixon said, "The present has links with the past and the future. We are building on the foundations of the past but we are laying down the foundations of the future church. In our graded Sunday School of 200 scholars we have material to shape for tomorrow. If the future is to be safe there must be no jerry-building." Mrs A Kirk responded. Mr J O Hughes (society steward) proposed the toast to the future and Miss Jean Calvert responded. She made an appeal for parents to send their children to the Primary Department of Sunday School at the age of three. "That is the best way to ensure the future," she said.

Musical items were rendered by Miss Bessie Galley and the Misses Joan and Irene Lewis.

Wheatley Hill Missionaries

With the acceptance of two more of its members as missionaries, Wheatley Hill Youth Fellowship, which next year celebrates its 21st anniversary, has the proud record of having provided five members for the mission field.

The latest two to be accepted, Nurse Lilian Craggs, only daughter of Mr and Mrs P Craggs, Red Barns, Hart Bushes, South Wingate, and the Rev Fred Stainthorpe, B Sc, son of Mr and Mrs J Stainthorpe, Shotton Colliery, are to be married at Wheatley Hill in July. They will then undertake special training as missionaries, and, under the Baptist Missionary Society will go out next year to the Belgian Congo.

They will be the second pair from the Fellowship to be married before leaving for the mission field. The other pair, Mr Fred Hobbs and Miss Paddy McAloon (Seaham) who were also married at Wheatley Hill, are now missionaries in a leper colony in Tanganyika, East Africa. The other member of the fellowship to take up missionary work- Mrs Boshier (formerly Miss Mary Chisholm, of Wheatley Hill)-has been engaged in the work for some years now. She was married while home on furlough last year. Mrs Boshier and her husband serve in Ibadon, Western Nigeria.

Local Preacher

Nurse Craggs, who underwent her nursing training at Hartlepools Hospital, is at present employed at the Nose, Throat and Ear Hospital in London. She has been there 12 months. For two years running Nurse Craggs, who was formerly a local preacher in the Thornley Methodist Circuit, won the North of England speaking competition for nurses.

THEIR MINING CAREER ENDS

On reaching the age of 65, eleven workmen at Wheatley Hill Colliery-three officials, one deputy and seven miners- are retiring this week-end. The officials are Mr John White (colliery cashier), Mr Lance Hird (Master's weighman), and Mr Joseph Brown (head painter), and the deputy is Mr John Gillings, Durham Street, Wheatley Hill.

The other workmen who have reached the end of their mining career are Messrs William Laverick (tub mender), Robert Hutchinson (stone-man), Alfred Brown (bank hand), Maurice Waddy (gardener), and Ernest Glanville, John Cain and Robert Richardson (datal workers). With the exception of Mr Waddy, who lives in Thornley, and Mr Glanville, of Wingate, these workmen all live in Wheatley Hill.

RETIREMENT OF MR C A SMITH

Having calculated miner's wages at Thornley Colliery for 47 years, Mr Charles Arthur Smith, chief wages clerk and deputy cashier, has seen many changes in the rates of pay, and in the complicated modes of calculation. In the process he became an expert on miners' wages. Having reached the age of 65, he retired on Wednesday. He was a committee member and librarian of the old Miners' Welfare Institute at Thornley, until it was burned down in 1944. A keen supporter of local football and cricket, he was financial secretary of the old Albion football club, and is now deputy chairman of the Welfare cricket club, following a period as chairman. A member of the Smith family, formerly of

Thornley Hall farm, he still follows country pursuits, including duck shooting and badger watching.

2 April 1954

THORNLEY
Fire in Church Hall

The Vicar of Thornley, the Rev H W Jackson, noticed from his study window shortly after midday on Sunday that smoke was coming from the outer asbestos wall of the church hall, about 200 yards from the vicarage. He hurried to the building and in the hall, which was full of smoke, he found Mr T H Holder, who had been passing and had gone into the hall to investigate. While Mr Holder telephoned from Mr Norman Gowland's house for the fire brigade, the Vicar, joined soon afterwards by

Mr William Hetherington, worked hard to quell the flames which were now visible outside and inside the hall. The brigade soon got to the seat of the fire, caused by the stove, which had been lit for the Sunday School in the afternoon, setting alight to the wooden lining. Some damage to the outer asbestos wall and the inner wooden wall was caused, partly by the fire and partly through having to hack away asbestos sheeting behind the stove.

9 April 1954

CLUB ALTERATIONS

Extensive alterations are being made to Wheatley Hill Workmen's Club. New toilet accommodation has been provided for both men and women and a new reading room and library are being built on the lower floor. The old reading room has been converted into an office for the secretary, Mr Thomas Storey.

New Club Steward

Mr Harold Armstrong took up his new duties as steward of Wheatley Hill Workmen's Club this week in succession to Mrs Florence Williams, who recently retired from the position after 20 years' service and has left the district for Blackpool. For the past eleven months Mr Armstrong has been steward at Tursdale and Metal Bridge Workmen's Club near Spennymoor. He was formerly a miner at Blackhall, where he lived for many years, and a well-known billiards player in that village.

16 April 1954

TOP TOWN TEAM

A team of twenty children was chosen to represent Wheatley Hill in the annual Top Town contest organised by the Easington Rural Area Road Safety Committee, at a concert in Wheatley Hill Welfare Hall organised by the local Road Safety Committee. Fourteen variety items were judged by Mr J C Hunter (Wingate) and Mr and Mrs R Wilson, and the programme was compered by Mrs R Slater (secretary of the Road Safety Committee) and Mrs T Fox. The winning team comprised the following, Melvyn Peters, M Foster, Edward Smart, Pamela Vincent, Gregory Warrier, Beverley Clogg, Colin Shearsmith and Marjorie Moore (minuet), Lorna Newton, Margaret Thubron, Ettie Watson and Valerie Smith (acrobats), Drydon Fox (mouth organ solos). Pamela Bell (soloist), Jean Musgrave, Jean Saiger and J Craggs (play) and Faith Thornton, Margaret Carr and Ann Marshall (song and dance). P C. J L Jackson, Accidents Prevention Officer for the Castle Eden Division presided, and the accompanist was Miss Hutchinson, who also assisted in training the competitors. The team will compete against Horden in the first round of the competition on Thursday night. Wheatley Hill Boy Scouts were chosen from eight teams to represent the village in the Rural Area road safety quiz (senior section) and Wheatley Hill Junior School will compete in the junior section.

CHARMIAN WELSH STILL ON TOP
RETAINS ONE-METRE DIVING TITLE

Many swimming enthusiasts at Durham City Baths saw Charmian Welsh, Durham's Olympic diver retain the Woman's One-metre springboard title with a classic exhibition of precision diving. Still at school Charmian, who belongs to Thornley, is a member of Durham A S C. She gained 80.71 points, four fewer than when she won the championship for the first time last year.

This is the first time that this international event has been staged at Durham, and its success well rewarded the tremendous efforts on the part of the swimming club officials and the support of the City Council.

The men's one-metre championship was also included in the programme and went to the holder, Tony Turner of Highgate Diving Club (London).

In the ladies event, Miss Eunice Millar of Islander Ladies Diving Club (London) who finished third to Miss Welsh last year was again a close rival, and this time finished second. Turner's victory was a comfortable one of 102.31 points in spite of the challenge of K Collin, Isleworth Penguin S C who came second.

Perfect Dive

Thunderous applause greeted Charmian Welsh's superb final dive in her series, the finest individual dive of the whole programme. It was a perfect one-and-a –half somersault with tuck, which brought her the score of 13.20 points.

Also taking part in club events with which the programme was interspersed were her two 15 year old brothers, twins Peter and Anthony, and her14 year old sister Hilary. Peter and Anthony were first and second respectively in the Coyne Cup for junior men's club champion-ship, and Hilary was second to Miss J Stout in the Smith Cup for the ladies club breast stroke championship.

There were only two competitors from the north east who quali-fied for the finals of the woman's championship. The Durham City Club had two contestants in the final of the men's championship. They were J Harris who gained 72.08 points and J Lucas who gained 59.70 points.

Prizes were presented after each event by Mr Arthur Mothersdale, Shildon, this year's president of the Amateur Swimming Association.

23 April 1954

LECTERN BIBLE GIFT

At evensong in All Saints' Church, Wheatley Hill, on Sunday, the Vicar the Rev Arthur Preston, dedicated a new lectern Bible to the memory of Flight-Sgt George A Atkinson, of Wheatley Hill, who lost his life while on operations over Germany on November 23, 1943. Flight-Sgt Atkin-son was serving as a pilot in the R A F. The Bible was the gift of his parents, Mr and Mrs J Atkinson, well-known business people, of Front Street, Wheatley Hill.

OVER 60 CLUB

Several new members were enrolled at the meeting of Wheatley Hill Over-60 Club in the Church Hall on Tuesday. The entertainment was provided by club members, highlight being the T V panel game "What's My Line," with Mr William Luke as chairman. Mrs Turner, Mrs Taylor, Mr C Raffell and Mr W Snowden formed the panel and Mr G Charlton, Mr J T Robinson, Mrs Amies and Mrs Carter were the challengers.

Winners of the mystery prizes were Mr N Smithson, Mrs N Cook and Mrs B Venables.
30 April 1954

WHEATLEY HILL MAN RETAINS POSSESSION OF HOUSE
Because his daughter was waiting for a house before being married, a Wingate builder applied at Durham County Court on Monday for possession of a house he built 15 years ago, and which he alleged was being used to store furniture.

Refusing the application, Judge Clifford Cohen told George Sandwick, Brookfield, Front Street, Wingate: "As a landlord who is in a position to build houses, you are in a different position to many others who apply for possession. It seems almost unfair to builders, but I think you could build another house for your daughter, and I don't think it would hurt her to wait for a few months. I am satisfied that the balance of hardship is with the defendant."

Mr Sandwick said he built the houses in Sandwick Terrance, Wheatley Hill, in 1939, and he wanted his daughter to have one. She had waited for 10 years, and was now 32. The tenant was using the house only to store his furniture, and was living with his mother, he alleged.

Cross-examined by Mr R Reed, Mr Sandwick said he was building houses, but only on order. None of his houses had become vacant in the past year, and his daughter was to be married when he got possession of the house.

Leslie Cairns, 8, Sandwick Terrace, told the court he moved into the house in 1941, and since parting from his wife had been living between his mother's home and his own house. Because his mother had been ill recently, and was unable to look after his 12-year-old son, he had been living at Sandwick Terrace. He had tried at various times to buy the house, and Mr Sandwick had agreed to sell at £1,250 three years ago, but later changed his mind.

VICAR'S WARDEN AT THORNLEY FOR 25 YEARS
In accepting with regret the resignation of Mr Henry Hetherington, the Vicar of Thornley (the Rev H W Jackson), said his 25 years of service as Vicar's warden had been "an example of faithfulness." The Vicar was thanking Mr Hetherington at the annual parochial meeting, at which

there was an attendance of 33 electors. He said that Mr T Woodward would succeed Mr Hetherington.

Mr R Brandling was re-elected people's warden, an office he has held for ten years. Others elected were: Diocesan Conference, Mr T H Holder; Easington Rural Deanery Conference, Mesdames H Hetherington and R Brandling; Church Council, Messrs S Gutteridge, R Heads, W Hetherington, A Hutchinson, W Shutt, Mesdames Amos, Heads, Long, Muir, Plant, Tully, T Woodward, Swinburne, Walton, D Hutchinson, Parker, Luke and Jackson, Miss Swinburne. Others are to be co-opted.

Mr Brandling (treasurer) said the total church and hall income was £969 against a total outlay of £956. There had been a loss of £48 on the church hall account. As the collections and free-will offering were far short of meeting running expenses of the church, it would be necessary to keep up their special efforts, increasing them if possible. Other sections, such as the Mothers' Union and the Sunday School, all showed satisfactory balances.

The Vicar mentioned the interesting point that the confirmation candidates this year included ten adults, but he was sorry that at Thornley, as in all parts of the country, so many newly confirmed young candidates did not take Communion regularly. Of the 16 confirmed in1952, six were regular, and of 16 in 1953, nine were regular.

OVER-60-CLUB FORMED

The chorus of the song, "Keep right on to the end of the road," was chosen by the 45 who attended the inaugural meeting of Thornley Over 60 Club, presided over by Mrs Bessie Bosomworth, who gave an address on the aims and objects of the club. She made a strong appeal to members to bring the club to the notice of old people they knew to be lonely, as one of the chief aims of the club was to bring happiness and friendliness into the lives of old people. The life membership fee was fixed at a shilling, plus threepence at each meeting. All aged 60 and over are eligible. Wives under 60, whose husband are Over 60 or over, and husbands under 60 whose wives are over 60, will also be eligible. Mr A Welsh, senr, and Mr J H C Scott are to be invited to become president and chairman respectively. Elected were: Secretary, Mrs Ellen Brownless; treasurer, Mr R Slater; assistant treasurer, Mr T T Ridley; vice-chairman, Mr James Davies. A committee was also chosen. It is intended to have a "What's My Line" programme and to serve refreshments at a meeting on May 17, when it is hoped to welcome more new members. Mrs B Bosomworth and Mrs H Slater are to be the entertainment organisers.

Over –60 Club

Excellent entertainment was provided by Mrs Castor's children's concert party from Thornley, at the weekly meeting of Wheatley Hill Over-60 Club in the Church Hall on Tuesday. Mr R Taylor presided over a gathering of about 150 members in the unavoidable absence of Mr W Luke. The party of 20 children gave a colourful display of dancing and singing and individual items were contributed by Ernest Peachey, Derek Castor and Kitty Hall (songs), Jim Rutter (cornet solo), Valerie Wright (ballet dance), twins Joan and Joy Mathews (song and dance) and Ivy Castor (solo tap dance). The accompanist was Mr E Kitto jun. Thanks to the party were expressed by Mr R Taylor and Mr W Williams (entertainments organiser), Winners of the mystery prizes were Mrs Mitchell, Mr J P Brown and Mr T Carr.

AGED PEOPLE'S TRIP

Wheatley Hill Aged Miners' Homes Committee, at their meeting on Monday, decided upon Whitley Bay as the venue of the summer outing for retired miners over 65 and their wives, widows of retired miners and widows over 55 whose husbands were employed at Wheatley Hill colliery. The trip will be on Tuesday, July 13, and about 300 old folk are expected to qualify for it.

7 May 1954

THORNLEY ST GODRIC'S WIN TROPHY

To mark the Coronation of Her Majesty the Queen, Mr Baldasera, Wheatley Hill, presented a cup to be competed for annually by junior school football teams in the area. The final of this year's competition was staged by Thornley St. Godric's and Cassop junior teams. Keen hard fought tussles resulted in a win for Thornley St. Godric's. A big crowd watched this entertaining match.

Cassop won the toss and took advantage of the wind. The first half provided a rousing tussle with fast end to end play. Cassop were first to score with a disputed goal. The home side drew level when Morton, from the outside right position swung over a lovely centre for Regan to put into the net.

The second half saw defences predominate but both forward lines made valiant efforts to score.

Ten minutes from time Hoban shot a ball low into the far corner of the net to give the Thornley boys victory and the coveted Coronation Cup.

The cup was presented by its donor, Mr Baldasera, who complimented the winners and praised both sides for a finely fought exciting game.

21 May 1954

THORNLEY ST GODRIC'S R.C. JUNIOR SCHOOL
WINNERS OF BALDASERA CHALLENGE CUP
1953 - 1954 SEASON

Back L-R Mr Morgan, Eddie Lennox, Robert Burke, John Knowles, Peter Hepple,
John Ramshaw, Terry Smith, Mr Ellis
Front L-R Mr Finnerty, Michael Regan, Laurence Morton, Harry Morton (capt),
Jimmy Hoban, Miss McKearnan
Terry Hoban and Michael English

CARS COLLIDE HEAD-ON
Wheatley Hill and Ferryhill People Injured

Two young children-one from Wheatley Hill and the other from Ferry-hill-were severely injured and a number of other holiday-makers were injured when there was a terrific head-on collision between two cars on the narrow winding road between Hesleden and High Hesleden about tea time on Monday.

The two children; Colin Parkin (4) 1 Ninth Street, Wheatley Hill, and Beryl Ross (3) 21 Mainsforth Road, Ferryhill, were taken to West Hartlepool General Hospital. Colin who received a fractured skull, was later stated to be "very poorly," and Beryl, who received a suspected fracture of the skull was said the following day to have had a "fairly comfortable night". Both children suffered severely from shock.

Returning From Crimdon

With six other people- four adults and two children- the two children were returning home from Easington Rural Council's holiday lido at Crimdon in a car driven by Colin's father, John Thomas Parkin (34), when the collision occurred with a car travelling from the direction of Hesleden and driven by Joseph Bellingham (44) 31 Dene Villas, Horden, the sole occupant.

Both drivers were taken to Hartlepools Hospital together with the other passengers in Parkin's car, but after treatment for shock, cut and bruises, these passengers were allowed to return home. They were Mr Parkin's seven-year-old son, Frank, who had a small bone broken in his hand, Charles Quinn (25) a brother-in-law of Mr Parkin, of Moor Cottage, Wheatley Hill, and his wife Sheila Quinn 22, Mrs Lilian Coates (19), 12 Rutherford Terrace, Ferryhill, and the latter's two-year-old son Brian.

Mr Parkin received injuries to his chest and was later transferred to Shotley Bridge Hospital. Bellingham was detained in Hartlepools Hospital suffering head injuries, a suspected fracture of the jaw, and cuts to his knee and chin. The following day he was stated to have had a "fairly good" night.

Mrs Coats and her husband were spending the holiday week-end with her parents, Mr and Mrs Jack Ross, at Rose Cottage, Wheatley Hill. After lunch she had gone to Crimdon lido with her husband, on his motor-cycle, while their young son and niece, Beryl Ross, were taken there by Mr Parkin, a friend of the couple.

Cars Inter-Locked

When, some two hours after they had reached Crimdon, it began raining heavily, Mrs Coates decided to return in the car with the children.

In the collision both cars became inter-locked and were virtually wrecked. The windscreens were smashed and the steering wheel in Bellingham's car was ripped off. Broken glass was scattered about, and for some hours the road was blocked to public service vehicles.

A passing motorist, Maurice Woolfe, 127, Grange Road, West Hartlepool, rushed the boy Colin Parkin to hospital and others were taken by ambulance after attention on the spot had been given by police and others.

Mr Parkin, who is employed as a miner at Thornley colliery, has only recently recovered from a broken arm. His wife Mrs Doreen Parkin, has been a patient in Dryburn Hospital, Durham nearly a fortnight.

NEW PLAYING FIELD FOR THORNLEY

Thornley sports folk are anxiously awaiting for work to commence on the construction of their new playing field behind the welfare institute. At the presentation of prizes to the Thornley Welfare billiards and dominoes teams, Mr H Tunney, Deputy Labour director of the Durham Division of the N C B referred to the field. He said the N C B was keen on outdoor sports, and he would do all he could to assist in getting the work started on the new field.

Mr Tunney and Mr James Hesler, undermanager of Thornley Colliery, shared in handing over the prizes to the competitors. Coun. John Williams, a trustee of the Thornley Welfare Institute, presided. Mr W Henderson, Welfare secretary, and Mr Ivan Jones, of the No 3 Area Welfare department, were also present.

Mr Hesler congratulated the billiards team on winning the championship of the Northern Amateur Billiards League in their first season without losing a match.

In the gathering were representatives of the various Thornley trade union branches and supporters who had travelled with the teams on their away matches.

PRIZE LIST
The awards were:

*Winners of the No 3 Area Billiards &
Snooker Tournament*

League championship shield and five miniature cups: also casserole dishes for winning the NCB No 3 Area billiards and snooker tournaments: L Williamson, J Watson, J Lennox, G Wake, J McCoy. L Williamson received two cups for being runner-up in the individual snooker and billiards tournaments run by the league.

Messrs T Lennox, W Race, J Watson, J Abbs, and E Luke received thermos jugs and beakers for winning the Area dominoes tournament and table dishes for being runners-up in the Divisional tournament.

Mr Jack Watson returned thanks on behalf of the teams.

An entertainment was given by the Wheatley Hill Lyric Party (Mrs L Green, Mrs C English, Messrs W Williams, B Blenkinsopp, T King).

11 June 1954

ROAD SAFETY FINALS
Attractive Programme At Crimdon

Large crowds were attracted to Easington Rural Council's holiday lido at Crimdon on Saturday when the finals of the annual cycling proficiency test, road safety "quiz" and "Top Town" competition, organised by Easington Rural Area Road Safety Committee, were staged.

Six villages were represented in the finals: Shotton Colliery, Horden, Thornley, Haswell, Wheatley Hill and South Hetton.

They had all "battled their way" through early rounds and competition was keen in the finals, only a narrow margin separating the winners from the runners-up in each case.

The day's programme began with the cycling proficiency test in the picturesque dene in the afternoon. Winners were a team from Shotton Colliery, comprising Judith Smith, Marion Nicholson, John McCallum and Ronald Akenhead, while a team from Horden, comprising Alan Cook, Jean Stephenson, Lilian Main and Dennis Cockerill, were runners-up.

Police Team

Music was by Shotton Lads' Brigade Band, under the conductorship of Mr J Blunt, and the Brigade also gave an excellent display of P T under the leadership of Mr L Robson. And the main theme of the day's programme was spotlighted with a road safety demonstration by a police team from Aycliffe Police headquarters, in charge of Inspector G M Jarvis.

P C John L Jackson, Accidents Prevention Officer for Castle Eden Police Division, who was responsible for making arrangements for the programme, carried out the duties of compere in a most efficient and laughter-making manner when the quiz and "Top Town" finals were staged in Crimdon Pavilion at night.

A well-known West Hartlepool musician, Mr T I Phizacklea, a member of Hetton Lyons Male Voice Choir, Mr T Clish and Mr Osborne Mennear, of Easington Lane, were adjudicators for the "Top Town" contest. Sgt C Hathaway, Durham County Police Accident Prevention Department, was question-master for the quiz finals and the judges were Mr A Goodrich (Easington Colliery), Coun R Twitty (Horden) and Mr Fred Smith (Blackhall Colliery).

"Top Town" Contest

A galaxy of talent was provided by the teams from Thornley and Wheatley Hill competing in the final of the "Top Town" contest. Both gave a non-stop variety programme of dancing, vocal and musical items, and the adjudicators must indeed have had a most difficult task to name the winning team. The decision was given to Thornley. They were awarded

503 points compared with 484 points won by Wheatley Hill. Both teams consisted of young children- both boys and girls.

"There's certainly no difference between them so far as beauty is concerned," smiled Coun R Smith, Deaf Hill, chairman of Easington Rural Council, when he presented the prizes, "and there is very little so far as talent goes. They have both given us excellent entertainment."

The Thornley team which was presented with an £8 voucher, had Mrs J Walton as their accompanist and a dancing troupe was led by Glenice Ramshaw. Eight-year-old twins, Joan and Joy Mathews, gave songs and dances, Jimmy Rutter played the cornet and songs were by Irene Horner and Earnest Peachey, Janice Moore was a charming ballerina.

Wheatley Hill, runners-up, who received a voucher for £4, were in charge of Mrs O Slater, and Miss A Huthinson was their accompanist. Their programme consisted of an acrobatic display, an original play, old-fashioned dance, harmonica solos, and singing and dancing.

A team from Thornley, comprising Joseph Noble, Charles Harrison, Robert Baker and Jack Scott, also won the senior road safety quiz, defeating Haswell, last year's winners. They were presented with a shield and each member received a voucher for one guinea. The Haswell team, who were presented with a half-guinea voucher each, comprised Anthony Turner, John Jones. Malcolm Crow and Noreen Downing.

Junior Quiz Final

Defeating South Hetton in the junior quiz final, Wheatley Hill team, comprising Jean Patterson, Irene Armstrong, Alan Wilson and Melvyn Peters, were also presented with a shield and a guinea each. The South Hetton team consisted of Thomas Kitchen, George Robinson, John Fairley and James Graham.

Winners of a road safety poster design contest were: over17 years,1 and 2 Joseph Sanderson (Haswell), 3 B T Robinson (Thornley); 11-17 years, 1 Miss Margaret Bartram (Thornley), 2 Fred G Telford (Haswell). 3 John E Williams (South Hetton); under11 years,1 Michael Styles (Littlethorpe), 2 Peter Rochester (Easington Village), 3 Joan Monk (Easington Village).

Thanking the police, Special Constables, local road safety committees and others who had helped to make the day an outstanding success, Coun Smith said he hoped none of them would ever forget that the programme had been really organised to make people-both adults and children- more road safety minded. "On the roads, prevention is better than cure," he added, "and if everyone would only remember this we would see a big reduction in accidents on our roads today.

GIFT DEDICATED

Presented to All Saints' Parish Church, Wheatley Hill, by Mrs Foster, in memory of her son, Kenneth, who was killed in a motor- cycling accident near Crimdon last September, an oak table was dedicated at evensong in the church on Sunday by the Rev Arthur Preston (vicar of Wheatley Hill).

"KNIGHTS" CEREMONY

At a special session of the No 123 Wheatley Hill encampments of the Knights of the Golden Horn, Sir Knight Councillor J Cowperthwaite, G W T, of No 38 Wyngate encampment, raised Companions M Telford, J Dodds and B Aitken to the degree of Knighthood. Sir Knight Councillor J Bedford, also of the Wyngate encampments, presented Knight Ayre, the district scribe, with his meritorious Jewel. Vocal items were contributed by members and refreshments were provided by the Wheatley Hill encampment. Visiting encampments were West Hartlepool, Hartlepool, Spennymoor, Ferryhill, Horden, Wyngate, Easington, Trimdon Grange, Trimdon Colliery, Hetton-le-Hole, S J Slade (Spennymoor), Stockton, Sedgefield and Newton Aycliffe.

FIRE AT THE VICARAGE

Awakened by the smell of smoke about half-past two on Tuesday morning, the Vicar of Wheatley Hill, the Rev Arthur Preston, rushed down stairs and found smoke and flames pouring out of the kitchen. He immediately telephoned for the Fire Brigade and roused his wife and young son. Petelee and Wheatley Hill Units of the Durham County Fire brigade quickly reached the scene and got the fire under control but not before several articles of furniture had been destroyed and considerable damage done to the kitchen walls and ceiling. Damage was estimated at more than £100.

18 June 1954

CONSTABLE'S RETIREMENT

After 25 years' service in the police force-17 of which have been spent with the Durham County Constabulary – Police Constable James J Irving, of Wheatley Hill retires next Wednesday. The last seven years of his career have been spent at Wheatley Hill, in the Castle Eden Division. P C Irving, who is married with three daughters, began his career with the Hull City Police, and after eight years there was transferred to the County Constabulary at Darlington. After 18 months at Darlington and a brief spell at Woodland, near Barnard Castle, he was transferred to Washington. He served there for eight years and then after three months at Birtley made his final move to Wheatley Hill.

A keen bowler, he has been a member of the Castle Eden Divisional Police team since going to Wheatley Hill and formerly played for the Chester-le-Street Division. P C Irving was born just outside Whitehaven, and it is to the West coast town that he is returning in his retirement. After only a week's holiday he is taking up a new civilian post with the security police at an atom bomb station in Cumberland.

25 June 1954

TO WORK SATURDAYS

Following a special appeal from the Durham County Mining Federation Board miners employed by Wheatley Hill Colliery are to work the Saturday shift. The decision was made at a special meeting of the miners' lodge on Sunday, presided over by Mr H Bradshaw, when the appeal was fully discussed. It is over two years since the Saturday shift was worked at the colliery. After the meeting, Coun E Cain J P, lodge secretary, told our reporter that the decision to work on Saturday was a unanimous one. "When the Saturday shift was first worked at the colliery under the extra hours agreement it was stopped after a time by the Coal Board itself because it was considered an uneconomic proposition," said Coun Cain. "Later the miners responded to a special appeal to resume the Saturday shift, but absenteeism became so acute that eventually the lodge decided to end Saturday working. The miners at Wheatley Hill still adhere strictly to the five-day week agreement. They firmly believe that five days a week is sufficient for any man to work underground, but owing to the urgency of the recent appeal to resume Saturday working they are willing to give it another trial.

PREACHERS

Many circuits in Methodism may claim to have at least one octogenarian local preacher on its plan, but few will equal the distinction of Thornley circuit, which can point to three preachers in that category: Mr M F

Stephenson (Wheatley Hill), Mr I Barker (Trimdon Grange) and Mr D Galloway (Quarington Hill).

Mr Mathew F Stephenson, Eastfield, Cemetery Road, Wheatley Hill, said to our reporter, "I was 80 on Whit Sunday, and have been on the local preachers plan for 63 years. If I was asked to give young preachers a last message based on the experience of an old man it would be this: spend adequate time in preparation; it reveals itself in the pulpit if you don't. Seek to widen your outlook and deepen your mind by reading all types of literature. Unless the mind is well stored the preacher cannot give out to his congregation. Spend part of your time for preparation in earnest prayer for the services you are to hold.

Born At Haswell

Mr Stephenson was born at Haswell on June 6, 1874. He attended a private school run by Mr Waggott. His schooling ended at 12½, when he was apprenticed to the drapery trade. At the age of 20 he joined the staff of Haswell Co-operative Society. In 1912, he opened Wheatley Hill drapery branch of Sherburn Hill Co-operative Society, and remained buyer and manager till he retired in 1939.

While Mr Stephenson has held every office in church and Sunday School, in circuit life he served as Home Missions lay secretary and treasurer of the Preachers' Travelling Fund; he is still a valued member of the circuit finance and general purposes committee. He was appointed an associate member of Sunderland and Durham Methodist District Local Preachers' Committee, yet it is by his work as a local preacher that he will always be remembered.

Speaker At 14½

"I gave my first address in public at Haswell Band of Hope when I was 14½," said Mr Stephenson. "Before I was 15 I had spoken at the Sunday School, and when I was 16 I preached my first sermon. I came on to plan as a 'star' with my father, and was received on to 'full plan' in 1891. I have always taken a full share of the work, taking about six Sundays a quarter on my own plan. Then there were a few 'specials'. This continued till I had a major operation in 1951. Since then I have fulfilled some engagements."

When our correspondent asked Mr Stephenson whether it was harder to become a preacher 60 years ago, he replied, "It is certainly easier today. When I started to preach, at my ordinary work I had a

66-hour week. Studies for the plan then were much stiffer. We had to study history, geography and arithmetic. We also had to satisfy the examiners in Church history, Bible teaching and theology. Then we had to submit a written sermon and preach a trial sermon.

"Then the Thornley Circuit had 21 preaching places, with two ministers. So we had to work hard to get on to the plan, and there was more than enough work when we did qualify. In those days there was no room for the 'honorary preacher'- the man whose name appears on the plan, but does not preach."

A Comparison

On the Thornley Circuit, Mr Stephenson was known as a preacher of great talent. He was a gifted, successful exponent of the art of expository preaching. He mastered the theology of Christian doctrines and expounded the Christian faith with certainty and understanding.

When asked to compare preachers and congregations today Mr Stephenson said "There are as good preachers today as there were in the past. But in modern preaching it is noticeable that there is a lack of general reading. Congregations today are as attentive, or even more so than they were in my younger days. A congregation will listen when the message meets its needs."

Mr Stephenson has his own opinions on Church evangelism. "I do not approve of special missions unless the missioners are to be our own ministers and laymen. The efforts of the special missioners often result in too much emotion and excitement, with conversions that do not last. Evangelism is the ordinary work of minister and local preacher. In the early days of Methodism conversions followed nearly every service. Lack of united prayer by the Church as a whole. I think, is the explanation of why conversions are not an ordinary experience today."

Remembers Peter McKenzie

Looking back over the years, Mr Stephenson recalled hearing some of Methodism's great presidents and preachers. He particularly remembers the Rev Peter McKenzie, who was a miner converted in Haswell Wesleyan Methodist Chapel, because his mother was sitting in the same seat as Peter on the night he was converted.

Mr Stephenson referred to the quaint, forthright speech of men in his early days on the plan. Sometimes the prayer-meeting was used to express the congregation's views of the sermon. He remembers on one occasion the minister conducting the Sunday evening service and preaching a "milk-and-water" type of sermon. An old miner in the prayer meeting, longing for a more satisfying spiritual diet prayed, "O Lord, give us stronger meat than we've had today. We've been fed on the titty-bottle long enough."

It would appear that ministers in those days needed to be made of sterner stuff than their brethren of today.

Shorter Sermons

Mr Stephenson is a member of Thornley Bow Street Methodist Church, where he regularly worships with his wife. He said" Having to lay down my tools as a preacher has been hard to do."

A humorous smile lit up his face as he went on, "But becoming a hearer has taught me one thing. Sermons could well be shorter than they were in my day."

A treasured document hangs on the wall of his living room. It is the illuminated address on attaining his diamond jubilee as a local preacher.

2 July 1954

THORNLEY'S MINER ESSAYIST
Topped List At Edinburgh

Colleagues of unassuming Mr Tom Wetherell, 42-year-old secretary of Thornley branch, Colliery Deputies' Association, did not know that he was an essayist. They have been pleasantly surprised to learn that he has topped the list of three awards of a week at a summer school at Edinburgh for his essay on "What in your opinion, could be done to make trade union members more interested in their unions?" The awards are by the Durham County Deputies' Association.

In his essay of about 600 words, which is marked by a sincerity which may have had some weight with the adjudicators, Mr Wetherell says he is not surprised that in routine matters there is little interest, but is pleased to know that in anything affecting the whole of the members of a union there is plenty of interest.

Some Suggestions

He puts forward quite a number of suggestions for consideration, such as qualified speakers talking on debateable subjects affecting union members. He wonders, too, whether it would not be advisable to hold social events which would tend to make women folk more "union conscious." He asks that the fact each person in individual in thought and action should not be overlooked.

Mr Wetherell won a place at a secondary school, but instead preferred to start his pit career at 14. Now a deputy at Thornley Colliery, he sits on the pit consultative committee and permanent relief committee. For two years he has been secretary of Thornley Working Men's Club.

The others to receive the awards are Mr J Scorer, Brancepeth and Mr J E Parker, Seaham. Mr J T Brighton the reserve will take up the place if either of the others falls out.

9 July 1954

CATHOLIC CHILDREN'S DAY AT THORNLEY

The Rev Dr H McNeill presented the prizes at the fifth annual garden fete and field day of Thornley St Godric's Schools on Saturday. Many complete families were among the large attendance. Chief items were the finals of the children's sports. There was also kicking at goal, bowling at wicket, coconut shy, treasure hunt and a number of stalls. The "mystery man" (Mr Edward Ord, of Wheatley Hill) was named by Mrs Peggy Quinn, of Thornley. Thornley Colliery band played selections.

Children'S Sports

Flat racing: 5 years, 1 John Filon, 2 George Hoban and Terry Swan, 1 Aileen Hennessy, 2 Joan Regan: 6 years, 1 Peter Luke, Freddie Graney, 1 Anne Regan, 2 Anne Steel; 7 years, 1 David Howe, 2 Thomas Fleetham, 1 Doreen English, 2 K Hennessy; 8 years, 1 David Luke, 2 Thomas Elward: boys, 8 to 10 years plus, 1 M English, 2 A Bonar; 11 to 13 years, 1 H Morton, 2 M Regan; 14 and 15 years, 1 H Hepple, 2 H Morton; boys three-legged races, 8 to 10 years, R Ewens and J Lennox; 11 to 13 years, H Morton and L Morton; 14 to 15 years, H Morton and J Hoole.

16 July 1954

HASWELL'S COURAGEOUS MAN
Lost Both Legs In Colliery Accident

I have met a Bader of the pits, and it was an inspiring experience. Handsome Arthur Bonar, now 24, met me at the front door of his comfortable home in Pesspool Terrace, Haswell, and led me to the sitting room where we talked for an hour.

When I left I felt that he had successfully bridged the alarming gulf that must have faced him on losing both his legs when they became entangled in a coal-cutting machine in Thornley pit, when he was barely 20. He was five feet 11 inches in height, 13 stones in weight and a promising footballer and athlete.

It took three hours to extricate him. Doctors in the hospital almost despaired of him.

But Arthur never despaired of himself. It is probably because of this that he is alive today.

Poultry and Pigs

Since that fateful day he has married, set up a nice home, become a father, of eight-month-old Maureen, and is now the proprietor of a poultry and pig farm covering 3½ acres. Arthur and Gwendoline Turnbull were courting before the accident occurred, but they continued to look hopefully forward to marrying.

Their hopes were realised. Indeed, as I talked with Arthur I felt that the Bonar home has all the atmosphere of a happy and contented young couple. There was Gwendoline telling me about the cleaning she had been doing, tiny little Maureen kicking and gurgling as she lay on a pink shawl on the hearth rug in front of a nice fire (Arthur receives free coal from the N C B), and there was Mitzi, the Alsatian dog, who used to pull Arthur's wheelchair before his pre-car days.

Son of a Headmaster

Mr John Bonar, Arthur's father, was headmaster of Thornley St Godric's school. He died shortly before Arthur was born. Arthur attended St Godric's until he was nine, and then he went to St Bennett's School at Sunderland. Between being 12 and 16 he was a pupil at St Joseph's Secondary School at Stoke, with an ambition to becomea sea going engineer. Instead he became an apprentice fitter at Thornley pit, and was soon learning a great deal about modern coal producing machinery. It was in the recesses of Million's district at Thornley pit where he was so cruelly maimed.

He did not and could not take any employment for two years. Early in that interval three Johns of Thornley- John Kirk, John Callighan and John Tunney- raised funds and bought him a car. The National Insurance people provided him with two pairs of the most modern artificial legs.

Sitting-Down job in fitting Shop

Anxious to co-operate, the Coal Board gave him a sitting down job in the fitting shop at Thornley, which he already knew so well. It was an important productive job-sharpening the cutting bits for the coal-cutting machines.

Then came his marriage with Gewndoline. "Naturally we wanted a home of our own," he said. "And so we went to the new town of Peterlee. But somehow I couldn't settle there-and that is how we came to be here."

I feel that this state of unsettlement came from his strong individuality. It was an urge to action and a refusal to compromise with his disability.

But Preferred Poultry

It was behind his decision to give up his pit job and take on the poultry and pig farm. Without the slightest knowledge of pigs and poultry this was surely a most courageous and daring action. "It's wonderful how you learn as you go on," he said, smiling.

His 3½ acres are at the back of the terrace he lives in. "There's plenty of room for development," he said, smiling again. A year and half in the open-air has turned him dead against indoor work. All day long-except when he is doing his van-round delivering eggs-he is on his artificial legs. He is proud of his legs and thankful to those who made them.

He usually has 500 birds in his batteries, but at the moment there are not so many. Chicks run on the land until they are pullets. Sometimes he has 60 pigs. He talks prices like an old farmer. "They have dropped," he said. "But that cannot be helped." Though only 24, he is apparently learning to meet awkward situations as they arise.

Growing Tomatoes

He speaks highly of the wonderful help he has received from officials of the Durham County agricultural department, "All I have to do is write or give them a ring and they come out and help me," he said.

Another of his ventures in starting from rock-bottom is that of growing tomatoes in his two greenhouses, and in this also he is learning as he "goes on."

Gwendoline has her five- roomed house and little Maureen to look after, but when he needs help he has only to let her know, and she is by his side. He revealed his progress towards rehabilitation when he told me that for quite a time after his accident he wanted to do all the things he used to do – play football and carry on as a professional runner. "But that feeling has gone now," he said.

Keen Rifleman

Every Tuesday evening he drives over in his car to the shooting range at Wheatley Hill. He is keen on the rifle, "It has taken the place of all the other things I wanted to do."

This calm, intelligent young man looks forward with a smile on his face. In the hour I talked with him I did not detect the slightest sign of fear for the future. And Gwendoline too will keep her half of the bargain.

THORNLEY CATHOLIC SCHOOL PRIZE-GIVING

There were some interesting features connected with the annual speech day and prize-giving at Thornley St Godric's Mixed R C School. The Rev Dr McNeill, the school manager, was present, together with Rev Fr Robinson, curate at the Church of the English Martyrs; the Rev Fr Scanlon, home on furlough from India; and the Rev Fr Adamson.

Proceedings began with choral and drama entertainment. The headmaster, Mr J Finnerty reviewed the year's work saying that the cultural standard was being well maintained and referred to the fact that the school had won the Baldasera Cup, a trophy presented for annual competition to commemorate the Coronation.

He also paid a tribute to the work of Father McNeill. "In Father McNeill we have a school manager who is keenly interested in every activity of the school; whether that interest be educational, sport or religious." He also referred to the excellent service rendered to the school by Mr Morgan B A, who at the end of this term leaves Thornley to take up a teaching appointment on the staff of the De la Salle Grammar School, Sheffield. He presented Dr McNeill and Mr Morgan with enlarged photographs of the School team which had won the Baldasera Cup.

The school manager then presented the team with souvenir plaques. After congratulating the boys on their great win he turned to Father Adamson and said "It gives me great joy to see one who was a former pupil of this school ordained into the priesthood of our church. I hope it may be an inspiration for others here to follow his example."

Father Adamson, who has been appointed to the teaching staff of a Liverpool College, presented the school prizes. He said "The splendid groundwork I received in this school was the foundation of any success which has come to me in later years."

Prizewinners were: Head prefect, Catherine McKenna, Needlework: Margaret Conway. Rural science: Brian Bell and Joseph Knowles. General proficiency: Catherine Connolly and Jane Swan. Mathematics: Gordon Dockerty. Proficiency in games: Henry Morton. Good conduct: James Hoban. Religious knowledge: Dorothy Trisnam, Peter Knowles Catherine Connolly and Ann Wilson.

23 July 1954
WHEATLEY HILL SCHOLARS IN CAMP

Many would think that the advent of the school holidays would bring welcome respite for teaching staffs and that they would be glad to say goodbye for the time being to their pupils.

Such is not the case at Wheatley Hill where the staff of the Modern Boys' School have taken 50 of their pupils to camp. On Friday, the advance party left by lorry to take equipment to a site near Wolsingham. The main party left on Saturday.

Mr Arthur Harris, the Headmaster, told our representative: "Living together and working together under canvas is good training in co-operation for the lads. After being cooped up in school during the term, they will appreciate the pleasures of outdoor life."

The trip will not be without interesting educational outings. Tunstall reservoir and filter beds will be visited and arrangements have been made to look over local steel works and sawmills.

The members of the party are looking forward to a visit to Frosterley Limestone quarry and a trip has been organised to Bollihope Common. This is one of the few places in the country where the Sundew plant, an insect-eating flower can be found.

The boys, who will return tomorrow, are accompanied by the Headmaster, and Messrs Ward, Potts, Jones, Brown, Hornsby, Etherington, Dent, Stabler and Holder.

AMERICAN VISITS "NEW ENGLAND"
Former Thornley Man's Impressions

Mr William Tunney, former miner at Thornley Colliery, who emigrated to Ambridge ,P A (United States) 28 years ago, and is an American citizen, has just completed a month's visit to this country and flew back home at the week-end. He has been accompanied on his holiday by his wife and youngest son, age 20. Mrs Tunney will be remembered by many Thornley and Wheatley Hill people as Miss Celia O'Donnell, who was a teacher at St Godric's School. There are three sons and one daughter.

Although holding a good position in the States, Mr Tunney, who has toured Ireland, Scotland and England, during his holiday, declared "You in England have as good a 'sitting-down' as anybody in America."

He was amazed and delighted to see the great housing developments at Thornley and Wheatley Hill. "You've got a new England," he said. Among the places he visited were Davy Lamp, Kelloe, his birthplace, and the Trimdons.

He is a regular reader of the "Durham Chronicle," sent to him by a relative ever since he emigrated. "I don't think I have missed getting the paper in one single week," he said, with evident pleasure. "Every copy gets passed on to various Durhamites we know."

30 July 1954

WHEATLEY HILL GIFT

Twenty-one-year-old Billy Marshall, of Gowland Terrace, Wheatley Hill, who is leaving the village for Blackburn, where he is taking up a new post in the technical department of a valve factory, received the good wishes of his cricketing colleagues on Monday when, after Wheatley Hill's victory over Marsden, they presented him with a propelling pencil and cheque.

Billy, only son of Mr and Mrs W Marshall, has played cricket for Wheatley Hill for six years. A slow left-arm bowler, he has played a big part in the team's success this season – they are firmly established at the top of Division 1 of the Durham Coast League and he hopes to return each weekend from Blackburn until the end of the season.

Mr Joseph Soulsby presided at the presentation, supported by the club secretary and captain, Sid Wilson, and the gifts were handed over by the president, Mr J L Snaith (manager of Wheatley Hill colliery) It was only recently that Billy gained his B Sc degree at Durham University.

6 August 1954

NEW PLAYING-FIELD FOR THORNLEY

After long negotiations a start has been made with the levelling by bulldozer of land at the east end of Thornley Miners' Welfare Institute for a cricket and football ground.

The land is being leased to Thornley Miners' Welfare Committee by Easington Rural Council and the trustees of the late Mr George Linton. As it is not large enough for separate football and cricket pitches, one pitch will impinge slightly on the other.

The cost of the new field will be in the region of £4,000. The larger sum will come from the headquarters fund of the miners' welfare organisation and the local committee will provide a substantial amount.

Local sporting enthusiasts are expecting that when the new pitches are in use-but not this year- the standard of football and cricket in Thornley will be improved, and that both cricket and football clubs may be able to join leagues of higher status than those they are playing in at present. It may be possible for Thornley to resume its place in the Wearside League.

Grant Reduced

The new ground scheme was started by Thornley Parish Council shortly after the last war, when there was much justifiable dissatisfaction about the lack of playing fields in Thornley. The Ministry of Education promised a substantial grant, ratepayers agreed to contribute £200 through the rates, and negotiations for help from the Miners' Welfare Fund were in progress.

Restrictions in capital expenditure by the Government then caused the Ministry of Education to reduce their proposed grant to a figure which made it impossible for the Parish Council to go on with the scheme.

The Miners' Welfare Committee then took over. Mr W Henderson, the local secretary, has taken a considerable part in furthering the project to its present satisfactory stage.

When the new ground is in use the situation regarding playing fields will be enormously improved upon from what it was at the end of the war. Since then St Godric's A F C supporters have provided, by much hard work, a reasonably good and level football ground. Supporters of the Welfare Football Club did the same with some waterlogged ground, and a bright idea for cricket was that which resulted in a pitch being laid in the basin of the "Hilly," a beauty spot which will, unfortunately, be eventually filled up with waste stones from Thornley pit.

TERRY CULLEN IS MARRIED

Well-known in boxing circles in Durham County – he has fought as a professional for the past six years – Mr Terry Cullen, elder son of Mr and Mrs M Cullen, 16, Ashbrooke Estate, Shotton Colliery, was married in the Church of the English Martyrs, Thornley, on Saturday, to Miss Gladys May Peacock, second daughter of Mr and Mrs H Peacock, 18, Wheatley Terrace, Wheatley Hill, Father Robinson officiated.

The bridegroom, a welter-weight, has fought in many towns in the North-East. He is employed as a blacksmith at Wheatley Hill colliery. The bride has been employed in a radio factory at Spennymoor for the past three years.

Given away by her father the bride wore white figured satin, with a bridal veil and coronet of diamante and orange blossom and carried a bouquet of roses. She was attended by her sister, Miss Audrey Peacock, and Miss Eileen Cullen (sister of the 'groom), who were dressed, respectively, in green and pink tulle and velvet, with headdresses to match. They carried bouquets of sweet peas.

Best man was Mr Tony Hall (Shotton Colliery), and the grooms-man Mr Maurice Cullen (brother of the 'groom). A reception was in Wheatley Hill Welfare Hall, and later the happy couple left for the Lake District.

13 August 1954
SHERBURN AND DISTRICT ALLOTMENTS ASSOCIATION
Held their show in the Welfare Hall and Parish Field on Saturday
VEGETABLE CLASSES: **Pot Leeks**: 1, A Hutchinson Thornley; 2 N Wood; 3 J Defty, Trimdon. **Collection of vegetables**; A Hutchinson. **Celery**: 1 and 2 A Hutchinson; 3, J Defty **Onions**: 1, A Hutchinson; 2 J Defty. **Parsnips**: A Hutchinson G Watson. **Carrots**: 1 and 2 A Hutchinson. **Garden peas**; J Watson, Sherburn; Summers and Brown, Shadforth; Olga Ward, Sherburn. **Broad beans**; A R Wills Summers and Brown; J Watson. **Cauliflower**; 1 and 2 J Defty; A Hutchinson. **Kidney potatoes**;1and 2 W Irving, Gilesgate; S Satterley, Pittington. **Coloured**, W Irving, S Satterley. Round, 1 and 2 W Irving, S Satterley. **Coloured**, J Defty. **Tomatoes**; C Stead, Sherburn; G Nicholson, Sherburn N Percival, Pittington

416

Flowers:

Cut flowers; 1 and 2 T W Johnson, Nevilles' Cross; J Gibson, Pittington. **Gladioli**; 1 and 2 W Lovegreen, Durham. **Asters**; A R Wills, Durham. **Roses**; R Gleason, Gilesgate Moor; 2 and 3 T W Johnson. **Chrysanthemums**; A Hutchinson. **Antirrhinums**; 1 and 2 J Gibson, Pittington. **Dahlias(pom-pom)**; 1 2 and 3 W -Caveney, Fence Houses; **decorative**, W Lovegreen; 2 and 3 F Hunter, Easington. **Gent's button-hole**; T W Johnson; 2 and 3 J Cuny, Kelloe. **Lady's spray**; T W Johnson, J Gibson, J Hunter, Sherburn. Sweet Peas; A Hutchinson, F Hunter, T W Johnson. **Border carnations**; J Curry.

20 August 1954

WHEATLEY HILL PRIEST

A former "Bevin Boy" at Thornley Colliery – he was called up for service in the mines shortly before the end of the war – has just been ordained a Roman Catholic priest. He is Father Colum Adamson, only son of Mr and Mrs James Adamson, 9, First Street, Wheatley Hill. Father Adamson, whose father is a surface worker at Thornley Colliery, has had a life-long association with the Sacred Heart and English Martyrs Church at Thornley and is the first parishioner to become a priest.

After being a pupil at Thornley St Godric's R C School, Father Adamson began his studies for the priesthood at Freshfield College, Liverpool, in 1940. He was there five years before his "call-up" as a Bevin Boy and after nine months down the mine resumed his studies in philosophy in Holland. After two years in Holland he returned to England to complete his training at the College of Theology, Mill Hill, London.

Father Adamson's ordination took place, together with that of 31 other students of St Joseph's Missionary Society, in the Chapel of St Joseph's College, Mill Hill. Four of the students-including Father Adamson- came from the Hexham and Newcastle Diocese and the ceremony was performed by His Eminence Cardinal Griffin. It was the largest single ordination of priests from Great Britain this year.

Father Adamson is returning to Freshfield College – this time as a tutor – on September 13. His only sister, Veronica, is a health visitor in Sunderland.

27 August 1954

MINERS' LODGE

0fficials of Thornley Miners' Lodge elected unopposed for the next 12 months are: Chairman, Mr E Carter; corresponding secretary, Coun J Williams; financial secretary, Mr D Swallow; treasurer, Mr J Cherry; delegate, Mr D Gott; average takers, Messrs J R Barron (fillers) and T Lennox (stonemen). Coun Williams, a former corresponding secretary, takes the place of Mr W Downing, who is opposing Mr J Webb for the post of compensation secretary. Other nominations; Lodge committee (10 wanted), Messrs J Walker, J R Barron, W Heale, P Gott, M Kirk, W Anderson, T Barron, J Joicey, H Gill, M Kell, J Walls, J Maddison, A Hunter; Welfare Committee (5 wanted), Messrs D Swallow, W Quin, T Barron, R Saunders, M Kell, J Greener, J Storey, J Walls, J Maddison, W Heale, J Nicholson, H Gill; Federation Board, Messrs J Storey, J Walker and T Lennox.

FIFTY-FOUR YEARS AT THORNLEY COLLIERY
Retirement of Mr R Bosomworth

Mr Robert Bosomworth (67), has just retired after working 54 years at Thornley Colliery. He worked on the screening belts first, but was soon transferred to the blacksmith's shop, where he worked the rest of his time, beingoften employed on important development jobs. After the first World War, when various types of houses were built, he was engaged on "hoop" houses, devised by Mr J T Simpson, Thornley chief engineer, some of these being erected as far away as Tweedmouth. He also worked on the house named "Bede' Rest," at Durham, which was built by the Durham Miners' Association for Mr Peter Lee.

Seven Colliery Agents

Mr Bosomworth worked under seven colliery agents and managers; Messrs
W B Wilson, J W Laverick, G A Curry, J Rivers, M Barrass, A Welsh senior and A Welsh junior.

He recalls blowing the organ at Thornley Parish Church when Miss Ada Wilson, daughter of Mr W B Wilson, was married. At that time his father was sexton.

Mr Bosomworth was a member of the first Thornley Parish council. In His early thirties he became secretary of the mechanics' lodge, and was treasurer of the colliery hospital fund when the first motor ambulance was bought, the motor replacing the horse ambulance.

He was 16 years secretary of Thornley Workmen's Club, one year as chairman, and one year as treasurer.

A Busy Wife

While he himself lived a busy life, it can be said that his wife, Mrs "Bessie" Bosomworth, has been even busier. She has been associated with numerous committees, and is at present a member of the parish council and entertainments secretary of the Over-60- Club, in the founding of which she took the leading part.

Mr Bosomworth claims that there is nobody working at Thornley Colliery now who was working there when he first started.

3 September 1954

FELL FROM A LADDER
Inquest On Sherburn Hill Man

A verdict of "Accidental death" was recorded at a Durham Inquest on Friday on a Sherburn Hill man who died in Durham County Hospital on August 31, the day after he was admitted as the result of injuries received when he fell from a ladder at Thornley.

William Wignall, George Street, Sherburn Hill, a 54 year-old electrician, employed at Thornley Colliery, was working on a street light in Thornley when he slipped and fell to the ground,

Arthur Newton Woodward, assistant foreman electrician at the colliery, told the Coroner (Mr W Carr) that although it was the usual practice for electricians to wear safety belts, while working on poles, Wignall was not wearing one.

17 September 1954

CONCERT

Over 300 attended a concert at Thornley Welfare Hall, given to raise funds to buy a television set for Mr E Jones, who received spinal injuries at the colliery last year. The entertainment was provided by the Thornley Mothers' Club and Legionaires Combined Concert Party, Jackie Toye (accordionist) and John Dodds (tympanist). Guest artistes were Irene Horner, Ronnie Oswald, John Tunney and Johnny Quinn. Compere was Mrs Hobbs and organiser Mrs Chapman. The effort was expected to raise about £20 10s.

MOTHERS'S CLUB

There was a good attendance at the meeting of Thornley Mothers' Club, Mrs M Hobbs presided. The programme for the evening took the form of a display by six St John Ambulance Cadets, under their senior officer, Mrs E Stever, superintendent of the Spennymoor Brigade. An interesting programme was devised, showing the special brand of first aid required for all types of accident, including artificial respiration. Mrs Stever also gave a talk covering the work done by the St John brigade and thanked the members of the club for knitted squares received for the making of blankets. Mrs Stever and her team were thanked by the president. Lucky prizes were won by Mrs E Raine and Mrs D Etherington.

24 September 1954

ON HOLIDAY FROM CANADA
Former Resident Of Wheatley Hill

Two and a half years ago, Mr Robert Davison, a Wheatley Hill bricklayer, emigrated to Canada with his friend Mr Eddie Grosvenor, of Shotton. Both felt that there were more opportunities in a young country like Canada and proceeded to put their ideas to the test. Six months later their wives joined them.

Mrs Davison is now at her mother Mrs Prince's house, 5, Stephen Terrace, Wheatley Hill, on five months' holiday. She returns home on October 28.

Mrs Davison said, "I am glad of the opportunity of seeing my mother and family again but Canada is a good country to live in. The standard of living is good. Canada certainly has good prospects and offers good prizes but if anyone thinks they can do well without working, they had best remain here. My husband has had to work hard but is reaping the reward of his toil. At any rate, while I am here on holiday, my husband, with the help of his friend, Eddie Grosvenor, is building our new bungalow in George Street, Oak Ridges, Ontario."

Mrs Davison stated that the housing situation was bad in Canada. Rented self-contained flats were quite expensive so people went in for building or buying their own homes. "The flat we lived in for two years in the city of Toronto costs us between £25 and £30 a month.

Grand Life For Children

Speaking of medical services Mrs Davison said that Britain definitely had the pull. Facilities varied from province to province. Some have a form of National Health Service but others have not.

Mrs Davison said that children had a grand life in Canada. Skating, swimming, ice-hockey and fishing gave them a good physical training.

She said, "The children have a wonderful time at Christmas. The highlight is the 'Santa Claus' procession at the beginning of December. Students of the colleges and universities take part. People come from the country in their hundreds to see the procession.

"The people of Canada," she went on, "take their religion more seriously than people do here. Nearly everyone attends some place of worship. Those who do not worship are the exception rather than the rule. When work ceases in the shops on Saturday, all goods are cleared from the windows and a placard in a central position reads, "This is God's Day. You are called to rest. So worship God in the church of your choice".

1 October 1954

RETURN FROM "EXILE"
To Spend Retirement At Wheatley Hill

"America is a great country for a man who is prepared to work. There is plenty of employment and the pay is exceptionally good. In the States, the bricklayer, joiner and plumber are the men in demand. Bricklayers earn 23s an hour while joiners and plumbers receive 20s an hour. These workmen go to their work in smart cars." So said Mr Thomas Stogdale, 5, Wingate Lane, Wheatley Hill, who has just recently returned to this country after spending 32 years in the U S A.

Mr Stogdale was born in Castle Eden Colliery 72 years ago and started work at Station Town pit. He worked 10 hours a day and received a shilling a shift.

"I must be one of the few remaining people who worked at the Station Town pit. There can't be many of us left now," said Mr Stogdale. From Station Town he went to the old Trimdon Colliery mine, now closed, and served his apprenticeship as a fitter.

He gained his deputy certificate and went on to Armstrong College, Newcastle, where he gained his manager's ticket.

Deputy

Mr Stogdale worked as deputy at Wheatley Hill Colliery for a few years and then secured a post as overman at Dunston where his two daughters were born. He came back into the Durham coalfield to serve as under-manager at Ludworth Colliery. With troubled days in the industry Ludworth pit closed down in 1923.

Mr Stogdale and his wife Margaret, then made their great decision to emigrate to America. Mr Stogdale said, "I viewed conditions on the Durham Coalfield with misgiving. In fact, I felt that locally, the situation was bad and there was no future in mining. The standard of life and living conditions generally was low and depressing. So we made our minds up to leave it all and branch out again in a young and coming country. The U S A, was our immediate choice. We never regretted it."

In America Mr Stogdale did well and as the result of hard work rose to the top. He became engineer to an important concern. He retired in 1948.

The couple would have liked their two daughters, Mrs R T Bell and Mrs C Wood, to go out to the States. This was not practicable so Mr and Mrs Stogdale decided to come back to the Old country and be near their daughters.

Proved Wrong

Now that they have returned from 'exile', Mr Stogdale said, "My estimate of the mining industry in County Durham made in 1923 has proved to be wrong. I pay tribute to the work of the British miner and those in charge of the work for the transformation and progress that has been made.

"I compliment the housing authority too. I remember the rows of miners' cottages, with little comforts and practically no amenities. It is a pleasure to see the fine, modern, commodious dwellings that are going up today, which cater for the needs and well-being of family life."

Commenting on America Mr Stogdale said, "The country's vastness is impressive. From coast to coast there are 3,500 miles of varied scenery. While generally the climate is good we have to face the extremes of cold and heat. In the summer the temperature often reaches 110 degrees in the shade and in winter fall to below 25 below zero."

Giving his viewpoint on the American people he went on, "The population is cosmopolitan. On the whole they are quite friendly to British immigrants. While the rank and file work people have a high regard for Sir Winston Churchill and Mr Eden personally, they are quite suspicious of British policy and aims.

"There is a suspicion that Britain is willing to use America for her own ends. It is in higher circles of American life that our views and aims are thoroughly understood and appreciated."

Woman's Country

Taking up the story. Mrs Stogdale said, "America is a woman's country. Every house is designed to save her labour. The housewife can stand in the centre of her kitchen and not move more than a few steps. Every electrical device and labour-saving gadget is to her hand; fridge, cooker, washing machine etc. In modern houses in the States, each kitchen sink has a garbage disposal unit attached to it. Refuse is ground into powder and then washed away."

She also said that women's clubs attached to the churches did a good deal for women's social life. Mrs Stogdale is the daughter of Mr Ralph Terry, a well-known Wheatley Hill business man.

The couple are looking forward to happy years of retirement in this country. Their seven grandchildren and seven great-grandchildren are a great source of pleasure to them. They have entered into the life of Wheatley Hill by becoming associated with All Saints Church and they are members of the Over-60-Club.

8 October 1954

HOLIDAY IN CANADA
But No Place Like Home, says Thornley Woman

"After all, there's no place like home," said Mrs Jane Walls, of School Square, Thornley, "even though it is only 200 yards from the pit shaft."

She has returned from a visit to her son, William, and his wife and two children in their newly-built modern-style home on the southern tip of the island of Vancouver on the western side of Canada.

Before sailing across the Atlantic her experience of being "on the water" was limited to going over the Tyne ferry. But she enjoyed the Atlantic trip in weather which was a mixture of good and bad. What she liked about it was the good food, the comfortable quarters, and, most of all, the friendliness of the people on board.

After a night in the port of Montreal, she had practically four days of train travel. She had never slept in a train before, but after the first night she settled down to sleep comfortably. Meals and amenities on the train, with equally good service by attendants, made the journey enjoyable. The Canadian scenery, especially in the Rockies, was very impressive.

This was followed by another sea trip- a few hours only- from the Vancouver mainland over to her destination in Victoria.

This long journey of twice 7,000 miles has not given Mrs Walls a passion for travelling. "I had been thinking about making the journey for some time- hesitating now and again you know," she said. "But I made up my mind all of a sudden, and I didn't change it. All I wanted was to see my son and his wife and family. And now I am satisfied."

Married Canadian

Her son, William, now 33, was a butcher in the Wheatley Hill branch of Sherburn Hill Co-operative Society before he joined the R A F in the last war. While serving in Canada he met Bernice Hull, the Canadian girl who is now his wife. She came to England for the wedding. Under the name of Bill Walls on his shop front he is now in business on his own in Victoria and doing quite well. His new home, three miles away, has central heating, for which coal and wood are used at a rather expensive figure.

"But the climate is very similar to our own," says Mrs Walls. "They were complaining of having a bad Summer out there, but I though that, compared with what I saw of ours in the early summer and what I have heard about it since I came back, it was wonderful."

She got the impression that while wages are high in British Columbia, prices are also high and she isn't at all sure that the margin left over is better than it is here. "But everybody seems prosperous," she says. "At any rate, most folk run their own cars. In Victoria it is very difficult to find parking places.

Bill took a holiday while his mother was there, and the family went in their car by the coast route to San Francisco, a return journey of something over 1,000 miles. En route they stayed at "hotels," comfortable chalets dotted in clusters here and there for the convenience of travellers.

Mrs Walls says that all the people she met were friendly and kind, extremely interested in how the Old Country was going on, and delighted with the visit of the Queen and the Duke of Edinburgh. She didn't see the Queen, but she watched the Duke land from a plane after he had been touring while the Queen was resting.

Her absence from home lasted a little more than four months, including a fortnight's travelling each way. "I am pleased I made the trip. It has been a great pleasure-more so because I found my son and his family so happy and comfortable," she said.

LOFTHOUSE MUSEUM
Ludworth Man's Hobby

Seventy-three-year-old Bob Lofthouse has been counting up the number of visitors to his museum this year. It comes to nearly 200.

They have come, not only from many counties of England, but from abroad. Americans and Canadians have been among them, and a few days ago three young Germans called. They are in Durham studying mining. One of them is an expert butterfly collector; and he took his two friends along to Mr Lofthouse's Council house in Barnard Avenue, Ludworth.

Bob's is an odd museum. It is located in his bedroom. A stuffed wild cat, its fangs bared, glares from a case by the bedside. This is the first sight that greets Bob when he wakes in the morning.

Stuffed Fox and Cub

Walls are hidden by glass cases containing birds and animals- ducks, hawks, crows, woodpeckers, cuckoos, stoats, rabbits and weasles. On the floor, curled up, are a stuffed fox and cub.

Crocodiles' eggs are kept safely in a cabinet with scores of birds' eggs. Two ostrich eggs are strung up at the head of his bed. A swordfish's saw hangs on the wall. Brilliantly coloured butterflies and other insects from many parts of the world fill drawers.

Bob is getting short of space for his museum, but he is not worried about that. "I am content with my collection," he says. "The only collecting I do now is to pick up a few beetles now and again." Rest of his time is occupied in keeping his glass cases and cabinets spotless. Each carries a card with the name of each specimen in copper-plate handwriting.

"Gave Me the Creeps"

Miss Lily Lofthouse, Bob's sister - he is a bachelor- has got used to the odd museum upstairs. "It used to give me the creeps," she says

Roaming the fields, woods and hedgerows, Bob's lifetime hobby has been the study of birds, animals and plants. He does not wander so far now, for this ex-Thornley pit banksman is now 73, but he has a fair sized garden to cultivate. And this ornithologist, artist and humorist has so many callers that he finds he cannot travel far.

15 October 1954

CONCERT AT THORNLEY

"Something for everyone" was the slogan of St Godric's Choral Society for their annual concert on Tuesday at Wheatley Hill and last night at Thornley. Heading the vocal section were John Quinn, Doris Surman, Anthony Cavanghan, Marie Mitchell and Pat Hoban. Newcomers were Patrick and Paul McCoy and Anne Wilson. In the drama section a short thriller was given by Anne Connelly, Isabel Luke, Marie Mitchell, Anne Craig, Paul McCoy, John Corbett, David Shutt and Bernard Dryden. In the general production were Anne Lister, Mary Smythe, Fred Graney and Jack Toye (blind accordionist). John Tunney was compere.

Dances arranged by Ann Linten were performed by Ruth, Mary and Pat Hoban. In a children's corner of singing and dancing there were Anne Atkin, Monica Quinn, Dorothy Trismen, Michael Regan, Brian English, Keith Shutt, Peter Corbett, James Hoban, Terence Smith, Andrew Bonner, James Lister, Terence Hoban, Joseph Doyle, James Doyle and Harry Morton.

Miss Mary Scully was producer, and the Rev Father Robinson thanked all for their successful effort, the proceeds of which will go to the Church Building Fund.

THORNLEY SPORT SPOTLIGHT

"Spotlight on Sport", held in Thornley Miners' Welfare Hall on Thursday night by the staff of Wheatley Hill Boys' Modern School under the leadership of Mr A Harris, the head teacher, included well-known footballers Ted Purdon, Ken Chisholm and Tommy Wright, Sunderland, and Johnny Wright and Bob Hardisty, Bishop Auckland.

But there was disappointment, especially for the large number of schoolboys in the 400 audience, when Bob Hardisty had to apologise for the unavoidable absence of Len Shackleton. But the blow was softened when Bob produced Frank Brennan from the wings. The smiling centre half, given a good reception, obliged with a song.

The other footballers, in playing kit, played a "foot and head" match, titled "Sunderland v Bishop Auckland," designed to show the youngsters how easy it all is.

A highlight of the evening was the appearance of the popular little boxer, Teddy Gardener. First he gave a display of shadow boxing, and then took on a local youth, Kenneth Harvey, for three rounds. Not only did Teddy amuse the large audience, but he also caused the local youth's face to alternate between very serious looks and smiles.

SKATER'S DISPLAY

Sheila Gardner, Middlesbrough, 1953 champion skater of Great Britain, and who was due in Germany this week, gave an excellent display of grace and skill in the rather circumscribed area of the stage.

Other items by experts included some breathtaking weight lifting, gymnastics and judo. Two sturdy Wellfield Grammar schoolboys - Alan Hardy, Trimdon Village, and Gordon Forster, Wheatley Hill - showed great promise in their own gymnastic turn. Country dancing by girls and club swinging by boys of Wheatley Hill schools were pleasing items.

A football, duly autographed by the celebrities present, was won, appropriately enough, by Barrie Thubron, centre forward of Wheatley Hill Senior boys' team. It was presented to him with congratulations by County Coun Jack Andrews, Wheatley Hill, who thanked the performers and school staff for putting on such a fine show. "The school is badly in need of a sports pavilion," he said, "and the proceeds of this show will go a long way towards getting it."

Mr A Turner, Durham, representing the Central Council of Physical Recreation, displayed a wide knowledge of the various sports in his able performance of the duties of compere.

THORNLEY CLUBS' DARTS LEAGUE

Games played on Monday night under the auspices of the newly formed Thornley and District Workmen's Clubs Darts and Domino League resulted:

Darts; Quarrington Hill 2, Haswell Plough 1; Cassop 0, Coxhoe 3; Thornley 2, Wheatley Hill 1. **Dominoes**: Quarrington Hill 2, Haswell 0; Cassop 2, Coxhoe 0; Thornley 2, Wheatley Hill 0.

Officials of the league are: chairman, Coun J Cairns, Quarrington Hill; secretary, Mr J S White, Thornley; treasurer, Mr E Crangle, Haswell. More clubs are expected to join in the near future.

Darts Table	P	W	L	P
Thornley	6	6	0	14
Quarrington Hill	6	5	1	13
Coxhoe	6	4	2	11
Haswell	6	2	4	7
Wheatley Hill	6	0	6	4
Cassop	6	1	5	4

Dominoes Table	P	W	L	D	P
Quarrington Hill	6	5	0	1	11
Thornley	6	4	1	1	9
Cassop	6	3	0	3	6
Coxhoe	6	2	1	3	5
Haswell	6	1	1	4	3
Wheatley Hill	6	1	0	5	2

LUDWORTH CHURCH HALL

Sir - Although the Church Council had wished to hand over the old church school to Ludworth Village two years ago and in fact a Village committee has been running it, for reasons beyond the control of the Church Council, the Church Hall must be sold. So Cannon Tillard explained to a public meeting in Ludworth. The position now is that either the Village committee has to find £250, or a buyer has to be found elsewhere. The old school is the only social centre in the village and lack of funds has allowed the hall to get dilapidated. Many people feel that it can still be made a worthy village hall providing the local inhabitants are sufficiently interested. At least one local organisation is prepared to put money into renovating the building as a memorial hall. But as in most small communities considerable voluntary effort is required. Has Ludworth got the effort?

LOVE OF THE BIBLE
Bishop's Address at Thornley

People from all the parishes in the Easington Deanery filled Thornley Miners' Welfare Hall to hear the Bishop of Durham (Dr A M Ramsey) and the Rev N J Cockburn, of London, general secretary of the British and Foreign Bible Society, speaking in celebration of the 150 years of work of the society.

Canon R H Tillard, Rural Dean, introduced the Bishop on his first visit to Thornley. Many clergy of the Deanery were on the platform.

The Bishop said that love of the Bible had always been a marked feature of the North of England. "Go back to the beginning – to Venerable Bede, at Jarrow, a great lover of the Bible. No one did more than he did to spread the love of the Bible and the knowledge of the Christian religion in this part of the country.

"Scandal and Disgrace"

"It is likely that some of you here tonight belong to the people called Methodists – to give them their ancient and most honoured name. It was love for the Bible and its teaching that inspired John Wesley and his brother Charles to preach the Gospel in many parts of England.

"From 1879," went on the Bishop, "you had a series of three Bishops of Durham-Lightfoot, Westcott and Moule-who stood out in Christendom for their learning and love of the Bible."

The Bishop thought it would be a scandal and disgrace if people in the North of England did not know and love the Bible. He was afraid, however, that the position was strangely different now from what it was a hundred years ago. At that time there was a Bible in countless homes. It was known and read and quoted. We had only to read novels of that time to see that allusions to the Bible were frequently made and understood.

Many people now did not know that "Am I my brother's keeper?" and "A camel going through the eye of a needle," were Bible allusions. In the old days it was known what was intended when one talked of "Agag walking delicately." "I wonder how many of us today know why Agag was walking delicately and what it meant," said the Bishop.

Three Ways

In past days the reading of the Bible moulded and created the pattern of life of very many people of this country. Today there were many homes in which there was no Bible at all. And in many schools the teaching of the Bible was "scandalously bad."

In asking the audience to renew their gratitude for the Bible and their love and use of it, the Bishop pleaded, first, that the Bible be regarded as the book of the Church and God's people, second, that it be read historically, and, third, that it be read devotionally. He gave advice on how this was to be done.

Canon Cockburn gave much information on former and future translations and editions of the Bible.

22 October 1954

CRICKET CLUB

Flooding turned the "Hilly" cricket pitch into a children's bathing pool towards the close of last season, preventing the novices' competition from being completed, reported Mr J R Taylor, financial secretary, at the annual meeting of Thornley Colliery Welfare Cricket Club. Nevertheless the club gained the sum of £30, which formed the larger part of the closing balance. It was decided to assure the four semi-finalist teams that the competition would be played out early in 1955, possibly on the new ground at the east side of the Miner's Welfare Institute. It was decided to again compete in the Coxhoe and North-East Durham Leagues. Officers elected; President, Mr A Welsh, jun; chairman, Mr E Green; vice-chairman, Mr C A Smith; financial secretary, Mr J R Taylor; captain first eleven, Mr J R Taylor, vice-captain Mr T Robinson; captain, second eleven, Mr J Nicholson, vice-captain, Mr M Warrior.

5 November 1954

BISHOP OF DURHAM AT WHEATLEY HILL
CHURCH EXTENSIONS DEDICATED

Long before the service was due to begin, All Saints' Church, Wheatley Hill, was filled to capacity on Sunday evening for the visit of the Bishop of Durham (Dr A M Ramsey) to dedicate extensions carried out to the church during the past three years.

The scheme of alterations and renovations began with the building of a new entrance porch and an extension to the sanctuary and then seating capacity was considerably improved with the building of a new south aisle.

Cost £4,500

The interior of the church has been completely re-decorated and new carpetings have been added to its beauty together with an up-to-date system of electric lighting. The organ has been given a thorough overhaul, the outer walls of the church have been re-pointed, and altogether a "new look" has been given to this 80-year-old church.

The work has been carried out at an approximate cost of £4,500 and it is a tribute to the hard-working efforts of the Vicar (the Rev Arthur Preston) his wife, and the officials, members and friends of the church that the church is not a penny in debt. Most of the money has been raised in the parish by voluntary subscriptions and special efforts, and donations, which were greatly appreciated, were received from many local organisations, including workmen's and social clubs.

Included in the large congregation on Sunday night were representatives of Wheatley Hill miners' lodge and the local workmen's clubs-it was in appreciation of their support of the improvements scheme that they were specially invited together with local members of Easington Rural Council and the chairman of the Council, Coun R Smith, of Deaf Hill.

The service, with the choir playing its full part, was conducted by the Rev Arthur Preston, and Mr J Atkinson was at the organ.

Present-Day Saints

It was fitting, said the Bishop, who was visiting the church for the first time, that the dedication should come at the Festival of All Saints-at a time when we thought of thegreat family of the church of God in this world and in the unseen world. The Christian life was really a process of becoming more like the Lord Jesus. "Christians," continued the Bishop, "are meant to be like mirrors, resembling the Lord Jesus, reflecting His love, His brightness, His character. And the more we truly reflect Him like mirrors in this life, the more we are getting ready for the day when we shall be allowed to see Him, and shall dare to see Him, boldly and with unveiled face.

Those whom we called the saints were, and are, men and women like ourselves, said the Bishop. They were of the same flesh and blood, who really were like the Lord Jesus and reflected Him amongst their fellows. "Some of our Lord's first disciples were like that," went on the Bishop, "and so were some of the saints whom we remember especially in the North of England, saints who spread the Gospel when this part of the country was heathen, dark and barbarian."

But, continued Dr Ramsay, there were not only "the official saints." "There are those known to us," he added, "who did, or do, show us something of the love of Christ in the nature of their lives- in their charity, their patience or courage, their unselfishness and sometimes in the wonderful joy that fills them even when things are black and painful."

LUDWORTH

Led by Thornley Colliery Band, under Mr M Morgan D C M members of Ludworth British Legion, W I , and Wolf Cubs marched to the War Memorial where a service was conducted by Mr T T Johnson, who gave a simple and moving address. The "Last Post" and "Reveille" were sounded and the two minutes' silence observed. Poppy wreaths were laid on behalf of the Legion by Mr R Gibson, M M , Women's Section by Mrs C Gibson (vice-president) and Mrs Foster (Women's Institute). Relatives placed their floral tributes. There was a large attendance at the service.

12 November 1954

WOMEN BOWLERS
Trophies Presented To Wheatley Hill Winners

Trophies won by members of Wheatley Hill Welfare Women's Bowls Club during the past season were presented by a former president of the club, Mrs G Nicholson, of Chester-le-Street, who was among the guests at the annual presentation supper and social evening in the Welfare Hall, Wheatley Hill, on Friday night. The function was attended by a gathering of 130,including representatives of eight clubs which compete in the same league as Wheatley Hill, the North-East Coast Ladies' Bowls League.

Mrs Nicholson, who was introduced by Mrs S Hodson, chairman of the club,

presented the trophies and prizes as follows: Club Cup, Mrs E Atkinson; runner-up,

Mrs E Poulson; William Jones Cup, Miss A Hutchinson; runner-up, Mrs S Hodson;

Festival Bowl, Mrs E Hall; runner-up, Mrs S Hodson; mixed pairs Mrs S Hodson and

Mr W Kendall; runners-up, Miss A Hutchinson and MrT Blackett.

Thanks to Mrs Nicholson were expressed by Mrs E Hall, secretary of the club' who

also presented the former president with a bouquet of pink chrysanthemums.

Supporting Mrs Nicholson in her congratulations to the winners , was Mrs Frankland,

of West Hartlepool, president of the league.

An excellent supper was served and Mrs Hall officiated as M C for whist and

Miss A Hutchinson for dancing. Dance music was provided by Mr Jack Cain.

Prizes were presented to the following winners by Mrs G Nicholson:

Mesdames A Kendall, E Nicholson and E Hayes and Messrs W Snowdon, A Bramfitt

and R Taylor, and Mrs Alderton and Mrs Nixon (consolations).

3 December 1954

NEW WHEATLEY HILL GROUNDSMAN

From a short list of six, 34-year-old Mr Walter E Myers, of Rectory Row, Sedgefield has been appointed groundsman at Wheatley Hill Welfare Park, in succession to Mr Thomas W Alderson, who is retiring at the end of the year after filling the position for the past 28 years. There were originally 21 applicants for the post.

Mr Myers, who will take up his new duties next month, is at present employed on similar duties at Winterton Hospital, Sedgefield. The possessor of a Durham County horticultural certificate, he has been engaged on groundsman's duties since leaving school 20 years ago and has had considerable experience in the maintenance of bowling greens and tennis courts.

10 December 1954

SCOUT SINGERS

To raise funds to buy Christmas presents for the children's ward of Durham County Hospital, which they "adopted" two years ago, the 2nd Wheatley Hill Troop of Boy Scouts have been organising carol singing parties in the village.

MECHANICS' OFFICERS

Officers elected at the annual meeting of Wheatley Hill lodge, County Mechanics' Association, are Chairman, Mr W Gibson: secretary, Mr W S Ruth; treasurer, Mr E Snowdon; committee, Messrs J Jordon, S Scott, R Fawkes, F Horner and R Scott; delegate, Mr W Gibson.

SHIFTS ADVANCED

By a decision of Wheatley Hill Workmen's Federation Board, the miners and other grades of workmen at the colliery will work as usual on Christmas Eve and take the Boxing Day holiday on Monday. So that no one will be working late on Christmas Eve the management have agreed to advance all three shifts that day. The fore-shift will start three hours earlier, the back shift four hours earlier and the night shift five hours earlier. All the workmen will be out of the pit by 6.30 pm on Christmas Eve.

CLUB PARTY

About 40 retired members of Wheatley Hill Discharged and Demobilised Soldiers' and Sailors' Club were entertained to their annual Christmas party by the club management. They were welcomed by Mr Stan Hall, secretary of the County branch of the Workmen's Club Union, and Mr S Lavers, chairman of the Northern Clubs' Federated Breweries. Tea was followed by entertainment by local artistes, with Mr John Cain as accompanist. Each retired member received a Christmas gift of £1, and his wife 10s.

24 December 1954

NEW CHURCH LECTERN

A new oak lectern made by local craftsmen associated with the church and presented as a gift to All Saints' Church, Wheatley Hill, is to be dedicated by the Rev Arthur Preston (Vicar of Wheatley Hill) at evensong on Sunday.

31 December 1954

1955

FIRE AT LUDWORTH
Prompt Actions Praised

The prompt action of a young miner, who raised the alarm, was praised by a Ludworth householder, whose council house home caught fire in the early hours of Monday morning, and in turn, the quick-thinking of the householder who, after getting his wife and family of four to safety, shut all the doors, was praised by a fire officer at the blaze.

The householder, Francis Cordner, 135 Barnard Avenue, was asleep when fire broke out in the front living room downstairs. The flames were noticed by a young miner, Anthony Gavaghan, 110 Barnard Avenue, as he was returning home shortly after 4.30am. Quickly he banged on the front door and aroused Mr Cordner and then ran some 300 yards to the nearest telephone kiosk to summon Peterlee and Wheatley Hill Units of the Durham County Fire Brigade.

Furniture Blazing

When he dashed downstairs, Mr Cordner found the living room a mass of flames and the heat in the hallway and staircase was intense. He was able, however to run back upstairs and help his wife and family of four children – three boys and a girl – to safety, and then he shut all the doors. "If he had not had the presence of mind to shut the doors, confining the blaze to the living room, the whole house would probably have been gutted", Station Officer G W Price, in charge of Peterlee Unit of the Durham County Fire Brigade, told our reporter later. "It was quick thinking on Mr Cordner's part and he undoubtedly helped to save the major part of his home".

Furniture in the living room was blazing furiously when the firemen reached the scene and the intense heat had spread upstairs and along the hallway but they soon got the blaze under control. They were unable however to prevent most of the contents of the living room, including a television set, radio, three piece suite and other furniture, from being destroyed, together with floor coverings and some clothing.

Pets Died

Three pets of the family – two dogs and a budgerigar unfortunately perished. The dogs, one of them a pedigree Yorkshire terrier had sought refuge in a bedroom from the heat. When called they were apparently too frightened to leave the room and firemen found them lying suffocated.

The firemen were on duty for about two hours. The cause of the outbreak is unknown, though it is thought it may have been a spark jumping out of the fireplace.

Full of praise for Mr Gavaghan's timely warning, Mr Cordner said it had undoubtedly saved both their home and their lives.

7 January 1955

CLUB ELECTIONS – As a result of the half-yearly ballot of Wheatley Hill Soldiers' and Sailors' Social Club and Institute at the weekend, Mr W Hackworth was re-elected secretary for the ensuing year and Mr A Carr, Chairman. Mr A Wood was re-elected treasurer, unopposed. From 14 nominations the following were elected to the committee: Messrs J Hackworth, C Curry, J Gair, G Hedley, A Wood senior and H Walker. Mr T Cain was re-elected doorman.

WOMEN'S PARTY – Friends of the members were invited to the annual party of Wheatley Hill women's section of the Labour Party held in the Girls' Modern School, Wheatley Hill. An excellent supper was served by members of the committee, and Mrs R Watson and Mrs J Andrew were MC's for a whist and beetle drive. Prizes were won by Mrs Million (whist) and Mrs Powell (beetle drive). Games and competitions were also organised and suitable prizes awarded.

DIED IN YORKSHIRE – The funeral has taken place at Blidworth, near Mansfield, of a former Wheatley Hill resident, Mr John Brown, 63, who left Wheatley Hill 13 years ago. Mr Brown was employed for many years at Wheatley Hill colliery as head ropeman and a wagonwayman. He continued in the same employment at Blidworth Colliery, but six years ago lost a leg in an accident at work and had never worked since. Mr Brown is survived by his wife, three sons and a daughter. The sons, John, James and William all live in the Blidworth area and the daughter, Mrs R Soulsby, at Thornley.

21 January 1955

THORNLEY PARISH COUNCIL

Councillor J Nicholson referred, at the meeting of Thornley Parish Council on Tuesday, to the rapid conversion of houses into shops in The Villas, Thornley, for many years regarded as residential and situated on the main road. He said he was speaking from a road safety point of view.

Coun. Mrs Anderson, agreeing, said The Villas was their narrowest street and was not the place for lorries to wait about to deliver goods.

436

Coun. J H C. Scott: It's spoiling The Villas as a residential place. Everybody will be seeking a reduction of rates. We need houses just as we need shops, I'm afraid the building of shops is going to be rather overdone.

Coun. J Hoban: But surely they must get into touch with the planning officers.

Coun. M Murray (Chairman) offered the opinion that if the Rural Council had provided shops something could have been done about the present trouble. He was informed that land had been set aside for shops and that the shops had been allocated but that the District Council had done nothing further about this.

Although it was generally agreed that road safety would be adversely affected, the Council did not reach a decision as to what action should be taken.

POST OFFICE: SATURDAY OPENING

The head postmaster at Durham (Mr J Mawson), wrote informing the Council that their request for a post box in the vicinity of Cooper's Terrace and a stamp machine at Thornlaw post office would be granted, though there might be some delay in getting the necessary material.

On the request for one of the two sub-offices to be open on Saturday afternoons he said the Thornley office (the office in Hartlepool Street) had been closed on Saturday afternoons for many years. In 1951 the Council had agreed to the early closing of the Thornlaw office being changed from Wednesdays to Saturdays.

Coun. Mrs Bosomworth, supporting Saturday closing, said, "These men like to get away on Saturday afternoons as well as we do". Several members emphasised that this was not a personal matter, but that it was a matter of the convenience of the public.

One councillor spoke of a businessman having to go to Cassop for a postal order to send away money he had collected that day. Another spoke of a journey to Durham to post an urgent parcel.

It was agreed to continue negotiations with the head postmaster.

Other Matters

A letter was received from Wingate Parish Council asking that consideration be given to repairing the Thornley Council's portion of the path leading from the colliery railway to the Gassy Gutter. Wingate Council were asking the County Surveyor to supply an estimate for the portion of the path from the Thornley boundary to the Wheatley Hill Council houses, and they thought it would be "rather futile" to repair the Wheatley Hill portion without the Thornley portion being repaired. It was decided that an inspection be made pending further discussion on the matter.

An estimate of amounts to be raised from the rates during the year ending March 31 1956 was agreed upon. This provides for £240 for the general account, £450 for burial expenses and £1220 for lighting expenses, the total of £1910 being the same as for the current year.

Easington RDC wrote sanctioning an expenditure of about £55 for the renewal of street name plates. This does not include the council houses, which will receive the attention of the Surveyor.

4 February 1955

MINER RETIRES – After having worked 52 years as a miner, Mr Alfred Dobbin, of Thornley, has retired. Except for a period of ten months at Urpeth in his early teens, the whole of his service has been at Thornley. He went through the usual grades of trapper, putter, hewer and for the last 30 years as a stoneman. In the First World War he was an onsetter in the No 1 pit. He started at a wage of a shilling a day and worked under five colliery managers.

LEGION WOMEN – Mrs E Clark presided over a social evening organised by Thornley Women's Section of the British Legion in the Club Hall and welcomed visitors from Wheatley Hill and Trimdon branches. Mesdames P Luke, E Converry and H Slater and Mesdames E Clark, D Wright, P Luke, E Middleton and E Gordon took part in sketches. Mesdames M Barrass and M Mitchell sang duets. Refreshments, served by members of the committee, were given by members. Games and dancing followed. The weekly prize was won by Mrs M Thompson.

WOMEN'S FELLOWSHIP – The annual meeting of Thornley Circuit branch of the Methodist Women's Fellowship was held in Thornley Bow Street church, when the Rev H Ireland presided. Mrs J W Smedley, reported an income of £19.10s. After donations had been made to the Women's Fellowship Home for Mothers and Babies and Homes for the Aged funds, there was a credit balance of £5.8s. Interesting reports were submitted on the Quiet Day at Wheatley Hill by Mrs Johnson (Fishburn), the Saltburn three-day school by Mrs Partridge and the Circuit Retreat held at Thornley by Mrs C T Gladstone (Wingate). It was agreed that this year's retreat should be at Wheatley Hill Patton Street on September 22 and the Quiet Day at Coxhoe Central on October 17. The following officials were elected: President, Mrs J W Bragan (Kelloe); Treasurer, Mrs J W Smedley (Wingate North Road); Secretary, Mrs G Scott (Bowburn Durham Road); Magazine Secretary, Miss E Carrick (West Cornforth St Mark's).

11 February 1955

VILLAGE'S "ODD STREET OUT"
In Wheatley Hill: But Shadforth Parish

"Nobody there ever votes!" declared Coun A Bishop at Monday's meeting of Wingate Parish Council, referring to Lynn Terrace, Wheatley Hill – the street "across the beck" which is the "odd street out" in the village. Lynn Terrace excepted, the whole of Wheatley Hill comes within the area of Wingate Parish Council ... but this one street of 25 houses is in the Shadforth Parish Council area.

The colliery beck apparently forms the demarcation line between Shadforth and Wingate parishes. Only a few score yards from Lynn Terrace – at the other side of the beck - isSmith Street and this, like every other street in Wheatley Hill, is in Wingate parish.

But, on the whole, I found that few of the residents of Lynn Terrace seemed to mind being in a different parish to the rest of the village when I paid a visit there this week (write Norman Passfield).

"Not Worried"

Said 63 year old Mrs Ethel Laverick, of No 10, "I have lived here since I was married, 40 years ago, and it has never worried me one bit being in Shadforth parish and coming under Durham Rural Council instead of Easington Rural Council. Admittedly, it has sometimes meant a journey to Ludworth for the local elections instead of just a short walk up into the village at Wheatley Hill, but this has never troubled me. I don't think it is anything to make a fuss about!"

And Mrs Emma Natrass of No 12, who has lived there for 31 years, said it was not true to say that nobody in the street ever votes. "Cars come along to take us to Ludworth at election time and most of us go to vote!" she declared. "We are certainly not neglected!"

"Though the election candidates in the Shadforth parish may not, at first, be known to the residents of Lynn Terrace, they come along to introduce themselves before the voting", said Mrs Nattrass. "We have always taken an interest in the election, even though we are in a different parish to the rest of Wheatley Hill", she said, "and I for one, am not worried about not being in Wingate Parish!"

3-Mile Journey To Ludworth

There was the anomaly of having to make the three-mile journey to Ludworth to collect ration-books when rationing was in force, instead of collecting them at Wheatley Hill, but even this was not found "really inconvenient", went on Mrs Nattrass. "As a matter of fact", she added, "my son Robert generally used to collect books for the whole of the street!"

Bachelor John Henry Goyns, retired 67-year-old miner, who lives in No 5, said that as far as he was concerned it "made no difference" whether they were in Wingate or Shadforth parish. He has lived in the street since 1914. "And I have never found it inconvenient!", he declared.

But Wingate Parish Council have a strong supporter in 76-year-old Thomas Smith, who lives in No 19, in their efforts to have their boundaries altered so that Lynn Terrace is brought into their area.

"The sooner we are in Wingate parish the better!" he declared. "The street is in Wheatley Hill and yet it does not seem to be part of the village at all! For instance, the registrar for the Wingate parish regularly visits Wheatley Hill, but if anyone in Lynn Terrace wants to register a birth or death, off he has to go to Durham. It seems a ridiculous position!"

"A Canny Walk" To Ludworth

It was also "ridiculous" declared Mr Smith, who has lived in Lynn Terrace for 19 years, to have to go to Ludworth to vote. "I have only gone there to vote in the general election", he added. "I never vote in local elections – it's a canny walk you know!"

The Rev Arthur Preston (Vicar of Wheatley Hill) would also like to see the "anomalous" position of Lynn Terrace cleared up by the street being transferred to

Wingate parish. "It can, and has, caused confusion", he said. "The street has always been in the civic parish of Shadforth but, and this is not always realised by the people there, it is still in the ecclesiastical parish of Wheatley Hill. Anyone there wishing to have banns of marriage published must have them called in the parish church at Wheatley Hill – not Shadforth!"

One of the street's newest residents, Mrs Mary E Jordison of No 14 – she has only lived there two years – said it seemed "queer" for the people there to be in Shadforth parish. Strictly speaking, it seemed that their postal address should be Shadforth and not Wheatley Hill. "Often", she added, "I have received letters addressed to Lynn Terrace, Shadforth. It would be much better if the whole matter was cleared up and we were part of Wingate parish!"

Rural Council's Opinion

When the question of revision of Parish boundaries throughout the County was raised a few months ago, Wingate Parish Council expressed themselves satisfied with their present boundaries with the exception of Lynn Terrace.

They wrote to Shadforth Parish Council, enquiring whether they had any objection to the street coming into the Wingate parish but, Wingate Parish Council were told by their Clerk, Mr John Harper, on Monday, no reply had been received. As a result the Clerk wrote on the same subject to Durham Rural Council, who disclosed that Shadforth Council were not in favour of any alteration to their boundaries. Wingate Council are now to ask Easington Rural Council if they can assist in any way to have the "odd street out" transferred to the Wingate parish.

18 February 1955

Lynn Terrace, Wheatley Hill - in Shadforth Parish

MINERS LODGE DECISION – With the exception of the grading relating to coal-cutters and putters, Wheatley Hill Miners' Lodge, at a special meeting, presided over by Mr H Bradshaw, accepted the proposed new national wages structure. The new proposals, with emphasis on the grading, were outlined by the delegate, Mr J W Burrell, and the secretary, Coun E Cain. Most of the coal-cutters, Coun Cain told our reporter after the meeting, are grouped under Grade 2 in the wages structure, and the putters under Grade 4. "The meeting felt that both of these classes of workmen should be up-graded to Grade 1", he added.

OVER-60 CLUB – A year of excellent progress was reported at the first annual meeting of Wheatley Hill Over-60-Club, presided over by Mr R Taylor on Tuesday. Membership, it was revealed, had shown a steady increase and the club had become one of the most popular and successful organisations in the village. The financial statement showed a balance in hand of £52.13s.8d. Officers elected were: Chairman, Mr R Taylor; Vice Chairman, Mr J Hodson; Secretary, Mrs R Richardson; Treasurer, Mr T E Turner; Entertainment Secretary, Mr W Williams; Committee, Mesdames M Carr, T E Turner, J Hodson, B Murray, R Taylor and J Brown and Messrs C Raffell, T Robinson, W Snowden, T Lang, M Mahoney and H Smart. Mrs Shutt was congratulated on reaching her 80th birthday and birthday greetings were also extended to Mrs Farn and Mr N Snowden.

CHURCH OFFICERS – Sound progress in all departments was reported by the vicar, the Rev Arthur Preston, at the Vestry and Parochial meetings of All Saints' Church, Wheatley Hill. Over the past five years collections had shown a steady increase, and it was hoped this would continue. In the five years about £5,000 had been spent on repairs, renewals and extensions – during the year the Bishop of Durham had visited the church to dedicate the extensions – but the work done, the Vicar emphasised, was "only a beginning. Much more has yet to be done", he added, "and the need for giving on a generous scale is still as urgent". Mr J White, who has filled the position for some 30 years, was re-elected Vicar's Warden, and Mr W Marshall People's Warden. The sidesmen were all re-elected, with the addition of Messrs S Woodward and N Smithson and Mr A Robinson was re-elected auditor. Mrs Preston is secretary of the Council.

4 March 1955

FIRE AT THORNLEY
In Semi-Detached Council House

A young Thornley married woman had most of her new furniture, including a three-piece suite, a television set and radiogram, badly damaged when fire broke out late on Saturday night at her mother's semi-detached council house where she and her husband had been "living in" since their wedding eight months ago.

The young couple, Mr and Mrs Dyson Turnbull, occupied the front upstairs bedroom at 107 Thornlaw North, Thornley, where Mrs Turnbull's mother, 42 year old Clara Dunning, a widow, lives with her other four children. The fire was discovered by Mrs Dunning shortly after she and her 13 year old son Terence and two neighbours, Mr and Mrs Fred Farrell, 105 Thornlaw North, had been watching television in the married daughter's room.

Daughter a 'Bus Conductress

"My daughter had not got back from work – she is a 'bus conductress - and it was only about ten minutes after we had seen the end of the television programme and gone downstairs to my own living room that I smelt burning wood", Mrs Dunning told our reporter on Sunday. "I sent Terence upstairs to see if there was any sign of a fire and a few seconds later he came running down shouting that the room we had not long left was on fire".

Mrs Dunning found the room dense with smoke and flames. Quickly she got her three youngest children Ena, 11, Dorothy, 7 and Alan 6, who were sleeping in an adjoining bedroom, to safety, and willing neighbours arrived on the scene to fight the flames with buckets of water until the arrival of Peterlee and Wheatley Hill Units of the Durham County Fire Brigade.

Firemen's Prompt Work

The fireman quickly got the blaze, which spread to the living room downstairs, under control, their prompt and efficient work undoubtedly saving both Mrs Dunning's home and the house next door from being destroyed. Extensive damage, however, was done to the walls and ceiling and as the flames swept through to the rafters, from the upstairs room, a hole was burned in the roof.

Mrs Dunning and her family had to seek temporary accommodation with friends for the night, and the people next door, Mrs Gladys M

Kell, a widow, and her son and daughter, were warned that because of the damage to the dividing walls they would later have to vacate their home until repairs were carried out.

Though severe damage was done to the fireplace wall in the downstairs living room, only a chair in the room was burned together with several small articles, including some shoes. The greatest loss was sustained by Mrs Turnbull – the television set which was badly scorched was a wedding gift to her from her mother-in-law – and as well as the damage to her furniture, all her carpets and floor coverings were damaged.

Ran To Thornley

Mrs Turnbull was just finishing her shift, as a conductress on the G & B 'buses at Quarrington Hill, when told of the fire. Her husband had gone to Quarrington Hill to meet her. "There were no 'buses back home, it was so late," she said, "and we ran all the way back to Thornley".

Both Mrs Dunning and her daughter were full of praise for the help given by their neighbours, including Mr and Mrs Farrell and Mr Joseph Million, who lives opposite at 140 Thornlaw North. "They did everything possible both before the firemen arrived and afterwards", said Mrs Dunning, "and we cannot thank them too highly for their valuable assistance".

The fire is believed to have been started through a damaged fireplace in the upstairs room setting alight wooden joists in the wall cavity behind.

18 March 1955

THORNLEY CLUBS' GAMES LEAGUE

Quarrington Hill won the championship of the dominoes section of the Thornley and District Workmen's Clubs' Games League with a thrilling 2-0 victory over Thornley whom they entertained in the final fixture. A draw would have resulted in Thornley carrying off the double as they had already won the darts section.

A medal to be awarded for the highest individual score at darts has been won by G Clews (177) of Quarrington Hill. Awards are to be presented at a social evening to be held at Thornley on 12 April.

Monday's results: **Darts**: Quarrington Hill 2 Thornley 1; Coxhoe 2 Wheatley Hill Constitutional 1; Haswell 0 Wheatley Hill Soldiers and Sailors 3; **Dominoes:** Quarrington Hill 2 Thornley 0; Coxhoe 2 Wheatley Hill Cons 0; Haswell 2 Wheatley Hill S & S 0.

444

FINAL TABLES

DARTS	P	W	L	P
Thornley	24	20	4	55
Quarrington Hill	24	21	3	52
Coxhoe	24	16	8	43
Haswell	24	11	13	32
Wheatley Hill S&S	24	6	18	27
Wheatley Hill Constit	24	5	19	23
Cassop	24	5	19	20

Dominoes	P	W	L	D	P
Quarrington Hill	24	13	6	5	31
Thornley	24	14	8	2	30
Coxhoe	24	14	9	1	29
Wheatley Hill Constit	24	12	10	2	26
Cassop	24	11	12	1	23
Haswell	24	6	15	4	15
Wheatley Hill S&S	24	6	16	2	14

25 March 1955

WHEATLEY HILL FELLOWSHIP
DR SOPER AT THE COMING OF AGE CELEBRATIONS

When he visited Church Street Methodist Church, Wheatley Hill, on Friday night in connection with the coming-of-age celebrations of Wheatley Hill Young People's Fellowship, Dr Donald Soper, former President of the Methodist Conference, said the visit gave him particular pleasure because of his "long and deep" friendship with the founder of the Fellowship, Mr Jack Harrison.

It was around the fireside in the kitchen of the home of Mr and Mrs Harrison one Sunday evening 21 years ago that the Fellowship was founded. Young people of all denominations, not only from Wheatley Hill, but also from the surrounding villages, continued to meet at the Harrisons' home after attending Sunday evening worship at their own churches, and from that day to this not once has the weekly meeting been cancelled. Often Mr Harrison's home was packed to the door, and eight years ago it became necessary, because of the ever-increasing membership, to transfer the Fellowship to the Church Street Methodist Church, where the Sunday meetings have since been held.

Purpose of Dr Soper's visit was to address the first of a series of special meetings the Fellowship is holding during the next three months to mark its coming-of-age. The church was filled to capacity, with the Fellowship members occupying the choir stalls, and Dr Soper had many pertinent comments to make on various topics.

Both Archbishops

Referring to his remarks earlier in the week about the Archbishop of York and the hydrogen bomb, Dr Soper declared he was "quite prepared" to include the Archbishop of Canterbury in what he had said. "I don't mind people talking about the deterrent use of atomic bombs if they derive what they say from the Christian faith they possess", he said. "What does really bother me is Christians making speeches as Christians that could just as well have been made by agnostics!".

"I am so frightened that we parsons are not quite so honest in our pulpits as scientists are in their laboratories", went on the former Methodist President. "I am so anxious that what I say in the pulpit about the Bible or Christianity will not be contradicted by what my children or your children hear in their schools from their teachers. Not that science can overthrow religion – of course it can't!"

Out Into The World

The Reg Noel Catherall, resident Methodist minister who, with another official of the Church Street church, Mr Maurice Nixon, has given valuable assistance with the leadership of the Fellowship during recent years, presided and thanked Dr Soper for his inspiring address.

Telling the congregation of members of the Fellowship who had gone out into the world as missionaries, doctors, nurses and ministers, Mr Catherall said that two were now serving in a leper colony in Africa and another in a Methodist School in the same country.

"All these young people were inspired for Christian services at the Fellowship meetings", said Mr Catherall. "I think it is particularly challenging to say that the Fellowship is entirely devotional – and yet Sunday by Sunday there have been upwards of 80 or 90 young people who have met together in this church."

(We have omitted some of Dr Soper's speech as it is not necessary for the purpose of our book. The full speech can be seen at DCRO).

DURHAM MINERS FAVOUR THE AGREEMENT

Although some lodges had been critical of certain aspects of the agreement, delegates representing miners, enginemen and mechanics of the Durham coalfield voted by a big majority in favour of accepting the agreement reached between the NUM and NCB for a new wage structure for the mining industry. Mr Sam Watson, area secretary, NUM, explained the proposals at a meeting quoting the wages suggested for various grades. He answered questions before the vote was taken.

Afterwards, Mr Watson told our reporter, "The majority in favour of acceptance was in the ratio of 20 to one. This decision will now be sent to London, indicating that Durham coalfield has voted for the agreement. Steps can now be taken to put the new structure into effect".

1 April 1955

CLUB HALL OPENED
Dream Comes True at Wheatley Hill

Members of Wheatley Hill Workmen's Club saw the fulfilment of a ten-year dream when a new concert hall, built at a cost of about £12,000, was opened on Saturday.

At the end of the Second World War the suggestion was made that they should seek to extend their building to include a new hall and improved toilet accommodation. Much hard work has been put in by officials and committee.

At Saturday's opening ceremony unstinted praise was given to the "man behind the scenes", 63-year-old Mr Thomas Storey, who retired only in January after 29 years unbroken service as secretary of the club. In presenting a substantial cheque to Mr Storey as a token of appreciation of his services, on behalf of the management committee and members, the new secretary, Mr S Hughes, paid a glowing tribute to the "loyal and devoted" labours of his predecessor.

Praise For Mr Storey

Describing Mr Storey as the sponsor the concert hall project, Mr Hughes declared he was entitled to the full credit. "It was Mr Storey's ambition to see the expansion of the club and tonight I am sure you will agree with me that his ambition has been fully realised!" said Mr Hughes. "Let us hope that as the years go by his ambition will be realised further still as we seek to extend even further".

The idea behind the building of the hall was to give members and their wives the opportunity of "enjoying entertainment and a few hours leisure away from the dull monotony of everyday life". He hoped they would take full advantage of it and that as a result their lives would be brightened and their cares banished.

Mr Storey recalled the progress made by the Club during his long period of office and emphasised the important place a club filled in the life of working men. It was not just a case of coming to the club for beer, but for fellowship, comradeship and the brotherhood of man. Club-life offered many opportunities, especially for the younger members, and he hoped full advantage would be taken of them.

Vicar Attends Hall Opening

The doors of the new hall were opened by the Chairman of the Club, Mr Thomas Cowie, who was supported by Mr Robert Blythe, president of the County Club Union. Also present were Mr Stan Hall, county secretary, Mr Sid Lavers and Mr Harry Barrass, chairman and secretary, respectively, of the Northern Clubs Federated Brewery, Mr G Stainsby (architect) and Mr W Tomlin (contractor). Other guests at a luncheon preceding the opening, included the Rev. Arthur Preston (Vicar of Wheatley Hill), Mr J L Snaith, manager of Wheatley Hill Colliery, Mr F Simpson, Undermanager, Dr McLean and Mrs F Williams, the steward-ess of the club for 20 years until her retirement a year ago.

Club life, declared Mr Stan Hall, addressing the packed hall, was very much more than just bricks and mortar, no matter now magnificent or imposing the building.

In this "cock-eyed world" of ours today, went on Mr Hall, all sorts of people were seen divorcing themselves from society, travelling around in "their own little closed shops" and having little contact with the man in the street. It was essential to have some means whereby we could keep on a common footing and understand each other's point of view, even though we might disagree with the other person.

Tolerance

"The whole idea of club life", he said, "is summed up in the one word – tolerance. This is not a namby-pamby word. It means what it says. You can have different opinions about politics and different beliefs about religion and have a different way of life. You can be a businessman or a working man, but you can still have something in common with everyone else. If club life does nothing more than provide a reasonably comfortable place where people can meet in a friendly and sociable manner then apart from its other great ideals, it has an important place in the world!"

The Rev. A Preston declared that he felt he should be interested "in all that affects our community life. I should like to congratulate you on this splendid new hall", he added. "It is an asset both to your club and the village and I wish you all every happiness in your club life here".

Thanks to the speakers and all who had taken part were proposed by Mr Gordon Pryor, a member of the county club executive committee and seconded by Mr J Walton, another member of the same committee.

8 April 1955

CUP FOR WHEATLEY HILL

Following the excellent support given to the final of the competition on Wingate Welfare ground on Friday evening, officials of the Wingate Aged Miners' Football Cup have every reason to be highly satisfied. The competition was revived this season after a lapse of many years, and more than a thousand spectators saw the final between the Ferryhill and District League sides, Wheatley Hill Mechanics and Winterton Hospital. By virtue of a 3-2 victory the Mechanics carried off the trophy - it was presented to their captain, Les Goyns, by Coun J Bruce, Chairman of the local Aged Miners' Committee and, viewing the game as a whole, nobody would begrudge them their success. Though Winterton opened well, the Mechanics gradually got on top, and quarter of an hour from the end were winning by three clear goals.

Their opponents, however never gave up. Scoring two goals within ten minutes, their hopes were revived, and they stormed into the attack in a do-or-die effort to draw level. The Mechanics defence, where right back Betts and centre half, Marley made few mistakes, stood firm, however, and prevented any further scoring.

With the lively ball playing tricks on the hard ground, Wheatley Hill opened shakily but, fiercely though Winterton attacked, they found it difficult to get within shooting distance, and the "Hill" 'keeper, Harry Ainscough, was not unduly troubled. The few real shots that came his way he dealt with capably. Greatest threat from the hospital side came from their left-wing pair, Logstaffe *(sic)* and Greener.

The Mechanics eventually broke away with some well co-ordinated moves and with inside forwards, Goyns and Sid Slack, the inspiration of their attack, it came to Winterton's turn to fall back on defence. Just before half-time Blakemore, leading the Mechanics attack in place of the injured Humes, fastened on to a loose ball and put his side in front with a close-range drive, which left Willans, the Hospital custodian, helpless.

Shortly after the interval Winterton were awarded a penalty for hands, but Aiscough saved brilliantly from Arrowsmith. Wheatley Hill again took command, and after Goyns had shaken the cross-bar with a pile-driver from 35 yards, Blakemore headed in from the rebound to put them two up. When, after half an hour, Maddison further increased the Mechanics lead from the right wing, the game seemed all but over "bar the shouting".

But Winterton were not yet done! Following a spirited raid on their right they reduced the arrears through Wright – Ainscough got his hands to the ball, but it slipped from his grasp and rolled over the line into the net. This put new life into the Winterton side, for back they came again to score a second goal through Grieves, who smashed the ball into the net after Nicholson had struck the cross-bar.

With only a few minutes left for play anything could have happened. Winterton now had their "tails up" and were all out for the equaliser, but the Mechanics defence remained cool and collected and not another single chance came Winterton's way.

It was a hard-fought game, played sportingly throughout, and a "mention" must be given to the referee, Baxter Golightly, of Blackhall, who controlled it expertly.

The Mechanics after their rather tame beginning always had the measure of their opponents and fully deserved their victory.

TWELVE FOR MECHANICS!

Inspired by their cup success Wheatley Hill Mechanics enjoyed a runaway 12-0 victory over York Hill, whom they visited in the Ferryhill and District League on Saturday – this despite the fact that Ainscough, who normally plays in goal, turned out in the forward line. Benny Nicholson was given a "try-out" between the sticks and dealt efficiently with the few shots that came his way.

No fewer than six of the goals were scored by "Bram" Kelly, who led the "Hill" attack with dash and determination. Bobby Patterson netted a couple, and the other marksmen were Marley, Ainscough, Blakemore and Harris.

(We believe York Hill to be a district of Spennymoor)

THORNLEY DARTS PRESENTATION

The first presentation of trophies won in the Thornley and District Workmen's Clubs' darts and dominoes league took place in the Thornley Workmen's Club on Tuesday night. The clubs which had teams in the League were Thornley, Quarrington Hill, Coxhoe, Wheatley Hill Constitutional, Wheatley Hill D and DS, Haswell Plough and Cassop. All were represented at the presentation.

Mr James Quinn, Chairman of Thornley Club, presided and was supported by Mr F Arkwright of Coxhoe (league chairman), Mr Sid White of Thornley (league secretary); Mr F Crangle of Haswell Plough (league treasurer) and Mr T Wetherell (Thornley club secretary). Mr W Coxon of Sunderland presented the awards.

In the dominoes section of the league the winners were Quarrington Hill and their captain Mr F Carruthers received the Northern Echo Cup. In the darts section Mr Paul Smith (captain) received he Vaux Cup on behalf of Thornley Club. Mr G Clewes of Quarrington Hill club received the Milburn Medal for the highest individual score (177) in darts.

Miniatures

Miniature cups to Thornley players who had taken part in the tournament were handed to J Hoole, J Morland, J Ryan, T Millington, L Williamson, H Darby, R Forster, J Webb, J Hill, A Mole, J Dale, J Orton, D Taylor.

The Quarrington Hill captain thanked all the clubs for the part they had played in making that presentation possible. All the games had been played in the friendliest spirit. The Thornley captain spoke in similar terms. "To the losers better luck next time", he added.

Mr Coxon, who was thanked by the Chairman and Mr Arkwright called for a round of applause for the league officials and this was readily given. The chairman said he felt sure that more clubs would join the competitions.

Entertainment was provided by the Kitto Trio (Messrs E Kitto, jnr, J Boyle, J Kime), Mrs M Onion, Mr F Walker and Mr A Dove.

15 April 1955

CELEBRATIONS AT WHEATLEY HILL

On an Easter Monday afternoon 50 years ago two couples, who have spent the greater part of their married life in Wheatley Hill, were married in churches more than 100 miles apart. Neither couple knew the other, but later, when they came to live at Wheatley Hill, a common love for voluntary charitable work brought them together, and they soon became firm friends. Even then they did not realise they had been married on the same day – and at exactly the same time! Only a chance remark in a local shop ten years ago revealed this remarkable coincidence.

The couples who live within a few hundred yards of each other at Wheatley Hill, celebrate their golden weddings on Sunday. They are Mr and Mrs Peter Tyson of 14 Patton Crescent and Mr and Mrs Robert Taylor of 7 Greenhills Terrace. The Tysons are holding a celebration party at the home of their only daughter, Mrs Walter Baxter, Quilstile Road, Wheatley Hill and the Taylors too, are having a party for their relatives and friends at their own home.

"It was by the merest chance", Mrs Taylor told our reporter this week, "That we learned we had been married the same day. Mrs Tyson and I were in a chemist's shop at Wheatley Hill when she happened to say that she and her husband were celebrating their wedding anniversary that week. That was ten years ago. I told her my husband and I were also celebrating our anniversary – it was quite exciting when further conversation revealed the fact that we had both been married on 24 April, 40 years before!"

Married At Keswick

Both couples have been actively associated with Wheatley Hill Over-60 Club since its formation early last year. Mr Taylor is Chairman of the Club and both his wife and Mrs Tyson serve on the committee – Mrs Tyson as doorkeeper. All four enjoy quite good health and often their village activities bring them together.

Mr and Mrs Tyson were married at the parish church of St John's in the Vale, near Keswick. "Although it was early spring, it was like a mid-simmer's day!" recalled Mr Tyson, who celebrated his 78th birthday in October and is few months older than his wife – she was 78 in February. "We walked about a mile uphill to the church where we were wed – there were no wedding coaches those days – and then returned to my wife's home for the wedding reception. There was no honeymoon, but I enjoyed a week's holiday from work".

Both Mr and Mrs Tyson are natives of Cumberland, but they have lived in Wheatley Hill for the past 40 years. When he left school at the age of 11 Mr Tyson began "doing odd jobs on the farm," and then three years later got his first real job as a farm worker. He "lived in" with the farmer and his wife and was paid £4.10s a half year. By the time he was 21 he was earning between £10 and £11 a half year, but later he gave up farm work to begin employment at some steel works at Workington about the time of his marriage. "I got 24s a week at the works", said Mr Tyson, "and out of this we had to pay 4s.3d rent and rates".

A few years later the works closed down, whereupon Mr Tyson and his wife moved from Workington to Silecroft, near Millom, where he became groom-gardener to a local squire – Squire Walker. After five years in the Squire's service he left Cumberland for Wheatley Hill, where he carried out similar duties for the manager of the local colliery, Mr Matthew Barrass. For 19 years Mr Tyson served Mr Barrass, and then continued as groom-gardener for the manager's successor, Mr Joseph A Simpson, for seven years. "I then gave up gardening", said Mr Tyson, "and spent the last seven years of my working career in the powder house at the colliery, retiring when I was 71".

During the first world war, Mr Tyson werved for three years in the East Yorkshire Regiment. Most of the time he was abroad, in Macedonia.

Mr and Mrs Tyson have an only daughter and one grand-daughter. Their son-in-law, Mr Walter Baxter is a well-known local photographer. Their only son, Thomas Moffat Tyson was fatally injured in an accident Wheatley Hill Colliery 29 years ago, shortly before his 20th birthday – was crushed by a set of tubs.

Mr and Mrs Taylor

And what about the varied activities of Mr and Mrs Taylor? This couple who, like Mr and Mrs Tyson, are held in the highest esteem in the village have lived in Wheatley Hill since 1921, moving there from Easington Lane. All their life has been spent in East Durham. Both are 72 years of age, only a few months separating their birthdays. They were married at Houghton-le-Spring Wesleyan Methodist Church and they too, have had a strong link with Methodism.

Before he was 21 Mr Taylor was Sunday School Superintendent at Easington Lane Wesleyan Methodist Church where his wife was also a Sunday School teacher, and since coming to Wheatley Hill they have been associated with the Patton Street Methodist Church.

At the age of 12 Mr Taylor began work as a trapper-boy at Eppleton colliery, earning 1s.1d per day. Later he continued his mining career at Elemore colliery and became a fully qualified ambulance man. Shortly after the outbreak of the First World War he was one of the two members chosen from Hetton Ambulance Brigade to work in the St John Ambulance Hospital at Eataples in France. After two-and-a-half years' service there he went into the fighting line and shortly before the Armistice was severely wounded in the lungs. He spent nine months in hospital, before being discharged, and when he returned to Elemore pit found the work too heavy.

Mr Taylor hade to give up mining but soon found a new vocation, becoming one of the pioneers of a 'bus company, in the area, which ran a shuttle service between Thornley railway station and the neighbouring villages. "Four of us formed the one-'bus company", reminisced Mr Taylor, "and for a few years were kept quite busy. There were trains in and out of Thornley all day and our transport was more than welcomed to carry passengers to and from the station".

Eventually, however, a bigger 'bus company took over and Mr Taylor became an inspector the G & B 'Bus Company, filling this position for some 20 years until his retirement seven years ago. He made many friends in this capacity, becoming a familiar figure right along the different routes.

Keen Sportsman

All his life Mr Taylor has been a keen follower of sport – and in his younger days was particularly well-known as a cricketer in the Hetton area. He played for Hetton Lyons for many years and captained the side which won the Mid-Durham League in 1911. He and his wife were also two of the founders of the Tennis Club there and soon won considerable local fame in mixed doubles tournaments.

Mrs Taylor was born in Wingate but went to Easington Lane as a girl of 12. Like Mrs Tyson, she was one of the founder-members of the joint Wheatley Hill and Thornley WI and served on the committee of the Wheatley Hill branch when it was formed. Throughout her life she, too, has devoted much of her time to working for various charitable objects and at Wheatley Hill has been connected with many local organisations and committees.

On the outbreak of the Second World War Mrs Taylor took refresher courses in nursing and ambulance, gaining her medallion, and did her full share of voluntary service. She joined the staff of the ambulance station set up in Front Street, Wheatley Hill, and while she was on duty there during an air-raid warning her husband patrolled the streets as a Special Constable.

Both Mr and Mrs Taylor find happy recreation in a game of bowls at the local Welfare Park. Mr Taylor is chairman of the men's section and his wife, as recently as last season played in the women's bowls team. Mr Taylor is also a prominent Freemason, having been a member of the Caradoc Lodge at Castle Eden for the past 24 years – he attained the high distinction of Worshipful Master during the year 1946-47.

Mr Taylor is one of a family of six brothers and sisters whose average age is 78 – a seventh member of the family, Mr William Taylor died only last week at the age of 76.

Mr and Mrs Taylor have no family, but they will have quite a number of their relatives and friends at the celebration party on Sunday. That both they and Mr and Mrs Tyson may enjoy many more years of happiness and good health together is the golden wish of their countless friends throughout the area.

22 April 1955

FIREMAN AT WHEATLEY HILL

The twelve part-time fireman (all miners) who man the Wheatley Hill station came into their own on Thursday night. Since the war they and their appliances have been housed in two old cottages, now falling into decay. Their new centrally heated station provides them with a recreation room and a room for drying wet uniforms. The officer in charge (Mr Poulson) has an office to himself. This new station works in conjunction with the Peterlee and Durham City stations. It will serve Wheatley Hill and other mining villages in the immediate district.

Costing about £5,500, it is a compromise, by order of the Home Office, between a temporary and a more costly permanent building, but is substantial enough for a good many years. Its fire-fighting appliances are, of course, all modern. When one dials 999 for the brigade the call goes through to Durham, and the pressing of a button there calls the spare-time firemen in their homes, besides setting the local siren going.

DINNER – Members of Thornley branch of the Durham County Colliery Deputies' Association held their second annual dinner on Saturday at The Grand Hotel, West Hartlepool. Mr George Johnson presided. Guests included Mr J Brighton, BEM, President of the County Association, Mr James Hesler, Undermanager of Thornley Colliery and several retired members of the branch. In welcoming the guests Mr Johnson made particular reference to their old members who in the past had done so much towards making such social gatherings possible. He was sorry that all the members had not been able to attend. Taking part in entertaining the company were Messrs L Ellwood, T Tunney, G Champley, A Dove, J Brighton, W Parker and J Sandywell (pianist).

29 April 1955

PRESENTATION TO MR JACK HODGSON
Newsagents' Secretary for 35 Years

Members of the Durham branch of the National Federation of Newsagents, at a dinner at The Redhills Hotel, Durham, on Monday night, presented a gold watch to Mr Jack Hodgson (Wheatley Hill) in appreciation of 35 years devoted service as secretary of the branch.

Mr John Barrass (Hetton) chairman of the branch, made the presentation.

Appreciation of his work as a trade union organiser and negotiator were expressed by Mr S L Blair, general manager of the Durham County Press; Mr Harry Bousefield (Easington Lane), president of the North East District Council of Newsagents; Mr Franck Ferguson (Shildon), Secretary of the NE District Council of Newsagents and Mr John Barrass.

Mrs J Barrass presented Mrs J Hodgson with a dressing table petite-point set and Mr Blair handed a travelling clock to Mr Hodgson.

Mr Hodgson, a founder member of Durham branch, has been secretary for 35 years and served on the District Council and District Executive for 33 years, National Council for nine years and the Newsagents' Convalescent Home Committee for the past five years.

After dinner, entertainment was provided by Margaret Tulip (soprano), Tom Featonby (bass), Dave Mendel (entertainer) and Fred Watt (pianist)

6 May 1955

FINED –Simon H Hedley (35) of 5 The Avenue, Wheatley Hill, was charged with parking his van in a prohibited area in North Road, Durham, on 31 March. In a letter to the court he said he had pulled in behind a stream of cars. He was fined 10s.

MISS WHEATLEY HILL

Miss Freda Bradwell, a 16 year old clerk employed by a West Hartlepool firm, was chosen "Miss Wheatley Hill" at a well-attended "Beauty Queen" dance in the Embassy Ballroom, Wheatley Hill, on Saturday night, organised by Mr Gilbert Oliver, entertainments manager at Easington Rural Council's holiday lido at Crimdon. Miss Bradwell, who is the only daughter of Mr and Mrs G Bradwell, 17 Durham Street, Wheatley Hill, was presented with a prize of £2. Representing her village, she will now compete against other village "Queens" from the Easington Rural Area at Crimdon on August Bank Holiday Monday for the title of "Miss Crimdon 1955". Chosen runner-up was Miss Marian Smith (17), second daughter of Mr and Mrs S Smith, 34 Liddell Terrace, Wheatley Hill, who is employed as a shop assistant at Wheatley Hill branch of the Sherburn hill Co-operative Society. She was presented with a prize of £1. The judges were Coun R W Rowe (Shotton Colliery), chairman of the Rural Council Parks Committee, and his wife, and Coun and Mrs Gharters (Haswell) and the prizes were presented by Miss Valerie Johnson, daughter of Coun J Johnson, a Wheatley Hill representative of the Rural Council. Mr Oliver was compere and music was provided by the Embassy Dance Band.

13 May 1955

THORNLEY WELFARE FUNCTION

Members of the Thornley Miners' Welfare sports club were congratulated on their season's successes at a function presided over by Coun J Williams. Others who complimented the teams were Messrs D Hesler (under-manager of Thornley Colliery), E Carter (Chairman of the Miners' Lodge) and W Henderson (Welfare Secretary).

"We are here to show our appreciation", said Mr Williams. "This is the first year for the lads. Probably they will do better in the future".

Mr Hesler said, "We on the Welfare Committee are very proud". Apparently having the recent heavyweight boxing championship match in mind he suggested it might be a good idea for the Committee "to buy a goat to teach the boxers the butting game".

On behalf of the players, Mr John Watson thanked the Welfare Committee for the ready assistance they had given.

AWARDS

Senior snooker team (L Williamson, J Watson, E Dawson, T Alderson, H Taylor, G Wake, S Dickinson), winners of NCB No 3 Area tournament, and semi-finalists of the Divisional competition, L Williamson was individual champion of the snooker section of the Northern Amateur Billiards and Snooker League.

Senior billiards team (J Lennox, J McCoy, G Wake, J Watson, L Williamson) runners-up in Northern Billiards League and runners-up in No 3 Area competition. Best break in League by J Watson (102).

Junior billiards team (W Connelly, W Convery, R Dawson, J Morton). Winners of No 3 area competition and narrowly defeated in Divisional final. W Convery made break of 43.

Boxing. In the National Association of Boys' Clubs boxing competition, Ken Harvey (aged 16) was runner-up of all England and Wales. Beaten on points in final. Awarded trophy. A Kirby won the novices competition (seniors) in NCB Durham Divisional Competition.

There was an excellent display of trophies and prizes. The players presented Mr W Henderson (secretary), with a case of knives and forks.

WHEATLEY HILL VICTORIES

Both Wheatley Hill teams met with success in the Coast League on Saturday,. The first eleven collected maximum points for the first time this campaign with an easy home win over South Hetton – they nearly doubled the visitors score – while the second eleven, visiting South Hetton seconds, won by 17 runs.

A bright half century by their "skipper" Jack Martin, opening with George Allison, put the "Hill" well on the way to victory against South Hetton at the Welfare Park. Martin hit seven 4's. 89 runs were on the board before Wheatley Hill lost their fourth wicket but later wickets fell much more cheaply, the innings finishing at 108. Soakell was best of the visitors four bowlers, with six wickets for 19.

South Hetton's opening pair put on 17 before being separated, out against the deadly bowling of Allison, the succeeding batsmen found runs at a premium and they could only muster 56. Allison took eight wickets for 14 – seven of his victims were clean bowled and his last seven wickets, in a devastating spell, cost only three runs. Martin had one wicket for 20 and Chisholm one for 22. Details:

WHEATLEY HILL

G Allison	c Siddle	b Soakell	1
J K Martin	c Batey	b Soakell	50
D Alderton	b Soakell		4
H Simpson	Run Out		2
D Chisholm	Run Out		21
D Straughan	lbw	b Siddle	2
J Jordan	c Dickenson	b Anderson	9
E Simpson	b Soakell		0
A Fishwick	b Soakell		4
A Brierley	Not Out		1
T Clish	b Soakell		0
Extras			4
Total			**108**

SOUTH HETTON

W Short	lbw	b Chisholm	8
D Siddle	b Allison		0
J Dickinson	b Martin		13
D Soakell	c H Simpson	b Allison	8
A Anderson	b Allison		1
E Gray	b Allison		3
G Stewart	b Allison		5
H Batey	b Allison		8
R Richardson	b Allison		0
A Rogers	b Allison		1
J Laidler	Not Out		9
Extras			0
Total			**56**

After compiling 92 against South Hetton Second 11, Wheatley Hill Second 11 sent the home team back for 75, despite the fact that Hetton's opening bat, Hughes, had 27 to his credit.

Chief contributors to the "Hill" total were R Patterson (18), T Hall (17) and K Farn (17). Six wickets were taken by W Hutton for 34 runs while D Soakell took three for 26.

459

Bowling honours for Wheatley Hill went to Bobby Patterson, who took three wickets for only ten runs. T Hall, R Clish and G Carr had two wickets each for 14, 15 and 18 runs respectively.

27 May 1955

WHEATLEY HILL IMPROVEMENT

Strangers – and even local people themselves – are having difficulty finding an address in the colliery streets near Wheatley Hill cricket ground which run at right angles to the main road through the village.

The streets are named after towns and areas, such as Weardale Street, Stanhope Street, Durham Street and York Street, but with the absence of name plates at the end of each street, the postman was about the only person able to find his way about! But no longer will visitors have to knock at a door and ask the householder the name of the street. Wooden name plates have now been affixed – this will be to the mutual satisfaction of everybody!

OVER-60 CLUB – Mr P Moore presided over an attendance of 172 at a meeting of Thornley Over-60 Club. A vote of condolence was accorded to the relatives of two members, Mrs S Hoban and Mr W Davison, who have died since the previous meeting. Birthday greetings were given to Mrs J T Luke and Mr H Cowton. Messrs R Oswald, F Walker, N Iddon, Mrs B Bosomworth and Mr B Murray (pianist), provided entertainment. Mrs E Brownless also contributed. A prize given by Mrs Ainsley was won by Mrs P Lloyd and Mrs Heale.

WVS – Presiding at a meeting at Thornley, held for the purpose of forming a branch of the Women's Voluntary Services, Coun Mrs F M Peart said the Easington RDC was giving the movement its support and that she had been invited by County Headquarters to arrange the meeting. Miss Ainsley, West Hartlepool spoke on the work of the WVS. Mesdames Peart, H Slater, B Bosomworth, Carter, Taylor and E Brownless expressed their willingness to join.

MISS THORNLEY CHOSEN

At a beauty queen dance in Thornley Miners' Welfare Hall on Friday night, organised by Mr Gilbert Oliver, entertainments manager at Easington Rural Council's holiday lido at Crimdon, an 18-year-old factory worker, Miss Alice Stokoe of 13 Shinwell Crescent, Thornley, was chosen "Miss Thornley". She was presented with a prize of £2 and will now compete against other village "Queens" from the Easington Rural area at Crimdon on August Bank Holiday Monday for the title of "Miss Crimdon 1955". Chosen runner-up to Miss Stokoe was Miss Mary Stephenson aged 20 of 4 Thornlaw North, Thornley. Coun R W Rowe, Shotton Colliery, recently elected vice-chairman of Easington Rural Council and Mr Oliver were the judges, and the prizes were presented by Coun Mrs Peart, a local member of the Rural Council. Dance music was by the Embassy Dance Band.

10 June 1955

GOLDEN WEDDING
Celebration at Wheatley Hill

Esteemed in Wheatley Hill, where they have lived most of their married life, Mr and Mrs Ernest Rose, 28 Peter Lee Cottages, have celebrated their golden wedding. They were married in Holy Trinity Church, Wingate, and both still enjoy quite good health.

Mr Rose, who looks much younger than his 75 years, is a native of Aycliffe. His working career began at the age of 13 when he helped his father, a drainer in the fields. About 40 years ago he took up mining as a career – he was a sinker at Blackhall Colliery – and continued to work in the pits until his retirement at Thornley colliery at the age of 69.

Keen Gardener

Gardening now helps to fill in Mr Rose's0 spare time and both front and back gardens neat and trim are tribute to his work. "I put many a full shift in the garden in summer-time from nine o'clock in the morning until nine at night and I enjoy every minute of it" he told our reporter.

Mrs Rose, born at Hesleden, is 70. She does all her own housework and retains a bright and cheery outlook on life. Both she and her husband have a long and active association with All Saints Church, Wheatley Hill, where they were formerly members of the Church Council. Mr Rose is still a sidesman there and his wife a regular attender at the Mothers Union.

The couple have two sons and two daughters, all living in the area, and there are seven grandchildren. Their sons, Charles and Ernest, are in business at Wheatley Hill as painters and decorators.

17 June 1955

RABBIT FANCIER'S SUCCESS - Exhibiting three young Dutch rabbits, black, blue and grey, at the North Eastern Counties Dutch Rabbit Club young stock show at Stockton on Saturday, Mr George Ford, Wingate Lane, Wheatley Hill, a well-known rabbit fancier, won eleven firsts and five challenge cups as well as the prize for the best exhibit in the show.

GARDEN PARTY – A good company turned up for the annual Church Street Methodist Sisterhood garden party in the grounds of Weardale House, by permission of Mr and Mrs J L Snaith. Mrs P H Galley, sen, was organising secretary. The party was opened by Mrs A Gillett. Musical items included a solo and chorus by Mrs Jean Lang and the Sisterhood choir; and a quartet by Mr and Mrs Harold Lang, Mr Donald Lang and Miss Bessie Galley. The bran tub was in charge of Mrs J Hughes, a bring-and-buy stall in charge of Mrs W Hodgson and a gift stall manned by Mrs G Venables. Sisterhood members provided and served tea. About £15 was raised for Sisterhood funds.

MINERS' HOLIDAYS - Blackpool was again the most popular holiday destination for Wheatley Hill miners and their families when they began their annual fortnight's holiday last weekend. Many 'buses left the village for the Lancashire resort, though some holidaymakers went further afield to the south coast and to Scotland and Ireland. London was also a popular venue for some families and one party went as far as Cornwall. The local schools were on holiday and the stay-at-homes found enjoyment by joining day trips to resorts in the North-East or making the short journey to Crimdon lido, where some families booked camping sites. On Tuesday ten 'buses took some 200 scholars and about the same number of adults from All Saints Church on their annual outing to South Shields, where the sun shone all day and a most enjoyable time was spent. The arrangements were made by the Vicar of Wheatley Hill, Rev Arthur Preston. Members of the 2nd Wheatley Hill Troop of Boy Scouts spent this week in camp at Haltwhistle.

GOLDEN WEDDING
Wheatley Hill Couple's Celebration

Among the presents received by a Wheatley Hill couple, Mr and Mrs Thomas Frederick Williams of 10 Fifth Street, when they celebrated their golden wedding on Friday, was a beautiful bouquet from their youngest daughter, Esther, who lives in Holland. Their daughter, who met her husband, a Dutchman, while she was nursing in London during the last war, now lives at Delft.

Altogether Mr and Mrs Williams, who have lived in Wheatley Hill for the past 36 years, have living four sons and five daughters, 14 grand-children and two great-grand-children. All their family are married with the exception of one son, Robert, who lives with them. The couple who were married at Durham, both enjoy quite good health.

Hewing for 4½D a Ton

A retired miner, Mr Williams, who will be 77 next month, can recall the early days of his career when fellow workmen were hewing coals for 4½d a ton. "That," he told our reporter, "was when I was working as a putter at Heworth Colliery in Northumberland – and, mind you, the hewers then were filling up to a hundred tubs a shift for it was just like shovelling coal off a duff heap. Later at Thornley Colliery I have hewed coals myself for 1s.2½d a ton!"

Mr Williams was born in Gloucestershire but came North as a boy and began work at Coxlodge Colliery in Northumberland at the age of 14, earning tenpence a shift as a trapper-boy. Later he worked at a number of different pits in Northumberland and Durham before going to Thornley Colliery 53 years ago, and he has filled most jobs underground. He continued his career at Thornley Colliery until his retirement when he was 65. For 17 years he travelled there from Haswell Plough.

Mrs Williams, whose maiden name was Jane Anderson, was born at Sacriston 70 years ago, but spent her younger days until her marriage at Ushaw Moor, where she still has a number of relations. She has always led an active and busy life. "There was always plenty of work to do bringing up such a big family", she said,.

To mark their golden wedding anniversary the couple held a quiet family party at their home on Sunday.

24 June 1955

A CO-OPERATIVE PIONEER
Funeral of Mr Anthony Cairns

A Wheatley Hill man who had a 50 years association with the Co-operative movement until his retirement four years ago – he rose to be general manager of the Sherburn Hill Co-operative Society from being an apprentice at the society's first branch – was cremated at Sunderland on Tuesday.

He was Mr Anthony Cairns, Vernon House, Woodlands Avenue, who died suddenly on Sunday, his 69th birthday. Mr Cairns had enjoyed to the full his well-earned retirement and kept quite good health – only the day before his death, after being unwell for about a week, he was pottering about in the garden that he loved. He was taken suddenly ill that same night and died shortly afterwards.

Mr Cairns, whose death breaks a married partnership of 45 years, leaves a widow, two married daughters and one grand-daughter.

The First Apprentice

One of a family of eight born at Sherburn Hill, Mr Cairns won a Labour certificate at the Bluecoat School, Durham, and began working at the local colliery when he was only 12. He was them employed for a short spell at Chopwell Colliery, but when he was 15 became the first apprentice at the first branch of the Sherburn Hill Co-operative Society opened at Shotton Colliery. The branch at that time consisted of a single dwelling house.

Mr Cairns became one of the society's pioneers at Wheatley Hill, and at the age of 24 was appointed foreman at Sherburn Hill branch. He rose to be branch manager there and then filled a similar position for some six years at Wheatley Hill before being appointed to the responsible post of general manager of the whole society 13 years before his retirement.

On his retirement as general manager, Mr Cairns, at a large gathering of members of the society, was presented with a television set on their behalf, and this had filled in many happy hours for him.

Mr Cairns, after spending his younger days in the Sherburn Hill area, lived in Wheatley Hill for the greater part of his life. His brother, Mr Peter Cairns, has been president of the Sherburn Hill Society since 1939.

24 June 1955

UNTIDY CEMETERY
Complaint to Wingate Parish Church

Complaining about the "untidy state" of the Council's cemetery at Wheatley Hill, at the meeting of Wingate Parish Council, Coun N Cook declared that parts of it were "absolutely lost" for the want of attention. The condition of the cemetery was the cause of general complaint throughout the village, he added. Paths were overgrown with grass and weeds and it was practically impossible to get to some of the graves because of the height of the grass.

"Whether the cemetery is too big or not for one man to look after I don't know", went on Coun Cook, "but it is certainly in a bad way! At one time you could take pride in the cemetery but you cannot now!"

Mr J C Stott, the cemetery superintendent., remarked the Clerk, Mr J Harper, was instructed last year to keep the grass away from the paths. Coun A Bishop said he did not think there was anything "in bloom" at all in the cemetery, and Coun J Fenwick wondered if the Council thought it would be "unreasonable" to have the grass cut twice a year.

Joint Inspection

Coun Cook said it would make the cemetery look a little more "shipshape" if the grass could be cut more often – the grass, at any rate, should be kept away from all the paths.

It was agreed that the Wheatley Hill councillors should make a joint inspection, interview the cemetery superintendent, and report to the next meeting.

Misleading Clock

When Coun R Watson again complained about the unreliability of the public memorial clock in Wheatley Hill's Front Street, the Clerk said the matter had been taken up with the manufacturers, who said that the trouble was caused by the big variation in electrical current in the village. The clock had been stopped for some time, said Coun Watson, while Coun Fenwick said that even when it was going it was always showing wrong time.

"If you had to depend entirely on the clock you would not know whether it was night or morning!" declared Coun J H Charlton. For what good the clock was it might as well be "scrapped", commented Coun Cook.

It was decided that the Clerk should investigate the matter further.

CLUB COMMITTEE – From 36 nominations, Messrs G Henderson jun, who topped the poll with 137 votes, T Harper, G Cook, W Kears, J Frost and M Cain were elected to the committee of Wheatley Hill Workmen's Club for the ensuing year as a result of a ballot at the weekend.

VETERANS TRIP – Sunshine prevailed throughout the day for the annual outing to Redcar on Tuesday, organised by Wheatley Hill Aged Miners' Homes Committee, for retired miners at the local colliery and their wives and widows over 55. The party of about 400 were conveyed in 11 coaches and a most enjoyable day was spent by the sea. Each tripper received 7s.6d pocket money and in charge of the coaches were officials and members of the committee.

OVER-60 CLUB – Because many of the members were away on the annual retired miners' trip, Wheatley Hill Over-60 Club made their weekly meeting on Tuesday an "Open Night." Mr R Taylor presided and an excellent entertainment, consisting of choruses, duets, solos and sketches, was given by the Ushaw Moor Over-60 Club concert party. Mr J Deighton was compere and leader and Miss E Belshaw accompanist. Taking part were Mesdames Wright, Hurst, Foster, Kennedy, Burns, Race, Dodds, Kelly, Cavanagh, Nicholls, Henderson, Thompson, Deighton, Robson, Towns and Graham, Miss Johnson and Messrs Henderson, Hull, Foster, Wright, Bussey, Crozier and Mawson. Thanks to the party were expressed by the chairman and the entertainments secretary, Mr W Williams. Birthday greetings were extended to Mesdames Woodhead, Robinson and Turton and competition winners were Mesdames, Truscott, Robson, Turton and Harper and Mr J Hammond.

MR W BROWN – MISS A PEACOCK – When Miss Audrey Peacock, youngest daughter of Mr and Mrs H I Peacock, 18 Wheatley Terrace, Wheatley Hill, was married on Saturday to Mr Wesley Brown, youngest son of Mr and Mrs R W Brown, 60 Station Road, Easington Colliery, she was attended by six bridesmaids and a page. The ceremony took place at All Saints' Church, Wheatley Hill, the Vicar 'the Rev Arthur Preston' officiating. The bride, given away by her father, wore a gown of white net over figured taffeta with shawl collar; a full-length embroidered veil surmounted by a pearl headdress. She carried an ivory prayer book and wore a diamante necklace, the gift of the bridegroom. The Misses Barbara Howe and Ann Court (bride's cousin) were bridesmaids and wore dresses of blue taffeta with head dresses to match. They also carried prayer books. Small attendants were Carol Peacock (bride's niece), Margaret Brown, Peterlee (bridegrooms neice), Ann Hodgson (bridegroom's cousin) and Rosaleen Bowes. They all wore dresses of pink taffeta with headdresses to match and carried pink Dorothy bags.

Ronald Peacock (bride's nephew) was page. Best man was Mr Albert Owens. 200 guests attended the reception held in the Miners' Welfare Hall, after which the couple left for Weston-super-Mare.

15 July 1955

DOUBLE WEDDING AT WHEATLEY HILL

The Rev Noel Catherall officiated at a double wedding when two sisters, daughters of Mr and Mrs James Tipling, 13 Stanhope Street, Wheatley Hill, were married in Patton Street Methodist Church. Ada, their fifth daughter was married to Mr Thomas Ashwell, third son of Mr and Mrs M Ashwell, Edlington, Doncaster.

The bride wore a gown of white lace. bodice and net skirt with headdress of diamante and orange blossom and full-length embroidered veil. Miss June Wally (bridegroom's niece), wearing pale blue organdie with headdress to match attended the bride. Enid and Jean Mason (nieces of the bride), were small attendants. They wore dresses of lilac embossed organdie with headdresses to match. William (bridegroom's brother), was best man. The honeymoon is being spent at Rhyl.

The youngest daughter, June, was married to George W eldest son of Mr and Mrs G W Reay, 3 Weardale Street, Wheatley Hill. The bride, like her sister, was given away by her father. She wore white lace and full-length embroidered veil surmounted by a pearl headdress. The bridegroom's sister, Cissie, wearing a dress of lemon organza with headdress to match, was bridesmaid. Small attendants were Margaret and Marjorie Wilkinson, Peterlee (nieces of the bride), wearing dresses of pink embossed organza with headdresses to match.

Mr Thomas Hackworth was best man. A joint reception was held in Patton Street schoolroom attended by 200 guests.

CLUB COMMITTEE – With 90 votes, Mr Harry Syson 'topped the poll' in the ballot of Wheatley Hill Discharged and Demobilised Soldiers and Sailors Club to elect six committee members. Other elected were Messrs G Reay, T Dodds, L Hedley, B Miller and R Burnip. There were 15 nominations.

OVER-60 CLUB – Mr R Taylor presided over the Wheatley Hill Over-60 Club. Members stood in silence as a token of respect for Mr George Charlton, who died recently. Community singing was conducted by Mr C Raffle and birthday greetings were extended to Mrs Norman and Mrs Cammas. Enjoyable entertainment was by Wheatley Hill

Workmen's Club concert party comprising Messrs T Cowie (compere), E Evans (pianist), L Turnbull, W Foster, H Armstrong, Jones and F Walkers, assisted by Mrs Collingwood and |Mr E Edwards. Thanks were expressed by the chairman.. Competition winners were Mesdames Stoddard, Morris, B Bowes and White and Messrs E Barker, G Fawcett, J Hall and J Iveson.

WOMAN BOWLER'S SUCCESS – By reaching the final of the County Women's Bowling Association's four-wood singles, Mrs Edna Hall, 21 Jack Lawson Terrace, Wheatley Hill, who has been secretary of Wheatley Hill Women's Bowls Club since 1950, has qualified to compete in the All-England Women's Championships at Wimbledon during the week beginning 22 August. Mrs Hall meets Mrs Florence Wright, Horden, who will also be taking part in the Wimbledon Championships, in the county final at Durham today. To reach the final, Mrs Hall has fought her way through five rounds – in the semi-final at Cockton Hill on Monday she defeated Mrs Oates, Birtley, by 21 shots to six. It will be Mrs Hall's second appearance at Wimbledon, for she took part in the pairs championship three years ago after being runner-up with Mrs Adwick, West Hartlepool, in the county final. Mrs Hall, chairman of the North Eastern Ladies' Bowling League, has reached the final of the No 3 Area, NCB, pairs tournament with Mrs Hodson of Wheatley Hill and the semi-final of the singles tournament.

29 July 1955

THORNLEY CUP MEETING AT LUDWORTH

When the annual meeting of the Thornley Aged Miners' Cup competition was held at Ludworth on Saturday, it was stated by the secretary, Mr C Campbell, that the sum of £73.10s had been handed over to the Thornley Aged Miners' Homes Fund. In addition the Committee had allocated £7.13s to the Durham Football Association Benevolent Fund.

Two sets of trophies had been supplied to the last year's winners and runners-up - Cassop Victoria and Bearpark CW respectively. Over 20 clubs had entered the last year's competition.

Election of officers was as follows: President Mr A Welsh; Chairman, Mr J Hoban; Vice-Chairman, Mr G Briggs; Secretary, Mr Charles Campbell; Assistant Secretary, Mr Colin Campbell.

The meeting passed votes of thanks to the Thornley Band, the Thornley St Godric's Club for the use of the field and the St Godric's Ladies Committee for their assistance.

The secretary asks for entries for the ensuing year's competition which is open to 32 clubs within a radius of 12 miles from Thornley Post Office. The entries should be forwarded to Mr C Campbell, 2 Margaret Street, Ludworth.

LUDWORTH JUNIORS CELEBRATE

A presentation dance was held on Monday in the Ludworth Village Hall at which opportunity was taken to present to the successful players, of the Ludworth Juniors, their trophies won last season.

Mr C Campbell presided and stated that the team were winners of the NE Divisional Cup, the Browney and Meadowfield AP Cup and were joint runners-up in the Durham Junior League.

He added that Ludworth Juniors had won eight trophies in the last three seasons and it was the second time that the Divisional Junior Cup had been won.

Mr J Briggs, vice-president, handed miniature cups to the following players: G Greener, capt, N Graham, L Westgarth, R Appleby, C Smith, S Carr, T Thompson, A Fishwick, J Lowe, D Carr and J Goodchild. In addition a miniature cup from the Browney and Meadowfield Cup Committee was handed to Mr J Foster retiring secretary.

It was a successful dance the MC's for which were Messrs C Campbell and J Morrow. Music was by the Rhythmaires Dance Band.

WHEATLEY HILL BOYS IN CAMP

Most teachers and scholars in Durham County have said "goodbye" for six weeks, but this was not the case at Wheatley Hill Boys' Modern School.

A special 'bus drew up at the school and took on board 40 boys and seven members of the teaching staff. Messrs A Harris (head teacher), E Ward, H Holder, A Stabler, A Jones, L Dent and E Cherry. The party were setting out for a week under canvas at Frosterley in the West of Durham.

Mr Harris said, "Our idea is to take the boys away on a camping holiday, to let them live together in comradeship in other than school conditions. We shall get the most out of this cheap holiday by allowing plenty of time for relaxation and sport in beautiful country. Combined with this free-and-easy life we shall introduce elements of educational value".

Mr Harris stated that there would be a visit to Wolsingham steelworks. It was also intended to visit Tunstall Reservoir and filter beds. Frosterly quarries and lime kilns were to be visited while work is in progress and a trip would be taken to the historic Bollinghope Common.

Games and bathing would also contribute to the pleasures of openair life. Camp sing-songs will be an evening "tit-bit".

The spiritual side of education will not be forgotten. Mr Harris told our correspondent, "The boys will have church parade on Sunday. We shall attend worship in Frosterley Parish Church".

5 August 1955

OVER-60 CLUB –Mr J Hodson presided over about 250 members at the meeting of Wheatley Hill Over-60 Club in the Workmen's Club hall on Tuesday, when excellent entertainment was given by Thornley St Godric's concert party. Miss Scully was accompanist and music was by Mr Jack Toye, Thornley's blind accordionist. Taking part in the programme were Mrs Doris Surman, Marie Hood, Anne Wilson, Anne Atkin, Isabel Luke, Eileen Regan, Veronica and Anne Connolly and Messrs John Quin, Patrick McCoy, Pat Hoban, Robert Orchard, Paul McCoy, John Dickinson, Tom Kimmitt and Vincent Frain. In the absence of Mr John Tunney, Mr W Williams, entertainments secretary, was compere, and thanks to the party were expressed by Mr Hodson. Birthday greetings were extended to Mesdames Taylor, Robson and Bowes and Messrs H Smart and Stoddart. Winners of the "lucky" prizes were Mesdames W Brown, S Kime, R Jackson, R Kilburn and M E Hird and Messrs J Burdon, C Raffell and T Maddison.

FOOTBALLERS' PRESENTATIONS – To celebrate the team winning the Wingate Aged Miners' Cup last season, Wheatley Hill Mechanics Football Club held a dinner and presentation of miniature cups in the Miners' Welfare Hall. Presiding over a company of 100 players, members and friends of the club. Mr Stanley Johnson congratulated the team on winning the cup competition during the first season of its revival. The Mechanics had always proved themselves a force to be reckoned with and, added Mr Johnson, he was extremely sorry that, owing to the difficulty of finding officials to carry on, the club was likely to be disbanded. Miniature cups were presented to the following players by

Mr Fred Simpson, under-manager at Wheatley Hill Colliery: Wilf Goyns (captain), H Ainscough, R Betts, K Bowden, S Bell, G Marley, J Harris, M Maddison, L Blakemore, S Slack, L Raine and J Cowan. The club secretary, Mr John Davies, also received a miniature cup. Mr Simpson added his congratulations and also expressed regret that the club would not be able to carry on next season in local league football. Thanks to the players and all who had given loyal service to the club were expressed by Mr Davies. After dinner entertainment was provided by Mr John Quin, Miss Peggy Lawrence and Mr James Pyle (soloists) and Mr Clem Davison (comedian).

12 August 1955

FORMER THORNLEY MAN
Awarded The British Empire Medal

Sergeant Frederick Charles Greaves (28) of 15 Richard Street, West Hartlepool (a native of Thornley), who is serving in Kenya with the East African Army Service Corps, has been awarded the British Empire Medal by the Queen for rescuing his wife and a 10-year-old girl after his own and an adjoining chalet in Nairobi had been set on fire by Mau Mau terrorists.

The citation appearing in the "London Gazette" states that when the chalet in which Sergeant and Mrs Greaves were sleeping was set on fire early on the morning of 23 October last year, they were unable to escape through the front door because the veranda was burning furiously. Sgt Greaves therefore broke through the wire mesh on a window, pushed his wife through and then escaped himself.

Girl Was Trapped

In the adjoining chalet a 10-year-old girl was trapped and was screaming. Residents of other chalets, who by this time were organising fire-fighting, tried to get the child through the front window, behind which she could be seen, but were beaten back by the heat.

Sgt Greaves, with great presence of mind and at great personal risk, ran round the side of his own burning chalet to a small window at the rear of the room where the girl was trapped. With his bare hands he burst in the window and the protective expanding metal, climbed into the room and pushed the child out into the arms of one of the other residents.

While rescuing the child Sgt Greaves received cuts, second degree burns and lost much blood. He was detained in the British Military Hospital for 10 days.

Disregard Of His Own Safety

"Had it not been for his prompt action, quick thinking and complete disregard for his own safety", states the citation, "the child undoubtedly would have been burned to death". The chalet in which she had been sleeping was completely gutted.

Sgt Greaves, who was brought up at Thornley enlisted in 1948, and has been in Kenya for the last two years. His wife is still with him in the colony. Lieut-General Gerald W Lathbury, Commander-in-Chief, East Africa, has written to Sgt Greave congratulating him on his reward.

LATE MRS M A Carr – a Wheatley Hill widow who, though well turned 60, helped the national effort during the last war by working in a factory at the same time as all her nine sons were in uniform – three in the Army and six in the local Home Guard – was buried at Wheatley Hill cemetery on Saturday. She was Mrs Margaret Ann Carr (75) of 120 Wordsworth Avenue, who had been in failing health for the past few years. Mrs Carr was born at Middlesbrough but had lived in the Wheatley Hill and Thornley area for the greater part of her life – in Wheatley Hill for the past 47 years. While serving in the Army her fourth eldest son, Abraham, who was a regular soldier, was killed in the Middle East in 1942. The other sons in the Army were Christopher and Norman while Alfred, William, Luke, Jack, Herbert and George served in the Home Guard. Mrs Carr's husband, Alfred, died 34 years ago, and she is survived by her eight sons. The funeral service was conducted at "The Rest" by the Rev Noel Catherall and four of Mrs Carr's sons, Christopher, Norman, Herbert and Jack were under-bearers. There was a large cortege.

19 August 1955

CASTLE EDEN MAGISTRATES' COURT - TUESDAY 23 AUGUST 1955
LICENSEE FINED £10
Police Visit a Thornley Inn

When two police officers walked into the buffet of the Three Horse Shoes at Thornley at midnight on 22 June they saw glasses containing beer on the tables and the licensee, her husband and four other men in the room.

The magistrates were told this when the licensee, Maude Prince (34), was fined £10 for supplying intoxicating liquor during non-permitted hours. She pleaded "guilty".

The four men, who admitted consuming intoxicating liquor after hours, were each fined £5. They were Amos Bell (49) of Thornlaw North; Anthony Fahey (22) of Thornlaw South; Charles Anthony Mc-Quaid (40) of The Caravan and Joseph Lax (58) of Thornlaw South, all of Thornley.

"My God!"

Mr Stanley Lambert said Sgt Wright and PC Stokoe were walking along Hartlepool Street about midnight on 22 June when they saw lights in the Three Horse Shoes. They found the rear door open. Inside they saw the licensee's husband who, on seeing the uniforms, exclaimed "My God" and hurried back into the buffet. The officers followed him into the room where they saw his wife and four other men. There were bottles and glasses containing beer on the tables.

Mr Lambert alleged that Mrs Prince said to the policemen, "How did you get in here anyway? I thought the doors were all locked. You can't do anything: they are all my friends and I invited them". Mr Lambert alleged they had all "had plenty to drink" and described the offence as a "flagrant breach of the licensing Act".

Sgt Wright said all the people in the room, including the licensee, were under the influence of drink. There were bottles and glasses containing beer on the tables.

On behalf of Mrs Prince, Mr A N Levinson said the men were all friends of her and her husband. They had had supper with Mr and Mrs Prince in the private premises which adjoined the buffet. After supper because of the heat, they had retired to the buffet for a drink about 11.15pm. Mrs Prince had bought them each two drinks. It was not, in his opinion, a flagrant breach of the Act.

LEGION BIRTHDAY – 130 members and friends of the Thornley women's section of the British Legion celebrated the branch's 30th birthday in the Miners' Welfare Hall. Mrs E Clarke presided at the tea table and welcomed the guests. Guests of honour were Mrs Hedger (County Women's Section Secretary) and Mrs Robson, Fishburn (county representative). Tea was served. A birthday cake was baked and decorated by Mrs J Anderson. Mrs Hedger and Mrs Robson appealed for more generous support for the five rest homes and children's homes sponsored by the British Legion. Tea was followed by games and dancing. MC was Mrs H Slater. Musical items were by Mesdames M Chapmen, M Hobbs, E Middleton, M Mitchell, M Barrass, Misses Irene Horner and Jennie Robson and Mr Jack Toye.

OVER-60's – Mr J Hodgson presided at the weekly meeting of Wheatley Hill Over-60 Club in the Workmen's Club Concert Hall on Tuesday. Mr W Williams, entertainment secretary, conducted community singing and birthday greetings were extended to Mesdames Robson and Rowlands and Mr N Smithson. Mystery prize-winners were Mesdames W Poulson, Farn, Foster, Murray and Richardson. A splendid entertainment was provided by Thornley Legionaires. The programme consisted of choruses, songs, dances etc. Taking part were Mesdames Middleton, Barrass, Mitchell, Sandiwell, Convery and Pluck. Misses Redshaw, Campbell and Walls and Master R Pluck. Compere was Mrs B Bosomworth and the piano-accordionist Mr Jack Toye. Mr J Hodgson thanked the party, supported by Mr Williams. Mrs Bosomworth replied on behalf of the visitors.

26 August 1955

DEATH OF MR J H C SCOTT
Big Loss to Public Life

A Justice of the Peace and Chairman of the Juvenile Court at Castle Eden, Mr James Hamilton Christison Scott died on Monday afternoon at his home, Glenside, Thornley, after an illness of about four months. He was 62.

Prominent in the North-East as a Methodist, he was lay representative of the Sunderland and District Methodist Conference, and a member of the Sunderland and Durham Synod. He attended the London Conference last year and entertained the Sunderland and Durham Synod when they were in conference at Thornley some months ago. Like his parents, he late Mr and Mrs J T Scott, he regularly attended Waterloo Street Church at Thornley and had held several offices there and in the local circuit.

Member Of Council

A former member of Easington Rural District Council, he had also sat on Thornley Parish Council and was elected again this year but his illness prevented him from taking his seat.

A member of West Hartlepool Rotary Club, he served a term as president. Interested in the National Savings campaign, he was Chairman of the Easington South Committee. He served as a lieutenant with the Northumberland Fusiliers in the First World War and was mentioned in despatches. During the last war he was a leading special constable and chairman of Thornley Soldiers' Comforts Committee, afterwards becoming treasurer of the War Memorial Committee.

He was head of the firm of J T Scott and Sons, with drapery branches at Thornley, Wheatley Hill and Langley Park and a wholesale department centred at Thornley.

He leaves a widow but no family. Mrs Scott is president of the Thornley WI.

The Funeral

Thornley Waterloo Street Methodist church was crowded to capacity on Wednesday afternoon for the funeral service. The business, religious and social life of South-East Durham was widely represented.

The service was conducted by the superintendent minister, Rev George H Ireland. The prayers were taken by the Rev Harry Allen (secretary of the Sunderland and Durham District) and an address was given by the Rev John Crawford (District Chairman).

The hymns "O Love that wilt not let me go" and "Guide me O though great Jehovah" were sung. Cremation followed at West Hartlepool.

Mr Crawford said, "It is indicative of the esteem in which James Scott was held to see this large company of business colleagues, representative of the Church and social life of the district, gathered to pay tribute to one who was so greatly honoured and widely loved. His life held a two-fold emphasis; it was dedicated to the service of Christ and to his fellow men. He possessed a record of social service of which any man might be justifiably proud". Mr Crawford continued, "As parish and rural district councillor and as a magistrate, Mr Scott sought to promote the social wellbeing of the community. He often gave wise advice to people and boys and girls in all these capacities. James Scott carried his Christianity into the practice of his citizenship".

The minister continued, "Educated at Woodhouse Grove School, Mr Scott was proud of the Methodist tradition and sought by every means in his power to serve the Church he loved. He made a real contribution to Methodism in the Sunderland and Durham District and throughout the Connexion. He was a man of great generosity. He knew the meaning of the word, 'stewardship'. One of the most beautiful things about him was not so much the generous deeds he did, but the way in which he did them.

"Mr Scott had a lovable personality, possessed kindly good humour and had a real genius for friendship. The secret of his personality however, lay in something deeper than natural endowments. He was at heart a Christian gentleman whose life was consistent with his profession.

9 September 1955

WHEATLEY HILL CLUB
Extensions Cost about £6,000

"Very few people can deny that club life in Durham County is a very virile and fine thing!" declared Mr Stan Hall, secretary of the Durham County Workmen's Club Union and Institute, speaking on Wednesday night at the opening of extensions to Wheatley Hill Discharged and Demobilised Sailors and Soldiers Club which have cost in the region of £6000.

It was a very good thing, continued Mr Hall, for people in a village community to gather together in such a fashion and interest themselves in each other. Club life enabled them to learn the art of living together, it stood for tolerance and understanding. "If you have not got a spirit of tolerance ", the speaker went on, "and do not believe that everyone has the right to express himself and the right to be heard, then you are not going to get very far! The whole principle of club life is to be able to meet in fellowship, understanding and kindly tolerance".

Should Feel Proud

The responsibilities of club life were very simple, first of all they had a responsibility to themselves. "See that you carry on the club in a decent, friendly way" advised Mr Hall. "You also have an outside responsibility to see that nothing you do hinders the enjoyment of any other person who may not agree with your way of life. We believe that club life can be a decent way of life – I myself have found during the past ten years, in Durham County, magnificent changes in the spirit of clubs. The more tolerant you are of each other's feelings, the better you will enjoy your club life and the better will club life become known as one of the finest institutions in this country!"

Opening of new extension to
Wheatley Hill Discharged and Demobilised Sailors and Soldiers Club

Saying he felt "greatly honoured" to be present, Mr J L Snaith, manager of Wheatley Hill colliery, who performed the official opening, said the gathering that night spoke well for the happy relationship existing between the management and workmen at the local colliery.

"It is not so many years since this club was struggling to make ends meet" he added, "and it's a tribute to the work of the officials and committee that they should have been able to build this new hall – they should feel quite proud of their achievements. The days are now past when a man is content to take his refreshments at the bar – he wants comfortable surroundings, and here you certainly have them! The committee have been go-ahead and every credit is due to them".

Entertainment

Mr A Carr, Chairman of the Club, presided over a packed company in the new concert hall, which comprises the main part of the extensions, and thanks to Mr Hall and Mr Snaith were expressed by Mr F Simpson, under-manager at Wheatley Hill Colliery. "I hope you all have very many happy and pleasant times here", Mr Simpson addressed the members, their wives and friends. An excellent entertainment was provided by Mr James Pyle's party, comprising Mr Pyle, Mr R Armstrong, Mrs Peggy Hobbs, Mr W Forster and Mrs Mary Onion. The accompanist was Mr J Cain.

In addition to the new concert hall, which has seating accommodation for 150, the extensions include a secretary's office and new buffet bar. Furniture of the most modern design has been installed, a new piano has been bought and there is an up-to-date system of lighting, heating and ventilation. Renovations, including an extended bar counter and new floor coverings have also been carried out in the club buildings, which was opened in December 1938.

The club was founded by ex-Service men shortly after the end of the 1914-18 War, and in 1920 a wooden building was opened as its first headquarters. There were many "ups and downs" in the club's financial position after this – "I remember at one time we hadn't sufficient money to buy a barrel of beer", an old member recalled, but eventually sufficient money was raised for the premises to be opened in 1938.

Present membership of the club is about 300 and the officials are Messrs A Carr (Chairman), William Hackworth, (Secretary) and A Wood (Treasurer).

16 September 1955

WHEATLEY HILL FIRE TEAM'S SUCCESS

Competing teams were faced with the task of putting out a fire, which had broken out in three places in an improvised coal "seam" at Castle Eden on Saturday, when No 3 Area, Durham Division NCB held a contest for colliery fire brigades in the area. The winners of this "underground" test were Wheatley Hill fire team, who extinguished the blaze in 68.5 seconds. Runners-up were Horden Colliery team with a time of 80.9 seconds.

A surface fire test was won by Shotton Colliery with a time of 103 seconds – seven seconds less than the runners-up, Thornley Colliery.

The test was in charge of Chief Officer H Twist, of the NCB Fire and Rescue Brigade and Supt J J Smith, Houghton-le-Spring Unit. Mr R S McLaren, No 3 Area general manager, presented the prizes.

16 September 1955

CONCERT – There was a large and appreciative audience at a concert, given by St Godric's Concert Party in Thornley Welfare Hall on Monday, 3 October, in aid of parish funds. The show included light and modern tunes, dancing and items by guest comedian Stan Spowart. Artistes contributing solos and duets were John Quinn, Doris Surman, Marie Hood, Anne Atkin and guest singer Ruth Fishwick. The audience were delighted by the performance of Irish jigs and reels by Pat Hoban, Isabel Luke, Eileen Regan, Veronica Connolly, John Dickinson, Tom Kimmitt, Bob Orchard and Mat Thirlaway. Taking part in other dances were Anne Connolly and Vincent Frain. Dancing was not limited to traditional type and two surprises of the evening were a comic ballet by John Dickinson and Bob Orchard and a tango expertly performed by Patricia Hoban and Mat Thirlaway. Jack Toye, the blind musician, provided a lively selection on his accordion. Stage managers were Fred Graney, Agnes Fleming and Theresa Morton. The artistes were thanked by the Rev Dr McNeil, parish priest of Thornley.

WHEATLEY HILL WORKMEN'S CLUB

Prize-money totalling £150 was distributed at the first annual show on Saturday of Wheatley Hill Workmen's Club Leek Club, which has been revived after a lapse of about 12 years. With a pair of leeks measuring 72.47 cubic inches, Mr T Wilson was awarded first prize among the 16 stands. Other prize-winners, in order of merit were: R Cook (71.92 cubic inches), G Cooke (67.56 cubic inches), H Armstrong, W Symons, E Jones, G Rowbotham, T Kelly, A Sutherland, R Armstrong, S Smith, W Banks, J Wrighton, J R Hanby, R Hackworth and W Turton.

The show was judged by Mr H Smart, Wheatley Hill, and secretarial duties were carried out by Mr George Cook with Mr R Cook as treasurer.

7 October 1955

MINING IN INDIA
Wheatley Hill Man on Leave

A former Wheatley Hill man, who went out to Bengal 19 years ago as a colliery engineer and is now supervising engineer for six coal companies, embracing 28 collieries in India, has been spending a few week's leave at the home of his parents, Mr and Mrs J W Welsh, 24 Wellfield Road, Wingate.

He is Mr Kenneth J Welsh, who yesterday left with his Scottish-born wife and six-year-old son to return to India after a happy time visiting relatives and friends in this country.

Several of the collieries for which Mr Welsh is responsible as engineer are as far as 200 miles from his headquarters. "But", he told our reporter, "we are mostly concerned with those nearer at hand".

Mr Welsh's wife and son came back to this country in March – a few months ahead of his leave – and the son, who bears the same name as his father, has been attending Castle Eden village school.

After attending Henry Smith School, Hartlepool, as a boy, Mr Welsh studied electrical engineering at Armstrong College, Newcastle and gained his BSc degree. For some time after that he worked at Hebburn but was employed at Wheatley Hill colliery when he made the decision to go to Bengal.

FLEW TO KENYA – Miss Vera Liddell, younger of the two nursing daughter of Mr and Mrs George Liddell, of Shinwell Crescent, Thornley, has flown to take up a post as Sister in a hospital at Nanyuki, Kenya, about 150 miles from Nairobi. Her last post in England was as a Sister at Sedgefield General Hospital. A former pupil at Wellfield A J Dawson Grammar School, Miss Liddell received her training at the Royal Infirmary, Sunderland..

THORNLEY MOTHERS' CLUB – Mrs M Hobbs presided. The mothers made arrangements for a children's afternoon party to be followed by the mothers' own night out. Tea has been arranged to precede a social. It was announced that the secretary, Mrs T Mason, had received confirmation of the arrangements for Coxhoe Mother's Club to visit Thornley on 27 October. Mrs M Hobbs and Mrs T Mason were elected to represent the club on Thornley War Memorial committee. Lucky prizes were won by Mesdames G Lawson, E Raine and J Lennox.

14 October 1955

DRAMATIC SOCIETY – Pensioners from the village were invited free when Wheatley Hill Amateur Dramatic Society, who are staging a three-act thriller, "Dial M For Murder", in the Welfare Hall this week, held their final dress rehearsal on Wednesday night. There were only five players – four of them men – in the cast, but they gave an outstanding performance, and as the story unfolded the tension increased, and the audience was held spellbound. The leading roles were filled by Jean Willan and Leslie Barker and they received excellent support from Bryan Askew, Tom King and Don Willan. Mrs Nora Abbs and Mrs Millicent Askew were stage managers and the lighting effects were arranged by Mr Cyril Raffell. The play was presented to a large audience last night and is to be repeated tonight (Friday) and tomorrow (Saturday) night.

LATE MR J H HOLDCROFT – Well-known and esteemed in Wheatley Hill, where he had lived for the past 40 years, Mr John Henry Holdcroft died at his home in 4 Patton Crescent, on Tuesday at the age of 71. Mr Holdcroft had been in poor health during recent years. While employed at Wheatley Hill Colliery in 1929, Mr Holdcroft was severely injured by a fall of stone and was off work for about three years. He began his mining career at the age of 12 and was employed at a number of pits, including Dean and Chapter, Ferryhill, before going to Wheatley Hill where he retired at the age of 66. He was a member of the village's Over-60 Club. Mr Holdcroft is survived by his wife, three sons and two daughters. All his sons live in the village, but his elder daughter lives at Nuneaton, Warwickshire and his younger at South Hetton. Following a service in Patton Street Methodist Church, to be conducted by the Rev Noel Catherall, Mr Holdcroft is to be cremated at Sunderland tomorrow.

BOWLER'S PRESENTATIONS – At a whist drive, supper and social evening in Wheatley Hill Welfare Hall on Friday night, organised by Wheatley Hill Welfare Bowls Club, trophies won during the past season were presented by Mrs MacLean, wife of Dr W G MacLean, Wheatley Hill. Mr R Taylor was MC for the whist and Mr W Kendall for the dominoes and prize-winners were: Mrs J Johnson, Miss Dunn, Mrs Colvine and Messrs W Snowdon, J Starke and J Johnson (whist), and Messrs H Smart, T Lang and J Hodson (dominoes). Master Kenneth Shearsmith won a special prize. Supper was served, after which Mr W Craggs supplied radiogram music for dancing. During an interval Mrs MacLean presented the Club Cup to Mr W Kendall and the Moore Cup to Mr J W Burrell, who won this trophy for the third year in succession. Miniature cups were presented to Mr F Carr, who was runner-up in both competitions. Secretarial duties were carried out by Mr A Todd.

OVER-60 CLUB – At the weekly meeting of Wheatley Hill Over-60 Club in the Workmen's Club Hall on Tuesday night, members stood in silence as a mark of respect for a fellow member, Mr John Holdcroft, who died earlier that day. Mr J Hodson presided and community singing was conducted by Mr W Williams. Birthday greetings were extended to Messrs P Tyson, T E Turner, J Hodson, G Farrow, W Poulson and J Scott and Mesdames J Scott, L Adamson, J Gillings, J Hutler, Luke Todd, Mullen and E Richardson. An excellent entertainment was given by Crook Over-60 Club concert party, comprising Mesdames Askew, Asquith, Allen, Horseman, W Wilson, J Wilson, Ryecroft, Brown, Redman, Lister, Hall and Holliday, the Misses Stoker and M Holiday and Messrs J Brookes, Knowles, Holiday and Dewell. The party was under the leadership of Mr Peter Davis and Mrs Forster was accompanist. They were thanked by Mr Hodson, supported by Mr W Williams. Winners of the "lucky" prizes were Mesdames Todd, Robinson, Hutchinson, Snowden and Turton, Mr W Stannard and Mr T Robinson and Mrs Ayecroft and Mr Holiday (Crook).

21 October 1955

THORNLEY PARISH COUNCIL

Complaints were made at Thornley Parish Council on Tuesday night about damage to roadside seats. One member spoke of reprimanding some youths who were hammering a seat in a manner likely to cause damage. In view of the large amount of damage caused in the past and the inconvenience caused to the people – mainly old people – who use the seats, the Council decided to prosecute in cases where the necessary evidence could be obtained.

The re-numbering of council houses in Thornlaw South, asked for by the Parish Council, is to be carried out by Easington RDC. As an immediate change would entail much additional work in adjusting the Council's current rent collection and other records, it will not come into force until the next financial year which starts on 1 April.

LITTER NUISANCE

Information to the effect that a byelaw imposing a fine of not more than £5 is now in force in the Easington rural district is to be passed onto Thornley Women's Institute, who recently complained to the Parish Council of the litter nuisance in Thornley.

Other byelaws now in force relate to the control of bulls, throwing of stones and missiles in streets, fouling of footways by dogs, indecent language and the preservation of ornamental road margin.

The County Council Highways Committee have adopted the Parish Council's request that the front of Garden Terrace be made up instead of the back street. The adopted programme also includes the making up of the back streets between Bow and Galt Streeets, between Galt and Asquith Streets and between Asquith Street and Moor View. The Council is to be notified of estimated costs before the work is begun.

The NCB agrees with the Council that the old wall at the west end of High Street South prevents drivers coming out of Swinburne and Park Street seeing traffic on the adjoining road. The Board have therefore agreed to the wall being pulled down.

LEGION WOMEN – Mrs M Brain presided over the annual meeting of Wheatley Hill Women's Section of the British Legion. There was a good attendance. Business details were presented by Mrs E A Stainsby. In her secretarial report Mrs Stainsby reported on an increase in membership on the previous year. "We now have 109 members", said Mrs Stainsby, "Our meetings are attracting higher attendances. I think this is indicative of an increased interest in the British Legion by the women of our village". Mrs M Straughan presented a satisfactory financial statement. She intimated that there was every reason for believing their financial strength was sound. There were balances in hand in both the general fund and the petty cash account administered by the secretary.

The following officers were appointed: President – Mrs P Tyson; Vice-President – Mrs S Eddy; Chairman - Mrs M Brain; Vice-Chairman – Mrs M Forster; Secretary – Mrs E A Stainsby; Assistant Secretary – Mrs B Carter; Treasurer – Mrs M Straughan; Standard Bearer – Mrs E Bradley; Assistant Standard Bearer – Mrs M Brain; delegate to the County Conference – Mrs E A Stainsby; Committee Officials – Mesdames D Jackson, Eve Richardson, R Maughan, M Forster, N Briggs, M Kime and E Bradley.

4 November 1955

NEW MOBILE WINDER
Demonstrated at Wheatley Hill

Described by a Coal Board official as "extremely simple in operation" and a "wonderful asset" to the Division, a new mobile winder, bought recently by Durham Division of the National Coal Board for use in the event of an emergency at any colliery in the division, was demonstrated on Wednesday at Wheatley Hill colliery, one of the smallest of the eight in the No 3 Area.

The winder, which cost in the region of £20,000 and is a completely self-contained unit, was making its first appearance in the No 3 Area, where it is remaining a few days so that the 60-odd winding enginemen in the area can be instructed in its use. The full unit, consisting of the towing vehicle and the winder itself, weights over 33 tons and is more than 42 feet long. The towing vehicle as well as pulling the winder, carries a 183 hp diesel engine to generate the electricity for the winder.

"First Class Addition"

Incorporating the latest safety devices and system of electrical signalling, the winder, declared a Coal Board official, was a "first-class addition" to the safety aspects of a pit. It was a magnificent job quiet easy to handle. "And everyone is most enthusiastic about it", the official added.

As well as being used for emergency work to bring men to the surface should the pit winding machinery break down, the mobile winder can be used to examine shafts not equipped with winding engines.

Within a quarter of an hour of reaching a colliery after an SOS has gone out for its services, the winder can be anchored firmly to a specially-constructed concrete platform near the shaft for emergency winding operations to start.

From the winder a rope and attachment can be lowered at eight feet per second to a maximum depth of 3000 feet and a lift of two tons can be made. To haul men out of the pit an open bucket-type kibble is used at the moment. The kibble is about three-and-a-half feet deep and four feet in diameter. Later, a Coal Board official revealed, it is hoped to design a cylindrical type of cage which would be more comfortable for transport.

11 November 1955

GRIEVANCES BEFORE WINGATE COUNCIL

Poor domestic lighting at Wheatley Hill was again one of the main topics for discussion at the meeting of Wingate Parish Council on Monday when, despite a letter from the area chief engineer of the Coal Board saying that "some slight improvement" had been made, several councillors declared there had been no improvement.

Coun N Cook declared that in some houses during the week it was scarcely possible to read a newspaper, though he admitted there was a "good light" at weekends. "After a certain time at nights and at weekends we can generally get a good light, but during the week-days we can scarcely get a light at all"! he added.

The area chief engineer wrote that the Coal Board were hoping to continue the "slight improvement" already made, but the increasing use of electrical equipment in the village soon absorbed any benefits derived. Television sets alone, at the rate at which they were being installed, were creating an additional load problem. These, together with electrical appliances, had a severe effect on an already heavily-loaded system and the position was growing worse each year.

Growing Demand

"However", the letter continued, "we will continue to do whatever we can we can to improve matters but we would remind you that only a major reconstruction of the system, such as the North-Eastern Electricity Board will be instituting in the near future, will provide lasting benefit in face of the growing demand".

After Coun J H Charlton had declared that the Council appeared to be "batting their heads against a stone wall" in their efforts to get better lighting, it was agreed to write again to the Coal Board, asking what improvements they intended carrying out.

Message from Electricity Board

Coun J Fenwick declared he could not see where much improvement had been made. "I don't think the people of Wheatley Hill should have to suffer such poor lighting until the Electricity Board takes over ", he added "Everybody is dissatisfied and something ought to be done about it!"

It seemed, said Coun P Unsworth, that the Coal Board would not do anything because of the impending change-over. Coun Charlton said,

"They do not want to be involved in extra expense because they know they will soon be turning over the network to the Electricity Board".

The Electricity Board wrote that the change-over was proceeding "as well as could be expected". It was hoped that the work would be completed in the Deaf Hill area between July and August next year, in the Wingate and Station Town area between June and December, 1957 and in the Wheatley Hill area between August and December 1957. "It may well be that these dates can be anticipated by six months", the letter added.

18 November 1955

SCOUTS IN A ROAD CRASH
Unlucky Trip for Wheatley Hill Boys

Three Wheatley Hill Boy Scots were injured, but only one was taken to hospital, when a motor-cycle combination in which they were passengers, swung across the road at a narrow bend in Filpoke Lane, near High Hesleden, shortly before mid-day on Sunday and crashed over the grass verge into a hedge.

The driver of the combination, Leslie Barker (32) of 35 Liddell Terrace, Wheatley Hill, who was taking the Scouts to Crimdon for some signalling practice ,escaped with abrasions to his legs.

One of the boys in the sidecar, 13 year-old Gordon Cutty of 8 Patton Crescent, Wheatley Hill, received a severe scalp wound when he was thrown forward and struck his forehead against a piece of wood. After treatment by Dr Dixon of Horden, he was taken to a Sunderland hospital.

The other boy in the sidecar, Francis William Lowther (14) of 18 William Morris Terrace, Shotton Colliery, received abrasions to his right cheek and the boy on the pillion, Stephen Walker (15) of 11 Greenhills Terrace, Wheatley Hill, suffered from abrasions to his face and right hand. The injuries to these two boys were only slight and they were allowed to go home after attention.

When the accident occurred, a car travelling ahead with more Scouts stopped and the driver took Cutty, the worse injured, for medical treatment.

THORNLEY DRAMA GROUP
Appearing in "Suspect"

Thornley Drama Club are this week presenting "Suspect" before large audiences. The play is under the direction of the group's new producer, Bert Martin, a veteran actor of countless amateur and operatic productions, who is well-known for his work in this sphere in the Thornley, Horden and Rotherham districts.

Stage managers, Mrs Potts and Mrs Winter, have seen to it that the "set" is of the high standard usually associated with the group's productions and a cast of experienced players is headed by Eva Martin, who portrays the difficult role of a lonely woman haunted by the grim memories of her past.

She is admirably supported by Olive Lincoln, Marjorie Donald and Marion Swinburne. Others in the cast include Alfred Barnett, David Gott, Jimmy Bewick and John Watson. On Monday old age pensioners enjoyed the performance.

The group is grateful to Miss Flora Robson, who, when appearing in the same play at Newcastle, gave the group invaluable advice which has proved most helpful.

EASINGTON'S BEST OUTPUT THIS YEAR

Easington Colliery, the second biggest of the eight in No 3 Area (South East Durham) Durham Division, NCB, had its best output of the year last week when it produced 20,280 tons against a target of 17,000 tons.

Horden, the biggest pit, also passed its target by a big margin for the 15th successive week, and the other target-breakers were Blackhall, Thornley, Wheatley Hill and Deaf Hill. The area's total output of 91,977 tons exceeded the combined target by 5827 tons.

OUTPUT AT THORNLEY COLLIERY

With a target of 7500 tons per week, Thornley Colliery had an output of 9193 tons last week. In the previous week in was 9002 while 8000 had been exceeded several times.

Asked the reason for the rise to over 9000, a member of the colliery consultative committee said that the pit conditions were favourable at the moment. He believed that the recent outputs were the best the colliery had achieved since 1939.

A large building which is to house one of the new modern cleaning plants has been erected. It is the predominant building at the colliery. It is understood that this cleaner will serve Wheatley Hill Colliery as well as Thornley.

25 November 1955

WHEATLEY HILL

Mr and Mrs C G Dobbin of 2 Fred Peart Place, Wheatley Hill, have been informed that their son, Mr Arthur Dobbin, 45 Wykebeck Road, Leeds has been awarded his SRN certificate. Before the war Mr Dobbin worked in the pits. In the Army he served with the Royal Army Medical Corps in India and Singapore. He became keenly interested in nursing and made up his mind that on demobilisation he would make it his career. He was appointed a nursing orderly at St James's Hospital, Leeds, in 1945. Mr Dobbin will be remembered in the Wheatley Hill area as a goalkeeper in the local school team and with Wheatley Hill Juniors. His father was a well-known cornet player with Wheatley Hill Colliery band. Mr Dobbin married a Leeds girl and has a son and a daughter.

OVER-60 CLUB – There was a large attendance in Wheatley Hill Workmen's Club Hall for the meeting of the Over-60 Club. Mr J Hodson presided. Birthday greetings were extended to Mesdames Aitken, Kenny and Robinson; Messrs E Barker and S Gibson. Entertainment was provided by Mr Fred Gelson's party from Station Town. Mrs A Ayre was compere and the accompanists were Mrs Watts and Mrs Dixon. An excellent programme of choruses, songs, dances and monologues were presented by the following artistes: Mesdames Hays, Dixon, Watts, East sen., East jun., Gelson, Harry, Ward, Kyle, Trevena and Gaskell. Messrs G Gelson, W Gelson, Melvyn Harry, Stanley Gelson and the Misses P Dixon and R Wood. Thanks were expressed by the president and Mr W Williams, entertainments secretary, who also conducted community singing. Prize-winners were Mesdames J Scott, R Bowes, M Ayre, Vine, Earnshaw and Mr T Simpson.

THORNLEY NONAGENARIAN
Mrs Monaghan Looks Back to Early Days

Mrs Mary Ann Monaghan, Roseberry Crescent, Thornley, was 90 on Saturday. There was a celebration party in her little bungalow on Sunday when the guests included some of her 17 great-grandchildren. She lives by herself, but is attended to by a daughter, Mrs Cowan, who lives in a bungalow within a hundred yards.

Mrs Monathan's husband, who died 33 years ago, was well-known in Thornley. In remarkably good health for her age, Mrs Monaghan has lived all her life at Thornley except for the five weeks after she was born, when the family moved from Framwellgate Moor. She probably holds a record for long residence in the village.

She recalls for instance, the fire at Thornley pit in the seventies, when the heapstead was burned down and the men were thrown out of work for a long period.

Evictions Recalled

"A lot of people shifted to other collieries to get their living", said Mrs Monaghan. Another incident she remembers inspired the local poets to sarcastic rhyming. This was the eviction of some of the miners from their homes in the neighbouring village of Wheatley Hill, a job carried out by imported men who became known as 'candymen'. "We were expecting them to come to Thornley in the next week, but they didn't come", said Mrs Monaghan. "The strike was settled in time to prevent us from being turned out of our homes".

A more cheerful event was "The Big Dinner" at Thornley, when the local group of pits was being taken over by new owners. To celebrate the event, these new owners roasted an ox for dinner for the workmen.

Coal Owners Bankrupt

The famous occasion known as the "Putt Pay", when the men's wages were not forthcoming owing to the bankruptcy of the owners, is recalled by Mrs Monaghan. She says her husband got his wages in about three weeks after they were due, but that others, especially those who had gone away, had to wait much longer.

She was married when she was 21. Wages at that time were paid fortnightly. "Sometimes we had thirty shillings or two pounds", she said. "Two-pound-ten was a big wage, but that was a fortnight mind". To eke out their wages miners often turned to other things in their spare time, such as gardening and keeping pigs and poultry. Mrs Monaghan told how she and Ned, her husband, took the money that he had received from selling his ducks and hens and went to Durham.

Just outside the town they bought a pig. With a string tied to one of its legs they walked the pig all the way back to Thornley. On reaching the village they were 'observed' by the local policeman, the late Constable John Prior, sometimes called "the big black Bobby".

"I expected him to ask where we had got the pig", said Mrs Monaghan, "but he didn't. He just laughed at us". In telling this she laughed herself, as though she was again seeing herself, her husband and the pig walking together in the street.

Ned Was Injured In The Pit

Ned Monaghan was injured in the pit when he was 56 and was unable to return to work. He will be remembered by many of the older Thornley men as the collector for the Roman Catholic Church. The same people may remember that Mrs Monaghan was a McGuigan, sister of Frank, Charlie, Matt, Jim and Michael McGuigan. Her only sister was the wife of Mr 'Ferdie' Conelly, who was prominent for many years in Thornley Lodge and political affairs and could always be depended upon to liven up a political meeting by asking questions.

Like many very old people, Mrs Monaghan thinks that people used to be more homely than they are today. "We had to be homely. There was nothing else for us. We hardly ever got away from home, and so we had to make the best of it", she said. A trip to Sunderland in her day was a big event, not just the casual affair it is today.

Was Very Beautiful

"Paint and powder" was not used in her young days. As she sat in an old-fashioned arm chair and talked, one noticed an enlarged photograph of her hanging on the wall. She said she was about 18 when it was taken. It showed her to have been a very beautiful girl.

The recollection of most of the older members of Thornley RC Church can reach backward no further than Father Haggerty's days as parish priest, but Mrs Monaghan remembers Fathers Ross, Bolam, Foran, Smith, Brannen and Mulhally, as well as Father Haggerty and all those who have served the parish since his day.

WHEATLEY HILL WOMEN BOWLERS

Nine of the ten clubs in the North-Eastern Women's Bowling League were represented at the annual social evening and prize-giving of Wheatley Hill Welfare Women's Bowls Club in the Welfare Hall on Monday night. They were welcomed by Mrs S Hodson, who presided, and after supper Mr T W Alderson of Peterlee, retired groundsman at Wheatley Hill Welfare Park, presented the trophies and prizes won during the season by members of the Wheatley Hill Club.

Mrs E Hall, secretary of the club, was presented with the Club Cup, and her 16-year-old daughter, Miss Pamela Hall, who was playing her first season at bowls, was presented with the William Jones Cup. Mrs E Poulson was runner-up for the Club Cup and Mrs S Hodson for the William Jones Cup. The Festival Bowl was won by Mrs S Hodson with Mrs E Atkinson runner-up. The prize-winners were congratulated by Mr Alderson, supported by the league president, Mrs E Smurthwaite of Park Club, West Hartlepool.

Mrs Hall was MC for whist, prizes for which were won by Mesdames E Humphreys, A Marshall and R A Brown and Messrs T Simpson, L Anderson and W Snowdon. Miss Hutchinson was MC for dancing and music was supplied by Mr J Glancey and partner, West Cornforth. The function was attended by about 170 members and friends of the club.

9 December 1955

VICAR'S DEPARTURE

Many tributes to their work in the parish were paid to the Rev and Mrs Arthur Preston when they occupied the place of honour at a farewell social evening in Wheatley Hill Welfare Hall on Saturday, organised by the parishioners of All Saints' Church. After serving as Vicar of Wheatley Hill for the past six years, Mr Preston left this week for Gateshead, where on Monday he is to be inducted as Vicar of Christ Church. Mr W Marshall, people's warden, presided at the gathering and the Vicar's warden, Mr J White, on behalf of the parishioners and friends, presented Mr and Mrs Preston with a cheque, and their son Hilary, with a book. Best wishes were extended to all three for a happy stay in their new parish by the wardens, Mr J Atkinson (on behalf of the choir) and Miss D Richardson (on behalf of the Sunday School teachers). The Vicar and his wife suitably replied, thanking the parishioners for their gift and for their loyalty during the past six years. Supper was served by women members and the entertainment which followed included a potted pantomime "Cinderella", presented by members of Wheatley Hill Women's Institute, with Mrs R Woodward as producer. Solos were contributed by Messrs N Blakemore, A Alderton and B Blenkinsopp and with Mr G Crosby, they also sang quartets. Master Bernard English made a pleasing debut on the concert platform with two monologues and the accompanist was Mrs C English. Thanks to all who had helped to make the evening a success were expressed by Mr W Woodward.

16 December 1955

WHEATLEY HILL "GOOD DEED"

Popular visitors to the children's ward of Durham County Hospital on Saturday afternoon were a party of Wolf Cubs from the Wheatley Hill Pack who, together with the Scouts and Rovers at Wheatley Hill", adopted" the ward three years ago.

The Cubs were accompanied by 22 Girl Guides from the Wheatley Hill Company and they all sang carols for the young patients and distributed Christmas gifts. The Cubs were in charge of Cubmaster, A Watson and Scoutmaster Leslie Barker and the Guides had Lieuts Mrs R Watson and Miss Ruth Hedley in charge. The Guide Captain, Mrs L Barker, was unable to be present. The young folk, after entertaining the boys and girls in the children's ward, visited the men's and women's wards and sang a number of carols there.

Early in the New Year the Wheatley Hill Scouts and Rovers are to visit the children's ward with a gift of six nursery chairs they have bought for the use of the patients.

30 December 1955